CALIFORNIA PARALEGAL'S GUIDE

SECOND EDITION

Formerly
CALIFORNIA PARALEGAL'S HANDBOOK

By
Zella Mack

Parker & Son Publications, Inc.
Box 60001
Los Angeles, California, 90060

Printed in United States of America

Preface

This Second Edition is in response to the strong acceptance of this book since its original publication. It has been completely revised with addition of much new information of assistance to the paralegal plus innovative schedules to make the work easier and ever more accurate. The key researcher working with Zella Mack was Sheila Molnar, Esq.

The main purposes of the Paralegal's Guide are (1) to guide and assist paralegals or legal assistants working under the general supervision of an attorney; (2) to serve as a textbook for the paralegal student commencing the study of law whether by self-study, under the tutelage of an attorney or experienced personnel within the law office, or in a prescribed course of study for legal assistants; and (3) as a quick reference for many legal procedures, a permanent desk book for attorneys, paralegals and legal secretaries.

The material is highly selective and concise, the better to serve as a practical aid. In general only the usual and most typical procedures are covered. To explore every phase of legal procedure would make this book too voluminous to be handy; to discuss every variation would serve only to confuse. Entire books which cover the many subtopics include such excellent references as Dan Henke's *California Law Guide* (Parker & Son Publications) on legal research, and California Real Estate Sales Transactions (Continuing Education of the Bar) on sales of real property, for instance.

While the career of legal assistant is the newest one in the field of law, its tradition is as old as the law itself. For the past century and more, young would-be attorneys, striving to be accepted at the bar, not only "read the law" under the guidance of their mentor but performed the very tasks the paralegal is now handling. The great lawyers of the past, including Abraham Lincoln, journeyed to the county courthouse, researched the facts and the law, wrote complaints, writs, briefs and answers, served papers and, in so doing, learned the practice of law.

The rapid increase in litigation and the tremendous expansion of the legal profession to meet the needs of modern society has put heavy burdens on the attorney of today. Fortunately a large pool of highly trained legal aides is growing, available to handle many aspects of that load. Already thousands of legal assistants are employed throughout the country doing background work to provide their attorney-employers the information and time to handle clients and appear in court. Paralegal associations are springing up; in-service training programs are growing, not to mention the certificate programs in more and more colleges, junior colleges and law schools.

In this volume, Zella Mack has laid the foundation for learning how to become a legal assistant and has provided a useful procedure handbook. The Paralegal's Guide is arranged in four main parts: (1) the background of the law and courts; (2) Civil Litigation, including the preparation for the trial and the follow-up responsibilities and specialties within the general field; (3)

specialty fields of law such as Probate, and (4) clear steps to take in legal research and writing.

What will The Paralegal's Guide do for you?

As a legal assistant, it will:

1) make your work easier and save you time on the job,

2) increase your knowledge, and perhaps your status, in the law office,

3) make you more valuable to your employer, and

4) give you a feeling of confidence in this important new field of work.

As an attorney employing legal assistants or paralegals, it will:

1) define tasks paralegals can perform for you, freeing you for higher rate activity,

2) save your time training them on the job,

3) provide answers for their questions,

4) make them more efficient and increase billable time.

As a legal secretary, it will:

1) teach you to be a legal assistant so you can increase your income and status,

2) understand the work of the legal assistant and appreciate their problems.

As a teacher of paralegals, it will:

1) provide an entire pattern of a paralegal course of study,

2) provide reading assignments for your students,

3) save your time in preparing and finding material for your class,

4) serve as a reference work for your students on the job after graduation.

The Paralegal's Guide will be supplemented in the future to keep it up-to-date with the latest procedures and changes in the law.

What is a legal assistant or paralegal? At a panel of the California State Bar Convention in 1976 on the subject, the following succinct definition was made:

"The paralegal (is) generally defined as a non-lawyer working under the supervision of an attorney to deliver some legal services to the client. The paralegal operates with facts rather than legal theories, merely putting the facts together for the attorney. Areas of paralegal involvement vary. One suggestion offered for determining what tasks the paralegal should perform is that the attorney should decide what he or she does repetitively — for example, certain discovery procedures, filling out forms. Other possible duties: any activity involving a large number of documents (sorting, indexing, chronologizing), preparation of trial exhibits, certain investigative functions (interviewing witnesses and clients, developing correlative evidence to confirm or dispute). . . . The prognosis for the future was the demise of the traditional law office arrangement (lawyer-secretary-clerk), increasing use of the law office administrator, and the eventual licensing and regulation of paralegals." (State Bar of California Reports: Oct. 1976, p. 7.)

The American Bar Association has given its support to the concept of the legal assistant. The future of the highly trained paralegal is assured. Such professionals are an important part of the legal services of society. As the author, Mrs. Mack says, "The improvement of the administration of justice is the objective of the legal profession, and is brought about in many ways. I hope this book will, in some measure, contribute to that worthy end."

The Publishers

CONTENTS

The Author

Zella Mack is eminently qualified to write this book. She has had wide experience in the work of the paralegal or legal assistant and legal secretary both with private practitioners of law and the courts. She has a fine educational background and has for many years taught other legal aides. Mrs. Mack is a Certified Legal Assistant.

She is a graduate of the University of California at Berkeley, receiving her Bachelor of Arts degree. Mrs. Mack has had the opportunity of working in many types of law offices, ranging from partnerships to corporate law firms. She has been employed by some of the most prestigious law firms in the country such as Ropes & Gray in Boston; Pillsbury, Madison & Sutro in San Francisco; and the Sacramento firm of Mull & Pierce. The late Archibald M. Mull, Jr., was a past president of the State Bar of California; Justice Fred R. Pierce is a retired Presiding Justice of the Court of Appeal, Third Appellate District. In San Francisco she also worked for Sidney L. Weinstock and Roger Anderson when they were associated. While she was in Boston with Ropes & Gray she was assigned to James Barr Ames, who is a senior partner with the firm.

More recently Mrs. Mack was Judicial Secretary to Leonard M. Friedman, retired Associate Justice of the Court of Appeal of the State of California, Third Appellate District. She has also been employed in the office of the California Attorney General as secretary to Chief Assistant Attorney General Willard A. Shank and former Chief Deputy Attorney General Charles A. Barrett.

Mrs. Mack has taught legal secretarial training courses and fundamentals of legal assisting under the auspices of the Sacramento Legal Secretaries Association and the Sacramento County Bar Association. She is a member of the Sacramento Association of Legal Assistants, the National Association of Legal Assistants, the Sacramento Legal Secretaries Association, the California Writers Club, and is a Sustaining Member of the National Federation of Paralegal Associations. Her husband, Frank P. Mack, graduated from Harvard Law School. He is a member of the State Bar of California, and is an Administrative Law Judge for the State of California. As Zella Mack puts it, ''he has been a constant source of help and encouragement in writing this book.''

Acknowledgments

I wish to express my gratitude to all the following who have, in one way or another, contributed to the production of this book: James Aaron, Probate File Examiner, Sacramento County; Charles A. Barrett, former Chief Deputy Attorney General; Benjamin H. Brown; Miles Clark, Editorial Director; Honorable Leonard M. Friedman, Retired Associated Justice, Court of Appeal; Eva S. Goodwin, Judicial Staff Attorney, Court of Appeal, First Appellate District; Al Gottlieb; Antonia Hansen, CLA; Betty Foot Henderson; Wilfried H. Kramer, Clerk, Court of Appeal, Third District; Vincent P. Lafferty; Kenneth B. Lake, Lake Law Books, Inc.; Lawrence J. Loheit, Trustee, Chapter 13 Proceedings, Eastern District; Peggy O'Neill, Legal Assistant; Therese M. Nichols, Legal Assistant; Lloyd H. Riley; Craig Wesley Rimer, Paralegal Administrator & Investigator; Linda Roye, Legal Assistant; Willard A. Shank, Chief Assistant Attorney General; Tosh G. Yamamoto; Sarah N. Wristen; and my husband,

Frank P. Mack,
Adminstrative Law Judge.

Chapter 1

THE PARALEGAL ROLE

What is a paralegal?*

The term "paralegal" has been in use for over a decade. Yet a great deal of uncertainty as to what a paralegal is, or how the term should be defined, still exists. See the Preface for the definition made at the California State Bar Convention. The lay person may relate the word to the paramedical; others believe paralegals are really legal secretaries by another name.

Kenneth Severn, a Fellow of the Institute of Legal Executives in England, in an article in Facts and Findings (December 1976) had this to say about the "paralegal" designation: "Of all the American titles for legal executives, I like 'paralegals' the least. It sounds as if the persons were under a physical disability."

Indeed, this is not as far-fetched as one might think, as the following story illustrates. At one hotel where a paralegal group was meeting a room for a conference had been requested. When the paralegals arrived at this room, they reportedly found a room equipped with ramps for their wheelchairs!

Attempts to define "paralegal" or "legal assistant" end as exercises in futility. Perhaps at this time the concept of "paralegal" can best be conveyed by describing what a paralegal does — and they do many things, as the next chapter details. The scope of their work is growing every day, as attorneys earnestly look for work they can properly delegate.

---

*To date other terms used include nonlawyers, certified attorney assistants, paraprofessionals, and legal assistants. "Paralegal" and "legal assistant" are used interchangeably in this book, though in the writer's mind the term "paralegal" has a broader connotation, encompassing more fields.

PARALEGAL SPHERE DEFINED

One must view this profession in terms of three relevant factors which define and limit the sphere of influence of paralegal workers at the present time.

1. The first factor is the legal limitation imposed. This means the paralegal worker is bound by a legal sanction which limits his or her function. Participation in trial work or giving of legal advice is now precluded. This is as it should be, and not viewed by the writer as any handicap. Ultimate professional responsibility rests on the shoulder of the lawyer. He or she must supervise, if only in a general manner, all the work that is delegated. Nevertheless, *within* the lawyer's office, the boundaries of the law work the legal assistant can do — if permitted by the lawyer — need be limited only by the legal assistant's capabilities.

2. The second factor is the subjective considerations. Many lawyers simply cannot delegate authority. Many lawyers are overworked, but continue to waste their time performing standardized procedures. Lawyers need time to perform the work for which they were trained and do best. How many lawyers have picked up their briefcase in the morning to go to court and wished they had had more time to prepare the case? As long as the lawyer is responsible for the finished product, he is not shirking his responsibility by delegating work. A typist could make a mistake which, if overlooked, would be at least embarrassing, conceivably disastrous — but no one would contend the lawyer should do his or her own typing!

Not all lawyers are convinced that the use of paralegals would mean greater profits; they fear it would only add to their overhead. "If the use of paraprofessionals can save one hour of a lawyer's billable time per day, a lawyer with a 45-year practice can earn an additional half million dollars during his lifetime."* Lawyers have discovered that a legal assistant is profitable; their time is billable to a client.

Reluctance of a lawyer to delegate also stems in part from the fact that the practice of law, like the practice of medicine, develops a close personal relationship between attorney and client, and the lawyer may fear to have anyone but himself tread on this hallowed ground. What of the opinion of their esteemed clients? They need not worry. *If lawyers accord status and respect to their paralegal workers, so will their clients.*

The good paralegal worker acts as a liaison between the client and the lawyer, and stands in a better position than the lawyer to assure

---

*New Careers in Law: II (American Bar Association Special Committee on Legal Assistants (Conference Report, June 1971)), p. 13.

the client that he is "in good hands." The knowledgeable paralegal or legal assistant can act as a buffer on those occasions when clients tend to encroach upon the time of the lawyer, usually without realizing it. To the average client, there is but one case, and that one is his.

Opportunity to develop their capabilities is essential to function as a paralegal. Paralegals should be free from duties such as dictation, machine transcription and filing, to have the time and energy to fulfill their roles as legal assistants. Others can be readily hired to perform the mechanized tasks. To quote from Studs Terkel's book, Why Men Work, "The part of this task assigned to management is the provision of working conditions which will release the creative instinct of every worker, and which will give play to his divine-human ability to think." Mortimer J. Adler, the educator, has also said that most people do not know their limits of comprehension; that they have never tried their powers to the full.

3. The third factor consists of the objective considerations, meaning personal qualifications, the skill and ability of the particular employee. The exercise of initiative requires, first, *facts, or knowledge,* and judgment. The responsibility of a legal position, whether in a private general practice law office, a corporation law office, some other specialized field of law, a government office, or wherever, depends upon (a) the nature of the work of the employer, the actual duties, whether he must necessarily perform them himself, (b) willingness to assume responsibility, and (c) ability to act dependably and independently.

That ability, as noted, is built on facts, or knowledge. That knowledge is now being provided by training courses throughout the country. Curricula for legal paraprofessionals have been set up and are being offered in various colleges in California as well as in other states. (See Appendix for list of California schools.)

DEVELOPMENT OF THE PROFESSION

The first development which gave momentum to the paralegal profession was the creation of a systematic paralegal curriculum. Until very recently on-the-job training was virtually the only method by which one became a legal assistant. However, a few years ago, following the lead of the British (the British Institute for Legal Executives emphasizes qualifying for employment), American colleges and universities instituted training programs for legal assistants. The structured course of study gives the future paralegal a broader vision and deeper understanding of the legal concepts he or she will be dealing with on a daily basis. Previously, each legal assistant had to create his or her own system of information and organization, a process which could take many years. With the advent of the collegiate training program more and more men and women are attracted to a paralegal career.

The courses are generally taught by attorneys or paralegals with many years of practical experience, often with expertise in a certain specialized field.

Special courses are being offered in accounting for law offices, administrative agencies, bankruptcy, civil litigation, commercial law, communications skills, constitutional law, consumer protection, corporate securities, corporation law, creditor's and debtor's rights, criminal law procedure, domestic relations, environmental and poverty law, general law practice, interviewing/counseling techniques, investigation and case preparation, labor law, law office management, legal research, personal injury actions, probate, real estate specialization, tenant-landlord relations, torts, welfare law, wills and estate planning, and other subjects. New legislation has expanded the role of arbitration in the superior courts, and there are new developments in the settlement field.

All this training is producing paralegals proficient in many fields capable of performing a wide variety of tasks. Paralegals are being employed in the larger law offices at an increasing rate, in various legal specialty fields.

The second development which gave momentum to the movement is the training of paralegals by the federal government, commencing in 1965 with the establishment of the Office of Legal Services under the Office of Economic Opportunity (later the Community Services Administration). The National Paralegal Institute, originally established under that office in 1972, trained paralegals for four years and has played a pivotal role in promoting paralegalism. Beginning in 1975, it started to provide training and technical assistance in the area of legal services for the elderly. It receives grants and contracts to design and deliver training to paralegals and lay advocates employed in anti-poverty law offices. It does not operate a school, but conducts special training events around the country upon the request of federal or state agencies.

The National Paralegal Institute has developed programs in the following substantive areas: Social Security, Supplemental Security Income, Aid to Families with Dependent Children, Food Stamps, Landlord and Tenant Law, Public Housing Law, Medicare, Medicaid, In-Home Supportive Services, Employment Discrimination in Age, Race, Sex and Disability, Guardianship and Conservatorship, Patients' Rights, Consumer Law (finance, credit and liability), Wills and Probate Avoidance, Tribal Court Law, Agricultural Labor Law, Institutionalization (Nursing Homes), Disability Law, Handicapped Legal Rights,

Mortgage Assignment Remedies, and Unauthorized Practice Rules. In addition the National Paralegal Institute provides technical assistance to state units of government and to provider agencies on how to establish training programs, delivery systems for legal services, and programs which utilize nonlawyer advocates.

The National Public Law Training Center holds law and advocacy training events ranging from two days to two weeks. Its 1979-1980 program topic areas were Public Benefits and Entitlements, Legal Advocacy Skills, The Advocacy Spectrum, Housing Law for Non-Lawyers, Advocacy for Youth, Women and Immigrants, Mental Health and Handicapped Law, and Trainer Training.

What do the paralegals in the public sector do? Most of them interview clients and witnesses. Many of them deal with government agencies on behalf of their clients. They help the elderly and the poor in cases involving social security and appeals, Supplemental Security Income, taxes, wills, pensions, nursing home care, age discrimination and involuntary commitments. They might investigate cases and prepare reports. In legal services to the poor and other public sector work they actually represent clients, where authorized by statute, regulations, or by a court, including representation at state administrative hearings where representation by an attorney is not required by law.

The Legal Services Corporation is a private, nonprofit organization created and funded by Congress to provide legal assistance to the poor in civil matters. It was established by the Legal Services Corporation Act of 1974 and began operations in July 1975. The Corporation is funded by congressional appropriation and distributes its funds through grants and contracts to legal services programs that meet specific requirements.

The Corporation's offices are staffed by full-time attorneys and paralegal assistants — approximately 6,218 attorneys and 2,830 paralegals. Programs provide advice and advocacy for those who qualify for free legal assistance. Although most of the programs provide legal representation and counseling generally in civil matters, some specialize in problems relating to consumer affairs, the elderly, administrative benefits, housing and family law, health law, migrant workers, and American Indians. Many of the problems are disposed of through negotiation, consultation, and other out-of-court mechanisms, rather than litigation.

The Corporation has expanded its legal services programs into unserved and underserved areas.

NONPROFIT PRIVATE LAW FIRMS

One of the largest group of nonprofit private firms is the Legal Aid Society. Legal Aid Society offices employ one group of paralegals in the traditional role of preliminary interviewing, drafting pleadings, taking care of service and filing, and preparing witnesses for simple hearings. These paralegals are used frequently in the domestic relations area. The other group of Legal Aid Society paralegals have a less traditional role: that of advocates. These paralegals interview, investigate, research, draft pleadings and represent clients at hearings as allowed by the State Bar, mainly social security and welfare hearings.

The American Civil Liberties Union, also a nonprofit law firm, employs paralegals to do legal research (both case law and statutory), draft legal memoranda, and to manage entire cases where the issues do not require an attorney's expertise, such as school expulsion cases.

Government

Paralegals are found at all levels of government practice, in federal agencies, state attorney general offices and state agencies, county district attorneys and public defenders offices and city attorney offices, although proportionately fewer government attorneys have support paralegals than private law office attorneys. Although breakthroughs have been made which can be expected to increase utilization of paralegals in government in the future, several factors operate to constrain their use.

In private practice the paralegal's worth can be measured in terms of profit generated (and/or lower costs to clients). Government does not make a profit, though through streamlining and economizing of services performed taxpayers' money can be saved. But government does not have the freedom of private practice to experiment. It cannot simply add on paralegals and try out a program and judge its benefits — and then decide either to abandon or implement.

Civil service procedures must first be followed. Surveys and analyses must be made. Budgets must be prepared, justified and approved. Some may entertain fears of sacrificing attorney positions to obtain paralegal positions and then find themselves unable to have needed legal help. Too, the government's "clients" are other state agencies (or county and city agencies) who may protest the handling of their cases by paralegals which were formerly handled by attorneys. Also, there are fears their clients may choose to perform legal services in-house at, ostensibly, a lesser quality to taxpayers.

The utilization of paralegals in time-consuming work makes some government services possible where attorneys could not spend the time required, such as in collection work and victim assistance programs.

Government paralegals perform the same work as their counterparts in private practice. The most common usages of paralegals include performing legal research (most often involving codes and regulations, but sometimes case law research), assisting attorneys in preparation for trial, document control and docketing. There are tax specialists, worker's compensation specialists, probate and charitable trust specialists, antitrust specialists, criminal and civil investigation work and legislative monitoring.

Paralegals also perform work generated specifically from government practice, such as the preparation of administrative pleadings, regulatory and licensing agencies; consumer protection specialists and advocates, collection matters, including preparation of pleadings to collect moneys owed to the government (school loans, Medi-Cal liens, third party liens and tax liens), witness coordination, victim assistance, advocacy before certain boards and commissions, and extradition specialists.

FEDERAL GOVERNMENT

Federal government (as well as state and local governments) employs many paralegals and is exploring new ways to use them. It has two civil service classifications for paralegals: legal technician and paralegal specialist.

The legal technician class provides upward mobility for legal secretaries. The duties are legal clerical or technical and in some instances include typing. Legal technicians monitor cases in specific areas (e.g., social security disability complaints), set up files, collect information, draft form pleadings, calendar cases and maintain "tickler" files.

The legal technician class requires more responsibility and technical ability than is required of a secretary, but not as many legal skills as is required of a paralegal specialist.

The paralegal specialists, like the legal technicians, are often employed in offices of the United States Attorney. The paralegal specialist assists attorneys in complex litigation, especially criminal fraud cases, draft answers and monitors discovery documents, conducts legal research, drafts legal memoranda, interviews witnesses and handles collection cases.

Other paralegal specialists are employed by the Federal Trade Commission as research analysts and as consumer protection specialists. The Securities and Exchange Commission employs paralegals for litigation support, especially the review of legal corporate documents.

A Paralegal Specialist Series GS-950 has been established. The following is a description of the work of a Paralegal Specialist, GS-5 and above: "Paralegal specialist positions involve such activities as

(a) legal research, analyzing legal decisions, opinions, rulings, memoranda, and other legal material, selecting principles of law, and preparing digests of the points of law involved; (b) selecting, assembling, summarizing, and compiling substantive information on statutes, treaties, contracts, other legal instruments, and specific legal subjects; (c) case preparation for civil litigation, criminal law proceedings or agency hearings, including the collection, analysis, and evaluation of evidence, e.g., as to fraud and fraudulent and other irregular activities or violations of laws; (d) analyzing facts and legal questions presented by personnel administering specific Federal laws, answering the questions where they have been settled by interpretations of applicable legal provisions, regulations, precedents, and agency policy, and in some instances preparing informative and instructional material for general use; (e) adjudicating applications or cases on the basis of pertinent laws, regulations, policies and precedent decisions; or (f) performing other paralegal duties requiring discretion and independent judgment in the application of specialized knowledge of particular laws, regulations, precedents, or agency practices based thereon. These duties may or may not be performed under the direction of a lawyer.''

CALIFORNIA GOVERNMENT AND LEGAL ASSISTANTS

A class of Legal Assistant has been established in California civil service. The job description for that classification follows:
''Typical Tasks:

Under the immediate direction and control of an attorney who shall accept full responsibility for the tasks performed, assists in reviewing legal documents and appeals to determine whether they comply with specific requirements set forth in applicable legal codes; assists in reviewing for completeness information furnished by program staff in matters referred for legal proceedings; performs preliminary analyses of legislative bills; summarizes, organizes, and indexes prior opinions, testimony, depositions, documentary material from interrogatories, and abstracts; organizes trial documents and exhibits; researches legislative histories; gathers factual information and performs routine legal research to assist an attorney in determining appropriate action; assists in the preparation of roughs of complaints and pleadings; prepares legislative calendar; prepares fact sheets; prepares papers and arranges for service of process; assists in preparing drafts of documents such as motions to substitute parties, petitions, inventories, judgments, affidavits, certificates of readiness, requests for trial setting, reassignment of claims, decisions, orders of extension, notice of hearings, abstracts of judgment, returns of writs, certified copies, writs of execution, and satisfaction of judgments; prepares documents for opening and closing files for internal administrative purposes; prepares correspondence and reports; assists in preparing drafts of answers to inquiries regarding legal requirements and procedure relative to the appropriate legal code and answers to inquiries regarding status of cases and departmental procedures by attorneys, parties and the public; maintains liaison and exchanges legal and factual information with other legal units in the department and other State agencies.''

On March 13, 1975, the State of California established the class of Legal Assistant (above) and on July 2, 1981, it established another and higher class, Legal Analyst. The establishment of these classes is significant for the paralegal profession.

"Typical tasks for this class are described as follows: Under the general direction of an attorney who shall accept full responsibility for the tasks performed, the Legal Analyst investigates and analyzes facts and documents in connection with civil litigation; assists in criminal trial preparation by coordinating witnesses and processing subpoenas; coordinates with local law enforcement and judicial entities relative to ministerial problems; when delegated by the attorney, drafts interrogatories and responses to interrogatories; interviews witnesses, complainants and defendants concerning the facts of cases; drafts roughs of pleadings, complaints and motions for attorney review by the attorney; assists in the preparation of witness books and exhibit books; conducts historical research for the attorney by collecting and analyzing historical data with regard to cases and by summarizing deposition transcripts; assists in administrative proceedings by preparing drafts of accusations and statements of issues; prepares responses to routine procedural and/or large volume type inquiries; prepares legislative and follow ups on legislative and regulatory files; may also serve in a lead capacity over one or more Legal Assistants and clerical support staff as circumstances prescribe.''

ROLE OF WORD PROCESSING AND COMPUTERS

No discussion of the development of paralegalism would be complete without mention of word processing and computers.

A film, "The Information Society," produced in 1980 by the Aspen Institute of Humanistic Studies has the premise that as the Agricultural Age was started by the invention of the plow, and the Industrial Revolution by the invention of the cotton gin, so has the computer introduced the "information" age. It predicted that computer-connected employment is the wave of the future. We are only in the beginning phases.

The legal world has already been touched by this new era. Word processing and computer sales are on the increase. Law office management is perhaps the fastest growing field for paralegals. Changes in the legal field have heretofore been infrequent. One does not have to be particularly venturesome to suggest that the computer age will have a far-reaching effect on all our daily lives (not necessarily all to our liking) and that the legal field too will not escape.

CERTIFICATION — LICENSING

Paralegals are not licensed by any state, nor required to be certified in any state.

Arguments pro and con concerning certification are well known in the paralegal field. It appears that the issue of certification will have to be faced, sooner or later, and the outcome will depend upon the interaction of forces and events. But the goals of all paralegals are the same and the writer is confident that, working together, the role of the paralegal will continue to be enhanced. (See Appendix, Examination for Certified Legal Assistant.)

THE FUTURE

As was so aptly put by the late Mr. Justice William O. Douglas in a concurring opinion in *Johnson v. Avery* (1969) 393 U.S. 483, 491-492: "The increasing complexities of our governmental apparatus at both the local and the federal levels have made it difficult for a person to process a claim or even to make a complaint. Social security is a virtual maze; the hierarchy that governs urban housing is often so intricate that it takes an expert to know what agency has jurisdiction over a particular complaint; the office to call or official to see for noise abatement, for a broken sewer line, or a fallen tree is a mystery to many in our metropolitan areas.

"We think of claims as grist for the mill of the lawyers. But it is becoming abundantly clear that more and more of the effort in ferreting out the basis of claims and the agencies responsible for them and in preparing the almost endless paperwork for their prosecution is work for laymen. There are not enough lawyers to manage or supervise all of these affairs; and much of the basic work done requires no special legal talent. Yet there is a closed-shop philosophy in the legal profession that cuts down drastically active roles for laymen. . . .

"That traditional, closed-shop attitude is utterly out of place in the modern world where claims pile high and much of the work of tracing and pursuing them requires the patience and wisdom of a layman rather than the legal skills of a member of the bar."

"It is obvious to those who are familiar with [the paralegal] movement that it is mushrooming throughout the country . . .," writes Edward B. Winn, Esq., Chairman of the Committee on Legal Assistants for Lawyers, in its Annual Report to the State Bar of Texas, ''and it is important that lawyers through their bar associations not be bypassed but continue to maintain the lead in supervising and coordinating such growth and doing the following:

''(1) Educate the lawyer to the concept of the legal assistant and its growing importance in the practice of law;

''(2) Show the lawyer, particularly the small practitioner, how he can utilize such services to improve and expedite the value of his services to his clients at less cost with greater economic return and more leisure to himself. . . .'' (38 Tex. B.J. 593, 595 (June 1975).)

Since this writing, as we shall see in the next chapter, the paralegal field has been steadily and sturdily continuing to grow.

CALIFORNIA PARALEGAL'S GUIDE

Chapter 2

UTILIZATION OF PARALEGALS

Law firms of all sizes have found and are continuing to find, ways to utilize paralegals. If any firms or attorneys have not yet been convinced of the value of a good legal assistant, they should be asked: "Would you like to net a higher profit, eliminate many time-consuming daily tasks, and at the same time provide more efficient legal services for your clients?"

Other firms or lawyers are uncertain whether they can utilize paralegals, or *how* to do it. The first requirement for attorneys is a truly open-minded attitude. Attorneys generally are becoming more open-minded about utilizing legal assistants, but they may not know how to go about fitting them into their offices.

The first question is, "If I *could* delegate some of the work I am doing, would the extra time permit me to take on additional practice?"

If the answer is in the affirmative, the next questions are, "What kinds of work could I delegate to a *qualified* person? Do I really have to do everything I am now doing? Is there not at least *some* portion of every responsibility I could delegate? Which jobs are the most time-consuming?" And dare one suggest a further question: "What am I doing every day, that I'd rather not spend my time doing?" To answer these questions, the attorney must earnestly take a hard look at the problem. If necessary, he must pluck out one by one the duties he can delegate to a legal assistant. Many times has it been said that the good executive is one who can delegate.

This does not mean that the attorney loses control over how his or her work is done — any more than he or she is divested of responsibility for the end product, either by a client or the State Bar. Most experienced attorneys have devised their own methods of procedure and producing particular documents. And this brings us to

13

"systems." The use of "systems" is nothing more than a *recordation of that procedure of the attorney.*

New York attorney Bernard Sternin defines "systems" as a "way of doing something that follows a series of preestablished procedures and uses sets of prerecorded materials, in some prearranged way." In legal work each procedure differs or has particular nuances which must be thought through or worked out in detail. It is possible to systematize pleadings, usual letters, printed forms, instruments, instructions, and other related materials. A review of several closed files will provide material for systems in any field. Once the procedure is reduced to writing, only new ideas, or new procedures dictated by new laws, require changes. Systems can be created to deal with any substantive area of the law, and ordinary and repetitive tasks too, in any field, whether civil litigation, dissolution, probate, estate planning, workers' compensation, corporations, adoptions, and so on.

Systems can take different forms; the office manual, 3-ring binders, automatic typewriters with mag cards, word-processing.

At the time the work is done the problem and the solution seem etched in the mind — one thinks forever — but alas, time is an eraser. But once the attorney has *reduced the procedure to writing,* the next time the same or a similar problem comes up — which may be six months or a year or more later — it is like finding money in the bank. At the very least, giving instructions is easier.

The problem is that law offices are busy places. Time to do this work has to be found, or it will *never* be done. But if someone does it, in the long run the time and money saved is immeasurable. That someone may well be the paralegal — with minimum time from the attorney.

Systems, once established, provide in-house training for the legal assistant, are valuable as a reference and invaluable at the time a new employee is hired.

A reference book, "How to Create-A-System for the Law Office," by R. Ramo, may be obtained from the American Bar Association. This book outlines the steps in systematizing in detail. The American Bar Association has also issued Volume 1 of a two-volume work, "Working with Legal Assistants," which the attorney looking for ways to utilize paralegals will find of great interest.

Having decided upon the duties to be delegated to the paralegal by the attorney, and having embarked on a systems development plan, what now? The next step is to ask all the law office support persons to write a job description of the duties they are performing. With the descriptions, or specifications, in hand, an analysis of the jobs may be made.

If a paralegal is to be hired, which of the attorney's duties can be assigned to the paralegal? If the firm already has a legal assistant, the question should be asked, what additional tasks could he/she be freed from by reassigning them to a secretary or other support person.

The goal of everyone in a law office is the same: efficient, effective legal work; minimum cost to client; reasonable (or maximum?) profit to attorneys; commensurate salaries to support staff. To reach this goal a team approach should be realized. Everyone in the law office is important to its smooth operation. One's own work must be seen as of value and essential — and beyond just providing a living, if the job is to provide satisfaction.

Who needs paralegals? In the smaller firms one finds a belief that they are not large enough to have paralegals. Not so. True, in the larger firms a cursory view may more readily find duties to be delegated. But a closer look will show that the smaller firms need the assistant more than the larger firms. The smaller firm always has a time problem.

James Mize, Sacramento attorney, a sole practitioner, says "I personally believe that paralegals are already and will certainly be an integral part of the functioning of the efficient law office." Antonia Hansen, a Certified Legal Assistant in Santa Rosa, says: "If firms are large enough to take advantage of any of the word processing equipment, then they are large enough to use legal assistants. A mag card machine, if it is properly utilized, has a full-time operator. Anything less is a waste of money. So, the legal assistant coordinates and lays the work out for the mag operator, and the end product is twice the production of that turned out by two secretaries, using two Selectrics, and typing, and retyping and retyping."

Another point to be remembered by the attorney is that the good paralegal will *find* the work in the office that he/she can do. The attorney should, of course, permit the legal assistant to do such work if he/she has confidence in the legal assistant's capabilities.

The following pages of this chapter are devoted to the specific duties being performed by paralegals. Most all fields are covered in the charts, but by no means does this show all the work that can be done by legal assistants. Attorneys should nevertheless be able to get ideas for their own utilization of legal assistants. And the legal assistant should gain a better idea of what he/she might be expected to do when working in a particular field.

WHAT DO THEY DO IN A LAW OFFICE?

Legal Secretaries

Type correspondence
Take dictation, type dictated tapes
Type up forms based on attorneys' direction
Keep files up
File papers with proper court
Do not practice law
Receptionist
Meets, handles clients
Keep calendar for attorney
Keep time records
Make appointments
Keep appointment record

Paralegal or Legal Assistant

Interview clients
Research case law; Write memoranda
Attend depositions; Write briefs
Keep files up; Investigate
Prepare exhibits for trial
Do not practice law
Go to court with the attorney: keep track of case; check jury
A trained non-lawyer working under direction and supervision of a lawyer,
Design, develop, modify procedures, techniques, services, processes; prepare and interpret legal documents
Research, select, assess, compile, use information from law library
Analyze, handle procedural problems
May specialize in some area of law-litigation, probate, etc
Draft interrogatories, analyze transcripts of testimony
Index documents for trial
Keep records, inventories, accountings in probate
Prepare tax returns, deeds, contracts
Office accounting; Arrange escrows
Does NOT take dictation, type for others
Responsible only for his/her work/not supervisory/ keeps own calendar only
May not type (or know how to)

Law Clerk

Research cases
Shepardize cases
Investigate
Do not practice law
Go to court with attorney: check jury lists keep track of case
A trained (or intraining) lawyer working under a practicing lawyer
Write briefs
Take depositions
Interview clients

Law Office Administrator

Hire, fire staff
Manage finances
Set budget
Handle payroll
Do not practice law
Supervise billing, accts receivable, payable

Handle attorney time/cost sheets
Purchasing agent
Manage office, library or supervise
Set budget
Supervise staffs' set policies for non-lawyer employee
Keep trust accounts
Negotiate office space, furniture, phones, equipment
Set up office manual
Work with partners on policies, expenses
Set up files, or open files
Develop and improve systems

FUNCTION OF PARALEGAL

Complex Litigation

Some litigation paralegals work in firms which handle complex litigation involving large numbers of documents.

Paralegals who work on the complex litigation cases are generally part of a team composed of a senior partner-supervising attorney, one or two associates and one, two or several paralegals, depending on the magnitude of the discovery. Paralegal duties include drafting sets of interrogatories and responding to interrogatories, attending document productions, indexing, categorizing and analyzing documents in the context of the legal issues involved in the case, developing chronologies of events, preparing witness books for depositions and trial, summarizing, indexing and cross-referencing deposition transcripts, preparing exhibits and trial books, monitoring exhibits at trial, summarizing and analyzing trial transcripts while the trial is ongoing, and drafting the notice of appeal.

Types of cases involved might be antitrust suits, environmental lawsuits, shareholders' versus corporations, suits contractual suits for fraud, labor law, and others.

Paralegals are assigned to a case on a long-term basis and the knowledge gained of the case makes him-her invaluable at time of trial or hearing, or settlement of the case. They work with the attorney as a team.

Paralegals organize the bulk of evidentiary documents, which may comprise thousands of pages, and hundreds of pages of deposition transcripts — compiled over an extended period of time, maybe two to four years or longer. They index these documents, review and summarize them. Writing skills and analytical and problem-solving skills are most important in this work. Exercise of independent judgment is required a great deal of the time; the first-class legal assistant is increasingly being given more varied responsibilities.

As the computer becomes increasingly important for managing complex litigation, paralegals may be used to code documents into the computer, to supervise clerks who do the coding, and to work with the computer programmer to design the system for the litigation. Responsibility for designing the computer system would be delegated to an experienced lead litigation paralegal.

SUGGESTED DUTIES OF A PARALEGAL IN A COMPLEX CASE*

A. *Fact Research.* One of the most valuable contributions a paralegal can make to a complex case is the gathering of facts. The primary method of fact research is to review various sources of information in order to cull out facts that may be useful in the preparation of preliminary motions or ultimate preparation of the case for trial. This research could include review and summary of existing files and transcripts of depositions; review of documents produced or copied during discovery; research in public libraries; or even in-field observations of factual situations. It could also include such things as reviewing a client's correspondence files to find all letters on a particular subject; or reviewing trade journals to see if the president of a trade association has made any public statements on a particular subject. For any complex case there are many different bodies of information which contain facts potentially helpful to the plaintiff's or the defendant's case. The professional paralegal is well suited to the task of review and identification of these facts.

B. *Document Organization.* Most complex cases involve hundreds of thousands, and sometimes millions, of documents. These can include correspondence, computer printouts, invoices, photographs, magazines, contracts, or just about anything. One task that might be assigned to a paralegal is to help collect these documents and organize them in some rational system so individual documents can later be retrieved from the total collection with a minimum of effort. Here the paralegal functions much like a librarian. As the attorneys and others working on the case collect documents, the paralegal can be responsible for receiving them, identifying where they came from and when, cataloguing, and then organizing them in file folders, or in boxes, or transferring the information to some electronic data storage system.

If documents are to be put in some electronic storage system, the paralegal is a logical candidate to perform this task. A paralegal can be particularly useful if documents are to be summarized, either in connection with a transfer to an electronic storage system or as part of a manual system.

At some stage of the collection process the paralegal might also be charged with the responsibility of identifying and segregating doc-

*Excerpted from "Complex Litigation and the Role of the Legal Assistant in the Preparation of a Case for Trial," by John H. L'Estrange, Jr., and Charles W. Melville, November-December 1979, "Facts & Findings," published by the National Association of Legal Assistants and reprinted with their permission.

uments which are subject to the attorney-client privilege or the work product doctrine, or some other special handling requirement.

Despite efforts of paralegals to make the document process proceed smoothly, complex cases with many documents seem to spawn arguments among the lawyers about the production process. Frequently a party serves a formal request for the production and inspection of documents in the possession of another party in the case. After the production is completed, the party who made the original request then claims that certain documents were not included in the production, and that the whole process should be repeated, or that the producing party should be ordered to pay sanctions (usually in the form of a monetary fine or penalty) because he failed to fully comply with the written demand. The paralegals who were involved in the original production of documents are usually caught in the middle of these disputes. Sometimes they are even required to sign affidavits which are filed in court in connection with discovery motions.

Paralegals can be very helpful to the attorney who represents the party who is producing documents. They are usually charged with the responsibility of interviewing secretaries and other employees at the client's offices to make sure all documents which are responsive to the formal document request are gathered at the office where the inspection is to take place. During the inspection they are responsible for keeping the client's original files intact, especially when these files are used in the client's day to day operations. The paralegal also keeps an accurate record of exactly what the other side looks at, and what is copied. When the inspection is completed and after the copies have been made, the paralegal sees to it that the files are returned to the client.

Paralegals who work for the inspecting party have an equally important responsibility. They should maintain a record of everything produced and, if appropriate, the identity of the file it came from. After the inspection is completed, the paralegal for the inspecting party is responsible for verifying that all designated information was actually copied.

C. *Exhibit Organization.* Exhibits are nothing more than documents which have been selected for use during the pretrial proceedings, usually in depositions, and which ultimately may be introduced into evidence at the trial. This process of selecting exhibits from all the documents in a case is not something that should be put off until the eve of a deposition or a trial. The ideal way to handle the organization of exhibits is to reach an agreement with all parties in the case to use a uniform system for the identification of exhibits throughout the pretrial and the trial of a case. This means that once a document is marked as an exhibit at a deposition, at a pretrial evidentiary hearing, at the trial, or any other time during the case, the exhibit would be added to a master exhibit list; and it will always have the same number in any further proceedings in the case.

If such a uniform system of exhibit organization is used in a case, then the paralegal in that case can play a very important role in setting up and maintaining that system. His principal job is to collect and mark the exhibits as they are identified, and to coordinate with the paralegals who work for other attorneys on the case to make sure that everyone has the same set of documents with the same set of exhibit numbers.

Later at the trial, if the uniform system has been followed, the handling of exhibits and the presentation of documentary evidence should proceed very smoothly. The only exhibit responsibilities the paralegal will then have to worry about during the actual trial is to keep an accurate daily record of the exhibits offered and admitted into evidence and the rulings on objections. At the end of each day or week, the paralegal who is in the courtroom can coordinate with the paralegals for the other parties, and the deputy courtroom clerk, to make sure that everyone is in agreement on the exhibit rulings by the judge.

Civil Litigation

The civil litigation field is wide and varied, encompassing the countless pleadings and procedures in a civil action that may ensue from the time the client first comes into the office, through trial to judgment and collection and possibly an appeal, in many different types of actions. Under the general supervision and control of a lawyer, the paralegal should be familiar with and able to draft or prepare all legal documents involved, including proposed interrogatories and replies to interrogatories; digest transcripts of depositions and trial testimony; and index documents and exhibits for trial. During the initial interviewing the paralegal can take statements from clients and obtain information needed to prepare the required documents which provide the attorney with preliminary information. The paralegal can also aid in investigation and discovery work.

Function of Paralegal
Civil Litigation

Paralegal	Attorney
	Initial interview and advice to client; refer to legal assistant
Initial interview with client; gathering facts; analysis; checking statute of limitations	
Drafting pleadings	Review pleadings
Arranging for signature, filing and service; having copies conformed; calendaring	
Instructions to client and keeping him informed; conduct investigation; obtain documentary evidence; taking witnesses' statements	Review evidence
Draft documents for discovery: interrogatories, requests for admissions (or responses); draft questions for depositions; arranging for depositions and giving requisite notices	General instructions to legal assistant for discovery

Prepare for and take depositions |
Taking notes on testimony; summarizing depositions	
Prepare any motions required	Consider filing of any appropriate motions
Setting for trial, pretrial	Attend settlement conference; trial setting conference; pretrial conference
Legal research for any trial briefs and/or drafting briefs	Reviewing drafts of any trial briefs and finalizing briefs
Preparation for trial: notifying client, giving notice of trial, exhibits, evidence, witnesses, subpoenas, investigation of jurors	Review evidence and witnesses' statements; prepare for trial
Draft findings of fact if requested (or objections) and proposed Judgment	Review documents

Paralegal	**Attorney**
	Initial interview and advice to client; refer to legal assistant
Prepare Notice of Entry of Judgment and serve	
Prepare memo of costs (or objections)	
Prepare motion for new trial or notice of appeal if decided upon	Consider new trial motion if losing party (or prepare to oppose new trial motion)
If judgment for your client, obtain payment of judgment or arrange to levy execution; examination of debtor if necessary	Sign any notice of appeal
If appeal taken, legal research for appellate briefs	Finalize appellate briefs
Serve and file briefs within time limits	
	Prepare for and make oral argument
Draft any petition for rehearing or petition for hearing in Supreme Court, within time limits	Review draft of petition for rehearing or petition for hearing; finalize, sign
	Make oral argument

The above outline is not all-comprehensive. Litigation may extend for a number of years and require any number of pleadings, motions, and other filings. The above should serve to give a general idea of the role of the paralegal in civil litigation. See also the Function of Paralegal chart for Personal Injury actions, which are also civil litigation.

Personal Injury

Litigation paralegals who work in personal injury and insurance defense firms may work for a team comprised of attorneys and paralegals, or they may work alone where the work is task-oriented. Paralegals are mostly utilized in the discovery phase, especially with regard to propounding and answering interrogatories, noticing depositions, ordering medical records, summarizing medical records, summarizing depositions and preparing trial books.

Some litigation-oriented law firms specialize in such areas as medical malpractice, legal malpractice, aviation law, maritime law, and products liability. In those firms paralegals have also specialized and become paralegal litigation specialists where, in addition to the duties described above, they may also, at the lead attorney's discretion, prepare drafts of complaints, answers to complaints, demurrers and accompanying points and authorities, dismissals, and statements of damages. The latter responsibilities fall to experienced paralegals and are generated from cases which are highly specialized, allowing the paralegal to develop expertise in a narrow area of the law. For example, in the area of medical malpractice, paralegals, in addition to the duties mentioned above, are trained to review medical records for potential liability, locate and preliminarily interview expert witnesses and do medical library research concerning medico-legal issues.

Function of Paralegal
Personal Injury

This chart is intended only to give a general idea of the paralegal's function. The duties of the legal assistant in personal injury cases is in large part typical of the legal assistant's duties in any civil litigation lawsuit. The division of duties between the paralegal and the attorney will differ from law firm to law firm. The duties are not necessarily performed in the order given here, and all the documents referred to would not necessarily be required in a given action.

Some of the duties listed for the legal assistant should where feasible be delegated to other personnel in the larger law firms, or divided among a number of paralegals, to provide adequate time for the legal assistant to perform such tasks as legal research.

Again, local practice rules should always be checked.

Paralegal	Attorney for Plaintiff
Obtain from client all the facts of the accident (using comprehensive checklist)	Meet with client. Assess case and decide whether to accept
Give instructions for opening case file and starting a docket sheet	Have client sign retainer agreement specifying fee and complete agreement as to fee, expenses, etc.
Check on applicable statute of limitations, and time for filing claim if governmental agency involved	Explain to client collectible items of special damages and principal issues determining liability, collection, etc.

Paralegal

Give instructions to client and advise him of general procedure. Instruct client to advise of any change in address, phone number, employment, physical health, and to keep itemized record of his expenses.

Obtain client's signature on forms to obtain hospital and medical records and information from any governmental agency involved, and explain necessity of forms to client

Caution against signing any papers relating to the case or discussing the case with adverse party, investigator, witnesses or anyone

Write for accident report

Write to hospital for medical records

Write to attending physician for medical report and billing

Check with employer re loss of wages

Send letters to witnesses requesting statement or interview witnesses (by phone or in person)

Collect bills and lists of expenses

Collect photos and information as to insurance policies

Arrange for estimates of car repairs if car has not been repaired

Notify plaintiff if defendant has arranged for independent medical examination of plaintiff

Attorney for Plaintiff

Give general instructions to legal assistant as to any special problems involved in case

Paralegal	Attorney for Plaintiff
Follow progress of plaintiff's physical health; obtain any supplemental reports indicated	
Keep record of court costs	
If governmental agency involved, file notice of claim within prescribed period	
If plaintiff is a minor, prepare petition for guardian ad litem and order appointing guardian ad litem	Review and sign petition for guardian ad litem, obtain ex parte order appointing guardian ad litem
	Attend any criminal hearing with client
Arrange for investigator if so instructed	Discuss with legal assistant summary of all investigatory reports and determine whether further information or legal research on legal questions involved is needed; make determination whether to employ investigator; give general instructions re complaint
Determine jurisdiction, venue, parties, and dictate complaint and review	
Have client come in to read complaint and sign verification	
Give instructions for filing and for service	Review complaint in final form and sign
Send letter of representation to insurance carrier (if not done earlier)	Initial contact with insurance company to discuss settlement — discuss offers with client
Prepare plaintiff's response to any requests for amount of damages or, if none made, notify defendant of amount pursuant to Code Civ. Proc. §425.11	Fix amount of damages to be claimed
	Determine discovery to be done, interrogatories, dispositions, etc.
Draft interrogatories and serve	
Review answers and draft any requests for admission, and any responses	Review answers to interrogatories and responses to request for admission

Paralegal	**Attorney for Plaintiff**
Review responses to requests for admission and draft questions for any depositions desired by attorney	Take any depositions of witnesses or adverse party
If deposition of plaintiff to be taken, notify plaintiff of time and place; if deposition of defendant or witnesses to be taken, arrange for reporter, prepare and serve and file any notices and subpoenas required	
Summarize depositions, interrogatories and responses to requests for admission	
Draft any motions and points and authorities decided upon by attorney, and opposition to any motions filed by defendant	Determine any motions to be filed by plaintiff and give general instructions for preparation
Serve and file a Memorandum That Civil Case Is At Issue ("At Issue" Memorandum)	Appear in court at hearings on any demurrer or motions filed
Review file and consult with attorney re desirability of arbitration. If arbitration decided upon, prepare Election-Stipulation for Arbitration	Consult with legal assistant re arbitration Determine desirability of Arbitration
(If required in county in which action pending, after notice from clerk (CRC Rule 221(e)), file Certificate of Readiness within 20 days after mailing of clerk's notice (Certificate of Readiness is required in S.F., L.A., not in Sac.; check local rules)	
In Sac: Upon receipt of Notice of Trial Setting Conference calendar settlement conference; upon receipt of Trial Setting Conference Order, calendar trial date	
Organize file for settlement conference; update special damages	

Paralegal	**Attorney for Plaintiff**
Notify client of settlement conference date and arrange for client to attend	Attend settlement conference with client
Notify client of trial date and arrange for client to discuss case with attorney before trial	
Confirm trial date to defendant's attorney	

If case not settled:

Notify plaintiff's witnesses of trial date	
Arrange for any expert witnesses desired	Consider use of expert witnesses
Draft a statement of matters agreed upon and statement of factual and legal contentions	Discuss with opposing counsel matters to be agreed upon
Subpoena hospital bills and records by serving custodian	
Give instructions for preparation of subpoenas and subpoena duces tecum for witnesses; review same	
Subpoena adverse party if attendance desired (CCP 1987(b)). If case settled, draft release and request for dismissal. If plaintiff is a minor, obtain court approval of compromise	Advise legal assistant if adverse party to be supoenaed
Arrange for any jury investigative service desired	
Draft voir dire questions for jurors if desired by attorney	Instruct re any jury investigative service desired
Research for trial briefs on issues determined by attorney	Consider issues for trial briefs; finalize trial briefs
Prepare jury instructions	Review jury instructions
Draft proposed findings of fact and conclusions of law and judgment upon information from attorney; serve and mail to court	Review findings and judgment before presentment to court

Paralegal	**Attorney for Plaintiff**
	Prepare for, and hold trial
Serve and file notice of entry of judgment	
Prepare memorandum of costs and serve and file	Review and sign memorandum of costs
	If plaintiff prevails, prepare documents needed to comply; if defendant obtains judgment, decide whether to file motion for new trial and grounds
Draft motion for new trial if attorney wants new trial; serve and file	Decide whether new trial is in order and if so, instruct re grounds for motion
If new trial granted, prepare order	

If appeal is to be taken:

Draft notice of appeal	Review and sign notice of appeal
Serve and file notice of appeal within time limit	Discuss contents of record on appeal with legal assistant
Research for Appellant's Opening Brief and later Appellant's Reply Brief if filed	Finalize appellate briefs
Prepare, serve and file briefs within time limits	Prepare for and make oral argument

If appeal to Court of Appeal unsuccessful:

	Consider filing of petition for hearing in the Supreme Court; consider grounds for further appeal; instructions re petition for rehearing to legal assistant
Draft petition for rehearing; serve and file	Review draft of petition for rehearing; finalize, sign
	If petition for rehearing denied, decide whether to file petition for hearing, and advise legal assistant
Draft petition for hearing in Supreme Court	Finalize and sign petition for hearing in the Supreme Court
	Prepare for and make oral argument

Probate

Probate practice especially, requires a great deal of detailed paper work which is very time-consuming. To participate in the administration of estates the paralegal must become proficient in record-keeping, preparation of inventories and appraisements, valuation of assets, accountings, various petitions, real estate sales, summary administration of estates, distribution and closing of estates, forms to transfer stock and motor vehicles, applications for social security benefits and life insurance proceeds.

Probate work also involves the preparation of federal and state inheritance and income tax returns, fiduciary and individual. The greater the paralegal's expertise in taxation, the more invaluable the services to the firm. In large firms the tax work may be reviewed by, and the paralegal may need to consult, lawyers who are also tax experts.

Function of Paralegal
Probate (Estates)

In a typical estate, the legal assistant might be expected to perform the functions listed below. In a very large estate, or in a will contest proceeding, many other pleadings or procedures are usually necessary.

The functions of a legal assistant in a conservatorship or guardianship proceeding are similar.

Paralegal	**Attorney**
Interview with representative and collection of information	Initial interview with client
Have copies of will (if any) prepared. Mail decedent's will for filing	
Obtain certified copies of the death certificate	
Prepare petition for probate of will (or for letters of administration)	Review petition
Prepare Notice of Death and deliver to clerk	
Deliver conformed copy to newspaper for publication and obtain copies from newspaper for mailing, and mail to heirs, legatees, devisees	
Prepare and file declaration of mailing	
Check whether newspaper filed affidavit of publication	
If probating a will, arrange for testimony or affidavit or declaration of subscribing witness or witnesses, or deposition; if witness or his affidavit or declaration can't be produced, obtain proof	
Obtain application for surety bond and have petitioner sign, and arrange for issuance of surety company bond (unless representative furnishing)	Fix amount and type of bond to be issued

Paralegal	Attorney
Before hearing on petition for probate of will, prepare order admitting will to probate and letters testamentary, order appointing inheritance tax referee, letters testamentary; if hearing on petition for letters of administration, prepare order appointing administrator, letters of administration, and order appointing inheritance tax referee	Attend hearing for appointment of representative, have orders signed.
After hearing, publish Notice of Death; check on filing of affidavit of publication within 30-day period	
Obtain certified copies of letters testamentary (or letters of administration) needed in assisting representative to open estate bank account, safe-deposit box, transfer money, etc.	
Prepare inventory and appraisement except for value of items to be appraised; transmit to referee (if appointed, otherwise State Controller) with copy of will, IT-22 or IT-20 and IT-3 if required	Review inventory and appraisement and other forms to be delivered to referee
If securities to be sold, arrange for transfer	Consult with representative as to sale of securities if necessary or desirable
Review creditors' claims as received, present to representative for approval, then transmit to court; if claims rejected, prepare and serve Notice of Rejection	Instruct legal assistant re creditors' claims and review any questionable claims
Furnish representative with copies of pleadings as filed	
File Notice of Fuanciary Relationship and Application of Employer Identification number if Form 706 required	

Paralegal	**Attorney**
Prepare Form 706 (federal estate tax) if required, unless accountant is to prepare	Give instructions to legal assistant re Form 706, if required; decide whether to use alternative valuation date; review 706 in final form
Prepare decedent's final income tax returns and later fiduciary income tax returns or get data from representative for accountant to prepare; consult with attorney and accountant (if any) re fiduciary income tax periods	Consult with accountant (if any) and representative as to tax consequences to beneficiaries, in choosing periods of returns
Arrange for any sales of real property	Consult with representative and accountant (if any) as to any sales of real property
Prepare annual accountings (or First and Final Account and Petition for Distribution); mail requisite notices; compute fees	
Prepare order settling account (and for distribution if final account)	Attend hearings on accountings and for distribution, present orders for signature
Arrange with representative for distribution, payment of fees	Give legal assistant any special instructions on distribution
Prepare receipts of distributees to accompany checks of representative	
Prepare Affidavit for Final Discharge and Decree of Final Discharge; have representative sign Affidavit and arrange for judge's signature of Decree	
Notify bonding company of discharge	
Prepare Notice of Termination of Fiduciary Relationship and mail to IRS	

Corporations

Corporate legal work involves many diverse functions; to develop expertise in this specialty field requires extensive training and experience. Some legal assistants experienced in corporate work are setting up their own offices and operating independently, representing attorneys both in and out of state. Functions which the corporate legal assistant might perform include but are not limited to the following: consultation with incorporators concerning the details of organizing new corporations and preparation and execution of the many documents required, such as articles of incorporation, waivers and consents and by-laws, minutes of first meeting of directors, first meeting of incorporators, bank account resolutions, stock certificates, notices, and miscellaneous agreements; various other work such as preparation and filing of annual statements; amendment of articles of incorporation or by-laws; assisting in public sale of securities; qualifying corporations to do business in California or other states; qualifying corporations in foreign jurisdictions; legal research; updating corporate legislation; investigation of and extraction of information from corporate records and documents; obtaining financial data; drafting of various documents and assisting generally in mergers of corporations; dissolution of corporations. In public sector community work the corporate legal assistant helps groups that are in the process of organizing; encourages and assists the organization of the group either on a short-term basis as for a class action or on a long-term basis; and examines public records for lawsuits against particular corporations, among other duties.

Function of Paralegal
Corporations

Paralegal	Attorney
	Preliminary interview with client and perhaps accountant and advice re incorporation, expenses, fees and costs
Interview with client and attorney to obtain needed information	Interview with client and legal assistant; discuss possible names for corporation; incorporators, etc.
Check with Secretary of State on availability of corporate name; reserve name, send fee	
Draft Articles of Incorporation; make appointment with clients for signing	Review draft of Articles of Incorporation
Appointment with client at time of signing Articles	Appointment with client (incorporators or board of directors) for signing Articles; waiver of notice, adoption of bylaws; election of officers; adoption of stock certificates, seal, fix place of business, bank resolution, issuance of shares, Subchapter S election
Send Articles of Incorporation to Secretary of State for filing, with fee; order certified copies	
When returned, conform copies with date of filing (file stamp on first page)	
Order corporate outfit (the kit may contain seal, bylaws, waiver, minutes, minute book, stock certificates, book and stock ledger; Notice of Issuance of Share of Stock)	
If offering securities for sale, file Application for Qualification of Securities; include Consent to	

Paralegal	**Attorney**
Service of Process if a non-California corporation	
Prepare Notice of Issuance of Shares of Stock and file with Corporation Commissioner, with declaration	Sign Notice of Issuance of Shares of Stock
Draft Subchapter S Election and Consent of Shareholders	Review Subchapter S Election and Consent
Prepare minutes of first meeting of board of directors	Review minutes
Send Subchapter S Election to IRS and Statement to Secretary of State	
Draft transmittal letter for attorney of various documents, i.e., bylaws, minutes, stock certificates, Subchapter S Election, Statement, etc.	Review and sign transmittal letter and documents
Prepare a calendar for corporation as reminder	
Draft any later amendments of Articles of Incorporation or By-laws	Review any amendments
Prepare annual statements unless corporation doing its own	Review annual statement

Other Miscellaneous Duties
of the Corporate Paralegal

Draft documents for dissolution of corporations

Draft necessary documents to qualify corporations to do business in California or other states

Qualify corporations in foreign jurisdictions

Legal research

Update legislation affecting corporations

Other Miscellaneous Duties
of the Corporate Paralegal

Peruse corporation records and
documents and extract information therefrom

Obtain financial data

Draft various documents and
assist generally in mergers of
corporations

Criminal Law Procedure

In the field of criminal law the paralegal should be cognizant of
rights with regard to detention, entry, searches, arrests, bail, arraignment and hearings, plea bargaining, trials, probation, incarceration and
appeals.

Legal assistants can be valuable in jury investigation. During trial
they can assist in scheduling the witnesses and explaining to them the
developments of the trial, the controversies, the significance of points
in question. They can also conduct investigation of a criminal case;
can interview the defendant; develop recommendations to be made to
court as to alternatives to incarceration; make arguments for diversion
out of the criminal justice system to mental health system; do legal
research on parole and sentencing; and assist in bail reduction hearings.
They can also investigate grounds for litigation.

Law Office Administration

Law office administrators might have responsibility for staffing
— interviewing, hiring, training and supervision of nonlawyer personnel, setting salaries, overtime policy, holidays; assignments, work
distribution and workflow; docketing control; calendaring of court
dates and deadline dates for filing pleadings; process serving; timekeeping by attorneys and paralegals and billing of clients for their
services; collection of accounts; maintaining books on partners' accounts, trust accounts of clients and employees' accounts; inventorying
and purchasing office supplies and establishing procedures for budg-
etary control; maintaining personnel records; negotiation for space and
office equipment; purchase and maintenance of office equipment (typewriters, copying services, furniture); conferring with partners re policies and expenditures and for opening files and for file room maintenance; library management; checklists for interviewing and handling
different types of cases; setting up office manual; analysis of systems
and procedures. In short, the expert administrator can increase profits

of the law office by freeing the attorney from administrative chores to practice law and increase billable time.

The burgeoning use of word processors, computers and other electronic equipment makes one venture to guess that this may be the fastest area of growth for paralegals in the eighties.

Real Estate Law

As a real estate specialist the paralegal might handle preparation of deeds, deeds of trust, leases and contracts of purchase and sale; mortgages; make financial arrangements; arrange for escrows; and prepare actions to quiet title and foreclosure actions. The paralegal deals with brokers, escrow and title insurance companies, lenders, the Division of Real Estate, and municipal and other regulatory bodies. A knowledge of zoning laws, governmental regulations, covenants, conditions and easements, security instruments, and economic feasibility and tax consequences is needed.

Accounting

In a small or medium-sized firm a paralegal's duties might include accounting; in a larger firm the paralegal is apt to be a fulltime legal accountant. The duties might include issuance of salary checks, payment of social security, unemployment and disability insurance taxes; billing of clients; making deposits and writing checks on clients' accounts and partnership accounts; issuance of checks in payment of bills for rent, telephone, supplies, insurance, maintenance and repairs, dues and associations, entertainment, property taxes, postage meters; collection of bad debts; collection of costs recoverable on judgment, requiring knowledge of costs recoverable as court costs; preparation of trial balances, profit and loss statements and income tax returns.

FUNCTION OF PARALEGAL

The following pages contain more charts describing paralegal functions in a variety of civil actions.

Function of Paralegal
Independent Adoption

Paralegal	Attorney
Collect certified copies of documents verifying current marriages, previous marriages, and any dissolution of marriage of the adopting parents, and of the natural parent who claims custody of the child	Initial interview with adopting parents
Prepare release of natural mother	If representing both adopting parents and natural parent or parents, obtain consent from both (Civ. Code §225m)
Draft petition for adoption, agreement for adoption, and decree of adoption	Interview with parents advising re the investigation of the agency
Prepare a citation if required under Civil Code section 224 and serve on any nonconsenting natural parent	Obtain signature to release by natural mother (and presumptive father)
Draft transmittal letter to State Department of Social Services	Review drafts of petition, agreement and decree
Prepare itemized Declaration and Report of Expenses of petitioner (Civ. Code §224r)	Sign transmittal letter after reviewing documents collected
Draft transmittal letter to State Department of Social Services on county adoption agency	Review report when received from Department of Social Services
Write letter to client advising of hearing date, with instructions	Interview with adopting parents before court hearing
Obtain new birth certificate and send to Department of Vital Statistics	Appearance at hearing with adopting parents and child. Obtain signature to Agreement of Adoption and of Decree of Adoption
Prepare closing letter to client, with bill	

Function of Paralegal
Arbitration Proceedings in Superior Court — Plaintiff
(Check local rules for variances)

Paralegal	Attorney for Plaintiff
Review the file and consider: 1. Whether the arbitration award could exceed $15,000 2. Length of time since complaint was filed; if nearing 5 years, advise attorney 3. Whether investigation and discovery are complete 4. Documentary evidence 5. Time required for arbitration hearing	Review file and decide whether to file an election for arbitration or attempt to obtain a stipulation for arbitration, or neither
After consultation with attorney prepare election — stipulation for arbitration, if attorney decides to submit to arbitration	
Prepare letter to arbitration committee or administrator	Choose arbitrator or decide to ask for submission of names
File Plaintiff's election — stipulation for arbitration	
Prepare documents needed for further discovery (subpoenas, interrogatories, requests for admission)	Determine further discovery
When arbitrator-administrator checks for hearing dates, check calendar for possible hearing dates	
Consider with attorney: 1. Length of time the case would take for trial	Review case before hearing
2. Whether liability of the defendant is clear. Is it a case of simple negligence or is there culpability on the part of defendant?	Discuss amount of award with client Attend hearing
3. Amount to be offered to settle	
If award not acceptable to attorney, file request for trial within 20 days.	Review award. Decide whether acceptable

Function of Paralegal
Bankruptcy

Paralegal	Attorney
Initial interview with client with attorney	Initial interview with client
Give client questionnaire for data for filing	
Interview client to review questionnaire for completeness, get signature	
Confirm client's information discreetly	Review information with paralegal
Draft formal petition, statement, financial assets, liabilities	
Prepare formal pleadings for signing	
Act as creditor contact	
Inform debtor of first creditors' meeting	Advise on creditor contact
Prepare debtor for meeting	Prepare debtor for creditor's examination.
Keep informed of debtor's contacts with creditors	
Consult with debtor on debt reaffirmation agreement	Advise debtor on agreement
Monitor and aid in liquidating estate's assets if such action is necessary	

Paralegal Employed by Trustee

Review debtor's statement of affairs	Supervise case, direct paralegal
Collect cash held by debtor or other	
Send letters to banks, landlords, others to notify of bankruptcy, trustee appointment and request to turn over monies to trustee	

Paralegal	Attorney
Keep track of transfers of property	
Notify trustee of issues invoking trustee's powers; prepare pleadings if necessary	Confer on use of powers to act
Analyze property and best way to sell: prepare ads, find proper publications, appoint auctioneer if public sale	Reduce property to money by sale
Prepare accounting of each sale	Submit to court final report
Review creditors' claims, establish dispute basis, if any	Prepare pleadings
Notify trustee if bar to discharge	Oppose discharge if appropriate
Act as litigation paralegal	In litigation name attorney to act in trial
Prepare final proof of claim	
Determine if claim is secured; if so, determine collateral status	If Chap. 11 or 13, have paralegal monitor business' operation

Function of Paralegal
Dissolutions
(Uncontested)

Paralegal	Attorney for Petitioner
Initial interview with client. Complete detailed fact sheet	Initial interview with client. If case accepted, present retainer agreement to client for signature (or study). Discuss all aspects of fee
Deposit fee in client's trust fund for collection	
Have client prepare list of separate, community and quasi-community property, including retirement plans, life insurance and social security entitlement	Discuss source of properties owned by petitioner and respondent
Collect client's income tax returns	Collect retainer fee
	Instruct client on effect of reconciliation, etc.
Arrange for appraisal of any real property needed. (S.F. and L.A. can use inheritance tax referees, Sac. separate appraisers)	
Prepare Petition (Family Law), Summons (Family Law). Consider alternative of nullity, and joinder. If joinder, prepare Notice of Declaration re Joinder (Family Law). (If joinder of pension plan, use form in Rule 1291.15)	Review Petition (Family Law), Property Declaration and Income and Expense Declaration, and other documents prepared
	Attend any hearing on motion for joinder
Prepare Confidential Counseling Statement (mandatory in counties with conciliation court) (If in L.A. branch court, file Certificate of Assignment form) If custody action: Declaration under Uniform Custody of Minors Act	
If child support, spousal support, attorneys' fees or restraining order requested, prepare Order to Show Cause, also Application for Order and Declaration in Support of Order to show Cause, and	

Paralegal	Attorney for Petitioner
Property and Income and Expense Declaration	
Obtain judge's signature on Order to Show Cause	
Arrange for service of Petition (Family Law) and Summons (Family Law) and any of the above papers prepared. If Order to Show Cause signed, serve endorsed copy of same and supporting documents, 3 blank copies of Responsive Declaration, copy of Property Declaration and Income and Expense Declaration, and 1 blank copy Confidential Counseling Statement if used in County. Serve at least 10 days before hearing and if temporary restraining order granted, hearing on request for preliminary injunction must be not later than 15 days after order signed or 20 days upon good cause	File order granting temporary relief
	Counsel client re purpose of court procedure and significance of action taken; explain that Order to Show Cause can be decided on pleadings
	Consult with client in preparation for hearing, and attend hearing
File proof of service of above papers upon completion of service	
Calendar due date for Response (Family Law) (30 days from date of service)	
Send clients copy of all documents	
Arrange for any continuances (stipulation to keep any restraining order in effect)	
Record lis pendens if real property affected	
If children, instruct client to keep record of spouse's visits to children	

Paralegal	Attorney for Petitioner
Send regular bills to client	Give instructions for billing to legal assistant
Review Response (Family Law) or, if none filed, prepare Request to Enter Default (Family Law)	Review Response (Family Law)
File Marital Settlement Agreement (if not attached to petition) (should be acknowledged)	With client and counsel, arrive at terms of Marital Settlement Agreement, give instructions for preparation, and final review
Notify client when he is to appear, where he will meet attorney, etc.	
If stipulated judgment, answer must be acknowledged (in Sac. County) (Check local rules)	Transfer property as per agreement
Prepare Request to Enter Default (Family Law) and Request for Default Setting (in L.A.); arrange for entry of default. Check local rules re hearing	
or	
If Response (Family Law) and stipulation for judgment (Rule 1287) served and filed, set for hearing (Check local rules)	
Notify client of hearing date	
Before hearing prepare Interlocutory Judgment of Dissolution of Marriage and Notice of Entry of Default	
Notify client of hearing date	Prepare for hearing and attend hearing with client, present Interlocutory Judgment for signature of judge
Have respondent served with copy of Interlocutory Judgment	
Furnish client with copy of Interlocutory Judgment	
Record Interlocutory Judgment if real property affected	

Paralegal	**Attorney for Petitioner**
Calendar date on which Final Judgment may be obtained	
Prepare Request and Declaration for Final Judgment of Dissolution of Marriage, with Final Judgment (Family Law) and Notice of Entry of Judgment (Family Law)	
Have documents signed by judge, mail copy to respondent, furnish copy to client	

Dissolutions
(Contested)

In addition to the duties listed in the above uncontested cases:

Paralegal	Attorney for Petitioner
Prepare Memorandum That Civil Case Is At Issue and (in S.F. and L.A. and any county where required) Certificate of Readiness. In Sac: Upon receipt of Notice of Trial Setting Conference calendar settlement conference; upon receipt of Trial Setting Conference Order, calendar trial date	Prepare for and attend any hearing on motion to strike, quash or transfer filed by respondent
Arrange for any depositions and required notices	Take and review any depositions
Prepare subpoenas of any witnesses for trial	
Prepare and serve Notice of Trial unless pretrial held and determined at pretrial or trial setting conference	Attend trial setting conference and settlement conference
	Keep record of settlement negotiations. Dictate memoranda to file
Prepare property list for attorney to use in court	Review pleadings and inventory before trial. Discuss agreed statement with opposing counsel. Attempt to obtain agreement in division of assets. Examine data prepared by client. Determine whether children working when child support requested
After interlocutory prepare papers to place residence in tenancy in common and stipulate that it is community property if appropriate	Prepare for and present case at trial
Have respondent served with copy of Interlocutory Judgment and furnish client with copy	

Paralegal	**Attorney for Petitioner**
Record Interlocutory Judgment if real property affected	
Calendar date on which Final Judgment may be obtained	
Prepare Request and Declaration for Final Judgment of Dissolution of Marriage, with Final Judgment (Family Law) and Notice of Entry of Judgment (Family Law)	
Have documents signed by judge, mail copy to respondent, furnish copy to client	

Function of Paralegal
Unlawful Detainer
(After 3-Day Notice to
Pay Rent or Quit)

Paralegal	Attorney
Draft 3-day notice to pay rent or quit if not previously done by client	Initial interview with client
Arrange for service of notice	Instructions to legal assistant
Contact client; if tenant fails to move, draft complaint	Review complaint for unlawful detainer
Obtain signature of plaintiff to complaint	
Arrange for filing and service of complaint	
After answer filed, file memorandum to set	Review answer and documents and sign
Prepare notice of trial and serve	Prepare for trial
Prepare a declaration for judgment	Appearance at trial with client
Obtain plaintiff's signature	
Prepare a writ of possession and transmit to clerk for issuance	
Arrange for service of writ of possession	

Function of Paralegal
Workers' Compensation
By Therese M. Nichols, Legal Assistant

Paralegal	Attorney
Collect and record details of claim, Social Security claim or retirement application	Initial interview with client and legal assistant
Collect documents such as medical records, personnel records, list of employers and insurance carriers, employment records, etc.	
Review application, make any amendments necessary, obtain applicant's signature	
Explore necessity for rehabilitation with applicant	
Have applicant sign medical releases	
Request medical reports from defense attorney or insurance carrier	Discuss medical reports with legal assistant
Obtain information re past employers from applicant, or if not available, from Social Security	
Request from California Inspection Rating Bureau (C.I.R.B.) all information re insurance carriers of past and present employers	
Prepare proposed summary of issues	Review proposed summary of issues
Investigate possible serious and willful misconduct of employer (if grounds exist)	
If grounds exist, prepare Petition for Serious and Willful Misconduct of Employer	Discuss petition with legal assistant
Investigate possibility of Subsequent Injury Fund involvement	
Contact insurance carrier or rep-	

Paralegal	**Attorney**
resentative (or attorney) to determine whether matter can be resolved without litigation	
If liability denied, prepare and file a Declaration of Readiness to Proceed	
Request a Pre-trial conference	Attend pretrial conference
Obtain medical evaluation from an Independent Medical Examiner (IME) or Agreed Medical Examiner (AME) if possible in concurrence with defense, prior to requesting formal hearing. If not, obtain medical report from physician of attorney's choice	
Set up depositions of medical examiners and other witnesses or subpoena medical examiners for cross-examination. If depositions of lay witnesses not feasible, subpoena for the hearing	Take any depositions required
Evaluate doctor's reports	Review paralegal's evaluation of doctor's reports
Assess the Permanent Disability rating. If necessary, obtain Permanent Disability rating from Workers' Compensation Appeals Board Rating Specialist	Discuss rating with legal assistant
Draft evaluation of benefits due applicant	
Draft evaluation of medical liens	
Negotiate settlements with attorney (or representative) for the insurance carriers	Review and sign documents for settlement
Prepare settlement papers: Compromise & Release, Stipulations for Request of Award, as required	
Determine whether payment of	

Paralegal	**Attorney**
claimant's recovery and attorney's fee in compliance with award; if not, serve demand for proper payment.	
If payment not made within time period of Judge's Order — or 30 days have elapsed, draft Order for Penalty and Interest and send to Judge for his signature. Serve on all parties.	Confer with paralegal concerning late payment
Institute a "tickler" or "come-up" system to monitor the claim	
If Findings & Award made, advise client as to reopening of case if injury becomes greater, requires surgery, or in any way results in higher extent of Permanent Disability, within 5-year period from date of injury	Confer with paralegal concerning Findings and Award
If higher permanent disability arises, draft and file Petition to Reopen (or Petition for New and Further Injury)	
	Make any decision to file Petition for Writ of Review with the Court of Appeal, or later appeal to California Supreme Court
Assist in legal research for briefs; may draft briefs	If appeal(s) taken, prepare Petition for Writ of Review and any briefs, and attend oral argument
If appeal taken to Supreme Court, draft Petition for Hearing	

CALIFORNIA PARALEGAL'S GUIDE

Chapter 3

SCOPE AND SOURCE OF LAW

Paralegal study, being essentially the study of law and legal procedures, could appropriately begin with a definition of law. This is not easy to do. Many legal scholars are reluctant to define law. Instead they dispose of the question with comments to the effect that even great men of law have never been able to agree upon a definition. Hence, they say, to attempt more than a perfunctory definition would be presumptuous.

The following, then, is a presumptuous attempt to provide an idea of what the law really is, since it is felt that a definition of law is of importance to the paralegal student. It is unthinkable that anyone should embark upon a chosen career without some basic understanding of his field of endeavor.

TECHNIQUE OF THE LEGAL ORDER

The function of law, contrary to popular belief, is not to settle isolated disputes between A and B. Instead, the chief function, and result, of law is to lay the foundation for a feeling of security in our daily dealings. For in our daily lives we are totally enmeshed in the law.

One definition of law is supplied by one of the world's most eminent jurists, the late Professor Hans Kelsen:[1] "Law is an order of human behavior. An 'order' is a system of rules. Law is not, as it is sometimes said, a rule. It is a set of rules having the kind of unity we understand by a system. . . . Every rule of law [a norm] obligates human beings to observe a certain behavior under certain circumstances." To fail to

---

[1]Kelsen, Dr. Hans, professor emeritus at the University of California, Berkeley, *General Theory of Law and State*, p. 3.

behave in a certain way is to commit a "delict," for which the rule of law (the norm) provides a sanction.

By means of this specific technique, the legal order, as distinguished from the social order, seeks to bring about the desired behavior, to regulate human behavior. For example, the norm says you *ought* not to commit murder; if you do commit a murder, the norm (rule of law) provides a sanction, i.e., imprisonment.

SOURCE OF LAW

Our legal order did not spring into existence full-blown, completely organized and regulated. Substantive law (that law which creates, defines and regulates rights and duties) has its roots in common law, i.e., "the body of those principles, and rules of action, relating to the government and security of persons and property, which derive their authority solely from usages and customs of immemorial antiquity, or from the judgments and decrees of the courts recognizing, affirming, and enforcing such usages and customs; and in this sense particularly the ancient unwritten law of England." (Black's Law Dictionary (1957 ed.), citing 1 Kent, Comm. 492.) The authority of common law did not in its beginnings depend on legislative enactment, but on individuals acting in a certain way because they believed their acts had to be in conformity with a binding, not an arbitrary norm.

The common law of Medieval England was then, as it is today, the universal law of the land. But there were few records. The judges and lawyers cited the precedents from personal recollection, and from reliable hearsay as to the decisions before their time. While the common law began at this time to assume the pattern of case law, it was not until the early 1200s that adequate records of decisions began to be kept. These were the first law reports. It was not until 1292 that published reports of cases were inaugurated. It was at about this time that the term "common law" came into general use.

The common law of the various states, generally, then, is the common law of England, including English statutory law, as the two existed in 1776. That is the starting point.

COMMON LAW AND THE CONSTITUTION

The early common law was not universal. The common law owes its very existence to an organized government. And how is a government organized? By a constitution. The constitution is the basis of a legal order, of a state. But the constitution itself can, as a whole or in part, be unwritten, customary law. "If a legal order has a written constitution which does not institute custom as a form of law creation, and if nevertheless the legal order contains customary law besides statutory law, then, in addition to the norms of the written constitution, there must exist *unwritten norms of constitution,* a customary created norm according to which the general norms binding the law-applying organs can be created by custom. Law regulates its own creation and so does customary law."[2] The validity of all our laws depends upon the postulation that we ought to behave as the " 'fathers' of the constitution and the individuals — directly or indirectly — authorized (delegated) by the constitution command."[3]

The common law of the various states developed by judicial decisions as necessities arose from time to time demanding the application of common law principles to particular cases.

THE HIERARCHY OF LAW

Legislation and Statutory Law.

The general norms established by way of legislation or custom form a level which comes next to the constitution in the hierarchy of law. The statute is created by a decision of the legislature.

It is the legislature — according to the constitution — which is the authority competent to enact a statute. The procedure by which the legislature decides upon a statute consists essentially in a vote for a bill by a majority of the members.

a. STATUTORY LAW

"Statute" is derived from the Latin verb, *statuere,* meaning to set up or establish. And "statute law," used as a general term, is synonymous with "legislation." It refers to precisely worded rules of conduct established by legislative bodies. Both types of law, substantive and procedural, are exemplified in statutory law.

Substantive law is that law which creates, defines and regulates rights and duties; this includes all the rules and regulations under which we live, whether created by the legislatures or handed down by the courts as decisions.

Procedural law is that part of the law which prescribes a method of enforcing the rights granted by the substantive law. In other words, the substantive law may be thought of as the *rules,* and the procedural law constitutes the method to be followed in enforcing those rules. In their organic union they form the law, e.g., if a person has committed a crime, "then a certain organ (a court), appointed in a certain way, shall, through a certain procedure, especially on the motion of another organ (the public prosecutor) direct against the delinquent a certain

---

[2]Kelsen, *op. cit. supra,* p. 126.
[3]Kelsen, *op. cit. supra,* p. 116.

sanction.''⁴ Or, when a debtor, for example, fails to pay a just bill, he violates a rule of contract law. As a result, he may be sued. If the amount is small, he would probably be sued in a small claims court. The procedure which the creditor would have to follow in order to take that debtor into small claims court would be contained in the procedural law governing the filing of cases in the small claims court.

1) The California Legislature

The first California legislature had to set up an entire state government; specify the duties of various state officers; set up a system of courts; enact codes and statutes defining rights of persons and property, and crimes; and establish procedures for civil and criminal courts. At the same time there were conflicts between the mining, agricultural and commercial interests — and Indian attacks on the state's borders.

"The First Legislature adopted as the basic law of the state the common law of England, instead of the civil law derived from Roman-French-Mexican background. They appreciated the essence of the common law of England with its emphasis on the rights of the individual, as contrasted with the Roman law which emphasizes the right of the State, and its doctrine that 'the will of the Prince is the highest law.' ''⁵

The legislature functions to safeguard our liberties, through the means of the law. The legislature is responsive to the voice of the people, and the voice of concerned citizenry must remain active and alert.

2) The Legislative Process⁶

The Birth of a Law — All laws begin their existence as "bills." At the state level the bills are authored by members of the Legislature. At the federal level, bills are proposed by members of the House of Representatives or the Senate. In either case, the term "bill" is taken to mean the literary manifestation of the legislative process. If the bill is received favorably, a metamorphosis takes place which turns the bill into a law.

In California the process generally occurs in this order:
(1) Introduction and first reading
(2) Referral to committee
(3) Consideration by one or more committees of house of origin
(4) To floor of house of origin for vote

---

⁴Kelsen, *op. cit. supra*, p. 129.
⁵*The First Legislature of California*, published by the Senate of the State of California, p. 13.
⁶For an in-depth look at the legislative process see, Henke, *California Law Guide*, Parker and Son (2d ed. 1976, supp. 1981).

(5) To opposite house

(6) To one or more committees of opposite house for consideration

(7) To floor for vote

(8) If amended, back to house of origin (process is repeated until concurrence — to conference committee if amendments not acceptable to house of origin)

(9) Forwarded to governor

(10) Overriding governor's veto

(A) Although authored and introduced by members of the Legislature, all but a relatively few measures are drafted by the office of the Legislative Counsel of California. The Legislative Counsel is elected by the membership of both houses of the Legislature and has a staff of attorneys and clerical help. If a bill is not actually prepared by the staff, it is taken to the Legislative Counsel's office for checking before it is introduced. The drafting of legislative measures requires a highly specialized type of legal training. The draftsmen are not concerned with the policy or wisdom of a requested bill, but only in drafting it in such a manner that it will accomplish the desired objective, be constitutional, and administratively workable. This office also assists on amendments of the bill.

The subjects of bills are varied, many of little interest to the average man or woman. Legislative advocates are responsible for initiating many bills; legislative advocates include persons representing state governmental departments; representatives of civic, financial, religious and educational groups; and free lancers representing various groups. The common term for legislative advocates is "lobbyists." A lobbyist is anyone who for pay attempts to defeat or pass legislation. It is no crime for any citizen to seek to influence legislation; lobbying becomes a crime, and a felony, only when a lobbyist seeks to influence votes by "bribery, promise of reward, intimidation, or other dishonest means."

In any event, all bills must be formally introduced by a member of the Legislature. In California, since we have a bicameral legislature (meaning two houses), the bill may originate in either the Assembly or the Senate. "Introduction" consists of giving the bill a number and reading the title, or enough of it to identify the measure, aloud in each house of the Legislature. A copy of the bill is before each legislator at the time of the reading. Groups of members are formed into committees and charged with studying the many subjects of legislation. Once a bill has been introduced and read, it is referred to the appropriate committee.

(B) Bills are assigned to the proper committee by, in the Assembly, the Speaker of the House. In the Senate, the Committee on Rules makes the assignment. As soon as it is printed, it is delivered to the chairman or secretary of the committee to which it was assigned. The bill cannot be considered until 30 days have elapsed.

(C) The author interviews the chairman of the committee to determine when his bill may be taken up. At a hearing on the bill the author explains the bill and any opposition is heard. The committee reports it back to the house, usually with one of the four following recommendations:

    (a) Report it out with a ''do pass'' recommendation (indicates that a majority favors its becoming a law)

    (b) Amend and pass as amended (indicates a majority favors its becoming law with recommended amendments)

    (c) Amend and re-refer (indicates committee is not satisfied with bill, wants amendments printed into bill for further study, by same committee or another specified committee)

    (d) Without recommendation (indicates members do not believe in the bill but will let it stand or fall on its merits (not frequently used).)

The committee cannot amend the bill; it can only report it back to the house with the recommendation. The house (of origin) may or may not amend. The report is read and printed in the legislative journal and the bill is placed on the second reading file. During the second reading the committee amendments and proposed amendments from the floor are discussed and adopted. A bill may receive a ''second reading'' on three or four occasions.

(D) It then receives a ''third reading.'' Each of the three readings must be on different days. At the third reading floor debate begins and the bill is voted upon. A quorum must be present.

There are three options open at this stage: the bill may be passed, either with or without amendments; it may be referred back to committee; it may be rejected.

(There are many noncontroversial, uncontested measures and they may be placed, after the second reading, on the ''consent calendar.'')

(E) Once a bill is passed, it is sent to the second house.

(F)-(G) The same procedure is followed in both houses.

(H) If the second house passes the bill with amendments it goes back to the house of origin. If the house of origin doesn't want the amendments, a conference committee is appointed by both houses and a conference called. The conference committee attempts to iron out differences with a view toward passing an acceptable version. If after three such conferences the houses fail to agree, the bill dies.

(I) Once a finalized version is accepted by both houses and passed, it is referred to the Governor for signature. If the Governor signs it, the bill becomes law, and, if it is a nonurgency measure, becomes effective on January 1 of the following year. In the event the Governor refuses to sign a bill within 12 days after it is presented to him, it becomes law — unless the 12-day period has not expired by September 1, in which event he has 30 days within which to act on the bill. If the Governor wishes to formally veto a bill, he sends it back to the house of origin with a statement of his reasons.

(J) Bills vetoed by the Governor and returned to the Legislature can become law only if two-thirds of the members of each house vote to override the Governor's veto. Overriding the Governor's veto is rare, but it has happened at least 37 times in the last 100 years.

* * *

Bills are designated depending upon the house of origin; if the bill originated in the Assembly it is an Assembly Bill (AB), if it originated in the Senate it is a Senate Bill (SB).

The Governor sends all bills which are to become law to the Secretary of State, where they are given chapter numbers (e.g., ch. 1523). After the effective date of the bill it becomes a section in the appropriate code. So as a given bill becomes law it is catalogued in several ways. It will have a bill number (e.g., AB 11), a chapter designation (e.g., Statutes of 1970, chapter 1523, section 1, page 3427), and a code number (e.g., Code of Civil Procedure Section 688).

It should be borne in mind that an original bill may bear little resemblance to the bill at a later stage in this process, or as it is actually passed after many amendments. For this reason the legislators who originally supported the bill may withdraw their support at some stage; even the author of the original bill might vote against it.

Once a bill is passed, it may never be amended — or it may be amended many times. A search of all the volumes of statutes to find the current law would obviously be impracticable. This problem was alleviated by the codification of the statutes. This process simply entailed the collection of enactments related but scattered throughout different volumes.

Codification involves not only indexing, revision and expurgation of statute law, but also the creation of categories into which the consolidated statutes could be grouped. For instance, most criminal law is contained in the Penal Code. Laws relating to automobiles are contained in the Vehicle Code. California has 27 such codes.

California and the Common Law

Civil Code section 22.2 (enacted in 1951) provides: "The common law of England, so far as it is not repugnant to or inconsistent with the Constitution of the United States, or the Constitution or laws of this State, is the rule of decision in all the courts of this State." The common law encompassed by that statute is debatable. Nevertheless, except insofar as modified or changed by statutory law, the common law rule prevails in California. The common law rule is applicable and controls criminal proceedings in the absence of statutes at variance, and civil rights and duties when the Civil Code is silent upon a particular question and there is no other positive state or federal law which may be controlling.

In California, if the application of a common law rule should tend to cause injustice rather than justice, a different rule would be applied. Sometimes the reason for the common law rule has ceased; if a statute is enacted which makes application of the common law impossible, the statute has superseded it. In other words, the legislature can prevent the common law from being the decision in this state. Nevertheless, the statutes are presumed to state the common law rules, and unless they contain express declarations to the contrary, and unless the language of the statute makes it clear that it is departing from, altering or abrogating the common law rule, the statute will be construed in the light of common law decisions on the same subject. The mere repeal of a statute declaratory of a common law right does not negate the common law right.

Where a new right is created by a statute, the party aggrieved by its violation is confined to the statutory remedy if one is provided; otherwise, any appropriate common law remedy may be resorted to. But where the legislature has provided a statutory remedy which supplants, in whole or in part, a corresponding common law remedy, and has appended a limitation different from that applicable under the common law rule, a conflict exists between the two and the statutory remedy must prevail.

California courts must refer to the decisions of the English courts, and of American courts in states where the common law prevails; if there is a conflict between the American and English decisions, the American rule will ordinarily be adopted.

Courts and Case Law

Statutory norms are to be applied by the organs competent thereto, especially by the courts, but also by the administrative authorities. The law-applying organs must be instituted according to the legal order; the legal order likewise determines the procedure which those organs shall follow when applying the law. Generally, the courts show great deference to the laws promulgated by the elected lawmakers.

Chapter 4

THE COURTS

The United States has both federal and state court systems. Depending upon the circumstances of the case an action or proceeding may be commenced in either a federal court or a state court. In some instances, rights arising under state law may be asserted in federal courts, or Congress may have granted the federal courts exclusive jurisdiction. On the other hand, that jurisdiction which by law vests in a federal court, does not necessarily exclude the jurisdiction of a state court. The federal courts and the state courts may have concurrent jurisdiction in federal matters, in which event the plaintiff may decide to sue in either court. The best forum for the client can be an important decision. Federal-state court relationships can be very complicated. Here no more is done than to point to the question and to summarize generally the subject matter governing the jurisdiction of the various courts, the titles of the federal and state courts, and the territories over which they have jurisdiction.

In the majority of California law offices the bulk of lawsuits will be filed in either the state superior or municipal courts. The paralegal should know whether a suit belongs in the municipal or superior court (attorneys may not represent claimants in small claims court actions). The paralegal should be able to determine which county has jurisdiction over the lawsuit. If an appeal is to be taken, the paralegal should know to which court the appeal is to be taken. The paralegal should have at least a general understanding of the entire judicial system.[1]

The court headings as they appear herein, are the court headings to be used when filing documents in these courts.

---

[1]Recommended reading: "Choice of a Favorable Forum" Civil Trial Manual, McC. Figg, McCullough, Underwood, Reporters, Joint Project of the American College of Trial Lawyers and the American Law Institute-American Bar Association Joint Committee on Continuing Legal Education, ch. 3, p. 73 et seq. (1974); 16 Cal. Jur. 2d, Courts, p. 1 et seq.

FEDERAL COURTS

The Supreme Court of the United States

1 Chief Justice

8 Associate Justices

Mailing address: 1 First St. N.E., Washington, D.C. 20543

Jurisdiction (see Art. III, §2, U.S. Const.): Appellate jurisdiction in all cases in law and equity arising under Constitution, laws of the United States, and treaties made; all cases of admiralty and maritime jurisdiction; all cases affecting ambassadors, other public ministers and consuls; controversies in which the United States is a party, between two or more states, between a state and citizens of another state, citizens of different states, citizens of same state claiming lands under grants of different states, and state or its citizens and foreign states or citizens. Original jurisdiction in all cases affecting ambassadors, other public ministers and consuls, and those in which a state shall be a party.

See 18 U.S.C. 1332; 28 U.S.C. 1331-1346.

United States Court of Appeals for the Ninth Circuit

(Composed of Districts of California, Alaska, Arizona, Hawaii, Idaho, Montana, Nevada, Oregon, Washington, and District of Guam.) Mailing address: Post Office Building, San Francisco 94101.

The United States is divided into 11 judicial circuits. In each circuit there is a United States Court of Appeals for the circuit, having appellate jurisdiction as set forth in the United States Constitution. These courts have jurisdiction of appeals from all final decisions of the district courts of the United States (and of the United States District Courts of the Canal Zone, Guam, and Virgin Islands) — except where a direct review may be had in the United States Supreme Court.

Federal District Courts

States are divided into various federal judicial districts. In each such district there is a United States District Court for the district. The jurisdiction of these courts and the venue of actions to be brought therein are prescribed by the United States Code. (See 28 U.S.C. 1331-1361). Some of the cases over which the Federal District Courts have jurisdiction are stockholders' derivative suits; actions against the United States; eminent domain proceedings; actions for partition of lands where the United States is one of the tenants in common or joint tenants; any civil action whether or not of a local nature against defendants residing in different districts in the same state or involving property located in different districts.

The titles of the district courts in California are:

UNITED STATES DISTRICT COURT, EASTERN DISTRICT OF CALIFORNIA

(Counties of Alpine, Amador, Butte, Calaveras, Colusa, El Dorado, Fresno, Glenn, Inyo, Kern, Kings, Lassen, Madera, Mariposa, Merced, Modoc, Mono, Nevada, Placer, Plumas, Sacramento, San Joaquin, Shasta, Sierra, Siskiyou, Solano, Stanislaus, Sutter, Tehama, Trinity, Tulare, Tuolumne, Yolo, Yuba.)

Mailing address: 650 Capitol Mall, Sacramento 95814.

U.S. Post Office and Courthouse Building, Fresno 93721.

UNITED STATES DISTRICT COURT, NORTHERN DISTRICT OF CALIFORNIA

(Counties of Alameda, Contra Costa, Del Norte, Humboldt, Lake, Marin, Mendocino, Monterey, Napa, San Benito, San Francisco, San Mateo, Santa Clara, Santa Cruz, Sonoma.)

Mailing address: Post Office Box 3606 (450 Golden Gate Ave.) San Francisco 94102.

UNITED STATES DISTRICT COURT, CENTRAL DISTRICT OF CALIFORNIA

(Counties of Los Angeles, Orange, Riverside, San Bernardino, San Luis Obispo, Santa Barbara, Ventura.)

Mailing address: 312 North Spring St., Los Angeles 90012.

UNITED STATES DISTRICT COURT, SOUTHERN DISTRICT OF CALIFORNIA.

(Counties of Imperial, San Diego)

Mailing address: United States Courthouse Building, San Diego 92101.

* * *

SUMMARY AND COMPARISON OF FEDERAL RULES OF CIVIL PROCEDURE

The summary of federal rules below will serve as a ready reference in the law office. Beginners should perhaps first study the chapters on Civil Litigation, *infra,* which deal with California laws.

Civil law practice in the United States District Courts is governed by the Federal Rules of Civil Procedure (Fed.R.Civ.P.) and in addition by the Local Rules of each District Court (i.e., in California: Eastern District, Northern District, Central District, and Southern District). *It is to be emphasized that the Local Rules of the particular district should be consulted by the legal assistant.*

The Local Rules for the Eastern District are obtainable from the Sacramento court; the Local Rules for the Central District are obtainable from the Los Angeles Daily Journal; the Local Rules for the Northern District may be obtained from the court in San Francisco; and the local rules for the Southern District are available from the Daily Transcript newspaper.

The federal rules differ in many respects from the rules in state courts. Some attorneys have considerable practice in the federal courts and some only an occasional case. In any event, the legal assistant must become familiar with the applicable rules when working on a case in the federal courts. With one exception (discovery motions in the Central District) the rules following are from the Federal Rules of Civil Procedure. To repeat, it is to be emphasized that the legal assistant should obtain a copy of the Local Rules of the court in which the action is filed. While Local Rules must be in general conformity with the Federal Rules of Civil Procedure, they supersede the Federal Rules, so to speak, in dealing with the particular court.

Complaint

A civil action in the United States District Courts is commenced the same way as in any state trial court, by the filing of a complaint and the issuance of a summons by the clerk.

Service

Service on the defendants is made either by a U.S. marshal or his deputy, or a person specially appointed by the court, or by a person authorized to serve process in a state court action in which the district court is held or in which service is made. (Fed.R.Civ.P. 4(a), (c).)

Personal service of the summons and complaint is made in much the same manner as provided by state laws, as follows:

(1) Individuals other than infant or incompetent person	By leaving copies (1) at dwelling house or usual place of abode with person of suitable age and discretion residing therein, (2) by delivering to an agent authorized by appointment or by law to receive service (Fed.R.Civ.P. 4(1))*
(2) Infant or incompetent person	In same manner as prescribed by law of the state in which service is made
(3) Domestic or foreign corporation or partnership or other unincorporated association subject to suit under a common name	Delivering to an officer, a managing or general agent, or any other agent authorized by appointment or law to receive service *and,* if agent is authorized by statute to receive service and statute so required, by mailing copy to defendant (Fed.R.Civ.P. 4(3))*

*Under Rule 4(7), such defendant may also be served in any manner prescribed by U.S. statute or state in which the district court is held for the service of summons and complaint or other process.

Service of process on governmental agencies is provided in Rule 4(4)-4(6).

Service on Attorney

Service on an attorney is made by delivering a copy to him or by mailing a copy to him at his last known address (service is complete upon mailing) or, if address is unknown, by leaving it with the clerk of the court.

"Delivery" means one of the following:
1. Handing it to the attorney or the party
2. Leaving it at his office with his clerk or other person in charge
3. If no one in charge of office, leaving in a conspicuous place therein
4. If office closed or person has no office, leaving at dwelling house or usual place of abode with person of suitable age and discretion.

Filing

All papers after the complaint shall be filed with the court either before service or within a reasonable time thereafter, but the court on motion of a party or own initiative may order that depositions on oral examination and interrogatories, requests for documents, requests for admissions, and answer and response thereto not be filed unless on order of the court or for use in the proceedings.

The judge may accept papers for filing, in which event he notes the filing date thereon and transmits them to the clerk. (Fed. R. Civ. P. 5(e))

Computation of Time for Filing

The first day is excluded and the last day included, unless the last day is a Saturday, Sunday or a legal holiday, in which event the time expires at the end of the next day which is not a Saturday, a Sunday, or a legal holiday.

If the prescribed or allowed period is less than 7 days, Saturdays, Sundays and legal holidays falling within those 7 days are excluded.

"Legal holidays" include New Year's Day, Washington's Birthday, Memorial Day, Independence Day, Labor Day, Columbus Day, Veterans Day, Thanksgiving Day, Christmas, and any other day appointed as a holiday by the President, Congress or state where the district court is held. (Fed.R.Civ.P. 6.)

The court may extend the time with or without motion within the prescribed period or afterward upon motion for excusable neglect —

but not the time for action under Federal Rule of Civil Procedure 50(b) (motion for judgment notwithstanding verdict); Rule 52(b) (amendment to findings and judgment); Rule 59(b), (d) and (e) (motion for new trial; motion to amend judgment); or Rule 60(b) (motions for mistake, etc.), except to the extent and under the conditions stated therein.

Time for Filing Pleadings:

Answer	20 days after service of summons and complaint (except when service made on party outside state)
Answer to cross-claim	20 days after service
Reply to counterclaim	20 days after service of answer
Order of court for reply	20 days after service of order unless otherwise provided in order
Answer to complaint or cross-claim or reply to a counterclaim by U.S. officer or agency	60 days after service
Responsive pleading to motions under Rule 12:	
(a) If court denies motion or postpones disposition until trial on the merits	10 days after court's action
(b) If court grants a motion for a more definite statement	10 days after service of the more definite statement

Proof of Service

Return of service should be made promptly and in any event within the time for response and should be made by affidavit if by other than a U.S. marshal or his deputy. Failure to file proof of service, however, does not affect the validity of service. (Fed.R.Civ.P. 7.)

The court may allow any process or proof of service to be amended under such terms as it deems just. (Fed.R.Civ.P. 4(b).)

Party not inhabitant of or found within state	Summons, or an order in lieu of summons (provided for by a U.S. statute or an order of court or by a statute or rule of court of state in which district court held), under the circumstances and in the manner provided by the statute or order.
	The California provision of Code of Civil Procedure section 415.50 for proof of reasonable diligence to effectuate personal service does not appear in the federal rules.
Party in a foreign country	Either (1) under law of foreign country or (2) as directed by an authority in response to a letter rogatory (if service in either case reasonably calculated to give actual notice), or (3) upon an individual, by delivering to him personally, and upon a corporation or partnership or association, by delivery to an officer, a managing or general agent, or (4) by any form of mail, requiring a signed receipt, to be addressed and dispatched by the clerk of the court to the party to be served, or (5) as directed by order of the court.

As in state actions, service of documents subsequent to the summons and complaint (except ex parte motions), unless otherwise ordered by court, are served on each of the parties (except parties in default unless new or additional claims for relief are being made) if they are not represented by counsel, otherwise upon the attorney.

General Rules of Pleading

A pleading which is a claim for relief must contain a short and plain statement of

(1) grounds of jurisdiction (unless the court already has jurisdiction),

(2) showing that the pleader is entitled to relief,

(3) demand for judgment of the relief claimed, (Fed.R.Civ.P. 8(a).)

Signature of Pleadings

Pleadings must be signed by at least one attorney of record, and his address given.

The attorney's signature *constitutes a certificate* that he has read the pleadings; that to the best of his knowledge, information and belief there is ground to support it; and that it is not interposed for delay.

Pleadings need not be verified or accompanied by an affidavit.

Willful violations by an attorney, or the insertion of scandalous or indecent matter, subject him to appropriate disciplinary action.

If a party is not represented by an attorney he signs the pleading and states his address.

If the pleading is not signed, or signed with intent to defeat the purpose of Federal Rule of Civil Procedure 11 (signing of pleadings), it may be stricken as sham and false and the action shall proceed as if the pleading had not been served.

Defenses

Defenses should likewise be stated in short and plain terms and the averments admitted or denied as in state courts. If the defendant lacks sufficient information to form a belief as to the truth of an averment, he must so state, which operates as a denial.

If all the averments are denied, a general denial may be made.

Every defense in law or in fact must be stated in the responsive pleadings, except that the following defenses may be made by way of a motion:

1. Lack of jurisdiction over subject matter
2. Lack of jurisdiction over the person
3. Improper venue
4. Insufficiency of process
5. Insufficiency of service of process
6. Failure to state a claim upon which relief may be granted
7. Failure to join a party needed for just adjudication under Rule 19 (Fed.R.Civ.P. 12(b).)

Any affirmative defense should also be set forth. Some of the affirmative defenses listed in Federal Rule of Civil Procedure 8(a) are: accord and satisfaction, arbitration and award, assumption of risk, contributory negligence, discharge in bankruptcy, duress, estoppel, failure of consideration, fraud, illegality, injury by fellow servant, laches, license, payment, release, res judicata, statute of frauds, statute of limitations, and waiver.

Averments in a pleading which require a responsive pleading (i.e., averments other than those as to amount of damage) are admitted if not denied in the responsive pleading. Averments in a pleading which neither requires nor permits a responsive pleading, shall be taken as denied or avoided. (Fed.R.Civ.P. 8(d).)

Discovery

Discovery may be had by the following methods:
(1) Depositions upon oral examination or written questions
(2) Written interrogatories

(3) Production of documents or things or permission to enter upon land or other property, for inspection and other purposes

(4) Physical and mental examinations

(5) Requests for admissions

No limits are placed on the frequency of these methods, except that upon motion a protective order may be issued pursuant to Federal Rule of Civil Procedure 26(c).

As in California courts, parties may obtain discovery on any matter, not privileged, which is relevant to the subject matter and it is not ground for objection that the information sought may be inadmissible at trial, if reasonably calculated to lead to discovery of admissible evidence.

DISCOVERY CONFERENCES: At any time after commencement of an action the court may direct the attorneys for the parties to appear before it for a conference on discovery, or the court shall do so on motion of a party if the motion includes:

(1) A statement of the issues as they then appear

(2) A proposed plan and schedule of discovery;

(3) Any limitations proposed to be placed on discovery;

(4) Any other proposed orders with respect to discovery; and

(5) A statement showing that the attorney making the motion has made a reasonable effort to reach agreement with opposing attorneys on the matters set forth in the motion (Fed.R.Civ.P. 26(f).)

Failure to participate in framing a discovery plan as required by this section can result in payment of reasonable expenses including attorneys' fees.

Supplementation of Responses

Responses should be seasonably supplemented as to the following:

1. Questions as to identity and location of persons having knowledge of discoverable matters

2. Identity of expert witness, subject matter on which he is expected to testify, and substance of his testimony

3. If information is obtained that a response was incorrect when made, the response should be amended

4. Response, although correct when made, is no longer true and failure to amend is in substance a knowing concealment.

A duty to supplement may also be imposed by order of court, agreement of parties or new requests for supplementation of prior responses. (Fed.R.Civ.P. 26.)

Sanctions

An evasive or incomplete answer is treated as a failure to answer under Federal Rule of Civil Procedure 37.

Sanctions for failure to obey an order to permit or provide discovery include: (1) contempt of court (except as to an order to submit to a physical or mental examination), (2) taking the matters regarding which the order was made as established, (3) refusal to permit support or opposition of claims or defenses or prohibition of introduction of designated matters in evidence, (4) striking pleadings, and (5) payment of reasonable expenses and attorney's fees.

Central District Discovery Motions

Rule 3.15 of the rules for this district now requires attorneys to meet "in person" prior to the filing of any motion relating to discovery for possible elimination of the motion, or to narrow its scope. Counsel for the moving party must arrange for the meeting. Counsel for the opposing party is obligated to meet with counsel for the moving party within 10 days after service of a letter requesting the meeting and specifying the terms of the discovery order.

After the meeting, if they have been unable to settle their differences, the parties must file with the notice of motion a stipulation as to the remaining issues and the contentions, and points and authorities of each party as to each such issue.

New Rule 3.5.3 provides that attorney affidavits (or declarations) "shall contain only factual, evidentiary matter and shall conform as far as possible with the requirements of Federal Rule of Civil Procedure 56(e)," which establishes special requirements for affidavits used in connection with motions for summary judgment. These affidavits must be made on personal knowledge and set forth facts which would be admissible in evidence and show that affiant could competently testify to the matters stated therein. Responsive affidavits must likewise set forth basic facts showing a genuine issue for trial.

The notice period has been extended from 17 days to 21 days (same in Northern California district).

Motions

Unless made during a hearing or trial, motions must be in writing; the requirement of writing is met if the motion is stated in a notice of motion. (Fed.R.Civ.P. 7.)

Other than ex parte motions, written motions and notice of hearing of a motion must be served not later than 5 days before the date of hearing — unless a different period is fixed by an order of the court or by the rules.

Whenever a party has the right or is required to take some act or proceedings within a prescribed period after the service of a notice of other paper by mail, 3 days is added to the prescribed period.

Any supporting affidavit is served with the motion. Opposing affidavits may be served not later than 1 day before the hearing. (Fed.R.Civ.P. 6.)

Motion for Directed Verdict

The federal corollary of a motion for nonsuit is a motion for directed verdict. Either party may make such a motion at the close of evidence. If the motion is not granted, evidence may nonetheless be offered. The motion is not a waiver of trial by jury. (Fed.R.Civ.P. 50(a).)

Motion for Judgment Notwithstanding the Verdict

Within 10 days after entry of judgment only a party who has made a motion for directed verdict may move to have the judgment and verdict set aside and entered in accordance with the motion for directed verdict. If no verdict was returned, the motion must be made within 10 days after the jury is discharged. A motion for new trial may be joined or prayed in the alternative. (Fed.R.Civ.P. 50(b).)

Motion to Tax Costs

As in California appellate courts, the prevailing party is entitled to costs unless the court otherwise directs. The clerk may tax the costs on one day's notice, and review on a motion served within 5 days. (Fed.R.Civ.P. 54(d).) *Caveat:* See Local Rules for the particular district.

Eastern District of California Rule 122 allows filing of a motion within 10 days after notice of entry of judgment; the motion must be supported by a memorandum of costs certified by counsel as allowable costs, correctly stated, and necessarily incurred. Objection may be made within 10 days. The clerk will set a hearing and give notice.

The rules of the particular district involved should be checked. (In Northern District of California see Rule 265-1.)

Taxable costs for the most part are found in title 26 U.S.C. §1914, et seq., and include:

1. Clerk's fees (§§1914, 1920(1))
2. Marshal's fees (§§1920(1), 1921)
3. Court reporter's fees (§1920(2))
4. Docket fees (§1923)
5. Fees for exemplification and copies (§1920(4)) of papers necessarily filed or admitted into evidence (§1920(4))
6. Fees to masters, receivers and commissioners (Fed.R.Civ.P. 53(a))

7. Premiums on undertaking bonds or security required by law or by order of court or necessarily incurred by a party to secure a right accorded him in the action or proceedings

8. Other items allowed by any statute or rule or by the court in the interests of justice.

Motion to Dismiss

Unless a receiver has been appointed, a plaintiff may dismiss an action without order of court either (1) by filing a notice of dismissal (before an answer or a motion for summary judgment has been served) or (2) by filing a stipulation of dismissal signed by all parties who have appeared. The dismissal is without prejudice, unless otherwise stated, or if previously dismissed, in which latter event it operates as an adjudication on the merits. (Fed.R.Civ.P. 23(e), 41(a), 66.) Otherwise, an order of dismissal is required.

The defendant may move to dismiss if the plaintiff fails to prosecute or to comply with the rules or any order of court, or, after plaintiff has presented his evidence, on the ground that under the law and facts plaintiff has shown no right to relief. (Fed.R.Civ.P. 41(b).) If the court should then render judgment on the merits, findings must be made as provided in Federal Rule of Civil Procedure 52(a).

(See Fed.R.Civ.P. 52(c) for dismissal of counterclaims, cross-claims or third party claims.)

Findings of Fact

When the parties stipulate that a master's finding of fact shall be final, only questions of law arising upon the report may be considered. However, if a ruling requests findings of fact, the prevailing party must prepare them as in the state courts.

Local rules of the district should be consulted. In the Eastern District of California, for example, if the findings are approved as to form by all parties, they are filed with the clerk, who thereupon presents them to the judge. Otherwise they are filed with proof of service and the clerk holds them for 5 days before presentation to the judge, within which time a notice of disapproval, with proposed modifications and reasons, may be served and lodged. (LR 121.)

In the Northern District of California in nonjury cases findings of facts must be submitted in advance of trial or a trial brief may be accepted.

Bonds Costs on Appeal in Civil Cases

On civil appeal cases, the filing of a bond (amendment or the providing of other security) is within the discretion of the court, both as to form and amount. (Fed.R.Civ.P. 7.)

Jury Trial (Fed.R.Civ.P. 38, 39)

Except in an admiralty or maritime claim, any party may demand a jury trial, by serving a demand therefor in writing at any time after the commencement of the action and not later than 10 days after service of the last pleading directed to such issue. Or the demand may be indorsed upon a pleading of a party.

The demand must specify the issues to be tried by a jury or the demand will be deemed to apply to all the triable issues. (The court upon motion or of its own initiative may find that a right to jury of some or all issues does not exist under the Constitution or U.S. statutes.)

If the demand is for only some of the issues, any other party may serve a demand for jury trial on any or all of the issues. Once made, a demand may not be withdrawn without the consent of the parties.

Failure to serve or file a demand constitutes a waiver of the right to a jury trial. Issues not demanded for trial by jury are tried by the court. However, upon motion, the court has discretion to order a jury trial.

In actions not triable by a jury, the court upon motion or its own initiative may try any issue with an advisory jury or, with the consent of both parties — except in actions against the United States when a U.S. statute provides for trial without a jury — may order a trial with jury.

STATE COURTS

The highest court in each of the states is its Supreme Court.

A majority of the states have intermediate appellate courts; the states which do not are: Arkansas, Hawaii, Idaho, Maine, Minnesota, Mississippi, Montana, Nebraska, Nevada, New Hampshire, North Dakota, Rhode Island, South Carolina, South Dakota, Utah, Vermont, Virginia, West Virginia, Wyoming and District of Columbia. Two states, Connecticut and Delaware, utilize their superior courts as intermediate appellate courts.

THE CALIFORNIA JUDICIAL SYSTEM*

The Constitution of the State of California vests the judicial power of the state in a Supreme Court, Courts of Appeal, Superior Courts, Municipal Courts and Justice Courts (Const., Art. VI, §1). The Superior Courts, Municipal Courts and Justice Courts are the trial courts

---

*Excerpted from summary prepared by the Administrative Office of the Courts, which is the staff agency of the Judicial Council of California, 4200 State Building, 455 Golden Gate Avenue, San Francisco, California 94102 (March 31, 1981)

of the California judicial system; the Supreme Court and Courts of Appeal are appellate courts that primarily review trial court decisions.

The Constitution also provides for agencies dealing with judicial administration: the Judicial Council, whose principal function is to improve and expedite the administration of justice (Const., Art. VI, §6); the Commission on Judicial Appointments, which must confirm all gubernatorial appointees to fill appellate court vacancies (Const., Art. VI, §§7, 16); and the Commission on Judicial Performance, which deals with the admonishment censure, removal or retirement of judges for misconduct or disability (Const., Art. VI, §§8, 18).

Supreme Court

The Supreme Court is California's highest court and its decisions are binding on all other courts of this state.

The Supreme Court consists of a Chief Justice and six Associate Justices. It has original jurisdiction in proceedings involving special writs: mandamus, certiorari, prohibition and habeas corpus. It also exercises reviewing power under its constitutional authority to transfer to itself for decision, appeals taken to the Courts of Appeal either before or after the Courts of Appeal have handed down final decisions in these appeals (Const., Art. VI, §§10 and 12). This reviewing power enables the Supreme Court to pass on important legal questions and to maintain uniformity in the law. Any party may petition for a hearing in the Supreme Court after decision by a Court of Appeal, and if the hearing is granted the decision of the Court of Appeal becomes a nullity. All Supreme Court decisions are published in the Official California Reports.

Members of the Supreme Court are appointed by the Governor and must be confirmed by the Commission on Judicial Appointments. To be qualified for such an appointment, a person must be an attorney admitted to the practice of law in California or have served as a judge of a court of record in this state for 10 years immediately preceding his appointment (Const., Art. VI, §15). After confirmation, the judge serves until the next gubernatorial election when he must run unopposed for election on a nonpartisan ballot (Const., Art. VI, §16). The Supreme Court judges are elected for 12-year terms.

Regular sessions are held by the Court in San Francisco, Los Angeles and Sacramento. The Court may also hold special sessions elsewhere. . . .

In addition to its other responsibilities, the Supreme Court reviews the recommendations of the Commission on Judicial Performance and the State Bar of California concerning, respectively, the disciplining of judges and attorneys.

Courts of Appeal

The Courts of Appeal, established pursuant to a constitutional amendment in 1904, are California's intermediate courts of review and carry the main load of review work. They have appellate jurisdiction when superior courts have original jurisdiction, and in certain other cases prescribed by statute. Like the Supreme Court, they also have original jurisdiction in habeas corpus, mandamus, certiorari and prohibition proceedings (Const., Art. VI, §10). . . .

The state is divided into five appellate districts, each having a Court of Appeal composed of one or more divisions. Each division is composed of three or more judges appointed by the Governor and confirmed by the Commission on Judicial Appointments. Their qualifications, election and term of office are the same as for Supreme Court judges. The Legislature has the constitutional authority to create new appellate districts and divisions of the Courts of Appeal (Const., Art. VI, §3). Currently, the five appellate districts have 13 divisions and 59 judges. The headquarters for the five appellate districts are: First District, San Francisco; Second District, Los Angeles; Third District, Sacramento; Fourth District, San Diego and San Bernardino; and Fifth District, Fresno. . . .

Superior Courts

The superior court is the trial court of general jurisdiction in the California judicial system. It is sometimes called the trial court of residual jurisdiction; that is, it has original trial jurisdiction in all causes except those given by statute to other trial courts (Code Civ. Proc. §82). The superior court also sits as a probate court, juvenile court and conciliation court. (See Prob. Code §301 et seq.; Welf. and Inst. Code §500 et seq.; Code Civ. Proc. §1730 et seq.) In addition, the superior court has trial jurisdiction of all felony cases. The superior court tries all civil and criminal matters above the jurisdiction of the municipal and justice courts (Const., Art. VI §10; Code Civ. Proc. §86; Pen. Code §1462). [In any county where there is a municipal court, the superior court has jurisdiction in civil cases in which the amount involved exceeds $15,000 (Code Civ. Proc. §§82, 89).]

There is a superior court in each of the 58 counties and the number of judges is fixed by the Legislature (Const., Art. VI, §4). . . .

Superior court judges serve six-year terms and are elected at the general election on a nonpartisan ballot by voters of the county (Const., Art. VI, §6(b) and (c); Elec. Code §41). Vacancies are filled by appointment of the Governor. A judge of the superior court must be an attorney admitted to the practice of law in California or have served as a judge of a court of record in this state for at least 10 years immediately preceding election or appointment (Const., Art. VI, §15).

The superior court also hears appeals from decisions of municipal and justice courts (Const., Art. VI, §11). All appeals except in small claims cases are heard by a three-judge appellate department in each county. Appeals to the superior court are governed by rules adopted by the Judicial Council (Const., Art. VI, §6; Code Civ. Proc. §§77, 117.10, 901; Pen. Code §1468). Appeals may also be transferred from the superior court to the Courts of Appeal (Cal. Rules of Court, Rules 61-69).

Municipal Courts

The municipal court is one of two types of trial courts below the superior court; the other is the justice court. Currently, there are about 83 municipal courts and 472 judges. State legislation authorizes each county board of supervisors to divide the county into judicial districts. When the population of a judicial district exceeds 40,000, a municipal court is established in that district (Const., Art. VI, §5).

Municipal courts have original trial jurisdiction in criminal misdemeanor and infraction cases (Pen. Code §1462), and in all civil cases arising within the municipal court district in which the amount involved is $15,000 or less (Code Civ. Proc. §86). The municipal courts also exercise a simplified small claims jurisdiction in cases not exceeding $750 (Code Civ. Proc. §116.2). In addition, the judges act as magistrates to conduct preliminary hearings in felony cases to determine whether there is reasonable and probable cause to hold a defendant for further proceedings or trial in superior court. . . .

*   *   *   *   *

Municipal court judges are elected for six-year terms on a nonpartisan ballot by voters of the judicial districts in which their courts are located (Gov. Code §71145). Vacancies in the office of municipal court judge are filled by the Governor (Gov. Code §71180). Municipal court judges are required to be attorneys admitted to the practice of law in California for at least five years immediately preceding election or appointment (Const., Art. VI, §15).

Justice Courts

Justice courts are established in all judicial districts having a population of 40,000 or less (Const., Art. VI, §5). . . .

[Procedures in justice courts have been made the same as for municipal courts. (See Code Civ. Proc. §§431.30, 465.631; Gov. Code §§26824, 71601.)]

*   *   *   *   *

Judges of the Supreme Court, Courts of Appeal, superior courts and municipal courts may not practice law and are ineligible for other public employment and public office. A superior or municipal court judge may, however, become eligible for election to another public office by taking a leave of absence without pay before filing his declaration of candidacy for that office. Acceptance of that office is a resignation as a judge (Const., Art. VI, §17). A justice court judge who is an attorney may practice law, but not before any justice court in his own county (Gov. Code §§68082-83).

No judge or judicial officer may receive a court fine or fee for his own use.

Small Claims Courts

(Code Civ. Proc. §116 et seq.)

In each justice and municipal court there is a small claims division. The Judicial Council provides by rule for practice and procedure.

"Small claims courts" determine controversies involving $750 or less. Municipal court judges sitting as a small claims court have jurisdiction in unlawful detainer actions where there is a default in rent for residential property, tenancy is from month to month or less, and the total amount claimed is $750 or less. (Code Civ. Proc. §116.2.)

Small claims actions have been transferred to a higher court when the defendant filed an action against the plaintiff in a higher court based on the same facts but in an amount in excess of the monetary jurisdiction of the small claims court. Effective January 1, 1981, such a transfer is postponed until after judgment in the small claims court, unless the ends of justice would be served by a prejudgment transfer, in which event both actions shall be tried together in the transferee court.

The higher court is authorized to award the defendant in the higher court the costs of transfer, including attorney's fees and filing fees, if he prevails in the higher court.

The parties may not be represented by attorneys in small claims court, although nothing shall prevent an attorney from rendering advice to a party to such litigation either before or after commencement of the action. An attorney may appear to prosecute or defend an action by or against himself, or by or against a partnership in which he is a general partner and in which all the partners are attorneys, or by or against a professional corporation of which he is an officer or director and of which all the other officers and directors are attorneys at law.

A corporation may appear through employees, officers or directors. Any other entity may appear through employees.

No formal pleadings other than a claim and order are necessary. (See Code Civ. Proc. §§116.4, 116.8.)

Appeals From Small Claims Court

Only the defendant has the right of appeal (appeal is to the superior court) from the judgment, and only if he does not seek affirmative relief in the small claims court. In the event of an appeal the case is tried anew and there is no appeal from the decision of the superior court. (See Code of Civil Proc. §§117.1, 117.8, 117.10, 117.12.)

If defendant did *not* appear at the hearing in small claims court, the defendant, as *prerequisite* to appeal, must file motion to vacate judgment within 30 days after clerk has mailed by first-class mail notice of entry of judgment, and defendant must have appeared at the hearing on the motion or submit written justification for not appearing, plus written evidence in support of the motion. The court must have denied or failed to decide the motion within 60 days after filing. (Code Civ. Proc. §117.8, subd. (b).)

If defendant appeared at the hearing on the motion to vacate the judgment (or submitted a written justification for not appearing and written evidence supporting motion and motion was denied or not decided within 60 days), defendant may appeal to the superior court, but only as to denial of motion to vacate judgment. The appeal may be heard without recalendaring if the court finds that the motion to vacate should have been granted. (Code Civ. Proc. §117.8, subd. (c).)

If defendant did *not* appear at hearing and was *not* properly served with notice, he may move to vacate 180 days after he knows or should have known that judgment was entered against him. The motion shall be supported by a declaration.

TITLES OF CALIFORNIA STATE COURTS

California Supreme Court

IN THE SUPREME COURT OF THE STATE OF CALIFORNIA

Address: 350 McAllister St., Room 4050
            San Francisco, CA 94102.

Sessions of court are held in San Francisco, Sacramento and Los Angeles.

One Chief Justice
Six Associate Justices

Courts of Appeal

Five appellate districts. (First appellate district has four divisions; second appellate district, five divisions; fourth appellate district, two divisions.) Presiding justice and two associate justices sit in each court.

The titles of the courts are:

FIRST APPELLATE DISTRICT:

IN THE COURT OF APPEAL OF THE STATE OF CALIFORNIA, FIRST APPELLATE DISTRICT, DIVISION ONE

IN THE COURT OF APPEAL OF THE STATE OF CALIFORNIA, FIRST APPELLATE DISTRICT, DIVISION TWO

IN THE COURT OF APPEAL OF THE STATE OF CALIFORNIA, FIRST APPELLATE DISTRICT, DIVISION THREE

IN THE COURT OF APPEAL OF THE STATE OF CALIFORNIA, FIRST APPELLATE DISTRICT, DIVISION FOUR

(Clerk's office for First Appellate District is in the State Building, 350 McAllister St., San Francisco 94102.)

COUNTIES OF FIRST APPELLATE DISTRICT:
Alameda, Contra Costa, Del Norte, Humboldt, Lake, Marin, Mendocino, Monterey, Napa, San Benito, San Francisco, San Mateo, Santa Clara, Santa Cruz, Solano, Sonoma.

SECOND APPELLATE DISTRICT:

IN THE COURT OF APPEAL OF THE STATE OF CALIFORNIA, SECOND APPELLATE DISTRICT, DIVISION ONE

IN THE COURT OF APPEAL OF THE STATE OF CALIFORNIA, SECOND APPELLATE DISTRICT, DIVISION TWO

IN THE COURT OF APPEAL OF THE STATE OF CALIFORNIA, SECOND APPELLATE DISTRICT, DIVISION THREE

IN THE COURT OF APPEAL OF THE STATE OF CALIFORNIA, SECOND APPELLATE DISTRICT, DIVISION FOUR

IN THE COURT OF APPEAL OF THE STATE OF CALIFORNIA, SECOND APPELLATE DISTRICT, DIVISION FIVE

(Clerk's office for Second Appellate District is at 3580 Wilshire Blvd., Los Angeles 90010.)

COUNTIES OF SECOND APPELLATE DISTRICT:
Los Angeles, San Luis Obispo, Santa Barbara, Ventura.

THIRD APPELLATE DISTRICT:

IN THE COURT OF APPEAL OF THE STATE OF CALIFORNIA, IN AND FOR THE THIRD APPELLATE DISTRICT

(Clerk's office for Third Appellate District is in Room 119, Library and Courts Building, Sacramento 95814.)

COUNTIES OF THIRD APPELLATE DISTRICT:

Alpine, Amador, Butte, Calaveras, Colusa, El Dorado, Glenn, Lassen, Modoc, Mono, Nevada, Placer, Plumas, Sacramento, San Joaquin, Shasta, Sierra, Siskiyou, Sutter, Tehama, Trinity, Yolo, Yuba.

FOURTH APPELLATE DISTRICT:

IN THE COURT OF APPEAL OF THE STATE OF CALIFORNIA, FOURTH APPELLATE DISTRICT, DIVISION ONE

(Clerk's office is at 1350 Front St., San Diego 92101.)

IN THE COURT OF APPEAL OF THE STATE OF CALIFORNIA, FOURTH APPELLATE DISTRICT, DIVISION TWO

(Clerk's office is at 303 W. Third St., San Bernardino 92401.)

COUNTIES OF FOURTH APPELLATE DISTRICT:

Imperial, Inyo, Orange, Riverside, San Bernardino, San Diego.

FIFTH APPELLATE DISTRICT:

IN THE COURT OF APPEAL OF THE STATE OF CALIFORNIA, FIFTH APPELLATE DISTRICT

(Clerk's office is at 2550 Mariposa St., Fresno 93721.)

COUNTIES OF FIFTH APPELLATE DISTRICT:

Fresno, Kern, Kings, Madera, Mariposa, Merced, Stanislaus, Tulare, Tuolumne.

Superior Courts

SUPERIOR COURT OF CALIFORNIA, COUNTY OF_____

(There is a superior court in each county of the State. The superior courts are located at the county seats of each county.)

Municipal Courts

IN THE MUNICIPAL COURT, JUDICIAL DISTRICT OF THE CITY OF _____ COUNTY OF _____, STATE OF CALIFORNIA

(Similar titles are used for each of the municipal courts. The locations of the municipal courts are listed in the annual reports of the Judicial Council.)

JURISDICTION OF CALIFORNIA COURTS

Jurisdiction of Supreme Court

1. Issuance of extraordinary writs (such as writs of mandamus, supersedeas, habeas corpus, prohibition, certiorari).
2. Appellate jurisdiction:
   a. In equity — in all cases except those arising in municipal or justice courts.
   b. In all cases at law which involve title or possession of real estate, or legality of any tax, impost, assessment, toll, or municipal fine.
   c. In all appealable probate matters.
   d. In all criminal cases, on questions of law only, where judgment of death has been rendered.
   e. All matters ordered by the Supreme Court to be transferred to it from the Courts of Appeal.

Jurisdiction of Courts of Appeal

1. Issuance of extraordinary writs (same as Supreme Court).
2. Appellate jurisdiction:
   a. Appeals from superior courts (except where Supreme Court has appellate jurisdiction), in the following cases:
      (1) All cases at law in which superior courts are given original jurisdiction.
      (2) Forcible or unlawful entry or detainer (except those arising in municipal or justice courts).
      (3) Insolvency proceedings.
      (4) Prevention or abatement of nuisance.
      (5) Proceedings for mandamus, certiorari, prohibition, usurpation of office, removal from office, contesting elections, eminent domain, and such other special proceedings as may be provided by law.
      (6) All criminal cases, on questions of law only, except where judgment of death has been rendered.
3. All cases pending before Supreme Court which shall be ordered by the Supreme court to be transferred to a Court of Appeal.

Jurisdiction of Superior Courts

1. Issuance of extraordinary writs.
2. All civil cases and proceedings except cases where jurisdiction is given by law to municipal or justice courts. Superior courts have jurisdiction where amount sued for exclusive of interest is $15,000 or more, if there is a municipal court in county; if not, $1,000.

3. All criminal cases amounting to felony, and cases of misdemeanors not otherwise provided for.
4. Special cases and proceedings not otherwise provided for, as:
   a. Legality of tax, impost, assessment, toll, or municipal fine.
   b. Probate and guardianship cases.
   c. Adoption cases.
   d. Juvenile court cases.
   e. Condemnation cases.
   f. Escheat cases.
   g. Cases under Reciprocal Enforcement of Support Law.
   h. Dissolution of corporations.
   i. Naturalization.
   j. Cases involving title or possession of real property in a county having no municipal jurisdiction.
5. Appellate jurisdiction in such cases arising in municipal and justice courts as may be prescribed by law.

Each judicial district which has a population of 40,000 or more has a municipal court.

Jurisdiction of Municipal and Justice Courts

The jurisdiction of municipal and justice courts is the same and concurrent. (Cal. Code Civ. Proc. §83.)

1. Criminal cases where the offense is a misdemeanor and committed within the county in which court established, except where juvenile court has jurisdiction or other courts have exclusive jurisdiction. Violations of traffic laws are mostly misdemeanors. Usually violations of the penal and vehicle codes and city or county ordinances are involved.
2. Exclusive jurisdiction in all cases involving violation of ordinances of cities and towns situated within district in which court is established.
3. Civil cases where amount sued for, exclusive of interest, is not more than $15,000, in such cases as:
   a. Breach of contract.
   b. Nonpayment of promissory note.
   c. Automobile damages.
   d. Rent.
   e. Recovery of possession of real property.
   f. Foreclosure of liens.
   g. Recovery of personal property for which payment has not been made.
   h. Dissolution of partnership.

    i.   Forcible entry of unlawful detainer (rental value must be $1,000 or less a month, total claimed $15,000 or less or last rental charge $1,000 or less a month and total damages $15,000 or less) (see Cal. Code Civ. Proc. §86)

    j.   Personal injuries from wrongful act or negligence.

Appeals are taken to the appellate department of the Superior Court.

Jurisdiction — Municipal v. Superior Court

If a defendant in a municipal court cross-complains for an amount in excess of $15,000, the action must be removed to the superior court.

On the other hand, if a cross-complaint is filed in a superior court action and the claim in the cross-complaint is less than $15,000 *and* if it does not arise out of the same transaction, the superior court has no jurisdiction to give an award on the cross-complaint.

A single plaintiff or a group of plaintiffs can aggregate an amount in excess of $15,000 to bring an action into the superior court.

In an action for recovery of personal property, however, one may not add loss of use to the value of the property in order to bring the case into the superior court.

Chapter 5

COMMENCING THE LAWSUIT

The legal assistant is involved in every step of the lawsuit. By and large, all the documents described in this chapter may be drafted by legal assistants. Whether in a given instance the legal assistant will attempt to do research, draft briefs and prepare the more difficult and complex pleadings, will depend upon the skill, training, experience, and capability of the individual legal assistant, and upon the law firm employing the legal assistant. (See Chapter 2 for Function of Paralegal chart in Civil Litigation.)

Many of the forms referred to herein are printed forms which the legal assistant can learn to complete accurately. In some instances the author has set out certain language which the forms are required by statute to contain; such language may already have been provided for in the printed forms available, whether for optional or mandatory use.

Once the pleadings and forms are prepared, the legal assistant needs to know what to do with them, to arrange for signatures, conform the copies to original, when and how to serve and file the documents.

But the legal assistant must first learn what the procedure is, know what step comes next, and be prepared. To this end intensive calendaring is a must, not only of the last day to take a specified action, but two or three reminders in advance if necessary. The legal assistant should take the initiative and follow through in a case and not have to wait to be told before taking the next step. The valuable legal assistant THINKS, and THINKS AHEAD.

Let us take an automobile collision as a typical case. One of the persons involved consults an attorney and tells him the facts. The attorney believes the party has a *cause of action* and prepares a *complaint* against the other person involved. The complaining party is called to the attorney's office to read the complaint and to sign a *verification* attached to the complaint. The party bringing the complaint is called the *plaintiff*, and the party defending the action is called the *defendant*.

What happens then? Briefly, the steps that are taken to bring the case to trial are outlined in the following paragraphs. An outline is given here to develop a perspective of how a typical lawsuit might proceed. The various pleadings and procedures here mentioned are discussed in detail under the appropriate heading. Reference to this outline will show where a particular procedure fits into the larger pattern. Other common procedures, but procedures that are not necessarily a part of every lawsuit, are detailed in later chapters.

1. The *original complaint* is filed, i.e., lodged, with the clerk of the court in which the suit is brought. A filing fee is paid.

2. At the time of filing this original complaint the clerk *issues* the summons. (After service is made, original summons is filed.)

3. A *copy of the complaint and of the summons* is served on the defendant. (See Service of Documents, *infra*.)

4. The defendant has 30 days to serve on the plaintiff's attorney and file an *answer, demurrer, or to otherwise plead*.

5. If the defendant wants more time to prepare his pleading, his attorney asks the other party's attorney for a *stipulation extending time*. The attorney would probably grant the extension, but if for some reason he or she refused, the defendant could apply to the court for an *order extending time*.

6. If the defendant files a *demurrer, a hearing* (not a trial) is held on the demurrer. If the demurrer is held to be valid, that is, sustained, the attorney for the plaintiff will in all likelihood be given leave by the court to serve and file an *amended complaint*. Then the defendant's attorney could file a demurrer to the amended complaint, and repeat the process, or he or she could file an *answer*.

7. Once an *answer* is filed, the case is at *issue*, and may be set for trial.

8. Either attorney may file a *Memorandum That Civil Case is At Issue*, but it is usually filed by the plaintiff's attorney.

9. If any other party is not in agreement with the estimates, he or she may within 10 days serve and file a memorandum on his or her behalf.

10. If a pretrial conference is not requested in the Memorandum, a *Special Request for Pretrial Conference* may be filed by either party.

11. The clerk will give 60 days' notice of the *pretrial date* to all parties.

12. Before pretrial, counsel is required to have completed their *depositions*, i.e., testimony, of witnesses, and other discovery proceedings.

13. *Settlement conferences:* After a case has been on the civil active list, the clerk sends an invitation to attend a settlement conference. The case is placed on the *settlement calendar* if one of the parties accepts the invitation 20 days prior to date of pretrial or trial setting conference, if required (if not required, 20 days prior to trial date). The clerk notifies all parties of acceptance; the clerk may, upon joint request, order the case placed on settlement calendar. Settlement conferences are held informally before a judge.

[For rule regarding short causes (time estimated for trial 1 day or less), see Rule 207.1, California Rules of Court]

14. Counsel appear in courtroom or judge's chambers for pretrial (superior court only). At or before the conference a *joint written statement* is submitted to the pretrial conference judge. The court issues a *pretrial order* at or within 5 days after the pretrial is held. The *trial date* is ordinarily set at the pretrial (not earlier than 30 days) and appears in the pretrial order; no further notice is required. If it is not fixed in the pretrial order, the clerk will give at least 30 days' notice of trial.

15. Any witnesses to be called are subpoenaed in advance of the trial.

16. If trial is to be by jury, jury instructions are prepared in advance and *one day's jury fees deposited 14 days before trial.* Jury fees may vary from county to county.

17. *Trial* is held.

18. The court announces decision and may then designate the party to prepare *Findings of Fact and Conclusions of Law,* or may wait until request therefor is made and notify one of the parties to prepare them. Or the court may prepare the findings after request. The party designated or notified has 10 days after request to prepare them. Opposing counsel has 10 days in which to file objections. Usually a proposed *Judgment* is served and mailed to the judge at the same time, or the court may prepare the Judgment.

19. The judge signs (or modifies and signs) *Findings of Fact and Conclusions of Law* and *Judgment*, and the clerk files them and returns endorsed-filed copies. A *cost bill* is served and filed, not later than 10 days after judgment is entered.

20. clerk serves and files *Notice of Entry of Judgment* on all parties.

21. Losing party may file *Notice of Appeal.*

22. If no appeal is filed, case is closed. Losing party pays judgment (if a money judgment) and prevailing party thereafter files a *Satisfaction of Judgment.*

23. If losing party fails to pay the judgment against him, a *Writ of Execution* may be levied and satisfaction of the judgment obtained in this manner, if the losing party owns any assets.

Any action that is not a criminal case, is a civil case. Civil litigation embraces the whole spectrum of legal actions including tort actions, suits for personal injuries, for property damage and for breach of contracts; marriage dissolutions — to name only a few. Probate proceedings are civil proceedings.

Forms for Documents

Under California Rules of Court the use of certain forms (printed) is mandatory. The standard forms adopted by the Judicial Council for mandatory use are listed under Rule 982, mandatory family law forms under Rules 1281-1291.40. Other forms approved by the Judicial Council are optional.

In addition, other printed forms are available from the office of the county clerks (and clerks of municipal courts). The forms available vary from county to county so a check should be made in the county of practice for available forms. Ordinarily a list can be obtained from the clerk. In Los Angeles County certain probate orders are prepared by the Probate Commissioner.

Other documents are typewritten and dictated or prepared from form books, or forms set up in the law office manual are followed.

JURISDICTION

Before commencement of a suit it must be determined which court has jurisdiction over the persons and the subject matter of the case. "Jurisdiction" is the power or authority, granted to a court by the constitution (state and federal) and by statute, to hear and determine legal matters. Jurisdiction is an essential concept to grasp, for without jurisdiction a court does not have the power to adjudicate. There are two types of jurisdiction, subject matter jurisdiction, and jurisdiction over the person (or property).

Subject Matter Jurisdiction

Subject matter jurisdiction is the power to hear and determine a particular case. A decision rendered by a court without subject matter jurisdiction is void. This type of jurisdiction is determined by the amount of money damages sought (e.g., over $15,000 in Superior Court), or the value of property in dispute, or the nature of the proceeding (e.g., Superior Court has exclusive jurisdiction in certain matters, such as probate, adoption and Family Law).

For statutorily prescribed subject matter jurisdiction of the various California courts see Chapter 4. The Federal Courts have exclusive jurisdiction over certain subject matter such as bankruptcy and admiralty (see 28 U.S.C.A. §§1333-1338).

Personal Jurisdiction

Personal jurisdiction is the power of a particular court to adjudicate the rights of the person or the rights over the property named in the action. (See Code Civ. Proc. §410.10.) There are three types of personal jurisdiction: 1. in personam jurisdiction, 2. in rem jurisdiction, 3. and quasi-in-rem jurisdiction.

IN PERSONAM

Before liability can be imposed the court must have jurisdiction over the person of the defendant or respondent. The inception of this jurisdiction is a properly served summons. There are many bases for in personam jurisdiction; see Mason, *California Civil Procedure Handbook,* for a discussion of them and other questions of jurisdiction.

A corporation or an unincorporated association is a "person" for jurisdictional purposes and therefore may be a party to a lawsuit.

IN REM

An action in rem is instituted against a thing (i.e., property) rather than against a person with the object of determining the interests of persons in the property (which may be real or personal). Some types of in rem actions are bankruptcy, probate, and escheat.

QUASI-IN-REM

A suit is quasi-in-rem where the plaintiff cannot obtain jurisdiction of the person of the defendant but the person has property in the state out of which the plaintiff can satisfy his claim.

In other words, the suit is against a person but the claim is satisfied (or partially satisfied) against a thing.

Forum Non Conveniens

Under certain statutorily prescribed conditions a court in its discretion may decline to exercise jurisdiction (see CCP §410.30(a)).

VENUE

Venue signifies the geographic location where a cause shall be tried and depends on constitutional and statutory provisions.

An important responsibility of the legal assistant is checking to make certain the lawsuit is commenced in a proper county.

The place (i.e., the county, district) where an action is to be tried is spoken of as the "venue" of the action. Venue is not jurisdiction; jurisdiction refers to the power or authority of the courts to hear cases, whereas venue is merely a statutory designation of where a case may be heard. If a statutory venue provision is not complied with a judgment is not void as it would be if the court did not have subject matter jurisdiction. Venue, unlike subject matter jurisdiction, may be waived.

Venue is the neighborhood, place or county in which an injury is declared to have been done or a fact to have happened and determines the county or place wherein a court having jurisdiction of the action may properly hear and determine the cause. For proceedings in state courts the statutes (Code Civ. Proc. §§392-403) govern as to venue, the county in which an action may be brought. The parties may not confer venue on a particular court other than as provided by statute.

The venue statutes are contained in Civil Code sections 392 to 403 and are briefly summarized for reference as follows:

County	Action
If real property involved, county where realty is situated	Recovery of possession of real property
	Quieting title
If real property is situated in more than one county, in any one of the counties (CCP §392)	Enforcement of liens on real property
	Determination of claim to real property ejectment
	Forcible entry and detainer
	Foreclosure of chattel mortgage
	Foreclosure of mortgage on realty
	Foreclosure of liens
	Nuisance
	Partition
	Waste
	Injuries to realty
	Every other type of real property action
County where the injury occurs *or* county of residence of defendant (CCP §395)	Injury to person or personal property
County where contract was executed *or* where it was to be performed *or* county of residence of defendant (or some of the defendants if more than one) (CCP §395)	Actions involving contracts
County in which the cause of action arose (CCP §394)	Actions against public officials
	Actions to recover penalty, forfeiture or fine
	Actions on officials' bonds

STATUTES OF LIMITATION

One of the most important responsibilities a legal assistant has is making certain a lawsuit is filed within the time prescribed by law. A statute of limitations is a law which prescribes the period beyond which suit may not be brought, i.e., *filed*. Possibly the client has consulted an attorney too late, in which event nothing can be done. For example, if the client sustained personal injuries he must file a lawsuit against the other party within one year from the date of the accident. If, on the other hand, the only damages were to his automobile, he can file the lawsuit within 3 years, since the statute of limitations to recover for damage to personal property is 3 years.

The statutes of limitations are a critical area of operation for the legal assistant and attorney. Not only may the client sustain financial loss, the deadlines decreed by the statutes of limitation provide a fertile ground for legal malpractice actions. This problem may be avoided if proper precautions are taken.

First of all, if the client consults the attorney far enough in advance the attorney can and should avoid any running of the statutes (i.e., the end of the statutory time period). Sometimes the client comes into the office close to the end of the statutory time period. The *first question* a legal assistant should ask in looking at a new case is, does a statute of limitations apply? And if so *when does the statute of limitations run?* That date should be noted on the outside of the case file and should also be calendared. (See Chapter 6 for a more detailed look at calendaring.) Calendaring may involve writing several dates in advance of the final date on the appropriate calendars; in other words, if the statute runs on June 21, a notation only on that date is not sufficient. The statute of limitations is stopped by the commencement of an action, and an action is "commenced" *when the complaint is filed* (Code Civ. Proc. §350).

Some of the statutes of limitations are set out in Code of Civil Procedure sections 312-363, and others are scattered throughout the codes. A classification according to period of limitation is found in 2 Witkin, California Procedure, (2d ed.) pages 1104-1116. A few of the most common ones are listed below for ready reference, but the entire statute must be read for exceptions and beginning dates for the running of the statute.

1 Year

Assault	CCP 340
Bank — Forged or raised checks	CCP 340
Battery	CCP 340
False imprisonment	CCP 340

Forcible entry or detainers	CCP 1172
Forfeiture or penalty statute	CCP 340
Libel	CCP 340
Notary Public, misfeasance or malfeasance	CCP 338
Personal injury	CCP 340
Public official — bond	CCP 338
Seduction of person below legal age	CCP 340
Slander	CCP 340
Worker's Compensation, Medical Disability	Lab. C. 5405
Wrongful Death	CCP 340

2 Years

Contract, oral or implied	CCP 330
Lease (Oral), Breach of	CCP 339.5
Title Insurance Policy, Abstract, Guaranty	CCP 339
Worker's Compensation, benefits other than	
Medical Disability	Lab. C. 5405b

3 Years

Fraud or mistake (from date of discovery)	CCP 338
Liability created by statute	
(other than penalty or forfeiture)	CCP 338
Notary Public's notarial act	
(from date of act)	CCP 338
Personal property, recovery of property damage	
(as in auto accident)	CCP 338
Public officials' act — bond	CCP 338
Real property (trespass or injury)	CCP 338
Hazardous waste (from date of discovery)	CCP 338

4 Years

Actions not otherwise provided for	CCP 343
Book account or account stated	
(from date of last entry)	CCP 337, 343
Contract, written — rescissions	CCP 337, 343
Demand Note (from execution)	CCP 337, 343
Lease, Written — Breach or abandonment	CCP 337.2
Marriage (Nullity) (See CC 4425 & 4426 for	
beginning date of 4-year period)	CC 4426
Personal Injury damages from patent deficiency in construction	
on or improvement to real property	CCP 337
Wrongful death from patent deficiency in construction	
on or improvement to real property	CCP 337

Tolling of the Statute

If at the time the client consults the attorney it appears at first glance that indeed the statute has already run, all may not be lost. A look should be taken at the tolling provisions found at Code of Civil Procedure section 351, et seq. Under section 351, if the cause of action *accrues* when a defendant is outside of California, an action may be filed after his return to the state within the limited term or, if he departs from California after the cause of action accrues, the time of his absence is not part of the limited time (Code Civ. Proc. §351). An investigation may have to be made or discovery had to determine if in fact defendant was out of California.

Under Code of Civil Procedure section 352, if at the time the cause of action accrues a person is under the age of majority, insane, or imprisoned on a criminal charge or under sentence of a criminal court for a term less than life, the time of such disability is not part of the time limited. (This section does not apply to actions against public entities.)

If the defendant dies before the statute expires, an action against the surviving spouse pursuant to Probate Code section 205 (community property liability) may be commenced (1) within 4 months after the death of defendant *or* (2) before the expiration of the applicable statute of limitations if defendant were alive — *whichever occurs later* (Prob. Code §353.5).

Another consideration, especially in the insurance area, is does the equitable doctrine of estoppel apply? An estoppel may occur when one party has relied to his detriment on the acts, words or conduct of another party. An estoppel may arise where a plaintiff relies on statements made during negotiations with the claims department of an insurance company. "Various circumstances may give rise to estoppel, such as an admission of liability and an agreement to settle or a misrepresentation by the claims representative of the date of loss or the date on which the statutes will run." (Some Thoughts on Claims Prevention and Repair, Baughman, Claims Manager, Lawyers' Mutual Insurance Company Newsletter (Mar. 1981).)

Insurance Code section 11580.2, which provides for a one-year from date of accident statute for filing against an uninsured motorist, has its own tolling provisions.

COMPLAINT AND SUMMONS

A complaint is the legal document which commences the lawsuit and in which is set forth the facts upon which the suit is brought, the grounds for the complaint. These grounds are set forth in "allegations," in paragraphs which probably in most courts may be designated at option by arabic numbers (1, 2, 3) or roman numerals (I, II, III). However, Los Angeles local rules require arabic numbers. (Local rules should be checked for this as well as other procedural requirements.)

Drafting the Complaint

The complaint should be succinct, not spelled out in too much detail.

The causes of action should be separate and distinct. It is better to state causes of action against each defendant separately.

A "cause of action" is "composed of a primary right possessed by the plaintiff with a duty devolving upon the defendant and a breach of such right and duty." (Mason, *California Civil Procedure Handbook*, Parker & Son Publications, Inc. 1981, p. 114)

See form of complaint in chapter on Personal Injuries, *infra*.

Filing the Complaint and Issuing the Summons

Having determined the proper jurisdiction and venue and that the statutory period for filing the lawsuit has not run, the original complaint is filed with the clerk of that court and a filing fee paid. At the same time the clerk will issue a summons, which directs defendant to file with the clerk of the court in which the action is brought a written pleading in response to the complaint (defendant may plead to the complaint orally in a justice court) within 30 days, and states that unless the defendant does so, default will be entered upon application of the plaintiff and the court may enter judgment against the defendant for money or other relief requested in the complaint.

The complaint and summons must be served upon each defendant named (unless the defendant anticipates the suit and authorizes his attorney to accept service on his behalf). After service of the summons and complaint is completed, the original summons, with a return of service thereon or attached thereto, is filed with the court. The complaint may be verified (see Verification of Pleadings, *infra*).

A summons is a printed form, to be filled out before being presented to the clerk for issuance. The copies should thereafter be conformed as to date and signature before service is made. The legal assistant should make certain that this is done. (In some counties, and possibly all, the clerk will conform them if the copies are presented at the time he issues the summons.)

A summons form follows:

SUMMONS

NAME AND ADDRESS OF ATTORNEY:	TELEPHONE NO	FOR COURT USE ONLY

ATTORNEY FOR (Name): ATTORNEY BAR #

Insert name of court, judicial district or branch court, if any, and Post Office and Street Address

PLAINTIFF:

DEFENDANT:

SUMMONS

CASE NUMBER:

NOTICE! You have been sued. The court may decide against you without your being heard unless you respond within 30 days. Read the information below.

If you wish to seek the advice of an attorney in this matter, you should do so promptly so that your written response, if any, may be filed on time.

¡AVISO! Usted ha sido demandado. El tribunal puede decidir contra Ud. sin audiencia a menos que Ud. responda dentro de 30 días. Lea la información que sigue.

Si Usted desea solicitar el consejo de un abogado en este asunto, debería hacerlo inmediatamente, de esta manera, su respuesta escrita, si hay alguna, puede ser registrada a tiempo.

1. TO THE DEFENDANT: A civil complaint has been filed by the plaintiff against you. If you wish to defend this lawsuit, you must, within **30** days after this summons is served on you, file with this court a written response to the complaint. Unless you do so, your default will be entered on application of the plaintiff, and this court may enter a judgment against you for the relief demanded in the complaint, which could result in garnishment of wages, taking of money or property or other relief requested in the complaint.

DATED: _____, Clerk, By _____, Deputy

(SEAL)

2. NOTICE TO THE PERSON SERVED: You are served
   a. ☐ As an individual defendant.
   b. ☐ As the person sued under the fictitious name of: _____
   c. ☐ On behalf of: _____

   Under: ☐ CCP 416.10 (Corporation)   ☐ CCP 416.60 (Minor)
          ☐ CCP 416.20 (Defunct Corporation)   ☐ CCP 416.70 (Incompetent)
          ☐ CCP 416.40 (Association or Partnership) ☐ CCP 416.90 (Individual)
          ☐ Other:
   d. ☐ By personal delivery on (Date): _____

A written response must be in the form prescribed by the California Rules of Court. It must be filed in this court with the proper filing fee and proof of service of a copy on each plaintiff's attorney and on each plaintiff not represented by an attorney. The time when a summons is deemed served on a party may vary depending on the method of service. For example, see CCP 413.10 through 415.50. The word "complaint" includes cross-complaint, "plaintiff" includes cross-complainant, "defendant" includes cross-defendant, the singular includes the plural.

Form Adopted by Rule 982
Judicial Council of California
Revised Effective January 1, 1979

(See reverse for Proof of Service)

SUMMONS

CCP 412.20, 412.30, 415.10.

Summons (face)

PROOF OF SERVICE
(Use separate proof of service for each person served)

1. I served the
   a. ☐ summons ☐ complaint ☐ amended summons ☐ amended complaint

   b. On defendant (Name)

   c. By serving (1) ☐ Defendant (2) ☐ Other (Name and title or relationship to person served)

   d. ☐ By delivery at ☐ home ☐ business (1) Date of
      (2) Time of   (3) Address

   e. ☐ By mailing (1) Date of   (2) Place of

2. Manner of service (Check proper box)
   a. ☐ **Personal service.** By personally delivering copies (CCP 415 10)
   b. ☐ **Substituted service on corporation, unincorporated association (including partnership), or public entity.** By leaving, during usual office hours, copies in the office of the person served with the person who apparently was in charge and thereafter mailing (by first-class mail, postage prepaid) copies to the person served at the place where the copies were left. (CCP 415 20(a))
   c. ☐ **Substituted service on natural person, minor, incompetent, or candidate.** By leaving copies at the dwelling house, usual place of abode, or usual place of business of the person served in the presence of a competent member of the household or a person apparently in charge of the office or place of business, at least 18 years of age, who was informed of the general nature of the papers, and thereafter mailing (by first-class mail, postage prepaid) copies to the person served at the place where the copies were left. (CCP 415 20(b)) **(Attach separate declaration or affidavit stating acts relied on to establish reasonable diligence in first attempting personal service.)**
   d. ☐ **Mail and acknowledgment service.** By mailing (by first-class mail or airmail) copies to the person served, together with two copies of the form of notice and acknowledgment and a return envelope, postage prepaid, addressed to the sender. (CCP 415 30) **(Attach completed acknowledgment of receipt.)**
   e. ☐ **Certified or registered mail service.** By mailing to address outside California (by registered or certified airmail with return receipt requested) copies to the person served. (CCP 415 40) **(Attach signed return receipt or other evidence of actual delivery to the person served.)**
   f. ☐ Other (Specify code section)
      ☐ Additional page is attached

3. The notice to the person served (Item 2 on the copy of the summons served) was completed as follows (CCP 412 30, 415 10, and 474)
   a. ☐ As an individual defendant
   b. ☐ As the person sued under the fictitious name of
   c. ☐ On behalf of
      Under ☐ CCP 416 10 (Corporation)   ☐ CCP 416 60 (Minor)   ☐ Other
            ☐ CCP 416 20 (Defunct corporation) ☐ CCP 416 70 (Incompetent)
            ☐ CCP 416 40 (Association or partnership) ☐ CCP 416 90 (Individual)
   d. ☐ By personal delivery on (Date)

4. At the time of service I was at least 18 years of age and not a party to this action
5. Fee for service $
6. Person serving
   a. ☐ Not a registered California process server
   b. ☐ Registered California process server
   c. ☐ Employee or independent contractor of a registered California process server
   d. ☐ Exempt from registration under Bus & Prof Code 22350(b)

   e. ☐ California sheriff, marshal, or constable
   f. Name, address and telephone number and if applicable, county of registration and number

I declare under penalty of perjury that the foregoing is true and correct and that this declaration is executed on (Date) _____ at (Place): _____, California.

(For California sheriff, marshal or constable use only)
I certify that the foregoing is true and correct and that this certificate is executed on (Date): _____ at (Place): _____, California.

_____ (Signature)   _____ (Signature)

A declaration under penalty of perjury must be signed in California or in a state that authorizes use of a declaration in place of an affidavit, otherwise an affidavit is required.

Proof of Service

Verifying the Complaint

Verification of a complaint makes verification of the answer mandatory (except in justice courts) — and except where the amount sued for is under $1,000. (Code Civ. Proc. §431.40.) In a verified answer, defendant expressly admits certain allegations, denies others, and those he fails to deny are deemed admitted.

If the complaint is not verified, a general denial of each and every allegation of the complaint is sufficient under Code of Civil Procedure section 431.30(d). In a tort action, which is not required by statute to be verified, a verified complaint may yet be preferable, to require a specific answer. A general denial puts in issue only the material allegations of the complaint. (A "material" allegation is defined in Code of Civil Procedure section 430.10 as "one essential to the claim or defense and which could not be stricken from the pleading without leaving it insufficient.") The General Denial form, which is not verified, may be used even where the amount prayed for *exceeds* $1,000 *if the complaint is not verified.*

"[I]t is safer not to verify the complaint and thus avoid the danger of having an erroneous or unproved allegation used for impeachment purposes at trial or as admissions against interest." *Wennerholm v. Stanford Univ. School of Medicine* (1942) 20 Cal.2d 713, 128 P2d 522; quoted in Werchick, *California Preparation and Trial,* p. 253, Parker & Son Publications, Inc.

A pleading is said to be verified when it has appended thereto an affidavit (sworn to before a notary) or a declaration (statement made under penalty of perjury) as to the truth of the pleading. Under Code of Civil Procedure section 2015.5 a declaration may be used wherever an affidavit may be used. Code of Civil Procedure section 2015.5 requires that the declaration contain wording substantially as follows: "I certify (or declare) under penalty of perjury that the foregoing is true and correct. (Date and Place) (Signature)."

Operative July 1, 1981, a declaration executed outside the state may be used in California if in substantially the following form: "I certify (or declare) under penalty of perjury under the laws of the State of California that the foregoing is true and correct. (Date) (Signature)."

Verification is *required* only on the documents specifically designated by various statutes. However, since some attorneys may verify many pleadings and other only those required by statute or where they have a particular reason for doing so, the legal assistant should check with the attorney.

A cost bill *must* be verified (Code Civ. Proc. §1033) and a bill of particulars must be verified if a pleading is verified. (Code Civ. Proc.

§454.) Among other proceedings requiring verification are petitions for writs (review, mandamus, prohibition), certain probate petitions (to establish fact of death, to appoint trustee for estate of missing person, restoration to capacity), complaint in unlawful detainer, petition for involuntary dissolution of corporation, preliminary injunction, quiet title actions. Pleadings of governmental bodies and agents are excepted from the requirements of verification statutes. Where a complaint is not verified although required by statute to be verified, it may be stricken on motion.

Verification, however, is always *permitted*, and serves other purposes. For example, facts in a verified complaint may be used on motion in lieu of a separate affidavit, except when verified by the attorney. (Code Civ. Proc. §446.)

Who may verify: The party to the action or his attorney, if the parties are absent from the county where the attorney has his office or for some cause are unable to verify it, or the facts are within the knowledge of the attorney or other person verifying. If verification is by attorney or other person, the affidavit must set forth the reasons why the affidavit is not made by one of the parties. (Code Civ. Proc. §446.)

When a corporation is a party, the verification may be made by an officer thereof. (Code Civ. Proc. §446.)

When the State, any county thereof city or school district, or any officer of the State, county, city or school district in his official capacity, is plaintiff or defendant, the complaint or answer, as the case may be, need not be verified. (Code Civ. Proc. §446.)

Affidavit to Verify Complaint

A form of verification (in affidavit form) follows:

STATE OF CALIFORNIA
COUNTY OF SACRAMENTO   ss.

MARY PRICE, being first duly sworn, deposes and says:

I am the plaintiff in the above-entitled action; I have read the foregoing Complaint and know the contents thereof; the same is true of my own knowledge, except as to those matters which are therein stated upon my information or belief, and as to those matters, I believe it to be true.

signature/ Mary Price

Subscribed and sworn to
before me this 24th day
of May, 19____.*

(SEAL) s/ Roberta Caldwell
    Roberta Caldwell†
Notary Public in and for the
    County of Sacramento.
        State of California.

My Commission Expires March 24, 19____.
The "affiant" is the person who makes an affidavit, i.e., in the above
example, Mary Price.

Signatures

Clients should be instructed to sign documents as their names
appear therein, e.g., since the name appears as "Mary Price," the
signature should not be "Mary Esther Price" or "Mary E. Price."
Conversely, if the name in the document had been "Mary Esther
Price," a signature of "Mary E. Price" or "Mary Price" would not
suffice.

Clients are asked to read documents before signing and the legal
assistant should be alert that the document is properly signed.

Filing Fees

When a document is filed to initiate an action — usually a complaint
or a petition — or when a defendant makes his first appearance in a
case — usually by answer or demurrer — a filing fee is payable. The
term "filing fee" is used, although actually the "filing fee" is comprised of a basic filing fee, a law library fee, and the reporter's fee,
if any.

A complete list of the filing and other fees is contained in California
Courts Directory and Fee Schedules, obtainable either from your local
municipal court clerk's office or from the Business Manager, Municipal
Clerks Association, Post Office Box 460, Bellflower, California
90706.

(Under Government Code section 6103 the State of California is
not required, in most cases, to pay a *filing* fee on the commencement
of the action or a first appearance fee, but does pay the reporter's fee,
if the particular county charges one. Later, however, if the state obtains

---

*Starting with the word "Subscribed" and ending with "19____" is the portion
called "jurat," i.e., that portion of the affidavit which states when, before whom,
and where the affidavit was made.
†A rubber seal contains the name of the notary as required by Government Code
section 8207.

a judgment for money in the case, then, out of the first moneys collected on that judgment, under Government Code section 6103.5, the filing fee becomes payable, as well as the fees for service of process.)

SERVICE OF SUMMONS AND COMPLAINT
On Counsel

We have seen that the summons and complaint must be personally served on the defendant. Ordinarily a defendant will obtain an attorney, and the attorney will be served with any subsequent pleadings filed in the case. Proof must be made to the court that all the pleadings in the case have been actually served on the opposing counsel. This is obviously necessary, since otherwise the plaintiff could proceed to trial and judgment without the defendant's knowledge and therefore without an opportunity to defend himself.

Legal papers are served on opposing counsel either by leaving the same with a person in charge of the office of the attorney during regular office hours, or by depositing them, sealed and postpaid, in the mail directed to such attorney at his usual post office address.

Every copy served must bear a notation of the date and place of mailing, or be accompanied by an unsigned copy of the affidavit or certificate of mailing.

If a copy of the document is delivered to the attorney at his office, he (or his legal assistant or other person authorized by him) will sign a receipt typed on the original of the document, in the following or similar language:

Receipt of copy of the within Answer is hereby acknowledged this 25th day of May, 19____.

s/ Philip Brown
Attorney for Plaintiff

Proof of service by mail is usually made by a *Declaration of Service by Mail* (see Code Civ. Proc. §2015.5), made under penalty of perjury. A suggested form of Declaration follows:

Declaration of Service by Mail

I, _____ , declare as follows: I am a citizen of the United States, over the age of 18 years, and not a party to the within action; my place of employment and business address is ——————————————————————————————— ,

———————————————————————————— , California ——————.

On ——————————————————————— , 19——, I served the

attached———————————————————————————————
by placing a true copy thereof in an envelope addressed to each of the
persons named below at the address shown, and by sealing and depositing said envelope in the United States mail at Sacramento, California, with postage prepaid:
[Name and address as on envelope]

There is delivery service by United States mail at each of the places
so addressed, or there is regular communication by mail between the
place of mailing and each of the places so addressed.
I declare under penalty of perjury that the foregoing is true and
correct.
Executed on ————————————— , 19——, at ————————— ,
California.

———————————————————————————
Declarant

The proof of service forms may be completed by the secretary (or
legal assistant) or, under Code of Civil Procedure section 1013a, subdivision (2), by the attorney.

On Defendants

The initial pleading in a lawsuit (i.e., the complaint or petition and
summons) must be served on the defendants. (Subsequent pleadings
are served on the defendants' counsel, if an attorney is retained, as
discussed *supra*.) Service may be effected by one of the following
means, or as otherwise ordered by the court:
1. *Personal delivery* of a copy of the summons and complaint to
the defendant. The person making the service must be over 18 years
of age and not a party to the action. (Code Civ. Proc. §415.10.) *Service
is complete upon delivery*.
Section 415.10 requires that the date of delivery be entered on the
face of the copy of the summons at the time of its delivery, but that
service without such date is valid and effective.

2. *Substituted service on corporation, unincorporated association (including partnership, public entity).* A copy of the summons and complaint may be left with a person closely connected with the defendant, and apparently in charge of his office, at the defendant's place of business. The person with whom the summons and complaint are left must be at least 18 years of age and must be informed of the contents. The name of the person and his title should be obtained. (Code Civ. Proc. §415.20(a).)

Thereafter a copy of the summons and complaint are mailed by first-class mail, postage prepaid, to the defendant at the place where the copy of the summons and complaint were left. *Service is complete on the 10th day after such mailing.*

3. *Substituted service on natural person, minor, incompetent, or candidate for public office.* A declaration or affidavit must be prepared establishing reasonable diligence in first attempting personal service. In lieu of personal service (a preferable type of service), substituted service is made by leaving a copy of the summons and complaint with a person closely connected with the defendant, either at the defendant's place of business with a person apparently in charge of his office, or at his dwelling house or usual place of abode with a competent member of his household. The person with whom the summons and complaint are left must be at least 18 years of age and must be informed of the contents. The name of the person and relationship to defendant should be obtained. (Code Civ. Proc., §415.20(b).)

Thereafter a copy of the summons and complaint must be mailed by first-class mail, postage prepaid, to the defendant at the place where the copy of the summons and complaint were left. *Service is complete on the 10th day after mailing.*

4. *Mail and acknowledgment of receipt of summons.* Serve by mailing first-class mail or airmail, postage prepaid, the papers to the person to be served together with two copies of a form of Notice and Acknowledgment as provided by Code of Civil Procedure section 415.30(b) and a return envelope, postage prepaid, addressed to the sender.

NOTICE AND ACKNOWLEDGMENT OF RECEIPT OF SUMMONS

The notice and acknowledgment shall be substantially in the following form:

(Title of court and cause)

NOTICE

TO: (Name of person to be served)

This summons is served pursuant to Section 415.30 of the California Code of Civil Procedure. Failure to complete this form and return it to the sender within 20 days may subject you (or the party on whose behalf you are being served) to liability for the payment of any expenses incurred in serving a summons upon you in any other manner permitted by law. If you are served on behalf of a corporation, unincorporated association (including a partnership), or other entity, this form must be signed in the name of such entity by you or by a person authorized to receive service of process on behalf of such entity. In all other cases, this form must be signed by you personally or by a person authorized by you to acknowledge receipt of summons. Section 415.30 provides that this summons is deemed served on the date of execution of an acknowledgment of receipt of summons.

(Signature of sender)

ACKNOWLEDGMENT OF RECEIPT OF SUMMONS

This acknowledges receipt on (insert date) of a copy of the summons and the complaint at (insert address).

Dated: (date this acknowledgment is executed)

(Signature of person acknowledging receipt,
with title if acknowledgment is made on behalf
of another person)

Service is deemed complete on the date a written acknowledgment of summons is executed, if such acknowledgment is thereafter returned to the sender.

If the summons is not returned within 20 days, the defendant shall be liable for reasonable expenses incurred in serving or attempting to serve him and such costs shall be awarded whether or not the plaintiff is entitled to recover costs in the action.

5. *Service by Publication.* If an *individual* defendant cannot with due diligence be served in any of the foregoing ways, he may be served by publishing the summons in a California newspaper. (Code Civ. Proc. §415.50.) Such a defendant might have departed from California, or he might be concealing himself to avoid service.

Procedure on publication: An *affidavit* for publication of summons (Code Civ. Proc. §415.50) in which is recited all attempts to locate the defendant, that is, search of telephone directories, city directories, county tax collector's record, register of voters, details of inquiries made, and dates, is taken to a judge with an *order for publication of summons*. The newspaper in which publication is to be made should be named in the order and should be designated as most likely to give notice to the person to be served. (Code Civ. Proc. §415.50.)

Government Code section 6064 requires publication *once a week for four successive weeks*, in a newspaper published once a week or oftener, with at least 5 days intervening between the respective publication dates, not counting such publication dates. The court may order a long period of publication. (Code Civ. Proc. §415.50.) *Service is complete at the expiration of the time prescribed by the order for publication.*

The order for publication must direct that a copy of the summons and complaint be mailed to the defendant if his address is ascertained before the expiration of the time prescribed for publication of summons. (Code Civ. Proc. §415.50.)

Although an order for publication has been made, however, the papers may be served by any of the other methods provided above, in which event the service by the other means supersedes the service by publication. (Code Civ. Proc. §415.50(d); see Gov. Code §6064.) (See "Comment-Judicial Council" following Code Civ. Proc. §415.50, West's Ann. Code.)

6. *Proof of service.* Proof of service is made by the affidavit of the person making the service.

After service by publication, an *affidavit of publication* must be presented to the court (Code Civ. Proc. §417.10); the newspaper will furnish this affidavit.

Service is deemed complete on the last day of required publication.

Service On Certain Other Defendants.

Service on the following defendants may be made by personally delivering a copy of the summons and complaint as indicated:

1. *Minors and Wards:*	To his or her parent, guardian, conservator, or similar fiduciary, or if no such person can be found with reasonable diligence, to any person having care or control of such minor or with whom he or she resides or is employed, or to the minor if he or she is at least 12 years of age.
2. *Conservatees:*	To his or her conservator or similar fiduciary and to such person, but, for good cause shown, the court may dispense with delivery to such person.

3. *Political candidates:* As provided by Elections Code section 54 when authorized.

4. *Public entity:* To the clerk, secretary, president, presiding officer, or other head of its governing body. (Here "public entity" includes state and any office, department, division, or agency of the state, the Regents of the University of California, a county, city, district, public authority, public agency, and any other political subdivision or public corporation in this state.)

If personal service cannot be made on the above defendants, substituted service may be made as provided by Code of Civil Procedure section 415.20(b) (except a defendant public entity).

5. *Joint stock corporation:* See Code of Civil Procedure sections 416.10 and 416.20.

6. *Person outside state:* In any manner provided for service of person in California, or by mailing a copy of the summons and complaint by airmail requiring a return receipt. (See Code Civ. Proc. §415.40.) *Service is deemed complete on the 10th day after mailing.*

Service on Defendant Corporations

1. *Domestic Corporations.* Domestic corporations are served by delivering a copy of the summons and complaint to a person designated as agent for service of process (as provided by any provision in Corporations Code sections 202, 1502, 2105 or 2107 (or Corporations Code sections 3301-3302, 6500-6504), or by serving the president or other head of the corporation, a vice president, secretary or assistant secretary, treasurer or assistant treasurer, general manager, or person authorized by the corporation to receive service. If the corporation is a bank, service may also be made on the cashier or assistant cashier. (Code Civ. Proc. §416.10.)

If after reasonable diligence no such person can be located within the state, and if shown by an *affidavit* to the satisfaction of the judge that with reasonable diligence service of process cannot be made either by hand delivery (§415.10 subd. (a)), by mail as provided in Code of Civil Procedure section 415.30, or by substituted service as provided in Code of Civil Procedure section 415.20, subdivision (a), the judge may make an *order* that service be made upon the corporation by delivering to the Secretary of State (or person employed in his office in the capacity of assistant or deputy) *one copy of the process for each defendant to be served, together with a copy of the order authorizing such service.* Service in this manner constitutes personal service upon the corporation. (Corp. Code §§1701, 1702.)

Service is deemed complete on the 10th day after delivery of the process to the Secretary of State. (Corp. Code §1702, subd. (a).) The defendant must appear within 30 days thereafter. (Corp. Code §1702, subd. (b).)

The following language must be typed on the copy of the summons served on the person (Code Civ. Proc. §412.30):

> To [name of person served]: You are hereby served in the within action [or special proceeding] on behalf of [name of corporation or unincorporated association] as a person upon whom the summons and a copy of the complaint may be delivered to effect service on said party under the provisions of [state appropriate sections of ch. 4 of Code of Civil Procedure commencing with section 413.10].

(Judicial Council forms now cover this and other similar language requirements of the codes; appropriate boxes should be checked.)

When the person so served is also served as an individual, notice of such fact must appear on the copy of the summons. The proof of service must recite that such notification was given.

2. *Foreign Corporations.* (Corp. Code §§2110 *et seq.*) Foreign corporations are served by serving any officer or its general manager in this state (or if a bank a cashier or an assistant cashier), any natural person designated as agent for service of process, or designated corporate agent as evidenced by records in the Secretary of State's office. (Corp. Code §2110.)

If after diligent search no such person can be found and it is so shown by *affidavit* to the judge, the judge may make an *order* that service be made by personal delivery to the Secretary of State, or to an assistant or deputy secretary of state, of 2 *copies of process together with 2 copies of the order* (*except* that if the corporation has not designated a corporate agent as required by Corporations Code section 2105, only 1 copy of the process and order need be delivered but the order shall set forth an address to which such process shall be sent by the Secretary of State). (Corp. Code §2111.)

If a foreign corporation has forfeited its right to transact business in California, service may be made in the same manner as set forth above. (See Corp. Code §2114, subd. (c).)

Service on a foreign corporation which has *surrendered* or *withdrawn* its right to do business in California is made pursuant to Corporations Code section 2114 by personal delivery to the Secretary of State (or to an assistant or deputy secretary of state) and no authorizing court order is required. The process is then sent to the address in the certificate of surrender or address of the surviving domestic corporation.

The corporation must appear within 30 days after delivery of the process to the Secretary of State.

Service on Unincorporated Associations

Domestic unincorporated associations and partnerships: Service may be made by delivering a copy of the summons and complaint to a person designated as agent for service of process as provided by Corporations Code section 24003.

a. *Association that is a general or limited partnership:* May also be served by delivering a copy of the summons and complaint to a general partner or general manager.

b. *Association that is not a general or limited partnership:* May also be served by delivering a copy of the summons and complaint to the president or other head of the association, a vice president, a secretary or assistant secretary, a treasurer or assistant treasurer, a general manager, or a person authorized by the association to receive service of process. The following language must appear on the copy of the summons served on the person (Code Civ. Proc. §412.30):

> To [name of person served]: You are hereby served in the within action [or special proceeding] on behalf of [name of corporation or unincorporated association] as a person upon whom the summons and a copy of the complaint may be delivered to effect service on said party under the provisions of [state appropriate sections of ch. 4 of Code of Civil Procedure commencing with section 413.10].

When the person so served is also served as an individual, notice of such fact must also appear on the copy of the summons. The *proof of service* must recite that such notification was given.

Service on Individuals Sued Under Fictitious Name

Complaints frequently designate Doe defendants, as First Doe, Second Doe and Third Doe, because the names of some of the defendants are unknown or because of the possibility of discovering that someone else should have been named as defendant. Naming Does eliminates the necessity of amending the complaint to bring in the newly discovered defendant, provided the complaint contains all the allegations necessary to cover the new defendants.

When serving a person sued under a fictitious name, say as First Doe, there should be typed somewhere *on the copy of the summons being served on the defendant* the following language:

"To *(his real name):* You are hereby served in the within action as (or on behalf of) the person sued under the fictitious name of First Doe." (Code of Civil Proc. §474.)

The return of service (proof of service) must state the fictitious name under which such defendant was served and the fact that notice of identity was given by endorsement upon the document served as required by Code of Civil Procedure section 474. Compliance with Code of Civil Procedure section 474 is a requisite for taking default.

Service on Nonresident Vehicle Owners

Pursuant to Vehicle Code sections 17454, 17455, and 17456, nonresidents of California who become involved in automobile accidents while in California may be served in the following manner:

a. *Mailing of copy of summons and complaint to Director of Motor Vehicles* by certified or registered mail, addressee only, return receipt requested, or leaving a copy of the summons and complaint at the Director's office. (Service is effective the day the return receipt is received from the Director's office.) A $2 fee should accompany the papers.

b. *A notice of such service on the Director* must either

(1) be sent by registered mail to the defendant or

(2) served personally outside the state. *Proof of service of the notice* is made by attaching affidavit showing mailing and the return receipt bearing the signature of the defendant to the original summons *or,* if served outside California, by a due return.

Acceptance of a certificate of ownership or registration or acceptance or retention of a California driver's license constitutes consent to service within or without California and whether or not they are then residents of California in a cause of action arising in California out of the ownership or operation of a vehicle in California. When the summons is served outside California, it may be served as set forth above pursuant to Vehicle Code sections 17454, 17455, and 17456, or pursuant to Chapter 4 (commencing with section 413.10) (see paragraphs 1 through 5 under heading "On Defendants" hereinabove).

Proof of Service

Code of Civil Procedure section 417.10 contains the requirements for proof of service on a person within the State of California; Code of Civil Procedure section 417.20 contains the requirements for proof of service on a person outside California. The reverse side of the official form of Summons contains a form of Proof of Service.

An affidavit or certificate of service by mail must set forth the exact title of the document served and filed but need no longer be affixed to the original, or a true copy, of the document served and filed. (Code of Civ. Proc. §1013a.)

Return of service on the summons on the complaint (or cross-complaint) must be made within three years after the commencement of the action, unless the parties have extended the time in writing by stipulation or the defendant has made a general appearance, and the case shall be dismissed by the court. (Code Civ. Proc. §581a.) The legal assistant should be very alert to this important time requirement. (See Motion to Dismiss, next chapter.)

Lost Summons

The practice of issuing an "alias" summons when the original summons had been lost, has been abolished.

Now, if the summmons has been returned without serving defendant, or lost before service made, another original may be issued. (Code Civ. Proc. §412.10.)

A separate summons may be secured for service on one or more defendants, all of which are "original" summonses.

When an original summons is lost *after* service and *before* it is returned to the court to be filed, its return is excused. Code of Civil Procedure section 417.30 provides that an affidavit of the process server may be returned in lieu thereof.

A summons must be served and returned within three years from the commencement of the action, unless the parties have stipulated to extend the time, or unless the defendant has made a general appearance. (Code of Civ. Proc. §581a.)

The legal assistant should be aware of this limitation and calendar or otherwise keep check to make certain that the time does not lapse on any summons issued, which would make the case subject to a motion to dismiss.

SERVICE SUMMARY
Personal Service

1. Serve personally copy of summons and complaint on defendant(s).
2. File proof of service of summons and complaint.

Substituted Service

On natural person, minor, incompetent, or candidate for public office:

1. Leave copy of summons and complaint at usual place of abode with a competent member of household (over 18) or at place of business with person apparently in charge of office.
2. Mail a second copy of summons and complaint by first-class mail, postage prepaid, to address where papers left.
3. File proof of service of summons and complaint and affidavit or declaration showing reasonable attempt to effect personal service.
4. Service is complete 10th day after mailing.

Substituted Service

On corporation, unincorporated association (including partnership, public entity):

1. Leave copy of summons and complaint at defendant's place of business with person apparently in charge of office (at least 18 years of age). Inform such person of the contents and obtain title of person.
2. Mail a second copy of summons and complaint by first-class mail, postage prepaid, to address where papers left.
3. File proof of service of summons and complaint and affidavit or declaration showing reasonable attempt to effect personal service.
4. Service is complete 10th day after mailing.

Admission of Service

1. File written acknowledgment of receipt of summons and complaint. (Code Civ. Proc. §§417.10-417.20.)

   (A general appearance by a defendant is "equivalent to personal service of summons.") (Code Civ. Proc. §410.50.)

Mail and Acknowledgment of Receipt of Summons

1. Mail first-class mail or airmail, postage prepaid, summons and complaint to defendant with 2 copies of Notice and Acknowledgment, plus return envelope, postage prepaid, addressed to sender.

2. Proof of service must include Acknowledgment of receipt of summons.

3. Service is complete 20th day after Acknowledgment, *IF* the Acknowledgment is returned to sender.

Service by Publication

1. Prepare affidavit for publication of summons and order for publication of summons.

2. Present to judge for signature of the order.

3. Publish summons in newspaper once a week or more often (with 5 days intervening between publication dates) for four successive weeks — unless court has ordered longer period of publication.

4. Service is complete upon completion of publication as prescribed by order.

5. Obtain an affidavit of publication from the newspaper to file with the court.

AMENDMENT OF COMPLAINT AND ANSWER

(Code Civ. Proc. §§471.5-473;
Rule 205, California Rules of Court)

If an error or omission in the complaint is discovered, the complaint may be amended once as of course. (Code Civ. Proc. §472.) The procedure for amending may vary depending upon the status of the case, to wit:

If

(1) the complaint has not been served:

or

(2) the complaint has been served but no answer or demurrer filed (and defendant does not have an attorney):

An amended complaint is filed and a new summons on amended complaint issued and served on defendant

Defendant has 30 days after service to answer the complaint as amended

If

(3) the complaint has been served and an answer or demurrer filed

An amended complaint is filed:
(a) By stipulation of counsel
   or
(b) By filing a motion. A copy of the amended complaint is attached to the original motion and served; the original is filed after an order allowing its filing; then a copy is served on the attorney (or he may acknowledge receipt)

The motion is served 10 days before the hearing

If

(4) Answer is amended

Adverse party has 10 days after service (or such other time as court fixes) to demur to the amended answer

Amendment of Complaint for
True Name of Doe Defendant

[TITLE OF COURT AND CAUSE]

AMENDMENT TO COMPLAINT

On filing the complaint in this case plaintiff, being ignorant of the true name of a defendant, designated such defendant in the complaint by the fictitious name of FIRST DOE, and, having discovered the defendant's true name to be LAWRENCE WHITTINGTON BEN-CHLEY, plaintiff amends the complaint by inserting such true name instead of the fictitious name wherever it appears in the complaint.

Dated:

_____

Attorney for Plaintiff

DEMURRER

(Code Civ. Proc. §430.10)

After a complaint is served, the defendant usually files either an answer or a demurrer. An answer and a demurrer may be filed at the same time. Consideration should also be given to the filing of a motion to strike. (See next chapter.) A demurrer is a pleading objecting to defects appearing on the face of a complaint and putting at issue questions of law only. A demurrer (or answer or other pleading) must be filed within 30 days.

The grounds for a demurrer are specified in Code of Civil Procedure section 430.10. Briefly summarized, they are:

1. Court has no jurisdiction of the subject of the cause of action.

2. Plaintiff has no legal capacity to sue.

3. Another action is pending between the same parties for the same cause.

4. There is a defect or misjoinder of parties plaintiff or defendant.

5. Complaint does not state facts sufficient to constitute a cause of action.

6. Complaint is uncertain (includes "ambiguous" and "unintelligible").

7. In actions founded upon a contract, it is not evident on the face of the complaint whether the contract is written or oral or whether it is implied by conduct.

8. The complaint was not accompanied by the certificate required by Section 411.30 or 411.35. [Relates only to malpractice action against physician or surgeon or dentist.]

Grounds 1 and 5 above may be raised at any stage of the litigation, but the other grounds are waived unless timely raised by answer or demurrer. (Code Civ. Proc. §430.80.)

Use of a demurrer is an attempt to win on a cause of action or to force the plaintiffs to plead themselves out of part or all of the causes of action. It may force the plaintiff to plead facts that may be attacked later. Use of demurrer usually narrows the causes of action so that the parties have a clearer understanding of what will be litigable.

HEARING AND NOTICE

The party filing the demurrer must serve and file therewith a notice of hearing specifying a hearing date not less than 10 days and not more than 15 days from the filing and notice; if the Law and Motion Calendar in that county is not regularly heard on a date within the prescribed period, the notice of hearing must specify the date of the Law and Motion Calendar next following the 15th day. For good cause shown to the court, the hearing may be held on an earlier or later date. (Rule 202, California Rules of Court.)

The demurrer should contain supporting points and authorities of each ground. (Rules 202, subd. (a), 502, subd. (a), California Rules of Court.)

Demurrers are commonly referred to as *general* or *special* demurrers. A special demurrer will enumerate specific grounds, such as misjoinder of parties, lack of capacity to sue, failure to define whether they are partners, association, etc., a minor, or need for a guardian. A *general* demurrer usually states that the complaint does not state facts sufficient to constitute a cause of action against defendant (see ground 5 above).

At the hearing argument is made to the court by counsel. Then the court either (a) sustains the demurrer with (or without) leave to amend, or (b) overrules the demurrer with (or without) leave to answer. The court may take the demurrer under submission at the time of the hearing, in which case the clerk of the court will notify the parties of the court's ruling.

If the demurrer is held to be valid, i.e., sustained, then the plaintiff must amend his complaint or, if the plaintiff were not given leave to amend his complaint, the case would be closed — unless plaintiff appeals. If the demurrer is held to be invalid, then the defendant is usually given leave to answer within a specified number of days. If the time is not specified, leave to answer or amend within 10 days shall be deemed granted (Rules 202, 502, California Rules of Court). The *time to amend or answer* runs from the *date of service* of the notice of decision or order. (Code of Civ. Proc. §472b.)

Forms for general demurrer and notices of overruling demurrer and sustaining demurrer follow:

Demurrer

```
MANNING & FINCH
Attorneys at Law
Forum Building
Sacramento, CA 95814
Telephone:  447-3490

Attorneys for Defendants
```

SUPERIOR COURT OF THE STATE OF CALIFORNIA

FOR THE COUNTY OF SACRAMENTO

JOHN SMITH,)	NO. 126704
)	
Plaintiff,)	
)	
v.)	D E M U R R E R
)	
JAMES BROWN; WHITE CORPORATION,)	
a California corporation;)	
FIRST DOE; SECOND DOE; and)	
THIRD DOE,)	
)	
Defendants.)	
)	

Come now the defendants, JAMES BROWN and WHITE CORPORATION, a California corporation, and demurring to the complaint of plaintiff on file herein, for cause of demurrer, specify:

I

That said complaint does not state facts sufficient to constitute a cause of action against said defendants.

WHEREFORE, defendants pray that plaintiff take nothing by reason of his complaint and that they may be hence dismissed with their costs of suit herein incurred.

MANNING & FINCH

By *William Manning*

Attorneys for Defendants

POINTS AND AUTHORITIES IN SUPPORT OF DEMURRER

Code of Civil Procedure, Section 430.10.

Some local court rules require that a demurrer include the following statement signed by the attorney; check local rules:

I hereby certify that this Demurrer is filed in good faith, not for the purpose of delay, and in my opinion the grounds are well taken.

_____

(Name of attorney)

One Alternative Form of Demurrer to Complaint:

Defendant demurs to the complaint herein on each of the following grounds separately:

1. The first cause of action fails to state facts sufficient to constitute a cause of action.

2. It cannot be ascertained from the first cause of action whether the contract therein sued on was written or oral, or implied by conduct.

3. The second cause of action fails to state facts sufficient to constitute a cause of action.

4. The second cause of action shows on its face that Lillie Mercer is an heir of the plaintiff's decedent, Rene Carnation, and has not been joined in this action as a party plaintiff.

5. The complaint shows on its face that the court lacks jurisdiction of the subject of the cause of action set forth as plaintiff's third cause of action.

6. The third cause of action fails to state facts sufficient to constitute a cause of action in that it shows on its face that it is barred by a statute of limitations.

*7. With respect to the fourth cause of action, there is another action pending between the same parties on the same complaint. This court is hereby requested to take judicial notice of the records and files in the case of Buster Burns, plaintiff, v. Millie Wing, defendant, No. 11234, now pending in the Municipal Court of California, San Joaquin Judicial District. Certified copy of the records and files in this case are furnished herewith as required by section 453(b) of the Evidence Code to enable the court to take judicial notice of this matter.

---

*Code Civ. Proc. §§430.30(a), 430.70.

Notice of Overruling of Demurrer

```
1   PAUL D. BLACK
    Attorney at Law
2   926 J Street
    Sacramento, CA 95814
3   Telephone:  445-4567

4   Attorney for Plaintiff

5

6

7

8              SUPERIOR COURT OF THE STATE OF CALIFORNIA

9                  FOR THE COUNTY OF SACRAMENTO

10

11  JOHN SMITH,                    )        No. 126704
                                   )
12              Plaintiff,         )
                                   )
13       v.                        )     NOTICE OF OVERRULING
                                   )
14  JAMES BROWN; WHITE CORPORATION,)        OF DEMURRER
    a California corporation;      )
15  FIRST DOE; SECOND DOE; and     )
    THIRD DOE,                     )
16                                 )
                Defendants.        )
17  _____  )

18

19  TO THE DEFENDANTS ABOVE NAMED AND TO MESSRS. MANNING & FINCH,

20  THEIR ATTORNEYS:

21       PLEASE TAKE NOTICE that on Tuesday, July 6, 1976, the

22  above-entitled Court overruled the above-named defendants'

23  demurrer to the complaint herein, and that said defendants have

24  ten (10) days within which to answer said complaint.

25

26

27                              Attorney for Plaintiff

28
```

Notice of Sustaining of Demurrer

```
PAUL D. BLACK
Attorney at Law
926 J Street
Sacramento, CA 95814
Telephone:  445-4567

Attorney for Plaintiff
```

SUPERIOR COURT OF THE STATE OF CALIFORNIA

FOR THE COUNTY OF SACRAMENTO

JOHN SMITH,	)	NO. 126704
Plaintiff,	)	
v.	)	NOTICE OF SUSTAINING
JAMES BROWN; WHITE CORPORATION,	)	OF DEMURRER
a California corporation;	)	
FIRST DOE; SECOND DOE; and	)	
THIRD DOE,	)	
Defendants.	)	

TO THE PLAINTIFF JOHN SMITH ABOVE NAMED, AND TO PAUL D. BLACK,

ESQ., HIS ATTORNEY:

PLEASE TAKE NOTICE that on July 6, 1976, the above-
entitled Court sustained the above-named defendants' demurrer
to the complaint herein, with ten (10) days' leave to plaintiff
within which to amend said complaint.

MANNING & FINCH

By _William Manning_

Attorneys for Defendants

```
[1.  Prepare original and 3.
 2.  Serve 1 copy on attorney for plaintiff.  (Attach copy of
     affidavit or declaration of mailing.)
 3.  File with clerk original notice with original affidavit or
     declaration of mailing attached.  Have copy endorsed-filed.]
```

ANSWER

(Code Civ. Proc. §§430.10, 430.30)

An answer is a document filed in reply to a complaint.

The answer (or demurrer) must be filed within 30 days. If a demurrer is filed, the answer need not be filed until a ruling is made on the demurrer.

The answer denies that certain allegations or parts of them are true, denies other allegations for lack of information or belief, and admits those that are true. If the complaint is not verified, an answer may be simply a general denial of the entire complaint, in language such as: "Denies each and every allegation contained in the complaint herein." However, such a general denial only serves to put in issue the material allegations of the complaint or cross-complaint. If the complaint (or cross-complaint) be verified, the denials then have to be specific. (Code Civ. Proc. §431.30(d).)

Under Code of Civil Procedure section 431.40, in an action in which the demand exclusive of interest does not exceed $1,000, the defendant may file an unverified general written denial and a brief statement of any new matter constituting a defense, on a form prescribed by the Judicial Council. If the complaint is not verified, the General Denial form may be used pursuant to Code of Civil Procedure section 431.30 in actions where the demand or value of the property exceeds $1,000. The form follows:

GENERAL DENIAL

NAME AND ADDRESS OF ATTORNEY (OR DEFENDANT WITHOUT ATTORNEY)	TELEPHONE	FOR COURT USE ONLY
ATTORNEY FOR		
Name of court, branch, judicial district, mailing and street address		
PLAINTIFF		
DEFENDANT		
GENERAL DENIAL	CASE NUMBER	

> THIS GENERAL DENIAL MAY BE USED ONLY WHERE THE COMPLAINT IS UNVERIFIED OR WHERE THE COMPLAINT IS VERIFIED BUT THE DEMAND OR VALUE OF THE PROPERTY IN CONTROVERSY DOES NOT EXCEED $1,000.

1. Defendant (Name):
   generally denies each and every allegation of plaintiff's complaint.

2. Defendant asserts the following affirmative defenses (Set forth briefly the facts constituting each separate affirmative defense [See item 3a]. *Attach additional pages if necessary.*):

Dated: _____

_____
Signature of defendant

NOTICES TO DEFENDANT

3a. An affirmative defense is new matter constituting a defense to plaintiff's claim which must be stated in defendant's response. New matter is generally some fact or facts which would prevent the plaintiff from obtaining a judgment against you even if all of plaintiff's factual claims were proven to be true. Affirmative defenses recognized by law are of many kinds, such as self-defense, privilege, lack of capacity to sue, statute of limitations, and discharge of the debt by payment.

b. If you have a claim for damages or other relief against the plaintiff, the law may require that your claim be set forth in a separate pleading called a cross-complaint or your claim may be forever barred. (See Code of Civil Procedure Sections 426.10-426.40.)

The original of this General Denial must be filed in this court with proof that a copy was served on each plaintiff's attorney and on each plaintiff not represented by an attorney

Form Adopted by Rule 982 of
the Judicial Council of California
Effective January 1, 1978   **GENERAL DENIAL**   CCP 431.30, 431.40

Answer

<table>
<tr><td>1</td><td>MANNING & FINCH
Attorneys at Law</td></tr>
<tr><td>2</td><td>Forum Building
Sacramento, CA 95814</td></tr>
<tr><td>3</td><td>Telephone: 447-3490</td></tr>
<tr><td>4</td><td>Attorneys for Defendants</td></tr>
</table>

1 MANNING & FINCH
   Attorneys at Law
2 Forum Building
   Sacramento, CA 95814
3 Telephone: 447-3490

4 Attorneys for Defendants

5

6

7

8   SUPERIOR COURT OF THE STATE OF CALIFORNIA

9   FOR THE COUNTY OF SACRAMENTO

10

11 JOHN SMITH,   )   No. 126704
)
12   Plaintiff,   )
)
13   v.   )   A N S W E R
)
14 JAMES BROWN; WHITE CORPORATION,)
    a California corporation;   )
15 FIRST DOE; SECOND DOE; and   )
    THIRD DOE,   )
16   )
            Defendants.   )
17 _____)

18

19   Defendants JAMES BROWN and WHITE CORPORATION, a Cali-

20 fornia corporation, answer the complaint herein as follows:

21   I

22   Admit the allegations contained in paragraphs I, II and

23 III of the complaint herein.

24   II

25   Defendants have no information or belief sufficient to

26 enable them to answer the allegations of paragraphs IV, V and VII

27 of said complaint, and basing their denial on that ground, deny

28 each and every allegation thereof.

III

Deny each and every, all and singular, generally and specifically, the allegations contained in paragraphs VI, VIII and IX of said complaint.

WHEREFORE, defendants pray that plaintiff take nothing by his complaint and that they be hence dismissed with their costs.

MANNING & FINCH

By *William Manning*

Attorneys for Defendants

Frequently an answer admits some of the allegations, denies the truth of others on information or belief, or simply denies them.

Affirmative Defenses in Answers

In an affirmative defense, even though the defendant or respondent admits facts alleged in the complaint, additional facts are asserted pointing to a judgment for the defense nevertheless. In personal injury cases the more experienced legal assistant who has analyzed the case should be able to recognize available affirmative defenses and include them in the draft of the answer. In some offices the attorney may give general instructions to the legal assistant as to the defenses to be included.

Any affirmative defenses must be set out in the answer or be forever waived. Some examples are set forth below as ready reminders:

1. *Comparative Negligence (sole proximate cause)*

As a *FIRST*, SEPARATE AND DISTINCT AFFIRMATIVE DEFENSE, this answering defendant alleges that the injuries and damages complained of by plaintiff are the direct result of his sole fault and negligence, thereby barring his claim completely.

2. *Comparative Negligence*

As a *FIRST*, SEPARATE AND DISTINCT AFFIRMATIVE DEFENSE, this answering defendant alleges that the injuries and damages, if any, sustained by plaintiff, were the direct result of the fault and negligence of plaintiff, and that the damages, if any, awarded herein should be diminished in proportion to the amount of fault and negligence attributable to the plaintiff.

3. *Facts insufficient to constitute a cause of action*

As a _____ DEFENSE, this answering defendant alleges that the_____ Cause of Action of the complaint on file herein fails to state facts sufficient to constitute a cause of action against this answering defendant. (Or: _____ this answering defendant alleges that neither plaintiff's complaint, nor any of the alleged causes of action therein, state facts sufficient to constitute a cause of action against this answering defendant.)

4. *Immunity of public entity*

As a _____ DEFENSE, this answering defendant alleges that this answering defendant is entitled to the various immunities set forth in the Government Code of the State of California; that the precise nature and extent of the immunities applicable to this defendant in these proceedings are not now known to this answering defendant, and said defendant prays leave to amend this answer to relate the full extent of said immunities when the same has been ascertained.

5. *Statute of Limitations*

As a _____ DEFENSE, this answering defendant alleges that said cause of action is barred by the provisions of the Code of Civil Procedure, section 340, subsection 3 (one year) [or Section 338 (three years).]

DEMURRER TO ANSWER
(Code of Civ. Proc. §§430.40 *et seq.*)

A demurrer may be filed to an answer, as well as to a complaint or cross-complaint, or to the answer to the cross-complaint, in whole or in part, within 30 days after service of complaint or cross-complaint. (Code Civ. Proc. §430.40.) A demurrer to an answer must be filed within 10 days of the service of the answer to the complaint or cross-complaint. (Code Civ. Proc. §430.40(b).)

Grounds for demurrer to answer are:

(1) Answer does not state facts sufficient to constitute a defense;

(2) Answer is uncertain (includes "ambiguous" or "unintelligible");

(3) If answer pleads a contract, cannot ascertain whether the contract pleaded is oral or written. (Code of Civ. Proc. §430.20.)

A demurrer shall distinctly specify the grounds upon which it is taken; otherwise it may be disregarded. (Code of Civ. Proc. §430.60.)

The party filing a demurrer serves and files therewith a notice of hearing specifying a hearing date not less than 10 days nor more than 15 days from the filing of the demurrer and notice, but if the Law and Motion Calendar in that County is not regularly heard on a date within the prescribed period, the notice shall specify the date of the Law and Motion Calendar next following the 15th day. (Rule 202(b), California Rules of Court.)

Points and authorities shall be served and filed with the demurrer. (Rule 202(a), California Rules of Court.)

The procedure as to hearing is the same as the procedure on a demurrer to a complaint. If the demurrer to the answer is overruled, the case would proceed as if it had never been filed, that is, the answer is on file and valid and the case would then be at issue and probably ready to be set for trial. A Notice of Overruling of Demurrer should be served and filed.

If the demurrer to the answer were sustained, then the party filing the demurrer to the answer (the plaintiff) would serve and file a Notice of Sustaining of Demurrer to Answer, and the answer would have to be amended.

CROSS COMPLAINT
(Code of Civ. Proc. §428.10)

The purpose of the cross-complaint is to allow the defendant to settle all matters of controversy between the parties in one action and avoid a multiplicity of suits.

Affirmative *defenses* are set up in the answer; affirmative *relief* is sought through the cross-complaint.

If the defendant files an answer, he must include, by way of cross-complaint, any related cause of action which at that time he has against the plaintiff, or he cannot thereafter in any other action assert such related cause of action. (Code Civ. Proc. §426.30.)

Exceptions are made if the defendant did not file an answer or if the court lacks jurisdiction to render a personal judgment against him.

In a cross-complaint the defendant may state a claim against a codefendant or a third party. If new parties are named, a summons on the cross-complaint must be issued and served in the same manner as in an original action.

The cross-complaint may be filed in addition to an answer at the same time, or, by permission of the court, subsequent to the filing of the answer and during the course of the action. (Code Civ. Proc. §428.50.)

If a cross-complaint can be filed at the time of filing the answer the necessity of filing a motion to file the cross-complaint is avoided.

A copy of the proposed cross-complaint is attached to the original motion as an exhibit; the original of the proposed cross-complaint is kept in the file until the motion is granted.

Plaintiff (or a defendant or third party after service) must answer a cross-complaint. In a cross-complaint the defendant prays for judgment against the plaintiff and cross-defendant (and any *new parties* named as cross-defendants).

Since the legal assistant may well be drafting the cross-complaint, a reading of Mason, *California Civil Procedure Handbook*, Chapter 8, on Responsive Pleadings and Cross-Complaints, is suggested.

The heading of a cross-complaint might be set up in the following manner:

Cross-Complaint

The cross-complaint may not be combined with the answer but must be a separate document. (Code Civ. Proc. §428.40.)

[TITLE OF COURT]

WAYNE AVALON,	)	No. 270160
Plaintiff,	)	
v.	)	
CARLOS COGAN, et al.,	)	
Defendants.	)	
_____	)	CROSS-COMPLAINT
CARLOS COGAN,	)	(Personal Injuries)
Cross-complainant,	)	
v.	)	
WAYNE AVALON; GEORGE LAMB; CENTRAL TITLE INSURANCE, a corporation; DOE I; DOE II, and DOE III,	)	
Cross-defendants.	)	

Note that an abbreviated form is used in the first part of the title, which conforms to the title on the complaint; the names of the other defendants need not be repeated. The answer to the cross-complaint would use the same title as the cross-complaint itself.

BILL OF PARTICULARS

The plaintiff is not required to set forth in his complaint the items of an account alleged. For example, perhaps a customer does not pay for goods purchased from a store from time to time over a period of months. The store owner may sue for the total amount due, without itemizing each sale. If, however, the defendant, after being served with the complaint, serves and files a *Demand for Bill of Particulars, within 10 days thereafter plaintiff must deliver to defendant a copy of the account,* or be precluded from giving evidence thereof. (Code Civ. Proc. §454.) This account is called a "Bill of Particulars."

If the complaint is verified, the Bill of Particulars must be verified. The party makes the verification, or an agent of the party or his attorney if the facts are within their personal knowledge, or if the party is not within the county where the attorney has his office or is for some cause unable to make the affidavit.

In representation of the defendant, the legal assistant may be called upon to prepare the Demand for Bill of Particulars; if representing the plaintiff, to prepare the Bill of Particulars. If the file does not contain sufficient information, the client will most likely have to be contacted to provide same. "Particulars" means just that; in the example above, the Bill of Particulars would list the dates, description of items sold, amounts of sales, etc.

DEFAULTS

If defendant fails to file an answer, demurrer, notice of motion to strike, notice of motion to transfer, notice of motion to quash service of summons or to stay or dismiss the action, or notice of filing of a petition for writ of mandate, within 30 days after service is complete (5 days in unlawful detainer action) — and no stipulation or order extending time to plead has been granted — defendant's "default" may be taken.

In *Nelson v. Southerland* (1960) 187 Cal.App.2d 140, 142, quoting 2 Witkin, page 1694, the court said: " 'There is no statutory or rule requirement that the plaintiff's attorney notify the defendant's attorney (if known) that he intends to take a default. But failure to do so will usually be a sufficient ground for setting the default aside on motion under C.C.P. 473.' "

A printed form is used for defaults, which appears below: "Request to Enter Default, Declaration Under CCP 585.5, Declaration of Mailing (CCP 517), Memorandum of Costs and Declaration of Non-Military

Status.'' The Request to Enter Default, it will be noted, contains four boxes for checking under ''2'' of the form.

Number 1 is completed to have the default entered, preliminary to having a judgment entered.

Default Only

2a is checked to enter the default and estop defendant from appearing in the action, when for some reason (possibly the other defendants have not been served) plaintiff is not ready to proceed to enter judgment.

Suit on Contract of Prior Judgment

2b may be checked if the service was other than by publication and the action arose upon a prior judgment of a California court or upon contract (other than contract or sale arising under Civil Code sections 1801, 2981; see and complete question 3 of form).

Attorney's Fees

2b(1) for attorney's fees is applicable to Code Civ. Proc. §585, subdivision 1, cases only if a schedule of attorney fees has been adopted by rule of court, and then only if the contract sued on provides for an attorney's fee in the event suit is brought thereon, *or* the plaintiff is entitled by statute to recover an attorney's fee in the action. The clerk fills in the fee from the schedule.

Under section 585, subdivision 1, plaintiff may ask the court to fix the amount of the attorney's fee, in which event 2c should be checked, rather than 2b(1).

Suits Other Than Contract or Service Made by Publication

2c is also to be checked in actions (1) where the suit is other than on contract or (2) where service was made by publication. (See Code Civ. Proc. §585, subdivisions 2 and 3.) Plaintiff must produce testimony, and the judgment is entered by the court, not the clerk. A date must be set for hearing. If the defendant is not a California resident, the plaintiff must be examined under oath.

Suit Involving Real Property

If the action relates to title or possession of real property, see the provisions of section 585, subdivision 3, which apply.

Under Code of Civil Procedure section 585, subdivision 4, an affidavit may be used to obtain judgment in lieu of personal testimony, in the cases referred to in Code of Civil Procedure subdivisions 2 and 3, except in cases involving dissolution or annulment of marriage, separate maintenance, custody of children, or application to have attorney's fee fixed.

The sum of the judgment should appear from the face of the complaint or be only a mathematical computation. The original summons with proof of service must be on file before default can be taken. Some counties have a printed form of *Judgment by Default by Court,* as in Los Angeles County.

The forms of *Request to Enter Default,* etc., and *Judgment by Default by Clerk* follow.

Request to Enter Default, Etc.

NAME AND ADDRESS OF ATTORNEY	TELEPHONE NO	FOR COURT USE ONLY
ATTORNEY FOR		
Insert name of court, judicial district or branch court, if any, and Post Office and Street Address		
PLAINTIFF		
DEFENDANT		
REQUEST TO ENTER DEFAULT	Case Number	

1. TO THE CLERK   Please enter the default of the following defendant on the (cross/amended) . . . . . . complaint
Defendant (Name. See footnote* before completing):

2. Check applicable items and apply credits, if any, below
   a. ☐ Enter default only.
   b. ☐ Enter clerk's judgment under CCP 585(1).
      (1) ☐ When authorized by law include attorneys fees below, per court schedule.
      (2) Complete declaration under CCP 585.5, below.

   c. ☐ I request a court judgment under CCP 585(2), (3), 989, etc. (Testimony required. Apply to clerk for hearing date, unless court will enter judgment on affidavit under CCP 585(4).)

   d. Judgment to be entered

	Amount	Credits Acknowledged	Balance
(1) Demand of Complaint . . . . $	$	$	
(2) Attorney Fees . . . . $	$	$	
(3) Interest . . . . $	$	$	
(4) Costs (see reverse side) . . . $	$	$	
(5) TOTAL . . . . $	$	$	

Dated: . . . .

_____ _____
(Type or print name of attorney)   Signature of (Attorney for) Plaintiff

DECLARATION UNDER CCP 585.5

3. This action: (Check applicable box for each of the following items)
   a. ☐ Is ☐ Is not   on a contract or installment sale for goods or services subject to CC 1801, etc. (Unruh Act).
   b. ☐ Is ☐ Is not   on a conditional sales contract subject to CC 2981, etc. (Rees-Levering Motor Vehicle Sales and Finance Act).
   c. ☐ is ☐ Is not   on an obligation for goods, services, loans or extensions of credit subject to CCP 395(b).

I certify (or declare) under penalty of perjury that the foregoing is true and correct and that this declaration is executed on (Date): . . . . , at (Place): . . . . , California

_____ _____
(Type or print name of declarant)   (Signature of declarant)

FOR COURT USE ONLY	Default entered as requested on . . . . By	☐ Default NOT entered as requested. (State reason on reverse side.)

(See reverse side for Declaration of Mailing, Memorandum of Costs, and Declaration of Nonmilitary Status)

* The word "plaintiff" includes cross-complainant, "defendant" includes cross-defendant, singular includes the plural and masculine includes feminine. Declaration must be signed in California (CCP 2015.5) Affidavit required when signed outside California

Form adopted by the
Judicial Council of California
Revised Effective July 1, 1975

REQUEST TO ENTER DEFAULT, DECLARATION UNDER CCP 585.5, DECLARATION OF MAILING, MEMORANDUM OF COSTS, AND DECLARATION OF NONMILITARY STATUS

CCP 585, 585.5, 587, 1033½

DECLARATION OF MAILING (CCP 587)

4. a. ☐ On (Date): . . . ., a copy of this Request To Enter Default was mailed (by first-class mail or airmail, postage prepaid) to each defendant's attorney of record, or if none, to such defendant at his last known address, addressed as follows:

   b. ☐ The address of the following defendant and of his attorney of record is unknown to plaintiff and his attorney (Name):

I certify (or declare) under penalty of perjury that the foregoing is true and correct, and that this declaration is executed on (Date): . . . . at (Place): . . . ., California.

. . . .
(Type or print name)   (Signature of declarant)

MEMORANDUM OF COSTS

5. Costs and disbursements are listed as follows (CCP 1033½):
   a. Clerk's Filing Fees. . . . . $
   b. Process Server's Fees. . . . . $
   c. . . . . $
   d. . . . . $
   e.   TOTAL . . . . $

I am (the attorney or agent for): . . . . the party who claims these costs. To the best of my knowledge and belief the foregoing items of cost are correct and have been necessarily incurred in this action.

I certify (or declare) under penalty of perjury that the foregoing is true and correct, and that this declaration is executed on (Date): . . . . at (Place): . . . ., California.

. . . .
(Type or Print Name)   (Signature of declarant)

DECLARATION OF NON MILITARY STATUS

6. Defendant (Name): . . . . is not in the military service or in the military service of the United States as defined in Section 101 of the Soldiers' and Sailors' Relief Act of 1940, as amended, and not entitled to the benefits of the Act.

I certify (or declare) under penalty of perjury that the foregoing is true and correct, and that this declaration is executed on (Date): . . . . at (Place): . . . ., California.

. . . .
(Type or print name)   (Signature of declarant)

Judgment (Default by Clerk)

No. C-6

Name, Address and Telephone No. of Attorney | For Use of Court Clerk Only

IN THE SUPERIOR COURT OF THE STATE OF CALIFORNIA
IN AND FOR THE COUNTY OF SACRAMENTO

Plaintiff(s)

vs.

No.

JUDGMENT BY DEFAULT BY CLERK

Defendant(s)

In this action, the defendant(s) hereinafter named, having been sued herein upon a contract for the recovery of money or damages only, having been personally served with summons and a copy of complaint, having failed to appear and answer the complaint within the time allowed by law, and upon application of plaintiff(s), default of said defendant(s) having been entered;

acknowledgement of credit having been made in the sum of $ _____ ;

Judgment is hereby entered that plaintiff(s)

recover from defendant(s)

the sum of $ _____ principal; $ _____ interest; $ _____ costs; and

pursuant to court schedule $ _____ attorney fees.

I certify this to be a true copy of the judgment entered on the date and in the Minute Book herein set forth.

J. A. SIMPSON, COUNTY CLERK

By _____
                                    Deputy Clerk

JUDGMENT (DEFAULT BY CLERK)

PROVISIONAL REMEDIES

In order to protect a claim from dissipation during the pendency of a lawsuit a plaintiff may avail himself of a variety of ancillary or collateral proceedings known as provisional remedies. These temporary remedies, which are used only in conjunction with a lawsuit, are attachment (Code Civ. Proc. §481.010 et seq.), claim and delivery (Code Civ. Proc. §511.010 et seq.), injunction (Code Civ. Proc. §525 et seq.), receivership (Code Civ. Proc. §564, et seq.), deposit in court (Code Civ. Proc. §572 et seq.), and undertaking of persons handling private property or funds. (Code Civ. Proc. §571.) It is a good idea for a legal assistant to become familiar with all of these statutory remedies, as they are used with some regularity. Attachment, one of the more commonly used and complex provisional remedies, is discussed in detail below.

Writs of Attachment

The provisional remedy of attachment is used where a plaintiff seeks to protect a possible judgment in his favor by having certain property (real or personal) of the defendant or respondent held in custody of the law. The right of the attaching creditor is only a potential one, contingent upon the outcome of the case.

The action which is the basis for an attachment must be for a fixed or readily ascertainable amount not less than a total of $500 exclusive of costs, interest and attorney's fee and must be based upon a contract, express or implied. (Code Civ. Proc. §483.010.)

The decision to levy a writ of attachment is made by the attorney handling the case. The legal assistant can assist in ascertaining the properties of defendant subject to attachment. Also the legal assistant should be able to complete all the necessary forms hereinafter discussed and set out, and follow up throughout the process. But first the paralegal must study the rules and procedure governing attachments in order to intelligently handle the procedure. To that end the author hopes the following discussion, and practice in completing the forms, in the classroom and on the job, will be sufficient. Additional self-study, however, may be undertaken, and is recommended.

ATTACHMENTS AGAINST INDIVIDUALS

An attachment may be issued against an individual only where the claim arises out of the conduct by the individual of a trade, business or profession. (Code Civ. Proc. §483.010, subd. (c).)

An attachment may *not* be issued against an individual where the claim is based on the sale or lease of property, a license to use property, the furnishing of services, or the loan of money when such property or money was used by the individual primarily for personal, family or household purposes. (Code Civ. Proc. §483.010, subd. (c).)

Nor may an individual defendant's property be attached if the claim is secured by any interest in real or personal property unless the security has become valueless or decreased in value below the amount claimed, in which event the amount of the attachment "shall not exceed the lesser of the amount of such decrease or the difference between the value of the security and the amount then owing on the claim." (Code Civ. Proc. §483.010(b).)

ATTACHMENT AGAINST CORPORATION, PARTNERSHIP OR UNINCORPORATED ASSOCIATION

An attachment may be issued against a corporation or a partnership or an unincorporated association without regard to whether the defendant was engaged in a trade, business or profession.

PROPERTY SUBJECT TO ATTACHMENT

Corporation, Partnership or Association

All corporate property where the defendant is a corporation, and all partnerships or association property where the defendant is a partnership or other unincorporated association (for which a method of levy is provided in Article 2 commencing with section 488.310) is subject to attachment.

Individual

Any property which is necessary for the support of the individual defendant and members of his family supported in whole or part by the defendant and all compensation for personal services, is exempt from attachment, whether called wages, salary, commission, bonus or otherwise. (Code Civ. Proc. §487.02.)

The following property may be attached where the defendant is an individual and the claim arises out of his conduct of a trade, business or profession and the subject of contract is not used primarily for personal, family or household purposes (Code Civ. Proc. §487.010):

1. Interests in real property except leasehold estates with unexpired terms of less than 1 year

2. Accounts receivable, chattel paper and choses in action except any such individual claim with a principal balance of less than $150

3. Equipment

4. Farm products

5. Inventory

6. Judgments arising out of the conduct by the defendant of a trade, business or profession

7. Money on the premises where trade, business or profession is conducted by the defendant, and all but $1,000 of money located elsewhere

8. Negotiable documents

9. Negotiable instruments

10. Securities

Persons Not Residing in State (Including Foreign Corporations Not Qualified To Do Business in California and Foreign Partnerships Which Have Not Filed a Designation Pursuant to Corporations Code Section 15700)

A writ of attachment may be levied upon any property for which a method is provided in sections 488.310 *et seq.* (See Code Civ. Proc. §§492.010 *et seq.*)

APPLICATION FOR ATTACHMENT; TEMPORARY PROTECTIVE ORDER, ETC.

Prior to the issuance of the first writ of attachment, plaintiff must file with the court an application accompanied by an affidavit (or declaration). (See Code Civ. Proc. §§484.010, 482.040, 484.030.) (The verified complaint may be used in lieu of or in addition to the declaration; a declaration is incorporated in the new form.) The declaration is signed by the plaintiff. An original and office copy should be prepared.

The application must include the following (Code Civ. Proc. §484.020):

1. A statement that the action is a proper one for issuance of a writ of attachment;

2. A statement of the amount sought to be recovered;

3. A statement that the attachment is not sought other than for the purpose of recovery on the claim;

4. A statement that the application has no information or belief that the claim has been discharged in a bankruptcy proceeding, or stayed.

5. A description of the property (see Code Civ. Proc. §484.020, subd. (e)) adequate to identify the property and a statement that plaintiff is informed and believes that such property is subject to attachment. Where the defendant is a corporation, a reference to "all corporate property which is subject to attachment pursuant to subdivision (a) of Code of Civil Procedure Section 487.010" satisfies the requirements; where the defendant is a partnership, a reference to "all partnership property which is subject to attachment pursuant to subdivision (b) of Code of Civil Procedure Section 487.010" satisfies the requirements. This information is included in the printed form.

HEARING

No order or writ may be issued except after a hearing. (Code Civ. Proc. §484.040.) At least 20 days prior to such hearing the defendant is to be served with:

1. Copy of the summons and complaint

2. Copy of *Application for Attachment, Temporary Protective Order, Etc.* and any supporting affidavit

3. *Notice of Application and Hearing for Right to Attach Order and Writs of Attachment.*

Section 484.050 provides for the contents of the notice of application and hearing. The application form incorporates all that is necessary to apply for a right to attach order, an order for writ of attachment, additional writs of attachment and a temporary protective order. The forms follow:

Application for Attachment, Temporary Protective Order, Etc.

NAME AND ADDRESS OF ATTORNEY	TELEPHONE NO	FOR COURT USE ONLY
Insert name of court judicial district or branch court if any and post office and street address		
PLAINTIFF		
DEFENDANT		

APPLICATION FOR

[ ] RIGHT TO ATTACH ORDER   [ ] ORDER FOR ISSUANCE OF WRIT OF ATTACHMENT

[ ] ADDITIONAL WRIT OF ATTACHMENT   [ ] TEMPORARY PROTECTIVE ORDER

   [ ] AFTER HEARING   [ ] EX PARTE   [ ] AGAINST PROPERTY OF NONRESIDENT

CASE NUMBER

1. Plaintiff (Name)

  makes application [ ] after hearing [ ] ex parte for

  a   right to attach order and writ of attachment

  b [ ] writ of attachment

  c   additional writ of attachment

  d   temporary protective order

  e [ ] an order directing the defendant to transfer to the levying officer possession of [ ] property in defendant's possession

     [ ] documentary evidence in defendant's possession of title to property [ ] documentary evidence in defendant's

     possession of debt owed to defendant

2. Defendant (Name)

  a   is a corporation qualified not qualified to do business in California

  b   is a California partnership or other unincorporated association is a foreign partnership which has has not

     filed a designation under Corp C 15700

  c   is an individual who [ ] resides [ ] does not reside in California

3.   Attachment is not sought for a purpose other than recovery on a claim for money which is not secured within the meaning

    of CCP 483.010 [ ] and is based upon a contract the facts showing plaintiff is entitled to a judgment are set forth in the

    [ ] verified complaint [ ] attached affidavit [ ] following facts

4. [ ] The claim arises out of the conduct by the individual defendant of a trade business or profession. The claim is not based

    on the sale or lease of property a license to use property the furnishing of services or the loan of money where any

    of the foregoing was used by the defendant primarily for personal family or household purposes

5. Plaintiff seeks to recover from defendant the amount exclusive of interest of $

  a   which includes estimated costs of $

  b   which includes estimated allowable attorney fees of $

6. Plaintiff has no information or belief that the claim is discharged or the prosecution of the action is stayed in a proceeding under

  the National Bankruptcy Act   **(Continued on reverse side)**

The word plaintiff includes cross complainant defendant includes cross defendant singular includes the plural and masculine includes feminine and neuter. Verified pleadings and affidavits supporting this application must comply with CCP 482.040. Declaration under penalty of perjury must be signed in California or in a state that authorizes use of a declaration in place of an affidavit otherwise an affidavit is required.

Form Approved by the
Judicial Council of California
Effective January 1 1977

**APPLICATION FOR ATTACHMENT,
TEMPORARY PROTECTIVE ORDER, ETC.**

CCP §§ 482.040 482.080
484.010–484.030 484.310
484.420 484.510 485.010
485.510–485.530 486.010

7 Plaintiff is informed and believes that the following property sought to be attached is subject to attachment

   a [ ] Real property standing in the name of defendant or any other person (Describe property, state name and address of other person in the manner required by CCP 488 310)

   b [ ] Tangible personal property in the possession of defendant or any other person (Describe property, state name and address of other person)

   c [ ] Farm products or inventory of a going business (Describe)

   d [ ] Motor vehicles or vessels which are equipment of a going business and for which a certificate of ownership has been issued by the Department of Motor Vehicles (Describe)

   e [ ] Equipment of a going business (Other than in item 7d. Describe)

   f [ ] Growing crops or timber to be cut, standing on the real property of the defendant or any other person (State location of and describe crops or timber, state name of other person)

   g [ ] Money of an individual defendant
       (1) [ ] located on the premises where a trade, business or profession is conducted by defendant
       (2) [ ] in excess of $1,000 located elsewhere than on the premises where a trade, business or profession is conducted by defendant and not in deposit accounts
       (3) [ ] located in a deposit account in excess of $1,000
       (4) [ ] in excess of an aggregate amount of $1,000 located [ ] in deposit accounts [ ] in a deposit account and money located elsewhere than on the premises where a trade, business or profession is conducted by defendant
   h [ ] Property covered by the bulk sales notice recorded in   County,
      on (Date)   or the proceeds of the sale of such property
   i [ ] Plaintiff's pro rata share of proceeds from an escrow in which defendant's liquor license (Numbered) is sold
   j [ ] Any corporate or partnership (California unincorporated association) property for which a method of levy is provided. (Use only for other than an individual defendant.)
   k [ ] Any property of a nonresident defendant for which a method of levy is provided (CCP 492.040)
   l [ ] Other property (CCP 488.370–488.430. Describe)

(Continued on page three)

8. ☐ Plaintiff is informed and believes that the property sought to be attached is not exempt from attachment.

9. ☐ The court issued a Right to Attach Order on (Date): . . . . ☐ pursuant to CCP 484.090 (On hearing)
   ☐ and Order for Writ of Attachment pursuant to CCP 492.030 (Nonresident)   ☐ and Order for Writ of Attachment
   pursuant to CCP 485.220 (Ex parte).

10. ☐ The court pursuant to CCP 485.240 found plaintiff is entitled to a Right to Attach Order on (Date): . . . .

11. ☐ Nonresident defendant has not filed a general appearance.

12. ☐ Plaintiff ☐ alleges on ex parte application for order for writ of attachment ☐ is informed and believes on application
    for temporary protective order that plaintiff would suffer great or irreparable injury if the order is not issued before the matter
    can be heard on notice because

    a. ☐ It may be inferred that there is a danger that the property sought to be attached would be

        (1) ☐ concealed

        (2) ☐ substantially impaired in value

        (3) ☐ made unavailable to levy by other than concealment or impairment in value

    and the inference is supported by facts set forth in the ☐ verified complaint ☐ attached affidavit
    ☐ following facts (Specify):

    b. ☐ a bulk sales notice was recorded in: . . . . County
        on (Date): . . . . and published pursuant to Division 6 of the Commercial Code with respect
        to a bulk transfer by the defendant.

    c. ☐ An escrow has been opened pursuant to the provisions of Bus & PC 24074 with respect to the sale by the defendant
        of a liquor license (Numbered): . . . .

    d. ☐ Other circumstances (Indicate):

13. ☐ Plaintiff requests the following relief in the temporary protective order (Specify):

14. Plaintiff a. ☐ has filed an undertaking in the amount of: $ . . . .
        b. ☐ has not filed an undertaking.

Dated: . . . . . .

. . . .
(Type or print name of applicant)   (Signature of applicant)

By: . . . .
        (Name and title)

15. ☐ All facts contained herein are within the declarant's personal knowledge as shown by the following:

DECLARATION

I certify (declare) under penalty of perjury that the foregoing is true and correct and that this declaration is executed
on (Date) . . . . at (Place) . . . . California.

. . . .
(Type or print name)   (Signature of declarant)

16. Total number of pages attached: . . . .

PAGE THREE

Form Approved by the
Judicial Council of California
Effective January 1, 1977

**APPLICATION FOR ATTACHMENT,
TEMPORARY PROTECTIVE ORDER, ETC.**

Notice of Application and Hearing for Right to Attach Order and Writs of Attachment

NAME AND ADDRESS OF ATTORNEY	TELEPHONE NO	FOR COURT USE ONLY
ATTORNEY FOR		
Insert name of court, judicial district or branch court, if any, and post office and street address		
PLAINTIFF		
DEFENDANT		

NOTICE OF APPLICATION AND HEARING FOR	CASE NUMBER
[ ] RIGHT TO ATTACH ORDER [ ] ORDER FOR ISSUANCE OF [ ] WRIT OF ATTACHMENT [ ] ADDITIONAL WRITS OF ATTACHMENT	

1. Notice to defendant (Name)

2. Plaintiff has filed an application for
   a [ ] a right to attach order and writ of attachment. (Check items 4a, 4b and 4d(1).)
   b [ ] a writ of attachment. (Check item 4d(2).)
   c [ ] an additional writ of attachment. (Check item 4d(2).)

3. A hearing on plaintiff's application will be held in this court as follows
   a. Date   Time   [ ] Dept   [ ] Div   [ ] Rm. No.
   b. Address of court

4. You are notified that
   a. [ ] A right to attach order will be issued if the court finds that plaintiff's claim is probably valid and the other requirements for issuing the order are established. This hearing is not for the purpose of determining whether the claim is actually valid. Determination of the actual validity of the claim will be made in subsequent proceedings in the action and will not be affected by the decision at the hearing on the application for the order

   b. [ ] If you desire to oppose the issuance of a right to attach order, you must file with this court and serve on plaintiff no later than five days prior to the date set for hearing in item 3, a notice of opposition and supporting affidavit as required by CCP 484.060

   c. If a right to attach order is or has been issued, a writ of attachment will be issued to attach your property described in plaintiff's application unless the court determines that such property is exempt from attachment or that its value clearly exceeds the amount necessary to satisfy the amount to be secured by the attachment. However, since the right to attach order will not necessarily be limited to your property described in plaintiff's application, a writ of attachment may later be issued to attach other of your nonexempt property.

(Continued on reverse side)

At least 20 days prior to the hearing, the defendant shall be served with a copy of this notice and other documents required by either CCP 484.040 or CCP 484.330, as appropriate. The word "plaintiff" includes cross-complainant, "defendant" includes cross-defendant, singular includes the plural and masculine includes feminine and neuter

Form Approved by the
Judicial Council of California
Effective Jan. 1, 1977

**NOTICE OF APPLICATION AND HEARING FOR
RIGHT TO ATTACH ORDER AND WRITS OF
ATTACHMENT**

CCP 482.120, 484.040-484.060,
484.330-484.350

Continued and end

d. If you claim that all or some portion of the property described in plaintiff's application is exempt from attachment, you must, no later than five days prior to this hearing

    (1) ☐ include your claim of exemption in your notice of opposition filed and served pursuant to CCP 484.060 or file and serve a separate claim of exemption with respect to the property as provided in CCP 484.070.

    (2) ☐ file with the court and serve on plaintiff a claim of exemption with respect to the property as provided in CCP 484.350.
If you fail to prove that such property is exempt, any further claim of exemption to such property will be barred in the absence of a showing of change in circumstances occurring after expiration of the time for claiming exemptions.

e. Claims of exemption resulting from a change of circumstances, whether after denial of a previous claim or expiration of the time for claiming exemptions, may be asserted as provided in CCP 482.100.

f. You may obtain a determination at the hearing whether property not described in the application is exempt from attachment. Your failure to claim that property not described in the application is exempt from attachment will not preclude you from making a claim of exemption with respect to such property at a later time.

g. Either you or your attorney or both of you may be present at the hearing.

h. YOU MAY SEEK THE ADVICE OF AN ATTORNEY AS TO ANY MATTER CONNECTED WITH PLAINTIFF'S APPLICATION. SUCH ATTORNEY SHOULD BE CONSULTED PROMPTLY SO THAT HE MAY ASSIST YOU BEFORE THE TIME SET FOR HEARING.

Dated: . . . .

                                     (Signature of (Attorney for) Plaintiff)

TEMPORARY PROTECTIVE ORDER

The preceding application form provides for application for a temporary protective order. The application includes language showing that the plaintiff would suffer great or irreparable injury if issuance of the order were delayed until the matter could be heard on notice. Such injury might occur by reason of concealment of the property, impairment in its value, or by the property's otherwise being made unavailable. (Code Civ. Proc. §§485.010, 486.010.)

Upon proper showing, when plaintiff makes a notice application for a writ of attachment, the court will issue the temporary protective order upon the filing of the undertaking (as provided by sections 489.210 and 489.220). (Code Civ. Proc. §486.020.) The temporary protective order may be issued in lieu of a writ of attachment (see Code Civ. Proc. §486.030), when plaintiff applies ex parte for a writ, in which case plaintiff must comply with the requirements of service in Code of Civil Procedure section 484.040.

A form follows:

Temporary Protective Order

NAME AND ADDRESS OF ATTORNEY TELEPHONE	FOR COURT USE ONLY
ATTORNEY FOR	
Insert name of court, judicial district or branch court, if any, and post office and street address	
PLAINTIFF	
DEFENDANT	
TEMPORARY PROTECTIVE ORDER	CASE NUMBER

1. The Court has considered the application of plaintiff (Name): . . . . for
   ☐ a right to attach order, order for issuance of writ of attachment pursuant to Chapter 4 (Commencing with CCP 484.010) and a temporary protective order.
   ☐ an ex parte right to attach order and order for issuance of writ of attachment pursuant to Chapter 5 (Commencing with CCP 485.010).

FINDINGS

2. The Court finds
   a. The claim upon which the application for attachment is based is one upon which an attachment may be issued.
   b. Plaintiff has established the probable validity of the claim upon which the application for the attachment is based.
   c. The order is not sought for a purpose other than the recovery upon the claim on which the application for the attachment is based.
   d. Great or irreparable injury will result to the plaintiff if issuance of the order is delayed until the matter can be heard on notice, based on the following
      (1) ☐ There is a danger that the property sought to be attached would be
         (a) ☐ concealed
         (b) ☐ substantially impaired in value
         (c) ☐ made unavailable to levy by other than concealment or substantial impairment in value.
      (2) ☐ A bulk sales notice was recorded in . . . . County on
         (Date): . . . . and published pursuant to Division 6 commencing with Sec. 6101 of the Commercial Code with respect to a bulk transfer by the defendant.
      (3) ☐ An escrow has been opened pursuant to the provisions of Bus & PC Code 24074 with respect to the sale by the defendant of a liquor license (Numbered): . . . .
      (4) ☐ Other circumstance (Indicate):

   e. ☐ The requirements of CCP 485.220 are satisfied, but a temporary protective order should issue instead of an ex parte right to attach order and order for issuance of writ of attachment.
   f. An undertaking in the amount of $ . . . . is required before a temporary protective order shall issue, and plaintiff has filed an undertaking in that amount.
   g. The property subject to the following order is (Describe):

(Continued on reverse side)

The temporary protective order shall be served on the defendant with the documents referred to in CCP 494.040. The word "plaintiff" includes cross-complainant, "defendant" includes cross-defendant, singular includes the plural, and masculine includes feminine and neuter.

Form Approved by the
Judicial Council of California
Effective January 1, 1977

TEMPORARY PROTECTIVE ORDER
(Attachment)

CCP 486.010–486.110

h. ☐ The following property is inventory or farm products held for sale (Specify):

i. ☐ Other (Specify):

ORDER

3. IT IS ORDERED
    a. Defendant (Name): . . . .
       shall not transfer, directly or indirectly, any interest in the property described in item 2g of the findings.

    b. ☐ Defendant shall not dispose of the proceeds of any transfer of inventory or farm products held for sale
       except under the following restrictions (Specify):

4. ☐ It is further ordered:

5. It is further ordered that this order shall have no force or effect as to any property after levy thereon by plaintiff,
    nor in any event after (Date): . . . .
6. Total number of boxes checked in items 3 and 4: . . .

Dated: _____ . . . . _____

                             (Type or print name)   (Signature of Judge)

NOTICE TO DEFENDANT: An undertaking has been filed with the court by plaintiff. You may object to the undertaking on the grounds of the insufficiency of the sureties or the amount of the undertaking (CCP 489.070).

If the property is farm products held for sale or is inventory, the temporary protective order may not prohibit you from transferring the property in the ordinary course of business, but may impose appropriate restrictions on the disposition of the proceeds from such transfer.

You may issue any number of checks against any of your bank accounts in this state in any amount for the following purposes:
    (1) Payment of any payroll expense (including fringe benefits and taxes and premiums for workers' compensation and unemployment insurance) falling due in the ordinary course of business prior to the levy of a writ of attachment.
    (2) Payment for goods thereafter delivered to you C.O.D. for use in your trade, business, or profession.
    (3) Payment of taxes if payment is necessary to avoid penalties which will accrue if there is any further delay in payment.
    (4) Payment of reasonable legal fees and reasonable costs and expenses required for your representation in the action.
In addition, you may issue any number of checks for any purpose so long as the total amount of such checks does not exceed the greater of the following:
    *(1) The amount by which the total amount of deposit exceeds the sum of the amount of plaintiff's claim and the amounts permitted to be paid pursuant to this notice;
    (2) One thousand dollars ($1,000).

CLERK'S CERTIFICATE
I hereby certify that the foregoing is a correct copy of the original on file in my office.
           Dated: . . . .

Clerk of the Court by _____ Deputy

[Seal]

RIGHT TO ATTACH ORDER AFTER HEARING AND ORDER FOR ISSUANCE OF WRIT OF ATTACHMENT

After hearing, the *Right to Attach Order for Issuance of a Writ of Attachment,* and the *Writ of Attachment,* may be issued if the defendant does not claim that his property is exempt or, claiming exemption, fails to establish such exemption. If a right to attach order is issued but a writ is not issued because of a successful claim of exemption, plaintiff may apply for a writ against other property discovered which is nonexempt.

There are two forms which may be used on ex parte applications for writs (Code Civ. Proc. §485.220) or for additional writs (Code Civ. Proc. §485.440) : *Ex Parte Right to Attach Order and Order for Issuance of Writ of Attachment Resident; Ex Parte Right to Attach Order and Order for Issuance of Writ of Attachment (Nonresident).*

The form to be used in conjunction with a hearing is the *Right to Attach Order After Hearing and Order for Issuance of Writ of Attachment* form, which is set forth on the following pages.

Right to Attach Order After Hearing and Order for Issuance of Writ of Attachment

NAME AND ADDRESS OF ATTORNEY TELEPHONE NO	FOR COURT USE ONLY
ATTORNEY FOR	
Insert name of court judicial district or branch court if any and post office and street address	

PLAINTIFF	
DEFENDANT	

☐ RIGHT TO ATTACH ORDER AFTER HEARING ☐ ORDER FOR ISSUANCE OF WRIT OF ATTACHMENT AFTER HEARING	CASE NUMBER

1. The application of plaintiff (Name)

   for a ☐ right to attach order and order for issuance of writ of attachment   ☐ order for issuance of writ of attachment

   against the property of defendant (Name)

   came on for hearing as follows *(Check boxes in item 1 c and d to indicate personal presence)*

   a. Judge (Name)

   b. Hearing date   Time   ☐ Div   ☐ Dept   ☐ Room No

   c. Plaintiff (Name) ☐   Attorney (Name) ☐

   d. Defendant (Name) ☐   Attorney (Name) ☐

FINDINGS

2. The Court finds

   a. Defendant is a ☐ corporation ☐ partnership ☐ unincorporated association ☐ individual

   b. ☐ The claim upon which the application is based is one upon which an attachment may be issued

   c. ☐ Plaintiff has established the probable validity of the claim upon which the application is based

   d. ☐ The attachment is not sought for a purpose other than the recovery on the claim upon which the application is based

   e. ☐ Defendant failed to prove that all of the property described in plaintiff's application is exempt from attachment

   f. ☐ The following property of defendant, described in plaintiff's application, is exempt from attachment (Specify)

   g. ☐ The following property, not described in plaintiff's application, claimed by defendant to be exempt

      (1) ☐ is exempt from attachment (Specify)

      (2) ☐ is not exempt from attachment (Specify)

   h. ☐ An undertaking in the amount of $ is required before a writ shall issue,

      and plaintiff ☐ has ☐ has not filed an undertaking in that amount

   i. ☐ A Right to Attach Order pursuant to ☐ CCP 484.090 (On hearing) ☐ CCP 485.220 (Ex parte) was issued on

      (Date)

   j. ☐ The Court pursuant to CCP 485.240 found plaintiff is entitled to a Right to Attach Order on (Date)

   k. ☐ Other (Specify)

(Continued on reverse side)

The word "plaintiff" includes cross-complainant, "defendant" includes cross-defendant, singular includes the plural, and masculine includes feminine and neuter

Form Approved by the
Judicial Council of California
Effective Jan. 1, 1977

**RIGHT TO ATTACH ORDER AFTER HEARING
AND ORDER FOR ISSUANCE OF WRIT OF
ATTACHMENT**

CCP 482.040, 484.090,
485.240, 487.010, 488.010,
488.020, 488.310–488.430,
489.210 et seq.

ORDER

3. IT IS ORDERED

a. ☐ Plaintiff has a right to attach property of defendant (Name): . . . . in the amount of: $ . . . .

b. ☐ The property described in items 2f and 2g(1) of the findings is exempt and shall not be attached.

c. ☐ The clerk shall issue a writ of attachment ☐forthwith ☐upon the filing of an undertaking in the amount of: $ . . . . against the property of defendant described below or in attachment 3c.

   (1) ☐ Real property, standing in the name of defendant or any other person. (Describe property; state name and address of other person in the manner required by CCP 488.310):

   (2) ☐ Tangible personal property in the possession of defendant or any other person. (Describe; state name and address of other person):

   (3) ☐ Farm products or inventory of a going business. (Describe):

   (4) ☐ Motor vehicles or vessels which are equipment of a going business and for which a certificate of ownership has been issued by the Department of Motor Vehicles. (Describe):

   (5) ☐ Equipment of a going business (Other than in item 3c(4)). (Describe):

   (6) ☐ Crops growing on or timber to be cut standing upon real property in the name of defendant or any other person. (State location of and describe; state name and address of other person in the manner required by CCP 488.010 and CCP 488.360(c)):

   (7) ☐ Money of an individual defendant
      (a) ☐ located on the premises where a trade, business or profession is conducted by defendant
      (b) ☐ in excess of $1,000 elsewhere than on the premises where a trade, business or profession is conducted by defendant and not in deposit accounts
      (c) ☐ located in a deposit account in excess of $1,000
      (d) ☐ in excess of an aggregate amount of $1,000 located ☐ in deposit accounts ☐ in a deposit account and money located elsewhere than on the premises where a trade, business or profession is conducted by defendant.

   (8) ☐ Other property (CCP 488.370–488.430 and CCP 487.010 Describe):

   (9) ☐ Any property for which a method of levy is provided (Use only for other than individual defendant).

d. ☐ Defendant (Name). . . . . (☐ who was personally present when the following order was pronounced orally by the court) shall transfer to the levying officer possession of ☐any documentary evidence in defendant's possession of title to any property described in item 3c; ☐any documentary evidence in defendant's possession of debt owed to defendant described in item 3c; ☐ the following property in defendant's possession (Specify):

NOTICE TO DEFENDANT: Failure to comply with this order may subject you to being held in contempt of court.

e. ☐ Other:

f. Total number of boxes checked in item 3: . . .

Dated: . . . .

                (Type or print name)   (Signature of Judge)

VACATING THE TEMPORARY PROTECTIVE ORDER

The defendant may terminate the temporary protective order by application and filing of an appropriate undertaking. Or the defendant may obtain an ex parte order modifying or vacating the temporary protective order, in the interest of justice and equity to the parties, without filing an undertaking. Optional forms for this purpose are entitled:

> *Application and Notice of Hearing for Order to Vacate, Modify or Terminate Temporary Protective Order* and *Order to Terminate, Modify or Vacate Temporary Protective Order.*

Attach any supporting affidavit and points and authorities. (Code Civ. Proc. §489.320.)

NOTICE OF OPPOSITION TO RIGHT TO ATTACH ORDER AND CLAIM OF EXEMPTION (ATTACHMENT).

The defendant may use this form to oppose the issuance of the right to attach order (see Code Civ. Proc. §484.060) and/or to claim exemption of his property either after receipt of noticed application or on his motion due to change of his circumstances, or an ex parte levy pursuant to section 482.100 (see Code Civ. Proc. §§485.610, 487.020, 482.100, 690.50.)

This dual form of *Notice of Opposition to Right to Attach Order and Claim of Exemption,* together with any supporting affidavits and points and authorities attached, must be served no less than 5 days before the date of hearing, otherwise defendant may not oppose issuance of the right to attach order (Code Civ. Proc. §§484.060, subd. (a), 484.070) and may not claim exemption except as provided in section 482.100 where there has been a change of circumstances occurring after denial of a claim of exemption or after the expiration of the time for claiming the exemption earlier in the action. (See Code Civ. Proc. §482.100.)

The form is set forth on the following pages.

Notice of Opposition of Right to Attach Order, Etc.

NAME AND ADDRESS OF ATTORNEY: TELEPHONE NO.	FOR COURT USE ONLY
ATTORNEY FOR:	
Insert name of court, judicial district or branch court, if any, and post office and street address.	
PLAINTIFF:	
DEFENDANT:	

NOTICE OF ☐ OPPOSITION TO APPLICATION FOR RIGHT TO ATTACH ORDER ☐ CLAIM OF EXEMPTION ☐ MOTION (AFTER ISSUANCE OF WRIT) FOR CLAIM OF EXEMPTION ☐ **AND MOTION FOR CLAIM OF EXEMPTION**	CASE NUMBER:

1. To plaintiff (Name): . . . .

2. You are notified that at the hearing to be held in this court and set for
   Date: . . . . Time: . . . . ☐ Dept. ☐ Div. ☐ Room No.: . . . . . .

3. Defendant (Name): . . . .
   a. ☐ Will oppose the issuance of a right to attach order upon the following grounds (State grounds of opposition. CCP 484.060(a)):

   b. ☐ Will claim exemption ☐ move the court for an exemption from attachment of the following property:
      (1) ☐ Property exempt from execution under CCP 690 et seq. (Specify code section and describe property):

(Continued on reverse side)

This notice of opposition and claim of exemption, together with any supporting affidavits complying with CCP 482.040 and points and authorities, shall be filed and served on the plaintiff not less than five days before the date set for the hearing. If defendant fails to file and serve this notice, and supporting documents, within five days of the hearing date he will be denied the right to oppose issuance of the right to attach order (CCP 484.060(a)). If defendant fails to file and serve on plaintiff his claim of exemption of property described in plaintiff's application, he may not later claim the exemption except as provided in CCP 482.100. (CCP 484.070(a)). Defendant's motion for claim of exemption based on necessities (CCP 487.020(b)) pursuant to the procedure in CCP 482.100(c) requires service of this notice of motion on plaintiff not less than three days prior to the date set for the hearing.

Form Approved by the
Judicial Council of California
Effective January 1, 1977

**NOTICE OF OPPOSITION TO RIGHT TO ATTACH
ORDER AND CLAIM OF EXEMPTION
(Attachment)**

CCP 482.100, 484.010 et seq.,
487.010, 487.020(a) (b) (c),
485.610

(2) ☐ Property which is necessary for the support of an individual defendant or the defendant's family supported in whole or in part by the defendant. (CCP 487.020(b). Describe Property):

(3) ☐ Compensation paid or payable to a defendant employee by an employer for personal services performed by such employee whether denominated as wages, salary, commission, bonus, or otherwise. (CCP 487.020(c). Describe compensation):

(4) ☐ Property not subject to attachment pursuant to CCP 487.010. (Describe property):

(5) ☐ Other. (Describe property and specify grounds for exemption):

4. Defendant's affidavit supporting any factual issues and points and authorities supporting any legal issues is attached.

5. Total number of pages attached: . . . .

Dated: . . . .

. . . . (Type or print name) . . . .　　　　_____
　　　　　　　　　　　　　　　　　　　　　　　　　　　　　　　　　　(Signature of (Attorney for) Defendant)

By: . . . .
　　　　　　　　(Name and Title)

UNDERTAKING BY SURETIES FOR ATTACHMENT OR CLAIM AND DELIVERY

Before a writ or temporary protective order may be issued, plaintiff must file an undertaking, in the amount of $500 in the justice court, $2,500 in the municipal court, or $7,500 in the superior court. Upon objection of the defendant, the amount may be increased to the amount of probable recovery. (Code Civ. Proc. §§489.210, 489.220.)

The original undertaking is filed with the court (Code Civ. Proc. §515.010) and a copy attached to the writ of possession (Code Civ. Proc. §514.020) and a copy may be required to be attached to the temporary restraining order, if any (Code Civ. Proc. §513.010.)

For procedure for issuance of a temporary restraining order, see Code of Civil Procedure section 513.010, et seq.

The form for an undertaking is set forth on the following pages.

Undertaking by Sureties

NAME AND ADDRESS OF ATTORNEY	TELEPHONE NO	FOR COURT USE ONLY
Insert name of court, judicial district or branch court, if any, and post office and street address		
PLAINTIFF		
DEFENDANT		

UNDERTAKING BY ☐ PLAINTIFF'S ☐ DEFENDANT'S SURETIES FOR ☐ ATTACHMENT ☐ CLAIM AND DELIVERY	CASE NUMBER

1. ☐ Plaintiff (Name):
2. ☐ Defendant (Name):
3. Amount of undertaking: $
4. ☐ Address to which notice of exception to sureties may be sent *(Applicable to Claim and Delivery)*:

5. This undertaking is for ☐ attachment ☐ claim and delivery. We, the undersigned, hereby submit to the jurisdiction of the court in all matters affecting our liability on this undertaking and obligate ourselves, jointly and severally, to and including the amount specified in item 3.

ATTACHMENT

a. ☐ to pay defendant any amount the defendant may recover for any wrongful attachment by the plaintiff in the action pursuant to CCP 489.210.

b. ☐ to pay the plaintiff the value of the property released not exceeding the amount of any judgment which may be recovered by the plaintiff in an action against the defendant pursuant to CCP 489.310.

c. ☐ to pay the plaintiff the amount of any judgment that may be recovered by the plaintiff in the action against the defendant pursuant to CCP 489.320.

d. ☐ to pay any person other than the defendant whose interest is sought to be attached and who is rightfully entitled to such property any amount recovered for wrongful attachment pursuant to CCP 489.240.

CLAIM AND DELIVERY

e. ☐ to plaintiff, that if plaintiff recover judgment in the action, defendant shall pay all costs awarded to plaintiff and all damages that plaintiff may sustain by reason of the loss of the property, not exceeding the amount of this undertaking pursuant to CCP 515.020.

f. ☐ to defendant, in the amount of the undertaking for the return of the property to defendant if a return thereof be ordered, and for the payment of any sum defendant may recover against plaintiff, not exceeding the amount of this undertaking pursuant to CCP 515.010.

6. a. Surety (Name):   b. Surety (Name):

(1) Residence address: (1) Residence address:

(2) Business address: (2) Business address:

(3) Address for service: (3) Address for service:

(Continued on reverse side)

The word "plaintiff" includes cross-complainant, "defendant" includes cross-defendant, singular includes the plural, and masculine includes feminine and neuter. The declaration under penalty of perjury must be signed in California, or in a state that authorizes use of a declaration in place of an affidavit, otherwise an affidavit is required. A copy of plaintiff's undertaking must be attached to the writ of possession (CCP 514.020), the original filed with the court (CCP 515.010), and may be required to be attached to the temporary restraining order (CCP 513.010). In Claim and Delivery Proceedings a copy of defendant's undertaking must be mailed to levying officer and plaintiff, and the original together with a proof of service by mail filed with the court (CCP 515.020(b)).

Form Approved by the
Judicial Council of California
Effective January 1, 1977 **UNDERTAKING BY SURETIES** CCP 489.010–489.420,
515.010, 515.020, 1012,
1013a, 1056, 1057, 1058a

7. I am not an officer of the court nor a member of the State Bar of California and am a ☐ resident and householder ☐ freeholder within California and I own assets worth the sum specified above, over and above all my just debts and liabilities, exclusive of property exempt from execution.

8. *(To be completed when undertaking exceeds $2,000.00)*
   a. I rely on the following described property belonging to me as qualifying me on the undertaking (Describe property and nature of declarant's interest, and specify best estimate of actual cash value of each such property):

   b. The charges, liens, impediments or clouds against such property known to me, and the amounts thereof, are as follows (Specify):

9. I certify (declare) under penalty of perjury that the foregoing is true and correct, and that this declaration is executed on (Date): at (Place): California.

(Signature of surety)

(Type or print name)

10. *(Applicable to attachment)* My estimate of the market value of the property qualifying the sureties specified above is: $

(Signature of Party)

7. I am not an officer of the court nor a member of the State Bar of California and am a ☐ resident and householder ☐ freeholder within California and I own assets worth the sum specified above, over and above all my just debts and liabilities, exclusive of property exempt from execution.

8. *(To be completed when undertaking exceeds $2,000.00)*
   a. I rely on the following described property belonging to me as qualifying me on the undertaking (Describe property and nature of declarant's interest, and specify best estimate of actual cash value of each such property):

   b. The charges, liens, impediments or clouds against such property known to me, and the amounts thereof, are as follows (Specify):

9. I certify (declare) under penalty of perjury that the foregoing is true and correct, and that this declaration is executed on (Date): at (Place): California.

(Signature of surety)

(Type or print name)

10. *(Applicable to attachment)* My estimate of the market value of the property qualifying the sureties specified above is: $

(Signature of Party)

COURT APPROVAL *(Applicable to Attachment)*

The undertaking is approved.

Dated:

(Signature of Judge)

WRIT OF ATTACHMENT

The writ of attachment is issued by the clerk of the court after the court has signed an order for issuance of a writ of attachment. The writ of attachment is the authority for the levying officer to levy upon the property of the defendant.

A writ of attachment may be issued by the court at the time of issuance of summons or at any time prior to judgment. Several writs may be issued simultaneously or from time to time, whether or not any writ previously issued has been returned to the court. An *alias writ* is issued if a writ is lost. (Code Civ. Proc. §§482.080; 482.090.)

A writ of attachment ceases to be of force and effect three years after date of issuance of the writ of attachment — if not sooner released or discharged.

Upon motion of plaintiff made not less than 10 nor more than 60 days before the expiration of the three-year period, and upon not less than 5 day's notice to defendant, the writ of attachment may be extended for a period up to 1 year. The maximum period of the attachment, including such extensions, shall not exceed 8 years from date of issuance.

In the instances specified in Probate Code section 732, an attachment lien may be converted to a judgment lien upon the property of a decedent's estate.

Notice of Attachment

A *Notice of Attachment* is served informing the defendant of all of the following:

"(a) The capacity in which he has been served.

"(b) The specific property which is sought to be attached. [This requirement is complied with by serving a copy of the order for issuance of the writ of attachment with the *Notice of Attachment*.]

"(c) His rights under the attachment, including the right to make a third-party claim pursuant to Section 689.

"(d) His duties under the attachment." (Code Civ. Proc. §488.020.)

A form for *Writ of Attachment* follows:

Writ of Attachment

NAME AND ADDRESS OF ATTORNEY TELEPHONE NO	FOR COURT USE ONLY
Insert name of court, judicial district or branch court, if any, and post office and street address	
PLAINTIFF	CASE NUMBER
DEFENDANT	FOR RECORDER'S USE

WRIT OF ATTACHMENT   [__] AFTER HEARING   [__] EX PARTE

1 TO THE SHERIFF OR ANY MARSHAL OR CONSTABLE
   OF THE COUNTY OF
2 This writ is to attach property of defendant (Name)

   and the attachment is to secure $
3 YOU ARE DIRECTED TO ATTACH the following property or so much thereof as is clearly
   sufficient to satisfy the amount to be secured by the attachment
   (Describe property and state its location, itemize by letter)

4 [__] An interest in the real property described in item 3   stands upon the records of the county, in the name of the following
       person other than the defendant
       a Name
       b Mailing address, if known, as shown by the records of the office of the county tax assessor

5 [__] The real property on which the [__] crops described in item 3   are growing [__] timber described in item 3   to be
       cut is standing stands upon the records of the county in the name of
       a Name
       b Address

[COURT SEAL]

Dated

Clerk of the Court by   Deputy

A copy of the Notice of Attachment must be served with this writ

Form Approved by the
Judicial Council of California
Effective January 1, 1977   **WRIT OF ATTACHMENT**   CCP 488 010

Opposition to Writ

Whenever a writ is issued, a defendant who has appeared in the action may apply to the court, by noticed motion, for an order permitting him to substitute an undertaking for any of the property subject to being attached. (Code Civ. Proc. §489.310(a).)

The notice of attachment or temporary protective order must include a statement informing defendant of his right to object on the grounds that the sureties are insufficient or that the amount of the undertaking is insufficient. (Code Civ. Proc. §§489.230, 489.070.)

A combined form of the Judicial Council may be used to apply to:

(1) Substitute an undertaking for the property attached;

(2) Determine whether plaintiff's sureties are sufficient;

(3) Increase the amount of plaintiff's undertaking;

(4) Release the property attached because its value exceeds the amount secured by attachment;

(5) Where writ of attachment issued ex parte: for order to set aside the right to attach order, quash the writ of attachment, and release the attached property. This form, and its corresponding form of order, are entitled: *Application to Set Aside Right to Attach Order and Release Attached Property, Etc. and Order to Set Aside Attachment, to Substitute Undertaking, Etc., Instructions to Levying Officer (Marshal, Sheriff, or Other Levying Officer).* (Code Civ. Proc. §488.010 et seq.; 488.370, et seq.)

The writ of attachment should identify the defendant whose property is to be attached, state the amount to be secured and describe the property being levied upon.

If the writ does not adequately describe the property for the levying officer to execute the writ, the plaintiff must give instructions, signed by the plaintiff or his attorney of record, to the levying officer containing a description which is adequate and the name and address of any person to be served with copy of the writ and notice of attachment. (Code Civ. Proc. §488.010.)

If the defendant's interest in real property is being attached, the writ shall identify any person other than defendant in whose name the real property or interest stands upon the county records and shall describe the real property. (Code Civ. Proc. §488.310.) If growing crops or timber to cut are being attached, the writ must disclose the identity of any person in whose name the property stands in the county records. (Code Civ. Proc. §488.310.)

The levying officer will also serve the summons and complaint if they have not previously been served upon the defendant. (Code Civ. Proc. §488.030(c).) The paralegal should prepare original office copy, and 1 copy for levying officer. (a) If real estate is being attached, give legal description of property and street address, and name and address of owner of record. (If the property stands in the name of a third person, whether alone or with the defendant, the writ of attachment should identify such third person.) (b) Personal property should be fully described, giving street address where it is located, name of person in possession, etc. (c) If a bank account is being levied on, a special bond is provided and the levying officer directed to deliver at the same time as levy is made. (A bond in twice the amount of claim is needed to deliver to the bank at the time of levy.) The levying officer's fee is forwarded with the transmittal letter.

CALIFORNIA PARALEGAL'S GUIDE

Chapter 6

LEGAL CALENDARING

CALENDAR SYSTEMS

Accurate and dependable calendaring is vital to the proper operation of any office or firm. Responsibility for calendaring is a proper function of the paralegal. If a good system of calendaring is not already operating, the paralegal in consultation with the attorney should set up a system suitable to the particular office. In a smaller office more simple methods can be used than in a large law firm with a file room and file clerks.

In all law offices each attorney has his or her own desk calendar or day book on which notations are made of all court appearances, appointments, and whatever notes as reminders of upcoming dates is desired. Someone, whether the paralegal if in a small office, or a personal secretary in a larger firm, should be charged with the responsibility for writing all such dates on the attorney's calendar — and should keep a duplicate calendar with any additional reminders needed.

Incoming mail should be checked upon receipt for any dates noted. When a pleading is filed, usually some future date is indicated for taking some action in a particular case, or that a court hearing or trial is on a particular date. For example: John Jones was served with summons and complaint in a lawsuit on May 2. Today, May 6, he asked the attorney to represent him in this case. Looking at the calendar following this section, under "ANSWER," etc., how many days does the attorney have to file an answer or other pleading for defendant John Jones? The defendant has 30 days after May 2 to file his answer. Thirty (30) days after May 2 is June 1. On the calendar for June 1 a notation should be made, such as "Last day to answer, Smith v. Jones." A notation should be made on the calendar two or three days in advance of the deadline date to allow time for preparation and to have Mr. Jones come into the law office and sign a verification. By this type of advance calendaring last-minute rushes and pressure jobs are avoided and — most important of all — no important date is ever overlooked!

Trials should be calendared two or three weeks in advance of the trial date. If a brief is to be prepared, a week or two may be required. If the brief is to be printed, time should be allowed for the printer to prepare a galley proof (this is discussed in the Chapter on Appeals), for its correction and return to the printer, before the final printing. A client may ask the attorney to prepare a complaint a short time before the statute of limitations runs against his cause of action. New cases should be checked and any such dates calendared to guard against the running of the statute. (See Statutes of Limitations, Chapter 5, for further discussion.)

The Tickler File

Instead of a calendar a "tickler file" may be used. One "tickler file" is a card index with a set of monthly guides and a set of day guides. Cards with notations of what is to be done are placed behind the date involved, and each day the cards are checked to see what needs attention.

Another type of "tickler file," which perhaps properly should not be called a tickler file at all, can be used in conjunction with the calendar. It is perhaps more suitable to a smaller office. This method is to mark a date on the cover of the file itself — the date on which the file needs attention — and the name of the case written on the calendar of the person responsible on that date. Each day the desk calendar is checked and the files noted there are pulled and given to the attorney or paralegal, as the case may be. *No file is ever placed in the cabinet drawer without a future date on it.* If this procedure is followed, no case is ever overlooked.

Time Computation

The time within which any act provided by law is to be done is computed by *excluding the first day* and *including the last day,* unless the last day is a holiday, in which case the period is extended to the next day which is not a holiday. (Code Civ. Proc. §12.)

"If any city, county, state, or public office, other than a branch office, is closed for the whole of any day, insofar as the business of that office is concerned, that day shall be considered as a holiday for the purpose of computing time under Sections 12 and 12a." (Code Civ. Proc. §12b).

Section 12a provides in part. ". . . The term 'holiday' as used herein shall mean all day on Saturdays, [and] all holidays specified in Sections 6700 and 6701 of the Government Code'' The State holidays listed in Government Code Sections 6700 and 6701 are:

Every Sunday
The third Monday in February
The last Monday in May
First Monday in September (Labor Day)
The second Monday in October (Columbus Day)

February 12 (Lincoln Day)	
July 4	On following Monday
September 9 (Admission Day)	if date falls on
January 1	Sunday
December 25	
November 11 (Veterans Day)	On Friday if date falls on Saturday and on the following Monday if date falls on Sunday

Good Friday, 12 Noon to 3 p.m., is also listed, but a court decision has nullified the holiday.

Banking holidays include Saturdays; optional bank holidays will also include the Monday following a January 1, July 4, or September 9 which falls on Saturday, and the Friday preceding a December 25 which falls on Saturday.

Service of any document by mail is complete at the time of the deposit in the postoffice, or a mail box, mail chute, etc. (Code Civ. Proc. §1013.) Reference should be made to the affidavit of mailing attached to a document, then, and the time computed from that date rather than the date of receipt by the law office, unless it is personally delivered to the law office.

Note: A document required to be served *and filed* within a certain period is not "filed" until the date the clerk receives the document, whether by personal delivery or by mail; therefore the filing requirements cannot be met by mailing a document to the clerk on the last date for serving and filing since in all probability the document would not reach the clerk until at least the following date, one day late.

Illustrations of Computation of Time:

1. The client, the defendant, was served with a summons and complaint on Friday, July 31, 1981, in the county in which the action was brought. Hence he has 30 days to plead. July 31 — the first day — is excluded in computation. Counting 30 days starting with August 1, 2, 3, and so on — makes Sunday the 30th of August the last day.

Sunday is a holiday. The client therefore has through Monday, August 31 to plead.

2. Say receipt is acknowledged on Friday, October 30, 1981, of a copy of proposed Findings of Fact and Conclusions of Law. The attorney has 10 days within which to file objections. Counting 10 days after Friday, October 30 — 1st day Saturday, October 31, 2d day Sunday, November 1, 3d day Monday, November 2, 4th day Tuesday, November 3, etc., makes Tuesday, November 10, the last day to serve and file objections.

3. The attorney files a demurrer. A hearing is held and the judge overrules his demurrer, with 10 days' leave to answer. The attorney for the plaintiff serves a Notice of Overruling of Demurrer on Monday, November 16, 1981. Counting the 17th as the 1st day, the 10th day falls on Thursday, November 26, 1981, which is Thanksgiving, a holiday. Hence the last day to serve and file an answer is Friday, November 27, 1981.

The following calendar is not a complete list of all dates to be noted but is a fairly comprehensive list of the more common dates in general pleadings in civil cases.

THE LEGAL CALENDAR
Civil Cases
Superior and Appellate Courts

ADMISSIONS, REQUESTS FOR	After 10 days from date of service of summons; leave of court required if within 10 days. CCP §2033.
DENIAL OR OBJECTIONS TO ADMISSIONS	Deemed admitted unless denial or objections made within 20 days after service (court may enlarge time up to 15 days without notice; shorten or extend time on motion and notice. CCP §2033).
AMENDED COMPLAINT	30 days to answer, demur or otherwise plead to amended pleading after service. CCP §§471.5-473, Rule 205.*
AMENDED ANSWER	10 days after service of amended answer or the as court may direct, to file a demurrer. CCP §471.5.

*All references to Rules are to California Rules of Court.

ANSWER (or DEMUR or otherwise plead) to Complaint	30 days after service. CCP §412.20.
ANSWER (to Petition for Hearing in Supreme Court)	20 days after decision becomes final as to Court of Appeal. (Decision becomes final 30 days after filing in Court of Appeal.) Rule 28(a)
ANSWER to Petition for Rehearing (Supreme Court or Court of Appeal)	23 days after filing of decision. Rule 27(c).
APPEAL (from Superior Court):	
Notice of appeal	File within 60 days after date of mailing notice of entry of judgment by clerk pursuant to CCP §664.5, *OR*
	Within 60 days after date of service of written notice of entry of judgment by any party upon the party filing the notice of appeal, *OR*
	Within 180 days after date of entry of judgment.
	WHICHEVER IS EARLIEST. Rule 2(a), (c).
	If motion for new trial is made and denied, time for filing notice of appeal is extended until 30 days after either (a) entry of order denying motion or (b) denial thereof by operation of law, but in no event later than 180 days after date of entry of judgment. Rule 3(a)
	See Rule 3(b) for time when motion to vacate is made.
	For time for cross-appeals, see rule 3(c).
Notice designating record on appeal	10 days after filing notice of appeal. See Rule 5(a).
Notice designating additional records	10 days after service of appellant's notice of designation. See Rule 5(b).

BILL OF PARTICULARS	Defendant has 10 days after demand for bill of particulars to deliver a copy of the account to plaintiff. CCP §454.
FINDINGS OF FACT and CONCLUSIONS OF LAW and JUDGMENT	Within 10 days after oral announcement of decision, or if none made, within 10 days after clerk mails notice of decision, findings of fact and conclusions of law must be requested or will be deemed waived (in municipal courts request must be made at time of trial or will be deemed waived, and in any event cannot be required if amount sued for exclusive of interest and costs or value of property in controversy does not exceed $1,000. CCP §632. Rule 232.
Designation or notice to prepare findings	At time of decision court may designate party to prepare findings if requested, or may, within 5 days after request made, notify counsel to prepare. Rule 232(a), (c).
Time to prepare findings	Preparation by court: Within 15 days after request.
	Preparation by counsel: If *designated* by court, within 15 days after request made. If *notified* by court after request, within 15 days after notice. Rule 232(c).
Objections:	15 days after date of service of findings to serve and file objections or submit counter findings, etc. Rule 232(d).
INTERROGATORIES	Serve on any party at any time after 10 days from date of service of summons; leave of court required if within 10 days CCP §2030.
ANSWERS TO INTERROGATORIES	30 days after date of service of interrogatories (time may be enlarged by court) CCP §2030.
JURY FEES	Deposit 1 day's jury fees 14 days in advance of trial (2 days in advance in justice court). CCP §631(5).

MOTIONS (In General) (See special types of motions below.)	10 days before the hearing on the motion. CCP §1005. (Court may prescribe a shorter time.) If served by mail: 15 days in California; outside California but in U.S., 20 days; outside U.S., 30 days. (CCP §1013(a) does not apply under CCP §1005.)
MOTION FOR NEW TRIAL	Serve and file Before entry of judgment OR Within 15 days of the date of mailing notice of entry of judgment by clerk of court pursuant to CCP §664.5, OR Within 15 days of service by any party of written notice of entry of judgment, OR Within 180 days after entry of judgment, WHICHEVER IS EARLIEST. Rule 203(b). CCP §659.
Affidavits:	When new trial motion made on grounds specified in first four subdivisions of CCP §657, must be made on affidavit (CCP §658), within 10 days after serving the notice (CCP §659a).
Counter-Affidavits:	Adverse party has 10 days after service of affidavits to serve and file counter-affidavits. CCP §659a.
Oral argument:	After expiration of time for counter-affidavits, a notice of oral argument (*if any*), 5 days' notice given by clerk. CCP §661.
MOTION TO QUASH SUMMONS	Notice of motion must be served and filed within the time to plead. Notice must designate a time for making the motion not less than 10 nor more than 20 days after filing of the notice. CCP §418.10. Service of notice extends defendant's time to plead until 15 days after service of written notice of order denying motion. See CCP §418.10.

MOTION TO STRIKE	Must be served and filed within time required to answer and prevents a default being taken but does not extend time to demur. CCP §§435, 585.
	Must specify a hearing date not more than 15 days from the filing of the motion (plus any additional time required to be given). See CCP §§435, 585.
MOTION FOR SUMMARY JUDGMENT	Serve at least 10 days before the hearing date. CCP §437c.
MOTION TO TAX COSTS	File within 10 days after service of the cost bill. CCP §1033.
MOTION TO VACATE JUDGMENT	Serve and file
	Before entry of judgment *OR*
	Within 15 days of date of mailing notice of entry of judgment by clerk of court pursuant to CCP §664.5, *OR*
	Within 15 days of service by any party of written notice of entry of judgment, *OR*
	WHICHEVER IS EARLIEST. CCP §663a.
PETITION FOR REHEARING (Court of Appeal or Calif. Supreme Court)	15 days after filing of decision. Rule 27(b).
ANSWER TO PETITION FOR REHEARING	23 days after filing of decision. Rule 27(c).
PETITION FOR HEARING (Calif. Supreme Court)	File within 10 days after decision of Court of Appeal becomes final as to Court of Appeal (which is 30 days after filing in Court of Appeal). Rule 28(b).
ANSWER TO PETITION	20 days after decision becomes final as to Court of Appeal (which is 30 days after filing of decision in Court of Appeal). Rule 28(c).

Superior courts:

TRIAL, NOTICE OF TIME AND PLACE	Short causes (time estimated for trial 1 day or less) are exempt from any pretrial, settlement conference or trial setting conference. Rule 207.1. [If case not completely heard in 5 hours, judge may complete the trial or he may declare a mistrial, in which case a new memorandum must be served and filed and proceed as for other causes.]
If pretrial conference held:	If time is fixed by pretrial order, no further notice of time and place of trial need be given. Rule 219(b). If time and place not fixed by pretrial order, clerk gives 30 days' notice by mail (unless time shortened). Rule 219(b).
If no pretrial conference held:	*In courts having more than 10 judges:* Clerk gives 60 days' notice of *trial setting conference.* *In courts having less than 10 judges:* Clerk gives 90 days' notice of trial.

If adverse party fails to appear at trial, the other party may not proceed with case, if the issue to be tried is an issue of fact, unless proof first made either that clerk of court gave 20 days' notice to adverse party or, if such notice not served by clerk, that 15 days' notice has been given by any party (in unlawful detainer action, 5 days' notice, 10 days if served by mail). CCP §594.

Where service is made by mail in an unlawful detainer action, the 10 days' notice is not extended by Code of Civil Procedure section 1013.

Code of Civil Procedure section 1013:

Service of mail is complete at the time of deposit in the United States post office, or a mail box, sub-post office, substation or mail chute, or other like facility, etc.

Section 1013 also provides:

> The service [by mail] is complete at the time of deposit, but any prescribed period of notice and any right or duty to do any act or make any response within any prescribed period or on a date certain after the service of such document served by mail shall be extended five days if the place of address is within the State of California, 10 days if the place of address is outside the State of California but within the United States, and 20 days if the place of address is outside the United States, but such extension shall not apply to extend the time for filing notice of intention to move for new trial, notice of intention to move to vacate judgment pursuant to Section 663a of this code or notice of appeal.
>
> The copy of the notice or other paper served by mail pursuant to this chapter shall bear a notation of the date and place of mailing or be accompanied by an unsigned copy of the affidavit or certificate of mailing. The provisions of this subdivision are directory.

An affidavit or certificate of service by mail must set forth the exact title of the document served and filed but need no longer be affixed to the original, or a true copy, of the document served and filed. (Code Civ. Proc. §1013a.)

Legal Newspapers

Legal newspapers publish the courts' calendars for each day. If the calendar in the law office shows that a matter is to be heard that day, one of the first items of business for the day is to check the newspaper, first, to confirm that the matter actually appears as being on the court's calendar and, secondly, its position on the calendar. *Then the legal assistant should find out how each particular calendar is actually handled.*

For example, reference to one Law and Motion Calendar in the San Francisco Recorder shows 37 motions calendared for one day. The paper shows 9:30 a.m. as the time of the law and motion calendar. Obviously 37 matters cannot all be heard at one and the same time. The case that is the 37th is not going to be heard until much later than 9:30 a.m. and the calendar may continue over into the afternoon. If it appears that the matter will not be heard until mid-morning, the attorney *might* not need to rush to be there at 9:30. However, some of the matters on the calendar might be continued over, or may already have been taken off calendar, so ample time must be allowed.

The same is true of other calendars. All matters are set for the same hour. The reason for this, of course, is to make the best use of the court's time. There is no foretelling how long a matter may take and therefore cases could not be set for a fixed amount of time. The most feasible way is to set the number the court thinks it can hear, and have counsel present and ready. This may take an undue amount of the attorney's time, but no better way has been found.

Court trials and jury trials are likewise listed in the paper and watch must be kept as to how close the court is getting to a case, and check made with the court as to what the outlook is. Legal newspapers also publish probate notices and other forms of notice, and it is well to check the newspaper on the dates scheduled for publication.

Chapter 7

PREPARATION FOR TRIAL

I. DISCOVERY

"Civil Discovery is . . . the most important area in the job function for the litigation paralegal. Legal assistants are working with interrogatories, depositions and other discovery materials to assist the lawyer to present a most effective case possible for his/her client."*

Independent legal assistants who are litigation specialists are finding this to be true as they continue to do substantial work in the field of discovery.

Within the law office more litigation jobs are being performed by legal assistants, such as drafting of interrogatories and answers to interrogatories; summarizing and indexing answers to interrogatories; drafting motions to compel further interrogatories, drafting requests for admissions and responses to requests; summarizing and indexing responses to requests for admissions; drafting Notices of Requests to Produce documents and summarizing and reviewing the documents received in response and responses to Notice to Produce; preparation of documents re depositions, as Notices of Taking of Deposition, Subpoena Duces Tecum, and supporting declarations; and drafting of other motions for physical, mental or blood examinations; arranging for medical examinations, etc.

What Is Discovery, and Why Have It?

Discovery consists of the prescribed legal procedures by which any attorney attempts to find out before the trial all he or she can about the case to ascertain the truth and prevent perjury. Who are the witnesses for the adverse party? What do they know about the facts of the case? Upon what documents are they relying to prove their case?

---

*"Para Legal Update," published by the National Legal Assistant Conference Center, 2444 Wilshire Blvd., Suite 600, Santa Monica, CA 90403.

In the process of discovery all parties become better educated as to the strengths and weaknesses of their claims or defenses. False, fraudulent or sham claims or defenses are exposed. When discovery is complete, the attorneys should have the information necessary to better assess their client's case.

Their evaluation of a case influences them when discussing a possible settlement. The net result of discovery is to encourage settlement. If settlement negotiations should fail and the case go to trial, the attorneys will be better prepared to argue the case. They know what evidence will be presented; the chances of surprise evidence are lessened.

Discovery also serves to preserve evidence for use at trial and to commit parties to a position.

The attorney has a wider scope during the discovery stage and the evidence rules are more relaxed. Any question may be asked which is not privileged and which is relevant to the subject matter involved. "Relevancy to the subject matter" has been interpreted to be a broader concept than "relevancy to the issues;" the relevancy is more loosely construed than when applied at trial. (*Greyhound Corp. v. Superior Court* (1961) 56 Cal.2d 355, 390.) (See Werchick, *California Preparation and Trial,* pp. 271-272.)

Opposing counsel may not object on the ground that the testimony would be inadmissible at trial, as long as the testimony seems reasonably calculated to lead to the discovery of admissible evidence. (Code Civ. Proc. §2016; Fed.R.Civ.P. 26(b)(1).)

The work product of an attorney is privileged, and therefore not discoverable, under Code of Civil Procedure section 2016(b) "unless the court determines that denial of discovery will unfairly prejudice the party seeking discovery in preparing his claim or defense or will result in an injustice. . . ." This is a qualified privilege against discovery of the attorney's work product. "Work product" is not defined in the code and must be interpreted under the facts of each case. (See *Southern Pacific Co. v. Superior Court* (1973) 34 Cal.App.3d 270.) The courts have held that to disclose the identity of a nonexpert witness in a personal injury case violated this qualified work product privilege. (*City of Long Beach v. Superior Court* (1976) 64 Cal.App.3d 65.) (See Mason, California Civil Procedure Handbook, p. 238, et seq.)

Materials held by California courts to be discoverable under the work product rule are listed on page 282 of Werchick, California Preparation and Trial, and materials held *not* to be discoverable are listed on page 283, *et seq.*

An absolute privilege is created under Code of Civil Procedure section 2016(b) as to an attorney's impressions, conclusions, opinions, or legal research or theories, which are *not* to be discoverable under any circumstances.

The writer believes that Code of Civil Procedure section 2016 would apply to protect the work product of the paralegal because it is a part of the work product of the attorney.

The principal devices for discovery are depositions, interrogatories and requests for admissions. In addition, by means of motions for production of documents and subpoenas duces tecum, evidentiary documents may be inspected. Code of Civil Procedure section 2021 deals with waiver of errors and irregularities relating to depositions or interrogatories.

DEPOSITIONS

A deposition is a statement (as of a witness or of a party) taken orally before an officer authorized to administer oaths, as a notary public. The witness is questioned by opposing counsel and the statement is transcribed by a reporter and signed by the witness.

The deposition may be used at trial if the witness is absent. The deposition may also be used to impeach the testimony of a witness. Depositions also make it possible to avoid calling witnesses who are not going to be useful in the case.

Procedure for Taking Depositions

The deposition of a party to an action or any other person, e.g., a witness to an automobile accident, may be taken at any time after the service of the summons or appearance of the defendant (or before an action upon petition in the manner provided by Code of Civil Procedure section 2017). If the notice of the taking of the deposition is served by the plaintiff within 20 days after service of the summons or appearance of the defendant, leave of court to take the deposition must be obtained.

Code of Civil Procedure section 2019, subdivision (a)(6), provides that a corporation, partnership, association, or governmental agency may be named as the deponent, and the matters on which examination is requested described with reasonable particularity. The organization shall then designate one or more officers, directors or managers, agents, or other persons who consent, to testify on its behalf.

A notary public or other authorized person administers the oath of the person whose deposition is being taken. Counsel for the parties are present and opposing counsel also may ask questions of the witness. A reporter takes the questions and answers verbatim in shorthand (or stenotype) and later transcribes his notes.

A party may also videotape the deposition if the notice of taking deposition states that the deposition will also be videotaped. The cost of the videotaping is not, however, a recoverable court cost.

After the reporter completes the deposition, the witness is notified that the deposition is available for reading, correcting and signing. If within 30 days thereafter the witness does not correct, approve — or refuse to approve — by means of a letter, or otherwise refuse to approve or sign it, the officer before whom it was taken is required to so indicate on the deposition. The deposition then may be used in the same manner as though the witness had read, corrected and signed it.

Ordinarily the witness reads the transcript, makes any necessary corrections, and signs it, before a notary public.

Promptly upon correction, approval, or refusal to approve, the deposition, or upon expiration of 30 calendar days following notification to the witness that the deposition is available for reading, correcting and signing, the officer taking the deposition seals the deposition in an envelope endorsed with the title of the case and identified as the deposition of the witness.

Sometimes the parties are agreeable to the taking of a deposition of the witness; sometimes they are not. The procedure is simpler if they agree because then, by written stipulation, the parties may take depositions before any person, at any time or place, and upon any notice. (Code of Civ. Proc. §2019(a)(2).) If the parties are not willing to stipulate, the documents needed are:

a. *Notice of taking of deposition.* The notice must state the name and address, if known, of the person to be examined and the time and place for taking the deposition.

This notice should be served on every other party to the action (Code Civ. Proc. §2019(a)(1) (a party is served by serving his counsel, if he has an attorney, otherwise, personally on the party). Such notice must be served at least 10 days before the date of the deposition, plus 1 day for every 300 miles of distance of place of examination from the residence of the person to whom notice is given (court may enlarge or shorten this time). The original notice with proof of service are filed in the deposition.

b. *Subpoena re deposition* (printed form). A subpoena re deposition is served personally on the person whose deposition is being taken. *A subpoena re deposition is not needed to take the deposition of a party, or officer, director, managing agent of any such party or person, or of a person for whose immediate benefit an action is prosecuted or defended,* if proper notice of the taking of the deposition is given to the attorney for such party, or to the party himself if he has no attorney.

A deponent may be required to attend only in his county of residence if the place of taking the deposition is not more than 75 miles from his residence. A party may be required to attend in the county of place of trial if the place of deposition is not more than 150 miles from his residence. However, a party, or a person for whose immediate benefit said action is prosecuted or defended, or an officer, director or managing agent of such party or person, may be required to attend at a place more than 150 miles from his residence — upon court order and upon 10 days' written notice. (CCP §2019.)

A form for *notice of taking of deposition,* and the combined form of *subpoena re deposition* and *subpoena duces tecum re deposition* used in Los Angeles County, follow.

Notice of Taking of Deposition

```
 1 │ PAUL D. BLACK
   │ Attorney at Law
 2 │ 926 J Street
   │ Sacramento, CA 95814
 3 │ Telephone:  445-4567

 4 │ Attorney for Plaintiff

 5 │

 6 │

 7 │

 8 │             SUPERIOR COURT OF THE STATE OF CALIFORNIA

 9 │               FOR THE COUNTY OF SACRAMENTO

10 │

11 │ JOHN SMITH,                    )         NO. 126704
   │                                )
12 │           Plaintiff,           )
   │                                )
13 │    v.                          )      NOTICE OF TAKING OF
   │                                )
14 │ JAMES BROWN; WHITE CORPORATION,)         DEPOSITION
   │ a California corporation;      )
15 │ FIRST DOE; SECOND DOE; and     )
   │ THIRD DOE,                     )
16 │                                )
   │           Defendants.          )
17 │ _____ )

18 │

19 │ TO EACH PARTY AND TO THE ATTORNEY OF RECORD FOR EACH PARTY HEREIN:

20 │       NOTICE IS HEREBY GIVEN that the plaintiff John Smith

21 │ herein will take the deposition of JOHN DOYLE as a witness, whose

22 │ address is 5448 - 40th Street, Sacramento, California, upon oral

23 │ examination, on Monday, July 12, 1976, commencing at 10:00 a.m.,

24 │ at the law offices of Paul D. Black, 926 J Street, Sacramento,

25 │ California, before Mary Tiffany, or such other notary public as

26 │ may be present at said time and place.

27 │       If said deposition is not completed on said date, the

28 │ taking thereof will be continued from day to day thereafter at
```

1   the same place, Sundays and holidays excepted, until completed.

2

3   _Paul D. Black_

4   Attorney for Plaintiff

5

6

7

8

9

10

11

12   [Give this notice to every party to the action. This notice is
     the only document required if you are taking deposition of one
13   of the parties, or an officer, etc., thereof, i.e., you would
     not need subpena.]

14

15

16

17

18

19

20

21

22

23

24

25

26

27

28

Preparing for a Deposition

The legal assistant will be expected to set up the deposition, i.e., to arrange a time and place and for a court reporter, give the requisite notices and notify the deponent (person whose deposition is taken). A convenient time for the deponent should first be determined. Then the legal assistant can contact opposing counsel. Attorneys customarily work together to find a convenient date for the deposition. *Quid pro quo.*

In a lengthy case where more than one deposition is to be taken, or where unusual technical or unfamiliar terms are apt to be used, it is best to retain the services of the same court reporter, who will become familiar with the terminology. The reporter may call on the paralegal for assistance.

The experienced legal assistant after reviewing the pleadings and evidence should be able to identify the legal issues in order to assist the attorney in framing questions for the deposition. The legal assistant should confirm such identification of the issues with the attorney. Without an overview of the case, the legal assistant cannot properly function in this field.

Practical Aspects of Discovery and Taking Depositions

1. When taking depositions, most attorneys attempt to get the facts as soon as possible before opposing counsel does as it gets the freshest response from the deponent. As cost is a factor, this gives the legal assistant the information and time to work out the most convenient and most economical plan for taking depositions as well as the most workable total discovery plan, to find out what evidence is needed and how to collect it.

Usually the depositions of the adverse party and the key adverse witnesses should be taken, at the minimum, plus any expert of the adverse party. However, the attorney might not want to take a doctor's deposition in a personal injury case for tactical reasons because it helps the doctor to prepare for trial. When a doctor's deposition is taken, he or she knows what questions to expect at trial.

Usually, the attorney will prefer not to take the depositions of his or her plaintiff-client, or witnesses, particularly the best witnesses, unless they might not be available for trial.

2. In taking depositions in a distant city the legal assistant should check on the costs of a court reporter in that city. The attorney may find it cheaper to take a court reporter with him, or even to fly the witness to his home base if he is willing to make the trip. (An Easterner might welcome the opportunity for a paid trip to California.)

If the decision is made to take the deposition out of town, the attorney will decide whether to take the deposition himself, or to bring in a local attorney. Since the local attorney would be unfamiliar with the case, any temporary saving in this regard could prove costly in the long run.

When depositions are taken out of state pursuant to Code of Civil Procedure section 2024, or upon stipulation of the parties, the officer taking the deposition is presumed to be bound by the same laws as to the deposition as within California, unless otherwise agreed upon by the parties. If the deposition is taken before a shorthand reporter with a place of business in California where the deposition will be kept, the officer is to send the deposition to the court where the action is pending for filing, unless the parties otherwise agree.

3. When noticing a deposition and not sure of the names, such as the officers of a corporation, describe them as "the person most knowledgeable about a particular subject matter."

4. Copies of deposition usually required:
    1 for witness
    1 for each attorney
    1 for court reporter

5. When a deposition is held pursuant to stipulation of counsel for parties, no formal notice is required. In such event counsel should also stipulate that the rules of the Code of Civil Procedure apply.

6. In subpoenaing records, when you don't know who has them, name the "Custodian of Records."

If the documents are voluminous make arrangements to view them at the location where they are stored. Ask not only for the original documents but also for all copies of documents, as there could be "original" information on a copy. Ask the custodian for his index, and a copy of their document retention and destruction policy. If you find a document scheduled for destruction, a court order prohibiting destruction or a stipulation of the adverse party agreeing not to destroy the documents should be obtained. Stationery stores sell sequential stampers, which can be used for numbering the documents. Then if opposing counsel produces one without a stamp, you will know it was not produced for you.

A "reader-viewer" can be rented and a copy made of the documents wanted. If the records are out of town, you may want to microfilm them.

7. A request for admissions can be combined with a brief set of interrogatories in which the parties may be asked why they failed to admit any request for admission — if they did. They can be asked for

the facts that led them to deny the request for admission, or for any witnesses or documents which are the basis for denial.

8. Misuse of discovery: The attorney — and legal assistant — should be mindful of the power of the court if it finds a misuse of discovery. The court may: (1) strike pleadings, (2) stay proceedings, (3) award attorney fees, (4) rule out witness' testimony, and (5) dismiss the case — though in the client's interests the court usually wants to rule on the merits.

Deposition Stipulations

Usually the attorneys will agree on certain matters in connection with the taking of the deposition. The legal assistant can draft any agreements beforehand, or the firm may have a model stipulation ordinarily used. A sample of such a stipulation might read as follows:

"IT WAS STIPULATED BETWEEN COUNSEL for the respective parties that if the witness should refuse to answer any questions propounded by counsel, it shall be deemed that the Notary Public instructed the witness to answer, but that the witness still refused so to do.

"IT WAS FURTHER STIPULATED that all objections to questions propounded to said witness shall be reserved by each of the parties, save and except any objections as to the form of the questions propounded.

"IT WAS FURTHER STIPULATED that said deposition shall be taken pursuant to the provisions of Section 2016, *et seq.,* of the Code of Civil Procedure of the State of California.

"IT WAS FURTHER STIPULATED that said deposition shall be reported by ELSIE RATHER, Certified Shorthand Reporter, #1111, and a disinterested person, and thereafter transcribed by her into typewriting, to be read to or by the witness, who, after making such corrections therein as are necessary, will subscribe the same.

"IT WAS FURTHER STIPULATED that if this deposition has not been signed at the time of trial, it may be used at that time with the same force and effect as though signed by the witness, provided the witness has had a reasonable opportunity to read, correct, and sign the same."

These stipulations will be typed into the deposition by the reporter.

Preparation of the Witness

The client should be prepared for the taking of the deposition. This may be done by the attorney but might be done by the legal assistant if so instructed. An appointment with the client-deponent should be scheduled several days in advance of the deposition.

The client should be advised to answer all questions directly, not to digress, and to tell the truth. He may ask the reporter to repeat a question if he is uncertain. *If the question can be answered "Yes" or "No" he should answer "Yes" or "No." He should not volunteer information.* Nor should he guess at the answer if he does not know. He may answer a question where he is uncertain of his recollection but should so state that it is to the best of his memory. What we cannot clearly remember at one time — and especially under the stress of a deposition — may clearly be remembered at a later date. If this same question should be asked of the witness at the trial, and he has in the meantime, or does then, remember the correct answer, he may lose credibility if he was too positive in his answer in the deposition, when his memory was less accurate.

The client should dress appropriately and conservatively for the occasion. Too casual dress should be avoided.

The witness should not, of course, be flippant, or appear hostile, or argue.

The client should be forewarned that opposing counsel may attempt to elicit information not directly involved in the case at hand. In a personal injury accident case, for instance, opposing counsel may seek to discover if the witness had sustained injuries in a previous accident and been treated for them, in the hope of proving incapacity related to the first case. Opposing counsel may be looking for admissions of previous arrests, other litigation, and in a personal injury case, activities since the injury. Again, such information should not be volunteered, though it may not be hidden. But the client should be apprised of the possibility that such questions may be asked.

The client should also be forewarned that he may be asked if he discussed his testimony with his attorney. The client unprepared for this question may not know what to say. If opposing counsel tries to infer the witness' attorney told him what to say and asks him if the lawyer told him what to say, he can honestly say no, he only told him to tell the truth.

A sample list of questions to defendant which may be used in a deposition for a automobile accident case follows:

Suggested Questions for Deposition of a Defendant in an Automobile Accident Case

What is your name?

What is your address?

What is your occupation?

What was your occupation on the date of the accident?

What was the date of the accident?

At what time of day did the accident take place?

Where did the accident occur?

What is the nearest landmark?

What was the condition of the weather that day (night)?

What was the condition of the highway — was it wet or dry?

(If nighttime) What were the lighting conditions?

Were you familiar with that highway? Do you regularly drive it?

What kind of highway was it — paved, oiled, dirt?

Can you describe the scene generally (topography of terrain on both sides)?

What arterial markers are there or other signs, markings on pavement, speed warnings, painted lines, street or intersection lamps?

What kind of vehicle were you driving [make, type]?

Who owned the vehicle you were driving?

Who were the occupants besides yourself?

In what direction were you traveling just prior to the accident?

What was the position of your car with references to lanes and distance from the center line and curb line?

At what speed were you driving?

How do you know that was your speed?

Where were you when you first observed plaintiff in his car?

In what direction was plaintiff traveling?

What was the position on the highway of plaintiff's car when you first observed it?

Where were you when you first observed the plaintiff's car?

What was the make and type of plaintiff's vehicle?

At what speed was plaintiff traveling?

Did you see any other traffic just prior to the accident?

What did you do after you first observed plaintiff's car?

In what direction or directions were you looking up until the time of the impact?

Did you alter your speed at any time?

Did you alter the course of your vehicle?

When did you apply your brakes?

What movements of plaintiff did you observe of plaintiff after you first saw him?

Did plaintiff alter his speed?

Did plaintiff alter his course of travel?

When did plaintiff apply his brakes?

What was the lapse of time between your first observation of plaintiff and the moment of impact?

How far did your car travel during that period of time? Plaintiff's car?

Please describe the impact.

Was there any impairment of your vision by the sun, headlights of vehicles or objects?

At what point on the highway did the impact occur?

What portion of your car came in contact with plaintiff's car?

What portion of plaintiff's vehicle did your car strike?

What movement did your car make after the impact?

What movement of plaintiff's vehicle did you observe after the impact?

What happened immediately after the accident?

What conduct did you observe?

What conversation did you have with others after the impact?

What conversation did you have with plaintiff at the time of the accident or thereafter?

Did you overhear any conversations between plaintiff and others?

What was the origin of your trip that day?

Where were you going?

What was the purpose of your trip? [Determine whether defendant was acting within the course and scope of his employment as an agent for his employer (respondeat superior).]

Had you consumed any alcoholic drinks the day of the accident? [If answer is yes, "How many?"]

What was your speed as you approached the scene of the accident?

What lane were you traveling in as you approached the scene of the accident?

Did you have any liquor in your car?

What was the mechanical condition of your car?

The windshield?

Brakes?

Lights?

Horn?

Did you give any warning signal to plaintiff?

Describe the manner of giving the signal.

Did you apply your brakes?

How did your brakes respond?

What was your observation of the scene of the accident?

Did you see any tire marks? Where?

Did you see any gouge marks on the pavement? Where?

Did you see any blood on the pavement? Where?

Did you observe any marks on plaintiff's vehicle?

Did you observe any injuries by plaintiff?

Was there any impairment of any of your senses?

Do you wear glasses?

Do you have any hearing impairment?

Do you have the full and unimpaired use of your body, that is, do you have any physical handicap or illness of any kind?

How many years' experience have you had driving an automobile?

Do you have an operator's license? (Number of license)

Were there any eyewitnesses to the accident?

Did you observe any eyewitnesses to the accident?

Objections to Deposition Questions

The deponent should be further advised that if his own counsel makes an objection, he should not answer the question but wait for instructions from his attorney.

Proper grounds for objection to the form of a question are that it is: uncertain, ambiguous, unintelligible, compound, too general, a call for a narrative answer, already answered, a misquotation of a witness, leading, argumentative, an assumption of facts, or a call for specu-lation. (Werchick, *California Preparation and Trial*.) Other grounds for objection might be errors and irregularities in the notice of taking deposition (Code Civ. Proc. §2021(a)), disqualification of the officer before whom the deposition is taken (2021(b)), errors occurring at the oral examination (2021(c)(2)), and errors and irregularities in the manner in which the testimony is transcribed (2021(d)).

Objections to the competency of a witness or to the competency, relevancy, or materiality of testimony are not waived by failure to make them before or during the taking of the deposition, unless the ground of objection is one which might have been obviated or removed if presented at the time. (Code Civ. Proc. §2021(c)(2).) (See also, Code Civ. Proc. §§2019(e)(1) and 2021.)

A motion to compel an answer may be made under Code of Civil Procedure section 2034 but if the court finds that the refusal or failure was without substantial justification or that the answer does not comply with the requirements of section 2033, the court may require the payment of reasonable expenses incurred in obtaining the order including reasonable attorney fees; similarly, the party making the motion may be subjected to such payment.

If the court makes an order concerning an admission, and the order is not complied with within the time ordered by the court, it will be deemed admitted. (But see Code Civ. Proc. §§473, 2033.)

Attending the Deposition

The legal assistant may attend the deposition with the attorney and take notes as a basis for later discussion with the attorney before a transcript is received (sometimes the transcript may not be prepared), with a view to taking additional depositions, or preparing for trial.

Assuming the legal assistant does attend the deposition, the legal assistant's own evaluation of the witness can be of help to the attorney. What are the criteria? The following material may be of assistance in evaluating the deposition witness, or other witnesses interviewed in the course of investigation.

Evaluating Testimony of Witness

Are the witness's own statements consistent? Are they consistent with other objective evidence? Does he seem to remember other matters as keenly as he claims to remember that about which he is testifying (or giving a statement to the legal assistant)? Does his testimony coincide with objective findings in the case? Has he made contradictory statements elsewhere within your knowledge?

How does his conduct outside the room compare? Is he claiming personal injury? Consider his behavior, appearance, tone, body movements. Is his voice calm regardless of his words? How long does he actually sit during the questioning — if claiming personal injury, has he said he cannot sit for that long?

What might be his motivation and bias in the case? Does he have a financial interest in the outcome of the case? An emotional interest? Religious, political? Is he a friend, relative — an enemy?

Study his general demeanor. Is it open, frank? Or evasive? Intelligent? Frightened, ill at ease? Angry? What is his reaction to other witnesses or parties?

The Expert Witness

All of the above applies to the expert witness, who is usually paid to testify. The attorney will ask how complete and accurate is the foundation of the information on which he bases his opinion. What is his relative expertise in the field? Is he testifying in his own specialty field? His expertness does not extend beyond his own field of expertise; in an area beyond that field, without additional special qualifications in that area also, he is as any other layman. A person can have a minimal education but qualify as an expert on a subject on which he is well informed; it is the information, knowledge and skill, not the academic degree, which confers expertness.

Summarizing Depositions

The attorney should have a summary of a deposition for reference. During the trial when a witness is being examined, the attorney may need to refer quickly to the testimony of the witness made during his deposition, in order to impeach the witness. A summary of the salient facts was, until a few years ago, mostly prepared by attorneys. Now a legal assistant may find it his or her duty to make such a summary. While probably an attorney should make some kind of brief summary after every deposition if time permits and when his impressions are still fresh in his memory, there is a practical reason for a legal assistant to assume or accept such a task.

A legal assistant may be able to pay special attention to every detail of the deposition allowing the attorney to follow the general tenor, alert to questions of content which are of questionable nature and which should be objected to. Under any circumstance, however, it is well for a legal assistant to attend the deposition and take notes to compare ideas with the attorney afterward even if the attorney prefers to write the summary himself.

The presence of the legal assistant at the deposition has an added value in that it places the legal assistant in the position that the jury will take in trial. Impressions of the witness are gained in person that cannot be divined from reading the transcript of his testimony. The legal assistant may get ideas for questions for the attorney to ask at trial of the same witness or other witnesses. If the witness is the client or one who had been interviewed by the legal assistant, the legal assistant should point out any inconsistencies to the attorney.

A deposition in a simple case may not take much time. But many cases have lengthy and complex depositions. In recent years there are many more large cases, in the fields of antitrust litigation, job discrimination, labor law, environmental law, shareholders' suits, fraud, contractual disputes, etc.

Some of the legal assistants being hired for this work have just graduated from college. Larger firms are looking for the graduates with fine academic records, possibly with higher degrees. They need persons who can write well and concisely and who are quick to analyze and solve problems, and *who can see the relevance of the facts to the litigation*. Persons who have experience that demonstrates additional research and writing and analytical ability are being hired by these firms also.

Accuracy in the summary is vital to the attorney relying on it for the facts. In paraphrasing the testimony, choice of words is important and requires careful reading and writing. The legal assistant must be able to read and digest clearly, concisely and quickly, summarizing literally thousands of pages, over a long period of time. Sometimes hearing transcripts are summarized as well.

Summarizing depositions is time-consuming work if done well, and is often tedious. Any boredom can be lessened only by total involvement in the lawsuit. An overview of the whole case is imperative, not only to do the job well but to provide a sense of accomplishment, in seeing the end results of paralegal work. The legal assistant may possibly attend trial, and testify.

Methods of Summarizing Depositions

The forms of summaries vary. It has been said that there are as many systems for summaries and documentation as there are attorneys and law offices.

The purpose for which the summary will be used, and by whom, should be considered. The form should be one that best suits the purposes of the attorney who uses it. The legal assistant should request instruction from the attorney as to his or her preference of style. If such instruction is not forthcoming, the legal assistant may use one of the following models, or devise a summary best suited to the case.

The summary should reflect any inconsistencies in the testimony of the witness in the deposition, or in the answers to interrogatories. These can be interposed in brackets. Documentary evidence reviewed by the legal assistant may give rise to questions in the light of the testimony. The legal assistant's analysis can be the basis for further depositions by the attorney, or questions to be asked at trial, or other discovery to be undertaken.

Outline or Narrative Summary

A simple accident case might have a short summary such as the following:

FACTS

DATE:		March 4, 1980
TIME:		4:00 P.M.
DAY:		Wednesday
PLACE:		Country Club Plaza Shopping Center, Fulton Street, Sacramento, CA
PARTIES:	*Plaintiff:*	Renee Wills 28 years of age Driver; sole occupant of vehicle.
	Defendant:	Maury Carr; 75 Years of age, driver; wife was sole passenger.
VEHICLES:	*Plaintiff:*	1976 Chevrolet Station Wagon
	Defendant:	1973 Impala Chevrolet
WITNESSES:		None.
CHP REPORT:		None.
DESCRIPTION:		Plaintiff vehicle and Defendant vehicle were

in the Country Club Plaza Center parking lot. Both were proceeding toward the Fulton Street exit. Defendant vehicle approached Plaintiff vehicle, perpendicularly, from the right; Plaintiff vehicle preceded Defendant vehicle into the line of cars exiting the parking lot; Defendant vehicle, from Plaintiff's right, pulled into the line immediately behind Plaintiff. The line of cars then proceeded slowly, in a stop-start fashion, to the exit.

IMPACT: Plaintiff stopped.
          Defendant failed to stop.
Impact occurred between right rear bumper of Plaintiff vehicle and right front bumper of Defendant vehicle.

*   *   *

The above format is easy for the reader to follow.

In a more complex case a Narrative Summary might be utilized. This type of summary is a simple narration of the facts of the lawsuit. Also it might be tailored to the person who is going to use it. Some summaries have page references, but others are straight narration.

Chronological (Sequential) (Logical) Summary

In this type of summary the legal assistant goes through the deposition page by page and paraphrases it. Since the legal assistant can dictate it and move right along, it is perhaps less time-consuming to prepare.

On the other hand, the attorney may have to read through a lot of extraneous material to find the testimony on particular points. The summary could turn out to be almost as voluminous as the deposition, which would be impractical.

Each entry may be typed on a card and sorted alphabetically by subject. A large card index might become unwieldy, however. And a card could be lost or misplaced.

Instead of paraphasing the exact quote may be used. To indicate quotes some use ellipses (three dots). Quotation marks could be used. The legal assistant must be able to know when the exact wording might be important and when it can be paraphrased. Certainly if a witness is to be impeached, his exact words will be needed.

From this type of summary, however, an Index Summary can be prepared.

Chronological Summary — *Example*

Case: Roe v. Doe, Sacramento Superior Court 123456
         Deposition of Joe Mather 7/25/81

Page 1
Attorney: Bill Brown
L/A: Rae Burns

Page	Lines	
6	7-9	Joe Mather was passenger in car traveling westerly from Rocklin to Sacramento
7	11-12	Cars passing Mather's car did not have lights on
8	13-17	Mather did not see either a taillight or arm signal
9	12-16, 20-23	Mather could see ahead for a hundred yards

Category Summary

This type of summary might be prepared from a chronological summary. Or the legal assistant might start with headings for each subject and copy statements from the deposition while reading through.

The transcript may first be photocopied and a cut-and-paste method used; duplication more than once may be required if a statement pertains to more than one category.

Category Summary — *Example*

MARION v. MILLER
Outline of Deposition Transcript of
Robert Roberts
Taken: June 25, 1981

Subject	Pages	Tab Color
Meeting before Accident	65, 66, 67	Yellow
Accident	45, 50, 51, 61, 71	Pink
Dump Supervision	31, 32, 33, 34	Blue
Safety Procedures		
Dump Sites	14, 15, 24, 35, 37	III-A Orange
Heavy Equipment	16, 23	III-B Orange
Safety Equipment		
Vests	40, 41	I-A Green
Rearview Mirrors	16, 17, 19	I-B Green
Backup Warnings	72, 73, 74	Red

A variation in the above summary appears as follows:

		Page	Lines
Vests:	Safety vests are issued directly to the individual	28	12-18

Index Summary (Topical Index) (Alphabetical) — *Example*

Index to Deposition of Plaintiff
Taken 5/23/80

TOPIC	Page	Lines
1. Accident	6	6-9
2. Accident	7	11-12
3. Signals	8	13-17
4. Visibility	9	12-16, 20-23

Not all Index summaries are prepared in the same manner, as previously indicated. Some have the page number, the topic (or facts) and a short summary. For instance, the above summary could be set up as follows:

Page   *FACTS:*

6   Accident   Joe Mather was passenger in car traveling westerly from Rocklin to Sacramento

The summary is Alphabetical if the topics are alphabetized as they are above in the first brief sample.

Use of Computers for Depositions

Computers can be used in summarization of depositions and transcripts — as well as in control of documents. But the use of computers is beyond the scope of this chapter.

Suffice to say that the full text of a volume of transcript can be introduced into the computer for desk reference output, in which, down the center of the page, is every transcript word. To the left and right of the word being indexed is the actual context in which the word was used. To the far right is the transcript page citation. Such indexes can be produced by witness, by day, or cumulatively.

Word processing and computer use is growing rapidly. One of the best ways to educate oneself is to inquire of the many manufacturers.

Filing of Depositions

Depositions need not be filed with the court unless they become relevant to an issue in the trial or other pending proceedings and the court orders that the deposition be filed. (Federal rules allow judges to waive the filing of discovery documents. Such papers as depositions and internal company memos need only be exchanged by the two sides of the litigation.) A reasonable filing fee may be charged by the clerk. If a filing fee is charged, the fee shall be paid by the party noticing the deposition, or by stipulation, to the officer taking the deposition, and the officer pays the fee to the clerk at time of filing.

The officer taking the deposition is required to furnish a *certified* copy of the deposition to any party to the action or to the deponent, upon request made before the delivery or mailing of the deposition and payment of reasonable charges therefor.

Retention of Depositions

The officer taking the deposition is obligated to keep the deposition — whether or not it is actually signed — for six months following the "final disposition" of the case. If no order for filing is made within this six-month period, the officer would be required to file the deposition only if he discontinued his occupation. The officer must give all parties prompt notice of the availability of the deposition.

Destruction of Depositions

The court may destroy or otherwise dispose of any exhibit or deposition 5 years after the time for appeal has expired, if no appeal is taken; 5 years after the final determination of an appeal therein; 5 years after a motion for new trial has been granted and a motion to set the case for trial has not been filed, or a motion to set the case has not been made within such 5 years; where a case has been remanded to the trial court for trial and the case is not brought to trial 5 years from the date of filing the remittitur; 5 years after the dismissal of an action or proceeding.

Code of Civil Procedure section 1952.3 also permits the court on its own motion to destroy or otherwise dispose of any exhibit or deposition introduced in the trial, or filed in the action, after 10 years following introduction or filing where, in the discretion of the court, the exhibit or deposition should be destroyed or disposed of.

Any party may file a notice requesting the preservation of the exhibit or deposition for a stated time, up to 3 years; the exhibit or deposition may be destroyed after such time unless another notice is filed.

Any sealed file is retained for at least an additional two years past the date on which it would otherwise be destroyed. (Code Civ. Proc. §1952.3.)

PRODUCTION OF DOCUMENTS

Under Code of Civil Procedure section 2031 a party may make a motion, supported by a declaration or affidavit, for another party to identify documents, papers, books, accounts, letters, photographs or tangible things, of a category specified with reasonable particularity in the request, and to produce and permit their inspection, copying or photographing. Such motion may not be made to require a person other than a party to produce or identify documents.

If a party or other deponent refuses or fails to answer any question propounded upon examination during the taking of a deposition, or refuses or fails to produce books, documents or other things under his control pursuant to a subpoena duces tecum, or to identify documents, papers, books, accounts, letters, photographs, objects, or tangible things, section 2034 of the Code of Civil Procedure makes provision for application to the court for an order compelling answer or identification, not less than 10 nor more than 30 days from such refusal or failure. The original transcript of the deposition must be lodged with the court 5 days prior to the hearing on such a motion.

A subpoena duces tecum re deposition may be used to require either a party or a nonparty to produce documents. A supporting affidavit of declaration is required for its issuance. (Code Civ. Proc. §1985.) The supporting affidavit and the subpoena duces tecum re deposition must describe the documents in detail and state that the witness has the documents in his possession or under his control. The declaration must in addition set forth the materiality of the documents to the issues involved in the case. A copy of the declaration must be attached to the notice of taking deposition.

The printed form of *subpoena duces tecum re deposition* and the printed form of *Application for Subpoena Duces Tecum re Deposition* and *Civil Subpoena* follow:

Application for Subpoena Duces Tecum re Deposition

NAME, ADDRESS, AND TELEPHONE NUMBER
OF ATTORNEY(S)

ATTORNEY(S) FOR

SUPERIOR COURT OF CALIFORNIA, COUNTY OF LOS ANGELES

	CASE NUMBER
PLAINTIFF(S)	
VS	APPLICATION FOR SUBPOENA DUCES TECUM RE DEPOSITION
DEFENDANT(S)	

STATE OF CALIFORNIA, County of Los Angeles

The undersigned states: That he is attorney of record for   in the above entitled

action; that the deposition of   is noticed for hearing before

      at   M.,

in Room No.   , located at   in the City of

      , County of

State of California, on   , 19

That

has in his possession or under his control the exact matters or things designated below:

That the above documents are material to the issues involved in the case by reason of the following facts:

That good cause exists for the production of the above described matters and things by reason of the following facts:

WHEREFORE request is made that the Subpoena Duces Tecum issue

Executed _____ , 19___ , at _____ , California .

I declare under penalty of perjury that the foregoing is true and correct.

_____
(Signature of Declarant)

ATTORNEY OR PARTY WITHOUT ATTORNEY (NAME AND ADDRESS):	TELEPHONE NO.:	FOR COURT USE ONLY
ATTORNEY FOR (NAME):		

Insert name of court, judicial district or branch court, if any, and post office and street address.

PLAINTIFF:

DEFENDANT:

CIVIL SUBPENA ☐ COURT ☐ DEPOSITION	CASE NUMBER:
☐ **DUCES TECUM** ☐ OTHER (specify):	

THE PEOPLE OF THE STATE OF CALIFORNIA, TO (NAME):

1. **YOU ARE ORDERED TO APPEAR AS A WITNESS in this action as follows unless you make a special agreement with the person named in item 3:**

   a. Date: Time: ☐ Dept.:   ☐ Div.:   ☐ Room:
   b. Address:

2. and you are

   a. ☐ ordered to appear in person.

   b. ☐ not required to appear in person if you produce the records described in the accompanying affidavit in compliance with Evidence Code sections 1560 and 1561.

   c. ☐ ordered to appear in person and to produce the records described in the accompanying affidavit. The personal attendance of the custodian or other qualified witness and the production of the original records is required by this subpena. The procedure authorized pursuant to subdivision (b) of section 1560, and sections 1561 and 1562, of the Evidence Code will not be deemed sufficient compliance with this subpena.

   d. ☐ ordered to designate one or more persons to testify on your behalf as to the matters described in the accompanying statement. (Code of Civil Procedure 2019(a)(6))

3. **IF YOU HAVE ANY QUESTIONS ABOUT WITNESS FEES OR THE TIME OR DATE FOR YOU TO APPEAR, OR IF YOU WANT TO BE CERTAIN THAT YOUR PRESENCE IS REQUIRED, CONTACT THE ATTORNEY REQUESTING THIS SUBPENA, NAMED ABOVE, OR THE FOLLOWING PERSON, BEFORE THE DATE ON WHICH YOU ARE TO APPEAR:**

   a. Name: b. Telephone number:

4. **WITNESS FEES:** You are entitled to receive witness fees and mileage actually traveled, one way, as provided by law, if you request them **BEFORE** your scheduled appearance. **Request them from the person named in item 3.**

5. If this subpena requires your attendance at proceedings out of court and you refuse to answer questions or sign as required by law, you must attend a court hearing at a time to be fixed by the person conducting such proceedings.

6. You are ordered to appear in this civil matter in your capacity as a peace officer or other person described in Government Code section 68097.1.

   Date: Clerk of the Court, by _____, Deputy

DISOBEDIENCE OF THIS SUBPENA MAY BE PUNISHED AS CONTEMPT BY THIS COURT. YOU WILL ALSO BE LIABLE FOR THE SUM OF FIVE HUNDRED DOLLARS AND ALL DAMAGES RESULTING FROM YOUR FAILURE TO OBEY.

For Court Use Only	Dated: . . . . _____
	(Signature of person issuing subpena)
	. . . .
	(Type or print name)
	. . . .
	(Title)
	(See reverse for proof of service)

Form Adopted by Rule 982
Judicial Council of California
Revised Effective July 1, 1980

CIVIL SUBPENA

PROOF OF SERVICE OF CIVIL SUBPENA

1. I served this ☐ subpena ☐ subpena duces tecum and supporting affidavit by delivering a copy personally to the person served as follows:

   a. Person served (name):

   b. Address where served:

   c. Date of delivery:
   d. Time of delivery:
   e. Witness fees (check one)

      (1) ☐ were offered or demanded
           and paid. Amount: $ _____

      (2) ☐ were not demanded or paid.

   f. Fees for service . . . . $ _____

2. I received this subpena for service on (date):

3. Person serving

   a. ☐ Not a registered California process server.   e. ☐ California sheriff, marshal, or constable.
   b. ☐ Registered California process server.   f. Name, address and telephone number and
   c. ☐ Emplcyee or independent contractor of a   if applicable, county of registration and number:
       registered California process server.
   d. ☐ Exempt from registration under
       Bus. & Prof. Code 22350(b).

I declare under penalty of perjury that the foregoing is true and correct and that this declaration is executed on (Date): . . . . at (Place): . . . . , California.

(For California sheriff, marshal, or constable use only) I certify that the foregoing is true and correct and that this certificate is executed on (Date): . . . . at (Place): . . . . , California.

_____
        (Signature)

_____
        (Signature)

A declaration under penalty of perjury must be signed in California or in a state that authorizes use of a declaration in place of an affidavit; otherwise an affidavit is required.

Review of Procedure

Depositions

Where witness is a party to the action	Where witness is not a party to the action
1. Notice of intention to take deposition is served on all parties (if party has attorney service is made on attorney)	1. Same
2. Deposition is taken	2. Serve subpoena on witness
3. Notice of filing of deposition is served	3. Deposition is taken
	4. Notice of filing of deposition is served

Depositions With Production of Documents
(Duces Tecum)

Where witness is a party to the action	Where witness is not a party to the action
1. Declaration (or affidavit) to have subpoena duces tecum issued is filed	1. Same
2. Subpoena duces tecum served	2. Same
3. Notice of intention to take deposition and for production of documents is served on all parties, with copy of declaration (or affidavit) attached (prior to 1/1/82 attach to subpoena duces tecum, CCP §1987.5)	3. Same
4. Deposition is taken	4. Same
5. Notice of filing of deposition is served	5. Same

INTERROGATORIES

Code Civ. Proc. §2030

Interrogatories are written questions which may only be served upon opposing parties to the action or proceeding. (Code Civ. Proc. §2030.) The party served with a set of written interrogatories must furnish such information as is available. Interrogatories may be served on parties following their depositions. They are prepared, either by attorneys or legal assistants, in the same general format as other legal documents.

In preparing interrogatories, the number one rule is keep them short and concise. The chances of compelling an answer to an uncomplicated question are better.

Some questions can hardly be objected to, such as: What was the plaintiff's wage loss? Did you consult a doctor? What was the amount of the medical expenses incurred by plaintiff or on his behalf?

After drafting the questions the legal assistant should read them over. Has the same question been repeated in the same or slightly different form? Watch for form questions that may have been duplicated. There is no merit in being repetitive. Nor should the question be asked at all, if the answer is not really needed — unless a commitment from the witness is desired. A voluminous set of questions may reflect negatively on the attorney, if deemed by the court to be unduly burdensome.

Interrogatories may be served any time after 10 days from date of service of summons or appearance of the other party. Leave of court may be granted to permit earlier filing. The interrogatories must be answered separately and fully in writing, under oath, by the person making them, and will be served on the party making the interrogatories, within 30 days after service thereof (unless court on motion and notice extends or shortens the time (court may enlarge time up to 15 days)).

Interrogatories and answers must also be served on all parties who have appeared, unless the court has waived this requirement, having found that enforcement would be "unduly expensive, oppressive or burdensome."

A copy of the interrogatories or responses must be provided, within 30 days, to any party who for any reason was not previously served and who makes a written request therefor at any time prior to final judgment. The person making the interrogatories may move the court for an order requiring further response. Such a motion must be made upon notice given within 30 days of service of answers or objections, unless the court on motion and notice has enlarged the time.

When a motion to compel interrogatories is necessary, the original interrogatories have to be attached to the motion. A duplicate original photocopy can be signed and used.

The party serving the interrogatories is required to retain the original interrogatories, with original proof of service attached, and the original answers. These documents need not be retained after final judgment in the action. (Code Civ. Proc. §2030.)

Filing

The party serving the interrogatories retains the original, with proof of service, and also the original responses.

Interrogatories and any responses are not *filed* with the court except upon order of the court made after motion and notice and for good cause shown. They *may*, however, be *lodged* with the court, but not filed, unless the court determines they have become relevant to an issue in a trial or other proceeding. Check local rules re interrogatories.

REQUESTS FOR ADMISSIONS
Code Civ. Proc. §2033

Under Code of Civil Procedure section 2033, after the summons has been served or a party appeared, any other party who has appeared in the action may make a written request of such other party for the admission by the latter of the genuineness of any relevant documents described and request for admission of the truth of any such relevant matters of fact. If request for admission is made by plaintiff within 10 days after service of summons, leave of court must be obtained as for interrogatories.

Copies of the documents, unless already furnished, shall be served with the request, and inspection of the originals may be requested.

Each of the matters for which request has been made is deemed admitted unless within 30 days a sworn statement (by the client; the attorney cannot sign) is served specifically denying or setting forth the reasons why he cannot admit or deny, or objections are served on the ground of privilege or irrelevancy or impropriety. For good cause and without notice the court may enlarge the time up to 15 days; for good cause, a shorter time may be allowed by court motion and notice to the party to whom the request is directed, or extended with or without notice but in no event later than 60 days prior to date of trial.

The request for admissions must contain the following words at the end: "If you fail to comply with the provisions of Section 2033 of the Code of Civil Procedure with respect to this request for admissions, each of the matters of which an admission is requested will be deemed admitted."

If the party serving the request for admissions serves a notice in writing by certified or registered mail, return receipt requested, notifying the party that the genuineness of such documents or the truth of such facts has been deemed admitted, the other party shall not have the right to apply for relief under Code of Civil Procedure section 473 (mistake, inadvertence, surprise, excusable neglect) unless a motion requesting relief is served and filed within 30 days after service of notice.

A denial must fairly meet the substance of the requested admission, and if in good faith only a part should be denied, he must specify what is true and deny the remainder.

If a request for admission is denied, and the other side is able to prove the requested admission as a fact, at the conclusion of the case the other side is entitled to attorney's fees and costs for proving that fact.

The request for admission is a good tool that is sometimes ignored. Either party can make requests; all the burden is on the answering party.

Requests for admission, like interrogatories and responses, are not *filed* with the court except upon order of the court made after motion and notice and for good cause shown. They too may be lodged with the court but will not be filed unless the court determines they have become relevant to an issue in a trial or other proceeding. Check local rules concerning requests for admissions.

Effective January 1, 1982, the party responding to the request for admissions serves the original responses made under oath upon the party who serves the request for admissions, who is required to retain the original request for admissions with the original proof of service thereof annexed and the original responses, for at least six months after the judgment becomes final. (Code Civ. Proc. §2033.)

II. PRETRIAL INVESTIGATION

By Craig Wesley Rimer, Paralegal Administrator
& Investigator, and Zella Mack

No discussion on preparation for trial would be complete without a section on investigation. Good, conscientious investigation forms the basis for the trial of a case. Whether the client wins or loses his case may well depend upon the thoroughness of the job of investigation.

The discovery process discussed in the first division of this chapter is a part of the investigative process. But other investigation may precede and lead into the discovery procedures, or take place at the same time.

A legal assistant may be called upon to do investigative work at one time or another. The extent of the investigation duties will depend upon how much time the legal assistant can devote to any one case. The investigative role may be of four different kinds:

(1)   The legal assistant as the initial interviewer, with or without the presence and assistance of the attorney, will have identified the legal issues in the case and the relevant facts to be confirmed or developed. From this a report will be written up for the person who is to do the investigation — if that person is not also the legal assistant — with general instructions to the investigator as to what is needed.

(2)   If time permits, the legal assistant may do the actual investigation. He/she may be called upon to handle investigation including locating and identifying defendants, locating records and police reports, locating and interviewing potential witnesses, and taking photographs, as well as many other activities. At the minimum, most legal assistants in civil litigation are called upon to locate a defendant for service, or a witness who seems to have disappeared. In representing a criminal defendant, too, much can be done by the legal assistant by way of investigation.

(3)   If an outside investigator is utilized, the legal assistant will analyze and evaluate the report and information gained, which may lead to further discovery steps, or in any event will establish the facts for the attorney to use at trial. The same will be true if the legal assistant does the investigation.

(4)   Locating assets. Another form of investigation the legal assistant often has to make is to locate assets upon which to levy execution. Winning a judgment does not necessarily end the case. The judgment debtor may think the court was wrong in its decision and may try to evade payment.

Under Code of Civil Procedure sections 714, *et seq.*, a judgment debtor may be required to appear before a judge for an examination concerning his assets. This procedure can be helpful but does not stop the debtor from trying to dispose of his property in some way, by transferring funds or changing title.

Therefore an asset investigation without disclosure to the judgment debtor may give a better chance of collecting. The usual steps for background investigation discussed above can be used. Other creditors or other persons with animosities toward the debtor may be willing to share information.

Effecting Service

The legal assistant may on occasion, or in some offices frequently, be called upon to serve process. Personal service is not always easy. The witness or defendant who expects to be served may attempt to evade service.

Personal service of a summons means actual delivery to the defendant in person. The strict requirement of manual delivery is relaxed when the defendant attempts to flee the approaching process server. "Attempted delivery to a recalcitrant defendant, *in his presence,* is permitted. Examples are collected in *Sternbeck v. Buck* (1957) 148 Cal.App.2d 829, at page 833, and include flinging the process at a retreating defendant while telling him what it is, or putting it under the windshield of his retreating automobile. These cases do not rewrite the requirement of personal service and permit some other service, but rather, analyze the facts of service and find they are tantamount to a personal delivery. . . ." (*In re Abrams* (1980) 108 Cal.App.3d 685, 694-695.)

The original summons need no longer be shown to the defendant.

Most individuals of good reputation in the community can be first approached by telephone and an appointment made for service. The legal assistant should explain that this is a courtesy call, to avoid service under circumstances which may prove embarrassing.

No provision for substituted service of a subpoena is made, as for the summons. Code of Civil Procedure section 1987 states that the "service of a subpoena is made by delivering a copy, or a ticket containing its substance, to the witness personally. . . ."

A subpoenaed witness who fails to appear is subject to a fine of $500 (Code Civ. Proc. §1992) or a judgment of contempt or a fine up to $500 or five days' imprisonment under Code of Civil Procedure section 1218. Since the witness is subject to punishment for criminal contempt, not lightly invoked, personal service of the subpoena must be made.

However, in the case of a witness who is concealed "in a building or a vessel" to prevent service, an order that the county sheriff serve the subpoena may be made, upon an "affidavit of the concealment, and materiality, of the witness," under Code of Civil Procedure section 1988. This extra effort and expense might be deemed justified, but in certain cases could be felt necessary. Under the same code section the sheriff is authorized to break into the building or vessel to effect service, after such order is made.

Experienced investigators usually resort to more subtle ruses to reach the person to be served. Incidentally, the legal assistant is well advised to leave immediately once the papers have been served. The person served might become angry and vent his feelings upon the only person present, the legal assistant.

Preparing for Service on a Corporation

If a complaint is being prepared naming a corporation as a defendant, determine the exact name of the corporation in order to properly name the corporation as a defendant. The "United Face Co." may prove to be not a corporation at all but a partnership, associates doing business under a common name, or an individual doing business under a fictitious name.

Determine whether a defendant to be served is a California corporation or a foreign corporation qualified to do business in California, in order to incorporate the appropriate allegation in the complaint.

At the same time inquire as to the name of any person designated for service by the corporation, and the names and addresses of the officers on file so that service of the summons and complaint can be made.

All such information may be obtained by writing or phoning the Secretary of State's office in Sacramento.

Locating the Defendant or Witness

The legal assistant may be called upon to serve a defendant or witness who cannot readily be located. An address may or may not be given to the legal assistant. The legal assistant may find that there is no such person at the address given and no one at the address who has any idea where he or she is. Some people not only change jobs but move around a lot from city to city, or even from state to state. Younger persons can be expected to have gone elsewhere to school, or might be making a trip to a foreign country.

But before assuming the person is gone, the general area where he was last known to reside should be combed. There are some basic steps which should be taken first.

(1)   TELEPHONE DIRECTORY: The first place to look is in the telephone book. Is the person listed? Is there anyone of the same or similar name? One of the persons listed just might be a relative. (This won't work if the last name is Smith, but often there are only four or five of the same last name.) If they have an unlisted number, the legal assistant is out of luck.

(2)   THE POST OFFICE: Contact the post office for a forwarding address. A person who is hiding often leaves a forwarding address to a post office box.

If the person had a post office box and a business, government regulations permit the post office to release information on the post office box application; the application may include a current home address which the post office will give out. A check of the application will also reveal whether the person was using the post office box of his employer to receive mail. Then at least you will have the address of his employer, hopefully his current employer.

(3) LAST KNOWN ADDRESS: If time permits, drive to the last known address. Find out who is living there and for how long. Perhaps they have some information about the individual they will give you. Of course they may know the individual very well and simply be protecting him. He may still be there.

(4) NEIGHBORS: People living in the vicinity may be able to provide information as to present whereabouts, or his place of employment. They may be able to tell you what kind of automobile the person drives, whether he had out-of-state license plates, and if so, which state.

(5) DEPARTMENT OF MOTOR VEHICLES: The Division of Registration can check the records for a list of all vehicles registered in a certain name. If the legal assistant has a license plate number, the Department can furnish the name and address of the registered owner and the legal owner. If the person proves not to be at the address shown, contact should be made with the legal owner, usually a lending institution. The lending institution may or may not furnish his address; if not, they may at least be willing to deliver a message to the person. If they do, he may come forth; of course, if he does not wish to cooperate, nothing will be heard from him.

This information cannot be obtained by phone from the Division of Registration. It is necessary to obtain a form from the Division of Registration and mail it to them (Post Office Box 11319, Sacramento 95852) or go to their office and sign the form. A packet of forms may be purchased from the Division. There is a charge for the information (currently $3). In the form the reason must be given for wanting the information and it is signed under penalty of perjury. The Division has guidelines for deciding whether to furnish this information. If the person had been involved in an accident or service on him is desired, the information would presumably be furnished. However, the Division is required by law to notify the person that they have released such information to you. Obviously, if the person wished to make service difficult, this would be a hindrance. But if he can't otherwise be located, there is little choice.

(b) *Division of Drivers' Licenses:* If the legal assistant can furnish the driver's license number and name, a letter can be written to the Division of Drivers' Licenses (Post Office Box 11231, Sacramento 95852); with payment of $1 (the current charge), the driving record of any California individual will be furnished. The record will extend up to seven years from date of conviction on more serious charges such as drunk driving, five years on reckless driving charges, five years for hit-and-run, and 37 months for lesser offenses. (This may be done in person at their Sacramento office.)

The person involved is not notified of the release of this information.

The legal assistant may find a bureau which will get this information for an additional charge, and will have to decide which is the less expensive to the office, based upon time demands.

(6)   JAIL: The legal assistant should not miss checking the local jail. The person sought just might be there.

Keep a record of the investigation, with dates, to show a sequence of events, and when and where all evidence was obtained. Make adequate file notes.

Any evidence obtained should be kept in a safe place, in the custody of the legal assistant or one individual, so doubts cannot be raised as to whether it is an authentic piece of evidence. A note of where it is to be stored should be made in the legal assistant's file at the time of taking the evidence. Such evidence might include letters, contracts, negatives, slides, or almost anything.

Any evidence uncovered in a field investigation should be photographed on the spot.

Taking a Statement

The legal assistant in civil litigation will have an occasion to take statements of clients, witnesses, or defendants.

The legal assistant may wish to first talk to the witness briefly to see if the witness can add anything of value to a client's case. If it appears the witness' statement would be adverse or hostile, perhaps no written or recorded statement should be taken, since that would be discoverable. But on the other hand the legal assistant *may* be able to turn the hostile witness around into a friendly witness, by being friendly and cooperative with the witness. An interview or investigation serves to eliminate the necessity for calling any unfavorable witnesses to testify.

Statements serve a number of purposes. First, the facts have to be obtained from the client to decide whether there is a case at all, and secondly, the statements of the parties and witnesses will form the basis for the conduct of the case.

In setting up the appointment, the legal assistant should try to meet the convenience of the witness, as to time and place. A witness who has been treated considerately will tend to be more cooperative when giving a statement.

There is no mystique to the good interview. The legal assistant who is genuinely concerned and exhibits a friendly and serious interest in the client's case should have no real problem. In an initial interview with a client the legal assistant should have at hand a checklist of all the facts necessary to prepare the complaint. Let the client give his version of the facts forming the basis for the cause of action before launching into your questions. By letting the client tell his story in his own way and interrupting as little as possible so that you get a record in his own words, you will miss very little of what the client considers important facts in the case. *Listen* to what he is saying. Few people really listen. Never put words in the witness' mouth.

The legal assistant should expect that the client or witness will digress and must adroitly yet firmly get the conversation back on track. The legal assistant must not seem in a hurry (no matter what the pressures) or the interviewee will not relax.

The witness should be interviewed as soon as possible. Witnesses tend to forget with a lapse of time, and the case may not reach the trial stage for a few years. In all cases the legal assistant should obtain the age, date of birth, Social Security number, address, phone numbers for home and work, employment information, spouse's name, and name and address of nearest relative. This information will be needed if the case does not go to trial for a number of years and you wish to locate the witness at that time.

Accurate notes should be made of the oral interview. As much information should be gathered as possible; at a later date the witness may not choose to be as cooperative. Get admissions of the witness if possible, and appropriate.

Statements may also be taken over the telephone with recording devices, by the use of tape recorders, or on videotape. The name of the person who is being taped should be recorded, and the taping should be done only with his permission. Statements may also be taken on videotape.

A written statement of a witness can be used for impeachment of the witness who tells a different story during the trial. Even the credibility of your own witness can be impeached, in the interests of truth. (Cal. Ev. Code §785.)

A typewritten statement is best. Do not erase as the attorney for the adverse party might claim tampering. Give the witness a chance to correct mistakes himself, and then initial the change. Then he can't say he didn't read it. If the statement is in the language and style of the witness, impeachment if necessary is made easier.

The witness should be asked to sign each page. If he refuses to sign, ask him to initial it. At the end of the statement it is advisable to include some language such as the following: "I, the undersigned, do hereby declare under penalty of perjury under the laws of the State

of California that I have read the foregoing statement consisting of
_____ pages and I do hereby certify that it is true and correct to the
best of my belief. I further declare that this statement was executed
on the _____ day of _____, 19 _____.''

Inquiry should be made of the witness as to whether he has been
contacted by any other investigator or insurance adjuster.

Extended Investigation

Other good sources of information when developing a dossier on
an individual, whether a juror or client or witness are:

(1)   CITY DIRECTORY. This is usually found in the city or state
libraries. The occupation or business of the person being investigated
may be indicated.

(2)   REGISTRAR OF VOTERS. The voter's registration affidavit
indicates the place of birth, Social Security number, home address,
spouse's name, and general description. The birthdate and Social Security number may make it possible to identify other vital statistics.

(3)   COUNTY RECORDER'S OFFICE. Any recorded documents
relating to the person being investigated will reflect in abstracts of
judgments, liens, deeds, trust deeds, quitclaim deeds, etc.

(4)   BANKRUPTCY COURT. If the person has ever filed for
bankruptcy, the petition and schedules will disclose information and
sources of information. All assets and creditors are listed.

(5)   COUNTY CLERK'S OFFICE. Criminal and civil complaints
may be checked, as well as any probate of estates proceedings.

(6)   LICENSING AGENCIES. If the party has ever been issued
a license such as a contractor's license information can be obtained
from the agency.

(7)   SECRETARY OF STATE. Information concerning corporations may be obtained from the Secretary of State's office.

In short, the paralegal-investigator must use ingenuity and re-
sourcefulness in conducting an investigation. Many sources other than
those mentioned above are available, if the legal assistant has the time
and the case justifies the expense. Other sources are telephone company
employees, newspaper carriers, unions, government officials, insurance companies.

1	taken by:	accident or incident date:
2	date:	
3	taken at:	time:
4		location:
5	vs	
6		
7	witness name:	
8	witness address:	
9	witness phone:	
10	witness employed:	city:
11	date of birth:	county:
12	social security no.	state:
13		
14		
15		
16		
17		
18		
19		
20		
21		
22		
23		
24		
25		
26		
27		
28	page number_____	_____ signature

```
 1   page number_____ statement of_____
 2   _____
 3   _____
 4   _____
 5   _____
 6   _____
 7   _____
 8   _____
 9   _____
10   _____
11   _____
12   _____
13   _____
14   _____
15   _____
16   _____
17   _____
18   _____
19   _____
20   _____
21   _____
22   _____
23   _____
24   _____
25   _____
26   _____
27   _____
28   date:_____          _____
                                signature
```

III. EVIDENCE

In order to properly assist the attorney in preparation for trial, or on appeal, or in other duties, the legal assistant should (1) be able to identify the legal issues involved in a case and (2) have a familiarity with the basic rules of evidence. A consultation with the attorney handling the case at the outset can save the time of both. The attorney can verify the legal assistant's view as to the issues and advise the legal assistant of possible theories or strategy he or she has in mind.

In drafting complaints or answers, summarizing depositions and motions and other documents, and other preparation for trial, such knowledge of the rules of evidence is important. Will the evidence, once obtained, be useable, i.e., admissible in court? The legal assistant needs to learn what evidence is admissible.

However, the legal assistant should remember that inadmissible evidence may also be valuable, in that it may lead to admissible evidence. Or, although it may appear to be inadmissible, the attorney may find a way to use it. Therefore the attorney should always be informed as to all the evidence obtained or obtainable.

What Is Evidence?

Evidence takes the form of (1) documents and writings, or (2) testimony of witnesses, or (3) physical objects.

Evidence is defined in section 140 of the California Evidence Code as "testimony, writings, material objects, or other things presented to the senses that are offered to prove the existence or nonexistence of a fact." "Evidence" includes anything offered in evidence, whether or not technically inadmissible (such as inadmissible hearsay evidence admitted because a proper objection was not made).

Relevant Evidence

The purpose of evidentiary rules is to provide a systematic way of admitting into court the facts which the court or jury as trier of fact must decide. By using this system the possibility of error is decreased and the interests of justice are served.

To be admissible evidence must be relevant and material, that is, it must have some important bearing on the case at hand. Relevant evidence must have some tendency in reason to prove or disprove a disputed fact that is of consequence to the action. Relevant evidence includes evidence of the ultimate facts in dispute and also evidence of other facts from which such ultimate facts may be presumed or inferred. In determining the admissibility of evidence a wide discretion is given to the trial court. Generally the ruling of the lower court will not be disturbed unless there is a clear showing of abuse.

Burden of Proof

Evidence Code section 500 states that a party has the "burden of proof" as to each fact the existence or nonexistence of which is essential to the claim for relief or defense that he is asserting. In other words, if one party contends that such-and-such is a fact, it is up to him to prove it, that is, convince the trier of fact that the facts are as he says they are. If a plaintiff alleges the defendant made false statements, he has the burden to prove they were false.

"Burden of proof" is defined in Evidence Code section 115 as the "obligation of a party to establish by evidence a requisite degree of belief concerning a fact in the mind of the trier of fact or the court."

The facts alleged in the complaint must be proven, as well as any other facts presented during the trial that would support a party's case if proven. (Cal. Ev. Code §500.) For example, suppose a petition is filed under Civil Code section 224 to declare a child free for adoption on the ground that the father had wilfully failed to support his child. Whether the natural father had been guilty of such failure was a question of fact for the trial court to determine.

"Usually, the burden of proof requires a party to convince the trier of fact that the existence of a particular fact is more probable than its nonexistence — a degree of proof usually described as proof by a preponderance of the evidence." (Cal. Ev. Code §500; Comment, Law Rev. Comm.)

The statutes specify who has the burden of proof in certain instances, e.g., in criminal cases, the state has the burden of proving a person is guilty of a crime (Cal. Ev. Code §520), and in tort cases the party claiming that another did not exercise a requisite degree of care has the burden of proving lack of due care. (Cal. Ev. Code §521.)

In meeting its burden of proof a party must apply the proper standard. In civil cases the standard is generally proof by a preponderance of the evidence. In some civil cases the standard may be higher, that is, proof by clear and convincing evidence. In criminal cases the proof standard is the highest proof beyond a reasonable doubt. The court instructs the jury as to the burden of proof and the proper standard to be applied to each issue. (Cal. Ev. Code §502.) Jury instructions are found in CALJIC (for civil cases) and BAJI (for criminal cases).

When a party has met his burden of proof the burden shifts to his opponent.

Along with the burden of proof there is the burden of "going forward" or producing evidence. Although these burdens may coincide at the outset the burden of producing evidence may shift if the party with the burden of proof produces extremely probative evidence or establishes facts giving rise to a presumption. Then the burden of going forward will shift to the other party. (See Cal. Ev. Code §550.)

Categories of Evidence

As mentioned above there are several categories of evidence ranging from witness testimony to physical evidence. The legal assistant should have a familiarity with these categories of evidence so that he or she knows when they are admissible and when they are excludable. The paralegal should also be aware of the techniques of authentication used to bring items of evidence before the court. Evidence must not only be relevant, it must be trustworthy as well.

WRITINGS

Writing is defined in Evidence Code section 250 as "handwriting, typewriting, printing, photostating, photographing, and every other means of recording upon any tangible thing any form of communication or representation." This very broad definition includes pictures and sound recordings as "writings".

Before a writing may be introduced into evidence a preliminary showing of its relevancy must be made. This is done by showing that the writing is authentic. One way of demonstrating authenticity is to show that the writing was made and signed by the author. A writing may be authenticated by its contents, by its age (ancient documents rule — a writing many years old that was not prepared with trial in mind tends to be trustworthy), by stipulation of the parties, by a witness to the writing or by the handwriting itself. (See Cal. Ev. Code §1400 *et seq.* for the various means of authentication.) "Authentication of a writing is required before it may be received into evidence." (Cal. Ev. Code §1401.)

The writing may be either an original or a copy. However, under the "best evidence" rule, the content must be proved by the original writing and not by testimony as to its content or a copy of the writing, unless certain exceptional conditions exist. (Cal. Ev. Code §1500, Comment, Law Rev. Comm.) (See Cal. Ev. Code §§1501-1511, for exceptions to the best evidence rule — as to copies, secondary evidence, etc.)

WITNESSES

Under California law everyone is presumed to be qualified to be a witness (Cal. Ev. Code §700) except on grounds for disqualification found in the statutes.

A witness is disqualified if he lacks requisite mental or physical capacity (Cal. Ev. Code §701), lacks personal knowledge of the matter

(Cal. Ev. Code §702), is the judge presiding at the trial in which he is called to testify and a party objects (Cal. Ev. Code §703), or is a juror in the trial of an action and a party objects (Cal. Ev. Code §704).

There are two types of witnesses, the lay witness, who testifies from personal knowledge and whose testimony is limited to the relevant facts and the expert witness, who has "special knowledge, skill, experience, training or education sufficient to qualify him as an expert." (Cal. Ev. Code §720.) An expert must be qualified as such to the satisfaction of the court before he is allowed to testify.

An expert is permitted to testify as to his opinion in the area of his expertise. (Cal. Ev. Code §801.) A lay witness' opinion is usually not admissible unless it is "rationally based" on his perceptions and "helpful to a clear understanding of his testimony." (Cal. Ev. Code §800.) For example, he may give his opinion as to the value of his property or his services; but he may not testify that in his opinion B committed a murder, because he saw A and B with guns near the scene of a murder a short time after the crime was committed and that B was agitated, running and cursing. In the latter case his testimony would be limited to the facts he perceived.

Expert Witnesses

Not later than the 10th day after a trial date is selected, or 70 days prior to the date set for trial, whichever is later, a party may file and serve a demand to exchange lists of expert witnesses. Thereafter such a demand may be served only upon a notice motion showing good cause.

The demand must contain substantially the following language:

"You are requested to serve and deposit with the clerk of court a list of expert witnesses in compliance with Section 2037 of the Code of Civil Procedure not later than the date of exchange thereby established. Except as otherwise provided in that article, your failure to do so will constitute a waiver of your right to call unlisted expert witnesses at the trial." (Code Civ. Proc. §2037.)

The words "date of exchange" as used here mean the lists of expert witnesses shall be exchanged 20 days after date of service of the demand *or* 50 days prior to the date set for trial, whichever is later. (Code Civ. Proc. §2037.1.)

Other provisions governing expert witnesses appear in section 2037.2 *et seq.*: filing and service (§2037.2); addresses and qualifications of witnesses, substance of testimony (§2037.3); notice to parties (§2037.4); objections and impeachment (§2037.5); calling parties not on list (§2037.6); fees (§2037.7); protective orders and compensation (§2037.8).

Court-appointed experts

In the discretion of the court, the fees of court-appointed experts may either be paid by the parties as apportioned by the court or be payable out of the county treasury. If paid by the county treasurer, the county is entitled to reimbursement, as specified. (Code Civ. Proc. §1031.5; Cal. Ev. Code §730, as amended; effective January 1, 1980, and until January 1, 1983; see ch. 746, Stats. 1979.)

PHYSICAL EVIDENCE

Tangible objects include clothes, photographs, tape recordings, maps, weapons, and may be introduced in evidence if relevant (Cal. Ev. Code §350) and not excluded in the court's discretion (Cal. Ev. Code §352). For example, a particularly gruesome photograph of a murder victim may have a possible inflammatory effect upon a jury and be excluded by the court.

Before the evidence may be admitted, a proper foundation must first be laid which shows the relevancy and authenticity of evidence. (See Cal. Ev. Code §§400-406 for foundational evidence.) The attorney asks that the proposed exhibit be marked for identification for reference while the foundation is being laid.

DIRECT AND CIRCUMSTANTIAL EVIDENCE

Evidence may be either (1) direct, or (2) circumstantial.

"Direct evidence" means "evidence that directly proves a fact, without an inference or presumption, and which in itself, if true, conclusively establishes that fact." (Cal. Ev. Code §410)

Testimony of what a witness has seen or heard is direct evidence. The testimony of one credible witness is sufficient for proof of any one fact, although other witnesses may testify and contradict the testimony.

Circumstantial evidence is evidence applied to the principal fact indirectly, or from which the principal fact may be inferred. On a second degree burglary charge, a verdict of guilty would require evidence that defendant entered a building with the specific intent to commit theft. If the defendant had in his possession goods stolen from the burglarized building, that would be circumstantial evidence of the fact that he had intended to remove them from the building. Proof of specific intent to commit a crime usually rests on circumstantial evidence, since direct evidence of specific intent is seldom available. (1 Witkin, Cal. Crimes (1963) p. 424.)

JUDICIAL NOTICE

A court may take "judicial notice" of certain facts without requiring the usual proof.

The evidence must be a matter of common knowledge or facts which can be readily proved or which are so "universally known that they cannot reasonably be the subject of dispute." (Cal. Ev. Code §451(f).)

A California court may take judicial notice of the records not only of California courts but also of federal courts or any sister state. (Cal. Ev. Code §452(d).) Other matters of which the courts may take judicial notice are also set forth in California Evidence Code section 452. Mandatory judicial notice is required of the matters specified in California Evidence Code section 451.

Relevant Yet Excluded Evidence

Certain types of evidence may be excluded even though they are relevant. The trial judge may exclude relevant evidence in his or her discretion when the judge finds it to be more prejudicial than probative. (Cal. Ev. Code §352.) Other types of relevant evidence are statutorily inadmissible for public policy reasons (i.e. privileges) or because of problems with reliability and trustworthiness (hearsay and opinion evidence).

PRIVILEGED COMMUNICATIONS

Certain communications, even though they may be relevant, are not admissible into evidence for public policy reasons. A privilege is granted because it is considered more important to keep information exchanged in certain relationships confidential than it is to require that information to be exposed in court. Examples of privileged relationships are husband-wife, attorney-client and physician-patient. (See Cal. Ev. Code §§900-1040 for statutory law governing privileges.)

Work done by a paralegal for an attorney may be included in the attorney-client privilege. In *Upjohn Co. v. United States* (1981), 101 S.Ct. 677, 66 L. Ed. 2d 584, the court found that the attorney-client privilege covered not only the giving of professional advice by an attorney, but also the furnishing of information to an attorney to enable him or her to give sound and informed advice. But the court cautioned that the privilege extends only to communications; it does not preclude disclosure of underlying facts by those who communicated with the attorney.

A recent case has held that communications between a lay advocate and his client, a welfare recipient, whome he was representing at certain administrative hearings, are not protected by a privilege of confidentiality. A lay advocate is not authorized to practice law and hence does not fit the definition of lawyer set forth in California Evidence Code Section 950. See *Welfare Rights Organization v. Crisan* _____ Cal.App.3d _____, 175 Cal.Rptr. 687 (1981). It appears then that a paralegal working for an attorney may share that attorney's privilege but a paralegal working alone has no standing to claim a privilege. Developments in this area bears close watching by paralegals.

OPINION EVIDENCE

As stated above a lay witness' opinion testimony must be "rationally based on the opinion of the witness" and "helpful to a clear understanding of his testimony." (Cal. Ev. Code §800.) This rule requires that witnesses express themselves at the lowest possible level of abstraction, leaving conclusions to be drawn by the trier of fact.

An expert witness may give opinion testimony on his area of expertise if the court is satisfied with the witness' qualifications. (See Cal. Ev. Code §§800-897 concerning permissible opinion testimony.)

HEARSAY RULE

"Hearsay evidence" is defined in California Evidence Code section 1200 as "evidence of a statement that was made other than by a witness while testifying at the hearing and that is offered to prove the truth of the matter stated." A "statement" might be an oral declaration, a writing, or assertive conduct in lieu of words. Nonassertive conduct is not hearsay and is admissible if relevant.

The main objection to hearsay evidence is that, even though the evidence may be relevant, the person said to have made the statements sought to be introduced in evidence cannot be brought to the courtroom for cross-examination at the trial. Nor can the demeanor of the person when he made the statement be observed. The declarant may be dead or unavailable.

The rule excluding hearsay evidence is designed to guard against unreliable or prejudicial evidence being presented to the trier of fact.

Certain exceptions to the hearsay rule are found in the statutes or decisions. However, the fact that hearsay evidence may come within an exception does not *per se* make it admissible. Other rules of law — as "privilege" or the "best evidence" rule (discussed *supra*) may make the evidence inadmissible.

Some hearsay evidence may be admitted when there appears to be a necessity for that type of evidence or some circumstantial probability of its trustworthiness and it falls within a valid exception to the hearsay rule. (*People v. Brust* (1957) 47 Cal.2d 776, 785.)

The exceptions to the hearsay rule include dying declarations made under certain conditions (§1202); spontaneous statements made under stress of excitement (§1240); some business records (§1271); birth, death or marriage records (§1281); family history (§§1310-1316); confessions and admissions (§§1220-1227); former testimony (§§1290-1292); prior inconsistent statements (§1235); prior consistent statements (§1236); statements in writing when fact occurred (§1237); statements of identification (§1238). The exceptions are quite numerous, and complex; see California Evidence Code Sections 1200-1341 for laws governing hearsay and the exceptions.

If a legal assistant has a particular question as to admissibility it is suggested he/she consult Haight and Cotchett, California Courtroom Evidence, Exceptions to Hearsay Rule, contained in Chapter 21, and read the applicable decisions cited therein. Additional reading on this topic might include California Evidence Benchbook, Chapter 1, by Justice Bernard Jefferson.

Administrative Hearings

Government Code section 11513(c) deals with hearsay evidence applicable to administrative agencies governed by the Administrative Procedure Act. The section reads in part: "Hearsay evidence may be used for the purpose of *supplementing or explaining other evidence but shall not be sufficient in itself to support a finding* unless it would be admissible over objection in civil actions." (Emphasis added.)

The Unemployment Insurance Appeals Board is governed by Unemployment Insurance Code section 1952, which provides in part: "[UIAB and its administrative law judges] are not bound by common law or statutory rules of evidence or by technical or formal rules of procedure but may conduct the hearing and appeals in such a manner as to ascertain the substantial rights of the parties."

Title 22, California Administrative Code, section 5038, also applies to the Unemployment Insurance Appeals Board (discussed *infra*). That section provides in part that the administrative law judges may admit any relevant and material evidence regardless of any rule which might make improper the admission of such evidence over objection in civil actions, such as hearsay.

Similar provisions are found in Vehicle Code sections 14108 and 14112 (Department of Motor Vehicles) and Welfare and Institutions Code Section 1099 (Department of Social Services), and in Labor Code section 5708 (WCAB).

It is something of an anomaly in that the courts which review the decisions of these agencies are bound in *their* evidentiary findings by the hearsay rule as discussed in the preceding material.

The general rule in California is that, unless there is an express statutory exception to the contrary, a finding cannot be based upon hearsay alone. (*Walker v. City of San Gabriel* (1942) 20 Cal.2d 879, 881.) Where such a statutory exception exists, a finding may be based solely on hearsay. (*Sada v. Industrial Accident Commission* (1938) 11 Cal.2d 263.)

CALIFORNIA PARALEGAL'S GUIDE

Chapter 8

THE TRIAL

Before and during the trial the paralegal may be called upon to assist the attorney in drafting various pleadings and motions. Before the trial a paralegal may for example, work on pleadings such as a motion to sever an issue or a party, or a motion to bifurcate the trial.

This chapter discusses pleadings and motions that paralegals may assist in drafting, plus other duties a paralegal must undertake in order that a case may be properly prepared. (For discovery work see Chapter 7, Preparation for Trial.)

SETTING A CASE FOR TRIAL

Once a case is at issue, i.e., an answer to the complaint has been filed and no motions are pending hearing, a trial date may be set. Either party may set the case for trial, but usually the plaintiff's attorney does so, as in most cases the plaintiff is more interested in bringing the case to trial, and there are statutory limits on the time within which he must bring the case to trial or the case will be subject to dismissal. Plaintiff's attorney, then, files a Memorandum That Civil Case Is At Issue. This is a printed form.

Before the form can be filled out, the attorney must determine:
1. Whether he wants a jury trial.
2. How many days he estimates the trial will take.
3. How long he estimates the pretrial will take.
   (This is a shorter period than the time required for trial; maybe ½ hour to 2 hours, while a trial is apt to take 2 or 3 days or possibly much longer.)

Opposing counsel has 10 days to file a memorandum if he is not in agreement with the estimates.

A pretrial need not be held in "short causes" (cases in which the time estimated for trial is one day or less). However, if the trial should extend beyond five hours the judge may complete the trial or he may declare a mistrial, in which event a new Memorandum that Civil Case

Is at Issue must be filed and the case set as for other causes. (Rule 207.1, Cal. Rules of Court.)

The printed form also contains the question whether the case is entitled to priority in setting for trial. Most cases are not entitled to priority. Actions for declaratory judgment are entitled to priority in setting. (Code Civ. Proc. §§1060, 1062.3.) A hearing on an order to show cause on a preliminary injunction after an ex parte restraining order has been issued is entitled to priority for hearing. (Code Civ. Proc. §527.) Parties over age 70 who have a substantial interest in the case as a whole are entitled to preference, upon motion. (See Code Civ. Proc. §36.)

Cases in which the only contested issue is custody of a minor child are given preference, except matters to which special precedence may be given by law. In cases involving more than one contested issue, where one of the issues is custody of a minor child, the court is required to order a separate trial as to the custody, and the trial as to custody is to be given the same preference.

In counties requiring a *certificate of readiness,* no case on the civil active list may be set for pretrial conference, trial setting conference, or trial, until a certificate of readiness is filed. (See Rule 221, Cal. Rules of Court.)

PRETRIAL CONFERENCE

(Pretrial conferences are held in superior courts only)

A *pretrial* is an informal conference of counsel and pretrial judge held six to eight weeks before the trial date, either in the courtroom or in the judge's chambers, for the purpose of determining the matters on which the parties agree and the genuine issues. Counsel must request the pretrial conference, or the court may order it (except in "short causes"). (See Rule 208, Cal. Rules of Court.) A printed form of Special Request for Pretrial Conference may be filed.

Jurisdictional questions, the proper court, proper parties, Does, corporate or partnership or other entity capacity, are only a few of the matters that may be settled at a pretrial. Matters may be agreed upon and stipulated to, or facts are established as an issue. In an accident case, the time and approximate place of the accident, ownership of cars and drivers, and whether the driver was an agent of the owner, or an employee or independent contractor might be resolved. In a wrongful death case such matters as occupation, ages, marital status, lawful heirs and the length of time the decedent lived after the accident can usually be resolved. The amount of hospital bills and the doctor's reports can usually be agreed to. The issues may be narrowed by establishing the applicable charges of negligence. Whether or not an executor or administrator or guardian or conservator is validly appointed and has the right to sue can be determined. The laws which govern the case may be established, as well as the effect of instructions.

In other words, the genuine issues should emerge from pretrial.

California Rule of Court 212 lists the matters which the judge may consider and act upon, without adjudicating controverted facts.

Thus the time spent by attorneys in preparing for presentation of evidence is materially cut down and the time required for trial is lessened. The pretrial conference judge may also inquire of the attorneys as to the possibility of a settlement of the case (Rule 213, Cal. Rules of Court).

Cases are set for pretrial at least once a month. The clerk is required to give not less than 60 days' notice by mail of the time and place of the pretrial conference in each case to all parties. (Time may be shortened by stipulation or court order upon noticed motion.) (Rule 209(b), Cal. Rules of Court.)

The attorneys are required to prepare and submit to the pretrial conference judge, at or before the conference, a joint written statement of the matters agreed upon and a joint or separate written statement of the factual and legal contentions to be made as to the issues remaining in dispute. (Rule 210(c), Cal. Rules of Court.)

At the pretrial conference, or within 5 days afterward, the judge makes a *pretrial order,* which is a statement of the nature of the case, the matters agreed upon, etc., and the clerk serves this pretrial order upon the attorneys.

The attorneys have 5 days within which to serve and file with the clerk a request for any correction or modification of this order. (Rule 215, Cal. Rules of Court.) This time limitation should be kept in mind, in the event any corrections or modifications are desired before the pretrial order is filed.

If a request for correction or modification is denied, the clerk gives notice thereof and of the date the order denying was filed; if a request is granted, the clerk mails an endorsed-filed copy of the corrected or modified order.

Once filed, the pretrial order becomes a part of the record in the case and, where inconsistent with the pleadings, controls the subsequent course of the case. The clerk gives notice of its filing by mail to all parties in the case.

The case must be set for trial at a time and place not earlier than 30 days after the filing of the pretrial order (court may shorten time) but within 12 weeks after the pretrial conference. (Rule 219, Cal. Rules of Court.)

Ordinarily the date and place of the trial is fixed at the pretrial and then no further notice of trial is required. Otherwise, the clerk of the superior court is required to give 30 days' notice of trial to all parties. (Rule 219(b), Cal. Rules of Court.) When the pretrial order arrives it should be checked to note whether the date of trial has been fixed, and if so, the date should be calendared.

In a case where the adverse party fails to appear, and the issue to be tried is an issue of fact, Code of Civil Procedure section 594 requires the clerk of the court to give notice by mail 20 days prior to the trial date. If the clerk does not serve notice, any party may serve notice by mail not less than 15 days prior to the date set for trial. Proof of service may be made either by certificate or affidavit or other competent evidence. Thereafter the court may proceed to dismissal, verdict, or judgment, as the case may require. A notice might read as follows:

Notice of Time and Place of Trial

TO DEFENDANT_____ AND

TO_____, HIS ATTORNEY:

PLEASE TAKE NOTICE that the above-entitled case has been set

for trial (by jury) at ____m., on _____, 19____, in

Department No. ____of the above-entitled court, at the Courthouse,

_____Street, _____, Califor-

nia.

Dated:_____, 19____.

_____
                    Attorney for Plaintiff

TRIAL SETTING CONFERENCE

If no pretrial conference is held, a *trial setting conference* is held, at about the same time as pretrial would have been held. In a court where there are more than 10 judges the court clerk gives 60 days' notice of the trial setting conference (unless court shortens time or parties agree to a shorter time). (Rule 220(a), Cal. Rules of Court.) In a court where there are 10 or less judges, 90 days' notice must be given by the clerk. (Rule 220.4.) The trial date is set at the trial setting conference, on a date not later than 12 weeks of the date of the conference. (Rule 220.1, Cal. Rules of Court.) The parties or their counsel must attend and advise the court if the case is ready to be assigned a definite trial date. The parties or counsel must also inform the court as to discovery completed, what further discovery may be required, and when such discovery can be completed. (Rule 220.2, Cal. Rules of Court.)

SETTLEMENT CONFERENCE

As a part of its pretrial facilities the superior court establishes and maintains a *settlement calendar*. (Rule 207.5, Cal. Rules of Court.) When a civil case has been on the civil active list for 30 days, the clerk sends all parties an invitation to attend a *settlement conference*. The case is placed on the *settlement calendar* if one or more of the parties, not later than 20 days prior to the pretrial conference date (or if no pretrial is required, not later than 20 days prior to the trial date) advises the court that he accepts the invitation. The clerk notifies all parties of the acceptance. Settlement conferences are held informally before a judge. In San Francisco, see Superior Court Rule 2.6. In Los Angeles, see Rules 10, *et seq.*, Civil Trials Manual.

STIPULATIONS

In order to speed up the evidence gathering process the parties may stipulate as to certain facts not in dispute. Stipulations are agreements entered into by the parties, usually through their respective counsel. Counsel may stipulate as to agreed facts, evidence, to file an amended complaint, to extend the time to answer, and to many other matters incidental to the case.

The general form of all stipulations is the same. A stipulation to extend time to plead follows:

Stipulation Extending Time

```
 1
 2
 3
 4
 5
 6
 7
 8                SUPERIOR COURT OF THE STATE OF CALIFORNIA
 9                     FOR THE COUNTY OF SACRAMENTO
10
11   JOHN SMITH,                    )
                                    )
12              Plaintiff,          )
                                    )
13        v.                        )        NO. 126704
                                    )
14   JAMES BROWN; et al.,           )   STIPULATION EXTENDING TIME
                                    )
15             Defendants.          )
     _____)
16
17
18          IT IS HEREBY STIPULATED by and between the respective
19   parties hereto that the defendant James Brown may have to and
20   including the 5th day of June, 1977, within which to answer,
21   demur or otherwise plead.
22          This stipulation need not be filed.
23          Dated:  May 25, 1977.
24
25          _____
                    Attorney for Plaintiff
26
27
28
```

SUBSTITUTION OF ATTORNEYS
(Code Civ. Proc. §§284-286.)

A change of attorneys of record in an action may be necessary or desirable for a number of reasons. New attorneys may be employed in place of the former attorney, or another attorney may be associated as counsel of record. A change of attorneys may be made at any time if client and attorney agree, or upon the order of the court upon application of either client or attorney after notice from one to the other. If the attorney has been employed on a contingency fee basis, the court determines the amount of fee he should be paid.

A Substitution of Attorneys and Notice of Substitution of Attorneys must be served on opposing counsel and the originals thereof filed; until such service is made opposing counsel must recognize only the original attorney of record. Either service by mail is made and proof of service attached to the original documents, or an acknowledgment of receipt of copies is made on the originals before filing.

An additional attorney may be associated as counsel of record in a case, perhaps because he is a specialist in a particular field, or because he lives in the city where the trial will be held. The same form of substitution is used except that the names of the two attorneys are substituted in the place of one.

When an attorney dies or otherwise ceases to act as such for his client, the adverse party must give written notice to the party to appoint another attorney or to appear in person. (Code Civ. Proc. §286.)

See Code of Civil Procedure section 285.1 as to withdrawal of an attorney in domestic relations proceedings.

If a printed form is not available, a Substitution of Attorneys is typed on the same paper as any other legal pleading, with the title of the case and number, and might read as follows:

Substitution of Attorneys

(Plaintiff or Defendant) hereby substitutes (name of new attorney) as his attorney of record in place of (name of former attorney).

Dated:_____.

_____
(Signature of plaintiff or defendant)

(I) (We) consent to the above substitution.

Dated:_____

_____
(Signature of former attorney)

Above substitution accepted.

Dated:_____

_____
(Signature of new attorney)

SUBPOENA
(Code Civ. Proc. §1986, *et seq.*)

A subpoena is an order of the court directing a witness to appear in court. The county clerk or deputy clerk issues the original subpoena.

The witness is not always required to testify on the date set in the subpoena. Therefore the following language must appear in the subpoena: "Contact the attorney requesting this subpoena, listed above, before the date on which you are required to be in court; if you have any question about the time or date for you to appear, or if you want to be certain that your presence in court is required."

An attorney of record in an action or proceeding is authorized to sign and issue a subpoena to require attendance of a witness in court or to compel a person to appear for the taking of a deposition relative to a pending action or proceeding. The subpoena need not be sealed. (Code Civ. Proc. §1985; see Code Civ. Proc. §1986.)

A copy of the subpoena is personally served, i.e., delivered to the witness.

A return of service is made on the original subpoena, if the form bears one, or attached to the original. The original subpoena may be filed, or retained in the office file, unless the witness fails to appear.

Parties, beneficiaries and officers of parties may be compelled to attend in court upon written notice served on the party's attorney at least 10 days before the time designated to appear, as an alternative to being subpoenaed.

If subpoenaing a public employee, see Government Code sections 68097-68097.10.

A witness may demand a fee and mileage one way to court. He is entitled to a fee of $12 for each day's attendance and mileage one way at 20¢ per mile. (Gov. Code §68093.)

A witness may not be compelled to attend if the distance from his place of residence to the place of trial is not less than 500 miles. (Code Civ. Proc. §1989.) Commencing January 1, 1982, this limitation will not apply; the witness need only be a resident of California at the time of service.

An expert witness whose deposition is being taken (except for worker's compensation case) is entitled to an enhanced fee only if the deposition is desired solely for the purpose of obtaining any expert opinion which he holds upon the basis of his or her special knowledge, skill, experience, training or education. (Code Civ. Proc. §2037.7.)

Subpoena Duces Tecum
(Code Civ. Proc. §1987.5.)

A *subpoena duces tecum* is an order of the court directing a witness to appear in court and bring with him certain papers, files and records described in detail in the subpoena duces tecum. Some counties have a printed form.

A *declaration* (or *affidavit*) is required for the issuance of the subpoena duces tecum. The declaration must likewise describe the documents and state (1) that they are material to the issues involved and (2) that the witness has the documents in his possession or under his control.

A witness may not be subpoenaed if he resides more than 500 miles from place of trial. (Code Civ. Proc. §1989.) Commencing January 1, 1982, the witness need only be a resident of California at the time of service.

If the witness demands a witness fee, payment is made to him for each day's attendance ($12) and for travel to and from the place designated (20 cents per mile) one way. (Gov. Code §§68093-68097.)

Witnesses in either civil or criminal actions, or administrative proceedings, must be given written notice in the subpoena that they may be entitled to receive fees and mileage. (Code Civ. Proc. §2065; Pen. Code §1329.) New forms of subpoenas have been issued.

The party requesting a subpoena of business records must pay the custodian of the records, upon demand, all reasonable costs required to deliver the records before delivery.

"Reasonable costs" are defined as "actual copying costs plus any additional reasonable clerical costs incurred in locating and making the records available." Such clerical costs are based on a computation of the time spent multiplied by the employee's hourly wage. (Code Civ. Proc. §1987.4.)

Upon the filing of the original declaration, the subpoena duces tecum is issued. A copy of the subpoena duces tecum and a copy of the declaration are served on the witness personally. Anyone can make the service. A return of service is then attached to the original subpoena duces tecum showing that the subpoena and declaration were served; a copy of the declaration is attached.

The original subpoena duces tecum should be filed with the court not later than 5 days before the time designated for the production of documents, unless otherwise ordered.

See Code of Civil Procedure sections 1987.1 and 1987.2 providing for motions to quash or modify subpoenas duces tecum that make unreasonable or oppressive demands.

Production of Personal Records of Consumers

When seeking the records of a "consumer" (as defined in the act), at least 15 days prior to date of production, a copy of the subpoena duces tecum, the affidavit (or declaration) and a notice to the consumer, must be delivered to the consumer, at the consumer's last known address, or, if the consumer is a party, to his attorney, or by certified mail, return receipt requested, to his last known address, in accordance with Chapter 5 (commencing with Code Civ. Proc. §1010) of Title 14.

"Personal records" means the original or any copy of books, documents or other things pertaining to a consumer and which are maintained by any "witness" which is a physician, hospital, state or national bank, state or federally chartered savings and loan association, state or federal credit union, trust company, insurance company, attorney, or accountant." (Code Civ. Proc. §1985.3.)

"Consumer" means any individual, partnership of 5 or fewer persons, association, or trust which has transacted business with or has used the services of such witness or for whom the witness had acted as agent or fiduciary.

A certificate signed by the subpoenaing party or his attorney and attesting to compliance with the aforesaid service requirements, must also be served upon the witness at the same time.

A notice must also accompany the subpoena duces tecum and affidavit complying with Code of Civil Procedure section 1985.3, subdivision (c).

The notice required to be served shall be in a typeface designed to call attention to it and indicating that

(1) records about the consumer are being sought from the witness

(2) if the consumer objects to furnishing the records, he must file papers with the court within 10 days from the receipt of the subpoena, and

(3) if subpoenaing party will not agree in writing to cancel or limit the subpoena, an attorney should be consulted about the consumer's interest in protecting the right of privacy.

A consumer may, prior to the date for production, bring a motion under Code of Civil Procedure section 1987.1 to quash or modify the subpoena duces tecum.

MOTIONS

A motion is an application to the court for an order of the court. A motion may be made at any time during the pendency of the action or proceeding, when the relief sought would be appropriate. Any party may make a motion. A few of the more common motions are: *motion to strike; motion for change of venue; motion to amend complaint; motion to dismiss; motion for judgment on the pleadings; motion for summary judgment; motion for new trial;* ad infinitum. These motions are discussed separately herein. The *general* requirements for *all* motions are:

1. Every motion must contain:
a. The *grounds* upon which it is made
b. The *date and hour* the motion will be heard, and
c. The *papers* upon which the motion will be based.

2. *Points and authorities* must accompany a motion (except a motion for new trial — see motion for new trial discussed below). (Rule 203, California Rules of Court.) Within 10 days after filing a notice of intention to move for a new trial, points and authorities must be filed. Within 10 days the adverse party may serve and file points and authorities in reply. (Rule 203(b), Cal. Rules of Court.)

A most helpful set of books in preparing points and authorities is California Points and Authorities, Law and Motion Practice, published by Matthew Bender and Company. "The design of 'Points and Authorities' is to provide for the attorney the applicable decisions and citations required for motions and procedures at the trial level, and, in so doing, to supply the basic material for the preparation of appellate briefs. To make for easier use, the editors have presented the points and authorities in the form of special motions and procedures. Commentaries lead the attorney to the broader legal area of the relevant subject matter. The editors have listed the prime authorities after the statement of the point." (Vol. 1.)

3. *Service:* A motion must be served on opposing counsel within 10 days (15 days after 1/1/82) before the hearing on the motion, unless the court prescribes a shorter time; if served by mail, the time is extended to 15 days if mailed to an address within California, to 20 days if mailed to an address outside California but within the United States, or 30 days if mailed outside the United States. (Code Civ. Proc. §1005.) The provisions of subdivision (a) of Code of Civil Procedure section 1013 extending the time for exercising a right or doing an act when service is made by mail, do not apply to notices of motion governed by section 1005.

Service of motions on attorneys is made as provided in Code of Civil Procedure section 1011.

Proof of service by mail by affidavit or certificate must set forth the exact title of the document served and filed. The proof of service need no longer be attached to an original or true copy of the document served and filed.

Motion for Change of Venue
(Code Civ. Proc. §§396-397.)

The grounds for change of venue (i.e., transfer of case to another court) are:

1. Court is not the proper court
2. There is reason to believe an impartial trial cannot be had
3. Convenience of witness and ends of justice would be promoted by change
4. No judge of court qualified to act
5. When proceeding for dissolution filed in county in which petitioner resident for 3 months and respondent resident of another county in state, and ends of justice would be promoted by transfer to county of respondent's residence

A motion for change of venue on ground 1, that the action is brought in the wrong court, must be made at the time the answer or demurrer is filed, and must be accompanied by:

1. An affidavit or declaration of merits
2. Notice of motion. Also, the plaintiff must pay transfer costs. If the motion is made on grounds 2, 3, 4 or 5 set forth above, the party requesting the change must pay transfer costs at the time the notice of motion is filed.

Motion for Judgment on the Pleadings

Motion for judgment on the pleadings are governed by case law; no statutory authority exists. This motion is a legal test of the pleadings and is useful where there is a defect of the pleadings which cannot be corrected by amendment.

Either plaintiff or defendant may file the motion, although usually the plaintiff is the party filing. The court simply determines as a matter of law either (1) upon motion of plaintiff, that the complaint states a cause of action which justifies the relief prayed for and that the answer raises no defense, or (2) upon motion of defendant, that the complaint does not state a cause of action.

A motion for judgment on the pleadings may be made at almost any time in the proceedings prior to the entry of judgment, except that the plaintiff, of course, could not make such a motion until the defendant had filed his answer. The best test for determining whether or not it is too late to make the motion, is whether or not it is too late to amend the pleadings that are attacked.

In a motion for judgment on the pleadings, *an affidavit or declaration is not filed,* as the court considers only the pleadings.

Motion for Summary Judgment
(Code Civ. Proc. §437c;
California Rules of Court, Rule 203(a).)

A motion for summary judgment is filed when the moving party — either plaintiff or defendant — contends that the complaint or answer, as the case may be, is without merit as a matter of law. If the judge decides that issues of fact exist, the motion will be denied.

The motion may be made at any time after 60 days have elapsed since the general appearance in the action of each party against whom the motion is directed or at such earlier time as the court, with or without notice and upon good cause shown, may direct.

This motion is used only when it is necessary to rely on facts outside the present record to show the invalidity of the claim or defense

— otherwise a demurrer or motion for judgment on the pleadings is used.

1. The notice of the time and place of the hearing on the motion, and supporting points and authorities, must be served at least 10 days before the hearing on such motion.

2. The motion must be supported — or opposed — by affidavits, declarations, admissions, answers to interrogatories, depositions and matters of which judicial notice shall or may be taken.

Evidentiary objections, not raised in writing or orally at the hearing, shall be deemed waived.

The court is required, in making its determination, to consider all of the evidence set forth in the supporting papers except that to which objections have been made and sustained by the court.

The court is required to grant the summary judgment if it finds no triable issue as to any material fact and that the moving party is entitled to judgment as a matter of law. (Code Civ. Proc. §437c.)

3. The motion shall be heard no later than 45 days before the date of trial, unless the court for good cause orders otherwise.

A summary judgment is an appealable order.

When summary judgment has been granted or a nonsuit dismissing the moving party granted, a defendant or cross-defendant may make a motion for defense costs, prior to the discharge of jury *or* entry of judgment.

"Defense costs" include reasonable attorney's fees, expert witness fees, cost of services of experts, advisers and consultants in defense of the proceeding, where reasonably and necessarily incurred. The court may direct a separate trial on the issue of costs. (See Code Civ. Proc. §1038.)

Motion to Dismiss
(Code Civ. Proc. §§581-583.)

The court may dismiss an action for various reasons. (See Code Civ. Proc. §§581-583.) For example, the court may dismiss without prejudice when no party appears for trial following 30 days' notice of time and place of trial. (Code Civ. Proc. §581, subd. 6.)

Also, under Code of Civil Procedure section 583 a court may in its discretion dismiss an action if it is not brought *to trial within 2 years* after filing (subd. (a)) and shall (i.e., mandatory) dismiss action, upon motion of the defendant or by the court on its own motion after notice to plaintiff, if the action is not brought to *trial within 5 years,* unless the parties have stipulated in writing that the time may be extended (subd. (b)). (See Cal. Rules of Court, Rule 203.5.)

The legal assistant should guard against a dismissal of the action under this provision. For one reason and another a suit may be prolonged, and if the necesary steps to protect the client's case are not taken, the case may be dismissed.

The legal assistant should likewise become familiar with the provisions of subdivisions (c), (d) and (e) of section 583 relating to cases where a new trial has been granted, remanded for new trial after appeal, or a mistrial declared.

Motion to Strike

(Code Civ. Proc. §435; California Rules of Court, Rule 503(c).)

A motion to strike is a motion to delete the whole or part of the pleading (usually the complaint) and is used to reach pleading defects (such as defamatory statements) not subject to a demurrer.

Unless the motion is to strike an entire paragraph, cause of action, count or defense, it shall quote in full the portion or portions sought to be stricken (Rule 503(c), Cal. Rules of Court).

A motion to strike must be filed within the time required to plead and prevents a default being taken (see Code Civ. Proc. §§585, 586), but does not extend the time to demur. (Code Civ. Proc. §435.) If a demurrer is interposed, concurrently therewith, the motion shall be noticed and heard at the same time as the demurrer. (Rule 503(c), Cal. Rules of Court.)

A motion to strike must specify a hearing date not more than 15 days from the filing of said motion, plus any additional time required to be given. (Code Civ. Proc. §435.)

The motion to strike should be supported by an affidavit or affidavits of the persons having knowledge of the facts.

If the motion to strike is granted, the entire complaint could be dismissed, without the necessity of filing an answer.

Before making a motion to strike, the attorney should consider whether he might not thereby be inducing his opponent to get the information in some other way.

When an attorney makes a motion to strike, he should be careful to state the exact words he wishes to strike and give the legal grounds. Later, should an appeal be taken and an appellate brief be prepared, the legal assistant must examine the record and definitely ascertain the records which were objected to or stricken.

A motion to strike must specify a hearing date not more than 15 days from the filing of said motion, plus any additional time required to be given. (Code Civ. Proc. §435.)

The motion to strike should be supported by an affidavit or affidavits of the persons having knowledge of the facts.

If the motion to strike is granted, the entire complaint could be dismissed, without the necessity of filing an answer.

Motion for Nonsuit

Jury Trial: Under Code of Civil Procedure section 581c, after plaintiff has completed his opening statement at the trial, or after he has presented his evidence in a jury trial, the defendant may orally make a motion for nonsuit. In doing so, defendant does not waive his right to offer evidence if the motion is not granted.

"Under the law applicable to nonsuit cases of this type, in a case tried before a jury a motion for nonsuit may be granted only when, viewing the evidence in the light most favorable to the plaintiff, the result is that there is no evidence in the record of sufficient substantiality to uphold a verdict for plaintiff, and in making this determination the trial court must disregard the conflicting evidence and must give to plaintiff's evidence all the probative force to which it is legally entitled. [Citations.]" (*Ferreyra v. E. & J. Gallo Winery* (1964) 231 Cal.App.2d 426, 429-430.)

If the defendant succeeds in having his motion granted as to some issues but not all, the action will proceed on those other issues and no final judgment may be entered as to any of the issues until the action is terminated, at which time judgment is awarded as determined by the motion.

A judgment for nonsuit operates as an adjudication upon the merits, the same as if the case had actually been tried.

Motion for Judgment — Nonjury Trials

Under Code of Civil Procedure section 631.8, after a party has presented all of his evidence in a trial by the court, the other party — without waiving his right to offer his evidence if his motion is not granted, may move for a judgment. Such a motion may also be made on a cross-complaint. If the court renders a judgment for the moving party, the necessity of defense evidence is eliminated. The court may decline to render judgment until the close of all the evidence.

Findings must be made as provided in Code of Civil Procedure sections 632 and 634. The judgment operates as an adjudication on the merits. (*Garber v. Los Angeles* (1964) 226 Cal.App.2d 349.)

The party against whom the motion is made is given the opportunity to present additional evidence which the presenting party deems to be adverse to him, and to rehabilitate the testimony of a witness whose credibility has been attacked.

If the court finds that the evidence presented supports the granting of the motion as to some but not all the issues involved in the action, the court grants the motion as to those issues, and proceeds on the remaining issues. No final judgment may be entered prior to the termination of the action, but the final judgment shall — in addition to any matters determined in the trial — award judgment as determined on the motion.

Section 631.8 was probably intended as a substitute for nonsuits in nonjury trials; however, a judgment rendered on such a motion does not constitute a judgment of nonsuit. (*Stockton v. Ortiz* (1973) 36 Cal.App.3d 472; see also, *Pack Estate* (1965) 233 Cal.App.2d 74.)

Motion to Dismiss for Failure to Bring New Trial

When a motion for a new trial has been made and granted and no appeal has been taken, the action shall be dismissed upon motion of defendant after notice to plaintiff or by the court on its own motion unless brought to trial within 3 years after entry of an order granting a new trial unless the parties have stipulated to extend the time. (Code Civ. Proc. §583(c).)

If a judgment is reversed on appeal and cause remanded for a new trial (or when an appeal has been taken from an order granting a new trial and the order is affirmed on appeal), the court must dismiss upon motion of defendant after notice to plaintiff if not brought to trial within 3 years from the date the remittitur is filed by the clerk of the trial court. (Code Civ. Proc. §583(c).)

However, nothing in subdivision (c) of section 583 requires the dismissal of an action prior to the 5-year period prescribed by subdivision (b).

An action may likewise be dismissed upon motion of defendant after notice to plaintiff or by the court on its own motion when a case is not brought to trial within 3 years after an entry of an order declaring a mistrial or a jury's inability to reach a decision, in the absence of a stipulation extending time. (Subd. (d).)

The time during which the defendant was not amenable to process and the time during which the jurisdiction of the court was suspended is not to be included in computing time under section 583. (Subd. (e).)

The format for all motions is basically the same. On the pages following is a Motion to Dismiss for failure to bring to trial within five years, and the accompanying Declaration of the attorney. The Points and Authorities have not been included. They could have been included at the end of the motion after the attorney's signature, or they could be set out as a separate document, which is assumed here. If there are only a few citations they are generally included on the motion; extensive citations and quotations are more appropriately presented in a separate document.

See *United Shippers, Inc. v. Superior Court* (1980) 104 Cal.App.3d 359, 362-363.

```
1  ROGER RANDALL
   Attorney at Law
2  1924 - 13th St.
   Sacramento, CA 95814
3  Telephone:  (916) 232-2722

4  Attorney for Defendant

5

6

7

8            SUPERIOR COURT OF CALIFORNIA

9               COUNTY OF SACRAMENTO

10

11 RUTH ANN WHITE,        )         NO. 263263
                          )
12         Plaintiff,     )
                          )
13    v.                  )      MOTION TO DISMISS
                          )
14 JEFFREY JONES,         )   (Code Civ. Proc., § 583(b))
                          )
15         Defendant.     )
   _____)

16

17 TO RUTH ANN WHITE, AND TO LESTER LEDBETTER, ESQ., HER ATTORNEY:

18         NOTICE IS HEREBY GIVEN that Defendant Jeffrey Jones

19 will move the above-entitled court for an order dismissing the

20 above-entitled case for lack of prosecution pursuant to the

21 provisions of the California Code of Civil Procedure section

22 583(b).

23         Said motion will be made on _____, 1981,

24 at _____ _.m., or as soon thereafter as counsel can be heard,

25 in Department ____ of said court located at 720 - 9th Street,

26 Sacramento, Calfiornia.

27         Said motion will be based on all the papers and files

28 in the above-entitled case and on the Declaration of Roger
```

1   Randall, a copy of which is served herewith, and on the further

2   ground that plaintiffs have failed to prosecute said action and

3   bring the same to trial within five (5) years after it was filed.

4   No stipulation has been filed in this action extending

5   time.

6   Dated:_____, 1981.

7

8   _____

9   Attorney for Defendant

10

11

12

13

14

15

16

17

18

19

20

21

22

23

24

25

26

27

28

1   ROGER RANDALL
    Attorney at Law
2   1924 - 13th St.
    Sacramento, CA 95814
3   Telephone: (916) 232-2722

4   Attorney for Defendant

5

6

7

8   SUPERIOR COURT OF CALIFORNIA

9   COUNTY OF SACRAMENTO

10

11 RUTH ANN WHITE,   )   NO. 263263
)
12   Plaintiff,   )
)
13   v.   )   DECLARATION OF ROGER
)   RANDALL IN SUPPORT OF
14 JEFFREY JONES,   )   MOTION TO DISMISS
)
15   Defendant.   )
    _____)

16

17   I, ROGER RANDALL, state:

18   1. I am the attorney for the defendant, Jeffrey Jones,

19 in the above-entitled action.

20   2. This declaration is in support of defendant's

21 motion for an order dismissing the above-entitled action.

22   3. This action was filed by plaintiff on January 5,

23 1976.

24   4. This action has not been brought to trial for more

25 than five years and the defendant has not been absent from or

26 concealed within the State of California since the above-entitled

27 action was filed, and neither the defendant nor his attorney has

28 stipulated in writing or otherwise that the time for bringing the

                                -1-

1   said action to trial may be extended.

2   Executed _____, 1981, at Sacramento,

3   California.

4   I declare under penalty of perjury that the foregoing

5   is true and correct.

6

7   _____

8   Attorney for Defendant

9

10

11

12

13

14

15

16

17

18

19

20

21

22

23

24

25

26

27

28

-2-

JURY INSTRUCTIONS

Who may request: A jury trial may be demanded by either the plaintiff or the defendant, in either a civil or a criminal trial.

Fees: The party requesting the jury must deposit one day's jury fees *14 days in advance of trial.*

Jury instructions are prepared by counsel for both plaintiff and defendant. If the judge approves the jury instruction, it is read to the jury at the conclusion of the trial, that is, after the hearing of the evidence. He may modify the jury instruction. "Given," "Modified" and "Refused" are typed at the bottom of the instruction and checked. The instructions bear the heading either "Plaintiff's Instruction No. __" or "Defendant's Instruction No. __." The instructions should not be numbered until the time of trial, since only the instructions allowed are numbered.

Jury instructions should start on line 1 of the page. A jury instruction follows:

Jury Instruction

```
 1                           PLAINTIFF'S INSTRUCTION NO._____

 2

 3              In resolving any conflict that may exist in the

 4        testimony of expert witnesses, you should weigh the opinion of

 5        one expert against that of another.  In doing this, you should

 6        consider the relative qualifications and credibility of the

 7        expert witnesses, as well as the reasons for each opinion and

 8        the facts and other matters upon which it was based.

 9

10                           _____

11                                          Judge

12

13

14

15        Exact copy of Form 21-B, B.A.J.I.

16

17

18

19

20

21

22

23

24

25

26        GIVEN

27        GIVEN AS MODIFIED

28        REFUSED
```

"B.A.J.I. No. ___" should be noted on the form when the instruction is copied from California Jury Instructions (Book of Approved Jury Instructions). If the instruction is modified by the judge to apply to the case "B.A.J.I. No. ___as modified" should be typed on the instruction.

Sometimes cases are cited on the instruction as the basis for the instruction. Any quotations or citations of cases are single spaced.

Jury trial dates should be calendared so that jury instructions may be prepared in advance of trial.

The legal assistant should be able to prepare jury instructions under the general guidance of the attorney and subject to his or her review. While the B.A.J.I. and C.A.L.J.I.C. instructions serve as a guide, attorneys and judges are free to modify and supplement the instructions if they can prepare a different instruction which would "more adequately, accurately or clearly state the law." (Appendix, Cal. Rules of Court, §5.) If the trial judge determines that the jury should be instructed on a subject on which there is no B.A.J.I. or C.A.L.J.I.C. instruction, or one which can be modified to submit the issue properly, the instruction on the subject should be "simple, brief, impartial and free from argument." (§5, supra.) Modifications of the instructions should be indicated by parentheses or other appropriate means on the instruction. (§5, supra.)

According to an article in the September 1979 issue of the California State Bar Journal (Goebel, Defects in Jury Instructions: Can They Be Eliminated?), there are approximately 35 B.A.J.I. instructions customarily requested by trial lawyers and given by the judges in every trial.

DISMISSAL

(Code Civ. Proc. §§418.10, 581-583;
California Rules of Court, Rule 203.5.)

The plaintiff may have a case dismissed at any time before the trial commences, if defendant has not filed a cross-complaint. A plaintiff has an "absolute right to dismiss an action after a demurrer to his complaint has been submitted to the court for decision, assuming that in all other respects such a dismissal complies with the conditions imposed by section 581, subdivision 1." (*United Shippers, Inc. v. Superior Court,* 104 Cal.App.3d 359, 361; see Supplement to vol. 4 Witkin, Cal. Procedure (2d ed. 1971) Proceeding Without Trial, §51, p. 15.)

The plaintiff need only file a Request for Dismissal. This is a simple printed form in which the plaintiff merely requests the clerk to enter a dismissal of the case. The dismissal may be "with prejudice" or "without prejudice."

To dismiss *with prejudice* may mean that an agreement has been reached or a release signed. The defendant and plaintiff may have compromised and settled the case out of court and the plaintiff therefore be willing to dismiss.

To dismiss *without prejudice* means tht the plaintiff may sue again on the same cause of action.

The dismissal by the court must be in the form of a written order signed by the court and filed in the action. (Code Civ. Proc. §581d.)

ARBITRATION AND SETTLEMENT

Once a lawsuit is filed, how may it finally be disposed of?

1. The complaint may be pursued to trial and judgment, after which the judgment may be paid and a satisfaction of judgment filed, closing the case.

Payment of the judgment may be obtained but only after levy of a writ of execution. Or it might never be paid, if the defendant has no assets upon which to levy.

2. An appeal may be taken from the judgment by one of the parties and the case finally decided on appeal.

3. The party bringing the action, the plaintiff, could decide not to proceed and file a dismissal. This occasionally happens.

Or, the case may be settled, or arbitrated. In fact, an overwhelming majority of all the lawsuits filed are settled! Trials are time-consuming for the lawyer and the courts, and expensive for the clients and the courts, ergo the public. Occasionally personal feelings, bitterness, are so great as to make any thought of settlement futile. How and when may the case be "settled?"

1. The attorneys, with the consent of their clients, may settle the case before it reaches trial.

The settlement could occur anytime after the filing of the complaint and up to 10 days prior to commencing trial, if the attorneys discuss the case and reach an agreement, or a settlement might be reached at the time the settlement conference is held.

Plaintiff's counsel should give consideration to Code of Civil Procedure section 998 before declining an offer of settlement in writing and deciding to request a trial. Under Code of Civil Procedure section 998, if plaintiff does not accept defendant's offer and thereafter fails to obtain a more favorable judgment for plaintiff, the plaintiff will not recover any of his costs, and also will have to pay the defendant's costs, from the time of the offer, and further, the court, in its discretion (except in eminent domain actions), may require the plaintiff to pay the defendant's costs from the date of filing the complaint and the costs of the expert witnesses reasonably necessary.

Similarly, Code of Civil Procedure section 998 provides that if defendant does not accept plaintiff's offer and the defendant fails to obtain a more favorable judgment, the court has discretion to require that defendant pay costs of service of expert witnesses who are not employees, actually incurred and reasonably necessary, in either, or both, the preparation or trial of the case by plaintiff — in addition to plaintiff's costs.

2. The case may be arbitrated and a decision rendered which, unless a request for trial is thereafter made, is final.

3. An appeal may be taken and the case settled thereafter by the attorneys.

4. An appeal may be taken and the case may be settled at a settlement conference held by an appellate court judge, before oral argument and submission for decision.

Trial procedure and appeals are discussed in other parts of this book so the discussion at this point will center on arbitration in the superior court.

Mandatory Arbitration Law

In 1975 legislation was enacted providing for arbitration of certain superior court actions. Those statutes were repealed and new mandatory arbitration law added (new sections commencing with Civil Code section 1141.10).

Also, California Court Rules 1601-1617 were supplemented and amended and should be read in conjunction with the act.

The law provides that in each superior court with 10 or more judges (Counties of Alameda, Contra Costa, Fresno, Los Angeles, Orange, Riverside, Sacramento, San Bernardino, San Diego, San Francisco, San Mateo and Santa Clara) all civil actions must be arbitrated where the amount in controversy in the opinion of the court will not exceed $15,000. The amount in controversy is determined on the basis of the damages, not on questions of liability, or comparative negligence or other defenses. (Rule 114.16(b).) The court's decision is not appealable.

No determination of the amount in controversy need be made, however, if all defendants stipulate in writing that the amount exceeds $15,000.

Superior courts with fewer than 10 judges may adopt the mandatory arbitration feature by local rule, where the amount in controversy does not exceed $15,000. (Rule 1600(d).) Municipal court districts may also provide by local rule for mandatory arbitration. (Rule 1600(e).)

Since on July 1, 1979, the jurisdictional limit for municipal courts was increased to $15,000, no conference is necessary to determine whether the amount in controversy exceeds $15,000.

Further, in any superior, municipal or justice court arbitration is mandatory where the parties stipulate to arbitration regardless of the amount in controversy. (Rule 1600(a).) Any stipulation to arbitrate must be filed not later than 30 days before the date set for trial. (Rule 1601(a).)

Any case in any court must be arbitrated if the plaintiff files an election and agrees that the arbitration award shall not exceed $15,000. (Rule 1600(b).) Plaintiff may file a written request to arbitrate at the time the at-issue memo is filed, or at such later date permitted by court. (Rule 1601(b).)

The form of Election-Stipulation for Arbitration used in Sacramento County follows; other counties may provide a similar form.

IN THE SUPERIOR COURT OF THE STATE OF CALIFORNIA

IN AND FOR THE COUNTY OF SACRAMENTO

-o0o-

Plaintiff(s), vs. Defendant(s).	NO. **ELECTION - STIPULATION FOR ARBITRATION** (C.C.P. §1141.10)

Pursuant to Rule 1602, California Rules of Court, Plaintiff [and Defendant(s)]

_____ that the above-entitled matter may be submitted to arbitration,
stipulate/elects
and further _____ that the arbitration award shall not exceed
               stipulate/agrees
$_____ .

[ ] It is stipulated that _____
     shall be designated to serve as arbitrator.

[ ] It is requested that an arbitrator be appointed pursuant
     to the California Rules of Court.

Nature of Case: _____

Number
of Sides_____   Estimated Time
                                          for Hearing _____

DATED: _____ , 19___ .   _____

                                          Attorney(s) for _____

                                          _____

                                          Attorney(s) for _____

Names, addresses and telephone numbers of all attorneys in action:

_____   Representing _____

_____   Phone Number _____

_____   Representing _____

_____   Phone Number _____

When a stipulation or election is filed, the case is suspended from the civil active list and placed on an arbitration hearing list forthwith. (Rule 1601.) Such stipulation or election shall be filed not later than 30 days before the date set for trial. (Rule 1601(a).)

Local Rules

Local rules should be ascertained. In Sacramento, for example, in long cause matters, after an at-issue memo is filed the court mails to the parties a Notice of Trial Setting Conference 70 days prior to the conference. After receipt of the notice, all parties must file an Arbitration Determination Statement (printed form) at least 40 days prior to the conference date, on which date the Arbitration Administrator determines whether the case should be assigned to arbitration, and if so, mails a Notice of Assignment to Arbitration (which cancels the trial setting conference date).

Such rules are subject to change, as experience with the new program dictates.

Any court may adopt its own rules as long as they conform to the law and the California Rules of Court. The legal assistant should first determine the local rules. A check for sanctions should be made at the same time.

Cross-Complaints

Superior courts will remove a case from the arbitration hearing list on motion of a cross-complainant made within 15 days after plaintiff's election to arbitrate if the court determines that the amount in controversy in the cross-complaint exceeds $15,000. (Rule 1601(b).)

Exemptions

Exempt from arbitration are small claims actions or trials de novo on appeal from small claims courts, actions seeking equitable relief that are not "frivolous or insubstantial," unlawful detainer proceedings, and Family Law Act proceedings. (Rule 1600.5.)

A 1979 law (ch. 46, SB 275) exempts actions in courts participating in a pilot project on economic litigation (as, e.g., in the Municipal Court, Los Angeles Judicial District) and removes class actions from the list of exceptions to arbitration. A later law (ch. 948, Stats. 1979) permits such courts the option to provide by local rule for mandatory arbitration for actions pending on or filed after July 1, 1979.

Public construction contracts may contain specified provisions relating to judicial review of any arbitration. (Code Civ. Proc. §129.)

Particular actions and categories of actions may be exempted if arbitration would not reduce the probable time and expense of resolving the litigation. (Cal. Rules of Court 1600.5(f)(g).)

Placement on Hearing List

In superior courts, absent a stipulation or a request by plaintiff, actions shall be placed on the superior court arbitration hearing list "at the conference when the court determines the amount in controversy, which conference shall be held no sooner than nine months after the action has been placed on the civil active list and no later than 90 days before the date set for trial, whichever occurs first; . . ." (Rule 1601(c).)

The total amount of damages is the criteria; questions of liability or comparative negligence are not considered at the conference. All parties are present or represented by counsel. The court also determines at this conference whether a prayer for equitable relief is frivolous or insubstantial. (Code Civ. Proc. §1141.16(a).) No determination is made pursuant to this section (§1141.16) if all parties stipulate in writing that the amount in controversy exceeds $15,000.

Municipal court actions can be placed on the hearing list after they are at issue at such time as is designated by local rule. (Rule 1600(e).)

Dismissal for Failure to Bring to Trial

Subdivision (d) of Rule 1601 provides; "When pursuant to subdivision (c) (i.e., *absent* a stipulation of request by plaintiff to submit to arbitration) an action is placed or remains on the arbitration hearing list more than four years and six months after the date the action was filed, the time during which the action is pending on the arbitration hearing list shall not be included in computing the time periods specified in section 583 of the Code of Civil Procedure." Code of Civil Procedure section 583, subdivision (b), provides that a case may be dismissed if not brought to trial within 5 years after the filing of the action. Plaintiff's attorney should watch the time limitations closely, in deciding to stipulate to or request arbitration.

Award and Trial De Novo

The arbitrator must make the award in writing. He need not make findings of fact or conclusions of law. The award is filed with the clerk within 10 days after the conclusion of the hearing, with proof of service on each party to the arbitration. In cases of unusual length or complexity the arbitrator may apply for additional time and the court may allow up to 20 additional days for the filing and service of the award. Within the time permitted for filing the award, the arbitrator may serve and file an amended award. (Rule 1615(a)(b).)

The arbitration award is entered as a judgment if a request for a trial de novo, with proof of service on other parties appearing in the case, is not filed within 20 days after the date the arbitrator *files* the award with the court. This 20-day period to request trial may not be extended. Code of Civil Procedure section 1013(a) does not extend the time as it has been held not to apply. (See *Amoroso v. Superior Court*, 89 Cal.App.2d 240.)

Trial may be either by the court or by jury and will be calendared so far as possible in the same place on the active list as before the arbitration. The party who elects a trial de novo and does not receive a judgment more favorable than the arbitration award is subject to imposition of certain costs and fees under Code of Civil Procedure section 1141.21.

Failure of Arbitration

However, nothing in the act prohibits an award in excess of $15,000. And a party requesting a trial de novo after an award in excess of $15,000 is *not* subject to imposition of costs under Code of Civil Procedure section 1141.21 if the judgment is in excess of $15,000.

If arbitration fails, the case is restored to the superior court's civil active list for prompt disposition in the same place it would have had without arbitration, unless the court orders otherwise for good cause. (Rule 1616(b).)

Motion to Vacate

A motion to vacate a judgment entered pursuant to an arbitration award may be made within six months after its entry on specified grounds. (See Rule 1615(d); Code Civ. Proc. §1286.2(a)(b)(c).)

Arbitrator

The parties may by stipulation designate any person to serve as arbitrator. The designated party must file a written consent and the oath required within 15 days of the date of the stipulation, whereupon the designation becomes effective if the presiding judge does not disapprove within 5 days. (Rule 1602(b).)

If the arbitrator is not designated by stipulation, Rule 1605 provides a process for selecting the arbitrator from the appropriate panel. The composition of the arbitration committee is detailed in Rule 1603(b) for a court having 10 or more authorized judges; in Rule 1603(c) for a court having less than 10 authorized judges. Rule 1604 sets forth the composition of the panels of arbitrators.

No ex parte communication by counsel or the parties with the arbitrator may be made except for the purpose of scheduling the hearing or requesting a continuance. (Rule 1609.) The merits of a case may not be discussed with a judge: the merits of a case may not be discussed with an arbitrator. Nor may offers of settlement be disclosed to the arbitrator. (Rule 1609.)

Notice of Hearing by Arbitrator

The arbitrator sets the time, date or place of the hearing and is required to give notice to the parties at least 30 days prior to the date set for hearing. The hearing may not be set on Saturday or legal holidays except by agreement of all parties and the arbitrator. (Rule 1611.) Cases are to be scheduled not sooner than 35 days nor later than 60 days from the date of the assignment of the case to the arbitrator. (Rule 1611.)

The powers of the arbitrator are detailed in Rule 1614.

Discovery

The parties have the right to take depositions and obtain discovery, which must be completed not later than 15 days prior to the date of the arbitration hearing unless the court grants an extension of time. Rule 1612 supersedes Rule 222 providing for discovery up to 30 days preceding the trial date. (*Zinn v. Superior Court* (1980) 108 Cal.App.3d 583.)

A party may demand in writing that the other party produce a list of witnesses, and designating any expert witnesses, and a list of documents, excepting in matters arising out of collective bargaining agreements, actions involving personal injury or death, or as provided in the parties' agreement to arbitrate, and agreements described in Code of Civil Procedure section 1283.05, where the amount in controversy exceeds $50,000.

Evidence

Rule 1613 contains the rules of evidence at the hearing. Provided copies are delivered to all opposing parties at least 20 days prior to the hearing, the arbitrator must receive in evidence the following: written medical and hospital reports, records and bills (including physiotherapy, nursing and prescription bills), documentary evidence of loss of income, property damage repair bills or estimates, and police reports concerning an accident which gave rise to the case; any repair estimate offered as an exhibit (the copies delivered to opposing parties shall be accompanied by a statement indicating whether the property was repaired, and if it was, whether the estimated repairs were made in full or in part, and by a copy of the receipted bill showing the items of repair made and the amount paid); written statements of witnesses made by affidavit or declaration under penalty of perjury (unless the opposing party delivers to the proponent of the evidence a written demand to produce the person to testify at least 10 days before the hearing). Witnesses may be subpoenaed and depositions may be offered in evidence.

Record

The arbitrator may — but is not required to — make a record of the proceedings. Any such record is the arbitrator's personal notes, not subject to discovery. No other record may be made and the arbitrator may not permit the presence of a stenographer or court reporter or recording device, except as expressly permitted by Rule 1614(b).

The law remains in effect only until January 1, 1985, unless the date is extended.

Chapter 9

PROCEDURES AFTER TRIAL

FINDINGS OF FACT AND CONCLUSIONS OF LAW
(Code Civ. Proc. §§632, 634;
California Rules of Court,
Rules 232, 520.)

"Findings of fact" are the findings of the court as to the facts of a case after a trial is held. From these findings are drawn the conclusions of law by the court. The document is entitled "FINDINGS OF FACT AND CONCLUSIONS OF LAW." The conclusions of law indicate what the judgment is to be.

In superior court findings are not required unless requested by counsel. (In municipal court, on the other hand, findings are deemed waived unless expressly requested at time of trial, and in any event cannot be required if the amount sued for exclusive of interest and costs or the value of the property in controversy does not exceed $1,000 (Code Civ. Proc. §632).)

In the superior court, if the decision is announced in court with all parties present, the parties have 10 days within which to request findings. At that time the court may designate a party to prepare the findings if they are requested. The party so designated has 15 days after a request is made to serve and file the findings.

If the decision is not announced in court the clerk will thereafter give notice to the parties of the decision and the parties then have 10 days from the time the notice is mailed within which to request findings. Findings will be deemed waived unless requested within the prescribed time.

Within 15 days after the request for findings, if the court did not previously designate the party to prepare the findings, the court may either (1) prepare the findings (within 15 days from the date of request), or (2) request counsel to prepare them; counsel has 15 days after such notice to prepare, serve and submit them.

The experienced legal assistant should be able to draft proposed Findings of Fact and Conclusions of Law (and a proposed Judgment). If the court does not prepare the findings, either (1) the decision has been announced, in which event the attorney can advise the legal assistant of the decision, or (2) the court has mailed a notice of intended decision, which will form the basis for the findings of fact.

The findings, whether prepared by the court or the attorney, may have their basis in the following sources:

1. Testimony at the trial, and other evidence (a very good basis);

2. Stipulations made by the parties;

3. Admissions of the parties in the answer or other pleadings in the case;

4. Judicial notice of other actions, etc., which a court is permitted to take (see section on Evidence);

5. Observations of the witnesses at the trial;

6. Burden of proof on one of the parties, requirements of ''burden of proof;''

7. Failure of a party to answer allegations of pleadings when required to do so; and

8. Presumptions (see Cal. Evid. C. §500, *et seq.*).

Findings serve to separate the law from the facts. Findings should be made on all material, factual issues and support the judgment. ''Findings shall fairly disclose the court's determination of all issues of fact material to the judgment in the case and shall be concisely and chronologically stated whenever practicable.'' (Rule 232(e), Cal. Rules of Court.) ''However, the failure to find on a material issue is not ground for reversal when no substantial right of the appellant is prejudiced thereby.'' (*Kerr Land & Timber Co. v. Emmenson* (1965) 233 Cal.App.2d 200, 223.) Further, a finding need not be made on a specific issue if there is no substantial evidence to support it.

The language of the pleadings may be used in some instances but the findings may not refer to the truth or falsity of the allegations.

The findings and judgment are ''proposed'' because they are presented by the attorney for signature by the judge and the court is not bound to sign them as presented. They might also be objected to by the opposing counsel before being signed.

The legal assistant must be able to identify the issues and know what findings of fact are necessary to justify the conclusions of law drawn from the findings, and the proposed judgment. Once the findings of fact are correctly pinpointed, the preparation of the conclusions should flow logically from the findings.

The legal assistant who has been working on the case should not have too much difficulty preparing these documents. The legal assistant who attends the trial is in a better position to know how to proceed. Otherwise, he/she will have to rely on the notice of intended decision and perhaps general instructions from the attorney.

The attorneys will be in a better position on appeal if a good set of findings was prepared in the lower court.

A reading of 40 California Jurisprudence III, Judgments, page 439, *et seq.*, is recommended for the legal assistant, as well as the section on Findings of Fact in California Forms of Pleading and Practice.

* * * *

Usually a copy of the proposed judgment is served on opposing counsel with the proposed findings. An affidavit of mailing should be attached to the original, and the original mailed to the judge who presided at the trial; copies of each document should be sent to the clerk to be stamped and returned to the law office.

Opposing counsel has 15 days within which to serve and file objections.

If no objections are filed, the court may hold a hearing for argument as to the findings.

The court may, on motion, order a hearing on the objections — or on the proposed Judgment if no findings are required.

If a lack of finding is brought to the attention of the lower court, then a lack of finding on a material issue is not to be inferred upon appeal as being in favor of the prevailing parties.

After the Findings of Fact and Conclusions of Law are signed and filed, a Judgment will be signed and filed by the judge. (See Judgment, *infra*.) The clerk will return copies endorsed-filed if submitted.

A brief form for findings follows:

Findings of Fact and Conclusions of Law

```
 1  PAUL D. BLACK
    Attorney at Law
 2  926 J Street
    Sacramento, CA 95814
 3  Telephone:  455-4567

 4  Attorney for Plaintiff

 5

 6

 7

 8           SUPERIOR COURT OF THE STATE OF CALIFORNIA

 9              FOR THE COUNTY OF SACRAMENTO

10

11  JOHN SMITH,                   )       NO. 126704
                                  )
12          Plaintiff,            )
                                  )
13      v.                        )       FINDINGS OF FACT
                                  )
14  JAMES BROWN; WHITE CORPORATION, )            AND
    a California corporation;     )
15  FIRST DOE; SECOND DOE; and    )       CONCLUSIONS OF LAW
    THIRD DOE,                    )
16                                )
            Defendants.           )
17  _____)

18          The above-entitled cause came on regularly for trial

19  on _____, 19__, in Department ____ of the above-

20  entitled Court, before the Honorable _____,

21  judge presiding, sitting without a jury, a jury having been

22  expressly waived, PAUL D. BLACK appearing as attorney for

23  plaintiff, and MANNING & FINCH, by William Manning, appearing

24  as attorneys for defendants, and oral and documentary evidence

25  having been introduced on behalf of both parties, and the Court

26  having considered the same and hearing heard the arguments of

27  counsel and being fully advised in the premises, makes the

28  following findings of fact:
```

II

None of the allegations contained in paragraphs ____,
____ or _____ of defendants' answer is true.

III

Each allegation and denial in paragraph ___ of
defendants' answer is untrue, except it is true that
_____.

CONCLUSIONS OF LAW

From the foregoing facts the court makes the following conclusions of law:

I

Plaintiff is entitled to judgment against defendant
_____ decreeing that he recover from defendant
$_____.

II

_____ etc._____

Dated: _____, 19__.

_____

Judge of the Superior Court

JUDGMENT

(Code Civ. Proc. §664.)

A judgment is the formal opinion or decision of the court. The judgment may be either in favor of the plaintiff and against the defendant, or vice versa.

If findings are not requested and a written judgment is required, the court will prepare and mail a proposed judgment to all parties within 10 days after the expiration of the time for filing requests for findings.

If findings are waived, the court will prepare and mail a proposed judgment within 10 days from the time it announces its decision in open court or mails notice of its intended decision, or it may, in its discretion, notify either party (ordinarily the prevailing party) to prepare, serve and submit the proposed judgment to the court. The party so notified has 10 days after such notice to submit the proposed judgment.

Objections to the judgment may be filed within 10 days after filing. Within 10 days after the time for filing objections, or within 10 days after the hearing on any objections filed, the court signs and files its judgment.

The judgment is not effective for any purpose until it has been entered. A simple form of Judgment follows:

Judgment

1	PAUL D. BLACK Attorney at Law
2	926 J Street Sacramento, CA 95814
3	Telephone: 455-4567
4	Attorney for Plaintiff
5	
6	
7	
8	SUPERIOR COURT OF THE STATE OF CALIFORNIA
9	FOR THE COUNTY OF SACRAMENTO
10	
11	JOHN SMITH,) NO. 126704
12	Plaintiff,)
13	v.) J U D G M E N T
14	JAMES BROWN; WHITE CORPORATION,)
15	a California corporation;) FIRST DOE; SECOND DOE; and)
16	THIRD DOE,)
17	Defendants.)
18	
19	The above-entitled cause came on regularly for trial
20	on _____, 19__, in Department __ of the above-entitled
21	Court, before the Honorable _____, judge pre-
22	siding, sitting without a jury, a jury having been expressly
23	waived, PAUL D. BLACK appearing as attorney for plaintiff and
24	MANNING & FINCH by William Manning, Esq., appearing as attorneys
25	for defendants, and evidence, both oral and documentary, having
26	been introduced and the cause submitted for decision, and the
27	Court having heretofore made and caused to be filed its written
28	findings of fact and conclusions of law:

1   IT IS ORDERED, ADJUDGED AND DECREED that plaintiff

2 John Smith recover from defendant _____ $_____,

3 together with costs amounting to $_____.

4   Dated: _____, 19__ .

5

6   _____

7   Judge of the Superior Court

8

9

10

11

12

13

14

15

16

17

18

19

20

21

22

23

24

25

26

27

28

Cost Bills

The party who obtains judgment usually is entitled to recover his costs of suit from the other party. To do this, he must serve and file a "cost bill" or "memorandum of costs" within 10 days after *entry* of the judgment. (Code Civ. Proc. §1033.)

Caveat: The prevailing party in the superior court may not recover costs if the amount of his judgment could have been rendered in a court of inferior jurisdiction (i.e., under $15,000) unless the judge who presided at the trial (or other judge of the court) makes an order allowing costs or a part of such costs as he deems proper. (Code Civ. Proc. §1032.)

Similarly, costs may be denied in a municipal court if the judgment was for less than $750, if the action could have been brought in the small claims court. If the action could have not have been brought in the small claims court, recoverable costs are limited to actual filing fee and cost of service of process, *provided* the prevailing party satisfies the court that he informed the defendant *in writing* that he intended to commence legal action which could result in a judgment against defendant which would include costs and necessary disbursements allowed. (Code Civ. Proc. §1031.)

In an action for recovery of wages not over $300, the court shall add to costs an attorney's fee up to 20 percent of the amount recovered. (Code Civ. Proc. §1031.)

The cost bill must be verified by the party, his attorney, or the attorney's clerk. (Code Civ. Proc. §1033.) In the cost bill the items, the date paid and incurred, the nature of the item, and the amount, should be listed. The items must have been actually incurred. Some items generally allowable are:

1. Filing fees
2. Reporter's per diem
3. Reporter's transcription
4. Depositions — original and 1 copy
5. Notarial fees
6. Jury fees and mileage
7. Witness' fees and mileage
8. Expert witnesses' fees, if witnesses appointed by court — as court determines
9. Sheriff's, constable's and marshal's fees for service of summons or subpoena and for service of attachment or execution. (See Gov. Code §§26722, 26725.)

If opposing counsel objects to the inclusion of any of the items, he files a motion to tax costs within 10 days after service of the cost bill (Code Civ. Proc. §1033), specifying the items to which he objects.

A hearing on the motion to tax costs will be held and the judge will decide which items are to be included.

Within 2 days after the actual amount of the costs allowed is ascertained, the clerk is required by Code of Civil Procedure section 1033 to insert the total amount in the blank provided therefor in the judgment.

Notice of Entry of Judgment
(Code Civ. Proc. §664.5.)

The clerk of a justice, municipal or superior court is required by Code of Civil Procedure section 664.5 "promptly upon entry of judgment" to mail notice of entry of judgment to all parties who have appeared in the action; in a special proceeding he must mail such notice to all parties who have appeared at the trial or hearing of the particular petition, motion or matter, and file an affidavit of such mailing. "Judgment" as used in this section means any judgment, order or decree from which an appeal lies.

Also, upon order of the court the clerk shall mail notice of entry of any judgment or ruling, whether or not appealable.

California Rules of Court 204 and 504 provide that such notices given by the clerk pursuant to Code of Civil Procedure section 664.5 shall constitute service of notice.

MOTION FOR NEW TRIAL
(Code Civ. Proc. §§655 et seq.)

Code of Civil Procedure section 657 permits the losing party to ask for a new trial on the following grounds:

1. Irregularity in the proceedings	Supporting affidavit required if made on any of these 4 grounds. Must be served within 10 days after service of notice of intention to move for new trial. Opposing counsel has 10 days to serve and file counter-affidavits.
2. Misconduct of the jury	
3. Accident or surprise which could have been guarded against	
4. Newly discovered evidence	
5. Excessive damages, given under influence of passion or prejudice	May be made on minutes of court.
6. Insufficiency of the evidence to justify verdict or decision	
7. Error in law	

Points and authorities supporting the motion for new trial must be filed within 10 days after filing the notice of intention to move for a new trial. Within 10 days thereafter the opposing party may serve and file memorandum of points and authorities in reply. (Cal. Rules of Court, Rule 203(b).)

A motion for new trial must be served and filed

(a) Before entry of judgment OR

(b) Within 15 days of the date of mailing notice of entry of judgment by clerk of court pursuant to Code of Civil Procedure section 664.5, OR

(c) Within 15 days of service by any party of written notice of entry of judgment, OR

(d) Within 180 days after the entry of judgment, WHICHEVER IS EARLIEST,

> EXCEPT, that upon the filing of the first notice of intention to move for a new trial, each other party has 15 days after the service of such notice upon him to serve and file a notice of intention to move for a new trial.

Time provisions may not be extended by order or stipulation, and Code of Civil Procedure section 1013, extending time where service is by mail, does not apply. (Code Civ. Proc. §659.) After expiration of the time to file counter-affidavits, the judge sets the motion for hearing. (See Code Civ. Proc. §§660, 661.) Clerk gives both parties 5 days' notice of the hearing by mail.

After hearing, a notice of the ruling of the court (denying or granting of motion for new trial) is given.

WRITS OF EXECUTION
(Code Civ. Proc. §§681, *et seq.*)

In general, the discussion as to the role of the legal assistant as to attachments, is the same for executions. For a discussion of attachments see Chapter 5. The function of attachments and executions is the same, to secure the payment of judgment. The main distinction procedurally is that writs of attachment are issued before judgment, writs of execution after judgment.

After judgment is entered in a case, the losing party should make payment forthwith unless he intends to move for a new trial or appeal from the judgment. As a matter of practice the prevailing party (i.e., the party who obtains judgment, who "wins" the case) will allow the losing party a reasonable period of time within which to make payment. But he may, at any time after the judgment is entered and up to 10 years after the entry of judgment, ask the court to issue a *writ of execution*.

What is a writ of execution? A writ of execution is an order issued by the clerk of the court commanding a sheriff, constable, marshal or other officer to seize the property of the losing party for satisfaction of the judgment against him. In short, the property is seized, sold at a public sale, and the judgment paid.

The writ is returnable not less than 10 nor more than 60 days after its receipt by the officer to whom directed. If the officer is unable to find any assets of the party within the 60-day period, he will return the writ to the court unsatisfied and notify the attorney.

At a later date the attorney may learn of other assets of the defendant and wish to attempt to levy execution again; in this event a new writ of execution may be issued, *if the previous writ is on file*.

A levy on earnings is made by service of an earnings withholding order upon the debtor's employer. Such order generally would be in effect for no longer than 90 days, and the creditor who obtained such order is precluded for 10 days thereafter from serving another based on the same debt. However, other creditors may do so within this 10-day period, thereby gaining priority.

If the levying officer receives proceeds resulting from a levy he made but received after he has made his return to the court, the clerk will redeliver the writ to the levying officer to make an alias return as in the case of an original writ of execution, upon request of the person in whose favor the return runs.

When levying against a bank account or property in a safe-deposit box of a judgment debtor which also stands in the names of persons who are not judgment debtors, a special bond is required by Code of Civil Procedure section 682a, and, when the amount sought to be reached is less than the amount of the judgment, may be posted in twice the amount sought to be reached.

If the property to be levied upon is in the hands of a third party and the levying officer will not be required to sell, deliver or take custody of the property, the writ of execution may be sent to a registered process server.

Preparation of Writ of Execution

1. A *writ of execution* (a printed form) is prepared. Suggested number of copies:

1 original
1 copy for levying officer
  (Prepare an additional copy for each item
  to be levied upon)
1 office copy

Judgments bear interest on the total amount (i.e., principal and costs) from date of entry of judgment until paid. The amount of interest accruing per day must be computed and filled in on the printed form of Judgment in the space provided. An affidavit or declaration of the attorney must be filed with the court giving the interest accrued, i.e., the amount on which it is computed, the dates, etc. If any costs are incurred after the entry of judgment, an itemization should be included in the affidavit.

2. The original writ of execution is sent to the court for issuance, together with the cost for issuance of the writ.

3. *Instructions to levying officer* are prepared. (Some counties have a printed form; if none is available, the instructions are typed with title of court and cause as in any other legal document.) Prepare at least 1 original, 1 office copy.

The property being levied upon should be described in detail. Automobiles being levied upon should be described by the make, model number, year, license number, serial number, engine number, and how registered.

When levying on a bank account which is in more than one name, the levying officer should be provided with the special bond required by Code of Civil Procedure section 682a.

4. To levying officer (sheriff, constable or marshal) should be sent:

a. Original writ of execution

b. Copy or copies of writ of execution (1 copy for each item to be levied upon)

c. Original of Instructions to Levying Officer

The levying officer should be asked the amount of the deposit he will require as a fee, or his fee determined beforehand and sent with papers. If there are sufficient assets he will collect his fee as well as the amount of the judgment and his fee will be refunded to the law office. (Code Civ. Proc. §682.2.) Interest from the date of issuance of the writ to the date of levy of execution will be computed by the levying officer and likewise collected if possible. (Code Civ. Proc. §682.2.)

Property subject to execution:

"All goods, chattels, moneys or other property, both real and personal, or any interest therein, of the judgment debtor, not exempt by law, and all property and rights of property levied upon under attachment in the action, are subject to execution. . . ." (Code Civ. Proc. §688.)

Exempt from execution is a dwelling house or mobile home in which debtor or family of debtor actually resides to same extent and in same amount as debtor or spouse of debtor could select as homestead.

Heads of families and persons aged 65 or over may claim a homestead exemption, or claim for exemption from execution a dwelling house, housetrailer, mobile home, houseboat, boat, or other waterborne vessel in which such person or the family of such person actually resides, up to $45,000 in actual cash value, and all persons may claim exemption from execution up to $30,000 in actual cash value — over and above all liens and encumbrances. (Civ. Code §1260; Code Civ. Proc. §690.3.)

Code of Civil Procedure section 690.31 provides for a notice to the homeowner in a specified form in each application for a writ of execution against real property containing a dwelling house or mobile home.

Code of Civil Procedure section 690.31 provides a grace period of 2 days, during which period a keeper is installed when personal property is removed, or a dwelling or a business is levied upon.

Code of Civil Procedure section 690.2 also provides for exemption of one motor vehicle with a value not exceeding $500 over and above all liens and encumbrances.

Code of Civil Procedure section 690.18 has been amended to exempt from execution (and attachment or garnishment) money held, controlled, or in process of distribution by any private retirement plan or any profit-sharing plan designed and used for retirement purposes, or the payment of specified benefits from such retirement or profit-sharing plan, and all contributions and interest returned to any member of such retirement or profit-sharing plan.

Employees' Earnings Protection Law

"The amount of earnings of a judgment debtor exempt from the levy of a earnings withholding order shall be that amount provided by federal law in 15 U.S.C. Sec. 1673." (Code Civ. Proc. §723.050.) 15 U.S.C. section 1673 reads, in pertinent part: "(2) The maximum part of the aggregate disposable earnings of an individual for any workweek which is subject to garnishment to enforce any order for the support of any person shall not exceed

"(A) where such individual is supporting his spouse or dependent child (other than a spouse or child with respect to whose support such order is used), 50 per centum of such individual's disposable earnings for that week; and

"(B) where such individual is not supporting such a spouse or dependent child described in clause (A), 60 per centum of such individual's disposable earnings for that week; except that, with respect to the disposable earnings of any individual for any workweek, the 50 per centum specified in clause (A) shall be deemed to be 55 per centum and the 60 per centum specified in clause (B) shall be deemed to be 65 per centum, if and to the extent that such earnings are subject to garnishment to enforce a support order with respect to a period which is prior to the twelve-week period which ends with the beginning of such workweek."

Service of earnings withholding orders may be by personal delivery or by first-class mail, postage prepaid. (See Code Civ. Proc. §723.101.)

A writ of execution may be served by any registered process server where the property to be levied upon is in the hands of a third party and the levying officer is not required to sell, deliver, or take custody of such property. All other duties in connection with execution and processing shall continue to be performed by a sheriff, constable or marshal.

The allowable cost for such service by the process server shall not exceed $1.50.

The form for writ of execution follows:

Writ of Execution

NAME AND ADDRESS OF ATTORNEY	TELEPHONE	FOR COURT USE ONLY
ATTORNEY FOR (Name)		
Insert name of court, judicial district or branch court, if any, and post office and street address		
PLAINTIFF		CASE NUMBER
DEFENDANT		FOR RECORDER'S USE ONLY

WRIT OF EXECUTION ☐MONEY JUDGMENT ☐JOINT DEBTOR ☐POSSESSION OF ☐REAL ☐PERSONAL PROPERTY

1. To the Sheriff or any Marshal or Constable of the County of:
You are directed to satisfy the judgment described below, with interest and costs and your costs and disbursements, as provided by law. This writ may not be used for a levying officer's sale of a dwelling house as defined in CCP 690.31

2. To any registered process server: You are authorized to serve this writ only, in accord with CCP 687

3. Judgment creditor (Name)

4. Judgment debtor (Name and address)
☐ Additional name and address on reverse

5. Judgment entered on (Date)

6. Notice of sale under this writ ☐ has not been requested
☐ has been requested as set forth on the reverse

7. ☐ Joint debtor information set forth on the reverse

8. ☐ Real or personal property described on the reverse

(SEAL)

9 Total judgment as entered
  a Principal . . . . $
  b Attorney fees . . . . $
  c Interest . . . . $
  d Costs . . . . $
  e Total (Add 9a,b,c,d) . . . . $
10 Total judgment and accruals
  a Interest (On item 9e) as adjusted for payments and partial satisfactions (Per filed affidavit CCP 682 2) . . . . $
  b Costs (Per filed memo of costs after judgment) . . . . . . $
  c Total (Add 9e.10a,b) . . . . $
11 Net balance due on judgment
  a Payments and partial satisfactions . . . . $
  b Net balance due before issuance of writ (Subtract 11a from 10c) $
  c Fee for issuance of writ . . . . . $
  d Net balance due on date of writ (Add 11b,c) . . . . $
12 Levying officer. Add the following daily interest from date of writ to date of levy (7% per year on 9e or 11b, whichever is less) . . . . $

Dated   Clerk. By   , Deputy

NOTICE TO JUDGMENT DEBTOR: SEE REVERSE FOR IMPORTANT INFORMATION

(Continued on reverse)

Do NOT use this form for levy and sale of a dwelling house as defined in CCP 690.31 The singular includes the plural
Form Approved by the
Judicial Council of California
Revised Effective January 1 1979

WRIT OF EXECUTION

JC-5 (12/78) FRONT

15 USC §1673, CCP 681 et seq.
690 1 et seq. 690 50, 692a,
989-994. 1032 6, 1033 et seq

Writ of Execution (face)

Continued Items

4. ☐ Additional judgment debtor (Name and address):

6. ☐ Notice of sale has been requested by (Name and address):

7. ☐ Joint debtor was declared bound by the judgment (CCP 989-994)

    a. On (Date):   a. On (Date):
    b. Name and address of joint debtor: b. Name and address of joint debtor:

    c. ☐ Additional costs against certain joint debtors (Itemize):

8. ☐ Judgment was entered for possession of the following
    a. ☐ Real property.
    b. ☐ Personal property ☐ if delivery cannot be had, then for the value (Itemize in 8c) specified in that
          judgment or supplemental order.
    c. Description:

NOTICES TO JUDGMENT DEBTOR

YOU MAY BE ENTITLED TO FILE A CLAIM EXEMPTING YOUR PROPERTY FROM EXECUTION. IF SO, YOU MUST DO SO WITHIN 10 DAYS FROM THE DATE YOUR PROPERTY WAS LEVIED UPON BY DELIVERING TO THE LEVYING OFFICER AN AFFIDAVIT OF EXEMPTION, TOGETHER WITH A COPY THEREOF, AS PROVIDED IN SECTION 690.50 OF THE CODE OF CIVIL PROCEDURE. IF YOU WISH TO SEEK THE ADVICE OF AN ATTORNEY IN THIS MATTER, YOU SHOULD DO SO PROMPTLY SO THAT AN AFFIDAVIT, IF ANY, MAY BE FILED ON TIME.

PERSONAL PROPERTY REMAINING ON THE PREMISES DESCRIBED IN ITEM 8a AT THE TIME OF ITS RESTITUTION TO THE LANDLORD WILL BE SOLD OR OTHERWISE DISPOSED OF IN ACCORDANCE WITH SECTION 1174 OF THE CODE OF CIVIL PROCEDURE UNLESS THE TENANT OR THE OWNER PAYS THE LANDLORD THE REASONABLE COSTS OF STORAGE AND TAKES POSSESSION OF TH   PERSONAL PROPERTY NOT LATER THAN 15 D   'S AFTER THE TIME THE PREMISES ARE RESTORED TO THE LANDLL

                                         ● JC-5 (12/78) BACK

Writ of Execution (reverse)

ABSTRACT OF JUDGMENT
(Code Civ. Proc. §674.)

The party who wins a lawsuit and obtains a money judgment against the other party, does not necessarily collect it. The losing party may not have the assets with which to pay, or he might either sell his assets or transfer ownership, perhaps to a member of his family, before execution can be levied. Often there is reason to suspect that the losing party will attempt to evade payment. If he owns any real property, he can be prevented from selling or transferring it by recording of an *abstract of judgment* in the county in which his real property is located. Once recorded, the abstract acts as a *lien* against any real property owned by the debtor in that county. He cannot deliver clear title to the purchaser of any property without paying the judgment. And since he cannot deliver title, he cannot sell.

An *abstract of judgment* is a document (a printed form) describing the judgment involved and must contain the "title of the court and cause and number of the action; date of entry of the judgment or decree; names of the judgment debtor and of the judgment creditor; the address at which the summons was either personally served or mailed to the judgment debtor or the judgment debtor's attorney of record; amount of the judgment or decree, and where entered in judgment book or minutes." It shall also contain the social security number or driver's license number or both of the judgment debtor if they are known to the judgment creditor, and if they are not known, that fact shall be indicated on the abstract of judgment. (Code Civ. Proc. §674.) (See Code of Civil Procedure, section 668.5, re requirement of entry of judgment.)

An abstract of judgment is issued by the county clerk upon request, accompanied by his fee. After the clerk issues the abstract he will return it to the law office, and in turn it is forwarded, along with the required recording fee, to the county recorder for recording. If the judgment debtor owns property in more than one county, the abstract of judgment should be forwarded in turn to the county recorder of *each* county in which his property is located.

The county recorder is required to notify the person (or his attorney) against whom the lien is recorded.

Any state agency which records a state tax lien against real property is also required to notify the tax debtor of such recordation.

Failure to notify does not affect the constructive notice of the recordation, however.

If a judgment is paid, a Satisfaction of Judgment, duly acknowledged, is filed in the record of the action and a copy furnished to the county recorder for release of the abstract of judgment. See title Satisfaction of Judgment, *infra,* for form thereof.

The legal assistant should consult the attorney handling the case. Perhaps law office policy will dictate a request for abstract of judgment and recordation as soon as possible after entry of judgment. On the other hand, the attorney probably has a good idea as to whether payment of the judgment will be made, and if payment is expected, may feel the expense and work of recording an abstract is unnecessary. The legal assistant can make the request for abstract by letter and arrange for the recording, and subsequently for the Satisfaction of Judgment.

ATTORNEY OR PARTY WITHOUT ATTORNEY (name and address):	TELEPHONE NO	FOR RECORDER'S USE ONLY
☐ Recording requested by and return to:		

ATTORNEY FOR (Name):

NAME OF COURT AND BRANCH, IF ANY:

STREET ADDRESS:

MAILING ADDRESS:

CITY, ZIP CODE:

PLAINTIFF:

DEFENDANT:

ABSTRACT OF JUDGMENT	CASE NUMBER:

	FOR COURT USE ONLY

1. The judgment creditor applies for an abstract of judgment and represents
   a. Judgment debtor's

   ⌐   Name and address   ⌐

   ☐ Address unknown
   Driver's license state and number: . . . . ☐ unknown.
   Social Security number: . . . . ☐ unknown.
   b. Summons was personally served at or mailed to (address):

   ☐ Information regarding additional judgment debtors is shown on the reverse.
   Dated: . . . .
   _____
   (Type or print name)
   _____
   (Signature of Judgment Creditor or Attorney)

2. **I certify that the following is a true and correct abstract of the judgment entered in this action.**
3. Judgment creditor (name):
4. Judgment debtor (full name as it appears in judgment)

5. Total amount of judgment as entered
   a. Principal: $ . . . .
   b. Attorney fees: $ . . . .
   c. Interest: $ . . . .
   d. Costs: $ . . . .
   e. Total: $ . . . .
6. Judgment was entered
   a. on (date):
   b. ☐ in judgment book, minute book or docket
      (1) Volume no.:   (2) Page no.:

7. A lien in favor of a judgment creditor pursuant to CCP 688.1 is
   a. ☐ not endorsed on the judgment
   b. ☐ endorsed on the judgment as follows:
      (1) amount $
      (2) in favor of (name):

(Seal)

8. A stay of execution has
   a. ☐ not been ordered by the court
   b. ☐ been ordered by the court effective until (date):

This abstract issued on (date) . . . .   Clerk, By _____ , Deputy

Form Adopted by the
Judicial Council of California
Revised Effective January 1, 1981

**ABSTRACT OF JUDGMENT
(CIVIL)**

C C P 674, 688 1
Evid C 1531

PLAINTIFF (name):	CASE NUMBER:
DEFENDANT (name):	

ABSTRACT OF JUDGMENT (CIVIL) Reverse Side

Information regarding additional judgment debtors:

9.

Name and address

☐ Address unknown
Driver's license number is: . . . . ☐ unknown.
Social Security number is: . . . . ☐ unknown.
Summons was personally served at or mailed to (address):

10.

Name and address

☐ Address unknown
Driver's license number is: . . . . ☐ unknown.
Social Security number is: . . . . ☐ unknown.
Summons was personally served at or mailed to (address):

11.

Name and address

☐ Address unknown
Driver's license number is: . . . . ☐ unknown.
Social Security number is: . . . . ☐ unknown.
Summons was personally served at or mailed to (address):

12.

Name and address

☐ Address unknown
Driver's license number is: . . . . ☐ unknown.
Social Security number is: . . . . ☐ unknown.
Summons was personally served at or mailed to (address):

13.

Name and address

☐ Address unknown
Driver's license number is: . . . . ☐ unknown.
Social Security number is: . . . . ☐ unknown.
Summons was personally served at or mailed to (address):

14.

Name and address

☐ Address unknown
Driver's license number is: . . . . ☐ unknown.
Social Security number is: . . . . ☐ unknown.
Summons was personally served at or mailed to (address):

15.

Name and address

☐ Address unknown
Driver's license number is: . . . . ☐ unknown.
Social Security number is: . . . . ☐ unknown.
Summons was personally served at or mailed to (address):

16.

Name and address

☐ Address unknown
Driver's license number is: . . . . ☐ unknown.
Social Security number is: . . . . ☐ unknown.
Summons was personally served at or mailed to (address):

17. ☐ Continued on attachment 17.

SATISFACTION OF JUDGMENT
(Code Civ. Proc. §675.)

After a judgment has been paid, the judgment creditor must acknowledge satisfaction thereof. (Code Civ. Proc. §675, subd. (a).)

If an abstract of judgment has been recorded, the acknowledgement of satisfaction must, in addition to being filed, be either personally delivered or sent by first-class mail postage prepaid, to the judgment debtor or his attorney. (Code Civ. Proc. §675, subd. (b).)

If the judgment creditor fails to acknowledge satisfaction within 15 days after receipt of a demand in writing for acknowledgment, he is liable for damages and shall also forfeit the sum of $100. (Code Civ. Proc. §675, subd. (c).) A judgment creditor who unduly conditions delivery of an acknowledgement of satisfaction upon the performance of any act or the payment of any amount in excess of the amount to which he is entitled under the judgment, is liable for no less than $250. (Code Civ. Proc. §675, subd. (d).)

Satisfaction may be entered upon an execution returned satisfied, or the following form may be used:

Satisfaction of Judgment

To the clerk of the above-entitled court:

Payment having been made, you are hereby authorized and directed to enter, and I hereby acknowledge, full satisfaction of the judgment in the above-entitled action entered in Volume _____, page _____, of the official records of said county on the _____ day of _____, 197 _____.

_____
Attorney for Plaintiff

ACKNOWLEDGMENTS

An *acknowledgment* is the declaration by a person that he signed the document to which the acknowledgment is attached. The person making the acknowledgment signs the document involved, the notary public signs the acknowledgment itself. An acknowledgment is used on deeds, satisfactions of judgment, papers in business transactions, etc.

Any acknowledgment taken outside California in accordance with the laws of the place where an acknowledgment is made, is sufficient in California. (Civ. Code §1189, as amended 1980.) Printed forms of acknowledgment may be obtained from office supply stores.

Acknowledgment

STATE OF CALIFORNIA

COUNTY OF SACRAMENTO   ss.

On this 12th day of October in the year one thousand nine hundred and eighty-one before me ROBERTA CALDWELL, a Notary Public in and for the County of Sacramento, personally appeared RALPH JONES, known to me to be the person whose name is subscribed to the within instrument, and he duly acknowledged to me that he executed the same.

IN WITNESS WHEREOF, I have hereunto set my hand and affixed my official seal the day and year in this certificate first above written.

signature/Roberta Caldwell
Roberta Caldwell

Notary Public in and for the county of
Sacramento, State of California
My Commission Expires March 1983

Chapter 10

APPEALS-CIVIL

PREPARING AN APPEAL

Appeals in civil matters from the superior courts to the Supreme Court of California and the Courts of Appeal may be taken as specified in Code of Civil Procedure section 904.1 (and listed in the Appendix to the California Rules of Court). It should be noted that section 904.1 provides for an appeal from an order *granting* a new trial but *not* for an appeal from an order *denying* a new trial.

Since attorneys frequently *do* file appeals from nonappealable orders, one of the first things the legal assistant might do should the attorney indicate filing an appeal, is to check the statutes to see whether an appeal may be taken. Otherwise the nonappealability is not discovered until the case is reviewed; often such an appeal is combined with a valid appeal; in any event, the court can take no action on a nonappealable order.

An appeal should be meritorious. The court may assess a penalty if an appeal is a sham, frivolous or taken for purposes of delay. Rule 26 provides in part: "Where the appeal is frivolous or taken solely for the purpose of delay or where any party shall have required in the typewritten or printed record on appeal the inclusion of any matter not reasonably material to the determination of the appeal, or has been guilty of any other unreasonable infraction of the rules governing appeals, the reviewing court may impose upon offending attorneys or parties such penalties, including the withholding or imposing of costs, as the circumstances of the case and the discouragement of like conduct in the future may require."

Notice of Appeal

The notice of appeal from a judgment in the superior court is filed with the county clerk of the county where the judgment was entered. The time for filing a notice of appeal is fixed by the California Rules of Court and cannot be extended beyond the time provided therein. (See Appeals Timetable, *infra*.)

The legal assistant can prepare the notice of appeal for the attorney's signature. In a case where an unfavorable judgment has been entered, the legal assistant, being aware of the time limit for filing a notice of appeal, should check with the attorney to determine whether an appeal is contemplated.

If an election is made to proceed under Rule 5.1 (option of appendices in lieu of clerk's transcripts), a notice of election and notice to prepare reporter's transcript may be included in the document containing the notice of appeal. However, the appellant has 10 days after filing the notice of appeal within which to make the decision to proceed under Rule 5.1.

Appendix

Under Rule 5.1(b), an appendix prepared by the appellant or jointly by the parties shall contain copies of:

(1) those documents listed as items (1) through (5) in subdivision (d) of Rule 5 as are essential to the proper consideration of the issues, including such documents as the appellant should reasonably assume will be relied upon by the respondent in meeting the issues raised; (3) the appellant's notice of election to proceed under the provisions of this rule; (4) any motion opposed to proceeding under this rule, documents filed in connection with the motion, and the court's ruling thereon; (5) in the case of a joint appendix, the stipulation designating its contents; and (6) required indices.

The appendix shall conform to subdivisions (a), (d) and (e) of Rule 9 in form. Copies must show the date of filing in the trial court and the appendix must be bound separately. The cover is to contain the same material as the cover of a brief and be entitled "APPELLANT'S APPENDIX IN LIEU OF CLERK'S TRANSCRIPT" or "JOINT APPENDIX IN LIEU OF CLERK'S TRANSCRIPT" or "RESPONDENT'S APPENDIX" or "APPELLANT'S REPLY APPENDIX." Copies must show the date of filing in the trial court.

Counsel must confer and attempt to reach an agreement concerning a joint appendix.

The appellant's appendix shall be served and filed no later than appellant's opening brief. The respondent's appendix shall be served and filed no later than respondent's brief and may contain any document which could have been included in appellant's appendix but was not. The appellant may serve and file a reply appendix no later than the time for filing a reply brief.

Upon completion of the reporter's transcript and any clerk's transcript, the clerk mails notice to all parties, who may file request for correction within 10 days after mailing of the notice. If no such request is filed, the clerk certifies the record as correct.

Filing Fee

Rule 1 provides for payment of the filing fee (currently $50) simultaneously with the filing of the notice of appeal. Payment should be in the form of a check or money order payable to the clerk of the court of appeal. Cash will be accepted.

When the clerk of the court of appeal receives the notice of appeal, if the filing fee has not been paid, he will notify the appellant and payment must be made within 15 days from the date of the notice or good cause shown for nonpayment or being excused. See Rule 10, subdivision (a).

Record on Appeal

The *notice designating record on appeal* filed by the appellant may be filed at the same time as the notice of appeal but must be served on the respondent and filed within 10 days after filing of the notice of appeal. This notice designates all the papers, records, etc., that the appellant wishes to incorporate in the record on appeal. The record on appeal should include all documents, testimony, and exhibits essential to a decision by the reviewing court. However, the reviewing court may on its own motion order augmentation of the record whenever it is necessary to prevent a miscarriage of justice. (See Rule 5(f), Cal. Rules of Court.)

If appellant includes only portions of the reporter's transcript he must state the grounds which are being raised on appeal and is thereafter precluded from claiming any other errors or raising any other grounds for appeal without special permission of the appellate court. (Rule 4(b).)

Respondent's *notice designating additional records,* which he files if he wishes to include additional records not requested by appellant, is served and filed within 10 days after service of appellant's notice designating record on appeal. (Rule 5(b).)

The legal assistant should check with the attorney concerning the documents to be designated in the record on appeal.

Rule 10 provides that if appellant defaults in procuring the record on appeal within the time limits permitted, the clerk of the superior court shall forthwith notify him in writing (with a certified copy to the reviewing court including date of mailing) and that the appeal will be dismissed unless good cause is shown to the reviewing court within 15 days. If he fails to comply, the appeal will be dismissed.

Exception to foregoing rules: In the Third District Court of Appeal in Sacramento *only*, a new procedure for expediting record on appeal has been instituted. The Court of Appeal mails counsel a Stipulation for Use of Original Court File in Lieu of Clerk's Transcript, together with covering letter of instructions. It is the appellant's responsibility to obtain the necessary signatures and send the stipulation to the court for approval. Upon receipt the Court of Appeal will issue an order, and when the county clerk receives that order, the clerk will number the pages in the entire superior court file, paginate and prepare and attach a chronological index and provide counsel with copies of the index so they can paginate their own files accordingly. (This is to permit the appropriate citation to the record as required by Rule 15(a).) The only cost involved is for preparation of the chronological index.

Counsel need not file a clerk's transcript if the stipulation is returned to the Court of Appeal within the time provided for filing designation of the record (10 days after filing notice of appeal). The time within which to file the stipulation for use of the original file can be extended if the required signatures cannot be obtained within the 10 days provided. (A Designation of Reporter's Transcript must still be filed if such is required.)

By this procedure the entire record is sent to the Court of Appeal within about 10 days of receipt of the stipulation.

Reporter's Transcript

Within 10 days after filing notice of appeal, appellant files a notice to prepare reporter's transcript. The clerk of the court transmits this notice without delay to the reporter, who within 10 days files his estimate with the clerk, or advises the clerk that he notified the appellant directly of the estimated cost. Unless the reporter waives a deposit, the appellant must deposit cash with the clerk in the amount of the estimated cost. The reporter has 30 days to prepare the transcript.

Agreed Statement on Appeal

If the parties can agree on the facts and issues, an appeal may be presented by an agreed statement prepared by appellant and approved by all counsel. Within 40 days after filing the notice of appeal, the appellant files two copies with the county clerk for transmittal by him to the appellate court. (See Rule 6 for the contents of the agreed statement.)

Settled Statement on Appeal

In lieu of a clerk's transcript, or in lieu of a clerk's transcript and a reporter's transcript, the appellant may prepare a condensed narrative statement of the facts and issues. Appellant first files a notice of proceeding by settled statement, within 10 days after filing a notice of appeal. He then has 30 days within which to file a proposed narrative statement; respondent has 20 days thereafter to file proposed amendments. The trial court sets a date for hearing by the trial judge who heard the case.

As in the agreed statement, if the narrative statement does not cover all the oral proceedings, appellant must state the points to be raised on appeal and cannot then raise other grounds or claim other errors except by permission of the appellate court.

The legal assistant may be able to draft both the agreed statement on appeal and the settled statement on appeal, after discussion with the attorney and general instructions.

See Rule 7 for the contents of the settled statement in lieu of both transcripts, in addition to the condensed statement of the oral proceedings. Subdivision (d) of Rule 7 covers the rules as to settlement and engrossment.

Record on Appeal — Costs, Extensions, Corrections

The reporter will file an estimate of the cost of preparing the reporter's transcript, or he may notify appellant directly and also inform the clerk. Within 10 days after notification of the cost, appellant must arrange for payment of the estimated costs. If respondent designates additional material to be included in the clerk's transcript, he must make arrangements for payment of the clerk's fee for preparation of the additional material.

Within 30 days after payment has been arranged, the reporter and clerk prepare the transcripts, unless an extension of time has been granted. The clerk and reporter may obtain extensions of time up to a total of 90 days (30 days at a time) from the superior court; any further extensions must be obtained from the appellate court.

[In a criminal case the transcripts must be prepared within 20 days after payment of fees, and only the appellate court can extend the time for preparation of the record and any extensions may not exceed 60 days.]

A notice of completion of the clerk's and reporter's transcripts is sent to all parties, who have 10 days within which to propose corrections. The court makes a ruling on any proposed corrections, certifies the record and sends it to the appellate court. If none are proposed, the record is certified by the clerk and reporter and sent to the appellate court.

After the record has been filed in the appellate court, only the appellate court may consider its augmentation or correction.

Dismissal of Appeal

Appellant may dismiss his appeal at any time prior to the filing of the record in the appellate court by filing a written abandonment of the appeal or a stipulation for abandonment *with the superior court.* (Rule 19(a).) Once the record is filed, such a document must be filed with the appellate court. The court prepares the order of dismissal.

Respondent may file a motion to dismiss appeal (typewritten) with the appellate court either before or after the record is filed, but if filed afterward, the motion is to be accompanied by a certificate of the clerk of the superior court as provided in Rule 42.

FILING THE BRIEF

The *appellant's opening brief* must be filed within 30 days of the date of the filing of the record (date on the receipt aforesaid) *or* the filing of the reporter's transcript if there was an election under Rule 5.1, *or* within 70 days after filing election under Rule 5.1 if the appellant did not serve and file a reporter's transcript.

The *respondent's reply brief* must be filed within 30 days after the date the appellant's opening brief is filed.

The *closing brief of appellant* (the filing of which is optional with the appellant) must be filed within 20 days after the date of filing of respondent's reply brief.

The filing of each of these briefs may be extended for a period not more than 60 days, by stipulation of the parties filed with the court of appeal; thereafter the time may be extended only for good cause shown, by the Presiding Justice. (Rule 16(a).) Counsel presents an affidavit giving reasons for his inability to file his brief within the prescribed time, with an order following the affidavit and merely stating "IT IS SO ORDERED," for signature of the Presiding Justice. (An original and 2 copies should be presented to the court of appeal.)

A stipulation extending time must, of course, be filed *before* the expiration of the time to file the brief.

If *appellant* fails to file a brief when due, the parties will be notified in writing by the clerk of the court that the brief is overdue and that if it is not filed within 30 days the appeal will be dismissed, unless good cause is shown for relief. (Rule 17(a).) If an extension is then obtained and the brief not filed within the time granted, the appeal is subject to dismissal forthwith. (Rule 17(a).)

If *respondent* fails to file his brief within 30 days after the filing of appellant's opening brief, he will be notified by the clerk that the case may be submitted for decision on the record and on appellant's opening brief unless his brief is filed within 30 days or good cause shown. If respondent does not file his brief within the 30 days allotted or within the period to which his time is extended, the court may accept as true the statement of facts in the appellant's opening brief and, unless the appellant requests oral argument, submit the case for decision on the record and appellant's opening brief. (Rule 17(b).)

Calendaring — Legal Assistant

If the legal assistant is employed in the office of attorney for respondent, a date 30 days after receipt of appellant's opening brief will be calendared for respondent's brief.

The legal assistant in the office of appellant's attorneys should calendar the date for appellant's opening brief 30 days after the filing of the record, or the reporter's transcript if an election was made under Rule 5.1, or 70 days if no reporter's transcript.

If the attorney for appellant intends to file a reply brief — the filing of which is optional — a date of 20 days from the filing of respondent's reply brief will be calendared.

The legal assistant should be alert that the briefs are filed before the due date, and request an extension of time to file the brief in advance of the due date, if it appears that the brief cannot be filed in time.

The participation of the legal assistant in the research and drafting of briefs will depend upon the capabilities and training of the legal assistant and the expectations of the attorney in that regard. The attorney might ask the legal assistant to do some additional research at the time he is preparing for oral argument.

Amicus Curiae Briefs

"Amicus curiae" literally means "friend of the court." A person other than a party to the action may have an interest in the outcome of the case and may wish to file a brief supporting the position of one of the parties. Such a brief may be filed only by permission of the court (whether trial court or appellate court). (See Rule 14(b).)

Oral Argument

After the briefs have been filed the case is placed on the court's "ready for calendar list" and counsel are notified as soon as their case is ready for oral argument. The judges familiarize themselves with the facts and issues prior to the time of oral argument and therefore oral argument should have a purpose and not be requested merely for the purpose of repeating what has already been said in the briefs. If oral argument is to be waived, it is better done at this time than later, precluding another case from being placed on the calendar.

Each side is allowed a maximum of 30 minutes for oral argument (Rule 22), or such time as may be ordered by the court. The appellant opens the argument and may reserve a portion of his time for closing the argument.

When counsel are notified that their case is ready for oral argument they should file a designation of any exhibits in the lower court which they wish sent to the appellate court.

Also, either prior to or at the time of oral argument, counsel may present any new or additional cases intended for use at oral argument. This presentation may be in letter form but an original and 3 copies should be filed, with proof of service on the opposing counsel.

At oral argument, counsel are sometimes granted leave or directed to file supplemental letters or memoranda covering specific points of the law. Time limits are set by the court. The legal assistant should be alert to determine any such time limits set.

Decision

Subsequently, after any such supplemental material is filed and the case is submitted, the court renders its decision. Rule 22.5 provides that when oral argument on a case in the Court of Appeal has been heard, or a waiver of oral argument has been approved, and the time for filing all briefs and papers has passed, the cause is submitted. Submission may be vacated only by an order giving the reasons therefor and providing for resubmission. Copies are mailed by the court to all counsel, in a criminal case to the defendant and the Public Defender, to the Superior Court judge who presided at the trial, to the printer if published, to the Reporter of Decisions if unpublished.

PETITION FOR REHEARING AND
PETITION FOR HEARING

A *petition for rehearing* may be filed in the court of appeal within 15 days after the date of decision. The rehearing provides a way for the party to point out any factual errors in the opinion, to challenge the correctness of a statement of law, and to suggest modifications before the decision becomes final (30 days after the decision).

An answer to the petition for rehearing may be filed within *23 days after date of the filing of the decision.* (For instance, if the petition for rehearing were filed as late as the 15th day after the date of the decision, responding counsel would have only 8 days to file an answer to the petition.) The court may not extend the time for filing the petition for rehearing or the answer thereto. The petition for rehearing must be acted upon by the court no later than 30 days of the date of filing of their decision, at which time the opinion becomes final and the court of appeal loses jurisdiction of the case. Usually the court will make an order either denying or granting the petition for rehearing; if the court should not make an order within that time, the petition would be deemed denied.

It should be noted that if the court of appeal modifies its decision within the 30-day period after the filing of the decision, the 30-day period specified runs anew from the date of modification, i.e., the court's decision becomes final 30 days from the date of filing of the modified opinion (or 30 days from the date of filing the opinion on rehearing). (See Rule 24(a).)

If the court of appeal denies the petition for rehearing (or grants a rehearing and issues a new opinion on rehearing), a *petition for hearing* in the Supreme Court may (see Rule 29 for grounds for hearing) be filed by the losing party within 10 days after — *and not before* — the decision of the court of appeal becomes final in the court of appeal (30 days after filing). In other words, a petition in the Supreme Court must be filed within the 31st to 40th days after the date of the decision in the court of appeal. Briefly stated, a petition for hearing will be ordered (1) where it appears necessary for uniformity of decision or settlement of important questions of law; (2) where the court of appeal was without jurisdiction or (3) where, because of disqualification or other reason, the court of appeal decision lacks concurrence of required majority of qualified judges.

The *answer* to a petition for hearing in the Supreme Court must be filed within 20 days after the date the decision becomes final in the court of appeal (i.e., within 50 days from date of decision filed in the court of appeal). (For example, if the petition were filed on the 10th day after the decision, the responding party would have only 10 days to file his answer to the petition for hearing.)

The Supreme Court may grant or deny the petition for hearing within 30 days after a decision of the court of appeal becomes final as to that court (i.e., 60 days after date of decision in the court of appeal), and the Supreme Court may for good cause extend its time for an additional 30 days. If no order is made within the time specified, the petition for hearing is deemed denied. When a hearing is granted, the cause is placed on the calendar for oral argument, unless waived, or cause transferred to a court of appeal.

If the legal assistant is employed in the office of the attorney for appellant, the last day for filing appellant's opening brief should be calendared upon receipt of notice that the clerk's and reporter's transcripts have been completed.

If the attorney for the appellant is not the prevailing party on appeal, he may decide to file a petition for rehearing, and if that petition is not granted, a petition for hearing in the Supreme Court. The legal assistant should be alert to the dates involved for filing, set out in the following chart.

Appeals Timetable — Civil Cases

(The Appendix to the California Rules of Court contains a timetable for filing records, briefs and papers in the appellate courts.)

Notice of appeal from judgment	File within 60 days after date of mailing notice of entry of judgment by clerk pursuant to Code Civ. Proc. §664.5, OR
	If clerk does not give notice, within 60 days after date of service of written notice of entry of judgment by any party upon the party filing the notice of appeal, OR Within 180 days after date of entry of judgment, WHICHEVER IS EARLIEST. (Rule 2.)
	If a motion for new trial is filed and *denied*, time for filing notice of appeal is extended until 30 days after either (a) entry of order denying motion or (b) denial thereof by operation of law, but in no event later than 180 days after date of entry of judgment. (Rule 3(c).)
Notice of cross-appeal	Within 20 days after notification by the superior court clerk of the filing of the first appeal. (Rule 3(c).) When appeal taken from order granting new trial or vacating judgment, within 20 days after mailing notification of appeal from order. (See Rule 3(c).)

Time Period	*Reporter's Transcript*	*Clerk's Transcript*
Within 10 days after filing notice of appeal	Serve and file *notice* to *prepare reporter's transcript*, if appellant wants to present any point requiring consideration of oral proceedings. (Rule 4(a).)	Serve and file *notice designating the record on appeal*. (See Rule 5(a) for documents included.) (This notice lists the papers or records on file or lodged with the clerk to be incorporated in the clerk's transcript.)

	(Notice to prepare clerk's transcript and reporter's transcript may be included in same document, and in notice of appeal. Rule 5(a).)
Without delay	Clerk transmits a copy of the notice to reporter. (Rule 4(a).)
Within 10 days after notice from clerk	Reporter files an estimate of cost of preparing reporter's transcript, or notifies appellant directly and informs clerk. (Rule 4(a).)

Within 10 days after service of notice by appellant	Respondent designates any additional material he wants transcribed. (Parties may stipulate to material to be included.)	Respondent designates any additional material he wants included. (Rule 5(b).) (See Rule 5(d) re furnishing of copies by appellant.) (Parties may stipulate to material to be included.)
Within 10 days after notification of estimate of cost	Appellant deposits reporter's fee. Rule 4(c).	Appellant makes arrangements for payment of clerk's fee; respondent makes arrangement for payment of clerk's fee for additional material designated. Rule 5(b), (c).
Within 30 days after payment of fees	Reporter prepares transcript. Rule 4(d).	Clerk prepares transcript. See Rule 5(d).
Immediately on completion of clerk's and reporter's transcripts	Clerk of superior court gives notice of completion. (Rule 8(a).)	Clerk of superior court gives notice of completion. (Rule 8(a).)
Within 10 days after mailing of notice of completion	Any request for correction of transcript is made. (Rule 8(a).)	Any request for correction of transcripts is made. (Rule 8(a).)
	(See Rule 8(b) for hearing and certification if request for correction filed.)	
Within 30 days after filing of the record or the reporter's transcript if election under Rule 5.1, or 70 days after filing election under 5.1 if no notice to serve and file reporter's transcript	File Appellant's Opening Brief	
Within 30 days after filing of Appellant's Opening Brief	File Respondent's Brief	
Within 20 days after filing of Respondent's Brief	File Appellant's Reply Brief (Filing of this brief is optional with appellant.) (Rule 16(a).)	
_____	ORAL ARGUMENT HELD UNLESS WAIVED BY BOTH PARTIES.	

——	OPINION FILED. Becomes final in 30 days if no petition for rehearing filed.
Within 15 days of filing of decision in Court of Appeal	Petition for Rehearing may be filed
Within 23 days after filing of decision in Court of Appeal	Answer to Petition for Rehearing may be filed
Within 10 days (and not before expiration of 10 days) after decision of Court of Appeal becomes final (becomes final 30 days after date of filing). [In other words, file Petition for Hearing within 31st to 40th days after date of decision in Court of Appeal.]	File Petition for Hearing in California Supreme Court. Include copy of opinion of Court of Appeal in petition. [Proof must be made of delivery of 1 copy to the Court of Appeal rendering the decision.] (Rule 28(b).)
Within 20 days after decision of Court of Appeal becomes final as to Court of Appeal (i.e., 50 days from date of decision in Court of Appeal)	File Answer to Petition for Hearing in the Supreme Court. (Rule 28(b).) Supreme Court either denies or grants the petition for hearing within the 30 days after the decision in the Court of Appeal becomes final, or any extension of said period (may not exceed 60 days). (Rule 28(b).) If the petition is granted, the case is placed on calendar for oral argument and an opinion thereafter issued.
Within 15 days after filing decision	File Petition for Rehearing in Supreme Court
Within 23 days after filing decision	File Answer to Petition for Rehearing in Supreme Court
REMITTITUR	The clerk of the court of appeal issues a remittitur after the final determination of any appeal, which is usually at the end of 60 days after the filing of the opinion in the court of appeal but could be 60 days later if the Supreme Court extended its time as above.
COST BILL (on appeal)	Serve upon adverse party and file cost bill for allowable costs on appeal *in lower court* within 30 days after remittitur is filed in the lower court. (See Remittitur above.) Remittitur MUST BE ACTUALLY ON FILE before cost bill is filed. (Code Civ. Proc. §1034.)

COSTS ON APPEAL
(Rule 26, California Rules of Court.)

Certain items are allowable as costs on appeal in most cases. See Rules 26(a) and (b) for right to costs and entry of judgment for costs.

A remittitur issued by the Court of Appeal is sent down to the lower court 60 days after the date of the decision, and a *verified* cost bill must be filed *in the lower court within 30 days thereafter* (Code Civ. Proc. §1034); the remittitur must be *actually on file* before the cost bill is filed.

A remittitur is a sending back, as when a record is remitted, sent back, from a superior court to an inferior court. A remittitur goes down from the Courts of Appeal upon the expiration of the period during which a hearing in the Supreme Court may be determined (which is 30 days after the decision of the Court of Appeal becomes final). (Rules 25(a), 28(a), Cal. Rules of Court.) A decision of the Court of Appeal becomes final as to that court 30 days after filing, except in the case of a writ where the court has original jurisdiction, which becomes final immediately. (Rule 24(a), Cal. Rules of Court.)

Allowable costs on appeal (Rule 26(c), California Rules of Court):

1. By appellant, cost of preparing original and 1 copy of any type of record on appeal authorized by the California Rules of Court; by respondent, 1 copy of the record on appeal.

(EXCEPTION: If typewritten record parties must so stipulate and costs of copying exhibits and affidavits which could have been incorporated by reference are not allowable unless the court orders them copied.)

2. Reasonable cost of printing or reproduction of briefs by other process of duplication.

3. Cost of production of additional evidence.

4. Filing and notary fees and expense of service, transmission and filing of record, briefs and other papers.

5. Premium on any surety bond (unless court to which remittitur transmitted determines bond was not necessary).

Failure to Timely File Cost Bill

The time requirement for the filing of a cost bill is an important requirement of which the legal assistant should be very much aware. The legal assistant must know when the remittitur is filed in the lower court, since the time of its filing may be at the end of 60 days after the filing of the opinion in the Court of Appeal, but could be 60 days later if the Supreme Court extends the time (see Remittitur, *supra*).

A trial court has the power to grant relief upon a proper showing pursuant to the provisions of section 473 of the Code of Civil Procedure, where there has been a failure to file and serve a cost bill within the statutory time as provided in section 1034 of the Code of Civil Procedure. (*Soda v. Marriott* (1933) 130 Cal.App. 589; *Flores v. Board of Supervisors* (1970) 13 Cal.App.3d 480, 484; *Cornell University Medical College v. Superior Court* (1974) 38 Cal.App.3d 311, 315.)

The granting or denial of a motion made under Code of Civil Procedure section 473 for relief on account of a failure to serve and file a cost bill within the statutory time provided in section 1034 of the Code of Civil Procedure is largely a matter of discretion to be liberally exercised by the trial court in furtherance of justice. Appellate courts are reluctant to interfere with the exercise of such discretion and will only do so when it clearly appears there has been an abuse of discretion. (see *Lane v. Pacific Greyhound Lines* (1947) 30 Cal.2d 914; see also, *Beilby v. Superior Court* (1902) 138 Cal. 51.)

WRITS OF PROHIBITION AND MANDATE — SAN FRANCISCO COURT OF APPEAL*

A petition for writ of prohibition or mandate may be denied summarily if it is clear from the face of the petition that it has no merit. . . . The petitioner carries the burden of convincing the court that an alternative writ (which may be called an order to show cause) should issue. If the three-judge panel decides that the burden is not sustained, the petition is denied by a minute order signed by the Presiding Justice on behalf of the court. If the court concludes that a prima facie showing for relief has been made, and that the case is one which the court in the exercise of its discretion should consider on the merits, in most instances an alternative writ will be issued, fixing the date for the filing of a return and a date and time for oral argument.

Following the filing of a return, oral argument may be heard; the matter is submitted for decision and ultimately decided in a written opinion.

If the court is satisfied as to the merits of a petition after consideration of the petition and opposing points and authorities, the court will direct the issuance of a peremptory writ in the first

---

*From Internal Operating Practices, California Court of Appeal (1979), First Appellate District, San Francisco. The booklet, covering all the California Courts of Appeal, may be obtained without charge from the Administrative Office of the Courts, State Building, 3d Floor, 350 McAllister St., San Francisco, California 94102.

instance. (Code Civ. Proc. §§1088, 1105.) To permit the court to grant summary relief in this manner, the petition should contain a prayer for a peremptory writ.

It is often necessary for the Court of Appeal to take prompt action on a petition because delay would render the issue moot, to the prejudice of the petitioner. Such situations arise when the objective of the petition is, e.g., to prohibit commencement of a scheduled trial. Whenever a petition is filed that requires prompt action by the court, the urgency of the matter should immediately be brought to the attention of the Clerk. The court can then make a determination as to whether the challenged proceeding should be stayed temporarily in order to maintain the status quo pending consideration of the merits of the petition.

Motions

Motions must be made in writing and are ruled upon without hearing unless the court desires argument. (Cal. Rules of Court, Rule 41(b).) If the motion requires extensive examination of the record, the motion may be denied without prejudice; the motion may later be considered along with the merits on the appeal. See Chapter 8, for further discussion of Motions.

SETTLEMENT CONFERENCES IN APPELLATE COURTS

The number of appeals being filed — both civil and criminal — is ever-increasing. A growing backlog operates to reduce the time between the filing of an appeal and its calendaring for oral argument. Appellate courts like other courts are constantly looking for ways to meet the problems of their growing workloads. Criminal appeals are granted priority in calendaring over civil appeals. What happens to civil appeals?

In only a rather small percentage of cases do the attorneys agree on a settlement of the case and withdraw their appeal, or is an appeal dismissed for causes such as failure to file an opening brief or general unilateral abandonment.

As a result of experiments with settlement conferences in the Courts of Appeal, First and Third Districts, the adoption of a settlement conference rule similar to Rule 207.5 providing for superior court settlement conferences was advocated. Effective January 1, 1977, the Judicial Council adopted Rule 19.5, under which a presiding justice of the Court of Appeal may require counsel to attend a prehearing conference to consider the simplification of the issues on appeal, the possibility of settlement, and any other matters that may aid in the disposition of the appeal. Matters agreed upon are reduced to writing. Unless stipulated to, no reference may be made in any subsequent proceedings in the appeal, except a further prehearing conference or other settlement negotiations.

Under subdivision (b) of this rule, if a prehearing conference is ordered prior to the filing of appellant's opening brief, the period for filing the brief is extended 30 days after the conference date specified in the order.

On December 31, 1976, the Third Appellate District adopted rules applicable to that district.

COURT OF APPEAL
THIRD APPELLATE DISTRICT

Local Rules of Court*

[As adopted December 31, 1976.]

SETTLEMENT CONFERENCE PROCEDURES

Rule 1   SOURCE AND EFFECTIVE DATE

These rules have been adopted pursuant to Rule 19.5, California Rules of Court, and shall apply to all appeals in civil cases except appeals from proceedings under sections 600, 601 and 602 of the Welfare and Institutions Code. They shall operate upon cases in which the record on appeal (Rule 10, Cal. Rules of Court) is filed after January 1, 1977.

Rule 2   PRE-ARGUMENT STATEMENT

Within 20 days after filing of the record on appeal, every appellant and cross-appellant affected hereby shall serve upon all other parties to the appeal and shall file with the clerk of this court, along with proof of service thereof, a pre-argument statement containing the following:

a. Case title and number.

b. Identification of trial court.

c. Date of judgment or order appealed from.

d. Name of judge or judges who made the disposition or dispositions from which appeal is taken.

e. Date notice of appeal filed.

f. Name, address and telephone number of counsel for all parties to the appeal.

g. A brief description of the trial court disposition from which the appeal is taken.

h. A concise statement of the case, including a brief procedural history and all facts material to consideration of the issues presented by the appeal.

i. The issues to be raised in the briefs on the appeal or cross-appeal. (See form following these rules.)

Rule 3   SANCTIONS AND EXCUSE FOR NON-COMPLI-ANCE

A failure to file the pre-argument statement in accordance with Rule 2 shall result in dismissal of the appeal or cross-appeal. However, such statement need not be filed if a settlement conference is requested and held in accordance with Rule 4.

Rule 4   INVITATION TO ATTEND SETTLEMENT CONFER-ENCE

Immediately upon the filing of the record on appeal, the clerk of this court shall mail a copy of these rules (Rules 1 to 11) to counsel of record for all parties to the appeal. In addition, he shall extend to such parties a written invitation to attend a settlement conference; such invitation may be accepted by any party by so advising the court and all other parties in writing within 10 days of filing of the record on appeal. Upon receipt of such acceptance from any party, an appellate settlement conference will be scheduled no earlier than 30 days thereafter, and written notice thereof shall be given by the clerk to all parties.

Rule 5   POSTPONEMENT OF BRIEFING

Immediately upon the receipt by this court of an acceptance of the invitation to attend settlement conference, all further proceedings, including the filing of briefs, shall be suspended until after the settlement conference has been held and until such time as any settlement negotiations engaged in subsequent to the conference are terminated. Such termination shall occur when any party informs the court and all other parties in writing of such termination; or the court may terminate negotiations on its own motion. The next brief to be filed after such termination shall be due 30 days thereafter, and the clerk shall notify all parties in writing of the termination of negotiations and of the date the next brief is due.

Rule 6   COURT ORDERED CONFERENCE

In cases wherein no party has voluntarily accepted a settlement conference pursuant to Rule 4, the Presiding Justice may at any time after filing of the pre-argument statement required by Rule 2, order the parties to attend a settlement conference at a specified time and place. Upon the making of such an order, all further proceedings shall be suspended in the manner provided in Rule 5.

Rule 7   THE SETTLEMENT CONFERENCE

A Justice of the court will preside over every settlement conference. The primary purpose of the conference will be to endeavor to resolve the differences of the parties without further legal proceedings, to the end that there may be a prompt and just disposition of the appeal. Accordingly it is mandatory that counsel for every party attend a scheduled settlement conference. Counsel are further required to bring their client or clients to such conference except where hardship or other unusual circumstance makes it impossible or impractical to do so. Counsel shall confer with their clients in advance regarding settlement and shall be prepared to negotiate a settlement, whenever reasonably possible. Counsel shall be thoroughly familiar with the case and prepared to present their contentions in detail. Where complete settlement cannot be reached, partial settlement, or even the narrowing of issues on appeal, will be sought. The Justice presiding over the conference may in his discretion continue it from time to time to allow further opportunity for negotiation and agreement.

Rule 8   CONFERENCES WITHOUT APPELLATE RECORD

Ordinarily the court will not hold a settlement conference until after the appellate record is filed. Nonetheless it is recognized that at times an excessive expense of preparation of the appellate record or other extraordinary circumstance may justify a departure from the foregoing policy. Accordingly, the Presiding Justice shall have discretion to consider and grant a written application of any party to schedule a conference at any time after filing of the notice of appeal, where a sufficient showing of hardship or other unusual justification is demonstrated. Such application shall be supported by detailed reasons, and shall be served upon all other parties.

Rule 9   EXCLUSION FROM CONFERENCE REQUIREMENT

Notwithstanding the foregoing rules, the court may on its own motion exclude any case from settlement conference consideration. A party who believes that a scheduled conference, whether court ordered or invitational, will be oppressive or otherwise unjust to him, may so inform the court in writing (with a copy to all other parties), giving detailed reasons therefor, and requesting cancellation of the conference. The court shall promptly act upon such request.

Rule 10   LATE REQUEST FOR CONFERENCE

Notwithstanding the failure of all parties to accept the invitation to attend a conference within the time required by rule 4, any party may request a conference at any later time. Such request shall be in writing and shall set forth reasons justifying the delay, and a copy thereof shall be sent to all other parties. The court shall promptly consider and act upon the request.

Rule 11 DISQUALIFICATION OF CONFERENCE JUSTICE

Any Justice who participates in any settlement conference which does not result in settlement shall not thereafter participate in any way in the consideration or disposition of the appeal on its merits.

[If the invitation to a settlement conference is declined, appellants and cross-appellants must file a Pre-Argument Settlement. Failure to do so will result in dismissal of the appeal or cross-appeal.

IN THE COURT OF APPEAL OF THE STATE OF CALIFORNIA
IN AND FOR THE THIRD APPELLATE DISTRICT

PRE-ARGUMENT STATEMENT

a. Case title and number:

b. Identification of trial court:

c. Date of judgment or order appealed from:

d. Named of judges who made the disposition or dispositions from which appeal is taken:

e. Date notice of appeal filed:

f. Name, address and telephone number of counsel for all parties to the appeal:

g. A brief description of the trial court disposition from which the appeal is taken:

h. A concise statement of the case, including a brief procedural history and all facts material to consideration of the issues presented by the appeal:

i. The issues to be raised in the briefs on the appeal or cross-appeal.

CALIFORNIA PARALEGAL'S GUIDE

Chapter 11

EXTRAORDINARY WRITS

What Is a Writ?

The word "writ" was originally applied in English law to any of various instruments in letter form issued under seal in the king's name. It is now defined by statute as an order in writing, issued in the name of the people, or of a court or judicial officer. Writs are decrees issued by a court to an inferior court, board, public officer, or person either (a) commanding him to do something, or (b) to refrain from doing what he is doing.

Certain writs were often called "prerogative" writs, since they were issued originally, in England, by exercise of the royal prerogative, that is, a right the king had because he was king. Mandamus (a writ issued by a court to command performance of a duty) was originally a high prerogative writ, but it no longer depends on prerogative or sovereign power. It has come to be considered in the nature of an action at law between the parties, and is no more than an ordinary court process which anyone may use when it is appropriate.

The writ proceeding is sometimes referred to as an action at law because the general rules as to civil practice are applicable, but it is not an action at law in the ordinary sense, and while not strictly an equitable action in the usual sense, equitable principles are applicable. (The difference between common law jurisdiction and equity jurisdiction orginated in the differing practices of English common law courts and Chancery courts, respectively. Although these differences still exist today they are not as pronounced as they were in the early English system. Mandamus, for example, is an action at law where equitable principles may be applied). Mandamus is regarded as a special proceeding of a civil nature to afford a remedy where there is not a plain, speedy, and adequate remedy in the ordinary course of law; thus the remedy is an extraordinary one.

Only the procedure on petitions for writs of mandate (or mandamus) will be outlined, but a few other writs will first be mentioned briefly.

The *writ of prohibition* (Code Civ. Proc. §1102) is concerned solely with the question of jurisdiction. The writ is issued by an appellate court only to a judicial tribunal, a lower court (or to a "corporation, board, or person exercising judicial functions"), to prohibit it from further proceedings when it does not have jurisdiction to act.

A *writ of review* (*or writ of certiorari*) (Code Civ. Proc. §1068) may be issued when an inferior tribunal, board or officer, exercising judicial functions, has exceeded its jurisdiction and there is no appeal, nor any plain, speedy, or adequate remedy at law. The higher tribunal requests the lower court to certify the record of the proceedings before them to the higher court so the higher court can look at the record to determine whether the lower court has committed an error. However, this writ has fallen into disuse, and the writ of mandate has become much more common as a means of reviewing various decisions and adjudications of various governmental agencies, boards and commissions. It is not often used in California (except to review orders or awards of Worker's Compensation Appeals Board), but is used extensively by the Supreme Court of the United States to bring up cases from the lower courts to the Supreme Court.

The primary use of a petition for a *writ of habeas corpus* is to seek release from custody of persons who are either in prison or in constructive custody. It is brought on such grounds as improper sentencing, unfair trial, not having been advised of rights, etc.

Other writs are the writ of *supersedeas* and *error coram nobis*. These are not extraordinary writs. The petition for *supersedeas* is filed to delay the operation of a process of law and may be used only in a case where an appeal is pending, to stay the execution of the judgment where irreparable damage would be done, as in a foreclosure sale. The writ of *error coram nobis* is sought where there is an error in the record, where new facts have come to light which would have changed the judgment. The petition is filed in the trial court after judgment has been rendered but no appeal taken, and if denied may be appealed. If an appeal from the judgment has been decided by the appellate court, the petition should be filed in the appellate court.

The Administrative Hearing

A few comments on the administrative adjudicatory proceeding (Administrative Procedure Act) which precedes the filing of the petition for writ of mandate are in order.

An Accusation will have been prepared for the Contractors' State License Board and personally served (or served by mail) on the contractor, together with a blank form of the Notice of Defense and a copy of Government Code sections 11507.5, 11507.6 and 11507.7 pursuant to Government Code sections 11504 and 11505. (Gov. Code §11505(c).) The respondent (contractor) must file the Notice of Defense (signed either by himself or his attorney) within 15 days after service of the Accusation. (Gov. Code §11506(a).) The filing of the Notice of Defense operates as a denial of the allegations in the Accusation and as a request for a hearing. (The respondent may also elect to file an additional Notice of Defense under Government Code section 11506(a).) A Statement to Respondent is also served on the contractor. The Statement is an "instruction" to the contractor as to what he should do.

The agency is usually represented by the office of the Attorney General.

A Notice of Hearing must be given to the respondent at least 10 days before the hearing. (Gov. Code §11509.) A continuance may be granted only for good cause shown.

The agency has the burden of proof by a preponderance of the evidence. Applicants (as for a license) do not have vested rights to a license and the burden of proof is on them. (Gov. Code §11504.) The superior court on a petition would decide only whether substantial evidence justifies denial of the license.

If the contractor wishes to assert the defense of unconstitutionality or other defense, he must do so before the board. Otherwise, a petition for mandate on that ground will not lie.

After the hearing the hearing officer will propose a decision, which may or may not be adopted by the agency as its decision. (Gov. Code §11517.)

Petition for Writ of Mandate
(Code Civ. Proc. §1084 et seq.)

In a mandate proceeding in the superior courts the parties may be designated as "plaintiff" and "defendant" (see Code Civ. Proc. §1063) although in practice usually "petitioner" and "respondent" are used. In original proceedings in the appellate courts the parties should be designated as "petitioner" and "respondent." The plaintiff (or petitioner) asks the court (must be superior court or higher court) to compel the performance of an act by an inferior tribunal, corporation, board or person which under the law it is enjoined to do; for example, to compel a professional board to restore a revoked or suspended license to a licensee.

Let us refer back to our example of a contractor's license action. The Accusation has been filed against a contractor and a hearing held before a hearing officer and the Contractors' State License Board has revoked his license. The licensee's petition for reconsideration having been denied, he files a Petition for Writ of Mandate in the superior court to prohibit the board from revoking his license and asking the court to prohibit the board from making its decision effective (i.e., decision revoking his license) until a hearing can be held.

The Petition for Writ of Mandate must be filed within the 20 days after the last day on which reconsideration can be granted (usually 30 days after the decision is mailed or the effective date of the agency's decision). (Gov. Code §11521.) If a transcript of the hearing before the board is requested, the Petition for Writ of Mandate may be filed 30 days from date of its delivery.

(The time for filing a Petition for Writ of Mandate in a non-Administrative Procedure Act proceeding varies. Other Government Code sections should be checked for deadlines on certain kinds of cases.)

Document Preparation

The documents to be prepared are:
1. Petition for Writ of Mandate, which must be verified.
   (Prepare an original and 3 copies, plus one copy for each
                                                        respondent.)
2. Memorandum of Points and Authorities in Support of Petition for Writ of Mandate.
   The originals of these two documents are filed and copies presented to the judge as the basis for his signing, first;
3. Order Granting Alternative Writ of Mandate and Directing Issuance Thereof, and
4. Alternative Writ of Mandate. In this document the court commands the board to refrain from further proceedings in the matter specified until a further order of the court is made and to show cause at a specified time and place why it should not be permanently restrained from further proceedings in the matter. (In our example, where a contractor's license has been revoked, the court would order the Contractors' State License Board to refrain from making the revocation effective, and to show cause on the specified date why it should not be permanently restrained from revoking the license.) The alternative writ of mandate may be compared to the summons in an ordinary civil case, at least to the extent that instead of allowing 30 days within which to plead to the petition, it usually sets a specified time and date (at least 10 days thereafter — Code Civ. Proc. §1088) and is on the court's calendar for that date. The case must be heard by the court, whether or not the adverse party appears.

Copies of these four documents above listed are then personally served.

(Local rules of practice should be determined. Code of Civil Procedure section 1107 requires proof of service of the petition on respondent and real party in interest, but permits the court in its discretion and for good cause to grant an application ex parte. In practice, the alternative writ is granted ex parte and service of petition and alternative writ then made. The court also has discretion to issue a peremptory writ on filing of the petition without hearing, but not unless the petition has been served.)

The respondent (or real party in interest or both) *may* serve upon the plaintiff and file with the court within five days after service of the petition, points and authorities in opposition to the writ. (Code Civ. Proc. §1107.) Such points and authorities are in the nature of a brief and do not preclude the necessity for filing a return.

On the day of the return of the alternative writ the respondent may demur or answer (verified) or both. (Code Civ. Proc. §1089.) A demurrer is usually heard in the department of the court designated in the alternative writ on the return date. If a demurrer is to be interposed it is advisable to file an answer at the same time, since in the event the demurrer is overruled, while it may grant leave to file an answer, it has discretion to issue a peremptory writ without leave to answer.

If the return contains any affirmative allegations, the petitioner must file a *Replication to the Answer* denying the allegations of ultimate fact or they will be taken as true, become admissions, evidence; allegations that are mere conclusions, however, will not be deemed admitted. (See Code Civ. Proc. §1091.)

The court has the discretion to do one of three things: (1) Hear the matter on the return date, whether or not a return is filed; (2) if a return is filed set the matter specially (because the return has priority on the calendar); or (3) permit the matter to be handled by memorandum to set in the usual manner (either one of the parties may file a memorandum to set).

The trial in the superior court is not a trial de novo. The court is confined to the evidence in the agency's record. Therefore it is important that all witnesses be called and heard at the agency level.

However, if evidence has been improperly excluded by the agency, the court may hear it, or take new evidence that could not be heard before.

The superior court's test on review is stated in *Strumsky v. San Diego County Employees' Retirement Association* (1974) 11 Cal.3d 28, 520 Pac.2d 29:

We have concluded that there no longer exists any rational or legal justification for distinguishing with regard to judicial review between on the one hand, local agencies and state agencies of local jurisdiction and, on the other, state agencies of legislative origin having statewide jurisdiction. Accordingly, we hold that the rule of judicial review applicable to adjudicatory orders or decisions of the latter class of agencies — which was reaffirmed and explained to us in *Bixby* — is also applicable to adjudicatory orders or decisions of agencies in the former class. That rule is as follows: If the order or decision of the agency substantially affects a fundamental vested right, the trial court, in determining under section 1094.5 whether there has been an abuse of discretion because the findings are not supported by the evidence, must exercise its independent judgment on the evidence and find an abuse of discretion if the findings are not supported by the weight of the evidence. If, on the *other hand, the order or decision does not substantially affect a fundamental vested right*, the trial court's inquiry will be limited to a determination of whether or not the findings are supported by substantial evidence in the light of the whole record. (11 Cal.3d at p. 32) (Emphasis added).

Not all administrative decisions are appealed to the superior courts. Workers' Compensation decisions are subject to a writ of review by the appellate courts, not a writ of mandamus. Public Utilities Commission's decisions go directly to the Supreme Court by a writ of review. State Bar disciplinary matters go directly to the Supreme Court.

Exhaustion of Administrative Remedies

Courts continue to have to deny petitions for writs of mandate because the parties have failed to exhaust their administrative remedies, though this rule has been well established in California for many years. It is well stated in *Abelleira v. District of Appeal* (1940) 17 Cal.2d 280, 109 P.2d 942: "In brief, the rule is that where an administrative remedy is provided by statute, relief must be sought from the administrative body and this remedy exhausted before the courts will act. The authorities to this effect are so numerous that only the more important ones need be cited here as illustrations. [Citations.] . . ."

If the matter is heard on the return date, either the court will announce its decision at that time or the matter will be submitted, that is, the court will take the case under consideration and announce its decision later (the court may order briefs to be filed).

As in other civil cases, Findings of Fact and Conclusions of Law are not prepared unless requested. The request for findings must be served and filed within 10 days after the court's intended decision is orally announced or mailed. The announcement may designate a party to prepare the findings, if they are requested; the party so designated has 15 days after the request to serve and file the findings. Or, the court may notify one of the parties to prepare the findings after they are requested; the party has 15 days after such notification to serve and file the findings. Otherwise, the court must prepare and mail proposed findings to all parties within 15 days after the request for findings. Objections may be served and filed within 15 days after the proposed Findings of Fact and Conclusions of Law and Judgment are served. The court may hold a hearing on the objections. (Rule 232, Cal. Rules of Court.)

If the respondent is the prevailing party, the signing of the findings and judgment ends the case, unless an appeal is taken, in which event the writ and judgment are stayed.

If the petitioner is the prevailing party, he will prepare for the court's signature a Peremptory Writ of Mandate (that is, a writ requiring the board to do what the petitioner has asked that it do) which will be in accordance with the judgment which was entered and which must be served personally upon the adverse party or parties. Proof of personal service must be made and filed. The peremptory writ may have a return date, which is not a hearing date as in the alternative writ, but a date by which a return (usually called a Return to Peremptory Writ of Mandate) must be on file with the court telling the court that it has complied with the peremptory writ, and how it has complied.

The proceeding is closed after the Return to Peremptory Writ of Mandate is filed — unless an appeal is filed.

An appeal in a mandamus action is handled in the same manner as any other appeal to the appellate court, and the same rules for filing of notices of appeal, briefs, etc., apply.

Original Proceedings in Reviewing Courts (Courts of Appeal or Supreme Court)

The petition for writ of mandate may be an original proceeding in the appellate court rather than a proceeding in the superior court. Or the original proceeding may be a petition for a writ of habeas corpus, prohibition, supersedeas or the like.

The petition filed in a reviewing court must disclose:
1. Why it is proper that the writ issue from the reviewing court; and
2. Name of real party in interest.

The original petition must be accompanied by
1. Points and authorities and

2. Proof of service on respondent and real party in interest.

Within 5 days after service and filing of the petition, the respondent or real party in interest, separately or jointly, may serve and file points and authorities in opposition and a statement of any fact not in the petition which in his opinion is material. The court may allow the filing of the petition without service and may act without requiring prior filing of opposition.

If the petition is granted, the respondent or real party in interest may make a return by demurrer, verified answer or both — 5 days before the date set for hearing (unless other date specified by court).

If the return is by way of demurrer alone, and the demurrer is not sustained, peremptory writ may issue without leave to answer. (Rule 56, Cal. Rules of Court.) (Rule 56 does not apply to applications for a writ of habeas corpus or to petitions for review pursuant to Rules 57, 58 and 59.)

Petitions for writs in the appellate courts receive a preliminary screening and are usually presented to a panel of judges in conference in chambers. Parties and counsel are not present. If an "emergency writ," that is, one in which the court must take immediate action (as where trial is scheduled to start soon), the petition will be presented forthwith. Writs of nonemergency nature are usually presented at weekly "writ conferences." The petition is discussed and considered and often a final decision is made then and there. Or, final judgment may be deferred to obtain further information. The judges may put the case on calendar for oral argument, in which event it is submitted and treated in the same manner as an appeal.

Summary of Usual Steps in Petition for Writ of Mandate Proceedings in Superior Courts

1. Prepare:
   (1) Verified PETITION FOR WRIT OF MANDATE.
   (2) MEMORANDUM OF POINTS AND AUTHORITIES IN SUPPORT OF PETITION FOR WRIT OF MANDATE.
   (3) ORDER GRANTING ALTERNATIVE WRIT OF MANDATE AND DIRECTING ISSUANCE THEREOF.
   (4) ALTERNATIVE WRIT OF MANDATE.
2. File original PETITION FOR WRIT OF MANDATE and MEMORANDUM OF POINTS AND AUTHORITIES IN SUPPORT OF PETITION FOR WRIT OF MANDATE and have the Alternative Writ of Mandate issued.
3. Serve conformed copies of each of the documents listed in 1 above.

4. Adverse parties should serve and file a return (either a DEMUR-RER TO PETITION FOR WRIT OF MANDATE or a verified ANSWER TO PETITION FOR WRIT OF MANDATE, or both). The return may be filed at the time of hearing. The defendant-respondent (or real party in interest) *may* serve upon the plaintiff and file with the court within 5 days after service MEMORAN-DUM OF POINTS AND AUTHORITIES IN OPPOSITION TO THE PETITION FOR WRIT OF MANDATE. (Code Civ. Proc. §1107.)

5. If the answer contains any affirmative allegations, the petitioner should serve and file a REPLICATION to the answer, denying any untrue allegations.

6. The original ALTERNATIVE WRIT OF MANDATE with proof of service of the alternative writ, the order granting the alternative writ, the petition for the writ, and the points and authorities, should be filed before the return date.

7. Hearing is held. (Judge may or may not order briefs to be filed thereafter.)

8. Court announces its decision or forthwith mails to all parties a copy of the minute entry or written statement of intended decision. The announcement may state whether written findings of fact and conclusions of law, if requested, shall be prepared by the court or a designated party. (Rule 232(a), Cal. Rules of Court.)

9. Findings of fact are advisable. If findings of fact are desired, request must be served and filed within 10 days after the oral announcement of intended decision in open court, or within 10 days of mailing of announcement of intended decision.

10. If findings are requested, within 15 days after such request, court will prepare and mail proposed findings and conclusions to all parties, unless the court has designated a party to prepare the findings. Or the court may, after findings are requested, within 5 days notify counsel for any party to prepare the findings.

11. Party designated to prepare findings (under Rule 232(a)), must serve and file findings within 15 days after request for findings served and filed.

12. Party notified to prepare findings after request was made, must serve and file findings within 15 days after such notice.

13. Any party may object to proposed findings, conclusions or judgment within 15 days after service on him, and may include proposed counterfindings and conclusions. (Rule 232(d).)

14. FINDINGS OF FACT AND CONCLUSIONS OF LAW and JUDGMENT are signed by the judge and filed. (See Rule 232(h), Cal. Rules of Court.)

....

If plaintiff prevails:

11. Prepare a PEREMPTORY WRIT OF MANDATE. The peremptory writ usually (but need not) contains a date by which a return to the peremptory writ must be filed. Have the judge sign the peremptory writ.

12. Serve a copy of the PEREMPTORY WRIT OF MANDATE on the defendant or defendants, *personally*.

13. After the defendant has complied with the peremptory writ, a RETURN TO PEREMPTORY WRIT OF MANDATE is filed showing such compliance. (Attach a certified copy of any new Order and Decision of the administrative board involved to the original return.)

CASE IS CLOSED (unless appeal taken).

On the following pages are most of the forms mentioned in the foregoing Summary. These are intended not as model forms but as samples to make the discussion of the procedure more meaningful. All names and addresses are fictional.

1 | HARRY FORBES, Attorney General
   | of the State of California
2 | WILLIAM A. BADE, Deputy Attorney General
   | 555 Sunset Mall
3 | Sacramento, CA 95814
   | Telephone: (916) 445-5555
4 |
   | Attorneys for Complainant
5 |

6 |

7 |

8 | BEFORE THE REGISTRAR OF CONTRACTORS

9 | CONTRACTORS' STATE LICENSE BOARD

10 | DEPARTMENT OF CONSUMER AFFAIRS

11 | STATE OF CALIFORNIA

12 |

13 | In the Matter of the Accusation   )   NO. 13000
   | Against:)
14 |)
   | ROBERT PHELPS   )   ACCUSATION
15 | License No. 24689, Class B)
   | 1234 Massee Lane   )
16 | Elk Grove, California,   )
   |)
17 | Respondent.   )
   | _____)
18 |

19 | IVAN HINKLE, for causes for disciplinary action,

20 | alleges:

21 | I

22 | Complainant Ivan Hinkle makes this Accusation in his

23 | official capacity as Senior Deputy Registrar of Contractors,

24 | Contractors State License Board, Department of Consumer Affairs,

25 | State of California, and not otherwise.

26 | II

27 | On July 28, 1967, Robert Phelps was issued license

28 | number 24689 in classification B by the Registrar of Contractors.

1

1   Said license was in full force and effect at all times pertinent

2   hereto and has been renewed through August 1, 1976.

3   III

4   Business and Professions Code section 7090 provides

5   that the Registrar of Contractors may revoke or suspend the

6   license of any licensee who is guilty of or commits any one or

7   more of the acts or omissions constituting cause for disciplinary

8   action.

9   Business and Professions Code sections 118(b) and

10   7106.5 provide that the expiration or suspension of a license

11   by operation of law or by order or decision of the Registrar

12   shall not deprive the Registrar of jurisdiction to proceed with

13   disciplinary action against the licensee.

14   IV

15   On or about February 1, 1976, respondent Robert Phelps

16   entered into a written contract with Mr. and Mrs. Arthur Smith,

17   whereby he undertook to furnish all labor and material to furnish

18   a dwelling at 5678 Winding Way, Carmichael, for a contract price

19   of $40,000. Respondent Robert Phelps has been paid in full by

20   funds disbursed by Capitol Federal Savings and Loan Association

21   of Sacramento.

22   V

23   Respondent Robert Phelps has subjected his license to

24   disciplinary action under Business and Professions Code section

25   7109 in that he departed from or disregarded accepted trade

26   standards for good and workmanlike construction in material

27   respects on the Smith project without the owners' consent in

28   the following manner:

1. Failed to construct the floors in such a manner that they would not have creaks and squeaks in the vinyl covered areas in front of the kitchen sink, by the kitchen range, and by the hall-kitchen entrances.

2. Failed to properly grade the property and construct the project so that exterior surface would drain from the area in front of the garage and sidewalk.

VI

Respondent Robert Phelps has subjected his license to disciplinary action under Business and Professions Code section 7113 in that owners will be required to spend approximately $2,000 over the contract price which has already been paid to respondent Robert Phelps in full, in order to complete the Smith project in accordance with the terms of the contract.

VII

Respondent Robert Phelps has subjected his license to disciplinary action under Business and Professions Code section 7115 in that he failed, neglected or refused to give to the Smiths at any time during performance under the contract those notices required by sections 7018 and 7019, thereby violating those sections.

WHEREFORE, Complainant prays a hearing be had and if the allegations set forth above, or any of them, are found to be true, the Registrar of Contractors revoked or suspend license number 24689 issued to Robert Phelps; or take such other action as may be appropriate.

DATED:

IVAN HINKLE, Senior Deputy Registrar
Contractors' State License Board
Department of Consumer Affairs
Complainant

3

1
2
3

                              BEFORE THE
                        REGISTRAR OF CONTRACTORS
                    CONTRACTORS' STATE LICENSE BOARD
                          STATE OF CALIFORNIA

4   In the Matter of the Accusation   )   NO. 13000
     Against:)
5   )
             ROBERT PHELPS,   )   STATEMENT TO
6   )   RESPONDENT
                   Respondent.   )
7   _____)

8

9   TO THE RESPONDENT ABOVE-NAMED:

10   There is attached hereto a copy of an Accusation which
     has been filed with the office of the State agency named herein
11   and which is hereby served upon you.

12   Unless a written request for a hearing signed by you or
     on your behalf is delivered or mailed to the Agency named herein
13   within fifteen (15) days after a copy of the Accusation was
     personally served on you or mailed to you, you will be deemed to
14   have waived your right to a hearing in this matter and the
     CONTRACTORS' STATE LICENSE BOARD, DEPARTMENT OF CONSUMER AFFAIRS,
15   may proceed upon the Accusation without a hearing and may take
     action thereon as provided by law.
16
             The request for a hearing may be made by delivering or
17   mailing one of the enclosed forms entitled "Notice of Defense" or
     by delivering or mailing a Notice of Defense as provided in
18   section 11506 of the Government Code to: William A. Bade,
     Deputy Attorney General, 555 Sunset Mall, Sacramento, California
19   95814.

20   The hearing may be postponed for good cause. If you
     have good cause, you are obliged to notify the agency within 10
21   working days after you discover the good cause. Failure to
     notify the agency within 10 days will deprive you of a postpone-
22   ment.

23   You may, but need not, be represented by counsel at any
     or all stages of these proceedings. The enclosed Notice of
24   Defense, if signed and filed with the above-designated agency
     shall be deemed a specific denial of all parts of the Accusation,
25   but you will not be permitted to raise any objection to the form
     of the Accusation unless you file a further Notice of Defense as
26   provided in section 11506 of the Government Code within fifteen
     (15) days after service of the Accusation upon you.
27
             If you file any Notice of Defense within the time
28   permitted, a hearing will be had upon the charges made in the
     Accusation.

                              -1-

1   Copies of sections 11507.5, 11507.6 and 11507.7 of the Government Code are attached.

2

3   If you desire the names and addresses of witnesses or an opportunity to inspect and copy the items mentioned in section 11507.6 of the Government Code in possession, custody or control

4   of the agency, you may contact: WILLIAM A. BADE, Deputy Attorney General, 555 Sunset Mall, Sacramento, California 95814.

5

6

7

8

9

10

11   [Attachment: copy of sections enumerated above]

12

13

14

15

16

17

18

19

20

21

22

23

24

25

26

27

28

```
1                            BEFORE THE
                        REGISTRAR OF CONTRACTORS
2                   CONTRACTORS' STATE LICENSE BOARD
                    DEPARTMENT OF CONSUMER AFFAIRS
3                        STATE OF CALIFORNIA

4     In the Matter of the Accusation  )        NO. 13000
                                       )
5     Against:                         )        NOTICE OF DEFENSE
                                       )
6          ROBERT PHELPS,              )        (Pursuant to sections
                                       )        11505 and 11506,
7                   Respondent(s).     )        Government Code)
                                       )
8     _____)
```

9   I, the undersigned, the respondent named in the above-
entitled proceeding, hereby acknowledge receipt of a copy of the
10   Accusation, Statement to Respondent, Government Code sections
11507.5, 11507.6 and 11507.7, and two copies of a Notice of
11   Defense.

12   I hereby request a hearing in said proceeding to permit
me to present my defense to the charges contained in said
13   Accusation.

14   DATED:_____.

15

16

17   _____
                                    Respondent

18   Mailing Address of Respondent:

19

20   _____
                                (Street Address)

21

22   _____
           (City)   (State) (Zip Code)

23   Please indicate whether or not you intend to be represented by counsel. If you intend to have counsel, state his name,
24   address and telephone number.

25   The agency taking the action described in the Accusation
may have formulated guidelines to assist the administrative law
26   judge in reaching an appropriate penalty. You may obtain a copy
of such guidelines by requesting them from the agency in
27   writing.

28

```
1   ALBERT SIMPSON
    1234 Arden Way
2   Sacramento, CA 95825
    123-4567
3
    Attorney for Petitioner
4

5

6

7

8            SUPERIOR COURT OF THE STATE OF CALIFORNIA

9                    COUNTY OF SACRAMENTO

10

11  ROBERT PHELPS,              )      NO. 232582
                                )
12           Petitioner,        )
                                )
13      v.                      )      PETITION FOR WRIT OF
                                )
14  CONTRACTORS' STATE LICENSE  )          MANDATE
    BOARD, STATE OF CALIFORNIA, )
15                              )
             Respondent.        )
16  _____)

17

18          Petitioner, ROBERT PHELPS, hereby petitions this Court

19  for a Writ of Mandate under Code of Civil Procedure section

20  1094.5 directed to Respondent, CONTRACTORS' STATE LICENSE BOARD,

21  DEPARTMENT OF CONSUMER AFFAIRS, STATE OF CALIFORNIA, and by this

22  verified petition represents that:

23                              I

24          Petitioner, at all times mentioned in this petition, has

25  been and now is licensed as a contractor holding a B-1 Con-

26  tractor's license, under a license issued by Respondent, and

27  has engaged in the business of a licensed contractor in the

28  County of Sacramento.

                                1
```

II

At all times mentioned in this petition, respondent has been and now is the agency charged with administering the provisions of the State Contractor's License Law, California Business and Professions Code, section 7000, et seq. The presiding officer of the respondent agency is Tom Talleyrand.

III

An accusation was filed against petitioner pursuant to Government Code section 11503 alleging that petitioner had violated the Business and Professions Code, sections 7018, 7019, 7109, 7113, and 7115, and alleging the existence of cause for disciplinary action against petitioner under said sections. The accusation was served on petitioner and petitioner filed a Notice of Defense with respondent. A hearing was held in Sacramento County before a Hearing Officer, who then rendered his proposed decision. On November 7, 1976, respondent adopted that Decision as its own, making the Decision effective on December 7, 1976. Thereafter respondent mailed its Decision to petitioner; a true copy of the Decision is attached hereto and marked Exhibit A.

Thereafter petitioner moved the Court for reconsideration and the Court granted a stay in this matter, which stay terminates on January 2, 1977. Motion for reconsideration has been denied.

IV

The findings of the respondent's Decision, Exhibit A, are not supported by the weight of the evidence in that it was established at the hearing that the alleged defects did not exist and that petitioner built the homes according to the plans and

2

1 specifications provided to him. The specific findings that are

2 without evidence are set forth in the Petition for Reconsidera-

3 tion, which is attached hereto, marked Exhibit B, and incorporated

4 herein by this reference, and the Court is directed to the peti-

5 tion for the specific facts.

6   V

7   Petitioner has exhausted the available administrative

8 remedies required to be pursued by him.

9   VI

10   Petitioner does not have a plain, speedy and adequate

11 remedy in the ordinary course of law.

12   WHEREFORE, petitioner prays that:

13   1. An alternative writ of mandate be issued, ex parte,

14 and

15   2. An ex parte order be issued staying respondent's

16 Decision and ordering respondent to show cause why an order

17 should not be granted further staying that Decision; and

18   3. A Peremptory Writ of Mandate be issued ordering

19 respondent to set aside its Decision; and

20   4. Petitioner recover his costs in this action; and

21   5. Other relief be granted that the Court considers

22 proper.

23   DATED: December 27, 1976.

24

25 ROBERT PHELPS   ALBERT SIMPSON

26

27 [Add Verification]

28 [Attach Exhibits A and B]

                                    3

```
 1   ALBERT SIMPSON
     1234 Arden Way
 2   Sacramento, CA 95825
     123-4567
 3
     Attorney for Petitioner
 4

 5

 6

 7

 8              SUPERIOR COURT OF THE STATE OF CALIFORNIA

 9                       COUNTY OF SACRAMENTO

10

11   ROBERT PHELPS,              )          NO. 232582
                                 )
12            Petitioner,        )
                                 )
13        v.                     )      ORDER DIRECTING ISSUANCE OF
                                 )      ALTERNATIVE WRIT OF MANDATE
14   CONTRACTORS' STATE LICENSE  )            AND STAY ORDER
     BOARD, STATE OF CALIFORNIA, )      _____
15                               )
              Respondent.        )
16   _____)

17

18            GOOD CAUSE appearing from the verified petition for a

19   writ of mandate on file in this action,

20            IT IS ORDERED that an alternative writ of mandate

21   issue under the seal of this Court commanding the Contractors'

22   State License Board, respondent in this action, immediately after

23   receipt of the alternative writ of mandate, to set aside its

24   decision dated November 7, 1976, in the administrative proceed-

25   ings entitled "In the Matter of the Accusation Against Robert

26   Phelps, general contractors' license number 24689," or in the

27   alternative to show cause before this Court at a specified time

28   and place why it has not done so.
```

                              1

1   IT IS FURTHER ORDERED that the Contractors' State
2 License Board, respondent in this action, stay the operation of
3 its Decision pending the hearing on the alternative writ.
4   IT IS FURTHER ORDERED that a copy of this order, the
5 alternative writ of mandate and a copy of the petition for the
6 peremptory writ, and any supporting points and authorities be
7 served on respondent at least _____ days prior to the hearing on
8 the alternative writ.
9   Dated:_____.
10
11   _____
12   Judge of the Superior Court
13
14
15
16
17
18
19
20
21
22
23
24
25
26
27
28

                    2

```
 1   ALBERT SIMPSON
     1234 Arden Way
 2   Sacramento, CA 95825
     123-4567
 3
     Attorney for Petitioner
 4

 5

 6

 7

 8              SUPERIOR COURT OF THE STATE OF CALIFORNIA

 9                      COUNTY OF SACRAMENTO

10

11   ROBERT PHELPS,            )        NO. 232582
                               )
12           Petitioner,       )   ALTERNATIVE WRIT OF MANDATE
                               )
13           v.                )
                               )
14   CONTRACTORS' STATE LICENSE )
     BOARD, STATE OF CALIFORNIA,)
15                             )
             Respondent.       )
16   _____)

17   THE PEOPLE OF THE STATE OF CALIFORNIA:

18           To Contractors' State License Board, Respondent:

19           Good cause appearing from the verified petition for a

20   writ of mandate on file in this action,

21           YOU ARE HEREBY COMMANDED, immediately upon receipt of

22   this writ, to set aside your Decision dated November 7, 1976, in

23   the proceeding entitled "In the Matter of the Accusation Against

24   Robert Phelps, general contractors' license number 24689,"; or

25           IN THE ALTERNATIVE, to show cause before this Court on

26   _____ or as soon thereafter as counsel can

27   be heard, at the Law and Motion Department at the Courthouse,

28   City of Sacramento, California, why you have not done so, and

                                 1
```

1 whether or not the stay order heretofore issued should remain

2 in effect further staying that Decision until the matter may be

3 finally adjudicated.

4   Dated:_____.

5

6   _____, Clerk

7   By_____. Deputy Clerk

8

9

10

11

12

13

14

15

16

17

18

19

20

21

22

23

24

25

26

27

28

2

```
 1  HARRY FORBES, Attorney General
       of the State of California
 2  WILLIAM A. BADE, Deputy Attorney General
    555 Sunset Mall
 3  Sacramento, CA 95814
    Telephone:  (916) 445-5555
 4
    Attorneys for Respondent
 5

 6

 7

 8          SUPERIOR COURT OF THE STATE OF CALIFORNIA

 9                  COUNTY OF SACRAMENTO

10

11  ROBERT PHELPS,              )        NO. 232582
                                )
12            Petitioner,       )
                                )
13      v.                      )        ANSWER TO PETITION
                                )        FOR WRIT OF MANDATE
14  CONTRACTORS' STATE LICENSE  )
    BOARD, STATE OF CALIFORNIA, )
15                              )
              Respondent.       )
16  _____)

17

18          Respondent Contractors' State License Board makes a

19  return to the alternative writ and answers the petition for writ

20  of mandate filed in this action, and admits, denies and alleges

21  as follows:

22          1.  Admits each and every allegation in paragraphs I,

23  II, III, V and VI of the petition.

24          2.  Denies each and every allegation in paragraph IV

25  of the petition.

26          WHEREFORE, respondent prays that this Court:

27          1.  Deny the petition for writ of mandate.

28          2.  Discharge the alternative writ of mandate
                            1
```

1 heretofore issued.

2   3. Grant respondent its costs and such other relief

3 as may be appropriate.

4   Dated:_____, 1976.

5

6   HARRY FORBES, Attorney General
                          of the State of California
7   WILLIAM A. BADE, Deputy Attorney General

8   _____

9   WILLIAM A. BADE, Deputy Attorney General

10   Attorneys for Respondent

11

12

13

14

15

16

17

18

19

20

21

22

23

24

25

26

27

28

                                2

```
1   ALBERT SIMPSON
    1234 Arden Way
2   Sacramento, CA 95825
    123-4567
3
    Attorney for Petitioner
4

5

6

7

8              SUPERIOR COURT OF THE STATE OF CALIFORNIA

9                     COUNTY OF SACRAMENTO

10

11  ROBERT PHELPS,              )         NO. 232582
                                )
12              Petitioner,     )
                                )
13       v.                     )  JUDGMENT GRANTING PEREMPTORY
                                )
14  CONTRACTORS' STATE LICENSE  )       WRIT OF MANDATE
    BOARD, STATE OF CALIFORNIA, )
15                              )
                Respondent.     )
16  _____)

17

18          This matter came regularly before this Court on

19  January 25, 1977, for hearing.  Albert Simpson appeared as

20  attorney for petitioner and Bruce D. Benson appeared as attorney

21  for respondent.  The record of the administrative proceedings

22  having been received into evidence and examined by the Court, no

23  additional evidence having been received by the Court, arguments

24  having been presented, and the Court having made findings of

25  fact and conclusions of law, which have been signed and filed,

26          IT IS ORDERED that:

27          1.  A peremptory writ of mandamus shall issue from

28  this Court, remanding the proceedings to respondent and commanding
                                 1
```

respondent to set aside its decision dated November 7, 1976, in
the administrative proceedings entitled "In the Matter of the
Accusation Against Robert Phelps, general contractors' license
number 24689," and to reconsider its action in the light of this
Court's findings of fact and conclusions of law, and to take any
further action specially enjoined upon it by law.

      2. Petitioner shall recover his costs in this action,
in the amount of $_____.

      Dated:_____.

_____
Judge of the Superior Court

2

1

2

3

4

5

6

7

8   SUPERIOR COURT OF THE STATE OF CALIFORNIA

9   COUNTY OF SACRAMENTO

10

11 ROBERT PHELPS,   )   NO. 232582
)
12   Petitioner,   )
)
13   v.   )   PEREMPTORY WRIT OF MANDATE
)
14 CONTRACTORS' STATE LICENSE)
    BOARD, STATE OF CALIFORNIA,)
15   )
              Respondent.   )
16 _____)

17 THE PEOPLE OF THE STATE OF CALIFORNIA SEND GREETING:

18 TO: CONTRACTORS' STATE LICENSE BOARD OF THE STATE OF CALIFORNIA:

19   Judgment having been entered in this action, ordering

20 that a peremptory writ of mandate be issued from this Court,

21   YOU ARE HEREBY COMMANDED immediately on receipt of this

22 writ to set aside your Decision dated November 7, 1976, in the

23 administrative proceedings entitled "In the Matter of the

24 Accusation of Robert Phelps, General Contractor's License No.

25 24689," which proceedings are hereby remanded to you, and to

26 reconsider your action in the light of this Court's findings of

27 fact and conclusions of law, and to take any further action

28 specially enjoined upon you by law; but nothing in this writ

                                    1

1 shall limit or control in any way the discretion legally vested

2 in you; and

3   YOU ARE FURTHER COMMANDED to make and file a return to

4 this writ on or before _____, setting forth what you

5 have done to comply.

6   _____Clerk

7

8   By_____Deputy Clerk

9

10

11

12

13

14

15

16

17

18

19

20

21

22

23

24

25

26

27

28

2

```
 1 ║ HARRY FORBES, Attorney General
   ║    of the State of California
 2 ║ WILLIAM A. BADE, Deputy Attorney General
   ║ 555 Sunset Mall
 3 ║ Sacramento, CA 95814
   ║ Telephone:  (916) 445-5555
 4 ║
   ║ Attorneys for Respondent
 5 ║
 6 ║
 7 ║
 8 ║           SUPERIOR COURT OF THE STATE OF CALIFORNIA
 9 ║                    COUNTY OF SACRAMENTO
10 ║
11 ║ ROBERT PHELPS,              )          NO. 232582
   ║                             )
12 ║        Petitioner,          )
   ║                             )
13 ║   v.                        ) RETURN TO PEREMPTORY WRIT OF
   ║                             )
14 ║ CONTRACTORS' STATE LICENSE  )          MANDATE
   ║ BOARD, STATE OF CALIFORNIA, )
15 ║                             )
   ║        Respondent.          )
16 ║ _____)
17 ║ TO THE ABOVE-ENTITLED COURT:
18 ║           Respondent Contractors' State License Board by Tom
19 ║ Talleyrand, Registrar of Contractors, makes the following return
20 ║ to the Peremptory Writ of Mandate issued in this action.
21 ║           On the _____ day of _____, 1977, respondent
22 ║ issued its order setting aside the Decision dated November 7,
23 ║ 1976, and after reconsidering the case in the light of the court's
24 ║ judgment, issued a new decision in the administrative proceed-
25 ║ ings, substituting for the penalty imposed by its November 7,
26 ║ 1976, decision the following penalty:
27 ║           Suspension for a period of four months of license
28 ║ 24689, issued to Robert Phelps.  A true copy of that decision
   ║                              1
```

1   is attached hereto as Exhibit A.

2   Dated this _____ day of _____, 1977.

3

4   HARRY FORBES, Attorney General
                         of the State of California
5   JACK JOHNSON, Deputy Attorney General

6

7   By_____

8   Attorney for Respondent

9

10

11

12

13

14

15

16

17

18

19

20

21

22

23

24

25

26

27

28

                              2

Chapter 12

PREPARATION OF BRIEFS

The lawyers should decide on the best general approach, method of presentation and issues to be emphasized. Following orientation discussions with the assistant, they can delegate substantial portions of the factual and legal research and writing. . . . An assistant can also perform much of any necessary independent legal research under the lawyer's supervision concerning either issues not previously presented or issues that need to be reconsidered or expanded.*

A number of reference books which discuss legal research retrieval systems are listed in the ABA book (see footnote); it also features a bibliography of literature which lists books on how to write a good brief, writing style and appellate oral argument. In this book, chapter 13, Legal Writing, deals with writing the effective appellate brief.

The legal assistant also needs to know the essentials in the material following, which deals with the format, style and other requirements of briefs.

THE BRIEF

What is a brief? A brief is the *written* argument of the attorney. The main purpose of the brief, after setting out for the court the facts and legal issues, is to present the attorney's interpretation of the law, supported by pertinent authorities — cases, statutes, and texts — and quotations therefrom.

Briefs may be divided for our purposes into two main types: 1. the trial court brief; 2. the appellate brief.

1. *The trial court brief:* Briefs are usually filed in the trial court after a hearing or after the trial when the judge orders that briefs be filed. If an attorney returns from court and asks you to make a docket entry "Submitted on briefs 30-30-15," he would mean that the plaintiff

---

*Working with Legal Assistants, American Bar Association publication.

is to file an opening brief within 30 days from the date of the appearance in court, the defendant is to file a reply brief within 30 days after filing of the plaintiff's brief, and the plaintiff is to file a closing brief within 15 days after receipt of the defendant's reply brief. Sometimes an attorney on his own volition will file a "trial brief" at the time of the trial.

One copy of the trial court brief is served on the opposing counsel as any other pleading, and the original is sent to the judge who heard the case, and afterward filed.

Trial court briefs are now typed on 28-line paper and double-spaced. Quotations may be single-spaced, but double spacing is preferable.

A topical index and table of authorities cited, separately listed cases, statutes, court rules, constitutional provisions, and other authorities, are required.

2. *Appellate brief:* The appeal brief is filed in the appellate courts — the Courts of Appeal, the Supreme Court of the State of California, or the federal courts. (In our discussion here we do not include briefs in the federal courts.)

a. *Parties:* The party who appeals — the party who "lost" in the trial Court — is called the "appellant." He may, of course, be either the plaintiff or defendant in the trial court. The responding party — again either plaintiff or defendant — is called the "respondent." Usually they are designated as in the following example but the titles can be more complex (see California Style Manual, §§194, *et seq.*):

John Jones, _____ Plaintiff and Respondent,
v. Jane Doe, _____ Defendant and Appellant.

In the text of the briefs it is preferable to use the trial court terminology in referring to the parties, *i.e.*, "plaintiff" and "defendant."

For other rules as to style and titles of cases in the Courts of Appeal and Supreme Court of California, see California Style Manual: A Handbook of Legal Style for California Courts and Lawyers (Second Edition), by Robert Formichi, Reporter of Decisions, for sale by the Printing Division, Documents Section, State of California, N. 7th and Richards Blvd., Sacramento 95814.

Any petition or petition for rehearing filed in the courts of appeal, or petition for hearing filed in the Supreme Court, is set up in the same manner as a brief.

Appellate Briefs and Opinions

The format of original petitions or petitions for rehearing filed in the Courts of Appeal and of petitions for hearing in the Supreme Court of California is the same as for briefs.

Briefs, if they do not exceed 50 pages in length, may be either printed or prepared by other duplication process such as mimeograph, ditto, photocopy, etc. If the briefs do exceed 50 pages they must be printed unless special permission to file a typewritten brief or to prepare by other duplication process is obtained, either from the Chief Justice of the Supreme Court if filing in the California Supreme Court, or from the Presiding Justice of the Court of Appeal in which the brief is to be filed. (See Rules 15(b) (c), Cal. Rules of Court.)

Reasons given for requesting a typewritten brief might include poverty of clients, length of brief (*i.e.*, short), insufficient time to get the brief printed.

Exclude tables and index in counting the total number of pages. When filing in the Supreme Court of California, exclude opinion of Court of Appeal in counting total number of pages in a petition for hearing. (Rule 15(b), Cal. Rules of Court.)

One copy is served on each opposing counsel. One copy is deposited with the clerk of the superior court for delivery to the judge who presided at the trial of the case. Proof of such service and deposit must be made before the brief may be filed. (Usually the copy for the trial court judge is mailed to the county clerk with a short covering letter requesting that he hand it to the judge, and such service by mail is shown in the proof of service.)

DECLARATION OF SERVICE BY MAIL

I, _____, declare as follows:

I am a citizen of the United States and [a resident of *or* am employed in] _____ County, State of California, over the age of eighteen years, and not a party to the within action; my business address is _____.

On _____, _____, I served the foregoing _____ by depositing a true and correct copy thereof in an envelope addressed to each of the persons named below at the address set out immediately below each respective name, and by sealing and depositing said envelopes in the United States mail at _____, California, with postage thereon fully prepaid:

[*If criminal case, show service on District Attorney.*]

That on said date declarant also mailed by first-class mail, postage thereon fully prepaid, a true and correct copy of said _____ to the County Clerk in and for the County of _____, State of California, and ex officio Clerk of the Judge who presided at this matter in the lower court, addressed as follows:

[In civil cases, include the following paragraph:]

That on said date I caused _____ copies of the above named document to be deposited with the Clerk of the Supreme Court of the State of California.

[Paragraph below to be included when filing a petition for hearing, or answer to petition, in the Supreme Court, after decision by the Court of Appeal:]

That on said date I caused a copy of the above-named document to be deposited with the Clerk of the Court of Appeal of the State of California in and for the _____ Appellate District, Division _____.

There is delivery service by United States mail at each of the places so addressed, or there is regular communication by mail between the place of mailing and each of the places so addressed.

I declare under penalty of perjury that the foregoing is correct.

Executed on _____, at _____, California.

Attorney for _____

*Attach additional sheets if there is insufficient space provided on this form.

[Form for proof of service for briefs filed in the Supreme Court and Courts of Appeal. An affidavit of service may be used instead of a declaration. Most law offices will have forms on hand.]

Form of briefs not printed (typewritten or other process of duplication); (Rules 9(b), 15(c), (d)):

1. Briefs are prepared on paper not less than 13-pound weight, size 8½ × 11 inches.
2. Briefs are double-spaced (or 1½ spaced).
3. The headings should be capitalized or underscored, or both.
4. Quotations are indented.
5. Margins: 1¼ inches on left-hand side of page.
               1 inch on top and bottom of page.
               ½ inch on right-hand side of page.
6. The left-hand side of the brief is bound.

If stapled, the bound edge and the staples shall be covered with tape.

7. A cover is prepared (whether printed or typewritten) containing:

a. The title of the case
b. The name of the trial judge and county
c. The designation of the brief (e.g., Appellant's Opening Brief)
d. The name and address of the attorney filing the brief.

(The cover for a printed brief is typed on the same paper used to prepare the draft for the printer. Covers for typewritten briefs are called "manuscript covers" and purchased from stationery stores; the covers are a little heavier, to protect the other pages of the brief, and are usually blue, brown or gray. (Rule 15(b) (4).)

First page: The first page is headed by the title of the court and the cause the same as on the cover. The title of the document appears below the title of the cause and then the text of the brief commences. The number of the case also appears. (On a petition for hearing in the Supreme Court of California after hearing in the Court of Appeal, the petition and answer do not bear a number (except the Court of Appeal number on the cover), since a number is not assigned unless a hearing is granted.)

Topical Index: Briefs filed in the appellate courts must contain a topical index, prepared by listing the headings in the brief and the page numbers on which the headings appear. The Topical Index follows the cover page and is usually numbered in small Roman numeral (as i, ii, iii, etc.). An index might look like this one:

TOPICAL INDEX

NUMBER OF COPIES:

Printed, Typewritten or Other
Duplication Process

Number of copies for filing

*Proceedings in Supreme Court
(whether original proceeding or
after decision in Court of Appeal)*

All petitions, petitions for re-hearing, replies to petitions	File original and 14 copies. (Rule 44(b), California Rules of Court.)
Briefs	Original and 10 copies. (Rule 44(b).)
Motions, notices of motions, oppositions or response	Original and 7 copies. (Rule 44(b).)
Any other document or paper	Original and 1 copy. (Rule 44(b).)

Proceedings in Courts of Appeal

All petitions, answers, opposition or other response to a petition	Original and 3 copies. (Rule 44(b).)
Briefs	Original and 3 copies, and, in civil actions, proof of delivery of 7 copies to Supreme Court. (Rule 44(b).)
Motions, notices of motions, opposition or response	Original and 3 copies. (Rule 44(b).)
Any other document or paper	Original and 1 copy. (Rule 44(b).)

When any motion other than a motion to dismiss appeal is filed prior to the filing of the record on appeal, it shall be accompanied by such affidavits or other evidence in support of the motion as deemed necessary by the moving party. (Rule 42(b).)

Table of Authorities Cited: This table follows the Topical Index and is likewise numbered with small Roman numerals, continuing on from the last page number of the index (*i.e.*, the Topical Index might constitute pages i and ii and the Table of Authorities Cited pages iii and iv). This table may be divided into different categories, as Cases, Statutes, (or California Statutes and Federal Statutes), Codes, Texts, and Miscellaneous. An example follows:

TABLE OF AUTHORITIES CITED

CASES Page

STATUTES

TEXTS

Miscellany re Briefs

This section on ''Miscellany re briefs'' may be viewed as having no place in a paralegal book; it may seem elementary to some. However some of our readers will be beginners in the legal field. The attorney and/or the legal assistant are the ones responsible for the brief so they must be prepared to observe and correct errors. Occasionally, for example, secretarial errors will be made. Ideally, the correction of clerical errors should be left to the secretary. But the author's observations have been that attorneys do concern themselves with many such things. And if that be true of attorneys, then the paralegal too must do so. In this field, precision is essential.

None of the following rules are found in the statutes. None are absolutes. Many are subject to question, and where do you look for the final arbiter? The attorney — right or wrong — unless he or she can be dissuaded.

In the appellate courts the Reporter of Decisions is the final arbiter of the published decisions. And it is on the California Style Manual,

A Handbook of Legal Styles for California Courts and Lawyers, by Robert Formichi, Reporter of Decisions, that some at least of the following is based. A copy of this book is available from the State Document Section.

The brief should meet all the rules set forth in the foregoing section and be in the best presentable style. Otherwise, no matter how brilliant and scintillating the legal arguments, its appearance can detract.

1. INFRA, SUPRA

Whenever a case name is repeated in the same work, the word *"supra"* should follow the name of the case. The word *"supra"* may be used in lieu of repeating the citation; however, some authorities say that the citation should be repeated unless the case was previously cited in the same paragraph. *"Infra"* is used to denote that the citation of the case is to be found on a subsequent page.

2. QUOTATIONS

a. *Checking:* Quotations should be copied directly from the source book if possible, and carefully checked.

b. *Quotes within quotes:* In copying from a book, the quotation mark is added at the beginning of each paragraph. After quotation marks are once added, the opposite quotation mark from the one that appears in the book may be used, *i.e.*, if a single quote, a double quote, and vice versa. For example: Quotation as it appears in book:

In *Abels v. Frey*, 126 Cal.App. 48, . . . the court said: "By giving the notice prescribed by the statute, . . . ' "subject only to being reversed, set aside, or modified on appeal." ' " In copying this citation it would appear:

"In *Abels v. Frey*, 126 Cal.App. 48, . . . the court said: 'By giving the notice prescribed by the statute, . . . " 'subject only to being reversed, set aside, or modified on appeal.' " ' "

c. *Emphasis:* Words appearing in italics in a book should be underscored in typing. If the emphasis is the attorney's, the words "Emphasis added" or "Emphasis ours" in parentheses are used to indicate that the emphasis is his, *e.g.*: "Neither can the State in its own person, nor as represented in its local subordinate governments, be summoned to answer before its courts, *nor can its property*." (Emphasis ours.) (*People v. Doe*, 36 Cal. 220, 223.) [220 is the number of the page on which the case commences; 223 refers to the page on which the quotation appears; 36 is the volume number.]

d. *Deletions:*

Short quotations: Deletions should not be used in short quotations that form that part of a sentence, as:

Rather, it involves "sovereign immunity from suit" (see 1 Witkin, Cal. Procedure, §314).

At the beginning of the quotation:

". . . Although these funds" etc.

". . . the federal government" etc.

Here if the word "the" were to be initial capped to start the quotation, it would appear in brackets, as "[T]he federal government" etc. However, the first word in a sentence may be changed to lower case without a bracket or other indication.

In the middle of a sentence and end of a sentence:

"Surveys, made exclusively for . . . aerial . . . photogrammetry . . . ."

Of a citation, or series of citations:

Indicate omission of citation or citations by brackets: [Citation.] or [Citations.]

Whole sentences within a quotation:

"Does this constitutional inhibition apply merely to such money as actually reaches the treasury, or does it apply to funds belonging to the state which have not yet reached the hands of the treasurer? . . . The attorney general contends for a construction whereby the provision shall be held to apply only to moneys after the same shall have reached the hands of the state treasurer."

When the quotation ends with a complete sentence, deletion marks are not necessary.

Paragraphs:

A line of dots may be used to indicate the omission of one or more paragraphs. Three or four spaced asterisks are also sometimes used.

3. PUNCTUATION

The period and comma are placed *inside* the quotes.

Question marks, semicolons, colons and exclamation marks are placed inside the quotation marks if they are part of the quotation, otherwise outside.

A comma, colon or semicolon should not be placed before a parenthesis.

The dash is made with one hyphen, with space before and after hyphen, not with two hyphens.

4. ABBREVIATIONS

Some of the abbreviations used in briefs are:

aka	also known as
App. Op. Br.,	
p. 15	Appellant's Opening Brief, page 15
App. Div.	Appellate Division
approx.	approximately
art.	article
ch.	chapter
cf.	compare
cl.	clause
Const.	Constitution
C.T. 16	Clerk's Transcript, page 16
dft., dfts.	defendant, defendants
div.	division
do.	(ditto) the same
dr.	debtor
ed.	edition
e.g.	for example
et al.	and others
etc.	(et cetera), and so forth
Ex.	Exhibit
ex rel.	upon relation or information
et seq.	and the following pages
et ux	and wife
ex vir	and husband
f.	folio
fn.	footnote
ibid	in the same place
id.	(idem) the same
i.e.	that is
l.c.	lower case
1., 11.	line, lines
loc. cit.	(loco citato) in the place cited
memo	memorandum
op. cit.	in the work cited
p., pp.	page, pages

par.	paragraph
Pet., Petn.	Petition
pro tem	(pro tempore) temporarily
P.S.	(post scriptum) postscript
Reh.	Rehearing
resp.	respondent
Resp. Br., p. 17	Respondent's Brief, page 17
rpm	revolutions per minute
R.T. 25	Reporter's Transcript, page 25
sec. or §	section
sic.	thus (used in brackets to indicate error in quoted material)
SOP	standard operating procedure
ss	(scilicet) namely
subd.	subdivision
subsec.	subsection
tit.	title
u.c.	uppercase
v. or vs.	(versus) against
viz	namely [no period]
vol.	volume

5. FOOTNOTES

One footnote may be marked with an asterisk (*); more than one should be numbered. The footnote must be gauged to end at the usual line on the page, *i.e.*, the 28th line if on ruled and numbered paper. If the footnote requires all the remaining space on the page, the footnote will commence after completion of the line on which a footnote is designated, and as many additional lines as space will permit will be on the same page. In the case of an exceptionally long footnote that will carry over to the next page and beyond, at least two lines of the text should appear on the following page before starting the footnote. An example of an exceptionally long footnote appears below:

24 join in any deed of trust given to secure construction

25 loans for improving the property.[1] The next month the

26 _____

27   [1]The full text of the subordination clause is:
"Lessor agrees to subordinate their title and interest to
any and all construction loans or loan obtained by Lessee
28 for the purpose of constructing improvements on said

-3-

[Next page]

1 Margot corporation sublet the property to Jones and

2 Smith. The sublessees wished to borrow money on the

3 _____
    1(continued):
4

  premises. Lessor will join on any deeds of trust re-
5 quired by lenders or lending institutions for the purpose of giving as security for said construction loans

     and
      continuing
       either to end of page, 28th line

     or
      continuing
       to end of page and beyond to the following page,
       in the same manner as above, but ending on the
       last line of the page

6. CITATIONS

A *citation* is a reference to a statute, or a case (a decision of the court), or a legal text, in support of the proposition set forth. For example, in the case of *Mudd v. McColgan* (1947) 30 Cal.2d 463, the book in which the case appears is California Supreme Court Reports. 30 is the number of the volume. 463 is the page number on which the case begins. Note the names are underscored (or italicized in printed material). Cases pending in municipal or superior courts should not be underscored (or italicized). The year is usually placed after the name. Some attorneys prefer to place it after the page number, as 30 Cal.2d 463 (1947).

This is a citation of a legal text: 27 Cal. Jur. 100. The text is California Jurisprudence. As above, 27 is the number of the volume, 100 the number of the page.

In citing a case thus, *Brown v. Kennedy* (1980) 73 Cal. 64, 68, we mean the language of the opinion appearing on page 68 supports our particular point.

Citation after quotation: In a *quotation* part of the case, or statute, or text, is copied into the document. The quotation mark is placed before the last word, followed by name of case in parenthesis, and *period inside* parenthesis, as: ". . . or legal rule from determining it." (*Arenas v. United States*, 95 F.Supp. 962, 972-974.) The following method is also permissible: ". . . or legal rule from determining it" (*Arenas v. United States*, 95 F.Supp. 962, 972-974).

Citation after statement which is supported by a case: Period goes at end of sentence and inside parenthesis, as: The claim involves an inroad or spoliation on the funds of the sovereign. (*Pensioners' Protective Assn. v. Davis*, 50 P.2d at p. 974.)

Introductory Words and Phrases:

No introductory word,
citation immediately following the parenthesis, case cited concerns same legal principle being discussed in document

Contra,
indicates the case cited holds directly against the position taken by the writer

Accord,
indicates case cited is directly in point but facts are distinguishable from facts in writer's case

See
indicates that the case cited appears to support the expression or conclusion of the writer

But see
indicates that the case cited raises a question as to, or is contrary to, the position asserted by the writer

Cf.
indicates that although the facts of the two cases are different, an analogy may be drawn between the writer's case and the cited case which will give some support to the writer's statement

But cf.
indicates that although the facts of the cases are different an analogy may be drawn between them; the cited case is directly opposed to the writer's statement

REFERENCE LIST

Examples of Citation	*Text*
151 A.L.R. 1110	American Law Reports
1 Am. Jur. 425	American Jurisprudence
40 A. 225	Atlantic Reports (reports decisions of courts in Connecticut, Delaware, Maine, Maryland, New Hampshire, New Jersey, Pennsylvania, Rhode Island, Vermont)
148 A.2d 300	Atlantic Reports, second series
Cal. Admin. Code, tit. 18, §2028	California Administrative Code
Cal. Const., art. VI, §4½	California Constitution
149 Cal.App. 47	Reports of decisions of California Courts of Appeal
276 Cal.App.2d 386	Reports of decisions of California Courts of Appeal, second series
80 Cal.App.3d 397	Reports of decisions of California Courts of Appeal, third series
27 Cal.Jur. 100	California Jurisprudence
49 Cal.Jur.2d 185	California Jurisprudence, Second Edition
10 Cal.Jur.3d 80	California Jurisprudence, Third Edition
6 Calif.L.Rev. 33	California Law Review
1 Cal.Rptr. 15	California Reporter
220 Cal.34	California Supreme Court Reports
71 Cal.2d 430	California Supreme Court Reports, second series
21 Cal.3d 349	California Supreme Court Reports, third series
7 C.F.R. 969	Code of Federal Regulations
7 Colum.L.Rev. 50	Columbia Law Review

66 C.J. 95	Corpus Juris
14 C.J.S. 9	Corpus Juris Secundum
300 F. 188	Federal Reporter (reporting decisions of U.S. Circuit Courts of Appeal and Courts of Appeal)
263 F.2d 478	Federal Reporter (reporting decisions of U.S. Circuit Courts of Appeal and Courts of Appeal, second series)
78 F.Supp. 914	Federal Supplement (reporting decisions of U.S. District Courts)
3 F.R.D. 37	Federal Rules Decisions
82 L.Ed. 252	United States Reports — Lawyers Edition
50 L.R.A. 17	Lawyers' Reports Annotated
1 Merrick's Probate 30	Merrick's Probate
200 N.E. 179	Northeastern Reporter (Illinois, Indiana, New York, Massachusetts, Ohio)
156 N.E.2d 75	Northeastern Reporter, second series
300 N.W. 411	Northwestern Reporter (Iowa, Michigan, Minnesota, Nebraska, North Dakota, South Dakota, Wisconsin)
94 N.W.2d 461	Northwestern Reporter, 2d series
273 N.Y.S. 15	New York Supplement (New York appellate cases only)
16 N.Y.S.2d 25	New York Supplement, Second Series
7 Ops.Cal. Atty.Gen. 108	Opinions, California Attorney General
300 P. 383	Pacific Reporter (reporting decisions of appellate courts of California and 12 other western states: Arizona, Colorado, Idaho, Kansas, Montana, Nevada, New Mexico, Oklahoma, Oregon, Utah, Washington, Wyoming)
335 P.2d 578	Pacific Reporter, second series
27 S.Ct. 384	United States Supreme Court Reporter
200 S.E. 304	Southeastern Reporter (Georgia, North Carolina, South Carolina, Virginia, West Virginia)

106 S.E.2d 315	Southeastern Reporter, second series
200 So. 373	Southern Reporter (Alabama, Florida, Louisiana, Mississippi)
109 So.2d 183	Southern Reporter, second series
10 So.Cal.L.Rev. 55	Southern California Law Review
300 S.W. 588	Southwestern Reporter (Arkansas, Kentucky, Missouri, Tennessee, Texas)
321 S.W.2d 485	Southwestern Reporter, second series
1 Stan.L.Rev. 10	Stanford Law Review
State Bar J.	State Bar Journal
356 U.S. 527	United States Supreme Court Reports (official reports)
17 U.S.C. sec. 19	United States Code
28 U.S.C.A. sec. 733b	United States Code Annotated
U.S. Const., art. IV, sec. 3, cl. 2 U.S. Const., 14th Amend. [federal Constitution]	United States Constitution
1 U.C.L.A.L.Rev.	University of California Los Angeles Law Review
10 Wall. 49	Wallace's Reports, United States Supreme Court
11 Wheat. 360	Wheaton's United States Supreme Court Reports
7 Wigmore on Evidence (3d ed. 1940) sec. 2097, p. 478	Wigmore on Evidence, Third Edition
1 Witkin, Cal. Procedure, Jurisdiction, sec. 83, p. 351	California Procedure
1 Witkin, Cal. Crimes Defenses, sec. 128, p. 123	California Crimes

1 Witkin, Summary of Cal. Law (7th ed. 1960) Contracts, sec. 225, p. 253	Summary of California Law
Witkin, Cal. Evidence, Witnesses, sec. 423, p. 473	California Evidence
Witkin, Cal. Criminal Procedure, Trial, sec. 441 p. 443.	California Criminal Procedure

7. CALIFORNIA CODE ABBREVIATIONS

California statutes are published in sets of codes. West Publishing Company publishes one set, commonly referred to as "West's" codes. Bancroft-Whitney Co. publishes "Deering's" codes. West's codes are all annotated, that is, each section is footnoted with references to decisions, texts, etc. Certain Deering's codes are designated as Annotated.

Abbreviations for the California codes are given below. Other abbreviations are sometimes used, however.

Agric. Code	Agricultural Code
Bus. & Prof. Code	Business and Professions Code
Civ. Code	Civil Code
Code Civ. Proc.	Code of Civil Procedure
Com. Code	Commercial Code
Corp. Code	Corporations Code
Ed. Code	Education Code
Elec. Code	Elections Code
Evid. Code	Evidence Code
Fin. Code	Financial Code
Fish & Gm. Code	Fish and Game Code
Food & Agric. Code	Food and Agricultural Code
Gov. Code	Government Code
Harb. & Nav. Code	Harbors and Navigation Code
Health & Saf. Code	Health and Safety Code
Ins. Code	Insurance Code
Labor Code	Labor Code
Mil. & Vet. Code	Military and Veterans Code
Pen. Code	Penal Code
Prob. Code	Probate Code

Pub. Resources Code	Public Resources Code
Pub. Util. Code	Public Utilities Code
Rev. & Tax. Code	Revenue and Taxation Code
Sts. & Hy. Code	Streets and Highways Code
Un. Ins. Code	Unemployment Insurance Code
Veh. Code	Vehicle Code
Wat. Code	Water Code
Welf. & Inst. Code	Welfare and Institutions Code

8. WORDS FREQUENTLY MISUSED

AFFECT is a verb only, meaning to act upon or produce an effect upon

EFFECT may be a verb meaning to produce, to bring to pass, or it may be a noun designating that which is produced by a cause, the immediate result. Example: "What he says will not affect my plans." "Automation is going to effect a change in all our lives." "The illness is the direct effect of her mental state."

CITE (verb):   To quote by way of evidence, as to cite a case

SITE (noun):   Position or place, as a building site

SITUS (noun):   The place where something exists

COUNSEL is an attorney, or attorneys. As a verb "counsel" means to advise, as "I will counsel you." Sometimes it is used as a noun meaning advice, as "Your counsel is of great help to me."

COUNCIL is an assembly summoned for consultation, advice, as a city council.

DEMUR is the verb, meaning to hesitate, or, in law, to interpose a demurrer.

DEMURRER is the noun, meaning a pleading objecting to the complaint and further proceedings in the case because of some defect on the face of the complaint or its insufficiency in law.

DEPOSITARY: The person receiving a deposit

DEPOSITORY: A place where anything is deposited, as a safe-deposit box

ELICIT: To draw out

ILLICIT: Not lawful; improper

EMINENT: Distinguished (as an eminent man in the community)

IMMINENT: Impending; soon

GUARANTY (noun, never a verb) an agreement to recompense; an express or implied assurance of satisfaction; (plural form) the constitutional guaranties

GUARANTEE (noun):   The one who makes the guaranty or who acts as surety or gives security, as for a debt
(vt) to be responsible for the agreement of another

PRINCIPAL is the head of a school, or a central figure (main character).

PRINCIPAL is also a monetary foundation (principal and interest).

PRINCIPAL as an adjective means primary, as "The principal reason" etc.

PRINCIPLE is a standard or rule, as a "legal principle."

SOMETIME — an indefinite date: "I'll phone you sometime soon."

SOME TIME (two words):   a considerable period of time: "It has been some time since I have seen you."

THEREFOR is used to avoid a repetition. ". . . and good cause appearing therefor, IT IS HEREBY ORDERED" etc.

THEREFORE: In view of these conditions, therefore we take this action, as "Now, therefore, it is hereby ordered, adjudged and decreed" etc.

9. DIVISION OF WORDS

A word improperly divi-
ded (like this), looks like a word miss-
pelled (correct, mis-spelled).

A number of books on division of words are available. A convenient little book to keep at hand for ready reference is Word Division, Supplement to Government Printing Office Style Manual, available from the Superintendent of Documents, Washington, D.C.

A few of the general rules follow:

1. Divide a word which ends in a double letter after the word in its original form, as process-ing.

2. Divide where a single vowel forms a syllable within a word, as authori-ties.

3. Divide between syllables, as defend-ant, but remember that one-syllable words cannot be divided, as "writ", "plea."

4. Divide between two vowels that are pronounced separately, as certi-orari.

5. Divide between doubled consonants, as rescis-sion.

6. Divide between prefixes and suffixes, as pro-prietary, argu-ment.

7. Divide hyphened words only after the hyphen.

8. Do *not* divide a word at the end of a page, nor a citation if it can be avoided.

9. Do not divide names, except between first and last but not at end of page.

10. Avoid too many consecutive lines with divided words at the end.

10. NUMBERS

The comma is used in writing the amount of one thousand or more, as $1,500, 1,400 acres, 8,640 persons.

"No." and "Nos." are abbreviations for "number" and "numbers."

When amounts of money are an even number of dollars, the .00 is not used, as $5, $37, $140.

A sentence should not begin with a numeral; the amount should be written out, as: Twelve men were at the meeting.

Common usage is words for figures up to 10 only and the figure for higher numbers; if figures are used for lower numbers, the numerals should appear consistently throughout the document.

Write:

twelve feet four inches (12' 4")
1 hour 35 minutes 20 seconds
65¢ or 65 cents or $0.65 or sixty-five cents
one-half mile
fifties or 1950's
2 million or 2,000,000
14 percent or 14%
5-percent salary increase
12-year-old-boy

11. TIME

3 o'clock
    or   but *not* 3:00 o'clock
three o'clock

3:10 a.m. — but *not* 3:10 o'clock a.m.

12 M for twelve o'clock Noon

Military time is written as if the clock were numbered up to 24:

1 a.m. is	0100
1 p.m. is	1300
12 M. is	1200
3 a.m. is	0300
3 p.m. is	1500
11 p.m. is	2300

12. PROOFREADING

Printed briefs are usually first typed in draft form on legal-sized paper, perhaps on yellow or green paper, and either double or triple spaced. This draft is sent to the printer. A copy of the draft should be retained in the office file.

The printer returns a "galley proof" together with the draft to the attorney before the final printing. The galley proof is compared with the draft. The responsibility for its accuracy is the proofreader's. The attorney may wish to re-read the draft.

Proofreading is usually the job of the secretary in the law firm. The legal assistant will have to decide whether he/she also wishes to re-read the brief. In the author's view, the more persons who read it, the better. Mistakes can remain after passing through many good hands. In any event, the legal assistant should be familiar with proofreading marks.

Proofreading marks are listed and explained in *The Random House College Dictionary* (Rev. ed., 1980) at page 1568 and in other dictionaries and books on the art of writing. It may be possible to obtain a list of proofreading symbols from a printer.

CALIFORNIA PARALEGAL'S GUIDE

Chapter 13

LEGAL WRITING

WRITING THE EFFECTIVE APPELLATE BRIEF

By *Leonard M. Friedman,*
Retired Associate Justice, Court of Appeal,
Third Appellate District

1. *Do not twist facts. Do not omit facts unfavorable or inflate some and hide others.*

Occasionally, because of such treatment of the facts, a case described in the brief will bear little resemblance to that considered by the jury in the case. A lawyer kids himself, not the judges.

Rule 15(a), California Rules of Court, requires that the statement "of any matter in the record shall be supported by appropriate reference to the record."

2. *Erroneous jury instructions.* Alert readers of advance sheets will recognize relative rarity of reversals for this kind of error. In the last several decades appellate courts are increasingly realistic in measuring the effect of jury instructions. Most agree that juries are guided not so much by precise phraseology of instructions as by general sense. If a body of instructions, taken as whole, fairly conveys general sense of guiding principles, the reviewing court will not be concerned over imperfections in individual instructions.

This does not say that the appellate brief writer should ignore erroneous jury instructions, but suggests that only rarely is he justified in pinning hopes to that kind of error.

In recent years there are leading cases where the Supreme Court has reversed for erroneous jury instructions, in civil cases, where the court has chosen jury instruction cases as a vehicle to announce or change a rule of law.

3. *Some lawyers fail to consider the California Constitution, article VI, section 13, requiring that "the court shall be of the opinion*

*that the error complained of has resulted in a miscarriage of justice''
before it may set aside a judgment, etc.*

To require reversal, it is not enough to demonstrate that error
occurred, but you must go on to demonstrate — in light of the entire
record — that a different verdict would not otherwise have been probable. If he overlooks or fails to fulfill his task, his assignment of error
is worthless.

(See *People v. Watson* (1956) 46 Cal.2d 818, 836.)

4. *Attorney representing respondent should not accept appeal as
shaped by opponent's brief. Should not slavishly and unimaginatively
limit reply to appellant's points 1-2-3 in order of presentation chosen
by appellant.*

It is a tactical error to view respondent's brief negatively, merely
as a defense. It should be affirmative, vigorous, an aggressive coun-
terattack, a vindication of the trial court judge. Respondent's attorney
should cover all bases and not necessarily in rotational order established
by opponent.

5. *Rule 15(a), California Rules of Court, should not be a "flower
born to blush unseen, wasting sweetness on the desert air." It should
be spotlighted, underscored, italicized, outlined in neon.*

The rule is an indispensable guide to the appellate brief writer:
"Each point in a brief shall appear separately under an appropriate
heading, with subheadings if desired. Such headings need not be technical 'assignments of errors' but should be concise headings which are
generally descriptive of the subject matter covered. The statement of
any matter in the record shall be supported by appropriate reference
to the record. Every brief shall be prefaced by a topical index of its
contents and a table of authorities, separately listing cases, statutes,
court rules, constitutional provisions, and other authorities.''

The rule says that a brief shall state its various points separately.
Each point should have a concise heading which shall be generally
descriptive of subject matter. If lawyer follows this direction, he will
create for himself a tangible structure of argument.

Establish a table of contents enabling him to see, as though in x-
ray, the basic skeleton of his case, showing him whether he can achieve
a telling, vigorous and persuasive presentation. Some briefs are filed
with their arguments headed with roman numerals only, no descriptive
statement. Or they are cryptic and practically useless. Example of brief
following Rule 15(a):

SUBJECT INDEX

Topic headings should be compact, forceful, epitomize series of arguments; individually, describing the various parts of argument; collectively, describing the entire structure of appeal.

6. Two fundamental questions an appellate lawyer must face: (1) What are principles fixing an appellate court's power to change or set aside duly reached decision of trial court? (2) Granting that the topic or question is open to appellate supersedure, what motivation will lead the appellate court to change its result? Too many leap into the second area without troubling to inquire into the first. The appellate court is, after all, a tribunal of limited powers and may superimpose its decision on trial court's only when and to the extent the law permits. The novice should read and absorb Witkin's chapter on Appeals in California Procedure. An hour or two of this general reading provides a basic understanding of limitations on appellate courts and scope of appellate review.

Most lawyers are aware as an abstract matter of the basic division of function of trial and appellate courts. They know the trial court decides facts; the appellate tribunal is limited to questions of law. Most are aware of the abstract principle that the appellate court may nullify a verdict or finding only when not supported by substantial evidence. One is guilty of wishful thinking to ignore these principles. The court is continually picking up briefs in which counsel for appellant is vociferous re strength of his own evidence, compares the relatively feeble evidence on the other side, winds up with the empty and meaningless assertion that jury's verdict was against substantial evidence! Such an argument is delusory, nothing but a disguised entreaty for appellate retrial of facts. Appellant who attacks an adverse fact determination wastes his breath in praising the strength and convincing power of his own evidence. One must concentrate fire on weakness of his opponent's evidence; one must demonstrate the opponent's evidence fails to support verdict.

7. All, judges and lawyers alike, are weaned in the tradition of common law. Adherence to precedent is ingrained in the thinking; habitual, taken for granted as though it were a bodily process. Of course, effective brief writing requires effective, discriminating use of precedent. But it can be carried too far. Carried to dry logic extremes, emphasis on precedent may cause loss of contact with reality. It becomes a devitalized process matching one case against another regardless of other influences bearing upon decision. What are these?

For centuries, British and American lawyers and judges had viewed common law as vast structure of ready-made precedents. They viewed common law decisional technique as matter of reaching into this structure to pluck out precedent most closely matching case at hand. Exactly 50 years ago Cardozo (The Nature of the Judicial Process) exposed a fallacy: the universal technique of decision in the common law world is the application of past judicial experience to the decision of current controversies. The first thing the appellate court does is to compare the case before it with precedents. Nevertheless, a system of living law cannot evolve by a mechanical process of matching precedents. We go forward with our precedents to a certain point. But where the paths diverge, where precedents do not match, choices must be made. At that point the court seeks the guidance of history, custom, social utility and of accepted standards of right conduct.

Appellate courts do not stand above the great tides and currents which engulf the rest of men. The final consideration of law, that is, the final consideration of legal principles and rules, is the welfare of society. Ethical considerations can no more be excluded from administration of justice than vital air from rooms we inhabit. In the main we consciously adhere to precedent. But beyond precedent are other forces, the likes and dislikes, the complex of instincts and emotions and habits and convictions which make the man, whether he be litigant, lawyer or judge — thus Cardozo's central thesis.

Brief writers should follow Hamlet's advice to players: ". . . Use all gently: For in the very torrent, tempest, and — as I may say — whirlwind of passion, you must acquire and beget a temperance, that may give it smoothness. . . . Be not too tame neither, but let your own discretion be your tutor: Suit the action to the word, the word to the action; with this special observance, that you o'erstep not the modesty of nature."

*   *   *

Some Additional Notes on Brief Writing

1. *Selection and Arrangement of Points*

Brief writer's first task is identification and selection of issues on appeal. Do not oversell by multiplying issues; don't dilute strength of sound contentions by including dubious claims. If three or four sound issues are available, eliminate others; latter are probably nonreversible anyway. State strongest points first (unless logical development indicates otherwise). Do not sandbag, *i.e*, appellant should not reserve issues for his closing brief.

2. *Tone*

Tone is an indefinable quality involving sensitivity to reader reaction. Avoid incendiarism, sarcasm, disparagement, heavy humor and pretentiousness; seek clarity and simplicity.

3. *Presentation of Precedent*

Avoid long quotations from decisions; the judges have access to the law books. Better to condense or paraphrase accurately. If short, apt quotation is available, use it. Show how a precedent applies but avoid lengthy description of facts and history of precedential decisions.

4. *When to Summarize*

When the argument is unavoidably lengthy and complex, it may be useful to include a summary and condensed closing argument in a "Conclusion" section. Where issues are simple, a summary is unnecessary.

Always conclude a brief by telling the court what relief you want, e.g., the judgment should be reversed, modified, affirmed or reversed with instructions.

CALIFORNIA PARALEGAL'S GUIDE

Chapter 14

LEGAL RESEARCH

THE PARALEGAL RESEARCHER

One of the tasks to which the paralegal is assigned is the job of legal research. Though this might appear to the newcomer as a dry and uninteresting task, it is of vital importance to the outcome of every case. Even those cases settled out of court are often settled in favor of the attorney who has done a thorough research job.

Consequently it is imperative for a lawyer or legal researcher to know where to find the law, and how to find it quickly. Because, if the lawyer is negligent, he may be disciplined by the courts. In addition, if damage results from deficiencies, he may be sued by his client. At best, any lack of skill may result in the loss of a favorable verdict or judgment.

Knowledge of law consists largely in knowing where to find it, as well as being able to understand and apply it when found. There is no more need to burden one's memory with all the points of law, than it is to carry all of one's money, when it is just as convenient to keep it in the bank. Besides, since there are millions of points of law, this would be impossible. So it is more important that the researcher know how to find and analyze the applicable law, than to remember it.

The Realm of Legal Research

The two main sources of law with which the legal researcher must become familiar are (1) statutory law, and (2) case law. Books containing statutory or case law are considered primary; books explaining or summarizing the law, secondary.

Classification of Law Books

The chart below is a graphic representation of the classification of all law books.

```
                                                    ⎛ Constitutions
                                                    ⎜ Treaties
                                                    ⎜ Statutes
                                ⎛ Statute Books ——⎨ Ordinances
                                ⎜                   ⎜ Administrative
                                ⎜                   ⎜    Regulations
              ⎛ Source Books ——⎨                   ⎝ Court Rules
              ⎜ (Primary)        ⎜
              ⎜                   ⎝ Reports of Court Decisions
              ⎜
 LAW BOOKS ——⎨                   ⎛ Digests
              ⎜                   ⎜ Legal Encyclopedias
              ⎜                   ⎜ Annotations
              ⎜ Auxiliary Books ⎨ Textbooks and Treatises
              ⎝ (Secondary)      ⎜ Law Reviews and Legal
                                 ⎜    Periodicals
                                 ⎜ Restatement of Law
                                 ⎜ Legal Dictionaries
                                 ⎜ Indexes
                                 ⎜ Table of Cases
                                 ⎝ Citators
```

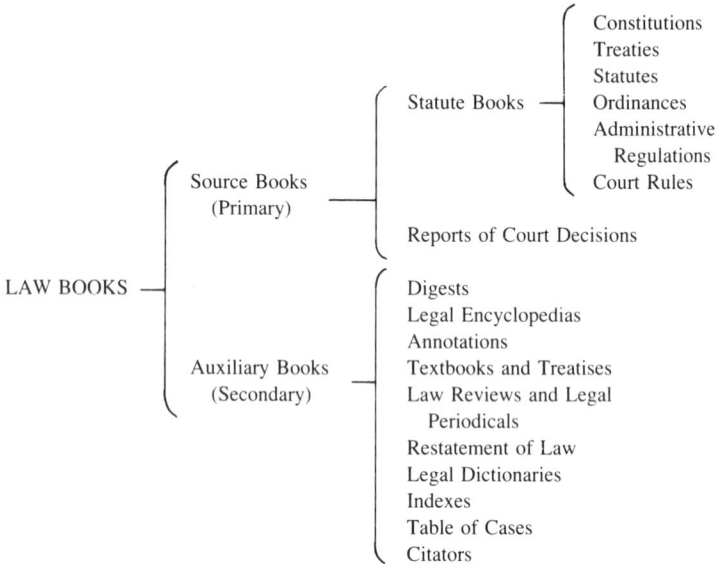

Statute Books

1. *Constitutions:*

Constitutions are concise and state fundamental principles only. Amendments to the Constitution follow the body of the Constitution.

a. United States Constitution.

b. California Constitution.

Many books contain a copy of the United States Constitution and of the California Constitution. The United States Code Annotated contains an annotated United States Constitution; West's and Deering's codes contain an annotated California Constitution.

2. *Treaties:*

Ordinarily, the general legal practitioner will not be called upon to interpret treaties (formal agreements between two or more nations relating to peace, alliance, trade, etc.). However, if it should be necessary to locate a treaty they may be found in a set called "United States Treaties and Other International Agreements."

3. *Statutes:*

A statute is formally enacted by a legislative body. U.S. Statutes are enacted by Congress; state statutes by the legislative bodies of the states. The federal statutes enacted by Congress are compiled in United States Code Annotated.

California statutory laws are compiled in codes. The following codes are available in unannotated paperbacks, convenient for desk or briefcase:

Civil Code
Code of Civil Procedure
Commercial Code
Corporations Code (with Corporate Securities Rules)
Evidence Code
Labor Code
Probate Code
Uniform Commercial Code (California)
>(Publisher is Parker & Son Publications, Inc.
>P.O. Box 60001, Los Angeles 90060)

There are two sets of annotated codes:

a. Deering's California Codes Annotated (commonly referred to as "Deering's codes") and

b. West's Annotated California Code (commonly referred to as "West's codes").

In these sets, first the statute is set forth, followed by annotations, that is, notes and headnotes from cases relating to the statute and other commentary on the particular statute. In addition, Deering's codes contain many forms, which follow the pertinent code section. The cases cited in the annotations are not the same in both sets of books; therefore reference to both sets affords additional leads to case law on a statute.

4. *Ordinances:*

Ordinances are local statutes, usually published by the city, town or county which enacts them, and are usually available in local libraries or the state law library.

5. *Administrative Regulations:*

The California Administrative Code contains the rules and regulations governing the many state professional and vocational boards and licensing agencies. Some of the decisions of administrative agencies are published. For example, selected decisions of the Unemployment Insurance Appeals Board are published as Precedent Decisions. All such decisions are usually available at state law libraries.

6. *Court Rules:*

The rules adopted by the Judicial Council of California and the Supreme Court are the California Rules of Court, are published separately, are also available in "LARMAC" (LARMAC INDEX TO CALIFORNIA LAWS (1975 Edition)). The rules are also published as part of West's and Deering's codes and in other books.

Reports of Court Decisions

California

The opinions in the California Appellate Reports and California Reports are "official" reports, which means that preparation of headnotes and publication of the cases are supervised by the courts through their Reporter of Decisions, and are to be distinguished from reports published by private companies.

1. California Reports contain the decisions of the California Supreme Court. Volumes 1 to 220 contain the decisions from 1850 to 1934; California Reports 2d, volumes 1 to 71, contain the decisions for the years 1935 to 1969. Cases since 1969 (California Reports 3d) are first issued in the Advance Sheets and later in bound volumes, when a sufficient number of decisions have been rendered to justify the publication of the next volume. In the third series, the cases bear the same page numbers in the bound volumes as in the Advance Sheets (for both Cal.3d and Cal.App.3d).

2. California Appellate Reports are the decisions issued by the California Courts of Appeal. Volumes 1 to 140 contain the decisions from 1905 to 1934, volumes 141 to 276, called California Appellate Reports 2d, the decisions for the years 1935 to 1969. Decisions issued since then are in the third series, first appearing in the Advance Sheets and later in the bound volumes. Their decisions are issued in the same Advance Sheets as the decisions of the California Supreme Court. Care should be taken when discarding, to be certain that bound volumes for both Supreme Court and Appellate Court have been issued, as the publication dates do not coincide.

Cases which are filed in the California Courts of Appeal and published, and in which the Supreme Court grants a hearing, will appear in the Advance Sheets but will not appear in the bound volumes. However, they do appear in bound volumes of:

3. West's California Reporter. Particular care should be taken to Shepardize a case appearing in West's California Reporter as the Supreme Court may have issued an opinion on the same case. Or, if the case is very recent, the Supreme Court might have "taken over" the case and the matter be pending in the Supreme Court; this can be determined by checking the Cumulative Subsequent History Table in the Advance Sheets.

Federal

1. Supreme Court Reports (cited, *e.g.*, 215 U.S. 312) are the official reports of the decisions of the United States Supreme Court.

2. Lawyers Edition (cited, *e.g.*, 23 L.Ed.2d 55) contains the unofficial reports of the United States Supreme Court and are published

by the Lawyers Cooperative Publishing Co. Page numbers in the Lawyers Edition and the United States Reports are not the same. In citing a case in the Lawyers Edition in a brief, it should be cited in this manner: 411 U.S. 233 [36 L.Ed. 2d 208].

3. The decisions of the Circuit Courts of Appeal appear in the Federal Reporter (cited "280 Fed. 420"); later cases appear in "F.2d."

4. Federal Supplement ("F.Supp.") contains the decisions of the federal district courts (comparable to trial courts in the state court system).

5. Federal Rules Decisions contains cases on procedural matters heard by the federal courts.

6. The National Reporter System of the West Publishing Company publishes unofficial reports of the United States Supreme Court in the Supreme Court Reporter.

7. For purposes of reporting cases in the various states, the 50 states are divided into seven sections and a reporting system is set up for a group of states, as follows:

Atlantic Reports (Connecticut, Delaware, Maine, Maryland, New Hampshire, New Jersey, Pennsylvania, Rhode Island, Vermont)

Northeastern Reporter (Illinois, Indiana, New York, Massachusetts, Ohio)

Northwestern Reporter (Iowa, Michigan, Minnesota, Nebraska, North Dakota, South Dakota, Wisconsin)

Pacific Reporter (Alaska, Arizona, California, Colorado, Hawaii, Idaho, Kansas, Montana, Nevada, New Mexico, Oklahoma, Oregon, Utah, Washington, Wyoming)

Southeastern Reporter (Georgia, North Carolina, South Carolina, Virginia, West Virginia)

Southern Reporter (Alabama, Florida, Louisiana, Mississippi)

Southwestern Reporter (Arkansas, Kentucky, Missouri, Tennessee, Texas)

Auxiliary Books

1. *Digests:*

A digest is an index of legal propositions naming the cases that support each proposition.

a. West's California Digest. This is a digest published by the West Publishing Co. for California. West's also publishes other national digests as well as digests of the regional reporter system.

b. McKinney's New California Digest.

The digests summarize the cases under subject matter categories. West's Digest has key numbers for cases which make it possible to locate similar cases.

2. *Legal Encyclopedias:*

An encyclopedia is also a treatise or commentary on law in which the topics are listed separately in alphabetical order, and comprehensively. There are two major national encyclopedias:

a. American Jurisprudence (2d series).

b. Corpus Juris Secundum.

California is fortunate in having its own California encyclopedia:

c. California Jurisprudence 2d and 3d.

Volumes of the third edition of California Jurisprudence are being issued as completed.

This set of books is arranged alphabetically by general subject matter, as Actions, Courts, Pleadings, Landlord-Tenant, etc.

3. *Annotations:*

An annotation is a critical or explanatory note. Annotations in West's and Deering's Codes may provide the statutory history, amendments to statutes and repeal of statutes, cross-references to other related statutes, and excerpts from pertinent cases. Two important annotated sets of books are:

a. American Law Reports Annotated (federal and state case law)

b. United States Code Annotated.

The laws passed by Congress are published unofficially in United States Code Congressional and Administrative News. However, the Statutes at Large have been codified much in the same manner as California laws have been codified into codes of varying titles, *i.e.,* they have been arranged by subject matter and given title numbers in the United States Code Annotated, a set of numbered codes. For example, whereas a tax law of California appearing in the Revenue and Taxation Code is cited "Rev. & Tax. Code §11314," a section involving a tax law of the United States would be cited by the volume number, as "26 U.S.C.A. §701."

4. *Textbooks (Treatises):*

A textbook is a treatise and attempts to present in narrative form the principle of law. Statements in textbooks are not the law; however, when an opinion quotes a textbook of established reputation in support of a principle, the textbook obviously has persuasive authority. Some textbooks are so well-known and established that they have become a weighty source of authority. Three such are: Williston on Contracts, Wigmore on Evidence, and Scott on Trusts.

A number of such books are published by Parker & Son Publications, Inc., some of which are:

Ballantine and Sterling, California Corporation Laws. (1976 fourth edition, with 1981 releases)

Haight and Cotchett, California Courtroom Evidence (1972, with 1981 supplement).

Johns, California Damages, Law and Proof (1977, with 1981 supplement)

Marsh, California Mechanics' Lien Law Handbook (1972, with 1981 supplement)

Werchick, California Preparation and Trial (1981, 3rd Edition)

Eisler, California Uninsured Motorist Law Handbook (1974, with 1981 supplement)

Herlick, California Worker's Compensation Law Handbook (1977, with 1981 supplement)

Cotchett and Elkind, Federal Courtroom Evidence (1975, with 1981 supplement)

The Continuing Education of the Bar books are treatises on practice and procedure, giving instructions and forms for instituting and conducting various proceedings. A complete list of their books can be obtained from their offices. A few of them that might be of particular use to the paralegal are:

Basic Personal Injury Anatomy

California Administrative Agency Practice

California Civil Appellate Practice (with supplement)

California Civil Procedure Forms Manual

California Civil Writs (with supplement)

California Conservatorships (with supplement)

California Decedent Estate Administration I,II (with supplement)

California Administrative Mandamus

5. *Law Reviews (and Legal Periodicals):*

Law review articles are usually issued in pamphlet form; later the law libraries bind them together. They are sponsored by the law schools and usually have a board of student editors. Commentary in the law reviews is written by law students. There are many law reviews from all the states, as Harvard Law Review. California has a number of law reviews, *e.g.*:

California Law Review (Cal. L. Rev.)

Southern California Law Review (So. Cal. L. Rev.)

Hastings Law Review (Hast. L. Rev.)

Stanford Law Review (Stan. L. Rev.)

University of San Francisco Law Review (U.S.F.L. Rev.)

Pacific Law Journal (Pac. L. J.)

The state bar associations publish state bar journals, as our California State Bar Journal. In addition, there are many other publishers of legal journals.

6. *Restatement of Law:*

Leading authorities on various topics of law have compiled materials over the years, which appear in a set of books called Restatements, *e.g.,* Agency, Conflict of Laws, Judgments, Property, Negligence, Restitution, Trusts. These authorities are often quoted with approval in court decisions.

7. *Legal Dictionaries:*

Legal dictionaries are of course collections of words used in legal writing, including many words of Latin derivation.

  a. Black's Law Dictionary
  b. Ballentine's Law Dictionary
  c. Bouvier's Law Dictionary
  d. Words and Phrases is a set of books. Definitions of a word as found in different cases are quoted.

8. *Indexes:*

Most sets of law books have a general index in a few volumes at the end of the set. For instance, the United States Code Annotated has such an index, so do West's Annotated Codes and Deerings' Annotated Codes, also California Jurisprudence 2d, Corpus Juris Secundum, and A.L.R.

A ready reference book is LARMAC, now issued annually, a complete subject index under one alphabetical listing to the Constitution, all the California codes and the General Laws.

9. *Tables of Cases:*

  a. A part of McKinney's New California Digest is a three-volume set of index of cases.

  b. West's California Digest likewise has an index of cases.

10. *Citators*

Shepard's Citations is published by Shepard Citations, Inc.; the publisher also furnishes upon request a pamphlet, "How to Shepardize Citations." This is a complete citation system, showing all citations by the California and federal courts to the California cases reported in the various series of California reports and in the California Reporter and Pacific Reporter of the National Reporter System, as well as to the California Constitution, codes, statutes, charters, ordinances, court rules and jury instructions. By use of these books the researcher can determine whether a case has been affirmed, modified, reversed, superseded, overruled, followed, questioned, etc.

*   *   *

We have attempted to provide a general classification of law books and references to the books of research more widely used in California. Many other books fall within these classifications and at one time or another will be needed by the practicing lawyer or paralegal. Research can be no better than the library. A paralegal will have available the library of his/her employer, plus local law libraries and perhaps a state law library. A ready source of law books for both lawyers and paralegals is of course the law book stores (such as Lake Law Books, 142 McAllister, San Francisco), where used as well as new books are sold. Complete sets of law books in excellent condition are usually available at substantial savings.

Researching

"Until very recently, no one paid much attention to the even greater and more prevalent incompetence in reading, except, perhaps the law professors who, ever since the introduction of the case method of studying law, have realized that half the time in a law school must be spent in teaching the student how to read cases. They thought, however, that this burden rested peculiarly on them, that there was something very special about reading cases. They did not realize that if college graduates had a decent skill in reading, the more specified technique of reading cases could be acquired in much less than half the time now spent."*

*   *   *

In his research, the lawyer checks on statutes, ordinances, court rules, and the rules of administrative authorities, as well as precedents. Administrative tribunals now are performing many functions which were formerly the exclusive business of courts. Their decisions are in many respects as authoritative within their sphere as decisions of courts in ordinary litigation.

If a lawyer is writing a brief, he or she must support his or her arguments by researching the problem and selecting the cases, *i.e.*, the precedents, which sustain his or her argument. Whether a lawyer is drawing up a contract or other legal document, the lawyer must know that what he or she is doing is supported by case law. Research is done in the law reports: California Reports, abbreviated "Cal." or "Cal.2d" (California Supreme Court decisions), California Appellate Reports, abbreviated as "Cal.App." or "Cal.App.2d" (California Courts of Appeal decisions), and other state reports.

---

*Mortimer J. Adler, How to Read a Book, p. 67.

Before starting research, the first thing to be done is to try to determine from the client the actual facts, the facts material to a successful determination of the case, the facts that can be proven. Think of the words descriptive of the main facts of the case at hand, and then consult an analysis of the topics. The leading word might come from the parties concerned (class, occupation, or relation), the subject matter, the cause of action or defense, object of the action, or the point of controversy other than the cause of action.

The new paralegal, or attorney, is not so apt to be certain of the legal principles applicable to the case, nor where they are to be found. The very latest decisions must be located. If the paralegal knows the principle of law applicable to his set of facts, he or she might look in a textbook or encyclopedia to find a case supporting the principle; if he or she doesn't know the principle, he or she will check in a digest to find it. Digests are better indexes to precedents, but the textbooks and encyclopedias are better adapted to studying the principles; after finding one case, other cases can be discovered.

If the subject sought is not found, check on synonyms and related subjects and consult the table of contents. If a valid statute applies to the case at hand, look for cases construing it. An annotated edition of the statutes or a citator (Shepard's) provides this information.

Jot down references that should be followed up, text, encyclopedia or case. Scan the case summaries in the digests under the word, phrase or topic heading. Read the case, analyze it and write out a summary. Then think about the case, its similarities or distinctions from the case at hand. (Never cite a case relying on an excerpt from a digest.)

Then "Shepardize" your case, making sure it has not been overruled, superseded, modified, etc. Shepard's Citations also lists cases bearing on a particular code section; for example, suppose Code of Civil Procedure section 396 is relevant to your case. You find:

"§§395 et seq.

17 Cal 69

83 Cal 501

24 P 160"

Some law books are called "finders," in other words, they are the books used as the starting point in researching a question. If you ask a California lawyer the law on a particular point, don't be surprised if his answer is "Look in Witkin." He is referring to one of the many series of excellent books written by B. E. Witkin which reliably and succinctly analyze legal points and lead the way to pertinent code sections and decisions supporting a particular point. His books provide a broad but condensed perspective on a particular subject. Some of his books deal with substantive law, others with court procedures. A few of his books are listed below, for a handy reference. The latest supplements to his works should always be consulted.

Summary of California Law
California Crimes
California Criminal Procedure
California Evidence
California Procedure

Case Summaries or Briefing a Case

A summary of a case should include:
1. The title, citation and date of the case
2. A statement of the question at issue
3. A statement of how the question arose

For example: Was it raised by demurrer, on a motion for change of venue, on a motion for summary judgment, by a ruling during trial, on a motion for judgment notwithstanding the verdict, or on a motion for a new trial?

4. A statement of the facts of the case
5. A statement of how the case was disposed of in the trial court

For example: Demurrer sustained without leave to amend; order denying or granting a change of venue; judgment of nonsuit; summary judgment; judgment on the verdict; or order granting a new trial

6. A statement of how the case came before the appellate court

For example: appeal; writ of mandamus, writ of prohibition

7. A statement of the errors assigned
8. The decision of the appellate court
9. Reasons for the decision.

Selective Reporting of Cases

A common misconception among lay persons, and also some law students, is that all court cases are reported. By "reported" is meant the cases are compiled in book form as legal decisions. But such is not the case, because the cases at the trial court level are seldom reported. A few selected cases of the appellate departments of the superior courts (which hear cases appealed from the municipal courts) appear in the California Supplement reports of cases in the California Appellate Reports. (They are cited "Cal.App.2d Supp.")

Probably the main reason for the confusion lies in the fact that a "court reporter" is often in attendance at a trial and records the proceedings every step of the way. Then the reporter, when requested by counsel, prepares a "transcript" of the trial, a verbatim reporting of everything said by the judge, counsel and witnesses. This transcript is called the "reporter's transcript" and when an appeal is taken, becomes a part of the record on appeal.

Court reporters are required to be present in all felony criminal matters. Counsel requests a reporter in the more important civil matters. If counsel requests a reporter in a civil municipal court case, he must directly pay the county for the reporter. All civil jury cases are covered by a reporter. Court reporters are not usually present, then, in misdemeanor cases, less important civil cases, or on motions, or in the small claims court.

It is the cases on appeal which fill the sets of law books. These cases are not step-by-step accounts, nor do they consist of a running chronology. The appellate cases are heard by a panel of three judges referred to as "justices." There is no jury in such cases, because it is not the function of such courts to re-try the cases, meaning they do not re-try the facts. If oral argument is held, the attorneys present their arguments; no witnesses are called and the parties need not be present.

All opinions of the California Supreme Court are published in the Official Reports. However, the reports of a given court, meaning the decisions which are assembled and printed in book form, do not always contain every case decided. Certain cases are intentionally omitted. To be published a case must meet certain criteria.

No opinion of a Court of Appeal or of an appellate department of the superior courts is published in the Official Reports unless such opinion (1) establishes a new rule of law or alters or modifies an existing rule; (2) involves a legal issue of continuing public interest, or (3) criticizes existing law.

A majority of the court must certify that it meets the above standard for publication. However, the California Supreme Court may order an opinion to be published that was not certified for publication by the authorizing court.

Opinions issued by the Courts of Appeal either bear the legend NOT TO BE PUBLISHED IN OFFICIAL REPORTS or (CERTIFIED FOR PUBLICATION).

Until 1964, after adoption of Rule 976 of the California Rules of Court, all decisions of the Courts of Appeal were published. An unpublished opinion of a Court of Appeal may not be cited by an attorney (Rule 977). The publication of opinions is a controversial question, as some attorneys feel that more or all of the opinions should be published.

Format of Reported Decisions

The paralegal, since he or she will have frequent occasion to refer to cases, should have a working knowledge of how the case is set up in the book of reported cases. Each case consists of several distinct parts:

1. Brief *summary* of the case.

2. *Syllabus or headnotes.* The term "headnote," being in common usage, consists of summary statements of the points of law (questions) decided in that case. This headnote is usually prepared by the Reporter of Decisions of the courts.

3. *Name of the judge* preceding the majority opinion is the name of the authoring judge.

4. *Facts of the case.* These may be stated in separate paragraphs usually following the headnotes. Or they may be embodied in either the opinion or the statements of counsel.

5. *Opinion.* The opinion includes all reasons set forth by the court as the basis for the decision. The opinion includes the reasons and conclusions reached, taken as one mental process.

6. *Decision.* This explicitly designates the precise decision reached, such as "Judgment affirmed" or "Judgment reversed," or it may be more explicit in the case of a remand or modification.

7. *Concurring and dissenting opinions,* if any. A concurring opinion may be written by a member of the court who agrees with the result reached but who wishes to state the reasons differently or give additional reasons, or, although he agrees with the result, he may not agree with the arguments that reach the result.

In the Courts of Appeal, 2 out of 3 justices must agree, to have a majority opinion. In the California Supreme Court, 4 out of 7 justices must be in agreement.

A dissenting opinion is one written by a judge who does not concur in the result reached by the majority opinion. Each dissenting member may write a dissenting opinion. Sometimes the reasons for the dissent are not given. Dissenting opinions are not binding opinions, not precedents.

Memoranda Decisions

Such decisions state only the conclusion of the court; the opinion is not printed.

"Technical" Knowledge

A certain amount of what we might call "technical" knowledge is required to check quotations and citations from cases and statutes.

Cases: All quotations, if only a few words, should be checked for 100% accuracy before using in a brief. *Go to the source.* Check *all* citations.

Checking quotations is easy. For example, in *Neet v. Holmes,* 19 Cal.2d 605, 607, the first number, 19, is the number of the volume of the reports; the case commences at page 605; and the quotation is to be found on page 607. The quotation on page 607 should support the statement made before the citation. if the quotation actually continues on to page 608, change the page reference to "607-608."

If the volume number is correct but the page on which the case begins is wrong, the index of cases in the front of the volume will give the page on which it will be found. More important is the particular page to which reference is made, since if that is incorrect, you have to read through or scan the entire opinion to locate the quotation. In this event, the numbered headnotes (brief statements of the points of law involved in the case) appearing at the beginning of the opinion may prove helpful, particularly if the opinion is long, if the quoted language seems to coincide in point with the headnote. The headnote numbers appear in boldface type and are easily spotted throughout the opinion.

If you have only the name of the case (and it is a California case or a Pacific Reporter case), check McKinney's Tables of Cases Digested or West's Table of Cases for the citation. Supplements listing the more recent cases are in the back of these books.

A citation to "Cal.App." may prove to actually be a citation from Cal.2d, or it may be a citation from Cal.App.2d, or Cal., and vice versa. If the citation proves incorrect, check in these other reports with the same volume number, or check the tables of cases in McKinney's or West's for the correct citation.

Statutes: If a crime were committed say in 1972, and one of the statutes (i.e., code sections) applicable to that crime had been amended by the Legislature since 1972, then the statute in effect would be the statute as it read prior to its amendment. The pocket supplements will contain the section as it currently reads, and immediately following the section are the dates of amendment, with the chapter number, and the page number in the statutes. The statute as it read in 1972 might be in the main text of the code itself, the amendment being in the pocket supplement, or reference to the Statutes of California may be necessary to find the statute as it read in 1972. The statutes are in bound volumes by the year, with chaptered numbers of the bill; usually the chapter number and page number will appear with the section. (See California Legislation, *supra.*)

The summary of the subject of a code section, the heading, which appears in boldface type after the number of the section, is not part of the section. Neither are the amendments which follow the section in parentheses, nor, of course, any of the annotations which follow the code section, in annotated volumes of the code, since they are not part of the sections.

The following books are recommended for legal research:
Cohen, *Legal Research in a Nutshell*

Henke, *California Legal Guide* (Parker & Son Publications, Inc., P.O. Box 60001, Los Angeles 90060)

California Law Office Handbook (Continuing Education of the Bar)

Pollack, *Fundamentals of Legal Research*

Price and Bitner, *Effective Legal Research*

Roalfe, *How to Find the Law* (West)

Rombauer, *Legal Problem Solving*

A course in Legal Bibliography if available would be helpful to the paralegal.

LEGAL RESEARCH COMPUTERS

The computer has moved into the daily life of lawyers and is being used to keep track of time spent on cases, bookkeeping functions, docket control, organization and management of evidentiary materials — and legal research.

The amount of time required for research is increasing because Congress and state legislatures, regulatory agencies and courts are increasing their output of new laws, rulings and decisions. The cost of thorough legal research strains the lawyers' budgets. Computer-assisted legal research can allegedly significantly reduce this burden and at the same time increase the quality of the research.

The LEXIS system, offered by Mead Data Central Inc., 200 Park Avenue, New York, N.Y. 10017 (San Francisco offices at 311 California St. and 1 Market Plaza; Los Angeles office at 707 Wilshire Blvd., 36th Floor), is presently one of two systems available to lawyers in private practice in the United States.

The other system is WESTLAW, offered by West Publishing Company, 50 W. Kellogg Blvd., St. Paul, Minn. 55165.

The paralegal with training in legal research can be readily trained to use LEXIS or WESTLAW. The productivity of the paralegal should be increased by their use. Employment of the paralegal for research, plus the increased productivity with computer research, should be an offset to the cost.

The quality of the research of both attorneys and paralegals should improve with the aid of computers.

CALIFORNIA LEGISLATION
BY EVA S. GOODWIN

Judicial Staff Attorney, California Court of Appeal, First Appellate District (based on manual for Judicial Attorneys, 1973).

Statutes and Legislative Materials

The attorney may be confronted with questions of statutory interpretation. An excellent brief review is in Chapter 8 of Newman & Surrey, Legislation; general definitions and Rules of Statutory Construction are found in Civil Code sections 4-23; Code of Civil Procedure section 1859; Government Code sections 1-23; but see also Llewellyn, *The Common Law Tradition Deciding Appeals*, pages 522-535. Unless the attorney has had a course on legislation or special experience in this field, he may be in strange and murky waters.

After a single version of a bill has been passed by both houses of the Legislature, it can be enacted into a statute in one of three ways. First, the Governor may sign it within certain time limits set forth in the Constitution. Second, the Governor may veto the bill and return it to the Legislature which may in turn enact the bill into a statute by a two-thirds vote in both houses. Finally, if the Governor fails to take any action on the bill within the constitutional time limits, it automatically becomes a statute. (Cal. Const., art. IV, §10, subd. (a).)

1. Time

With rare exceptions, all research must be based on the statute as it read at the pertinent time: for example, when the cause of action arose the offense was committed, or when the lower court acted. Subsequent amendments may throw light on prior legislative intent.* There is always a time lag. Until 1972, a statute became effective on the 91st day† after the final adjournment of the Legislature that passed it, unless a different date was prescribed by the statute.

As a result of the 1972 amendments to article IV of the state Constitution (providing for regular biennial legislative sessions commencing at noon on the first Monday in December of each even-numbered year and ending at midnight on November 30 of the following even-numbered year), a statute enacted at a regular session goes into effect *on January 1 next following a 90-day period from the date of its enactment;* a statute enacted at a special session goes into effect on the 91st day after adjournment of the special session at which it was passed, *except* that statutes calling elections, providing for tax levies or appropriations for usual current expenses and urgency statutes go into effect immediately* upon their enactment. (Stats. 1972, res. ch. 81, pp. 3350-3351; cf. Gov. Code §9516.)

---

*Or expressly so state — see Stats. 1980, ch. 132, effective May 29, 1980, and *People v. Harvey* 25 Cal.3d 754, 760.

†For legislation prior to December 1972, this date can be found on the page immediately following the title page of the first volume of statutes for each year.

*e.g., on filing with the Secretary of State.

As a result of the enactment of Government Code section 9510.5 that became effective on August 29, 1973, the effective date of all nonurgency bills will always be January 1, following the year designation for the chapter laws. (For example, a nonurgency bill that becomes Stats. 1973, ch. ..., is effective January 1, 1974.) Accordingly, for legislation enacted in 1973 and subsequent years, no reference to a table of effective dates will be required.

Consequently, the attorney should be alert to: 1) statutes that become effective immediately on their passage; 2) statutes that become operative as of a specified date; and 3) procedural statutes that may have retroactive or prospective application†. (For example, the Jurisdiction and Service of Process Act became effective on July 1, 1970; however, if a summons was served and not returned together with proof of service before July 1, 1970, the return may be made as provided by either the old law or the new law.)

The Pacific Law Journal since 1970 has published useful reviews of current legislative changes.†† Publications of the Continuing Education of the Bar and the California Law Revision Commission may be helpful. The Judicial Council and the Administrative Office of the Courts may have materials or reports relating to changes in procedure and court rules. The current amendments to the California Rules of Court are in the bound volumes of the California Reports.

2. *Legislative history*

Caveat: In contrast to federal legislative materials, California materials on legislative history are scarce and disorganized. Legislative debates are not reported. Often, no indication of legislative intent* can be gleaned; the area is one of great frustration and the attorney must rely on the sound analytical skills of a thoughtful lawyer, common sense, and the rules of statutory interpretation. Since 1955, some of the annotated codes have provided the Code Commissioner's notes.

a. To find legislative history of a particular statute, obtain the year, chapter and page number of the statute from the annotation ("Stats. 1959, ch. 1214, p. 1998"), the Table of Laws Enacted section of the Statutes and Amendments to the Codes, or the Final Calendar of Legislative Business.

---

†*cf.*, *In Re Marriage of Bouquet,*16 Cal.3d 583, holding retroactive the 1971 amendment of Civil Code section 5118.

††Before 1970, the State Bar Journal did so. Both sources are informative but not authoritative.

*See Steven A. Smith, *Legislative intent: In search of the Holy Grail* 53 Cal State Bar Journal 294 (Sept/Oct 1978, Vol 53, No. 5); James Delahanty, *Super Legislators: One Person Amendment of Statutes in California,* Los Angeles Daily Journal, Sept. 22, 1978.

b. Use the "Summary Digest of Statutes Enacted" or "Final Calendar" for the year the statute was enacted to: (a) ascertain the assembly and senate bill numbers from the cross-reference tables, listed by statute year, chapter and page; (b) the "Senate Bill" or "Assembly Bill" will show any changes in language subsequent to its introduction and prior to passage by both houses. Senate and assembly bills are indexed by the bill number. (*Caveat:* language changes of the bill are not shown in the "Final Calendar" or in the Summary Digest. Any changes in language subsequent to the introduction of a bill appear only in the *amendments*. All amendments should be checked.)

What happens when at any one session more than one bill affecting the same code section is enacted into statute? See Gov. Code section 9605 and *In re Thierry S.*, 19 Cal.3d 727, 738-743.

Note that the "Final Calendar" for each year also describes what code sections were "affected" that year, including amendments proposed but never passed. Often it is useful to know what did not pass in order to understand what did.

c. The "Senate Journal" and "Assembly Journal" show by year all activities of the senate and house on a *day-to-day* basis, including the letter of transmittal of the bill, reports on the bill, opinions of the Legislative Counsel, but no debates or texts of bills.

d. The Legislative Analyst's "Index to the Interim Committee Reports" shows whether a committee report was filed. Only interim (or fact-finding) and special committee hearings from 1937 to date are reported. (*Caveat:* the index lists the committees and subject matter but some volumes do not list the bill number. However, the Summary Digest, *supra,* and the Final Calendar, *supra,* will show whether a bill was referred to an interim committee.) Each house is indexed separately, by subject matter, alphabetically.

e. Legislative Counsel opinions. Published ones are in the Senate Journals and Assembly Journals, *supra,* and referred to in the Final Calendar as well as indexed in the "Legislative Digest." (Note that many of the opinions are not published. The office of the Legislative Counsel may release an unpublished opinion upon a request after consent by the state legislator who first requested the opinion from the Legislative Counsel.)

f. Opinions of the Attorney General. These are listed by statute number, subject matter, in each volume as well as in a separately bound index.

g. Reports of the Judicial Council, the State Bar and California Commission on Uniform State Laws are frequently helpful; for major procedural innovations, check the pertinent Continuing Education of the Bar volume.

h. Arguments made to the voters on statewide ballots are found in bound volumes "Constitutional Amendments and Arguments to the Voters" (published by the Secretary of State). This material may properly be cited to a court (*Crees v. California State Board of Medical Examiners* (1963) 213 Cal.App.2d 195).

i. For further information on California Legislative materials, see 4 Stanford Law Review 367; 42 C.L.R. 766; 3 Pacific L.J. 63; and Locating Legislative Intent by Extrinsic Aids, California State Law Library Paper No. 13, rev. October 1966, an unpublished manuscript on file at the Supreme Court library, an excellent compendium of sources and authorities, that is also the source of the legislative history check sheet below.

j. Since 1960, all legislators have maintained district offices. The district or Sacramento offices may have helpful information.

k. State Archives in Sacramento are the only permanent source of old bills and legislative documents. Minor libraries and those designated as a "state depository" also will have copies of bills and amendments, particularly during the session.

LEGISLATIVE HISTORY CHECK SHEET

Code section(s)_____

Statute and chapter number(s)_____

Bill number(s)_____

Committees bill referred:

    Assembly_____

    Senate_____

    Joint_____

Committee reports_____

Committee hearings_____

Other major sources:

    Legislative Journals_____

Code commission reports, notes and drafts of codes (1868-1953);
Law Revision Commission reports, recommendations and studies
(1953 to date)_____

Judicial Council reports (1926 to date)_____
Pacific Law Journal (1970 to date)_____
Review of code legislation (1955 to date)_____
State Bar of California's legislative program (Journal of the State
Bar of California, 1926 to 1970)_____
Minor sources:
Governor's messages and press releases; Legislative Counsel's re-
port on legislation necessary to maintain the codes; Commission
on Uniform State Laws reports; Legislative Counsel opinions; Ar-
guments to voters; Departmental reports; newspapers and news-
letters; committee files.
Separate indexes:
Final Calendar of Legislative Business
California interim legislative committees and reports
California state publications.

REFERENCE BOOKS

1. CALIFORNIA LAW GUIDE, by Dan Henke. Aids and techniques
   for finding state and federal law rapidly. Comprehensive list and
   description of sources. (Parker & Son Publications, Inc.)
2. THE PARA-LEGAL AND THE LAWYER'S LIBRARY, Cun-
   ningham. (Shepard's Citations, publisher.)
3. LARMAC INDEX TO CALIFORNIA LAWS (1975 Edition).
   One-volume index key-wording and cross-referencing to all codes,
   general laws and state Constitution. (Parker & Son Publications,
   Inc.)
4. CALIFORNIA PROBATE PROCEDURE (1973 with 1981 supplement), by Judge Arthur K. Marshall, Los Angeles Superior
   Court. Includes official Alameda County, San Francisco, Los
   Angeles and Judicial Council forms as well as the Probate Policy
   Memoranda of eight counties. (Parker & Son Publications, Inc.)
5. CALIFORNIA RULES OF COURT. Rules of practice and procedure adopted by Judicial Council and Supreme Court for the
   appellate courts, superior courts and municipal courts. (Available
   from Documents Section, Department of General Services, State
   of California, Sacramento.)
6. CALIFORNIA CODES. Unannotated paperbacks. Up-to-date
   with amendments. (Parker & Son Publications, Inc.)
   CIVIL CODE

CODE OF CIVIL PROCEDURE
CORPORATIONS (with Corporate Securities Rules)
EVIDENCE (with Committee Comments)
LABOR CODE
PROBATE CODE
UNIFORM COMMERCIAL (California)

7. CALIFORNIA CORPORATION LAWS, by Ballantine and Sterling. Text and index of Corporations Code, explanation of the law, forms, annotations and citations to leading cases. Five supplemented looseleaf volumes. (Parker & Son Publications, Inc.)

8. LEGAL CHECKLISTS (2 vols.), Becker, Sprecker & Savin. (Callaghan & Co.)

9. A GUIDE TO SERVICE OF PROCESS IN CALIFORNIA (1973), Peavey Co., (790 Pennsylvania Ave., San Francisco 94107.)

10. BLACK'S LAW DICTIONARY. (West Publishing Co., St. Paul, Minn.)

11. BOUVIER LAW DICTIONARY. (West Publishing Co., St. Paul, Minn.)

12. BLAKISTON'S NEW GOULD MEDICAL DICTIONARY. (Blakiston Co., Philadelphia.)

13. 20,000 WORDS, SPELLED, ACCENTED, DIVIDED. (McGraw-Hill Book Co.)

14. LATIN WORDS AND PHRASES IN EVERYDAY USE. (St. Louis Law Printing Co., Inc., 812 Olive St., Room 812, St. Louis 1, Missouri 63101.)

15. LEGAL SECRETARY'S HANDBOOK (1977-eleventh edition) edited by legal secretaries in collaboration with members of bench and bar. Comprehensive information on current procedures in California law practice. (Parker & Son Publications, Inc.)

16. STANDARD HANDBOOK FOR SECRETARIES, by Lois Irene Hutchinson. Not a legal text as such but excellent grammar reference for anyone. (McGraw-Hill Book Co.)

17. INTRODUCTION TO PARALEGALISM: PERSPECTIVES, PROBLEMS AND SKILLS (1974), by Statsky. (West Publishing)

18. PARKER DIRECTORY OF ATTORNEYS (annual edition). Lists active attorneys' names, addresses and telephone numbers in California. Revised each December. (Parker & Son Publications, Inc.)

19. MARTINDALE-HUBBELL LAW DIRECTORY. A listing of lawyers in the United States. (Published by Martindale-Hubbell Co.)

20. CALIFORNIA ROSTER. Contains names of state officials, lists counties with location of county seats, names of judges, officials and other information. (Available from Documents Section of State of California, Sacramento.)
21. CALIFORNIA COURTS DIRECTORY AND FEE SCHEDULES, compiled by Municipal Court Clerks Association of California, Business Manager, Municipal Clerks Association, Post Office Box 460, Bellflower, CA 90706.
22. CITATION, A UNIFORM SYSTEM OF. Forms of citations and abbreviations. (Published by the Harvard Law Review Association, Cambridge, Mass.)
23. CALIFORNIA STYLE MANUAL, A HANDBOOK OF LEGAL STYLE FOR CALIFORNIA COURTS AND LAWYERS (Second Edition) by Robert Formichi. (Published by Printing Division, Documents Section, Sacramento.)
24. A PRACTICAL MANUAL OF STANDARD LEGAL CITATIONS, Miles O. Price (2d ed. 1958). (Oceana Publications, Inc., Dobbs Ferry, New York.)
25. LAW WRITERS' GUIDE, by Paul W. Dwyer. (Bancroft-Whitney, San Francisco)
26. CALIFORNIA FAMILY LAW HANDBOOK, by L. Ryder Mason (Parker & Son Publications, Inc.)
27. CALIFORNIA CIVIL PROCEDURE HANDBOOK, by L. Ryder Mason (Parker & Son Publications, Inc.)
28. CALIFORNIA PREPARATION AND TRIAL, by Jack Werchick (Parker & Son Publications, Inc.)
29. USE OF COMPUTERS IN LITIGATION (A.B.A. 1979)

Chapter 15

CONTRACTS

CALIFORNIA CONTRACTS

In our daily lives contracts play an essential role. We enter into contracts when we take a job, rent an apartment, open a bank account, make a purchase, take out insurance, take or give a promissory note, and so on. Without contracts, it would be difficult to conduct our daily business.

Contracts have their effect and construction by the rules of civil law existing at the time the parties enter into the contract. The law defines the duty and the right, compels one party to perform the thing contracted for, and gives the other a right to enforce the performance by the remedies then in force.

In other words, the contract itself does not bind the parties to the contract; the law of the state binds the parties to perform according to their contract. " 'Contract' designates both the specific procedure by which the contractual duties and rights of the contracting parties are created and the contractual norm created by this procedure, an equivocation which is the source of typical errors in the theory of contract." (Kelsen, General Theory of Law and State, p. 137.)

The laws of contracts are indeed complex and voluminous, far beyond the scope of this chapter. Books and treatises have been written on the subject. The legal assistant should at least be aware of the basic general principles governing the law of contracts.

What might the legal assistant be called upon to do in connection with contracts, and what should the legal assistant know about these contracts? The legal assistant might be called upon to draft a contract; a client might ask for review of a contract by counsel before signing; a question of interpretation of the language of a contract might arise (interpretation is a matter for the attorney, the paralegal may supply the research upon which advice is based); a client may wish to sue for breach of contract, in which case a complaint for damages has to be drafted, or a complaint to compel specific performance of a contract may be needed.

The legal assistant should know what to look for in a contract, what questions to ask of the client, to determine the needed facts of the case. Only with some knowledge of applicable substantive law can the legal assistant adequately assist the supervising attorney.

Substantive law includes definitions and distinctions of various types of contracts; how contracts are formed; the parties; assent; consideration; formal requisites of contracts; illegal contracts; rules as to construction and effect of contracts; changes in status of contracts by modifying, terminating or novation; and the performance and breach of contracts.

California statutory law on contracts is found in the California Civil Code.*

General provisions relating to contracts are found in sections 1549-1701; capacity of parties and minors, sections 25-42; obligations in general and under contracts, sections 1427-1543; real property sales contracts, sections 2935 *et seq.*, 3306 *et seq.;* statute of frauds, section 1624; obligations imposed by law — fraud — negligence, sections 1708-1720; obligations arising from particular transactions: credit cards, consumer credit contracts, discount buying services, swimming pools, fine prints, etc., sections 1725-3268.

Suggested reading for a concise summary of contracts, is 14 California Jurisprudence III, Contracts (By James O. Pearson, Jr., J.D.) pages 153 *et seq.* Covered in his article are "the definitions of various types of contracts and the distinctions between them; the formation of contracts, including the requirements involving parties, assent, consideration, and the formal requisites for creating contracts; the nature and effect of illegality arising from a violation of statute or public policy; the rules governing the construction and effect of contracts; contracts for the benefit of third persons; changes in the status of contracts through modification, termination, or novation; and the performance and breach of contracts." (P. 153)

What is a Contract?

Many definitions have been propounded. A contract is defined in California Civil Code section 1549 as follows: "A contract is an agreement to do or not to do a certain thing."

Another definition commonly met is that a contract is a *promise* enforceable at law directly or indirectly or a contract is an *agreement*

---

*All references in this section on Contracts refer to Civil Code sections unless otherwise noted.

enforceable at law directly or indirectly. California Uniform Commercial Code section 1201 defines a contract as "the total legal obligation which results from the parties' agreement as affected by this code and any other applicable rules of law."

"Agreement" is defined as "the bargain of the parties in fact as found in their language or by implication from other circumstances including course of dealing, or usage of trade or course of performance as provided in this code (Sections 1205 and 2208). (Compare 'contract.')"

Creating a Contract — Offer and Acceptance

A popular theory of the nineteenth century was that there could be no contract without a "meeting of the minds". This theory first clearly emerged in the case of *Adams v. Lindsell* (1818) (1B and A1d 681). For over a century an *apparent* meeting of minds has sufficed to create a binding contract.

The parties must, then, appear to consent and agree upon the same thing. Simple declarations by the parties entering into an agreement — though identical — do not make a contract; the declaration of one party must be directed to, and accepted by, the other party. A contract is therefore said to consist of an offer and acceptance, plus consideration. (See below.)

That "offer" and "acceptance" are distinguished implies that they are not made simultaneously. The parties to a contract are not always in each other's presence during its creation. The law makes it possible for persons who are apart to create a contract by providing that the offeror is bound for a certain length of time or, if unspecified, a reasonable length of time — even if he has changed his mind!

Let us examine a common form of contract, an agreement to sell a parcel of real property. How do the parties arrive at a contract to purchase? Usually a broker shows the real property to a potential buyer. The broker quotes an "asking price," the price at which the seller has agreed to sell the property. (In a sense, the seller has made an invitation to negotiate to sell at a specified price to a qualified buyer.) The buyer may be willing to pay the "asking price," but knowledgeable buyers will usually at least try to buy it for less. So the buyer sets a price at which he is willing to purchase the property and an offer is drawn up and signed by the buyer for presentation to the seller. The offer may be made conditionally, *e.g.*, conditioned upon the buyer's ability to obtain a loan, in a certain amount, at certain interest rates, etc. That means that if the seller accepts this offer, but the buyer is unable to obtain the specified loan, the contract is not binding on the buyer. The broker presents this offer to seller — with a deposit as a demonstration of good faith.

The buyer may prescribe a period within which the seller must accept. The offer terminates at the time specified for the seller's acceptance or, if no time is specified in the offer, at the end of a "reasonable time," which is a question of fact in each case (§1587). The buyer may revoke his offer at any time before the seller has communicated his acceptance to the buyer (§1586).

Consent is deemed to be fully communicated as soon as the seller "has put his acceptance in the course of transmission [*e.g.*, in the U.S. mail] to the buyer" (§1583).

What are the Essentials of a Contract?

Four essentials to the existence of a contract are set forth in Civil Code section 1550: (1) the parties must be capable of contracting; (2) they must consent; (3) there must be a lawful object; and (4) there must be a sufficient cause or consideration. The contract is void if any one of these elements is missing.

(1) *Parties to a contract*

All persons are capable of entering into a contract except minors, persons of unsound mind, and persons deprived of civil rights (§1556).

Contracts of minors (under 18) for the necessaries of life are binding. Criminals who have lost their civil rights (felons) cannot make binding contracts. Nor can persons of mental incompetency. Incompetency includes intoxicated and insane persons.

(a) *Agency.* The incapacity of a principal to contract would not terminate an agency for a period not to exceed one year after the incapacity occurs if the instrument creating the agency provides that it shall not be affected by the subsequent disability or incapacity of the principal; this authority, however, is limited to transactions involving real property which comprises the principal place of residence of the principal. (§2356, §2307.1.)

(2) *Consent*

The consent of the parties to a contract must be free, mutual, and communicated by each to the other (§1565).

Consent obtained through duress, undue influence, fraud, misrepresentation, menace, or threats is not free and the consent is not real, and the contracts will not stand.

Other statutes relating to consent are found in sections 1567-1590.

Example: A and B negotiate an oral contract and A assumes the responsibility of reducing their agreement to writing for their signatures. A intentionally omits one of the terms they orally agreed upon and presents the document to B for signature. There is an implied representation on A's part that the document accords with their oral agreement, and A's intentional omission is fraud.

(3) *Lawful Object*

The thing agreed upon by the parties to the contract — to be done or not to be done — must be lawful or the contract is void (§1595). If the contract has several distinct objects, of which at least one is lawful and at least one is unlawful, in whole or in part, the contract is valid as to the lawful part and void as to the remainder (§1599).

For example, a contract for a gambling resort in California would not be binding because gambling is illegal in California.

In California some contracts are invalid per se. Some contracts may have a lawful object but yet are against public policy and so won't be enforced. Civil Code section 1667 provides: "That is not lawful which is:

"1. Contrary to an express provision of law;

"2. Contrary to the policy of express law, though not expressly prohibited; or,

"3. Otherwise contrary to good morals."

Civil Code section 1668 provides: "All contracts which have for their object, directly or indirectly, to exempt any one from responsibility for his own fraud, or willful injury to the person or property of another, or violation of law, whether willful or negligent, are against the policy of the law."

Certain agreements to fix prices are forbidden and so will not be enforced. An agreement with a person who is required by law to be licensed, but who is not licensed, such as a contractor or an attorney, cannot be enforced.

As a general rule, every contract that fixes the damages or compensation for a breach of the contract is void where it can be established that such a provision was "unreasonable under the circumstances existing at the time the contract was made" (§1671, subd. (b)).

A provision in a contract liquidating damages for the breach of a contract is void where the damages are sought to be recovered from:

"(1) A party to a contract for the real purchase, or rental, by such party of personal property or services, primarily for the party's personal, family, or household purposes, or

"(2) A party to a lease of real property for use as a dwelling by the party of those dependent upon the party for support" except when the nature of the case makes it impracticable or extremely difficult to fix the actual damage. (§1671, subds. (c) and (d).)

(4) *Consideration*

A promise in a contract is not binding, not enforceable, without "consideration."

The consideration is the value agreed upon. Consideration may consist of the payment of money but does not necessarily mean money.

"Consideration" is defined in Civil Code section 1605 as any benefit conferred, or agreed to be conferred, upon the promisor, to which he is not legally entitled, or any prejudice suffered, or agreed to be suffered, other than such as he is lawfully bound to suffer, as an inducement to the promisor.

Legal and moral obligations originating in some benefit conferred or judgment suffered, to the extent of the obligation, are good consideration (§1606).

Usually each party to a contract expects to receive something of value. Suppose A offers to sell his car to B for $500. B accepts and transfers title to the car. A agrees to pay for the car after the 1st of the month. The "consideration" is the car — and the money.

(a) *Detriment as consideration*

Or, the consideration may be a detriment. Suppose A owns a beautiful home with a view of the ocean. B owns the lot on the hillside below A's and is preparing to build a two-story home, which will block A's view of the ocean completely. B has a legal right to construct a two-story home on his lot. A says, if you will build a one-story home on that lot, I will give you $30,000. B agrees, forbearing his legal right. A's promise is binding upon him (A). A pays the $30,000 to B. B's forbearance of his right is a legal consideration.

(b) *Lawfulness of consideration*

The consideration of a contract must be a lawful one. If any part of the consideration is not lawful, the entire contract is void (§1608).

(c) *Sufficiency of consideration*

The consideration must not only be lawful but also "sufficient" and "adequate." To be "sufficient" the consideration must be either a benefit to the promisor or a detriment to the promisee. If a court holds that the consideration justifies the enforcement of a promise it is "sufficient;" if the court says it does not justify enforcement either you have (1) no consideration or (2) an insufficient consideration.

The American Law Institute has defined consideration as anything that is bargained for by the promisor and given by the promisee in exchange for the promise. It does not have to be equal in value. The courts are not apt to hold the consideration inadequate when bargained for; however, the consideration may seem so inadequate as to indicate the existence of fraud, or mistake or undue influence.

(d) *Consideration must actually be received*

The fact that a contract names a specific consideration is prima facie evidence of the consideration, but may be attacked on the ground that it was not received.

Oral and Written Contracts and Statute of Frauds

A contract may be oral or written. The contract may consist of an oral promise to act in a certain way, or to refrain from doing a specified thing, As noted above, an oral contract may relate to a job, month-to-month tenancy without a written agreement, etc.

"A contract may be in writing. An express contract is stated in writing." A promissory note is a contract, so are bank accounts, insurance, sales.

Certain contracts are not valid and enforceable unless they are in writing. California Civil Code section 1624 (known as the "statute of frauds") requires the following contracts to be in writing:

"1. An agreement that by its terms is not to be performed within a year from the making thereof.

"2. A special promise to answer for the debt, default, or miscarriage of another, except in the cases provided for in Section 2794 [specified obligations deemed to be original obligation of the promisor];

"3. A agreement made upon consideration of marriage other than a mutual promise to marry;

"4. An agreement for the leasing for a longer period than one year, or for the sale of real property, or of an interest therein; and such agreement, if made by an agent of the party sought to be charged, is invalid, unless the authority of the agent is in writing, subscribed by the party sought to be charged;

"5. An agreement authorizing or employing an agent, broker, or any other person to purchase or sell real estate, or to lease real estate for a longer period than one year, or to procure, introduce, or find a purchaser or seller of real estate or a lessee or lessor of real estate where such lease is for a longer period than one year, for compensation or a commission;

"6. An agreement which by its terms is not to be performed during the lifetime of the promisor, or an agreement to devise or bequeath any property, or to make any provision for any person by will;

"7. An agreement by a purchaser of real property to pay an indebtedness secured by a mortgage or deed of trust upon the property purchased, unless assumption of said indebtedness by the purchaser is specifically provided for in the conveyance of such property."

A contract required by law to be in writing, which through fraud is prevented from being in writing, may be enforced against the fraudulent party.

A written contract may be modified by an *executed* oral agreement.

A contract is an *executed* contract when all its conditions and objectives have been fully performed. All others are executory, or capable of being performed. (§1661.)

But a written contract supersedes all the negotiations or stipulations concerning its subject matter which preceded or accompanied the execution of the instrument and oral evidence of such prior negotiations or agreements in variance with the written contract is not admissible in evidence. This rule is commonly called the *"parol evidence rule."* (§1625.)

Express or implied contracts

A contract may be either express or implied, that is, manifested by conduct. The terms of an express contract are stated in words; the terms of an implied agreement are manifested in conduct. (See Civ. Code, §§1619-1621.)

It is legitimate to look at all the actions of the parties and glean from them whether or not it *appears* an agreement has been reached.

To constitute an implied contract, an agreement must be a transaction between two parties that ordinarily leads to contract. From the conduct of the parties their states of mind are inferred; their mutual assent and "meeting of the minds" is inferred from their bodily manifestations. *However, the legal effects of what a court decides is the agreement does not necessarily coincide with what one or both parties expected or presumed.*

Conditions Precedent, Concurrent, Subsequent

Obligations under contract may be conditional, depending upon the occurrence of uncertain events (§1434). The conditions may be precedent, concurrent, or subsequent (§1435). A condition precedent is one which "is to be performed before some right dependent thereon accrues, or some act dependent thereon is performed" (§1436). Conditions concurrent are those which "are mutually dependent, and are to be performed at the same time" (§1437). A condition subsequent is one "referring to a future event, upon the happening of which the obligation becomes no longer binding upon the other party, if he chooses to avail himself of the condition" (§1438).

In every contract, however, there is an implied covenant that neither party will do anything to destroy or injure the other's right to receive the benefit of the contract. In view of this implied covenant of fair dealing, it would, for example, be reasonable to imply a covenant than vendees would maintain buildings in approximately the same condition as when they took possession, reasonable wear and tear excepted.

This does not necessarily mean that to imply such a covenant *as a condition subsequent* permits forfeiture of a vendee's interest. California law construes contracts strictly against forfeiture. A contract is not to be construed to provide a forfeiture unless no other interpretation is reasonably possible. In the absence of an express covenant in the contract for forfeiture, Civil Code section 3275 provides a defaulting party relief against a forfeiture *if* full compensation is made. Alternative remedies to forfeiture might be receivership or injunction — or rescission.

The Contract

At this point is set forth a simple contract for the construction of a small apartment house. (The contract is not set forth in full and is not intended as a model form.)

ARTICLES OF AGREEMENT*
Contractor's License No. 1234567

THIS AGREEMENT, made this 25th day of October, one thousand nine hundred and seventy-nine, between JOSEPH GRIFFIN, hereinafter called the Owner, and THOMAS JESSUP, hereinafter called the Contractor (it being understood that the terms "Owner" and "Contractors" used herein in the single number shall include the plural, and the use of the masculine gender shall include the femine and neuter).

WITNESSETH:

FIRST: The Contractor, within the space of 180 working days from and after recording of loan agrees to furnish the necessary labor and materials, including tools, implements and appliances, required, and to perform and complete in a workmanlike manner, free from all liens and claims of artisans, materialmen and subcontractors thereon, all the work on attached plan and specifications, incorporated herein and made a part hereof; Contractor to be responsible for carpet, drapes, and furniture placement; this is a "turn key" operation; carpet, furniture, and drapery cost shall be borne by Owner; and all other works shown and described in and by and in conformity with, the plans and specifications for the same signed by the parties hereto; said plans and specifications to he furnished by Contractor.

---

*This is a simple contract for the construction of a small apartment house. There are 10 lengthy provisions which are printed on the reverse side of the contract which are not reproduced. The contract is not intended as a "model" form. Printed forms of contract are available from stationers, or the contract may be drafted based on systemized forms within the law office.

SECOND: Said construction work to be erected on a lot of land situated in the County of Sacramento, State of California, and described as follows: 1415 Baxter Street.

THIRD: The Owner agrees, in consideration of the performance of this agreement by the Contractor, to pay or cause to be paid to the Contractor, his legal representatives or assigns One hundred thirty thousand dollars ($130,000) in United States legal tender, at the times and in the manner following, to-wit: in the normal manner.

NOW, THEREFORE, the Owner hereby accepts the above proposal, and the Contractor agrees to perform the work comprehended thereunder, and by and between them as part and parcel of this contract the stipulations set forth in original writing on the reverse side hereof are understood and agreed upon.

Owner to pay contractor 7% ($9,100 maximum) fee outside of construction loan and as a monthly billed basis.

Any costs exceeding construction loan to be Joseph Griffin's, but not to exceed $5,000.

IN WITNESS WHEREOF, both parties have duly executed this agreement the day and year first above written.

_____   _____
        Witness   Owner

_____   _____
        Witness   Contractor

The contract should be signed by the parties exactly as their names appear in the contract. However, signatures by initials or a mark, by either the first names or the surnames of the parties, are valid.

Each party to a contract should read the contract before signing it. Unless the failure to read was due to fraud or trickery, however, failure to read it does not provide a defense. Excusable mistakes or confidential relationships between the parties may be defenses in some cases.

A party to a contract should not sign it unless he understands it. Each party should insist on being given a duplicate original of the contract (one signed by all the parties) instead of a copy.

Breach of Contract

A client may be involved in disputes over a contract to which he is a party. He may feel that the other party has breached the contract and wants to sue him. May a complaint for breach of contract be validly filed? First the following must be determined:

(1) Did plaintiff and defendant actually have a contract? (See "What is a contract?" and "Creating a Contract — Offer and Acceptance," *supra*.)

(2) Is the contract oral or written? The complaint must allege whether the contract is oral or in writing or it will be demurrable. The contract should either be copied into the complaint or incorporated by reference and a copy attached as an exhibit.

If the contract was subsequently modified or altered by any writing, a copy of such writing should be pleaded and attached as an exhibit.

Not only the contract but also any and all documents pertaining to the contract should be obtained from the client: any letters or memoranda between the parties relating to the contract, its performance or nonperformance; any written notice of rescission or purported rescission (the repeal or revocation of a contract, its extinguishment, see Civ. Code §1689; a number of other statutes also provide ground for rescission); any documents re damages or amount of damages; pleadings in any prior litigation pertaining to the contract — in short, any and all correspondence and papers in plaintiff's possession which might possibly pertain to the contract should be reviewed.

(3) Did the parties have the capacity to enter into a contract? In what capacity did the parties sign the contract, *i.e.,* were any of the parties a minor, conservator, guardian, corporation etc.?

Who are the potential defendants? The parties to the contract will of course be named as defendants, but has anyone acquired an interest in the contract through assignment or other succession in interest? Are there heirs to any of the parties to the contract who might have an interest in the contract?

The capacity of each defendant to be named should be ascertained.

(4) Was the agreement made for a lawful purpose?

(5) Was there consideration for the contract? Is the consideration sufficient and adequate as a matter of law?

(6) Has your client performed all the conditions which the contract requires him to perform? If not, has he been ready and willing to perform those conditions?

(7) Has the defendant failed and refused to perform the conditions of the contract required by the contract? Does he still fail and refuse to perform those conditions?

(8) Has the plaintiff sustained damages by reason of defendant's alleged breach?

(9) The jurisdiction and venue for your action must be determined.

In which county was the contract executed? Where was the contract to be performed? For example, if the contract was for the construction of an apartment house, in which county was it to be constructed? What is the county of residence of defendant? Actions involving contracts might be brought in any such county.

Other facts should be obtained from your client for your file, such as plaintiff's financial record. Is he solvent? Does he have a good reputation and standing in the community for his business dealings? Does he have good credit, bank and personal references? The same questions can be asked about the defendant.

A sample complaint for damages for breach of contract follows.

Complaint for Damages for Breach of Contract

```
 1 │ JOHN JONES
   │ Attorney at Law
 2 │ 670 Crown Street
   │ Sacramento, CA 95814
 3 │ (916) 345-6789
   │
 4 │ Attorney for Plaintiff
   │
 5 │
   │
 6 │
   │
 7 │
   │
 8 │                    SUPERIOR COURT OF CALIFORNIA
   │
 9 │                      COUNTY OF SACRAMENTO
   │
10 │
   │
11 │ JOSEPH GRIFFIN,              )         NO. 278901
   │                             )
12 │          Plaintiff,         )
   │                             )
13 │     v.                      )     COMPLAINT FOR DAMAGES
   │                             )
14 │ THOMAS JESSUP, and          )     (BREACH OF CONTRACT)
   │ DOES I through V,           )
15 │ inclusive,                  )
   │                             )
16 │          Defendants.        )
   │ _____)
17 │
   │
18 │
   │
19 │          Plaintiff alleges:
   │
20 │                              I
   │
21 │          Defendant Thomas Jessup is, and at all times herein
   │
22 │ mentioned was, a resident of Sacramento County, California.
   │
23 │                             II
   │
24 │          Plaintiff is ignorant of the true names and capacities
   │
25 │ of defendants sued herein as DOES I through V, inclusive, and
   │
26 │ therefore sues these defendants by such fictitious names.  Plain-
   │
27 │ tiff will amend this complaint to allege their true names and
   │
28 │ capacities when ascertained.
   │                              1
```

III

At all times mentioned defendant Thomas Jessup has been a general contractor duly licensed as such by the State of California.

IV

On or about October 25, 19　, in the City of Sacramento, County of Sacramento, State of California, plaintiff and defendants entered into a written agreement, a copy of which is attached hereto as Exhibit A and made a part hereof.

V

Plaintiff has at all times done and performed all the stipulations, covenants and agreements required by him on his part to be performed in accordance with the terms and conditions of the contract.

VI

On or about March 25, 19　, defendant Thomas Jessup failed and refused to perform said contract in that he abandoned said construction project; defendant Thomas Jessup still refuses and neglects and fails to perform said contract and to complete the construction of said apartment house project.

VII

As a result of defendant Thomas Jessup's breach of the contract, plaintiff has sustained damages in the sum of $75,000, no part of which has been paid.

WHEREFORE, plaintiff prays judgment against defendants, and each of them, as follows:

1.　For compensatory damages in the sum of $75,000;

2.　For interest on the sum of $75,000 from and after

2

1 │ March 25, 19 ;

2 │   3. For costs of suit herein incurred; and

3 │   4. For such other and further relief as the court may

4 │ deem proper,

5 │   *John Jones*
   │   _____

6 │   Attorney for Plaintiff

7 │

8 │

9 │

10 │   I, JOSEPH GRIFFIN, state:

11 │   I am the plaintiff in the above-entitled matter.

12 │   I have read the foregoing complaint and know the con-

13 │ tents thereof; the same is true of my own knowledge, except as

14 │ to those matters which are therein stated on information and

15 │ belief and, as to those matters, I believe it to be true.

16 │   Executed on April 5, 19 , at Sacramento, California.

17 │   I declare under penalty of perjury that the foregoing

18 │ is true and correct.

19 │   *Joseph Griffin*
   │   _____

20 │

21 │

22 │

23 │

24 │

25 │

26 │

27 │

28 │

                            3

CALIFORNIA PARALEGAL'S GUIDE

Chapter 16

PERSONAL INJURY (AUTOMOBILE ACCIDENTS)

Before starting the main topic of this chapter, automobile accident cases, which are actions in tort, let us digress to mention torts in general, and tort actions brought against the State of California.

TORTS

Tort actions, as do actions involving contracts, account for a substantial amount of civil litigation. The statutory basis for California tort law is rooted in Civil Code section 1708, which provides as follows: "Every person is bound, without contract, to abstain from injuring the person or property of another, or infringing upon any of his rights."

Specialists in the tort field find "torts" difficult to define. Black's Law Dictionary defines a tort as "[a] private or civil wrong or injury." A wide variety of conduct is regulated by tort law. Simple negligence, if it causes injury, is a tort. The defendant must commit a wrong, a wrong that violates a right of the plaintiff under a statute. A right in favor of the plaintiff must be protected by some law imposing a duty upon the defendant. The wrong done must cause injury or damage.

For a general discussion of torts, see 47 California Jurisprudence 2d, Torts, pages 691 *et seq.*

AUTOMOBILE ACCIDENT CASES

A look at new filings indicates that a high percentage of the lawsuits filed are for damages for personal injuries. Personal injury actions arise from a variety of accidents. On-the-job injuries sustained by employees in the course of their employment are covered by workers' compensation. Tort actions arise from products liability, *i.e.*, an implied warranty that the product is safe for the use intended and the product proved to be defective and caused damages. A tort action for personal injury is brought if negligence is involved in an accident.

According to National Safety Council reports, 18,100,000 auto accidents occurred in the United States in 1979. Of this number, 14,500,000 involved a collision between two vehicles. Other types of collisions accounted for 880,000, noncollision accidents accounted for 2,600,000, and pedestrians 120,000. A total of 51,000 deaths resulted from these accidents.

Reference books on personal injury cases are to be found in law libraries and the paralegal specializing in this field should become familiar with them. From these books the alert legal assistant may gain ideas for introducing new methods or improving the existing system.

Methodology is the key to efficient and successful law office administration. The smaller office as well as the big firm can be well organized. Valuable time is lost in searching for forms or information which should be at one's fingertips.

The first step is an office manual. Quite a number of forms are used in the typical accident case and these should be compiled in the office manual after approval by the firm. If the legal assistant finds that this has not been done, it is a project which he or she might well undertake. Reference can be made to form books in the law library and forms previously used found in the firm's files. *California Forms of Pleading and Practice Volumes on Damages and Personal Injuries* is one good reference source.

Some items the manual might contain relating to personal injury actions are:

Applicable statutes of limitation
Checklists (facts, personal injuries, property damage, insurance, etc.)
Any special instructions for handling
General instructions to be given client (by attorney and/or by legal assistant)
Forms:
　Retainer agreement
　Statement for client to complete
　Hospital authorization form
　Medical records authorization form
　Authorization for government agency
　Form of letter to witnesses
　Complaint allegations
　Answer allegations

At this point your attention is called to what has come to be known as "systems," defined by New York attorney Bernard Sternin as "a job-oriented collection of prerecorded materials,'' which consist of "data, documents, and instructions." "You extract and analyze the letters, documents and forms you routinely use when you do the job, and then you arrange them, give them code numbers so you can refer to them easily, and store them in ring books in the order in which they are usually used."* By the use of systems, attorneys can readily delegate their work to legal assistants. In those law offices having an automatic typewriter, the desire to take advantage of its potential has stimulated interest in the development of systems. Programmed materials are stored by recording onto magnetic cards.

How the accident cases are handled will depend upon the size of the law office and the division of duties. In a firm specializing in personal injury cases or handling a large volume of such cases, different paralegals may be designated to handle a particular aspect of each case. In such an office the degree of specialization will be higher, in contrast to the small office where one paralegal may be called upon to perform all these duties. In any event, one legal assistant should be responsible for the processing of the case and keeping the attorney — and the client — informed as to the status of the case.

The attorney will most likely meet the client initially and note a few salient facts, sufficient to enable him to decide whether he should take the case. He will question the client and formulate an opinion as to his veracity and as to the actual damages and liability. If it is obvious that there is no liability on the part of the adverse party, he would refuse the case.

A second meeting may be necessary to give the attorney time for investigation before finally accepting the case. He may decide that the legal theory upon which he could recover was not sound. Or he may find that injury is not shown. If the adverse party has no assets and no insurance — unless the plaintiff has insurance to cover — a lawsuit would probably be futile (though sometimes assets are later discovered or materialize). Occasionally a client's sole reason for wanting to bring suit is vengeance.

In assessing an auto accident case, about the first thing to do is to check the accident report. Was either driver cited? Citation of the

---

*A 20-page booklet, *What Automatic Typing Equipment Can Do For You,* is available free by sending a self-addressed envelope stamped with 40 cents, marked with the title, to Bernard Sternin, Attorney at Law, 5 Hawke Lane, Rockville Centre, New York 11570. An American Bar Association book, coauthored by Sternin, *How to Create-A-System for the Law Office,* may be ordered from the Section of Economics, American Bar Association, 155 East 60th St., Chicago, Illinois 60737, attention Donna Spilis, price $14.95. Sternin's column, the "Methods Box," appears in *Facts & Findings,* the official publication of the National Association of Legal Assistants.

adverse party for any violation indicates the officer at least thought the adverse party was at fault and is prima facie to the advantage of your client. If neither driver was cited, the accident report may indicate other contributing factors on the part of either driver. The primary collision factor may have come from some other source. If the weather was clear and it was daylight, other causes must be looked for. If the weather was not good, *i.e.*, cloudy, raining, snowing, foggy, does the report indicate the other party was driving too fast for such conditions? Was there a stop light or other controls? At what angle did they collide? If a pedestrian was involved, was he in the crosswalk when struck? If not, where was he? Was one of the parties turning? Who had the right of way? Had the other party been drinking or under the influence of drugs? Do you have a photo of the scene of the accident? Was it a "blind" intersection? All in all, who appears to be at fault? If both appear to have been guilty of negligence, how would you apportion respective fault?

Do you have witnesses? What is their version of the accident? Would they be good witnesses, *i.e.*, credible?

Having decided to accept the case, the attorney will generally ask the client to sign a retainer agreement, with specific provisions as to the fee. Generally the office will have its own form of retainer agreement. Care should be taken to make certain that the client understands the agreement. Malpractice claims sometimes arise with the client disgruntled about his fee. Personal injury cases are frequently taken on a contingency fee basis. This should be explained in detail. If the attorney expects to incur any expense for medical expenses, investigators, or other counsel, he should make it clear to the client and an agreement should be reached as to who is to bear the expense. A maximum amount might be set. The client might be given an opinion as to the amount of a reasonable verdict. To overestimate, however, might mean a disappointed client, and of course there is no foretelling what a court or jury might decide.

The legal assistant might be present at the first interview or, if not, will probably take additional information from the client before he leaves the office. A form or checklist should be devised for this purpose, if only for reference, and it should be designed to get the complete story. The client's version of the accident in narrative form should be obtained. A sketch should be made of the scene of the accident.

The statement taken from the client, then, should be detailed. It should contain information on any prior accidents the client may have had, any claims or lawsuits he may have filed, including any prior police record. Full information will prevent the attorney from being surprised in a disclosure in the courtroom, which could conceivably cause him to lose the case. Matters of public record about the client can be obtained by the adverse party. As a patient should disclose to his doctor, so should the client disclose to his attorney. It should be emphasized that information that may not seem pertinent to the client may nevertheless be important to the successful pursuit of his case. The legal assistant should cover the injuries in detail and specifically, i.e., the parts of body injured, whether broken bones, soft tissue injury, psychiatric injury.

The client should be advised that the adverse party's insurance carrier may be checking on him without his being aware of it, to discover whether he is actually disabled as claimed. Cases have been lost by production of photos of clients lifting, running, skiing, etc. Telescopic lens permit the taking of pictures from a distance without the subject's knowledge or awareness. This is not to suggest that a client should conceal the facts as to his true injuries or exaggerate them; a photo might nevertheless give a wrong impression should, for instance, the client be photographed attempting to do something he shouldn't have attempted, and for which he later suffered, or which was contrary to his doctor's orders.

The legal assistant should proceed to collect the necessary documents and investigate the case, either by collecting witnesses' statements or interviewing them. Interviews are frequently done by use of a recording machine over the telephone. (The telephone company can install a coupler making this possible.) The witness must of course be told that his conversation is being recorded and his consent given. If so instructed, the legal assistant may arrange for an investigator for the case, and then work with him.

A notebook of trial strategy material prepared by the legal assistant should list the witnesses, with their names and phone numbers, alphabetically, with a two or three-sentence synopsis of their expected testimony.

Refer to the section on discovery, in the chapter on preparation for trial for questions to witnesses.

Among the documents usually needed are: the accident report (either from the city police or the California Highway Patrol), any traffic citations; written statements by the client and witnesses; the plaintiff's medical history including past injuries and illnesses; copies of medical and hospital bills; bills for repairs of automobile; insurance policies of defendant. These may be compiled in a separate trial notebook for the attorney including all photographs, all other demonstrative evidence, and the pleadings. The notebook may also contain all discovery material developed through interrogatories, requests for admissions, and depositions.

A cross-examination list can be worked out by the attorney and legal assistant, as well as a voir dire list.

The attorney should set up a list of issues and then the legal assistant can help set out the evidence in direct proof of each issue thereunder.

A letter is sometimes sent to the adverse party by the attorney telling him of his representation and that if he is insured he should turn the letter over to his carrier and that if no reply is received by a specified date legal action will be taken. Some attorneys prefer to file suit first.

The paralegal should calendar the 100-day public entity statute, the one-year personal injury statute, and the 2-3-5 year dismissal statutes.

The Complaint — Personal Injury

Let us prepare a complaint based on the following facts:

Carol Smith, our client, and her 10-year-old daughter, Susan, were involved in an automobile accident at about 3:00 p.m. on May 18, 1978. Carol was driving her Ford Pinto automobile and was struck by another auto at the intersection of 23d and F Streets in the City of Sacramento, County of Sacramento, California. Susan was a passenger in the car. Carol was proceeding in an easterly direction on F Street and the other car was proceeding in a southerly direction on 23d Street at the time of collision. Ralph Roper was driving the other automobile, a 1975 Chevrolet. Ralph Roper was an employee of the Pacific Glaser Company and was driving his car on company business at the time. Carol's car was seriously damaged and was in the repair shop for a few weeks. Both Carol and Susan sustained physical injuries and Carol was unable to return to her job for some time.

The legal assistant should be able to draft the complaint. A checklist of basic facts appears in 4 Auerbach, Handling Accident Cases, §6, and checklists for essentials of a complaint appears at §23, for both personal injury and wrongful death actions.

Usually a law office will have systemized forms with preferred language they have approved. In other words, probably no two law firms would prepare an identical complaint on the same facts. The complaint in this case might look like the following:

Complaint

```
 1    H, ABE NOBLE
      Attorney at Law
 2    777 Beacon St.
      Sacramento, CA 95814
 3
      Attorney for Plaintiffs
 4

 5

 6

 7

 8            SUPERIOR COURT OF THE STATE OF CALIFORNIA

 9                   COUNTY OF SACRAMENTO

10

11    CAROL SMITH and SUSAN SMITH,    )        NO. 123456
      a minor, by and through her     )
12    Guardian Ad Litem, CAROL SMITH, )
                                      )
13             Plaintiffs,            )
                                      )
14        v.                          )    COMPLAINT FOR PERSONAL
                                      )
15    RALPH ROPER; PACIFIC GLASER     )         INJURIES
      COMPANY, a California corpora-   )
16    tion, and DOES ONE through FIVE, )
      inclusive,                      )
17                                    )
               Defendants.            )
18    _____)

19

20                 FIRST CAUSE OF ACTION

21        Plaintiff CAROL SMITH alleges:

22                        I

23        The true names or capacities, whether individual, cor-

24    porate, associate or otherwise, of defendants FIRST DOE, SECOND

25    DOE, THIRD DOE, FOURTH DOE and FIFTH DOE are unknown to plain-

26    tiff, who therefore sues said defendants by such fictitious names

27    and will ask leave to amend this complaint to show their true

28    names and capacities when the same have been ascertained;

                           1
```

1 plaintiff is informed and believes and thereon alleges that each

2 of said defendants is negligently or otherwise responsible in some

3 manner for the events and happenings herein referred to and negli-

4 gently or otherwise caused injury and damages proximately thereby

5 to the plaintiff as herein alleged.

6 II

7 Defendant RALPH ROPER is and at all times herein men-

8 tioned was a resident of the County of Sacramento, State of

9 California.

10 III

11 Defendant PACIFIC GLASER COMPANY is now and was at all

12 times mentioned herein a corporation duly organized and existing

13 under and by virtue of the laws of the State of California.

14 IV

15 Plaintiff is informed and believes and thereon alleges

16 that at all times and places herein mentioned the defendant RALPH

17 ROPER was driving a certain 1975 Chevrolet truck with the permis-

18 sion and at the direction of the defendant PACIFIC GLASER COMPANY

19 and upon its business and as its agent, servant and employee and

20 under its authority and within the scope and terms of said agency

21 and employment.

22 V

23 At all times herein mentioned plaintiff CAROL SMITH was

24 and now is the owner of a certain 1976 Ford Pinto, California

25 license number 687 ABC.

26 VI

27 At all times herein mentioned 23d Street was and now is

28 a public street and hghway running in a general northerly and

2

southerly direction in the City of Sacramento, County of Sacra-

mento, State of California; at all times herein mentioned F Street

was and now is a public street and highway in said city and

county, running in a general easterly and westerly direction and

intersecting said 23d Street.

VII

On or about April 18, 1978, at about the hour of 3:00

p.m. of said date, plaintiff CAROL SMITH was driving said Ford

automobile in a prudent and careful manner in a general easterly

direction upon and along said F Street in the vicinity of its

intersection with said 23d Street; at said time and place

defendants, and each of them, was driving a 1975 Chevrolet motor

vehicle along said 23d Street in a general southerly direction;

at said time and place defendants, and each of them, so negli-

gently and carelessly entrusted, owned, operated, maintained and

controlled said Chevrolet motor vehicle as to cause same to, and

same did, collide with the automobile which plaintiff CAROL SMITH

was driving as aforesaid with great force and violence, thereby

damaging the said Ford automobile and causing plaintiffs to

sustain the injuries hereinafter alleged.

VIII

By reason of said negligence and collision aforesaid,

and as a proximate result thereof, plaintiff CAROL SMITH received

injuries consisting of, but not limited to, severe injuries,

bruises, contusions, strain to all the muscles of her body, and

a fracture of the bone of her arm; the injuries thus received by

plaintiff have greatly impaired her health, strength and activity

and have thereby caused and continue to cause her great mental and

3

1   physical and nervous pain and suffering and an extreme shock to

2   plaintiff's nervous system; and said plaintiff is informed and

3   believes, and thereon alleges, that said injuries will result in

4   some disability to her, all to her general damage in an amount in

5   excess of the jurisdictional minimum of the superior court, which

6   will be shown according to proof at time of trial.

7   IX

8   As a further, direct and proximate result of the negli-

9   gence of defendants, and each of them, as herein alleged, plain-

10 tiff CAROL SMITH was required to and did employ and continues to

11 employ physicians, surgeons and others for medical examination,

12 treatment and care of said injuries, and did incur medical and

13 incidental expenses, which will be shown according to proof at

14 time of trial; plaintiff CAROL SMITH is informed and believes,

15 and on such information and belief alleges, that she will incur

16 further medical and incidental expenses for the care and treatment

17 of said injuries, the exact amount of which is unknown at this

18 time, all to her special damage in an amount to be proven at trial.

19   X

20   As a further proximate result of the hereinabove

21 alleged carelessness and negligence of said defendants, and each

22 of them, plaintiff lost the use of her automobile for a period of

23 time, all to her further special damage in an amount equal to the

24 reasonable value of said loss of use.

25   XI

26   As a further, direct and proximate result of the care-

27 lessness and negligence of defendants, and each of them, plain-

28 tiff CAROL SMITH was prevented from attending to her usual

                                     4

1 occupation or any occupation whatsoever and has been damaged in

2 an amount not yet ascertainable; plaintiff is informed and

3 believes and on such information and belief alleges that by reason

4 of said carelessness and negligence of defendants, and each of

5 them, plaintiff CAROL SMITH will, in the future, be prevented from

6 attending to her usual occupation for an undetermined period of

7 time, all to her further special damage in an amount to be proven

8 at the time of trial herein.

9

10   SECOND CAUSE OF ACTION

11   Plaintiff SUSAN SMITH, a minor, by her guardian ad litem,

12 CAROL SMITH, alleges:

13   I

14   For the purposes of this action, CAROL SMITH was duly

15 appointed by the above-entitled court on January 5, 1979, and

16 she now is guardian ad litem for said minor.

17   II

18   Said plaintiff by this reference hereby incorporates and

19 makes a part hereof as though fully set forth herein at length

20 all and singular the allegations contained in paragraphs I through

21 VII of the First Cause of Action herein.

22   III

23   On or about the 18th day of April, 1978, at or about the

24 hour of 3:00 p.m. of said date, plaintiff SUSAN SMITH was a

25 passenger in plaintiff CAROL SMITH's automobile being driven in

26 a general easterly direction on said F Street in the vicinity of

27 its intersection with said 23d Street in the City of Sacramento,

28 County of Sacramento, State of California.

5

IV

By reason of said negligence and collision aforesaid, and as a proximate result thereof, plaintiff SUSAN SMITH, a minor, received injuries consisting of, but not limited to, severe cuts and bruises on the face and head; the injuries thus received by plaintiff have greatly impaired her health, strength and activity and have thereby caused and continue to cause her great mental and physical and nervous pain and suffering and an extreme shock to plaintiff's nervous system; and said plaintiff is informed and believes and therefore avers said injuries are and each of them will be permanent, all to her general damage in an amount in excess of the jurisdictional minimum of the superior court, which will be shown according to proof at time of trial.

V

As a further, direct and proximate result of the negligence of defendants, and each of them, as herein alleged, plaintiff SUSAN SMITH was required to and did employ and continues to employ physicians, surgeons and others for medical examination, treatment and care of said injuries, and did incur medical and incidental expenses, which will be shown according to proof at time of trial; plaintiff SUSAN SMITH is informed and believes, and on such information and belief alleges, that she will incur further medical and incidental expenses for the care and treatment of said injuries, the exact amount of which is unknown at this time, all to her special damage in an amount to be proven at trial.

6

WHEREFORE, plaintiff CAROL SMITH and SUSAN SMITH, a

minor, by CAROL SMITH, her Guardian Ad Litem, pray for judgment

against the defendants, and each of them, for:

1. General damages in excess of the jurisdictional

limits of the superior court according to proof.

2. Special damages according to proof.

3. Costs of suit herein incurred.

4. Such other and further relief as the court may deem

proper.

Dated: January 8, 1979.

_____

Attorney for Plaintiffs

I, CAROL SMITH, state:

I am one of the plaintiffs in the above-entitled

matter.

I have read the foregoing complaint and know the con-

tents thereof; the same is true of my own knowledge, except as

to those matters which are therein stated on information and

belief and, as to those matters, I believe it to be true.

Executed on January 8, 1979, at Sacramento, Cali-

fornia.

I declare under penalty of perjury that the foregoing

is true and correct.

_____

7

A few comments regarding this complaint are in order. Two or more causes of action joined in the same complaint need not be separately stated. But some attorneys find it desirable for the sake of clarity and organization to separately state the causes of action. In the foregoing complaint the causes of action are separately stated. Numbers below correspond to the numbered allegations of the complaint.

Title of the Complaint

"Does" are ordinarily named in the title of a complaint as a matter of course.

If the plaintiff is a minor, a petition for the appointment of a guardian is necessary before filing suit. Note that the minor, not the guardian, is always named as plaintiff. In this suit, of course, the guardian is named as plaintiff in addition since she has her own cause of action for damages.

I

This is the allegation for Does, the so-called "fictitious name" allegation, based on Code of Civil Procedure section 474, which permits the plaintiff to bring suit against persons whose names have not been ascertained at the time of filing suit. This is particularly important when a statute of limitations would run out and bar filing suit. Charging allegations against the Does must be included. The naming of Does permits service on defendants discovered after suit is filed. The complaint must be amended to substitute the true name. Notice is not required.

III

This allegation shows that the employer is a corporation, in this case a domestic corporation (*i.e.*, incorporated under California laws.)

IV

Under the doctrine of respondeat superior, the employer is responsible for the actions of its agent when acting within the course and scope of employment. This paragraph alleges the agency.

VI

This allegation establishes the venue, in this case the county where the accident occurred. Our accident occurred in Sacramento County and the action is brought in Sacramento Superior Court.

VII

This allegation establishes the jurisdiction of the court, *i.e.*, that it is an action for property damage, over which the superior court has jurisdiction.

VIII

This allegation claims general damages sustained by plaintiff for personal injuries. The possibility that the total extent of injury may not be known at the time of filing the complaint exists and may be ascertained only at a later date. The allegation that injuries are permanent is usually based on the prognosis of the doctor.

Note the language that our plaintiff was driving "in a prudent and careful manner," *i.e.*, exercising ordinary care as is expected and required if she is to recover damages, and note the language as to the negligence of the defendants.

Code of Civil Procedure section 425.10 since 1974 has provided that the amount of damages demanded in a *superior court* action for personal injuries or wrongful death shall not be stated in the complaint.

However, the defendant may at any time after filing of the action request a statement setting forth the nature and amount of damages being sought and serve on the plaintiff (or cross-complainant) a request for a responsive statement. If the response is not served within 15 days thereafter, the court may be petitioned for an order compelling service.

If no such request is made, plaintiff is nevertheless required to give notice to the defendant of the amount of special and general damages sought (1) before a default may be taken, or (2) if an answer has been filed, at least 60 days prior to the date set for trial (Code Civ. Proc. §425.11).

Defense counsel needs to find out the damages because of insurance policy limits. If the defendant is being sued in excess of his policy limits he must be informed; he may want to obtain his own attorney rather than the insurance company's counsel.

A form of Request for Nature and Amount of Damages follows:

[Title of Court and cause]

TO PLAINTIFFS, AND EACH OF THEM, AND TO THEIR ATTORNEY, H. ABE NOBLE:

RALPH ROPER and PACIFIC GLASER COMPANY, a California corporation, defendants in the above-entitled action, pursuant to section 425.11 of the California Code of Civil Procedure, hereby request that you set forth, item by item, the nature and extent of the special and general damages which you seek by filing this action.

Dated:

s/ Clarence D. Paragon
_____

Attorney for Defendants

The Response to Request for Statement of Nature and Amount of Damages of plaintiff might simply read:

TO DEFENDANTS RALPH ROPER AND PACIFIC GLASER COMPANY, a California corporation, and to CLARENCE D. PARAGON, THEIR ATTORNEY:

The nature and amount of damages sought in the above-entitled action are as follows:

[list damages, 1, 2, 3, etc.]

Dated:

s/H. Abe Noble
Attorney for Plaintiff

Forms of request, response, notice of motion and order may be found in volume 5 of California Forms of Pleading and Practice, Damages.

IX

This is an allegation for the special damages for the expenses of physicians, surgeons, medical examination, treatment and care, sustained by plaintiff Carol Smith.

X

This an allegation for loss of use while plaintiff Carol Smith's automobile was being repaired. No claim for loss of use could be alleged if the automobile had been damaged beyond repair. Ordinarily a complaint would include an allegation for the damages to plaintiff's automobile, but is omitted here.

Other allegations for special damages might have been included, as for towing her car to a garage, damaged clothing.

XI

This paragraph is necessary to establish loss of wages. In this case plaintiff had not returned to work as of the time of filing the complaint.

Prayer

There are alternative ways of phrasing the prayer, as there are alternative ways of phrasing the language of the complaint.

Where there are multiple parties and/or multiple causes of action, the prayer is sometimes placed immediately following each cause of action.

Some attorneys use a separate numbered paragraph (arabic) for each type of damage prayed for in the complaint.

Verification

A complaint in negligence is not required by statute to be verified. Some attorneys do not verify negligence actions. The legal assistant should check with the attorney as to office policy as to verification. See Verification in Chapter 5, Commencing the Lawsuit.

The verification of our complaint is by plaintiff Carol Smith. The attorney could have verified under Code of Civil Procedure section 446 if the plaintiff had been absent from Sacramento County where the attorney had his office or if for some other reason plaintiff was unable to verify, or if the facts were within the knowledge of her attorney.

A form of verification if made by plaintiff's attorney would appear in the following or similar form:

"I, the undersigned, say:

"I am an attorney at law admitted to practice before all courts of the State of California and have my office in Sacramento County, California, and am the attorney for plaintiff in the above-entitled action, who is unable to make the verification because she is absent from said county and for that reason affiant makes this verification on her behalf; I have read the foregoing document and am informed and believe the matters therein to be true and on that ground allege that the matters stated therein are true.

"Executed on January 8, 1979, at Sacramento, California.

"I declare under penalty of perjury that the foregoing is true and correct.

Signature: H. Abe Noble

H. Abe Noble"

Other Frequently Used Allegations

There are a multitude of possible allegations, such as damages to clothing, employment of housekeeper, names of heirs in wrongful death action, loss of consortium, and so on. Here are included only a few of the more frequently used allegations:

Where a guardian ad litem is appointed for plaintiff:

Plaintiff _____ is a minor of the age of ____ years; heretofore by order of court duly given and made ___(name of guardian)___ the ___(relationship)___ of said minor was appointed as the guardian ad litem of said minor with authority to commence and prosecute this action for and on said minor's behalf, and by such appointment became and is now the duly appointed, qualified and acting guardian ad litem of said plaintff.

Where defendant is a corporation:

If a complaint is being prepared naming a corporation as a defendant, determine the exact name of the corporation in order to properly name the corporation as a defendant. The "United Face Co." may prove to be not a corporation at all but a partnership, associates doing business under a common name, or an individual doing business under a fictitious name.

Inquiry should be made as to the name of any person designated for service by the corporation, and the names and addresses of the officers on file so that service of the summons and complaint can be made.

All such information may be obtained by writing or phoning the Secretary of State's office.

If claim has been filed in estate:

If plaintiff had preliminarily filed a claim in the estate, the following allegation would also be necessary;

On _____, 19___, plaintiff forwarded a creditor's claim in the total sum of $_____ for the said damages sustained by plaintiff as a result of said accident to said defendant _____ as executor* of the estate of said_____, deceased; on _____ , 19___, said defendant _____as executor* of the estate of said _____, deceased, rejected said claim of plaintiff.
*Substitute "executrix," "administrator" or "administratrix" as appropriate.

Where defendant's automobile was owned by another but driven with defendant's permission (and not in course and scope of employment):

At all times herein mentioned defendant _____ was the legal and registered owner* of said automobile** which was then and there being operated by said defendant _____, and that said automobile* was at the time and place of the collision herein alleged being driven and operated by the said defendant with the consent, permission and authority of said defendant _____.
*Defendant is sometimes the registered owner but not the legal owner because title remains in the seller.
**Use "automobile," "motor vehicle," "motorcycle," as appropriate.

Where car has salvage value:

In the foregoing complaint the car was reparable. If the car was badly damaged but had some salvage value, the following paragraph would be used;

Plaintiff's said automobile at the time of said collision was of the actual and reasonable value of $_____; as a proximate result of said carelessness and negligence of said defendants and as a result of said collision said automobile was destroyed to the extent that (it was not economically reparable) or (repairs were estimated at an amount beyond its value); the reasonable salvage value of said automobile was and is the sum of $_____$; plaintiff was thereby damaged in the sum of $_____$.

Car Damaged Beyond Repair:

If plaintiff's car was damaged beyond repair (totaled), this allegation could be used:

Plaintiff's said automobile at the time of said collision was of the actual and reasonable value of _____ Dollars ($_____$); as a proximate result of said negligence and collision said automobile was destroyed beyond repair and rendered of no value; plaintiff has been thereby further damaged in the sum of _____ Dollars ($_____$).

When the car is damaged beyond repair, there is no loss of use allegation.

Wrongful Death — General Damages:

As a further proximate result of the hereinabove decribed negligence of defendants, and each of them, and of the resulting death of decedent, decedent's heirs at law have been deprived of the society, comfort, care, protection, services and support of decedent and have thereby sustained pecuniary loss, all to their pecuniary loss in an amount in excess of the jurisdictional minimum of the Superior Court.

Wrongful Death — Special Damages:

As a further proximate result of the hereinabove described negligence of defendants, and each of them, and of the resulting death of decedent, _____, as Executrix of the Estate of the decedent, has been required to pay funeral and burial expenses in an amount to be proven at the time of trial herein.

Procedure on Filing Complaint Where Guardian Ad Litem

On the date of filing the foregoing complaint in *Smith v. Roper,* et al., a petition of Carol Smith, as guardian ad litem of Susan Smith, a minor, and an Order Appointing Guardian of Minor is first presented to a superior court judge. The date the judge signed the order (page 5 of the complaint, line 15) is inserted on the original and all copies. After that has been done, the petition and order are presented to the County Clerk with a check for the filing fee.

Only then can the Complaint for Personal Injuries be filed and the summons issued. The lower portion of the summons is intentionally left blank. The box for 2a would be checked on the summons served on defendant Ralph Roper. On the summons for Pacific Glaser Co.

the boxes at 2c and beside CCP 416.10 (Corporation) would be checked.

The number of copies needed is:

1 original for filing with the court

1 copy for defendant Roper

1 copy for defendant Pacific Glaser Company

1 copy for client Carol Smith (and minor daughter Susan)

1 copy for office file (endorsed)

1 copy for office file (can be on plain paper), not to leave file when other copies taken to court; may be discarded when endorsed copy is returned

Answer

A checklist of defenses appears at pages 519-521 in Werchick, *California Preparation and Trial*, with which the legal assistant should become familiar. In point of fact, many of the chapters in this book should be of value and interest to the legal assistant in the civil litigation field.

Answer to Complaint

```
 1   CLARENCE D. PARAGON
     Attorney at Law
 2   999 Wright Way
     Sacramento, CA 95814
 3   (916) 474-9032

 4   Attorney for Defendants

 5

 6

 7

 8              SUPERIOR COURT OF THE STATE OF CALIFORNIA

 9                      COUNTY OF SACRAMENTO

10

11   CAROL SMITH and SUSAN SMITH,      )      NO. 123456
     a minor, by and through her       )
12   Guardian Ad Litem, CAROL SMITH,   )
                                       )
13              Plaintiffs,            )
                                       )
14        v.                           )      ANSWER TO COMPLAINT
                                       )
15   RALPH ROPER; PACIFIC GLASER       )
     COMPANY, a California corpora-    )
16   tion, and DOES ONE through FIVE,  )
     inclusive,                        )
17                                     )
                Defendants.            )
18   _____)

19

20        Come now defendants RALPH ROPER and PACIFIC GLASER

21   COMPANY, a California corporation, and each of them, and for

22   answer to plaintiffs' complaint on file herein, admit, deny and

23   allege as follows:

24                            I

25        Defendants deny each and every, all and singular, the

26   allegations contained in said complaint, denying generally and

27   specifically that plaintiffs, or either of them, were injured or

28   damaged as a result of the alleged conduct of these answering
```

                                    1

1 defendants as set forth in said complaint, or at all.

2

3   AS A SEPARATE, DISTINCT AND AFFIRMATIVE DEFENSE to

4 plaintiffs' complaint, these answering defendants allege as

5 follows:

6   I

7   That at the time and place referred to in said com-

8 plaint, and prior thereto, plaintiffs, and each of them, were

9 themselves actively negligent in and about the matters referred

10 to in said complaint and in their active negligence directly and

11 proximately contributed to and caused the incident alleged in

12 said complaint and the resultant damages sustained thereby, if

13 any there were.

14

15   WHEREFORE, these answering defendants, and each of

16 them, pray that plaintiffs take nothing by reason of their com-

17 plaint on file herein, that these defendants, and each of them,

18 be dismissed with their costs of suit incurred herein, and for

19 such other and further relief as the court may deem just and

20 proper.

21   Dated: January 25, 1979.

22

23   _____

24   Clarence D. Paragon

25   Attorney for Defendants

26

27

28

2

1   I, RALPH ROPER, declare:

2   I am one of the defendants in the above-entitled

3 matter;

4   I have read the foregoing Answer to Complaint and know

5 the contents thereof; the same is true of my own knowledge,

6 except as to those matters which are therein stated on informa-

7 tion and belief, and as to those matters, I believe it to be

8 true.

9   Executed on January 25, 1979, at Sacramento, Cali-

10 fornia.

11   I declare under penalty of perjury that the foregoing

12 is true and correct.

13   _Ralph Roper_

14   Ralph Roper

15

16

17

18

19

20

21

22

23

24

25

26

27

28

3

ANSWER TO COMPLAINT

The Answer to Complaint set out above is a general denial. Defendants might have elected to make a specific denial, in which event the introductory paragraph, the affirmative defense and the prayer of the answer would be the same, but in place of such paragraph one could have had two paragraphs reading like this:

I

Admit the allegations of paragraphs I, II, III, IV, V, and VI of the first cause of action of plaintiffs' complaint herein.

II

Deny all and singular, generally and specifically, each and every allegation contained in paragraphs VII, VIII, IX, X and XI of plaintiffs' complaint.

Similar denials as to plaintiffs' second cause of action would have been incorporated also. Since our complaint in this case was verified — and the amount sought exceeds $1,000 — defendants *must* verify their answer.

For ready reference, a few of the usual forms used in answers are set forth below:

1. *Admitting Portion, Denying Remainder*

Except as herein specifically admitted, defendant denies generally and specifically each and every allegation in paragraph ____ as though such denial is specifically set forth.

2. *Denial on Information and Belief*

Answering the allegations contained in paragraph ____, defendant is informed and believes and upon such information and belief denies each and every allegation contained therein.

3. *Denial for Lack of Information*

Answering the allegations contained in paragraph ____, defendant, for lack of information, neither admits nor denies each and every allegation contained therein.

4. *Denial by Reference*

Answering the allegations of paragraphs ____ and ____ of the ____ Cause of Action, defendant realleges and incorporates herein by reference, with the same force and effect as though set forth in full herein, each and all of defendant's allegations and denials contained in his answer to the First Cause of Action of plaintiff's complaint.

5. *Line-for-Line Denial*

Answering the allegations of paragraph ____, commencing with the word "____," line ____, page ____, and ending with the word "____," line ____, page ____, this answering defendant denies the allegations set forth therein.

6. *Straight Denial*

Answering the allegations of paragraphs ____ and ____, this answering defendant denies each and every, all and singular, generally and specifically, the allegations contained therein, and each and every part thereof.

SETTLEMENT

If the amount involved is small, economics demand that the attorney try to settle the case. A jury trial is expensive. The liability on the part of the defendant will influence the attorney's efforts to settle.

The attorney will discuss settlement with the client. The attorney will want to review all the pleadings, investigatory material accumulated, and special damages before the settlement conference and discuss with the legal assistant. A statement of the matters agreed upon may be stipulated by counsel.

The attorney will decide on what discovery should be made, interrogatories, requests for admission. One purpose of requests for admission is to give the attorney an idea of what to look for in depositions.

See Discovery section in Chapter 6, Preparation for Trial, for suggested questions in taking depositions in automobile accident cases.

Both attorneys will have the provisions of Code of Civil Procedure section 998 in mind in making an offer or accepting a defendant's offer, since either client may become subject to paying costs if an offer is refused. The attorney should keep a record of offers and counteroffers. If his client refuses an offer, the refusal should be obtained in writing from his client. A memorandum to file should be written at the end of negotiation.

In organizing a case for trial, the paralegal will arrange the file for the attorney to take to court. A means should be devised to make the documents in file and the proposed exhibits available for ready reference by the attorney. Index tabs might be used, or separate folders placed within the main file and labeled to separate the various reports, bills, photographs, proposed jury instructions, exhibits to be introduced, etc.

A few comments on the trial itself might not be amiss at this point. The trial itself is the highlight, or the climax of the entire proceeding.

Bifurcation of Trial

Code of Civil Procedure section 597 permits, upon the motion of a party, the trial of special defenses not on the merits of a case before the trial of other issues. Also the court, upon its own motion or the motion of a party, is authorized to require that the trial of any issue or any part thereof shall precede the trial or any other issue or part thereof.

Trial

Each side makes an opening statement, as a sort of preview, of what is to be presented. The client's case is presented through witnesses, documents, photographs and other evidence.

Attorneys draw out the facts of the situation from the witnesses. Under the rules of evidence they can ask only certain questions. For example, as a rule, lawyers may not suggest the answers to their own witnesses, but upon cross-examination may ask leading questions of their opponent's witnesses. A leading question is one which suggests the answer desired, as "Isn't it true, Mr. Brown, that you saw the defendant strike Mr. Jones?"

Nor is hearsay admissible evidence, because no cross-examination is possible. For instance, if Mr. Green says that Mr. White *told* him that he saw the defendant strike Mr. Jones, and Mr. White is not there in court, he cannot be cross-examined and therefore Mr. Green's testimony is not admissible in evidence.

The attorneys ask questions that bear upon the allegations made and the answers should be relevant. The plaintiff presents his case first and calls his witnesses. Then the defendant's attorney may cross-examine them to test their accuracy. When the plaintiff "rests," the defendant's attorney has the opportunity to present his side of the case. At this juncture the defendant's attorney might move for a nonsuit, in which event he would in effect concede the plaintiff's story but claim that no legal wrong had been done. Giving the plaintiff the benefit of the doubt, the judge must rule. If the motion for nonsuit is denied, the defendant would proceed to present his side. When he finishes, plaintiff may reply to the defendant with more evidence, and so on.

Both sides then argue their cases on the facts presented, reviewing, in their closing arguments, how the facts support their contentions. They may choose to present briefs. The case is then submitted, to await the judge's decision or the jury's verdict.

CLAIMS AND ACTIONS AGAINST PUBLIC ENTITIES AND PUBLIC EMPLOYEES
(Gov. Code §§810-996.6.)

Assuming for the moment that a particular tort action may be brought against a public entity (Gov. Code §§815 *et seq.*), the legal assistant should be familiar with the provisions of Government Code section 945.4, which prohibits, with certain exceptions, the bringing of a suit for money or damages against a public entity until a written claim therefor has been presented to the public entity and then acted upon by the board (governing board of local public entity or State Board of Control if against the State) or deemed to have been rejected by the board, in accordance with the applicable chapters of the code. The legal assistant should check the file, and with the client if in doubt, to determine whether the client has already complied with this requirement.

The filing of a claim is required to give the State (or other public body) an opportunity to make an early investigation of the facts and decide upon either settlement or litigation. A suggested form of a claim against a public entity appears on page 389 of Deering's Annotated Government Code. A little background as to the immunity from suit of a public entity is appropriate.

Sovereign Immunity

Sovereign immunity is said to have begun with the personal prerogatives of the King of England. In the feudal structure the lord of the manor could not be sued in his own courts and the king (the highest feudal lord) enjoyed the same immunity.

Under the doctrine of governmental immunity, or "sovereign immunity," the State of California and its political subdivisions were largely immune from tort liability. No public entity had been immune when it engaged in a proprietary function or in those cases where the legislature had waived immunity. The immunity of counties or local districts stemmed from an early American case which had adopted the rule of an English case.

On January 27, 1961, the California Supreme Court rendered two landmark decisions, *Muskopf v. Corning* (1961) 55 Cal.2d 211, and *Lipman v. Brisbane Elementary School Dist.* (1961) 55 Cal.2d 224, the net effect of which was that the State and its political subdivisions would not be held immune from tort liability except in some instances when its agent was immune, *i.e.*, when performing a discretionary rather than a ministerial act.

The *Muskopf* case discarded governmental immunity as mistaken and unjust and concluded: "Only the vestigial remains of such governmental immunity have survived; its requiem has long been foreshadowed. For years the process of erosion of governmental immunity has gone on unabated. The Legislature has contributed mightily to that erosion. The courts, by distinction and extension, have removed much of the force of the rule. Thus, in holding that the doctrine of governmental immunity for torts for which its agents are liable has no place in our law we make no startling break with the past but merely take the final step that carries to its conclusion an established legislative and judicial trend.'' (at p. 221.)

An onslaught of tort claims was anticipated and insurance was needed. A moratorium was declared in 1961 and in 1963 a statute was enacted entitled "Claims and Actions Against Public Entities and Public Employees," now popularly referred to as the "Tort Claims Act." (Gov. Code §§810 *et seq.*) Under this act public entities have no tort liability whatsoever *except* where expressly provided by the statute. While immunity is now the rule, there are, however, many exceptions provided by statute. (See sections following Government Code section 815.)

Tort Claims Act

As indicated above, Government Code sections now provide for the liability of governmental entities (the State (as defined in §900.6), the Regents of the University of California, a county, city, district, public authority, public agency, and any other political subdivision or public corporation in the State) and their employees under specified conditions and govern the procedure for filing claims and actions against them.

Sections 905-905.2 enumerate the classes required to be presented, and the exceptions.

Sections 910 and 910.2, *et seq.*, deal with the contents of the claims and signature, form, amendment, etc.

Sections 901 and 911.2, *et seq.*, relate to the time for presentment of claims.

Sections 911.4, *et seq.*, provide for a written application to present a claim that was not timely presented and for granting of the application under specified circumstances.

Section 912.4 covers the time for action on claims, extension of time by agreement, and effect of failure or refusal to act within the time specified.

Section 915 lists the method of presenting claims, any amendments to claims, or applications to file late claims.

Sections 940, *et seq.*, deal with actions against public entities and public employees.

Section 946.6 makes provisions for a petition to a court for an order for relief from the provisions of section 945.4 under certain circumstances.

Section 945.6 deals with the limitation as to the time for commencing suit against a public entity, which is generally six months after the claim has been acted upon or is deemed to have been rejected by the board; this section contains another time limitation for persons sentenced to imprisonment.

Section 950, *et seq.*, contain provisions for actions against public employees.

Special provisions relating to actions against the state (venue, transfer of action, service of claims and summons, etc.) are contained in section 955, *et seq.*, and special provisions relating to actions against local public entities are found in section 960, *et seq.*

All these interrelated sections should be studied carefully and any statutory amendments or additions noted.

LEGAL DOCTRINES AND COMMON TERMS — ACCIDENTS

Contributory Negligence

Two basic concepts relating to accidents stem from common law: "The first is that one whose negligence has caused damage to another should be liable therefor. The second is that one whose negligence has contributed to his own injury should not be permitted to cast the burden of liability upon another." (*Li v. Yellow Cab Co.* (1975) 13 Cal.3d 804, 822-823.)

Contributory negligence has been defined as negligence on the part of a person injured which, along with the negligence of another, proximately caused the tort of which the injured party complains.

In some states contributory negligence barred recovery to one guilty of *any* contributory negligence. The California legislature wished to make recovery possible to the negligent plaintiff under *some* circumstances. Therefore the legislature sought to include the concept of last clear chance in its rule of responsibility. (*Li v. Yellow Cab Co., supra*, 13 Cal.3d at pp. 822-823.) (See §12.2 under comparative negligence, Werchick, California Preparation and Trial, Parker & Son Publications. pp. 492-494.)

Last Clear Chance Doctrine

Under the last clear chance doctrine, defendant could be held liable although plaintiff may have been contributorily negligent. If defendant, immediately prior to an injurious act, had the superior [greater] opportunity to avoid the accident by the exercise of ordinary care, he had the "last clear chance" to avoid the accident. Under circumstances where this doctrine was properly applicable, the injured party was relieved from the rigid application of the rule of contributory negligence, with no recovery.

When the last clear chance doctrine was not involved, one who was guilty of any contributory negligence could not (prior to *Li v. Yellow Cab Co.*) recover from another for the injury suffered.

Under *Li v. Yellow Cab, supra,* 13 Cal.3d at pages 826, 829, the doctrine of last clear chance was abolished in California; along with contributory negligence it was subsumed under the general process of assessing liability in proportion to the parties' respective negligence (comparative negligence).

Comparative Negligence

The "all-or-nothing" rule of contributory negligence as it existed in California has been superseded by a system of "pure" comparative negligence, "the fundamental purpose of which shall be to assign responsibility and liability for damage *in direct proportion to the amount of negligence of each of the parties.* Therefore, in all actions for negligence resulting in injury to person or property, the contributory negligence of the person injured in person or property shall not bar recovery, but the damages awarded shall be diminished in proportion to the amount of negligence attributable to the person recovering." (Emphasis added.) (*Li v. Yellow Cab Co., supra,* 13 Cal.3d at p. 829.)

Under the theory of "comparative negligence," then a party's contributory negligence is not now nullified, rather, the damages are apportioned according to the degree of negligence, or fault, of each of the parties.

Li v. Yellow Cab Co. limited its retroactive effect, holding that the opinion applied to all cases in which trial had not begun before the decision became final. In cases commencing trial after May 1, 1975, the doctrine of comparative negligence applies and contributory negligence on the part of plaintiff will not act to completely bar recovery. *Li* also applies to the retrial of earlier cases reversed on appeal for other reasons.

Guest Statute

California's so-called "guest statute" was embodied in Vehicle Code section 17158, which before 1973 provided: "No person riding in or occupying a vehicle owned by him and driven by another person with his permission and no person who as a guest accepts a ride in any vehicle upon a highway without giving compensation for such ride, nor any other person, has any right of action for civil damages against the driver of the vehicle or against any other person legally liable for the conduct of the driver on account of personal injury to or the death of the owner or guest during the ride, unless the plaintiff in any such action establishes that the injury or death proximately resulted from the intoxication or willful misconduct of the driver.''

In *Brown v. Merlo* (1973) 8 Cal.3d 155, at page 873, the court said: ''The theory behind this 'compensation' classification appears to be that the driver who gives a free ride to a passenger does so because of a close relationship with his guest; because of the presumed closeness of this relationship, the driver may falsely admit liability so that his guest may collect from the driver's insurance company. To combat this risk of potential fraud, the guest statute eliminates all causes of action in negligence for automobile guests.''

In *Brown v. Merlo* the court concluded that these limiting provisions of the statute denied equal protection and held Vehicle Code section 17158 (except for its initial clause as to which no opinion was expressed) unconstitutional.

Whereas formerly the guest could recover only if the driver was intoxicated or guilty of willful misconduct, now in California a guest who is a passenger in an automobile stands in the same position as any other passenger and may recover if the driver be negligent. However, the owner-passenger presents a special problem. (See *Schwalbe v. Jones* (1976) 16 Cal.3d 514; *Monroe v. Monroe* (1979) 90 Cal.App.3d 388.)

Other states may still have "guest statutes" in effect.

Respondeat Superior

(Literally, "Let the master answer.")

In brief, this simply means that the principal is responsible for an agent who is acting within the course and scope of his employment by the principal. For example, the driver of a delivery truck for a store has an accident while driving the delivery truck. If he was delivering goods for the store at the time of the accident, and that delivery was within his employment, the store could be held responsible for the accident. Ordinarily, suit would be brought against both the driver and the store.

Res Ipsa Loquitur

Res ipsa loquitur literally means "the thing speaks for itself." In brief, it means that in the light of past experience such an accident would not happen unless someone (the defendant) had been negligent. In other words, ordinarily such an accident could only occur where ordinary care was not exercised. Therefore, on the face of the happening — and in the absence of any other explanation — the accident itself raises the presumption that someone was negligent.

Proximate Cause

" 'Proximate cause,' in the legal sense, is that cause 'which in natural and continuous sequence, unbroken by an efficient intervening cause, produced the injury or damage complained of and without which such injury or damage would not have occurred.' " (*Parker v. City and County of San Francisco* (1958) 158 Cal.App.2d 597, 607, quoting from 35 Cal.Jur.2d, page 551, §554.)

Preponderance of the Evidence

A jury is instructed that the plaintiff has the burden of establishing by a "preponderance of the evidence" all the facts necessary to prove certain issues involved in the case.

Preponderate means to surpass, to dominate. By a "preponderance of the evidence" is meant that body of evidence which is the more convincing and has the greater probability of truth.

If the evidence presented is evenly balanced on an issue, then the jury's finding on that issue must be against the party who had the burden of proving it.

Express Assumption of Risk

Defendant has available express assumption of risk as a defense to an action if, prior to the time of the accident, plaintiff and defendant have specifically agreed that plaintiff will not hold defendant responsible if an injury is caused by defendant's negligence, and plaintiff is injured.

Consortium

Consortium relates to the marital state and the rights obtaining to that association. Consortium embraces " 'love, companionship, affection, society, sexual relations, solace, and more.' " (*Rodriguez v. Bethlehem Steel Corp.* (1974) 12 Cal.3d 382, 405.)

Damages and Detriment

Civil Code section 3281: "Every person who suffers detriment from the unlawful act or omission of another, may recover from the person in fault a compensation therefor in money which is called damages."

Civil Code section 3282: "Detriment is a loss or harm suffered in person or property."

Civil Code section 3283: "Damages may be awarded, in a judicial proceeding, for detriment resulting after the commencement thereof, or certain to result in the future."

See Function of Paralegal chart in Personal Injury actions in Chapter 2.

Chapter 17

PROBATE

Perhaps in no other field is there such a wide latitude for the expertise of the paralegal as in probate administration. (See Chapter 2 for Function of Paralegal chart for Probate.)

Probate proceedings include (1) guardianships, (2) conservatorships, and (3) estate proceedings. All these probate proceedings are filed in the superior courts of California, in which jurisdiction is vested.

DIVISION I
ESTATE ADMINISTRATION

The purpose of probating an estate is to gather and preserve the property of a person who has died, to pay his debts, to determine and pay taxes owing, and to distribute the remainder to the persons entitled to it either by relationship as provided by law or by the will of the deceased.

All estates are subject to administration except estates valued at $300 or less. (See Prob. Code §§1143-1144.) A procedure is provided for eliminating probate where the estate does not exceed $30,000 (see Summary Administration, *infra*). In estates of persons dying after July 1, 1975, an optional procedure for administration with minimal supervision is available in certain circumstances (see The Independent Administration of Estates Act, Optional Procedure for Administration, *infra*), and provision is made for eliminating administration on community property passing to a surviving spouse (see Community Property Confirmation, *infra*).

The estate of a California *resident* must be administered in the county in which he was a *resident* at the time of his death, no matter where he died.

The estate of a nonresident who dies in California must be administered in the county in which he dies leaving an estate or, if he had no estate in that county, in the county in which he leaves an estate.

If he is outside California when he dies, any county in which he leaves property has jurisdiction. (Prob. Code §301.)

When a California resident dies leaving assets in a state other than California, it is frequently necessary that an ancillary administrator be appointed in the other state. The California representative of the estate may be appointed as the administrator unless the state in which the property is situated requires that personal representatives be resident of that state. The proceeding is known as an *ancillary administration*.

There are two basic types of estate proceedings:

1. When a person dies *testate, i.e.*, he leaves a will, and the executor (or executrix) named in the will petitions the court for letters testamentary. If he leaves a will but does not name an executor or executrix, a petition for letters of administration with the will annexed is filed.

2. When a person dies *intestate, i.e.*, he does not leave a will, and an administrator (or administratrix) petitions the court for letters of administration.

The procedure for each type of proceeding follows.

THE WILL

It might be said that there are three kinds of wills: a holographic will, a nuncupative will, and a witnessed will (ordinarily typewritten).

California law recognizes as valid a *holographic* will, that is, a will entirely written, dated, and signed by the testator himself. "It is subject to no other form, and need not be witnessed. No address, date or other matter written, printed or stamped upon the document, which is not incorporated in the provisions which are in the handwriting of the decedent, shall be considered as any part of the will." (Prob. Code §53.) Many controversies have arisen over the meaning of such wills. If not properly and clearly stated, the best possible interpretation under the law may not at all be what the testator really intended.

California also recognizes a *nuncupative* will, that is, one not in writing, made under certain circumstances, and for limited purposes. (See Prob. Code §§54, 55.)

A will is best prepared only after consultation with an attorney, in which the person who wishes to make a will informs the attorney how he wants to dispose of any property he owns, or may own at the time of his death, his marital status, his children, his heirs at law, etc. Many factors enter into the making of a will, many considerations, and a thorough knowledge of the law is necessary to ensure not only a valid will, but a good will, that is, one distributing the property of the testator as he wanted, and also with the best results tax-wise.

Another important reason for the services of an attorney is this need for tax planning. The attorney should be fully advised of the financial holdings of the party who is making a will. Frequently a husband and wife consult an attorney at the same time to have their wills drawn. The attorney needs to know whether their real property is community or separate, whether bank accounts and other holdings are separate or community, whether they hold their real property as community property or in joint tenancy, or otherwise. He needs to know who would succeed to their estates if they did not leave a will, and to whom they wish to leave their assets. An attorney must use his imagination to think of all the possible contingencies. Too often persons assume the order in which deaths will occur, if one is older or not in good health, or that they will predecease their children. The future of course is not predictable. A paralegal, too, must be aware of these variations.

Many factors enter into tax planning and considerable knowledge on the part of the attorney is required, to best advise his clients. Questions of taxation are complex; what might be beneficial to one person's financial interests, might prove costly to another. It depends upon the *tax identity* of each person, *i.e.*, his entire tax situation.

Although there is no "form" of will as such, a "simple" will is set out below for the purpose of illustrating *format only,* not as a model will, or as a model for the preparation of anyone's will.

Last Will and Testament

LAST WILL AND TESTAMENT

OF

EVA BAKER

KNOW ALL MEN BY THESE PRESENTS:

I, EVA BAKER, residing in the County of Sacramento, State of California, declare this to be my last will and testament, and revoke all prior wills made by me.

FIRST: I direct my executrix to pay all my just debts, expenses of last illness and funeral expenses as soon after my death as is convenient.

SECOND: I declare that I am unmarried and have no children living or dead.

THIRD: I hereby give, devise and bequeath to my sister, MARY SMITH, all of my property, whether real, personal or mixed and wheresoever situate. In case my said sister, MARY SMITH, predeceases me, I hereby give, devise and bequeath to my niece, MARGARET SMITH, all of my property, whether real, personal or mixed and wheresoever situate.

FOURTH: I have intentionally omitted to provide for my brother, RALPH BAKER.

FIFTH: I hereby nominate and appoint my said sister, MARY SMITH, the executrix of this my last will and testament, to serve without bond. If my said sister should not survive me or be unable to serve as such executrix, I then appoint MARGARET SMITH and direct that she serve without bond.

SIXTH: I have purposely made no provision for any other person, whether claiming to be an heir of mine or not, and if any person, whether a beneficiary under this will or not mentioned herein, shall contest this will or object to any of the provisions hereof, I give to such person so contesting or objecting the sum of One Dollar ($1.00) and no more, in lieu of the provisions which I might have made or which I have made herein for such person so contesting or objecting.

IN WITNESS WHEREOF, I have hereunto set my hand at Sacramento, California, this 30th day of June, 1981.

_____

The foregoing instrument, consisting of two (2) pages, including the page signed by us as witnesses, was on the date thereof, to wit, on the 30th day of June, 1981, signed by Eva Baker, the testatrix therein named, and declared by her to be her last will and testament, in the presence of us who, at her request and in her presence and in the presence of each other, have subscribed our names as witnesses to her said will; at that time the testatrix was over the age of eighteen (18) years, and appeared to be of sound mind and not acting under duress, menace, fraud, misrepresentation or undue influence.

We, individually, declare under penalty of perjury that the foregoing is true and correct.

Executed on June 30, 1981, at Sacramento, California.

_____Residing at_____

_____Residing at_____

We see that this will was signed, or "subscribed," at the end by the testatrix, Eva Baker. We see that it was signed by two witnesses, and two witnesses are required under California law. (Some states require 3 signatures and some firms use 3 witnesses.) The language before the witnesses' signatures, which is the usual language and which is referred to as "the testamentary clause," tells us that other requirements were met, to wit:

1. The testatrix, Eva Baker, signed the will in the presence of both witnesses, who were both present at the same time.

2. Eva Baker declared to both witnesses at the time of signing the will that it was her will.

3. The two witnesses signed the will at the request of the testatrix, Eva Baker, and in her presence. The witnesses' residences are included here, and should be included.

The requirements for execution and attestation of wills are set out in Probate Code section 50. The language constituting paragraph "SIXTH" of this will is commonly called "the disinheritance clause." Children, and the lineal issue of children, whether born before or after the making of the will, have to be named to be disinherited. (See Prob. Code §90.)

THE REPRESENTATIVE OF THE ESTATE

In an initial interview the paralegal should obtain the following information from the representative of the estate, to prepare a petition for probate of will:

1. Decedent's full name. Any other name by which decedent was known or held property.
2. Date of death of decedent.
3. Residence of decedent.
4. Description of property owned by decedent. (Property descriptions and detailed descriptions can be obtained later; sufficient to determine whether property valued at more than $10,000.) Any stocks, cash, bonds, personal property? Estimated annual income?
5. Date of execution of will.
6. Age of decedent at time will was executed.
7. Whether person named in the will as executor or executrix consents to act.
8. Names, ages and mailing addresses of the devisees named in the will. ("Adult" is sufficient for ages if over 18.)
9. Whether deceased left a spouse? any children? any child of a deceased child? parent or parents?
10. Names, ages and addresses of the heirs at law of the decedent. Blood relationship of each.

See Marshall, *California Probate Procedure,* page 2047, for a suggested form of letter to be written to a new representative by an attorney at the outset of the estate's administration.

The representative of an estate (executor, administrator) is an "officer of the court" and acts in a capacity of trust, *i.e.,* as a fiduciary. He signs an oath (in Letters Testamentary or Letters of Administration) that he will faithfully perform his duties.

If there is a will and no executor is named therein, the representative is called "administrator with the will annexed," commonly written "administrator c.t.a." (*cum testamento annexo*).

If there is more than one executor or administrator, they are coexecutors or coadministrators and sign all pleadings and perform their duties jointly.

Bank accounts must be opened in the name of the estate by the representative as executor or administrator. A certified copy of the letters testamentary or letters of administration are presented to the bank at the time of opening the account. Printed checks and an endorsement stamp may be needed.

Money in bank accounts in the name of the decedent must be either transferred to such an estate account or converted into an estate account.

A safe-deposit box in the name of the estate may be required for the safekeeping of securities of the estate.

Certified copies of the letters will be needed for transfer of any stock held by decedent. The representative needs the same insurance for the estate as would be needed for an individual — liability, fire, worker's compensation, auto, etc. Any existing policyholders should be notified of the death of the decedent and of the change in the name of the insured to the name of the estate.

Without prior court authorization, the representative may deposit any money belonging to the estate with one or more banks or savings and loans associations within the state. (Prob. Code §585.) Money deposited without an order of the court may be withdrawn without an order of the court. (Prob. Code §585.) Investments in direct obligations of the United States maturing not later than one year may also be made without prior authorization.

On petition of the executor or administrator, and upon good cause, the court may authorize the executor or administrator to invest money held for the benefit of the estate in units of a common trust fund described in Financial Code section 1564. The common trust fund shall have as its objective investment primarily in short-term fixed income obligations. (Prob. Code §585.1.)

When the claims have been paid or otherwise secured but the estate is not in a condition to be closed, surplus moneys may be invested in any manner provided by the will, after hearing and notice as prescribed by Probate Code sections 584.5 and 584.6.

The representative may not speculate with estate assets. The management and operation of a business may be continued either under the terms of the will, or after obtaining permission of the court. If the representative has advanced his own funds for payment of debts, to effect payment he must file a claim within the four-month period allowed for creditors to file claims.

If a request for special notice has been served upon the representative or his attorney pursuant to Probate Code section 1202, the representative must give special notice to such person of the filing of the petitions, accounts and reports mentioned in Probate Code section 1200. The notice shall be substantially in the form set forth in Probate Code section 1200.1 and must be given at least 10 days before the hearing. Proof of mailing of the notice should be filed with the court. (Prob. Code §1202.)

A similar request for special notice of the filing of the inventory and appraisement may be made under Probate Code section 1202.5, in which event the representative must give notice no later than 10 days after the filing of the inventory and appraisement. Proof of mailing should be filed with the court.

PROCEDURE FOR PROBATE OF WILL

To probate a will is to submit the will of the decedent for official certification by the court as being the genuine last will and testament of the decedent. *Local probate manuals for each county should be checked.*

Usually the executor named in the will petitions the court for appointment. No statute limits the time within which an application to probate a will must be made. However, an executor named in a will may be held to have renounced his right to act if he does not petition for letters testamentary within 30 days after date of death. (Prob. Code §324.)

If the executor does decline to act, or if the named executor has died, any devisee or legatee named in the will, or any other person interested in the estate (such as a creditor) may petition the court to have the will probated. The facts should be stated in the petition.

1. Several copies of the will should be prepared. (Heirs may request copies of the will.)
2. File original will with the county clerk of the county in which the probate proceeding is to be commenced (within 30 days of date of death). The original will is usually delivered to the county clerk

at the time of filing the petition for probate of will, and a copy of the will should be attached to the original petition.

If a will cannot be personally delivered to the county clerk it should be mailed by registered mail, return receipt requested, together with a letter of transmittal with endorsement for receipt on a copy of the letter for return, with a stamped, addressed envelope.

Petition for Probate of Will
(Prob. Code §326)

An original and 2 copies of the petition are prepared (minimum). Probate Code section 326 provides that a petition for probate of will must contain the following:

1. The jurisdictional facts

2. Whether the person named as executor of the will consents to act as executor

3. The street number, street, city, and county of the decedent's residence at the time of his or her death

4. Names, ages residences, and relation to decedent of heirs, devisees and legatees of decedent

5. Character of and estimated value of the property of the estate

6. Name of person for whom the letters are prayed.

A copy of the will is attached to the original petition and to each copy. The original petition is filed with the county clerk. A filing fee (the amount of which varies from county to county) is required to file the petition. The executor or the attorney's office should obtain certified copies of the death certificate. Usually the funeral director makes arrangements for the death certificate and will inquire of the family how many certified copies are needed and order them at that time.

The Judicial Council form of petition follows:

Petition for Probate

ATTORNEY OR PARTY WITHOUT ATTORNEY (NAME AND ADDRESS)	TELEPHONE NO	FOR COURT USE ONLY

ATTORNEY FOR (NAME)

SUPERIOR COURT OF CALIFORNIA, COUNTY OF SACRAMENTO
STREET ADDRESS 720 9TH STREET
MAILING ADDRESS
CITY AND ZIP CODE SACRAMENTO, CA 95814
BRANCH NAME

ESTATE OF (NAME)

Decedent

PETITION FOR	[ ] PROBATE OF WILL AND FOR LETTERS TESTAMENTARY [ ] PROBATE OF WILL AND FOR LETTERS OF ADMINISTRATION WITH WILL ANNEXED [ ] LETTERS OF ADMINISTRATION [ ] SPECIAL LETTERS OF ADMINISTRATION [ ] AUTHORIZATION TO ADMINISTER UNDER THE INDEPENDENT ADMINISTRATION OF ESTATES ACT	CASE NUMBER HEARING DATE DEPT TIME

1 Attorney requests publication in (name of newspaper)

(Type or print name)   (Signature of attorney)

2 Petitioner* (name of each):
   requests that
   a. [ ] decedent's will and codicils, if any, be admitted to probate
   b. [ ] (name).
      be appointed (1) [ ] executor   (3) [ ] administrator
                    (2) [ ] administrator with will annexed   (4) [ ] special administrator
      and Letters issue upon qualification
   c. [ ] authority be granted to administer under the Independent Administration of Estates Act
   d. [ ] bond not be required for the reasons stated in attachment 2d
      [ ] bond be fixed at $ to be furnished by an authorized surety company or as otherwise
          provided by law (specify reasons if the amount is different from the minimum required by section 541 of
          the Probate Code)
      [ ] deposits at (specify institution)
          in the amount of $ be allowed. Receipts will be filed
3 a Decedent died on (date)   at (place)
      [ ] a resident of the county named above
      [ ] a non-resident of California and left an estate in the county named above located at (specify location permitting
          publication in the newspaper named in item 1)
   b Street address, city, and county of decedent's residence at time of death

   c Character and estimated value of the property of the estate
      Personal property $
      Annual gross income from
          [ ] real property $
          [ ] personal property $
                        Total: $
      Real property $
   d [ ] Will waives bond
      [ ] All beneficiaries have waived bond and the will does not require a bond (affix waiver as attachment 3d)
      [ ] All heirs at law have waived bond (affix waiver as attachment 3d)
   e [ ] Decedent died intestate.
      [ ] Copy of decedent's will dated   [ ] and codicil dated
          is affixed as attachment 3e.

Form Approved by the
Judicial Council of California
Revised Effective January 1, 1981
DE-110(81)

(Continued on reverse)

PETITION FOR PROBATE

*All petitioners must sign the petition
Only one need sign the declaration

ESTATE OF (NAME):	CASE NUMBER:
Decedent	

PETITION FOR PROBATE

f. Appointment of personal representative
   (1) Appointment of executor or administrator with will annexed
     ☐ Proposed executor is named as executor in the will.
     ☐ No executor is named in the will.
     ☐ Proposed personal representative is a nominee *(affix nomination as attachment 3f(1)).*
     ☐ Other named executors will not act because of ☐ death ☐ declination ☐ other reasons *(specify in attachment 3f(1)).*
   (2) Appointment of administrator
     ☐ Petitioner is a nominee *(affix nomination as attachment 3f(2)).*
     ☐ Petitioner is related to the decedent as:
   (3) ☐ Appointment of special administrator requested *(specify grounds and requested powers in attachment 3f(3)).*
g. Proposed personal representative is a ☐ resident of California ☐ non-resident of California ☐ resident of the United States ☐ non-resident of the United States.

4. a. *(Complete in all cases.)* The decedent is survived by
   (1) ☐ spouse   ☐ no spouse.
   (2) ☐ parent   ☐ no parent.
   (3) ☐ child   ☐ no child.
   (4) ☐ issue of predeceased child ☐ no issue of predeceased child.
  b. No surviving child or issue of a predeceased child has been omitted from the list of heirs (item 6).
  c. *(Complete only if no spouse or issue survived the decedent.)* The decedent
   (1) ☐ had no predeceased spouse.
   (2) ☐ had a predeceased spouse whose heirs are named in the list of heirs (item 6).
   (3) ☐ had a predeceased spouse who had no heirs.
  d. *(Complete only if no parent or issue survived the decedent.)* The decedent is survived by
   (1) ☐ a brother or sister or issue of a predeceased brother or sister. None has been omitted from the list of heirs (item 6).
   (2) ☐ no brother or sister or issue of a predeceased brother or sister.

5. ☐ Decedent's will does not preclude independent administration of this estate under sections 591—591.7 of the Probate Code.

6. The names, residence or mailing addresses, relationships, and ages of heirs, devisees, predeceased devisees, legatees, and predeceased legatees so far as known to petitioner are ☐ listed below ☐ listed in attachment 6.

    NAME AND RELATIONSHIP   AGE   RESIDENCE OR MAILING ADDRESS

7. ☐ Number of pages attached:

Dated: . . . .

_____
(Signature of petitioner)

I declare under penalty of perjury under the laws of the State of California that the foregoing is true and correct and that this declaration is executed on (date): . . . . at (place): . . . .

. . . .
(Type or print name)

_____
(Signature of petitioner)

Notice of Death and of Petition to Administer Estate
(Prob. Code §§327, 333)

An original and 3 copies are prepared for delivery to clerk for issuance at time of filing petition. The clerk will set the petition for hearing on a date not less than 10 days nor more than 30 days from the date of filing the petition (15 days in Sacramento). In some counties a date may be preselected and filled in on the form before presentation to the clerk. The notice must be published in a newspaper of general circulation in the city where decedent resided at time of death, or where decedent's property is located if the court has jurisdiction over the estate pursuant to subdivision (3) of Section 301. If there is no such newspaper, the decedent did not reside in a city, or the property is not located in a city, then notice shall be published in a newspaper of general circulation in the county which is circulated within the community in which the decedent resided or the property is located. If there is no such newspaper, notice shall be given in written or printed form, posted at three of the most public places within such community. (Prob. Code §§327, 333.) ("City" means a charter city as defined in Government Code section 34101 or a general law city as defined in Government Code section 34102.) If the notice is published in a newspaper published once a week or oftener, three publications, with at least 5 days between the first and last publication dates, not counting such publication dates, are sufficient. (Prob. Code §333.)

PARALEGAL RESPONSIBILITIES

1. Deliver 1 conformed copy of notice to newspaper to publish.

2. Arrange to obtain from newspaper sufficient printed copies of notice to mail to all heirs, devisees and legatees.

3. At least 10 days prior to hearing, a notice of hearing (use Notice of Death, etc., form) must either be personally served or mailed, postage prepaid, to each heir, devisee and legatee, and nonpetitioning executor, at his or her respective place of residence or mailing address, if known to the petitioner, and if not known, to the county seat of the county where the proceedings are pending. (In Sacramento County local rule requires 15-day notice.)

This notice shall also advise the person receiving the notice of the right to request special notice pursuant to Probate Code sections 1202 and 1202.5.

If the estate involves testamentary trust for charitable purposes, notice of hearing and copy of petition and will must be personally served or served by mail on the Attorney General in Sacramento. A declaration or affidavit of mailing such notice is filed (on reverse of form).

Notice of Death and of Petition to Administer Estate

ATTORNEY OR PARTY WITHOUT ATTORNEY (Name and Address)	TELEPHONE NO.	FOR COURT USE ONLY
ATTORNEY FOR (Name)		

NAME AND ADDRESS OF COURT, OR BRANCH

SUPERIOR COURT OF CALIFORNIA, COUNTY OF

ESTATE OF

DECEDENT

NOTICE OF DEATH OF	CASE NUMBER

AND OF PETITION TO ADMINISTER ESTATE

1. To all heirs, beneficiaries, creditors, contingent creditors, and persons who may be otherwise interested in the will or estate of (specify all names by which decedent was known):

2. A petition has been filed by (name of petitioner):

   in the Superior Court of

   County requesting that (name):

   be appointed as personal representative to administer the estate of the decedent.

3. ☐ The petition requests authority to administer the estate under the Independent Administration of Estates Act.

4. ☐ A petition for community property determination pursuant to section 650 of the Probate Code is joined with the petition to administer the estate.

5. A hearing on the petition will be held

   on (date):   at (time):   in ☐ Dept.:   ☐ Div.:   ☐ Room:

   located at (address of court):

6. IF YOU OBJECT to the granting of the petition, you should either appear at the hearing and state your objections or file written objections with the court before the hearing. Your appearance may be in person or by your attorney.

7. IF YOU ARE A CREDITOR or a contingent creditor of the deceased, you must file your claim with the court or present it to the personal representative appointed by the court within four months from the date of first issuance of letters as provided in section 700 of the California Probate Code. The time for filing claims will not expire prior to four months from the date of the hearing noticed above.

8. YOU MAY EXAMINE the file kept by the court. If you are a person interested in the estate, you may file a request with the court to receive special notice of the filing of the inventory of estate assets and of the petitions, accounts and reports described in section 1200 of the California Probate Code.

9. ☐ Petitioner ☐ Attorney for petitioner (name):

   (address):

   (Signature of ☐ petitioner ☐ attorney for petitioner)

10. This notice was mailed on (date): . . . . at (place): . . . ., California.

    (Continued on reverse)

NOTE: If this notice is published, print the caption, beginning with the words NOTICE OF DEATH, and do not print the information from the form above the caption. The caption and decedent's name must be printed in at least 8-point type and the text in at least 7-point type. Print the case number as part of the caption. Print items preceded by a box only if the box is checked. Do not print the instructions in parentheses, the paragraph numbers, the mailing information or the material on the reverse.

Form Approved by the
Judicial Council of California
Effective January 1, 1980

**NOTICE OF DEATH AND OF PETITION
TO ADMINISTER ESTATE**

Prob C 327, 328, 333,
361, 441, 654,
1200

CLERK'S CERTIFICATE OF ☐ POSTING ☐ MAILING

I certify that I am not a party to this cause and that a true copy of the foregoing Notice of Death and of Petition to Administer Estate

1. ☐ was posted at (address):

      on (date):

2. ☐ was mailed, first class, postage fully prepaid, in a sealed envelope addressed to each person whose name and address is given below and that the notice was mailed and this certificate was executed on (date): . . . . at (place): . . . . , California.

                              Clerk, by   . . . . , Deputy

PROOF OF SERVICE BY MAIL

I am over the age of 18 and not a party to this cause. I am a resident of or employed in the county where the mailing occurred. My residence or business address is:

I served the foregoing Notice of Death and of Petition to Administer Estate by enclosing a true copy in a sealed envelope addressed to each person whose name and address is given below and depositing the envelope in the United States mail with the postage fully prepaid.

(1) Date of deposit: (2) Place of deposit (city and state):

I declare under penalty of perjury that the foregoing is true and correct and that this declaration is executed on (date): . . . . at (place): . . . . , California.

. . . .
(Type or print name)   (Signature of declarant)

NAME AND ADDRESS OF EACH PERSON TO WHOM NOTICE WAS MAILED

A declaration under penalty of perjury must be signed in California or in a state that authorizes use of a declaration in place of an affidavit; otherwise an affidavit is required.

NOTICE TO RELATIVES OF DECEDENT

Code sections will state that notice is to be sent to relatives of decedent of the first degree, second degree, etc. If the statute directs service on relatives of the first and second degree, you would serve the persons listed in those columns below, and so on.

DECEDENT

1st Degree	2d Degree	3d Degree	4th Degree	5th Degree	6th Degree
Children	Grandchildren,	Nephews,	Grandnephews,	First Cousins	First Cousins
Parents	Grandparents,	Nieces, Aunts,	Grandnieces,	once removed	twice removed
	Brothers, Sisters	Uncles	First Cousins		

BEFORE HEARING

Check:

1. That newspaper has filed its Affidavit of Publication of Notice of Probate of Will, *or*
2. That clerk has filed an affidavit of posting (if posting of notice is required by statute because there is no newspaper)

Arrange for Proof of Will

In an uncontested case the will may be admitted to probate:

1. On the testimony of one of the subscribing witnesses. Arrangements should be made for the witness (or witnesses if more than one is to testify) to appear in court and testify.

2. Affidavit or declaration of the witness or witnesses to which a photographic copy of the will is attached (Proof of Subscribing Witness form)

3. If no witness could be produced or his affidavit or declaration obtained:

   (a) Proof of the handwriting of the testator and one of the subscribing witnesses,
   (b) Proof of the handwriting of the testator and receipt in evidence either of
      (1) "writing at the end of the document offered as a will bearing the purported signatures of all subscribing witnesses" or
      (2) Affidavit of person having personal knowledge of the execution of the will and reciting facts showing due execution.

4. Upon direction of the court, deposition of witness outside the county, with photographic copy of the will being presented to the witness, and the same questions being asked as if personally present in court. (Prob. Code §§329, 1233.)

5. Upon an affidavit in the original will which may include or incorporate the attestation clause.

Unless the will requires a bond, if a verified petition for letters testamentary or administration alleges that *all* beneficiaries under the will, or *all* heirs at law of the decedent, have waived the filing of a bond, the court shall direct that no bond be filed. (Prob. Code §541.)

Determine the approximate value of the property in the estate, the probable value of the annual rents, issues and profits of all the property, to determine the amount of the surety bond required. Have application for bond signed by petitioner; arrange with insurance company for issuance of bond.

The bond may be an authorized surety company's bond, or, in the alternative (Prob. Code §§541.3, 1480.5), a representative may file:

(a) A cash bond

(b) An assigned interest in an account or accounts in a bank or insured savings and loan association; or

(c) Bearer or endorsed bonds of the United States or of the State of California.

Amount of bond (Prob. Code §541)

(a) If two individuals are sureties: 2 × value of personal property and 2 × value of probable annual income from real property.

(b) Surety company bond: No less than value of personal property and probable value of annual rents, issues and profits of property.

The following documents (printed forms) should be prepared before the hearing:

1. *Order for Probate* (Original and 5 copies)

2. *Order Appointing Referees and Inheritance Tax Referees* (Original and 1 copy)

3. *Letters* (Original and 5 copies minimum) One certified copy will be needed for each bank account, safe-deposit box, issues of securities, etc.

4. *Proof of Subscribing Witness*

Order For Probate

J.C. 2

NAME AND ADDRESS OF ATTORNEY TELEPHONE NO	FOR COURT USE ONLY
ATTORNEY FOR	

Name and address of court, or branch:
SUPERIOR COURT OF CALIFORNIA, COUNTY OF

ESTATE OF:

                                                            DECEDENT

ORDER FOR PROBATE:	CASE NUMBER

☐ ORDER APPOINTING   ☐ EXECUTOR
                        ☐ ADMINISTRATOR WITH WILL ANNEXED
                        ☐ ADMINISTRATOR
                        ☐ SPECIAL ADMINISTRATOR
☐ ORDER AUTHORIZING INDEPENDENT ADMINISTRATION OF ESTATE

1. Date of hearing: ☐ Dept. ☐ Div. ☐ Room No.   Judge

   THE COURT FINDS

2. a. All notices required by law have been given.
   b. Decedent died on (date)
      (1) ☐ a resident of the above-named county of the State of California
      (2) ☐ a nonresident of California and left an estate in the above-named county

3. ☐ The decedent's will dated:
     and each codicil dated:
     was admitted to probate by Minute Order on (date)

   IT IS ORDERED:

4. (name):
   is appointed
   a. ☐ Executor of the decedent's will   d. ☐ Special Administrator
   b. ☐ Administrator with will annexed   (1) ☐ with general powers
   c. ☐ Administrator   (2) ☐ with special powers as specified in Attachment 4d
                                                     (3) ☐ without notice of hearing

   and letters shall issue on qualification.

5. ☐ Authority is granted to administer estate under The Independent Administration of Estates Act

6. Bond is
   a. ☐ not required.
   b. ☐ fixed at $ to be furnished by an authorized surety company or as otherwise provided by law.

7. ☐ The inheritance tax referee appointed is (name):

Dated: . . . .
                                              Judge of the Superior Court
                                              ☐ Signature follows last attachment

8. Total number of pages attached:

No attachment permitted on less than a full page (California Rule of Court 201(b))

Form Approved by the
Judicial Council of California
Effective July 1, 1977   **ORDER FOR PROBATE**

Prob C 329, 351, 362
407, 409, 410
461, 462, 465, 541
591, 605, 1220–1224
1240

Order Appointing Referees and Inheritance Tax Referees

SUPERIOR COURT OF THE STATE OF CALIFORNIA IN AND FOR THE COUNTY OF _____

No.   Department

IN THE MATTER OF THE ESTATE OF

Deceased.

ORDER APPOINTING REFEREES AND INHERITANCE TAX REFEREES:

IT IS HEREBY ORDERED, that

a duly appointed, qualified and acting Inheritance Tax Referee in and for the County above named, and

they are

a disinterested person   , competent and capable to act, be and he is hereby appointed   *referee of

the estate of   , deceased.

IT IS FURTHER ORDERED, that said

be, and he is hereby designated and appointed as Inheritance Tax Referee to ascertain and report to this court the amount of inheritance taxes due out of said estate or which may be a lien or charge upon any property or upon the interest of any person herein, as provided in the Inheritance Tax Act.

Date ....

....
Judge of the Superior Court

*Insert "sole" if only one referee be appointed.

Letters

J.C. 3

NAME AND ADDRESS OF ATTORNEY	TELEPHONE NO	FOR COURT USE ONLY

ATTORNEY FOR:

Insert name of court, branch court if any, and Post Office and Street Address

ESTATE OF:

DECEDENT

LETTERS

☐ TESTAMENTARY ☐ OF ADMINISTRATION
☐ OF ADMINISTRATION WITH WILL ANNEXED ☐ OF SPECIAL ADMINISTRATION

Case Number:

STATE OF CALIFORNIA, COUNTY OF

1. ☐ The last will of the above-named decedent having been proved, the court appoints (Name):

   a. ☐ Executor.
   b. ☐ Administrator with will annexed.

2. The court appoints (Name):

   a. ☐ Administrator of the decedent's estate.
   b. ☐ Special administrator of decedent's estate
      (1) ☐ with the special powers specified in the Order for Probate
      (2) ☐ with the powers of a general administrator.

3. The personal representative ☐ is ☐ is not authorized to administer the estate under The Independent Administration of Estates Act.

WITNESS, the clerk of the above-entitled court, with seal of the court affixed.

Dated:

Clerk, by _____ , Deputy

[S E A L]

4. **AFFIRMATION**

I solemnly affirm that I will perform the duties of personal representative according to law.

Executed on (Date): _____ , at
(Place): _____ , California.

_____
(Personal Representative)

5. **CERTIFICATION**

I certify that this document is a correct copy of the original on file in my office, and that the letters issued the above-appointed person have not been revoked, annulled, or set aside, and are still in full force and effect.

Dated:

Clerk, by _____ , Deputy

[S E A L]

Form Approved by the Judicial Council of California Effective July 1, 1975   **LETTERS**   Prob C 463, 465, 501, 502, 540 CCP 2015.6

Proof of Subscribing Witness

NAME AND ADDRESS OF ATTORNEY	TELEPHONE NO	FOR COURT USE ONLY
ATTORNEY FOR		
SUPERIOR COURT OF CALIFORNIA, COUNTY OF		
ESTATE OF		
		DECEDENT
PROOF OF SUBSCRIBING WITNESS		Case Number

I, the undersigned, state (See footnote* before completing)

1. I am one of the attesting witnesses to the instrument of which Attachment 1 is a photographic copy. I have examined Attachment 1 and my signature is at the end of it.

   a. The name of the decedent was subscribed at the end of the instrument in the presence of the attesting witnesses present at the same time by
      (1) [ ] The decedent personally
      (2) [ ] Another person in the presence of, and by the direction, of the decedent

   b. The decedent acknowledged in the presence of the attesting witnesses present at the same time that the decedent's name was subscribed at the end of the original instrument by
      (1) [ ] The decedent personally
      (2) [ ] Another person in the presence of, and by the direction, of the decedent

2. At the time of subscribing or acknowledging the instrument the decedent declared to the attesting witnesses that it was decedent's [ ] will [ ] codicil. Then at the decedent's request and in the decedent's presence, the other attesting witnesses and I, in the presence of each other, signed as witnesses at the end thereof.

3. At that time the decedent was over eighteen years of age and appeared to be of sound mind.

4. I have no knowledge of any facts indicating that the instrument, or any part of it, was procured by duress, menace, fraud, or undue influence.

I certify (or declare) under penalty of perjury that the foregoing is true and correct and that this declaration is executed on (Date) _____ at (Place) _____ California

(Type or print name and address)   (Signature of witness)

ATTORNEY'S CERTIFICATION
(Check local court rules for requirements for certifying copies of wills and codicils)

I am an active member of The State Bar of California. I certify (or declare) under penalty of perjury that Attachment 1 is a photographic copy of each and every page of the [ ] will [ ] codicil presented for probate and that this declaration is executed on (Date) _____ at (Place) _____ California

(Type or print name)   (Signature of Attorney)

* The declaration must be signed in California (CCP 2015.5); affidavit required when signed outside California. No attachment permitted less than on a full page (California Rule of Court 201 (b))

Form Approved by the
Judicial Council of California
Effective July 1, 1975
Revised Printing Jan. 1, 1976   **PROOF OF SUBSCRIBING WITNESS**   Prob C 20, 50, 329

Petition For Letters of Administration

The petition for letters of administration must state the facts essential to give jurisdiction. Petitioner must also allege that he is a resident of the United States. Probate Code section 422(a) lists the order of priority of right of persons entitled to letters, to wit:

(1) The surviving spouse, or some competent person whom he or she may request to have appointed.

(2) The children.

(3) The grandchildren.

(4) The parents.

(5) The brothers and sisters.

(6) The next of kin entitled to share in the estate.

(7) The relatives of a previously deceased spouse, when such relatives are entitled to succeed to some portion of the estate.

(8) The public administrator.

(9) The creditors.

(10) Any person legally competent.

(b) A relative of the decedent who is entitled to priority under subdivision (a) is entitled to priority *only* if either of the following facts exist:

(1) The relative is entitled to succeed to all or part of the estate.

(2) The relative is a parent, grandparent, child, or grandchild of the decedent and either takes under the will of, or is entitled to succeed to all or part of the estate of, another deceased person who is entitled to succeed to all or part of the estate of the decedent. (Emphasis added.)

Under the above section, the relatives named (children, grandchildren, parents, brothers and sisters, next of kin, of decedent) have priority, in the order named, *if* they *also* are entitled to succeed to the estate of decedent; in addition, a parent, grandparent, child or grandchild of decedent who is entitled to succeed to the estate of another decedent (such as the deceased husband) who is entitled to succeed to the estate of the decedent.

If no one comes forth, the public administrator has a duty to petition for letters of administration. (Prob. Code §1140.)

The procedure on petitions for letters of administration, that is, where no will is involved, is substantially the same as on petitions for letters testamentary, with the following exceptions:

1. Prepare a notice entitled the same as the notice used when probating a will, *Notice of Death* and of *Petition to Administer Estate*.

(a) The clerk will set the petition for hearing and cause the *Notice of Death* to be published pursuant to Probate Code section 333 the same as in a testate estate.

(b) Clerk will mail this notice to the heirs named in the petition, at least 10 days before the hearing, either to each heir's residence or mailing address as set forth in the petition, otherwise at the county seat of the county where the proceedings are pending. (Prob. Code §441.) Such mailed notice shall also advise the person receiving such notice of the right to request special notice pursuant to sections 1202 and 1202.5. Clerk is furnished with the notices and stamped, addressed envelopes for this purpose.

(c) Clerk will file his affidavit of mailing and posting, if posting becomes necessary under Probate Code section 333.

2. The same printed forms are used to appoint either an executor or administrator; the appropriate boxes on each are to be checked. The forms are printed under Petition for Probate of Will, *supra*.

(a) *Petition For Probate*

(b) *Order For Probate*

(c) *Letters* The box for letters of administration is checked rather than Letters Testamentary.

Creditors

Probate Code sections 701 and 702 have been repealed; a notice to creditors has not been required since January 1, 1980. Probate Code section 700 as amended specifies that publication of Notice of Death and of Petition to Administer Estate, published pursuant to new Probate Code section 333, constitutes notice to the creditors.

CREDITORS' CLAIMS. (Printed forms available.) The creditors of the estate have the obligation to file creditors' claims, within 4 months after the first issuance of letters. (Prob. Code §700.) The claim must be verified or the executor cannot allow it. (Prob. Code §705.) If the executor allows the claim, it is then presented to the judge for his approval, and if the judge approves the claim, it should be filed within 30 days. If the executor rejects the claim, he must serve a notice of rejection of the claim, and it is advisable to send the Notice of Rejection by registered mail, return receipt requested. *Statutes of limitation run on creditors' claims from time of service of the Notice of Rejection.* (Prob. Code §714.)

Following is the Judicial Council *Creditor's Claim* form:

Creditor's Claim

NAME AND ADDRESS OF ATTORNEY: TELEPHONE NO.:	FOR COURT USE ONLY
	FILED FOR APPROVAL (DATE) (DEPUTY)
ATTORNEY FOR:	DUPLICATE MAILED (DATE) (DEPUTY)
SUPERIOR COURT OF CALIFORNIA, COUNTY OF	
ESTATE OF:	PRESENTED TO COURT FOR APPROVAL (DATE) (DEPUTY)
DECEDENT	
CREDITOR'S CLAIM*	CASE NUMBER

THIS CLAIM MUST BE PRESENTED TO THE PERSONAL REPRESENTATIVE OR FILED IN THE OFFICE OF THE CLERK OF THE COURT IN DUPLICATE WITHIN FOUR MONTHS AFTER THE DATE OF FIRST ISSUANCE OF LETTERS OR AS PROVIDED IN PROBATE CODE 700.

DECLARATION OF CLAIMANT

1. Total amount of the claim is: $

2. Claimant (Name)_____
   a. ☐ An individual.
   b. ☐ An individual doing business under the fictitious name of:
   c. ☐ A partnership.
   d. ☐ A corporation.

3. The claimant's address is:

4. I am authorized to make the claim which is justly due or may become due. To my knowledge there are no offsets or payments which have not been credited. I certify (declare) under penalty of perjury that this creditor's claim, including any attachments, is true and correct and that this declaration is executed on (Date):............................ at ...., California.

5. ....
   (TYPE NAME AND TITLE) (SIGNATURE)
   (ITEMS 6 — 9 TO BE COMPLETED BY THE PERSONAL REPRESENTATIVE)

6. a. Date of first issuance of letters: b. Date of death:

7. This claim was presented on (Date):

8. Claim is ☐ allowed for: $ ☐ Rejected for: $

9. Estimated value of estate:

   ....
   (TYPE OR PRINT NAME OF PERSONAL REPRESENTATIVE) (SIGNATURE OF PERSONAL REPRESENTATIVE)

10. ☐ Approved for: $ ☐ Rejected for: $

    Dated: ....
                                                 (Signature of ☐Judge ☐ Commissioner)

11. Total number of pages attached .... (Continued on Reverse Side)

* See reverse side for instructions before completing. The declaration must be signed in California (CCP 2015.5); affidavit required when signed outside California. No attachment permitted less than on a full page (California Rule of Court 201 (b)).

Form Approved by the
Judicial Council of California
Rev. Eff. January 1, 1980   **CREDITOR'S CLAIM**   Prob C 705–708, 710
Form PR-17 Co. Clk. (1-77)   712–714, 717

INSTRUCTIONS TO CLAIMANT

Claims must be itemized showing the date the service was rendered, or the debt incurred. The item or service should be described in detail, and the amount claimed for each item indicated. If any debt was incurred after the date of death, except funeral claims, it must not be included as an item on this claim form.

If the claim is based upon a note or other written instrument, a copy of such note or instrument must be attached. If secured by mortgage, deed of trust or other lien on property that is of record, it is sufficient to state the date, book and page and county where recorded.

DESCRIPTION OF CREDITOR'S CLAIM

Date of Item	Item	Amount Claimed
	TOTAL	$

CREDITOR'S CLAIM

PR-17 (8-80)

Certain creditors not receiving notice because they were out of state or who in good faith filed a claim in another nonconsolidated proceeding in which letters were not issued may file their claims within 1 year after expiration of the prescribed period and before the petition for final distribution has been filed. (See Prob. Code §707.)

Payment of Debts

Certain debts of decedent have priority for payment over other debts. If an estate does not have sufficient assets to pay all the debts, then the debts are paid off in the order of priority, to the extent of funds available, and the remaining debts are not paid. (Prob. Code §952.)

If all the debts for which priority is established are paid and there are some assets remaining but not enough to pay all the creditors, these creditors are paid on a pro-rata basis, since they all have equal claim.

The order for priority for payment is established in Probate Code sections 950 and 951, to wit:

(1) Expenses of administration
(2) Funeral expenses
(3) Expenses of last illness
(4) Family allowance
(5) Debts having preference under federal laws
(6) Wages up to $900 per employee for services rendered within 90 days prior to death (or pro rata payment)
(7) Mortgages, judgments that are liens, and other liens
(8) Judgments rendered against decedent that are not liens

If other debts are paid without claims, they must be paid within the four-month period permitted for filing of creditors' claims. Approval of the court is discretionary. (Prob. Code §929.)

Inventory and Appraisement

The inventory and appraisement (a printed form) should be prepared and filed within 3 months, or such further time as the court allows. (Prob. Code §600.) The clerk of the court transmits a copy to the county assessor "if timely requested" by the assessor. (Prob. Code §600.)

The personal representative is liable for damages for delay in filing inventory. (Prob. Code §610.)

Within 15 days after filing of the inventory and appraisement, any interested person may file written objections to any or all appraisals. The clerk sets such objections for hearing not less than 15 days after the filing and gives notice as provided in Probate Code section 1600. The party objecting must serve a copy of the objections upon the personal representative, upon all relatives within the second degree, and the inheritance tax referee, together with a copy of the notice of hearing, at least 10 days before the hearing. (Prob. Code §1550.1.)

The Inventory and Appraisement is prepared for the referee complete except for the value of the items which the referee must himself appraise, that is, all items except the items specified by Probate Code section 605 to be appraised by the executor or administrator. (See Prob. Code §605.) The values are *as of the date of death*. Income from real property, bank interest, dividends accruing after the date of death, are *income* to the estate.

The items should be listed and numbered. Joint tenancy assets should be listed separately. Federal Estate Tax Form 706 contains suggestions for listing and describing assets. Examples of a few items follow:

1. Savings account No. 242 at Central Bank
    NA, 12th and J Streets, Sacramento.
    Balance as of date of death .... $ 8,000.00
2. Commercial account at United California
    Bank, 10th and K Streets, Sacramento.
    Balance as of date of death .... $ 3,000.00

Give inheritance tax referee (if appointed); otherwise, State Controller, Division of Inheritance and Gift Tax:

1. Original and 2 copies of Inventory and Appraisement. (1 of these copies is for inheritance tax referee; 1 of these copies is for county assessor if timely requested by the assessor. (Prob. Code §600).)
2. 2 copies of any will, including any codicils.
3. Original and 3 copies of Form IT-22 (Inheritance Tax Affidavit). (Form is available from State Controller's office, Inheritance Tax Division.) (A Form IT-20 may sometimes be used in place of the IT-22 in a simple estate to obtain a release of lien on real property or consent to transfer provided that the applicant personally applies for it at the offices of the Inheritance Tax Division.)
4. Original and 3 copies of Form IT-3 (Affidavit Concerning Community Property). When date of death is prior to January 1, 1976, IT-3 is required when decedent survived by spouse and all properties in IT-22 are of a value of $10,000 or more. Where date of death is on or after January 1, 1976, and decedent is survived by spouse, IT-3 is required where the value of all property in IT-22 is $100,000 or more and the entire amount passes to surviving spouse, or if any of estate passes to persons other than surviving spouse. In determining $100,000 limitation, value of interest of both spouses in community or quasi-community property is taken into account.
    Where the date of death is on or after January 1, 1981, the IT-

3 is required where the decedent and surviving spouse entered into an agreement concerning the status of their property as either community or separate, and in cases where the will puts the surviving spouse to an election to either take under the will or take his/her one-half of the community property, or where the will disposes of any part or all of the surviving spouse's interest in the community property. Form IT-3 may also be required by the Controller's office in specific instances.

Give original and 1 copy of the IT-3 with IT-22 and any required supplementary documents to the inheritance tax referee if one has been appointed, otherwise to the inheritance tax district officer for area of residence of decedent.

No late filing penalty or particular filing date but inheritance tax cannot be determined until IT-3 filed — if it is required — and inheritance tax is delinquent 9 months after date of death.

5. Copy of petition.
See California Administrative Code, title 18, regulations 14501-14515(a) for other documents that might be required. The inheritance tax referee will return the original Inventory and Appraisement with his bill. His fees are computed as follows (Prob. Code §609):

Fees for referees appointed *prior* to September 13, 1976:

First $500,000	1/10th of 1% (but not less than $5)
All over $500,000	1/20th of 1%
	Plus actual and necessary expenses

Fees for referees appointed *after* September 13, 1976:

First $500,000	1/10th of 1% (but not less than $25)
All over $500,000	1/20th of 1% — maximum $5,000
	May apply to court for amount in excess of $5,000 if reasonable value of services exceeds $5,000
	Plus actual and necessary expenses

File original Inventory and Appraisement and copy with the county clerk (1 copy is for assessor) within 3 months after appointment of executor. (Prob. Code §600.) The executor (or administrator) appraises "at fair market value moneys, currency, cash items, bank accounts and amounts on deposit with any financial institution, and the proceeds of life and accident insurance policies and retirement plans payable upon death in lump sum amounts, excepting therefrom such items whose fair market value is, in the opinion of the executor or administrator, an amount different from the ostensible value or specified amount.'' (Prob. Code §605.)

Following is the Judicial Council form for *Inventory and Appraisement*:

Inventory and Appraisement

NAME AND ADDRESS OF ATTORNEY: TELEPHONE NO.:	FOR COURT USE ONLY
ATTORNEY FOR:	
SUPERIOR COURT OF CALIFORNIA, COUNTY OF SAN DIEGO	
ESTATE OF:	
☐ DECEDENT ☐ CONSERVATEE ☐ WARD	CASE NUMBER:
INVENTORY AND APPRAISEMENT* ☐ FINAL ☐ PARTIAL NO.: ☐ SUPPLEMENTAL ☐ REAPPRAISAL FOR SALE	Date of Death or of Appointment of Guardian or Conservator:

APPRAISALS

1. Total appraisal by representative (Attachment 1) . . . . $
2. Total appraisal by referee (Attachment 2) . . . . $
   TOTAL: $ _____

DECLARATION OF REPRESENTATIVE

3. Attachment 1 & 2 together with all prior inventories filed herein contain a true statement of ☐ all ☐ a portion of the estate that has come to my knowledge or possession, including particularly all money and just claims against me. I have truly, honestly and impartially appraised each item as set forth in Attachment 1 to the best of my ability.

I certify (declare) under penalty of perjury that the foregoing is true and correct and that this declaration is executed on
(Date): at (Place): , California.

_____ _____
(Type or print name of representative including title of corporate officer)   (Signature of representative)

STATEMENT OF ATTORNEY REGARDING BOND
(Complete if required by local court rule)

4. ☐ Bond is waived.
5. ☐ Bond filed in the amount of: $ ☐ Sufficient   ☐ Insufficient

Date: _____
(Signature of attorney for estate)

DECLARATION OF INHERITANCE TAX REFEREE

6. I have truly, honestly, and impartially appraised to the best of my ability each item set forth in Attachment 2.
7. A true account of my commission and expenses actually and necessarily incurred pursuant to my appointment is
   Statutory commission: $
   Expenses (Specify): $ _____
   Total: $
8. I certify (or declare) under penalty of perjury that the foregoing is true and correct and that this declaration was executed on
   (Date): at (Place): , California.

_____ _____
(Type or print name of referee)   (Signature of referee)

(Continued on Reverse Side)

*See reverse side for instructions before completing. The declaration must be signed in California (CCP 2015.5); affidavit required when signed outside California. No attachment permitted less than on a full page (California Rule of Court 201 (b)).

Form Approved by the
Judicial Council of California
Effective January 1, 1976
Form PR-21 Co. Clk. (9-76)

INVENTORY & APPRAISEMENT

Prob C 481, 600-611,
784, 1550, 1901

INSTRUCTIONS

See Prob. C. 601, 604, 608, 609, 611, 1550, 1606, 1702, and 1901 for additional instructions.

See Prob. C. 600–602 for items to be included.

If ward or conservatee is or has been confined in a state hospital during the guardianship or conservatorship, mail a copy to Director of State Department of Health at Sacramento. (Prob C. 1550, 1554.1, 1901)

The representative shall list on Attachment 1 and appraise as of the date of death or date of appointment of guardian or conservator at fair market value moneys, currency, cash items, bank accounts and amounts on deposit with any financial institution (as defined in Probate Code Section 605), and the proceeds of life and accident insurance policies and retirement plans payable upon death in lump sum amounts to the estate, excepting therefrom such items whose fair market value is, in the opinion of the representative, an amount different from the ostensible value or specified amount.

The representative shall list on Attachment 2 all other assets of the estate which shall be appraised by the Referee.

If joint tenancy and other assets are listed for appriasal purposes only and not as part of the probate estate, they must be separately listed on additional attachments and their value excluded from the total valuation of Attachments 1 and 2.

Each attachment should conform to the format approved by the Judicial Council.

Inventory and Appraisement (Attachment)

ESTATE OF:

CASE NUMBER:

ATTACHMENT NO:

(IN DECEDENTS' ESTATES, ATTACHMENTS MUST CONFORM TO PROBATE CODE 601
REGARDING COMMUNITY AND SEPARATE PROPERTY)

PAGE . . . . OF . . . . . TOTAL PAGES
(ADD PAGES AS REQUIRED)

Item No.	Description	Appraised value
1.		$

Form Approved by the
Judicial Council of California
Effective January 1, 1976

INVENTORY AND, APPRAISEMENT (ATTACHMENT)

Prob C 481,
600–605, 784,
1550, 1901

Valuation of Assets by Executor or Administrator and Inheritance Tax Referee

Probate Code section 605 provides for valuation of certain assets of the estate by the inheritance tax referee and of certain others for which the fair market value is readily ascertainable, such as cash items, by the executor or administrator.

The State Inheritance Tax Referees Association has made its interpretation of this section and in its Inheritance Tax Referees' Procedure Guide (January 1980) has listed categories to be appraised by the personal representative and by the referee, though not intended as an all-inclusive list. The lists are reproduced here by permission:

A. MONEYS AND CURRENCY:

To be appraised by Representative:

1. U.S. coin and currency in circulation and worth no more than face value.

To be appraised by Referee:

1. Coins and currency with a value other than face, including gold coin, foreign coin and currency, commemorative coins or medals, coin collections, and unusual or collector's items, such as old currency, bank notes, etc.

B. CASH ITEMS:

A 'cash item' is a check, draft, money order or similar instrument issued prior to decedent's death which can be immediately converted to cash and whose fair market value can be determined solely from its face without calculation or reference to other sources.

To be appraised by Representative:

1. Checks dated *before* decedent's death, including, but not limited to certified, cashier's, travelers checks, etc.
2. Cash dividends declared and payable to shareholder as of a date *before* decedent's death.
3. Bond coupons matured and redeemable in cash at face value *before* decedent's death.
4. Money orders dated *before* decedent's death.
5. Government warrants (checks) or similar instruments dated *before* decedent's death.
6. Drafts dated *before* decedent's death.
7. Social Security and Veterans lump sum death benefits.

The following are not cash items and are to be appraised by Referee:

1. Checks and drafts dated *after* decedent's death.
2. Cash dividends declared but payable to shareholder *after* decedent's death.
3. Bond coupons which mature *after* decedent's death.
4. Promissory notes and loans, secured and unsecured.

5. Accounts receivable of all types.
6. Contractual rights to receive money.
7. Refunds of all types, including but not limited to, taxes, insurance premiums, utilities, magazines subscriptions, auto clubs, medicare, hospital and medical reimbursement, etc.
8. Bonds, stocks and securities of all types, listed or unlisted, including Treasury notes, bills and bonds, whether or not they qualify for payment of federal estate taxes.
9. Bankers acceptance notes and bank capital notes.
10. Any item not in U.S. dollars.
11. Tax anticipation or registered warrants and notes.
12. Payments from escrow not closed before decedent's death.
13. Revolving funds on deposit with a cooperative or marketing organization.
14. Stamps and stamp collections.
15. Cash, cash items and any other assets which would be appraised by the Representative except for the fact that the item is an asset of a partnership, joint venture, trust or other entity, or is an asset of another decedent's estate.
16. A cash distribution from another decedent's estate *after* decedent's death.
17. Any item with a fair market value different from the ostensible value or specified amount.

C. BANK ACCOUNTS AND AMOUNTS ON DEPOSIT WITH ANY FINANCIAL INSTITUTION:

As defined by the code, 'financial institutions' include banks, trust companies, savings and loan associations and similar institutions and credit unions. Excluded from the definition are foreign financial institutions, industrial loan companies and thrift companies, such as Morris Plan.

To be appraised by Representative:
1. Bank accounts, and amounts on deposit in the name of the decedent, or in a fictitious name of the decedent, including (a) checking accounts, commercial, regular, personal, special, ten-plan, etc., and (b) savings accounts, passbook, share accounts or balances, time, demand, special plans, Christmas Club, etc.
2. Amounts on deposit with a 'financial institution' as defined including savings certificates, time certificates, certified time deposits, investment certificates, cumulative and accumulative investment certificates, investment thrift cerficates, installment thrift certificates, etc.
3. Totten trusts [bank account trusts].

To be appraised by Referee:
1. Any amount not in U.S. dollars.

2. Investment certificates issued by thrift companies, such as Morris Plan or Commercial Credit and any company having 'Thrift' in its title.

3. Amounts on deposit other than with a 'financial institution,'' as defined, such as U.S. Treasury certificates of indebtedness, certificates of deposit for state and municipal land, certificates of deposit issued for stock, certificates of beneficial interest, etc.

4. Any item with a fair market value different from the ostensible value or specified amount.

D. PROCEEDS OF LIFE AND ACCIDENT INSURANCE POLICIES AND RETIREMENT PLANS PAYABLE UPON DEATH IN LUMP SUM AMOUNTS:

To be appraised by Representative:

1. Proceeds of life and accident insurance and retirement plans payable upon death in lump sum amounts, even if not paid in a lump sum.

To be appraised by Referee:

1. Proceeds not payable in lump sum.
2. Annuities.

* * * *

A NOTICE OF FIDUCIARY RELATIONSHIP (Form 56, obtainable from the IRS) should be filed with the office of the Internal Revenue Service where the return is to be filed. (Regulation 301.6903-1.) It is supposed to be filed within 30 days after appointment. When the fiduciary capacity terminates, a written notice of the termination with satisfactory evidence thereof should be filed.

An APPLICATION FOR EMPLOYER IDENTIFICATION NUMBER (Form SS-4, obtainable from the IRS) should likewise be filed. The number issued should be used on all tax returns of the estate.

NOTICE OF TERMINATION OF FIDUCIARY RELATIONSHIP.

When the representative's duties in the estate are ended, the representative should notify the Internal Revenue Service of this fact, and mail a copy of the decree of discharge as proof. Thereafter the representative is relieved from liability for any acts occurring thereafter.

Joint Tenancy

Assets held in joint tenancy are not properly part of the estate and should not be listed in the inventory and appraisement; the representative does not account for the property held in joint tenancy. The joint tenancy property is, however, listed separately, in the inheritance tax affidavit and any federal estate tax return (706).

Termination of Joint Tenancy

Reprinted from State Inheritance Tax Referees Association Bulletin, Official Publication of the State Inheritance Tax Referees Association (Jan. 1, 1981):

Upon the death of a joint tenant, a Release of Lien and/or a Consent to Transfer from an authorized representative of the Controller of the State of California is required in order to clear title to a joint tenant's property. To accomplish this, it is necessary that an Inheritance Tax Declaration (Form IT-22) be completed, signed, and submitted.

EVERY ITEM OR QUESTION ON THE FORM MUST BE FILLED IN OR ANSWERED, AND THE FORM MUST BE SUBMITTED IN DUPLICATE.

This form may be acquired from the office of a State Inheritance Tax Referee in your county, or an office of the State Controller, Inheritance and Gift Tax Division, as set forth below.

State Inheritance Tax Referees are prohibited by law from giving legal advice regarding the completion of inheritance tax forms. Surviving joint tenants are advised to consult their attorneys in the preparation of these forms, since termination of joint tenancies involves legal questions and can result in substantial tax consequences.

If you wish to represent yourself, you should submit the completed Inheritance Tax Declaration with all related documents, including copies of: 1. Joint Tenancy Deed; 2. Wills and Codicils, (2 copies); and 3. Trust Agreements, if any, (2 copies).

OPTION 1: If you wish to select this option, you may submit the completed Inheritance Tax Declaration and other documents to a State Inheritance Tax Referee in your county. Upon receipt thereof the Referee will appraise the property and determine the inheritance tax due. The Referee is authorized to issue Releases of Lien and Consents to Transfer under appropriate circumstances.

The law provides that Referees shall charge $1.00 per one thousand dollars ($1,000.00) on the first $500,000 of property appraised. The fee for the portion of the property appraised in excess of $500,000 shall be .50 per $1,000 of property appraised. There is an additional charge for necessary expenses such as travel and mapping for this service. (Cash and bank accounts are not subject to Referees' fees.)

OPTION 2: If you select the second option you may submit the completed forms and other documents to an office of the State Controller, Inheritance and Gift Tax Division (see addresses below) where it will be processed as follows:

1) If an appraisal of the property is necessary to determine the inheritance tax due, the case will be assigned and documents transferred to an appropriate State Inheritance Tax Referee for handling.

2) If no appraisal of the property is necessary to determine the tax, you will be notified of the tax due, if any. Any necessary Release of Lien or Consent to Transfer can be issued by the Inheritance and Gift Tax Division. In this case, since no appraisal is made, no Referee fees or expenses are incurred.

NOTE: Before selecting option 2. it is suggested you consider that an appraisal of the assets can be for:

1. New tax basis for capital gains.

2. New depreciation schedule for income property.

3. Federal Estate Tax return, if required

4. A record of assets and values for the surviving joint tenants and heirs.

TAXATION OF ESTATES

The estate is subject to inheritance taxes, federal estate taxes, income taxes, and real property taxes. Many tax problems can arise in an involved estate, one where there is a trust or business, and so on. Tax considerations must be kept in mind by the paralegal at all times throughout the entire estate proceeding.

Tax planning for the estate starts in the preparation of a will, or in the setting up of a trust if that should precede the will, even in taking title to properties, and continues through the administration of the estate. Tax considerations confront the representative of the estate in the choice of valuation date, the selection of an accounting period for income taxes, the election to take deductions against either the federal estate tax or against the income tax, and timing of distribution, which can result in substantial tax savings to the estate and/or its beneficiaries. What would be best in a given situation, depends upon the *tax identity* of, first, the decedent when he was living, and later, of the estate and its beneficiaries. Tax expertise is essential to sound decisions.

Real Property Taxes

Real property taxes on real property held by an estate become delinquent on the same dates as an individual's property taxes, *i.e.*, December 10 and April 10.

Income Taxes

Decedent's Final Returns:
Federal (540) and state income tax returns (1040) for the decedent are due at the same time they would have been due had death not occurred; the same tests for filing as for individuals apply. In other words, if the decedent's returns would have been paid for the calendar year, the returns are due April 15; if decedent used a fiscal year, the returns would be due the 15th day of the 4th month after the end of that fiscal year.

Federal Income Tax for Estate:
A federal income tax is payable during administration if the gross income of the estate for the taxable year is $750 or over. (Int. Rev. Code §142.) A Form 1041 is filed with the Internal Revenue Service.
An extension of time to file may be granted for ''reasonable cause.'' (Form 2755)
Other federal returns which may be required of fiduciary are listed in the instructions for the Form 1041, where nonresident alien beneficiaries, estates and trusts, trade or business, and trusts, are involved.

State Income Tax for Estate:
State income taxes are payable for estate during administration if net (taxable) income amounts to $1,000 or more or the gross income exceeds $7,000, regardless of the net income (in case of a trust, if the net (taxable) income is over $100.
An extension of time to file may be granted upon furnishing a satisfactory explanation why the return cannot be timely filed.

Subsequent Returns (Due Dates)
The *first* subsequent return is for the adopted accounting period (calendar year or fiscal year, regardless of the basis on which decedent filed returns). The first taxable year for the estate may be any period (1) which ends on the last day of a month and (2) does not exceed 12 months from the date of death. For example, for a person dying on July 3, the last date that could be chosen to end the taxable year would be June 30 of the ensuing year. June 30 is less than one year from the date of death but the taxable year must end on the last day of the month and must not exceed one year, and July 31 would be *more* than one year.

Each subsequent return is made on the same basis (although a change can be made in the accounting period if approval is obtained).

The returns are due no later than the 15th day of the fourth month after the end of the estate's taxable year (whether calendar year or fiscal year is chosen).

Final Income Tax Returns:
"Final Return" should be written across the top of the last return filed for the estate (and statement (e) at the top of the Form 541 completed, for state income taxes).

Federal Gift and Estate Taxes

Prior to 1977 taxes were assessed separately on gifts of the estate transferred upon death. There was a lifetime exemption for $3,000 per year per donee. In addition, an individual could give $30,000 during his lifetime without being subject to tax.

Commencing in 1977, taxation on gifts and estates is unified, so that generally the tax will be the same on any transfer, whether by way of gift during a lifetime or upon death. Generally, annual gifts of $3,000 per donee may continue to be made without incurring any tax and will not be added back into the estate. Gifts made after December 31, 1976, and during the 3 year period ending on date of decedent's death, for which a gift tax return was required to be filed, are added back into the gross estate upon death and gift taxes will be added back into net value of the estate along with the amount of the gift itself. (See IRC §2035 (b)(2).)

Gifts made prior to 1977 are not included in the amount of transfers; reduction for prior tax is correspondingly limited. Special rules apply to gifts made between September 8, 1976, and January 1, 1977; and there is a limitation placed on the unified credit for gift taxes for gifts made before July 1, 1977.

Generally speaking, *any* transfer after 1976, whether by gift or from estate after death, will result in the same tax, *i.e.*, gifts and estates are taxed the same, the gifts on a cumulative basis. Upon death the amount of the gifts are added back into the estate and taxed. Credit is allowed for the tax previously paid on the gifts. Instead of a lifetime $30,000 exemption for gifts and the $60,000 exemption for an estate, a credit is allowed against the *tax* computed to be due as follows:

The unified gift and estate tax schedule applicable after December 31, 1976, follows:

In the case of decedents dying during	Amount of Tax Credit:	No tax on cumulative transfers (gifts and estate) not exceeding:
1977	$30,000	$120,666
1978	34,000	134,000
1979	38,000	147,333
1980	42,500	161,563
1981 and thereafter	47,000	175,625

Gift and Estate Tax Schedule

"If the amount with respect to which the tentative tax to be computed is:	The tentative tax is:
Not over $10,000	18 percent of such amount.
Over $10,000 but not over $20,000	$1,800, plus 20 percent of the excess of such amount over $10,000.
Over $20,000 but not over $40,000	$3,800, plus 22 percent of the excess of such amount over $20,000.
Over $40,000 but not over $60,000	$8,200, plus 24 percent of the excess of such amount over $40,000.
Over $60,000 but not over $80,000	$13,000, plus 26 percent of the excess of such amount over $60,000.
Over $80,000 but not over $100,000	$18,200, plus 28 percent of the excess of such amount over $80,000.
Over $100,000 but not over $150,000	$23,800, plus 30 percent of the excess of such amount over $100,000.
Over $150,000 but not over $250,000	$38,800, plus 32 percent of the excess of such amount over $150,000.
Over $250,000 but not over $500,000	$70,800, plus 34 percent of the excess of such amount over $250,000.
Over $500,000 but not over $750,000	$155,800, plus 37 percent of the excess of such amount over $500,000.
Over $750,000 but not over $1,000,000	$248,300, plus 39 percent of the excess of such amount over $750,000.
Over $1,000,000 but not over $1,250,000	$345,800, plus 41 percent of the excess of such amount over $1,000,000.
Over $1,250,000 but not over $1,500,000	$448,300, plus 43 percent of the excess of such amount over $1,250,000.
Over $1,500,000 but not over $2,000,000	$555,800, plus 45 percent of the excess of such amount over $1,500,000.
Over $2,000,000 but not over $2,500,000	$780,800, plus 49 percent of the excess of such amount over $2,000,000.
Over $2,500,000 but not over $3,000,000	$1,025,800, plus 53 percent of the excess of such amount over $2,500,000.
Over $3,000,000 but not over $3,500,000	$1,290,800, plus 57 percent of the excess of such amount over $3,000,000.
Over $3,500,000 but not over $4,000,000	$1,575,800, plus 61 percent of the excess of such amount over $3,500,000.
Over $4,000,000 but not over $4,500,000	$1,880,800, plus 65 percent of the excess of such amount over $4,000,000.
Over $4,500,000 but not over $5,000,000	$2,205,800, plus 69 percent of the excess of such amount over $4,500,000.
Over $5,000,000	$2,550,800, plus 70 percent of the excess of such amount over $5,000,000.

Federal Estate Taxes

In the estates of decedents dying after December 31, 1976, the following schedule is applicable in determining whether a return must be filed:

Decedents dying during:	File 706 if gross estate exceeds:
1977	$120,000
1978	134,000
1979	147,000
1980	161,000
1981 and thereafter	175,000

The Economic Tax Recovery Act of 1981:

This act will apply to federal estate taxes for decedents dying on or after January 1, 1982, and will have a substantial impact on estate planning. A review of wills executed prior to that date is imperative. Under this law, estates of decedents dying on or after January 1, 1982, will be transferred to surviving spouses free of estate and gift taxes. On the surviving spouse's death, the estate will be taxed if it exceeds the allowable exemptions, which will be phased in each year to a maximum of $600,000 for decedents dying after 1986. The top 70 percent brackets for large estates will be reduced gradually to 50 percent in 1985.

The new law also raises the $3,000 gift tax exemption for children or other donees to $10,000 per year commencing January 1, 1982.

This law will be covered further in future supplements.

TIME FOR FILING 706 AND PAYMENT OF TAX

The federal estate tax is due 9 months after the date of death.

Time can be extended up to 10 years for "reasonable cause."

Interest on the unpaid tax accrues at normal rates (currently 12%). (Other provisions are made for extensions if estate consists of an interest in a farm or closely-held business.) These provisions replace the previous more restrictive requirement of a showing of "undue hardship." (26 U.S.C. §6161)

EXTENSIONS OF TIME TO PAY

An extension of time to pay the tax does not extend the time for filing the return; applications for each must be made. Applications should be made well in advance of due date, at least 30 days, if possible, to give the IRS time for review and notification.

PENALTIES FOR LATE PAYMENT

Penalties may be imposed when a return is filed or tax is paid late, after the original due date or extended date. In any event, interest is charged on the tax underpaid or postponed. Therefore, if the return cannot be filed but the estate is in a position to pay the tax, it might be advisable to estimate and pay the tax, in which event interest would be charged only on the amount underpaid, if any.

Tax Assessment Period and Release from Personal Liability

FEDERAL ESTATE TAX — The estate tax must be assessed (1) within 3 years after the date the return (the 706) is filed or (2) within 3 years after the date the estate tax is due, whichever is later. This assessment period can be reduced to 18 months under certain circumstances (IRCA §6501(d)) by making a request for prompt assessment. (See 34 Am.Jur.2d, 9158, for form of letter.)

See Internal Revenue Code section 6501, subdivision (e), for the assessment period on fraudulent returns.

The executor or fiduciary of the estate may apply to the Internal Revenue Service for determination of the estate tax and for discharge from personal liability. Such application may be in the form of a letter requesting immediate determination of the amount of the federal estate tax and for discharge from *personal* liability for such tax, pursuant to Internal Revenue Code section 2204.

The determination must be made within nine months after such request or the filing of the return, whichever is later; within nine months the executor must be notified of the amount of the tax, and upon payment, shall be entitled to a receipt or writing showing such discharge. (IRC §2204.)

The estate remains liable for the tax during the three-year assessment period (or 18 months if shortened as above).

FEDERAL INCOME AND GIFT TAXES — A similar request for discharge from personal liability may be made for federal income or gift taxes. If the representative is notified of additional tax and makes payment he is discharged from personal liability, or, if no such notification is received, he is discharged 9 months after the date of the return if the date of death of the decedent was after December 31, 1973 (one year if date of death of decedent after December 31, 1970, and before December 31, 1973). (IRC §69051)

The estate is still liable for the tax within the applicable period.

STATE INCOME AND GIFT TAXES — A similar provision for California income and gift taxes is made in Revenue and Taxation Code section 19266.

STATE INHERITANCE TAXES — There are no similar provisions for release of personal liability for payment of state inheritance taxes.

Preparation of the 706

A helpful booklet, "Instructions for Form 706" is available from the Internal Revenue Service; also available are: "A Guide to Federal Estate and Gift Taxation" (Publication 448) and "Federal Tax Guide for Survivors, Executors, and Administrators (Publication 559). A copy of the Regulations should be at hand for reference, as well as the Internal Revenue Code. American Jurisprudence 2d annually publishes two taxation volumes which are an excellent reference. There are, of course, a number of tax services to which the law office may subscribe.

In general, the following deductions of a resident decedent are subtracted from the total amount in arriving at the taxable estate:

1. Funeral and administration expenses and claims against the estate (including taxes and charitable pledges).
2. Casualty or theft losses during administration of the estate (not compensated for by insurance).
3. Charitable transfers.
4. Marital deduction.
5. Unpaid mortgages or indebtedness.
6. Expenses of administering the estate (if not also deducted on the income tax return).
7. Expenses for selling property of the estate were formerly deductible if the sale was necessary in order to pay the decedent's debts, expenses of administration, or taxes, to preserve the estate, or to effect distribution. "Expenses for selling property" include brokerage fees and other expenses attending the sale. Selling expenses were also deductible against income taxes of the estate. However, in estates of persons dying after December 31, 1976, selling expenses *may no longer be deducted* for *both* estate and income tax purposes.

Marital Deduction (Federal)

In estates of decedents dying after December 31, 1976, the first $100,000 gift made by a spouse is not a taxable gift, the second $100,000 is fully taxable, and all amounts over $200,000 are subject to a 50% marital deduction.

In addition, the estate may deduct as a marital deduction either $250,000 or 50% of the amount of the adjusted gross estate, whichever is greater.

But an adjustment is made for the marital deduction previously claimed for gifts if it exceeded 50% of gifts to spouse. In other words, an adjustment is required where gifts to a spouse were under $200,000, since a tax would have been paid on the second $100,000 and a $250,000 marital deduction is allowed.

Carryover Basis — Federal

Prior to 1977, property was valued in the estate at its fair market value on the date of death (or alternate valuation date). Capital gains on a later sale was paid only upon the appreciation in value after the date of death. Commencing in 1977, the value of property was to be its value as of December 31, 1976 — subject to certain adjustments.

The Revenue Act of 1978 postponed the effective date of the changeover to December 31, 1979. In the Spring of 1980 the federal income tax law relating to these carryover basis rules was repealed.

California law conforms various provisions of the Inheritance Tax Law to the federal law as revised by the Tax Reform Act of 1976. This new law repeals the carryover basis rules to conform to present federal tax law and makes further conforming provisions relating to income from certain dispositions of property. (See Rev. & Tax. Code §§18046, 18051.1, and 18052, and §157 of Ch. 1079 of Stats. 1977; Revenue and Taxation Code sections 18047 and 18104 are repealed.)

Carryover Basis — California

For Decedents Dying After January 1, 1981

Neither half of real property held in joint tenancy by spouses — regardless of its source, whether community, separate or quasi-community — receives a stepped up basis on the death of one spouse.

As of this writing it appears that the Franchise Tax Board takes the position that where the death of a spouse occurs after January 1, 1981, neither half of the community property will receive a stepped up basis, *i.e.*, its fair market value. However, petitions for hearing in the California Supreme Court have been filed in *Mel v. Franchise Tax Board* (1981) 119 Cal.App.3d 898, and in companion cases decided by the Court of Appeal in the First Appellate District (opinions not published) *Bank of California* (1 Civ. 47334); *Levit* (1 Civ. 47337); and *Miller* (1 Civ. 47336).

If the deceased spouse left his one-half share to a third party the decedent's one-half share and the surviving spouse's one-half share might each get a stepped up basis.

Alternate Valuation Date

An election may be made on the estate tax return to value decedent's property on the date of death or six months after the decedent's death, with the exception that any property sold, exchanged or otherwise disposed of within the six-month period after decedent's death is valued as of the date sold, exchanged or otherwise disposed of.

The election must be applied uniformly to all of the property in the estate, e.g., you cannot value the real property as of the date of death and value securities that had depreciated six months after the date of death. If the alternate valuation date had been selected the IRS might try to prove that real property values had increased during that six-month period, and could result in increased tax if successful.

In some cases, where the assets consist of a substantial percentage of depreciated stock the alternate valuation date should definitely be selected, provided the tax saving will not be offset by appreciating assets.

There is one further facet to the alternate valuation rule: "Any property [including patents, estates for the lives of persons other than the decedent, remainders and reversions] that is affected by mere lapse of time is valued as of the date of the decedent's death, but adjusted for any difference in its value not due to mere lapse of time as of 6 months after the decedent's death, or as of the date of its distribution, sale, exchange, or other disposition, whichever date occurs first." (Publication 448, p. 16.) Examples of application of the lapse of time rule are also given on page 16.

Another consideration in making this election as to tax saving is the extra accounting that will be required. For California has no such provision for alternate valuation, and the estate will therefore be dealing with two sets of valuations in accounting and income tax reporting.

Valuation and Audits

The instructions which accompany the Form 706 and the publications mentioned above, provide detailed information and should be thoroughly studied by the legal assistant who works on 706s.

In the majority of cases the appraisals of the inheritance tax referee are used in the return and accepted by the IRS. If there is a sizeable holding of real property, commercial property, farm land, closely held stock, the IRS will want to be satisfied as to the basis of the valuation, or an audit may result.

For a substantial interest in mineral rights, an independent appraisal by a geologist is best and probably will not be questioned on review by the IRS engineers. Rights to receive income in the future are not worth what they are today and must be discounted.

Disclaimers

A disclaimer is a written instrument which declines, refuses, renounces or disclaims any interest which would otherwise be succeeded to by a beneficiary. (Prob. Code §§190-190.10, enacted in 1972.) Disclaimers are becoming more important as a consideration in post-mortem estate tax planning and the legal assistant in that field must become conversant with their possible uses, which is beyond the scope of this section.

Disclaimers have to be filed within a "reasonable time," as defined in Probate Code section 190.3.

Under the federal law (IRC §§2045, 2518, Revenue Act of 1978) applicable to transfers made after December 31, 1976, the refusal must be written and must be received no later than nine months after the transfer creating the interest (or 9 months after the disclaimant reaches the age of 21). None of the interest or its benefits may have been accepted and the interest once refused must go to a person other than the disclaimant, and the interest must pass to a person other than the disclaimant without any direction on the disclaimant's part. Apparently a disclaimer would be valid where a *spouse* disclaimed an interest which passed without the spouse's direction to a trust in which the spouse had an income interest. (Revenue Act of 1978, §702(m), amending IRC 2518(b)(4).)

California Inheritance and Gift Tax

Legislation making significant changes in California inheritance and gift tax law took effect January 1, 1981, with respect to decedents dying on and after that date and gifts made on or after that date; the provisions of the act relating to probate procedure and tax administration and collection apply to all estates, also effective January 1, 1981.

The level of exemption for all classes has been increased, and a total exemption provided for surviving spouses, whether community or separate property, unless the surviving spouse retains a "limited power of appointment" over the property, in which event the value of the property subject to such power is taxable to the surviving spouse.

A "limited power of appointment" is defined in Revenue and Taxation Code section 13693 as "a power which does not qualify under the preceding section [13692] as a general power of appointment." A limited power of appointment is one that generally permits the donee to appoint to a class that does not include himself, his estate, his creditors or the creditors of his estate. In other words, a limited power of appointment includes a power to appoint only to or among specified persons, but not including the donee holder of the power, nor his estate, his creditors or creditors of his estate. A power of appointment may be general as to part of the appointive property and limited as to the rest. Thus, where H is the donor and devises property to W (the donee) for life, and at W's death to be distributed, one-half to any person W by will directs, and one-half to X, Y or Z as W directs, W has a general testamentary power as to one-half the property and a limited power of appointment as to the remaining one-half. (Title 18, Cal. Adm. Code §13693.)

Surviving spouses are not, however, free from California taxes. Revenue and Taxation Code section 13442 provides as follows: "If no inheritance tax is payable to this State in a case where a federal estate tax is payable to the United States, a tax equal to the maximum state tax credit allowed by the federal estate tax law is hereby imposed." Thus, where there is an adjusted taxable estate calculated under federal law of say $240,000, for which is allowed a credit of state death taxes of $3,600, a California tax of $3,600 would be imposed under this section. If the adjusted taxable estate is $640,000, the tax imposed is $18,000 and would be payable by the surviving spouse. This is known as the "pickup tax."

If the inheritance tax payable in California is *less* than the maximum state credit allowed, a tax equal to the difference is imposed under Revenue and Taxation Code section 13441.

The safe-deposit box inspection required of county treasurers has been eliminated (Rev. & Tax. Code §14344, repealed).

A release from the Office of the State Controller indicates that all California banks, savings and loan associations and credit unions have been issued general (blanket) consents by the State Controller authorizing them to make transfers of accounts, deposits and certificates standing (A) in the name of a decedent, or (B) in the names of a decedent and any other person, or (C) in the name of a decedent as trustee or beneficiary, to the person or persons appearing to be otherwise legally entitled thereto up to the following amounts without obtaining individual consents, under the following conditions:

1. If the transferee is a resident of California
   and entitled to payment in his/her capacity as
   EXECUTOR OR ADMINISTRATOR
   of the estate of the decedent .... WITHOUT LIMIT
2. SPOUSE of the decedent .... WITHOUT LIMIT
3. LINEAL ANCESTOR OR LINEAL ISSUE
   of the decedent, *i.e.,* parent, grandparent, child,
   grandchild, etc. $15,000
4. BROTHER, SISTER OR DESCENDANT OF
   A BROTHER OR SISTER of decedent .... $ 7,500

5. Transferee NOT IN ANY OF THE FORE-
   GOING CLASSES .... $ 2,000
6. If funds are in a preneed trust account to be
   paid to a funeral director for funeral services
   for the decedent (Art. 9, Ch. 12, Div. 3,
   Bus. & Prof. Code) .... $ 2,000
7. Any payment or check certification pursuant to
   SECTION 4405(2) OF THE COMMERCIAL
   CODE, for each check or certification .... $ 1,000
8. CONTENTS OF SAFE DEPOSIT BOX. Any company,
   corporation, association or other person having in its
   custody or control a safe deposit box to which a decedent
   had a right of access is authorized to deliver custody or
   control of the contents of the box to the person or persons
   appearing to be legally entitled thereto.

The general consent to transfer in no way determines who is legally
entitled to the funds on deposit.

*   *   *   *

A life estate received by a spouse under an A-B Trust will not be
taxable under state law, but will be taxable under the federal "ter-
minable interest rule."

If the Controller finds that payment of inheritance taxes would
result in undue hardship (as defined in Revenue and Taxation Code
section 14143.5), he may in his discretion enter into a written agreement for payments on terms and conditions, provided he finds that
payment of the taxes and interest is adequately secured. (Rev. & Tax.
Code §14143.5.) If the written agreement is incorporated into the
decree of distribution, the tax may be paid in 10 annual installments
pursuant to section 14105. Under section 14180 the Controller may
for reasonable cause extend the period for payment 10 years from the
date prescribed by section 14103 (9 months from date of death) or,
in case of an installment amount referred to in this section, 12 months
from due date for last installment, including beneficiaries receiving art
work from a decedent-artist, where the art work comprises 35 percent
of the value of the gross estate or 50 percent of the taxable estate.

Farms and family businesses receive special consideration. Farms
and closely held (family) businesses may be valued in the estate on
the basis of current use of the property (an income approach), rather
than on its fair market value (highest and best use). (See Rev. & Tax.
Code §13311.5.) (See Special Use Valuation, *infra*.)

Beneficiaries receiving farms or closely-held businesses may be
allowed up to a maximum of 15 years to pay the taxes. (See Rev.
& Tax. Code §§14181, 14182.)

The inheritance tax referee will continue to value the property in the estate, within 60 days after receipt of the petition and necessary information and documentation, and to file a report with the probate court, which will officially fix the tax to be paid.

The provisions in the Probate Code prohibiting either a preliminary or final distribution of an estate (in Prob. Code §§1001, 1004) unless the inheritance taxes have been paid have been repealed. However, personal property taxes must be paid before distribution may be made. (Prob. Code §1024.)

Checks for inheritance taxes should be made payable to the State Treasurer; for fastest process, checks should be either mailed or delivered to the State Controller, Inheritance and Gift Tax Division (P.O. Box 1019, Sacramento, CA 95805); however, they will be accepted at the San Francisco and Los Angeles offices of the State Controller. For proper credit, when making payment, include (1) name of decedent, (2) date of death, (3) decedent's county of residence at date of death, and (4) decedent's social security number.

The inheritance tax is payable out of the property distributable to each beneficiary (unless the will otherwise provides); the receipt of the beneficiary should reflect the tax paid. California inheritance tax is delinquent if not paid within 9 months after date of death.

Penalty and interest are charged if the tax is delinquent.

Intestate Succession

The inheritance tax is essentially a succession tax, *i.e.*, a tax upon the right or privilege of inheriting the property, whether by will or laws of succession. The tax is measured by the share received by each particular beneficiary from the decedent's net estate. The amount of the inheritance tax payable will depend upon the relationship of the beneficiary to the decedent, whether or not the beneficiary takes under a will.

If decedent left no will, his estate is distributed in accordance with the California laws of succession. These laws are contained in Probate Code sections 200 *et seq*. The law of succession is different for separate property and community property. Therefore the legal assistant must first know to whom the property would pass in the absence of a will.

Laws of Succession

COMMUNITY PROPERTY

1. Upon death of either Husband or Wife:

½   ½

to surviving spouse   to surviving spouse if not
                                             otherwise disposed of by will

(Prob. Code §201)

SEPARATE PROPERTY

2. Decedent leaves surviving spouse and 1 child:

½	½
to surviving spouse	to child or issue of child

(Prob. Code §221)

3. Decedent leaves surviving spouse and more than 1 child living, or 1 child and lawful issue of deceased child:

⅓	
to surviving spouse	equal shares to children and lawful issue of any deceased child, by right of representation

(Prob. Code §221)

4. Spouse and no child:

⅔	
to surviving spouse	to lineal descendants in equal shares if of same degree of kindred, otherwise by right of representation

(Prob. Code §221)

5. No surviving spouse:
   Equal shares to issue, otherwise by right of representation
   (Prob. Code §222)

6. Surviving spouse and no issue:

½	½
to surviving spouse	to parents in equal shares, or survivor of parents, or, if no parents, to parents' issue by right of representation

(Prob. Code §223)

7. Surviving spouse and no issue, parent, brother, sister or descendant of deceased brother or sister: All to surviving spouse

(Prob. Code §224)

8. No spouse or issue: to parents in equal shares, surviving of parents; if no parents, equal shares to brothers and sisters and descendants of deceased brothers and sisters by right of representation

(Prob. Code §225)

9. No spouse, issue or immediate family:

Next of kin in equal degree except if 2 or more collateral

kindred in equal degree but claiming through different ancestors, those who claim through nearest ancestor
(Prob. Code §226)

Additional succession statutes, applicable to other situations, are found in Probate Code sections 228, *et seq.* If the decedent leaves no relative to take his estate under these laws, the property escheats to the State of California, in the absence of a will.

The rates for the various beneficiaries follow:

CALIFORNIA GIFT TAX'—RATES AND EXEMPTIONS

Effective as to gifts made on or after January 1, 1981

CLASSIFICATION	EXEMPTION	up to $25,000.00	$25,000 to $50,000	$50,000 to $100,000	$100,000 to $200,000	$200,000 to $300,000	$300,000 to $400,000	Over $400,000
Husband or Wife	ALL	EXEMPT						
Minor Child (Includes Adopted)	40,000		Rate of tax on amount left after deducting exemption from $50,000.00 **4%**	6%	8%	10%	12%	14%
Adult Child, Grandchild, Parent, Grandparent (Relationship may be by Blood or Adoption) Mutually Acknowledged Child Descendant of Mutually Acknowledged Child	20,000	Rate of tax on amount left after deducting exemption from $25,000.00 **3%**	4%	6%	8%	10%	12%	14%
Brother, Sister (Excludes Brothers- and Sisters-in-law) Descendant of Brother or Sister (Includes Descendant by Adoption) Wife or Widow of Son, Husband or Widower of Daughter	10,000	Rate of tax on amount left after deducting exemption from $25,000.00 **6%**	10%	12%	14%	16%	18%	20%
Strangers in Blood and Relationships not Specified Above	3,000	Rate of tax on amount left after deducting exemption from $25,000.00 **10%**	14%	16%	18%	20%	22%	24%

'GIFT TAX ANNUAL EXEMPTION. Value of $3,000.00 transferred to each donee in any calendar year is excluded from tax unless transfer is of a future interest.

IT-72 (REV. 1·81)

CONTROLLER OF STATE OF CALIFORNIA

15994-208 9-80 60M CAM ⊙● OSP

CALIFORNIA INHERITANCE TAX—RATES AND EXEMPTIONS

Effective as to decedents dying on or after January 1, 1981

CLASSIFICATION	EXEMPTION	up to $25,000.00	$25,000 to $50,000	$50,000 to $100,000	$100,000 to $200,000	$200,000 to $300,000	$300,000 to $400,000	Over $400,000
Husband or Wife	ALL EXEMPT*	3%	4%	6%	8%	10%	12%	14%
Minor Child¹ (Includes Adopted)	40,000		Rate of tax on amount left after deducting exemption from $50,000.00 **4%**	6%	8%	10%	12%	14%
Adult Child, Grandchild, Parent, Grandparent (Relationship may be by Blood or Adoption) Mutually Acknowledged Child Descendant of Mutually Acknowledged Child	20,000	Rate of tax on amount left after deducting exemption from $25,000.00 **3%**	4%	6%	8%	10%	12%	14%
Brother, Sister (Excludes Brothers- and Sisters-in-law) Descendant of Brother or Sister (Includes Descendant by Adoption) Wife or Widow of Son, Husband or Widower of Daughter	10,000	Rate of tax on amount left after deducting exemption from $25,000.00 **6%**	10%	12%	14%	16%	18%	20%
Strangers in Blood and Relationships not Specified Above	3,000	Rate of tax on amount left after deducting exemption from $25,000.00 **10%**	14%	16%	18%	20%	22%	24%

¹ Effective as to decedents with a date of death on or after January 1, 1981, minor orphans of a decedent are entitled to an exemption in an amount equal to $10,000 multiplied by the excess of 21 over the age of the orphan (in years) at decedent's date of death.
* If a surviving spouse receives a limited power of appointment in property, the property subject to the power is taxed at the rates indicated.

Inheritance Tax Declaration — Form IT-22

(Numbers beginning certain paragraphs in this discussion refer to Form IT-22, which follows on page 488.)

INHERITANCE TAX DECLARATION (Form IT-22) should be prepared. (Original and 4 copies.) (Original and 3 copies to inheritance tax referee as noted above.) If there is more than one executor, any one of the executors may make the affidavit. Affiant should be the person most familiar with the financial affairs of the decedent. Either a certificate of no tax due (a blue form) or a report of tax due (a white form) will be filed with the court by the inheritance tax referee (Rev. & Tax. Code §§14501, 14514), and a copy is furnished to the attorney.

Accurate and complete answers to the questions in Form IT-22 are particularly important since they form the basis for determination of tax. The Inheritance Tax Department supplies a helpful booklet of instructions, "Inheritance Tax Instructions," upon request. Information from the booklet is incorporated here, along with a few pointers and comments based on the statutes and regulations. *Numbers correspond to the question numbers in the IT-22.* Form appears at the end of this material.

Copy all the names of the decedent as in the title of the probate proceeding, which should include all the names by which decedent was known or in which he held property.

The IT-22 is required to be filed for (a) resident decedents, when a person residing in California at the date of death had interest in any type of property or who during his lifetime transferred by gift any property, (b) nonresident decedents, when a person not residing in California at date of death had an interest in any tangible personal or real property in California or who during his lifetime transferred by gift any such property; (c) in all cases where there is a court proceeding in California to probate an estate, terminate a joint tenancy or life estate, or to determine inheritance tax.

4a, 10b, 13. *Description of Assets.* "Joint tenancy" refers to ownership of property by two or more persons jointly, as "joint tenants," as real property or bank accounts; a joint tenant who is the surviving owner becomes the sole owner and has the right to immediate possession and enjoyment. Joint tenancies are reported here only (they do not belong in the Inventory and Appraisement). If the joint tenancy properties were community property of husband and wife, question 4b should be answered "Yes" but it is not necessary to give further particulars as required for joint tenancy property of decedent and other person.

Trustee bank accounts and United States bonds payable on death may be reported here (4a) or under question 13. Gift tax returns must be filed if non-community property transferred exceeds the statutory exemptions; attach copy of any gift tax return previously filed. Describe assets fully, so that the property may be readily identified. (See Cal. Adm. Code, tit. 18, Regs. 14501-14515(b).)

Real Property: Give date of deed, date of recordation and book and page number of record; county of location, street and number if in a city; name of person in whose name title stands; short statement describing improvements, if any. A copy of deed which includes the recording information may be submitted. If there is not enough space to describe all the property, use a separate sheet of paper and type "See separate list attached."

Promissory Notes: State (1) name of maker, (2) date of note, (3) face value, (4) rate of interest, (5) unpaid balance at date of death (principal and interest), (6) names of payees (beneficiaries) and manner in which title to note held, (7) date of maturity. If note was secured by a trust deed or mortgage, give brief description of secured property.

Bank, Checking, Savings and Certificate Accounts: Give name and branch of bank or savings institution, account number and nature of account.

Stocks: Give exact name of corporation, number of shares and class or series; common or preferred, and if preferred, the issue; par or no-par; certificate numbers. Value of securities traded on open market can be determined by any reputable stock broker, or newspapers.

Bonds: Give quantity and denomination, name of obligor, kind of bond, date of maturity, interest rate and interest due dates; series number (if more than one issue); name of exchange if listed or principal place of business of obligor if unlisted. Give year and month of purchase of U.S. savings bonds.

Life Insurance: The description should include the nature and type of the policy; name of insurer; name of beneficiary and relationship to decedent; number of policy; face value of policy and amount payable. Obtain IRS Form 938 from insurance carrier.

Judgments: If decedent had an interest in a judgment it is an asset of the estate and a description thereof should contain the following information: Title of court and cause in which judgment rendered; date rendered; name and address of judgment debtor and creditor; the amount unpaid. An abstract of the judgment will suffice.

Miscellaneous Assets: Jewelry, furs, automobiles, art objects, etc., should be described so they can be readily identified. Declarant's opinion (or expert's opinion if appropriate, as a jeweler's appraisal of jewelry or a furrier's appraisal of furs) of value of jewelry, furs, furniture, automobiles, mobile homes, tools and equipment.

Fractional Interests: If decedent owner held an interest as a co-tenant, give name of cotenant, relationship if any, fraction of interest, source from which the cotenants acquired interest.

If there is insufficient space to describe all the property, a notation should be made "See separate list attached" and the property described on a separate sheet of paper.

4a, 10b, 13. *Value of Assets:* Bank, checking, savings, certificate accounts: balance including any unposted interest. Promissory notes:

outstanding balance, including any accrued interest. Real Property: Fair market value of property; if no inheritance tax referee has been appointed, attach a copy of county property tax bill for the year of death for each parcel of property.

4b, 6a. Note necessity of attaching an affidavit (Form IT-16 (real property)) if claim is made that the joint tenancy property described in question 4a originally belonged to the surviving joint tenant. Form IT-15 is required for bank accounts. Property of a husband and wife held in joint tenancy, if it originated as community property, is treated as community property, for inheritance tax purposes. (Rev. & Tax. Code §13671.5.)

No formal proceedings are required to terminate joint tenancy on personal property unless tax is due; if tax is due on personal property see Revenue and Taxation Code sections 14551-14555. If no tax is due on real property, joint tenancy may be terminated by filing a certified copy of death certificate of the decedent and an affidavit of identity of the surviving joint tenant, followed by the filing of a tax release. If a tax is due on real property and no probate proceedings are pending, see Probate Code sections 1170 *et seq.*

5. Real property situated outside California and tangible personal property permanently located outside California, owned by California residents, is not subject to the California tax law. (Conversely, such property located in California is taxed although owned by nonresident decedents.)

Intangible personal property (including stocks, bonds, notes (secured or unsecured), bank deposits, accounts receivable, patents, trademarks, copyrights, good will, partnership interests, life insurance policies and other choses in action) of resident decedents, wherever situate, is subject to the inheritance tax law. (Rev. & Tax. Code §13303.)

Intangible personal property of nonresident transferor residing in United States is not subject to inheritance tax law. For nonresidents residing outside United States, see Regulation 13303, subdivision (3)(B).

6. Unless the trust instrument expressly states that the trust is "irrevocable," the trust is revocable and subject to inheritance tax. (See Civ. Code §2280; Rev. & Tax. Code §13646.)

Property transferred by decedent in trust: give name and address of trustee and each beneficiary. If completely described in inventory, refer to description, no need to describe.

See Revenue and Taxation Code sections 13692 and 13693 re powers of appointment.

4a, 7a, 8, 9c, 10b. Note the instruction requiring the tracing of the line of blood relationship.

Say

"descendant of a brother,_____ (or sister,_____) of the decedent"	not	"niece" "nephew"
"brother (or sister) of the father (or mother) of the decedent"	not	"uncle" "aunt"
"descendant of a brother,_____ (or sister,_____) of the father (or mother) of the decedent"	not	"cousin"

Beneficiaries not related by blood, other than spouse, should be designated as "Stranger." (See Rev. & Tax. Code §§13308-13309.)

When a surviving spouse is determining whether to elect to take under a will, consideration should be given to whether the interest in community property relinquished would be subject to gift taxes.

If decedent acquired, within 5 years of his death, assets taxed to him as a transfer (from spouse, lineal issue, lineal ancestor, adopted child or adopted child of lineal issue) a previously taxed property credit may be allowable if assets pass to a person who is exempt $5,000 or more.

Date of death of spouse (or other Class A beneficiary) is necessary to determine whether a "previously taxed property" credit is allowable (Rev. & Tax. Code §14071; see Cal. Adm. Code, tit. 18, Reg. 1407(a)). If probate proceedings were had, give the number of the proceeding and the name of the county.

8. An exemption of $50,000 applies to "true insurance" payable to named beneficiaries. This exemption does not apply to insurance payable to the estate — except G.I. insurance.

9. A full description of annuities, supplemental contracts and death benefits is important because usually these types of contracts are fully taxable because they are not "insurance" and therefore not entitled to the insurance exemption.

Proceeds of contributions to retirement funds are *not* exempt, but proceeds of State of California (and its political subdivisions) retirement funds are exempt.

10a. Value of any transferred asset at the date of gift and date of death is required; if sold prior to death, date of sale, amount and subsequent disposition of the proceeds of sale should be shown.

10a. Inter vivos trusts subject to inheritance tax are:

a. A transfer not a bona fide sale for an adequate and full consideration. (Rev. & Tax. Code §13641.)

b. Transfers made in "contemplation of death." (If the transfer is made more than three years prior to the death of the transferor, it is deemed not to have been made in "contemplation of death." (Rev. & Tax. Code §13642).)

c. A transfer made with the intention that it take effect in possession or enjoyment on death of transferor. (Rev. & Tax. Code §13643.)

d. A transfer where the transferor reserves income or interest in the property. (Rev. & Tax. Code §13644.)

e. A transfer where the transferee makes payments to or cares for the transferor. (Rev. & Tax. Code §13645.)

f. A transfer made as an advancement. (Rev. & Tax. Code §13647.)

Describe assets fully, as indicated under question 4 above.

(See Cal. Adm. Code, tit. 18, regs. 13641, *et seq.*)

13. If probate proceedings were instituted, and all of the property was listed in the Inventory and Appraisement filed therein, insert the notation "See Inventory and Appraisement" and attach a copy thereof.

15. if a claim was filed and allowed for an expense of the last illness of decedent, include it in the item "Debts of decedent (if probate, list only allowed claims)" but do not also include it in the first item "Expenses of last illness (paid after death by transferee or estate, net after any insurance reimbursement)," *i.e.*, do not report it twice.

"Funeral expenses" include burial, burial plot, either for the decedent alone or for the decedent and members of his family; tombstone, monument, or other memorial, and perpetual care of the burial plot. (Cal. Adm. Code, tit. 18, reg. 13986, subd. (c).)

If decedent carried insurance for the unpaid balance of his mortgage on real property, do not include the amount of the mortgage under "Encumbrances on real property."

"Costs of administration" includes costs of closing the estate, filing fees, publication of notice to creditors, cost of executor or administrator's bond (maximum $10 for bond $2,000 or less and ½ of 1% of amount of any bond in excess of $2,000); fee and actual and necessary expenses of inheritance tax referee (except fees on reappraisals). (See Prob. Code §541.5.)

DEDUCTIONS — FORM IT-22

Deductions which are allowable under Revenue and Taxation Code sections 13988 (ordinary expenses of administration) and 13988.1 (fees for certain extraordinary services) which are allowable against the inheritance tax, cannot be taken as deductions on the income tax returns unless there is filed with the return a statement to the effect that these items have not been allowed as deductions against inheritance tax and waiving right to have them allowed as deductions.

Extraordinary expenses during administration in connection with litigation or conferences in resisting federal income tax deficiency are not deductible. (Reg. 13988(g).) Costs incurred in maintenance of property during administration of estate, fire insurance, gardener's or caretaker's salary, or repairs or additions to property, are not deductible — but are valid deductions against income tax. (Reg. 13988(g).)

The following are nondeductible (Reg. 13988(g)):

1. Attorney's fees and costs of proceedings re contests or litigated claims or in connection with will contests.

2. Expenses including attorney's and representative's fees for objections to report of inheritance tax referee.

3. Expenses of sale of property (such as escrow, real estate agent's commission, attorney's fees, costs).

(However, these expenses are subtracted from the sales price to determine the net sale price when the will directs sale, sale is necessary to raise funds to pay taxes, debts or costs of administration, or the property is taken in a condemnation proceeding.)

4. Expenses of carrying on decedent's business. (These expenses are deductible on income tax return.)

5. Travel expense of executor or administrator or attorney except one-way expense to California to qualify.

15c. Professional fees and extraordinary fees may be included only if allowed under Revenue and Taxation Code section 13988.1 for tax work or joint tenancy.

* * * *

A copy of form IT-22 follows:

Inheritance Tax Declaration, Form IT-22

SUBMIT IN DUPLICATE

STATE OF CALIFORNIA

INHERITANCE TAX DECLARATION, FORM IT-22

ANSWER ALL QUESTIONS. If space insufficient, attach sheets of same size showing decedent's name, social security number and question number.

Full Name of Decedent (Show all names ever used)	Date of Death	Social Security No.
		Date of Birth

Place of Death. (Last usual address)	Cause of Death	Length of Last Illness

Attorney for Estate	Address	Telephone No.

Type of Court Proceeding	Case No.	Name of Executor/Administrator, If Any, and Title		
☐ Probate ☐ 650 Petition ☐ Other ☐ None	County and State	Address		Telephone No.

1. RESIDENCE OF DECEDENT AT TIME OF DEATH

County _____ State _____

NOTE: If claimed that decedent was not a California resident, attach completed form IT-2, Declaration Concerning Residence.

2. Did decedent leave a will? ☐ Yes ☐ No If yes, attach copy of will and any codicils.

3a. Was decedent survived by a spouse? ☐ Yes ☐ No

3b. Did decedent and surviving spouse ever enter into any written or oral agreement concerning the status of their property as community or separate? ☐ Yes ☐ No If yes, attach copy of agreement or affidavit proving oral agreement and completed form IT-3, Marital Property Declaration.

3c. Does decedent's will dispose of any part or all of surviving spouse's interest in community property? ☐ Yes ☐ No If yes, complete form IT-3, Marital Property Declaration.

4a. JOINT TENANCIES. Did decedent, at date of death, hold any assets in joint tenance or joint tenancy form? To obtain a release of Inheritance Tax Lien for real estate, it is necessary to submit date of deed, date of recordation and book and page number of record. ☐ Yes ☐ No If yes, list all jointly held personal property (including stocks, bonds, mortgages, checking and savings accounts, etc.) wherever located, and California real estate. Full amount must be shown, although portion has been released or transferred after death, and all assets must be included even if tax release or consent is not required.

Item No.	Name of surviving joint tenant	Relationship to decedent (See Instr. 5)	Description of each asset (See Instruction 7)	Market value at date of death (See Instr. 8)	FOR STATE USE ONLY

4b. Does surviving joint tenant claim contribution to any of the joint tenancy assets? ☐ Yes ☐ No If yes, give full particulars tracing source of funds, values, dates, etc., in attachment. (See Instruction 9)

NOTE: Survivor's burden of proof of claim of contribution: All joint tenancies are presumed to have been created from assets originally belonging to the decedent and subject to tax in full to the surviving joint tenant, except to the extent that the survivor can prove that the assets, or a portion, originally belonged to the survivor or that the survivor furnished consideration which was never received from the decedent. (Revenue and Taxation Code Sec. 13671.)

I DECLARE UNDER PENALTY OF PERJURY THAT THIS DECLARATION, INCLUDING ANY ATTACHMENTS, HAS BEEN EXAMINED BY ME AND TO THE BEST OF MY KNOWLEDGE AND BELIEF IS TRUE, CORRECT AND COMPLETE. IF PREPARED BY A PERSON OTHER THAN THE DECLARANT, HIS DECLARATION IS BASED ON ALL INFORMATION OF WHICH HE HAS ANY KNOWLEDGE.

Signature	Date	Address
Relationship to Decedent		
Signature of Person Preparing This Declaration	Date	Address

THE INHERITANCE TAX REFEREE MUST HAVE THIS FORM TO BEGIN DETERMINATION OF THE TAX. Send this form and all attachments to the Inheritance Tax Referee, if one has been appointed, otherwise to STATE CONTROLLER, Division of Tax Administration—Inheritance Tax.

P.O. Box 247 Sacramento 95802	107 South Broadway Los Angeles 90012	785 Market Street San Francisco 94103

IT-22 (REV. 1/81)

5.	ASSETS OUTSIDE CALIFORNIA. Excluding assets listed at item 4a, did decedent own tangible or intangible personal or real property outside of California?	☐ Yes	☐ No	**If yes,** describe property and give estimated value. (If probate is pending in another state, also attach copy of inventory.)

TRUSTS, LIFE ESTATES, POWERS OF APPOINTMENT			**(See Instructions 7, 8, 11)**
6a. Was decedent a trustee or beneficiary of a "trustee" bank or savings and loan or similar account?	☐ Yes	☐ No	**If yes,** attach a list of accounts giving balances at date of death, sources of funds and exact title in which each was held. (See Instruction 9)
6b. Did decedent enter into a declaration of trust, written or oral, or join in a trust agreement during his lifetime?	☐ Yes	☐ No	**If yes,** attach copy of trust document or proof of the oral agreement, and a list of trust assets at date of death with estimated market value of each.
6c. Was decedent beneficiary of a trust not created by him?	☐ Yes	☐ No	**If yes,** attach copy of trust documents and a list of assets at date of death and estimated market value.
6d. Was decedent a donee of a power of appointment?	☐ Yes	☐ No	**If yes,** attach a copy of document creating power of appointment and a list of assets at date of death and estimated market value.

7a. HEIRS, BENEFICIARIES, SURVIVING JOINT TENANTS AND TRANSFEREES. List all even if there is no court proceeding.

Item No.	Name	Date of Birth	Full Address	Relationship to decedent (See * below and Instr. 5)	Approximate value of interest or percentage of estate (See Instr. 10)

* **Relationship must be by blood,** except for surviving spouse, son-in-law, daughter-in-law, adopted or mutually acknowledged child or issue of adopted or mutually acknowledged child. List all others who are not blood relatives as "strangers".

* **Attach blood tracing** for niece, nephew, grandniece, grandnephew, great grandniece or great grandnephew.

* **Adoption or mutual acknowledgment of child.** Affidavit or other proof is required for transferee claiming through adoption or mutual acknowledgment. (Revenue and Taxation Code Sections 13307, 13310)

7b. Did any beneficiaries named in will predecease decedent?	☐ Yes	☐ No	**If yes,** list names, and if blood relatives list names of their children.

7c. Did decedent have any predeceased spouses? (Probate Code Sections 228, 229)	☐ Yes	☐ No	**If yes,** give name, county of residence and date of death of each.

7d. Is any divorced spouse a creditor of decedent or his estate or claiming an interest in the estate?	☐ Yes	☐ No	**If yes,** attach a copy of final decree and any property settlement agreement.
7e. Is California **previously taxed** property credit claimed?	☐ Yes	☐ No	**If yes,** give name, county of residence and date of death of prior decedent. (See Instruction 6)

8.	LIFE INSURANCE. Was there life and/or accident insurance in force on life of decedent?	☐ Yes	☐ No	**If yes,** list below.

Item No.	Insurance Company	Face amount and type of policy (term, endowment, mortgage, etc.)	Owner of policy (See * below)	Beneficiary receiving proceeds and relationship to decedent (See Instruciton 5)	Mode of payment and amount of proceeds received (See * below)

* **If owner was other than decedent or total proceeds exceed $50,000, or if decedent irrevocably selected mode of settlement, attach copy of IRS Form 712, obtainable from insurance company.**

ANNUITIES, SUPPLEMENTAL CONTRACTS AND DEATH BENEFITS

9a. Was decedent owner of annuity policies or supplemental contracts? ☐ Yes ☐ No   If yes, list under 9c.

9b. Did decedent have any interest in a "death benefit", "retirement plan", "profit sharing plan" or "stock purchase plan" or were any payments made under such plans by virtue of decedent's death? ☐ Yes ☐ No   If yes, list under 9c.

9c. Item No.	Company, or issuer of annuity, supplemental contract or death benefit	Type of policy or death benefit	Beneficiary and relationship to decedent (See Instruction 5)	Mode of payment	Lump sum or commuted value

9d. Is any item in 9c claimed to be nontaxable? ☐ Yes ☐ No   If yes, explain below or in attachment.

GIFTS AND TRANSFERS

10a. Did decedent transfer, at any time during his life, any real or personal property (stocks, bonds, notes, savings accounts, insurance policies, etc.) for other than money, for less than market value, or without any payment or consideration (including withdrawals or transfers from joint tenancy bank or savings and loan accounts)? ☐ Yes ☐ No   If yes, list under 10b and answer 10c through 10g. (See Instruction 12)

10b. Item No.	Name of transferee and relationship to decedent (See Instruction 5)	Date of transfer	Description of property and estimated market value at date of transfer (See Instructions 7, 8)	Market value at date of death (See Instr. 8)	FOR STATE USE ONLY

10c. Did decedent continue to receive all or part of the income after transfer, or continue to use property (including residing on real estate)? ☐ Yes ☐ No   If yes to 10c, 10d or 10e, explain below or in attachment.

10d. Was deed to any real property listed under 10b recorded after decedent's death? ☐ Yes ☐ No

10e. Was any restriction imposed by decedent on transfer of any property listed under 10b? ☐ Yes ☐ No

10f. Is it claimed that any property listed under 10b is not subject to inheritance tax? ☐ Yes ☐ No   If yes, explain below or in attachment. ("Payment of gift tax" or "exemption under Gift Tax Law" is insufficient.)

10g. Were California gift tax returns filed for any of the transfers listed under 10b? ☐ Yes ☐ No   If yes, identify transfer and give amount of gift tax paid (including penalties and interest).

11a. Did decedent receive any real or personal property by gift, bequest, devise, descent, proceeds of life insurance or joint tenancy survivorship? ☐ Yes ☐ No   If yes, complete 11b and 11c.

11b. Item No.	General description of each asset (See Instruction 15)	Full name and relationship of person from whom received	Date received	Approx. value on date received (See Instr. 16)

11c. IF RECEIVED BY GIFT	Item No.	State of residence of donor at date of gift

12. **ASSETS NOT OTHERWISE LISTED.** Assets standing in decedent's name alone, or in bearer form, including real property, stocks, bonds, mortgages, judgments, notes, accounts and loans receivable, cash, business or partnership interests, autos, farm equipment, interests in retirement funds, stock purchase plans or other employee benefits, furniture, furnishings, personal effects, insurance owned by decedent on life of any other persons, amounts due including tax or other refunds, and any other type of property. Also include assets in name of the surviving spouse which are community property. **(Probate cases.** If all property is listed in Inventory and Appraisement, do not list but make reference to Inventory and Appraisement.)

Item No.	Description of assets not otherwise listed **(See Instruction 7)**	Market value at date of death **(See Instr. 8)**	FOR STATE USE ONLY

13a. Was probate homestead granted or exempt personal property set aside by probate court? ☐ Yes ☐ No **If yes,** attach copy of court order.

13b. Was a family allowance ordered by probate court? ☐ Yes ☐ No **If yes,** attach copy of court order(s).

13c. Has there been litigation affecting the estate as to distribution, entitlement or value? ☐ Yes ☐ No **If yes,** attach copies of court orders. If litigation is pending, give case title, number, relevant issues and facts.

14. Will Federal Estate Tax Return, Form 706, be filed? ☐ Yes ☐ No **If already filed,** attach copy of page 1 of Form 706.

Federal Estate Tax	$	☐ Estimated	☐ Paid
Maximum allowable credit for State death taxes	$	☐ Estimated	☐ Determined

ALLOWABLE DEDUCTIONS (See Instruction 13) Any deduction over $1,000 must be itemized.

15a. All Cases

Expenses of last illness (paid after death by transferee or estate, net after any insuranceB reimbursement)_____

Funeral expenses (net after burial insurance, social security or other reimbursement)_____

Debts of decedent **(if probate,** list only allowed claims) _____

Encumbrances on real property (state exact balance for each parcel) _____

Liens or security agreements on personal property (state exact balance for each asset)_____

Taxes, a lien or due and unpaid at death: Income tax (net due at death) _____

          Real property (state exact balance for each parcel) _____

          Other taxes (itemize and explain) _____

Other deductions (itemize and explain)_____

15b. Probate Cases Only

Other debts (itemize and explain)

Ordinary executor's/administrator's commission ☐ Statutory ☐ Other ☐ Not claimed_____

Ordinary attorney's fees ☐ Statutory ☐ Other ☐ Not claimed_____

Costs of administration (filing fees, notices, etc.) _____

15c. **Additional Professional Fees—Probate and Other Court Cases.** (Show basis: tax work, joint tenancy, etc. Include only fees allowed under Revenue and Taxation Code Sections 13988.1)

Executor/Administrator _____

Attorney _____

Accountant _____

Itemization and detail of items under 15a, b, c.

16000-208 9-80 300M CAM○D OSP

Special Use Valuation — Farms and Closely Held Businesses

The special use valuation discussed below *APPLIES FOR INHER-ITANCE TAX PURPOSES ONLY. THE QUALIFIED REAL PROP-ERTY MUST STILL BE APPRAISED AT MARKET VALUE IN THE PROBATE INVENTORY AND APPRAISEMENT.*

Real Property

The value of real property is its fair market value at date of death. "Fair market value" is usually determined by the "highest and best use" to which the property can be put, though there are other approaches to valuation such as income capitalization, replacement cost minus depreciation, and comparable sales, or a combination thereof. Farm land frequently has a "highest and best use" in excess of its value as farm land, as for example a development site. However, to value the farm land in an estate as a development site can create a hardship for the heirs, who may be the decedent's children who intend to continue "in the footsteps of their father," and might well force them to sell the land as a development site to pay the taxes. This is against public policy which encourages the continued use of land for farming (and small business purposes). On the other hand, if the heirs intend to sell the property in any event for development, a windfall to them would result from a farm land calculation.

Therefore the Legislature enacted, for estates of decedents dying on or after January 1, 1981, Revenue and Taxation Code section 13311.5 to provide for a "special use" valuation for qualified real property used as farm for farming purposes or used in a trade or business other than the trade or business of farming. In addition, at least 50 percent of the adjusted value of the clear market value of the estate must consist of the adjusted value of real or personal property which, on the date of the decedent's death, was being used for a qualified use and was acquired from or passed from the decedent to a qualified heir of the decedent, and at least 25 percent of the adjusted value of the clear market value of the estate must consist of the adjusted value of the qualified farm or closely held business real property. In any event, the aggregate decrease in valuation shall not exceed $500,000 for any one decedent.

Section 13311.5 further provides for a recapture of the inheritance tax benefit if the heirs do in fact sell the property to nonfamily members or convert it to a nonqualifying use.

"Prematurely" means within 15 years after the death of the decedent and before the death of the qualified heir. "Qualified heir" means a member of the decedent's family who acquired such property (or to whom such property passed) from the decedent. If the qualified heir disposes of the property to a member of his or her family, that member will be treated as the qualified heir as to that interest. "Member of the family" means the individual's ancestor or lineal descendants, a lineal descendant of a grandparent of such individual, the spouse or the individual or of any such descendant. Legally adopted children are treated as children by blood.

If the recapture event occurs more than 10 years and less than 180 months after the date of death, the additional tax subject to recapture is reduced on a ratable monthly basis. If the recapture occurs within 10 years of the decedent's death, a recapture tax is assessed in an amount equal to the lesser of the adjusted tax difference attributable to this interest or the excess of the amount realized with respect to the interest over the value of the interest determined with the special use valuation.

The deceased owner and/or a member of the owner's family must materially participate in the operation of the farm or other business. Material participation is a factual determination to be made in each case. Passively collecting rents or making draws or other income is not sufficient for material participation, nor is merely advancing capital and reviewing a crop plan or other business proposal and financial reports each year. Also, the qualifying real property must have been owned by the decedent or a member of the decedent's family and used for a qualified use for periods totaling 5 years or more of the last 8 years prior to the date of death.

Further, the persons who have an interest in the real property must sign an agreement consenting to personal liability for any recapture tax. Qualified beneficiaries may post a bond in the amount required under Revenue and Taxation Code section 13311.5(e)(11) and avoid personal liability. This code section is lengthy and complicated and should be read in its entirety.

A special use election *may* so reduce the adjusted gross estate that elective deferral of tax payments will be available neither under Internal Revenue Code section 6166 (Rev. & Tax. Code §14181) nor section 6166A (Rev. & Tax. Code §14182) or may decrease the amount of tax which can be deferred. The executor has to balance the tax payable with a special use valuation against a higher tax deferred up to 15 years at the adjusted rate of interest. Also, consideration should be given to the possibility of a sale, and the tax aspects.

Transfer of an Automobile From Estate to a Distributee

To transfer an automobile to a distributee, the representative should first obtain the Certificate of Ownership ("pink slip"). The representative should then send a letter to the Department of Motor Vehicles enclosing:

1. Certified copy of letters testamentary (or letters of administration with the will annexed or letters of administration).
2. Certificate of Ownership of (describe vehicle, make, license number, engine number) issued in the name of the decedent.

   The personal representative signs the Certificate of Ownership in his official capacity as executor or administrator on lines 1 and 2. The name and address of the distributee (lines 5 and 7) should be typewritten. The person receiving the vehicle, the distributee, should sign on line 6.
3. Evidence of current registration.
4. Evidence of smog control.
5. The transfer fee.

If the automobile is sold from the estate, a Notice of Sale or Transfer of a Vehicle should be filed immediately, to avoid liability. Instructions for completing this form appear on its reverse side.

SALES OF REAL PROPERTY
(Probate Code §§754, *et seq.*)

Many sales of estate real property, probably the majority, are accomplished by private sale. The legal assistant should check the will. The executor has the option of private sale or public auction, whichever means he considers likely to obtain the highest possible price, with or without notice, if the will directs him or gives him authority to sell (Prob. Code §757) and the necessity of sale, or its advantage or benefit to estate or those interested need not be shown. In the private sale, offers are solicited independently rather than by open competitive bidding.

Pre-Sale

The executor or administrator should try for the widest possible exposure to the market. A notice that the property is for sale can be prepared describing the features of the property and mailed to several real estate brokers operating in the area. This notice or circular should state (1) that any sale is subject to confirmation of the court, and (2) that only such real estate commissions will be paid as are allowed by the court on confirmation of sale.

Notices to the brokers will be followed by requests for keys to inspect the property, and phone calls from the brokers asking questions about the property and conduct of the sale.

The paralegal rather than the executor or administrator might well send out the circulars and handle the phone calls from the brokers and inspection of the property.

A broker may actually be employed, but only by written agreement. The contract may grant an exclusive right to the broker to sell the property up to 90 days, *if* prior permission of the court is obtained by the executor or administrator. (Prob. Code §760.)

Section 584.3 authorizes an executor or administrator to grant an option to purchase real property.

Notice of Sale of Real Property at Private Sale

A Notice of Sale of Real Property at Private Sale must be published (if property being sold for not more than $1,000, posting is sufficient). If personal property as well is being sold (as in a furnished apartment house, residence with furniture), a Notice of Sale of Real and Personal Property at Private Sale as a unit would be published instead. The description in the notice should be the same as in the inventory and this description should be followed in the return of sale and order confirming sale.

The terms of sale specified in the notice fix the terms of the sale, *i.e.*, there cannot be a variance in the terms of sale as between the notice and the petition. (In Los Angeles county, if the notice specifies cash and the sale returned is upon a credit, higher offers made on either cash or credit shall be considered only if the representative in person or through his attorney informs the court prior to confirmation that the offer is acceptable; if the offer returned is for cash and a higher offer is made on credit, the representative must similarly indicate its acceptability before confirmation.) (Rule 409.) If not being sold for cash, language such as the following might be included: "Terms of sale cash in lawful money of the United States on confirmation of sale, or part cash and balance evidenced by note secured by Mortgage or Trust Deed on the property so sold."

The sale may take place at any time within one year from the earliest date stated in the notice (usually date of first publication). (Prob. Code §§780, 782.)

The Notice of Sale of Real Property at Private Sale is published at least three times during a 10-day period in a newspaper published at least weekly in the county where the property is located, and there must be at least 5 days (not counting the dates of publication) between the first and last publication date and the first publication must be at least 10 days before the date of sale. (Prob. Code §§780, 782; Gov. Code §6063a.)

Service of Notice of Hearing on Petitions for Sale of Real Property

Subdivision (b) of Probate Code section 1200.5, provides for service of notice of hearing on petitions for confirmation of sale or to grant an option to purchase real property 10 days before hearing, to any nonpetitioning executor or administrator, coexecutor or coadministrator, and all persons (or their attorneys if they have appeared by attorney) who have requested notice or given notice of appearance, in person or by attorney, as heir, devisee, legatee or creditors, by personal service, or by mail, addressed to them at the address in the request for special notice, if any, otherwise at their offices or places of residence, if known, and if not known, at the county seat of the county in which proceedings are pending.

Proof of giving notice shall be made at the hearing; and if the court is satisfied that notice has been regularly given, the court shall so find in its order, which is conclusive on all persons when it becomes final.

The clerk is also required to post notice pursuant to Probate Code section 1200.

Bidding

The notice should specify the place for submission of bids (e.g., the attorney's office). The form of the bid should conform to the notice. A form of bid may be found in California Decedent Estate Administration, Volume 1, page 518.

The sum offered must be 90 percent of the appraised value, which appraisal must have been made within one year from actual date of sale. The bids must be in writing and accompanied by 10 percent of the offer. The deposit should be held by the representative, not the broker. Or it might be deposited in the attorney's trust account in the name of the bidder.

Return of Sale

When a satisfactory bid has been received and a higher bid does not seem likely, the bid is accepted (subject to court approval) and a Return of Sale of Real Property at Private Sale and Petition for Confirmation is made to the court.

The petition must be verified and Probate Code section 755 requires that the report and petition be made within 30 days after such sale.

Notice of hearing on the petition for confirmation of sale is given pursuant to Probate Code section 1200. The clerk posts notice of the hearing at the courthouse at least 10 days before the hearing. Notices are sent by the attorney's office at least 10 days before the hearing to any nonpetitioning executor or administrator, coexecutor or coadministrator and all persons (or their attorneys) who have requested notice or given notice of appearance, in person or by attorney, as heir, devisee, legatee or creditor, by personal service, or by mail, addressed to them at the address in the request for special notice, if any, otherwise at their offices or places of residence, if known, and if not known, at the county seat of the county in which proceedings are pending. (Prob. Code §1200.5.)

If the real property had been specifically willed to someone, notice should also be sent to that devisee (unless, in Los Angeles County, consent of the devisee or legatee is filed).

A declaration of mailing should be prepared and filed. The preparation and sending out of notices referred to hereinabove can be handled by the paralegal — as well as preparation of the petitions — under the general supervision of an attorney.

The highest bidder should be informed of the time and place of the hearing on confirmation so that they may attend the hearing and prepare to protect their interests if increased bids are made. They may decide to pay more if they have to, to get the property. Others who have presented bids or indicated interest in the property should also be notified.

Court Hearing

Any increased bid made in court must be in writing and be accompanied by a 10% deposit. The first overbid must exceed the original bid by at least 10 percent on the first $10,000 of the sale price and 5 percent on the balance of the amount of the bid. Further overbids can be in any amount unless the court requires bids in higher multiples.

The attorney and the estate's representative should be present in court at the hearing. If the attorney is not present, the representative must advise court of approval.

Broker's Fee

If the sale is made on an increased bid, other than one holding a written contract, the court, under Probate Code section 761, allows a commission on the full amount of the sale as confirmed:

½ to the broker representing the original bidder whose bid was returned for confirmation

½ to the broker representing the person to whom sale was made, plus full commission on the excess over the original bid.

If the successful over-bidder did not have an agent, the full commission is paid to the agent holding the contract.

On the other hand, if the original bid was made direct to the estate, not through an agent, the agent responsible for the increased bid will receive a commission fixed by the court as reasonable compensation. (Prob. Code §761.5.) (In Los Angeles County, agent would receive 2½%.)

In Los Angeles County, local rules provide that upon confirmation of the sale of real property the court will not allow a broker's commission in excess of 5 percent (unless the sale is for less than $500), unless justified by exceptional circumstances. (Rule 403.) In some areas a 6 percent fee is allowed.

Finally, an Order Confirming Sale of Real (and Personal) Property should be prepared, signed and filed.

The Escrow

After the hearing is held and the court has approved a sale of the property, an escrow should be opened, although legally an escrow is not required. In effect, the sale is turned over to a neutral third party, the escrow holder, for completion. The escrow holder may be a title insurance company, a bank, a savings and loan association, or an independent escrow company. An escrow number will be issued and should be used for reference thereafter in all communications, oral or written, with the escrow holder.

The buyer and seller prepare their own instructions to the escrow holder. If there is a conflict between the instructions, the escrow holder has the duty to resolve them, at least by calling them to the attention of the buyer and seller so they can do so. A termite inspection of the property is usually made, usually requested by the purchaser, perhaps even before an offer or bid is made.

Various fees are payable from the escrow, as fee for issuing title policy, documentary stamps for transfer of property, recordation fees, reconveyance fees, escrow fee, etc., and the seller and buyer can make any kind of agreement as to their payment and give the escrow holder instructions in accordance therewith; ordinarily the seller pays for the cost of issuing the title policy.

A preliminary title report is usually requested and a title search made. A title insurance policy is ordered. If the property is mortgaged, the amount owing must be determined and paid. The interest on the loan must be computed. The requirements of any new lender must be determined and met. A proration of the taxes to the date of sale is usually made, per agreement. If the property is being rented, the rents are ordinarily prorated to the date of sale. Cleaning deposits and security deposits (as where an apartment house is being sold) are usually credited to the purchaser.

Arrangements must be made for insurance. If the purchaser wants to obtain insurance from his own carrier he will want to order it effective the date he becomes owner; the seller will want to cancel his insurance as of the time he is no longer the legal owner.

The escrow holder will pay the broker's fee before closing. If there are any special instructions for payment, the escrow holder should be advised. In any event, the names and addresses of the payee or payees should be furnished. An inventory of the personal property, if any, should also be furnished, and a bill of sale executed.

The paralegal can work with the escrow holder in obtaining any information desired from the executor or other persons in perfecting the sale. Before the escrow can be closed an administrator or executor's deed must be executed conveying the property to the purchasers.

When all the conditions of the sale laid down by the seller and by the purchaser are met, when all the money has been deposited in escrow, the escrow holder will "simultaneously" record the deed to the property and deliver the money to the estate, and then close the escrow. A settlement statement is delivered at the close of the escrow. By this means the purchaser can be certain of purchasing property to which the title is clear before his money is paid over; on the other hand, the seller's deed will not be delivered until all the purchase money has been actually collected. An increase in the representative's bond may be required to cover the sale price.

Summary of Procedure for Selling Real Property at Private Sale

Expose property to market.
Consider employment of broker by written contract.
Publish Notice of Sale of Real Property at Private Sale.
Inspection of property by prospective purchasers.
Receive bids.
Serve and file Return of Sale of Real Property at Private Sale and Petition for Confirmation.
Give notice of hearing on the Return of Sale.
File declaration of mailing (notice of hearing).
Advise purchaser and broker or brokers of hearing on petition.
Advise representative of hearing.
Attorney attends hearing with estate's representative.
Prepare Order Confirming Sale of Real [and Personal] Property.
Open escrow.
Prepare administrator's or executor's deed.
Check bond; increase bond if not covered to extent of sale price.

Defaults

If the successful purchaser fails to perform, the seller may either:

(1) Make a motion to the court to vacate the order of confirmation and order a resale of the property. The notice for the resale is the same as for the first sale. The defaulting purchaser is liable to the estate for any deficiency. (Prob. Code §788.)

(2) File a petition within 45 days showing that the petitioner has failed to keep the agreement and that a bid has been made in the same

or a higher amount, on the same or better terms, and in the manner prescribed in the original notice. The court may then vacate the order of confirmation and make an order confirming the sale to the new high bidder. Such notice as the court directs must be given to the defaulting purchaser, if his written consent to vacate the order confirming the sale has not been filed with the court. (Prob. Code §789.)

The forms for *Petition for Confirmation of Sale of Real Property* and *Order Confirming Sale of Real Property* follow:

Petition for Confirmation of Sale of Real Property

NAME AND ADDRESS OF ATTORNEY	TELEPHONE NO	FOR COURT USE ONLY
ATTORNEY FOR		
Insert name of court, branch court if any, and Post Office and Street Address:		

ESTATE OF	CASE NUMBER
	HEARING DATE
☐ DECEDENT ☐ CONSERVATEE ☐ INCOMPETENT ☐ MINOR	DEPT TIME
PETITION FOR CONFIRMATION OF SALE OF REAL PROPERTY	

1. Petitioner (Name of each. See footnote° before completing):

    is the ☐ Executor ☐ Administrator CTA ☐ Administrator ☐ Conservator ☐ Guardian
    of the estate and requests a court order for
    a. Confirmation of sale of estate's interest in the real property described in 2a below.
    b. ☐ Approval of commission of . . . .% (See local court rules).
    c. Additional bond ☐ fixed at $ . . . . . ☐ none.

PETITIONER STATES

2 a. Description of property sold
    (1) Interest sold ☐100% ☐ undivided . . . .%
    (2) ☐ Improved ☐ Unimproved
    (3) Street address and location:

    (4) Legal description (See Attachment 2a).

    b. Appraisal
    (1) Date of death or appointment of conservator or guardian:
    (2) Appraised value at above date: $ . . . . .
    (3) Date of sale:
    (4) Reappraised value within one year prior to sale:
        $ . . . .
        (If more than one year has elapsed from date b(1) to date b(2), reappraisal is necessary.)
    (5) Appraisal or reappraisal
        ☐ has been filed ☐ will be filed.

    c. Manner and terms of sale
    (1) Name of purchaser and manner of vesting title:

    (2) Sale was ☐ private ☐ public
    (3) Amount bid: $ . . . .
        Deposit: $ . . . .
    (4) Payment ☐ Cash ☐ Credit (See Attachment 2c)
    (5) ☐ Other terms of sale (See Attachment 2c)
    (6) ☐ Terms comply with Prob C 1532 and 1702.

    d. Commission
    (1) ☐ Sale without broker.
    (2) ☐ Written contract for commission was entered into with (Name): . . . .
        . . . .
        . . . .
        who is a licensed broker and secured the purchaser.

(Continued on Reverse Side)

° All personal representatives must sign the petition. Only one need sign the declaration. The declaration must be signed in California (CCP 2015.5).
Affidavit required when signed outside California. No attachment permitted less than on a full page (California Rule of Court 201(b)).

Form Approved by the
Judicial Council of California
Effective July 1, 1975

**PETITION FOR CONFIRMATION OF SALE OF
REAL PROPERTY**

Prob C 541, 542, 570
754, 755, 760, 786,
1200, 1532, 1702

e. Bond
  (1) Amount before sale: $ . . . . . . ☐ None
  (2) Additional amount needed: $. . . . . ☐ None
  (3) ☐ Proceeds to be placed in a blocked account
     (See Attachment 2e).

f. Notice of sale
  (1) ☐ Published ☐ posted as permitted by
     Prob C 780.
  (2) ☐ Power of sale in will.
  (3) ☐ Will directs sale of property.

g. Notice of hearing
  (1) Specific devisee ☐ None ☐ Consent to be filed
     ☐ Written notice will be given.
  (2) Special notice
     ☐ None requested.
     ☐ Has been or will be waived.
     ☐ Required written notice will be given.

h. Reason for sale (Need not complete if f(2) or f(3) checked).
  (1) ☐ Necessary to pay ☐ Debts ☐ Legacies
     ☐ Family Allowance ☐ Expenses.
  (2) ☐ The sale is for the advantage, benefit, and best interests of the estate and those interested in the estate.

i. Required amount of first overbid: $ . . . . . .

j. Petitioner's efforts to expose the property to the market were as follows (Specify):

_____
(Signature of each Petitioner)

I certify (or declare) under penalty of perjury that the foregoing, including any attachments, is true and correct and that this declaration is executed on (Date): . . . . at (Place): . . . ., California.

_____
(Type or print name)

_____
(Signature)

Order Confirming Sale of Real Property

NAME AND ADDRESS OF ATTORNEY: TELEPHONE NO	FOR COURT USE ONLY
ATTORNEY FOR:	
Insert name of court, branch court if any, and Post Office and Street Address:	

ESTATE OF:	
☐ DECEDENT ☐ CONSERVATEE ☐ INCOMPETENT ☐ MINOR	

ORDER CONFIRMING SALE OF REAL PROPERTY	Case Number

1. Date of Hearing: ☐ Dept. ☐ Div. ☐ Rm. No.:   Judge:

THE COURT FINDS

2. a. All notices required by law have been given.
   b. Good reason existed for the sale of the property commonly described as (street address or location):

   c. The sale was legally made and fairly conducted.
   d. The amount bid is not disproportionate to the value of the property.

   e. The amount bid is 90% or more of the appraised value of the property within one year prior to the date of sale, as appraised within one year of the date of sale.
   f. A sum exceeding the amount bid by the statutory percentages, exclusive of the expense of a new sale ☐ cannot be obtained ☐ was obtained in open court from the purchaser named below after complying with all applicable provisions of the law.
   g. The personal representative has made reasonable efforts to expose the property to the market. (Prob C 785)

THE COURT ORDERS

3. a. The sale of the real property described in Attachment 3a is confirmed to (Name):

   Manner of vesting title:

   for the sale price of $ . . . . and on the following terms (See attachment if necessary):

   b. The personal representative named below is directed to execute and deliver a conveyance of the interest in the property sold to purchaser on receipt of the consideration for the sale.
   (1) (Name):

   (2) (Name):

   c. (1) ☐ No additional bond is required.
      (2) ☐ Personal representative shall give an additional bond in the sum of $ . . . ., surety, or otherwise, as provided by law.
      (3) ☐ Net sale proceeds shall be deposited by escrow holder in the following depository:

      in a blocked account pursuant to Prob C 541.1, to be withdrawn only on court order.
   d. (1) ☐ No commission is payable.
      (2) ☐ A commission from the proceeds of the sale is approved as follows
          Amount: $ . . . .
          To:

   Date:

   _____
   Judge of the Superior Court
   ☐ Signature is at end of last Attachment.

Form Approved by the
Judicial Council of California
Effective July 1, 1975

ORDER CONFIRMING SALE OF REAL
PROPERTY

Prob C 760, 780–785.1

SALES OF PERSONAL PROPERTY

Personal property of a decedent which
(1) is perishable,
(2) will depreciate in value if not disposed of promptly,
(3) will incur loss or expense by being kept, or
(4) is necessary to provide the family allowance pending receipt of funds, may be sold without any kind of notice. Title passes without confirmation.

However, if the court does not later approve the sale, the personal representative is responsible for the value of the property. (Prob. Code §770.)

An official form of Ex Parte Petition for Approval of Sale of Personal Property and Order is provided.

Securities

Stocks and other securities may be sold upon obtaining an order of the court for sale.

The clerk sets such a petition for hearing and gives notice as provided by Probate Code section 1200 (or judge may prescribe shorter notice or dispense with notice).

Other Personal Property

Other personal property may be sold only after posting of notice at courthouse 10 days before the sale, or, if a private sale, 10 days before sale, or by publication pursuant to Government Code section 6063a, or both, as the representative may decide.

The notice must contain the time and place of sale and a brief description of the property.

If it is shown to be in the best interest of the estate, notice may be shortened to 5 days and posted or published pursuant to Government Code section 6061.

(See Probate Code sections 772 and 773 for other requirements.)

No notice is required when the will directs or authorizes the sale of property. (Prob. Code §757.)

With the exception of the procedure for sale of real property, the foregoing discussion considers only the "basic" pleadings used in probating an uncontested estate proceeding. Many other pleadings and procedures might be involved in the course of administering a single estate as, for example, petition for order to sell stocks (Prob. Code §771), petition for order to borrow money and mortgage property (Prob. Code §831), petition for order to lease property (Prob. Code

§841), petition for partial distribution (Prob. Code §1000), and petition for preliminary distribution (Prob. Code §1100) — to name only a few.

CLOSING THE ESTATE

Accounting and Petition for Distribution

At any time after one year from the issuance of letters, upon petition of any interested person, the court shall order the executor or administrator to render a full and verified account and report of administration. A final account praying for settlement must be filed if there are sufficient funds to pay all debts and the estate is in a proper condition to be closed. (Prob. Code §922.)

This section also provides for an attachment, after citation, if the accounting is not made.

Four months after issuance of letters, an executor or administrator or an attorney who has rendered services to an executor or administrator, may petition the court for an allowance upon fees. Notice of such a petition must be served 10 days before the hearing pursuant to Probate Code section 911.

If the estate were ready for distribution at the end of a year, a FIRST AND FINAL ACCOUNT AND REPORT OF REPRESENTATIVE, AND PETITION FOR DISTRIBUTION might be prepared at the same time, in one document. Probate Code section 1025.5, applicable to estates of persons dying on or after January 1, 1977, requires that either a petition for distribution be filed within 12 months after issuance of letters, if no federal estate tax return (Form 706) is required, or within 18 months if one is required, or file a verified report of status of administration showing the condition of the estate and the reasons why it cannot be discharged. The court may either require the filing of the petition for distribution or permit administration to continue upon specified terms and conditions.

If the executor is beneficiary of the entire estate, an accounting may be waived.

At least 10 days before any hearing on an account the executor or administrator must serve notice of hearing on the account upon.

(a) All persons requesting special notice pursuant to Section 1202 and the devisees and legatees whose interest in the estate is affected by the account and petition (or the heirs of the decedent in intestate estates) and the State of California if any portion of the estate escheats to it. (Prob. Code §926.)

Such notice shall be delivered personally or sent by first-class mail, or sent by airmail to any person residing outside the jurisdiction of the

United States, at his or her last known mailing address. (Prob. Code §926.)

(b) Any nonpetitioning executor or administrator, coexecutor or coadministrator, and all persons (or their attorneys if they have appeared by attorney) who have requested notice or given notice of appearance, in person or by attorney, as heir, devisee, legatee or creditors, or as otherwise interested. (Prob. Code §1200.5.)

Notices shall be addressed to them at their respective post office addresses given in their requests for special notice, if any, otherwise at their respective offices or places of residence, if known, and if not, at the county seat of the county where the proceedings are pending, or shall be personally served upon such person. (Prob. Code §1200.5.)

Proof of giving notice shall be made at the hearing; and if the court is satisfied that notice has been regularly given, the court shall so find in its order, which is conclusive on all persons when it becomes final. (Prob. Code §1200.5.)

(a) Notice is mailed to all persons requesting special notice and
(b) The clerk must post notice of hearing on account at the courthouse.
  (Prob. Code §1200.)

ATTORNEY'S FEES AND EXECUTOR'S OR ADMINISTRATOR'S STATUTORY FEES. If the executor's compensation is not provided for in the will, or if he does not renounce compensation, his fee for ordinary services is computed the same as the attorney's fees (Prob. Code §§910, 901), to wit:

Of the amount of the estate accounted for:

First	$15,000	4%
Next	$85,000	3%
Next	$900,000	2%
All over	$1,000,000	1%

The estate accounted for is the total amount of inventory, plus gains over appraisal value on sales, plus receipts, less losses on sales, without regard to encumbrances or other obligations on property and whether or not a sale has taken place. (Prob. Code §901.)

The fees for extraordinary services, such as sales or mortgages of real or personal property, contested or litigated claims against the estate, etc., as set forth in Probate Code section 902, are fixed by the court. Attorneys representing persons filing a petition under Probate Code section 650 may charge a reasonable fee, subject to approval of the court. Before hearing on final account an ORDER SETTLING FIRST AND FINAL ACCOUNT AND FOR DISTRIBUTION is prepared. (Original and 3 copies.) Vouchers are filed at time of hearing, if required. (See Prob. Code §925.) After this order is signed by the judge, the estate is distributed to the heirs, devisees and legatees. A receipt is obtained from each such heir for filing in court.

Then a DECLARATION FOR FINAL DISCHARGE AND FINAL DISCHARGE is prepared. (In some counties this is a combined printed form.) (Original and 3 copies.) After the receipts are obtained from the distributees, the executors signs this affidavit and the document is presented to the judge, who signs the decree. A copy is mailed to the bonding company to have the bond released. The estate is closed.

Declaration for Final Discharge

Name, Address and Telephone No. of Attorney(s)

Space Below for Use of Court Clerk Only

Attorney   for Petitioner _____

SUPERIOR COURT OF THE STATE OF CALIFORNIA
FOR THE COUNTY OF SACRAMENTO

Estate of

No.   Dept.

**DECLARATION FOR
FINAL DISCHARGE**

Deceased.

I am the _____ of the _____ of the above-
(executor, etc.)   (will/estate)

named decedent; I have paid all sums of money due from me as _____
(executor, etc.)

_____ , and have delivered up, under the judgment of distribution herein, all the property of the estate

to the parties entitled, and receipts of the respective distributees are on file. I have performed all the acts lawfully required of me

as _____
(executor, etc.)

I declare under penalty of perjury that the foregoing is true and correct.

Executed on _____ , 19 ___ , at Sacramento, California.

_____
(Signature of representative)

FINAL DISCHARGE

It appears to the Court, and the Court finds that the facts stated in the foregoing Declaration for Final Discharge are true.

IT IS ORDERED that _____ is discharged
(name of representative)

as _____ and that _____ and _____ sureties
(executor, etc.)   (he/she)   (he/she)

are discharged and released from all liability to be incurred hereafter.

Dated _____

_____
JUDGE OF THE SUPERIOR COURT

PROBATE CHECKLIST

The probate paralegal (in some firms called the "Probate Administrator") should keep a checklist (in file or 3-ring binder) of the various documents and procedures and check them off as they are completed in each proceeding. A separate checklist for testate and intestate proceedings is preferable. The following form may be customized to fit any special office procedures:

TESTATE PROCEEDING

Estate of _____

Probate No.: _____ Social Security No.: _____

ID#for Estate: _____ Date of Death: _____

Date

_____ Interview with client

_____ Petition for Probate of Will filed

_____ Notice of Death of [name of decedent] and of Petition to Administer Estate No. _____*

_____ Publication of Notice of Death of [name of decedent] and of Petition to Administer Estate No. _____ (first date: ___ last date: _____)*

_____ Affidavit of mailing to heirs filed

_____ Filed Affidavit of Publication of Notice of Death of [name of decedent] and of Petition to Administer Estate No. _____ (within 30 days after last publication)

_____ File proof of subscribing witness

_____ Bond obtained, personal or surety, amount: $ _____

_____ Order Admitting Will to Probate granted and Letters Testamentary issued (certified copies)

_____ Creditors' claims processed (Notices of Rejection served)

_____ Inventory of safe-deposit box

_____ Joint tenancy terminations

_____ Life insurance proceeds (Form 712)

_____ Application for Employer Identification No. (SS-4) to IRS

_____ Notice of Fiduciary Relationship (56) filed with IRS

_____ Order appointing inheritance tax referee

_____ Forward Inventory and Appraisement (90 days) (in triplicate) to inheritance tax referee

_____ Forward IT-22 and IT-3 to inheritance tax referee if required

_____ Review inheritance tax referee's report (10 days), check computation

_____ File Inventory and Appraisement (90 days)

_____ Order fixing inheritance tax

_____ Pay inheritance tax (or estimate) (within 9 months of date of death or within time as extended, up to 10 years of date of death)

_____ Receipt for inheritance tax

_____ Pay real property taxes (Apr. 10 and Dec. 10)

_____ Pay federal estate tax (if any) (9 months after date of death)

_____ Petition for preliminary distribution (if appropriate)

_____ Notice of hearing on petition

_____ Proof of notice of hearing on petition

_____ Order for preliminary distribution

_____ First and Final Account and Report of Representative and Petition for Distribution

_____ Notice of hearing on account and proof of notice

_____ Order Settling First and Final Account and for Final Distribution

_____ Distribution to heirs and beneficiaries

_____ Receipts signed and filed

_____ Carry-over basis letters to heirs if required

_____ Affidavit for Final Discharge and Decree for Final Discharge

_____ Notice of Termination of Fiduciary Relationship to IRS

_____ Copy of Decree of Final Discharge to bonding company

_____ Fees paid: Attorney's fee: _____
Executor's/Administrator's fee: _____

SUMMARY ADMINISTRATION
(Prob. Code §§630 *et seq.*)

Estates Consisting Entirely of Personal Property

Probate Code section 630 eliminates the necessity for probate of most estates that do not exceed $30,000, and where no real property is involved other than a right to or interest in a cemetery plot. Property held by the decedent in joint tenancy or as community or quasi-community property and passing to the decedent's surviving spouse under Probate Code section 202 is excluded in determining its value. Probate Code section 640 is authority for administration of estates where the net value over and above the value of any homestead interest does not exceed $20,000 and there is a surviving spouse or minor child.

When an estate consists entirely of personal property (exclusive of a motor vehicle, salary up to $5,000, and money due for service in the armed forces) and does not exceed $30,000, "the surviving spouse, the children, lawful issue of deceased children, a parent, brothers or sisters of the decedent, the lawful issue of a deceased brother or sister, or the guardian or conservator of the estate of any person bearing such relationship to the decedent, or the trustee named under a trust agreement executed by the decedent during his lifetime, the primary beneficiaries of which bear such relationship to the decedent, if such person or persons has or have a right to succeed to the property of the decedent, or is the sole beneficiary or are all of the beneficiaries under the last will and testament" may, without obtaining letters of administration, or awaiting the probating of the will (if any), collect any money due to the decedent and receive the decedent's property, upon furnishing an affidavit or declaration under penalty of perjury showing his right to receive such money or property. (Prob. Code §630.)

Where the decedent leaves a surviving spouse or minor child or children, and the net value of the estate over and above all liens and encumbrances and value of homestead does not exceed $20,000, the estate may be set aside to the surviving spouse or minor child or children. (Prob. Code §640.) The expenses of the last illness, funeral charges and expenses of administration have to be paid first.

If an estate does not exceed $5,000 and the spouse is entitled by succession or by will to receive the money on deposit and makes an affidavit so stating, the bank may turn over up to $500 to the spouse, without letters testamentary or administration. (Prob. Code §630.5.)

Community Property Confirmation and Set Aside
PROB. CODE §§202-206 SET ASIDE

Legislation applicable to estates of persons dying on or after July 1, 1975, provides that where a husband or wife dies intestate, or dies testate and by his or her will confirms, bequeaths or devises all or a part of his or her interest in the community property or quasi-community property to the surviving spouse, it passes to the survivor (subject to the provisions of Probate Code sections 203 and 205) and no administration thereon is necessary. (Prob. Code §202.) Probate Code Section 204 provides that a bequest or devise to a surviving spouse conditioned upon the spouse's surviving the deceased spouse by a specified period of time, is not to be considered to create such a qualified ownership as to necessitate administration, if the specific period of time has expired. The hearing date should be set after the time expires.

The surviving spouse may dispose of community real property or quasi-community real property 40 days after the death of the spouse, unless a notice has been recorded by someone other than the spouse claiming an interest in the property. The notice must describe the property and set forth the name or names of the owner or owners of record title.

The surviving spouse may elect to have the community property or quasi community property formally administered under Probate Code sections 300 *et seq.*, within four months of issuance of letters testamentary or of administration; this period may be extended upon a showing of good cause. (Prob. Code §202b.)

However, if decedent's will leaves all or part of his community property or quasi-community property to someone other than the surviving spouse or contains a trust or limits the surviving spouse to a qualified ownership in the property, probate administration of that portion of decedent's estate is required. (Prob. Code §204.)

If the surviving spouse elects to take under these sections without probate administration, a petition for confirmation is filed pursuant to Probate Code section 650 (see below).

PROB. CODE §650 SET ASIDE

Provision is made (Prob. Code §§650 *et seq.*) for the filing of a petition alleging that administration of *all or a portion* of the estate is not necessary because it is community property or quasi-community property passing to the surviving spouse. The petition may be filed by a surviving spouse, personal representative of surviving spouse, or guardian or conservator of the estate of the surviving spouse. Court approval is not required of the guardian or conservator. Probate Code section 651 provides that a 650 petition may be filed in pending administration proceedings without payment of an additional fee. (*Check local probate rules.*) A form Community Property Petition and Petition for Approval of Fees has been approved by the Judicial Council. Such petition shall contain:

1. Names, ages and addresses of the heirs, devisees and legatees of the deceased spouse, the names and addresses of all persons named as executor of the will of the deceased spouse, and the names and addresses of all persons appointed as executor of the will or administrator of the estate of the deceased spouse.

2. A description of the property of the estate which is alleged to be community property passing to the surviving spouse, including the name of the community property or quasi-community property business which the deceased spouse was operating or managing at the time of death.

3. The facts upon which the petitioner bases the allegation that all or a portion of the estate of the deceased spouse is community property passing to the surviving spouse.

4. The facts necessary to determine the county in which the estate may be administered if proceedings for administration are not pending.

5. A description of any interest in the community property which the court is being requested to confirm pursuant to section 201 or 201.5.

In Los Angeles County, see L.A. Probate Policy Memorandum section 8.02 for additional contents required in the petition.

If petitioner contends the community property passes upon the will, a copy of the will is to be attached to the petition. (Prob. Code §650(b).) (Question 5d.)

The election under section 650 does not apply if the petitioner has elected to have the interest in the community property or both the interest of the deceased spouse and the surviving spouse in the community property or quasi-community property administered pursuant to section 202(b).

Notice of Hearing on 650 Petition

If the petition under Probate Code section 650 is *not* included in the petition for probate of will or administration of estate, the clerk sets the petition for hearing and posts notice of the hearing as prescribed by Probate Code section 1200 (10 days before hearing). Better practice may be not to set the petition for hearing until the referee has completed the inheritance tax work, which may avoid a continuance. (See 2e in the Order.) The referee has 60 days from receipt to fix the tax. (Prob. Code §657.)

At least 20 days prior to hearing, a notice of hearing and copy of petition are personally served or mailed, postage prepaid, to: any non-petitioning personal representative, legatees, devisees and known heirs, all persons, or their attorneys, who have requested special notice or given notice of appearance, the Attorney General if decedent's will involves a testamentary trust for charitable purposes with a designated California resident trustee, or bequest or devise for charitable purposes without an identified legatee, devisee or beneficiary. (Prob. Code §653.)

Proof of service of a copy of the petition and a notice of hearing must be filed prior to the hearing.

See Probate Code section 205 for the surviving spouse's liability to creditors.

Attorneys are to be allowed a "reasonable fee" for their services. (Prob. Code §910.)

Notice of Hearing on Combined Petitions

If the 650 petition is joined with a petition for probate of will, notice of hearing is given as prescribed by Probate Code sections 327 and 328 and shall be included in the notice required by those sections; if the 650 petition is joined in a petition for administration, notice of hearing is given pursuant to Probate Code section 441 and shall be included in the notice required by that section. Notice of hearing on the petition for probate of will or for administration shall be given at least 20 days prior to the date of hearing and a copy of the 650 petition shall be personally served upon, or mailed postage prepaid, to all persons entitled to notice either under 328 (probate of will) or 441 (administration).

APPORTIONMENT OF DEBTS

Probate Code section 980 provides for the filing of a petition by the personal representative or anyone interested in the estate, prior to the filing of a petition for final distribution, for an order allocating the responsibility for those debts payable by the estate and also payable, in whole or in part, by the surviving spouse.

Notice of the hearing on such a petition and order to show cause is given under Probate Code section 1200 and copies served 10 days prior to hearing on the surviving spouse and the personal representative (if other than petitioner).

Brief Outline of Procedure

1. Prepare and file *Petition for Confirmation and Determination of Community Property* and have order appointing referee signed
2. Send Inventory and Appraisement and IT-22 (and IT-3 if required) to referee

3. Review Inventory and Appraisement for accuracy when returned, and if accurate, file original with court; send conformed copy to referee
4. Review inheritance tax referee's report when received and order fixing taxes, or certificate that no tax due
5. Have spouse pay federal estate tax, if any, due to IRS within 9 months from date of death
6. Have spouse pay any state inheritance tax (or pickup tax) to State Controller (check payable to State Treasurer) within 9 months from date of death
7. File *Notice of Hearing* (Probate) and proposed *Community Property Order and Order Fixing Fees* with court
8. Mail copy of petition and notice of hearing to:
   a. All devisees, legatees and known heirs
   b. Executor
   c. Personal representative who is not the petitioner
   d. All persons or their attorneys who have appeared or given notice of appearance or requested special notice
   e. Attorney General under certain circumstances
   f. All other persons named in will if petitioner bases his allegation that estate is community or quasi-community property upon the will
9. File proof of mailing with court
10. Obtain sufficient number of certified copies of *Community Property Order* from County Clerk to make any necessary title changes
11. Record certified copy of the *Community Property Order* in any office where real property is located
12. If any stock to be transferred, send certified copy of *Community Property Order* to stock transfer agent for transferring stock title
13. For decedents whose date of death is after January 1, 1980, send IRS information re carryover basis property (see IRC §6039A(a))

The above is not necessarily all-inclusive; the legal assistant may find the estate requires that other work be done, such as in connection with payment of claims, income tax, etc.

The Judicial Council forms of *Petition for Confirmation and Determination of Community Property* and *Community Property Order* are not used in Sacramento County. The Judicial Council printed forms follow. If quasi-community property is involved, the words "quasi-community property" must be inserted.

Community Property Petition and Petition for Approval of Fees

	FOR COURT USE ONLY
NAME AND ADDRESS OF ATTORNEY: TELEPHONE NO.:	
ATTORNEY FOR:	
Insert name of court, branch court if any, and Post Office and Street Address:	
ESTATE OF:	Case Number:
	HEARING DATE:
DECEDENT	
COMMUNITY PROPERTY PETITION AND PETITION FOR APPROVAL OF FEES	DEPT: TIME:

1. PETITIONER (Name):
   requests
   a. ☐ Determination of community property passing to the surviving spouse pursuant to Prob C 650 et seq.
   b. ☐ Confirmation of community property pursuant to Prob C 201.
   c. ☐ Approval of fees.
   d. ☐ This petition be joined with the petition for probate or administration of the decedent's estate.
   e. Immediate appointment of an inheritance tax referee.

2. PETITIONER is
   a. ☐ Surviving spouse of the decedent.
   b. ☐ Personal representative of surviving spouse.
   c. ☐ Guardian of the estate or conservator of the property of decedent's surviving spouse.

3. FACTS CONCERNING JURISDICTION
   a. Decedent died on (Date):
   b. ☐ a resident of the above named county of the State of California.
   c. ☐ a nonresident of California and left an estate in the above named county.

4. FACTS CONCERNING HEIRS, DEVISEES AND LEGATEES
   a. The names, addresses, relationships and ages of heirs, devisees and legatees so far as known to petitioner are:

Name and Address	Relationship	Age

(Continued on Reverse Side)

No attachment permitted less than on a full page (California Rule of Court 201(b)).

Form Approved by the
Judicial Council of California
Effective July 1, 1975

**COMMUNITY PROPERTY PETITION AND
PETITION FOR APPROVAL OF FEES**

Prob C 201–205,
650 et seq.

b. The decedent is survived by

   (1) ☐ child.   ☐ no child.

   (2) ☐ issue of predeceased child. ☐ no issue of predeceased child.

   (3) ☐ parent.   ☐ no parent.

c. No surviving child or issue of predeceased child has been omitted from the list of heirs.

d. *(Complete only if neither parent nor issue survived the decedent.)*

   The decedent is survived by

   (1) ☐ a brother or sister or issue of a predeceased brother or sister and none has been omitted from the list of heirs.

   (2) ☐ no brother or sister or issue of a predeceased brother or sister.

5. FACTS CONCERNING COMMUNITY PROPERTY

   a. Administration of all or part of the estate is not necessary for the reason that all or a part of the estate is community property passing or belonging to the surviving spouse.

   b. ☐ The legal description of the deceased spouse's property which is community property passing to the surviving spouse, including the trade or business name of any community property business which the deceased spouse was operating or managing at the time of death, is set forth in attachment 5b.[1]

   c. ☐ The legal description of the interest in the community property which petitioner requests the court to confirm to the surviving spouse as belonging to the surviving spouse under Prob C 201, is set forth in attachment 5c.

   d. The facts upon which the petitioner bases the allegation that the property described in attachments 5b and 5c is community property are stated in attachment 5d.[2]

   e. Names and addresses of all persons named as executors in decedent's will, or appointed as executors or administrators:

   f. Names and addresses of all persons named in decedent's will (in addition to those previously listed herein):[3]

6. ATTORNEY'S FEES

   The information regarding attorney's fees will be presented to the court at the hearing.

7. FACTS CONCERNING JOINDER

   A petition for probate or administration of the decedent's estate

   a. ☐ is being filed with this petition.

   b. ☐ was filed on (Date):

Dated:

              (Type or print name)   (Petitioner)

I certify (or declare) under penalty of perjury that the foregoing, including facts set forth in all attachments, is true and correct and that this declaration is executed on (Date): . . . .

at (Place): . . . . , California.

              (Type or Print Name)   (Signature of Petitioner)

8. Total number of pages attached: . . . .

---

[1] See Prob C Section 656 for required filing of list of known creditors of a business and other information in certain instances.

[2] See Prob C Section 650 for requirement that a copy of will be attached in certain instances.

[3] Required only as specified in Prob C 653(6).

Community Property Order and Order Approving Fees

NAME AND ADDRESS OF ATTORNEY:	TELEPHONE NO.:	FOR COURT USE ONLY
ATTORNEY FOR:		
Insert name of court, branch court if any, and Post Office and Street Address:		
ESTATE OF:		DECEDENT

COMMUNITY PROPERTY ORDER AND ORDER APPROVING FEES	Case Number:

1. Date of Hearing: ☐ Dept. ☐ Div. ☐ Rm. No.: Judge:

THE COURT FINDS

2. a. All notices required by law have been given.
   b. Decedent died on (Date):
   c. ☐ a resident of the above-named county of the State of California.
   d. ☐ a nonresident of California and left an estate in the above-named county.
   e. ☐ All inheritance taxes due by reason of the transfer of property described in the petition filed pursuant to Section 650 have been paid; ☐ the Inheritance Tax Referee has filed a certification that no inheritance tax is due; or ☐ the State Controller has, in writing, consented to the granting of this order without the prior fixing or payment of any inheritance tax.

THE COURT FURTHER FINDS AND ORDERS

3. a. ☐ The property described in Attachment 3a is community property and passes to (Name): ...., the surviving spouse and no administration thereon is necessary.
   b. ☐ See Attachment 3b for further order respecting transfer of the property to the surviving spouse.

4. ☐ To protect the interests of the creditors of (Business name): ...., a community property business, a list of all of the known creditors of which and the amount owing to each is on file;
   a. ☐ Within ... days from the date hereof, the surviving spouse shall file an undertaking in the amount of $ ...., conditioned that the surviving spouse shall pay the known creditors of the community property business the amount owing to each.
   b. ☐ See Attachment 4b for order protecting interest of creditors of the business.

5. a. ☐ The property described in Attachment 5a is community property that belongs to (Name): ...., the surviving spouse, under Section 201 of the Probate Code, and the surviving spouse's ownership thereof is hereby confirmed.
   b. ☐ See Attachment 5b for further order respecting transfer of the property to surviving spouse.

6. ☐ Attorney's fees are approved in the sum of: $

7. ☐ All property described in the community property petition which is not community property passing to the surviving spouse, or belonging to the surviving spouse under Section 201, shall be subject to administration in the above estate under Division 3 of the Probate Code.

Dated:

_____
JUDGE OF THE SUPERIOR COURT
☐ Signature follows last attachment

No attachment permitted less than on a full page (California Rule of Court 201(b)).

Form Approved by the Judicial Council of California Effective July 1, 1975 — COMMUNITY PROPERTY ORDER AND ORDER APPROVING FEES — Prob C 201, 203, 205, 650 et seq.

OPTIONAL PROCEDURE FOR ADMINISTRATION

The Independent Administration of Estates Act (Prob. Code §§591, *et seq.*) provides an optional procedure for administration of an estate with minimal supervision by the court.

Unless the decedent's will provides that his estate shall not be administered under the provisions of this article, an executor or administrator desiring to administer the estate under this article shall petition the court for such authority, either in the petition for appointment or by separate petition.

Notice is given as provided by Probate Code section 1200. At least 10 days before the date set for the hearing of the petition the petitioner shall cause notice of the hearing to be mailed to all legatees, devisees, all known heirs of the decedent and to all persons who have requested special notice under Probate Code section 1202.

After obtaining authority under this act the executor or administrator may seek court approval of any action taken but shall not be required to obtain court approval with respect to any actions during the course of the administration except for:

"(a) Sale or exchange of real property whether sold individually or as a unit with personal property.

"(b) Allowance of executor's and administrator's commissions and attorney's fees.

"(c) Settlement of accountings.

"(d) Preliminary and final distributions and discharge.

"(e) Granting options to purchase real property. (Prob. Code §591.2.)

Advice of Proposed Action.

However, notice of the following actions by way of an "advice of proposed action" must be given to all the persons to whom notice of the petition was given:

"(a) Selling or exchanging personal property, except for securities sold upon an established stock or bond exchange and other assets referred to in Sections 770 and 771.5 when sold for cash.

"(b) Leasing real property for a term in excess of one year.

"(c) Entering into any contract, other than a lease of real property, not to be performed within two years.

"(d) Continuing for a period of more than six months from the date of appointment of the executor or administrator of an unincorporated business or venture in which the decedent was engaged or which was wholly or partly owned by the decedent at the time of his death, or the sale or incorporation of such business.

"(e) The first payment, for a period commencing 12 months after the death of the decedent, and any increase in the payments of, a family allowance.

"(f) Investing funds of the estate, except depositing funds in banks and investing in insured savings and loan association accounts, and in direct obligations of the United States maturing not later than one year from the date of investment or reinvestment."

"(g) Completing a contract entered into by the decedent to convey real or personal property.

"(h) Borrowing money or executing a mortgage or deed of trust or giving other security.

"(i) Determining third-party claims to real and personal property if the decedent died in possession of, or holding title to, such property, or determining decedent's claim to real or personal property title to or possession of which is held by another." (Prob. Code §591.3.)

Service of this "advice" is given pursuant to Probate Code section 591.4. It shall be either delivered personally or sent by first-class mail (or airmail to any person residing outside of the United States) to each person described in Probate Code section 591.3 (devisees and legatees whose interests in the estate are affected by the proposed action; heirs of the decedent in intestate estates; to the State of California if any portion of the estate is to escheat to it; and to persons who have filed a request for special notice pursuant to Section 1202), at his last known address.

The date on which the action is proposed to be taken shall not be less than 15 days after the personal delivery, or mailing, of the advice.

Objection may be made to any proposed action, and the court must make an order. Thereafter the representative must comply with otherwise applicable code sections as to the proposed action, if he wishes to proceed.

DIVISION II
CONSERVATORSHIPS, GUARDIANSHIPS AND OTHER PROTECTIVE PROCEEDINGS
(Prob. Code §§1400 *et seq.*)

The terms "incompetent," "guardian," "ward," and "mentally ill," used in guardianships, have been objectionable when applied to loved ones who through illness and no fault of their own have become unable to care for themselves or their property. In 1957 legislation was enacted establishing conservatorships. A person who is under a conservatorship is called the "conservatee" and the person appointed to take care of his person is known as the "conservator of the person" and the person appointed to take care of his property as the "conservator of the estate." One person may be appointed conservator of both the person and the property.

Extensive changes were made in both the guardianship and conservatorship laws, effective January 1, 1981. The provisions concerning jurisdiction, venue, temporary appointments, oaths, letters, bonds, powers, duties, inventories and accounts for both guardianships and conservatorships are consolidated in the new law. The guardianship of an adult or of a married minor in existence on the operative date will be deemed to be a conservatorship and governed by the new conservatorship law. Under this new law guardianships are only for minors.

Other legislation enacted in 1980 repeals the Uniform Veterans' Guardianship Act as of January 1, 1981, and incorporates certain of its provisions in the general law relating to guardianship, conservatorship and other protective proceedings of Chapter 726 (Stats. 1979). (See Gov. Code §6107, as amended; Prob. Code §§1510, 1511, 1821, 1822, Prob. Code §1461.5.)

Probate Code section 1485 provides that the laws applicable to conservatorships shall govern guardianships "without petition or order," whether or not the letters of guardianship are amended. In Sacramento County the form of Letters of Conservatorship may be completed and box 2 checked and new letters will be issued, without notice. In Los Angeles County a petition is reportedly required. The legal assistant should check the local rules for his/her county.

CONSERVATORSHIPS

In a conservatorship a person may or may not be incompetent, but it is necessary to allege only that he is unable to care for himself or his property. The former law presented some questions as to a conservatee's legal capacity to enter or make transactions that bind or obligate the property in the estate. The new law is explicit that the appointment of a conservator of an estate is an adjudication that the conservatee lacks legal capacity to enter into or make any transaction that binds or obligates the conservatorship estate, with certain exceptions, and subject to the power of the court to authorize specific transactions by the conservatee. (Prob. Code §1872.)

The conservatee is not denied the right to control a personal allowance in an amount determined by the court upon petition (Prob. Code §§1871, 2421); the right to control his/her wages or salary as an employee (Prob. Code §§1871, 2601); the right to make a will, subject to limitations (Prob. Code §§1871, 20 et seq. (ch. 1, Div. 1); and the right to enter into transactions to the extent reasonable to provide the necessaries of life for the conservatee, spouse and minor children (Prob. Code §1871).

The court is also given authority to determine whether the conservatee has the capacity to enter into a valid marriage. If appropriate, the court is authorized to give the conservatee powers the conservator would otherwise have with respect to the conservatee's person.

Nomination and Petition

Probate Code section 1811 permits the spouse of an adult child, parent, brother or sister of the proposed conservatee to nominate a conservator in the petition or at the hearing on the petition. A nomination of a spouse or parent remains effective notwithstanding subsequent legal incapacity or death; a nomination by the spouse becomes void upon dissolution or adjudication of nullity of the marriage.

In the absence of such a nomination, of persons equally entitled in the opinion of the court to appointment, preference is to be given as provided in Probate Code section 1812:

(1) To the nominee of the conservatee
(2) To the spouse
(3) To an adult child or his or her nominee
(4) To a parent or his or her nominee
(5) To a brother or sister or his or her nominee
(6) To any qualified person or entity

The (verified) petition may be filed by anyone other than a creditor of the conservatee, "unless the creditor is a spouse, relative, or an interested state or local entity or agency or officer thereof or of a local public entity." (Prob. Code §1820.)

Certain nonprofit charitable corporations may be appointed as conservators of the person; a trust company may be appointed conservator of the estate only.

In most cases, the petitioner will be the client represented by the attorney. The legal assistant can work closely with the new conservator, who will need guidance as he becomes responsible for the management of the conservatee's property, or care of the conservatee. Therefore, in addition to the procedure leading to appointment, the legal assistant would do well to become acquainted with and study the duties of a conservator, who may have many questions that would be too time-consuming for the attorney.

A sample nomination form and the petition form and instructions for its completion follow:

Nomination

TO WHOM IT MAY CONCERN:

In the event that illness, physical misfortune, senility or incompetency shall befall me or, in the event that I shall become unable to handle my business affairs and/or to take care of my physical needs for any other reason, it is my request that the Superior Court of the County of my residence appoint _____ as Conservator of my person and _____ as Conservator of my estate.

I further direct that, in the event that _____ or some other friend shall determine the advisability of filing a Petition in Conservatorship with the Superior Court, they present this letter to the court and that the court shall consider it as a written nomination as provided for in Probate Code section 1810 of the State of California.

Dated this _____ day of _____, 19____

[signature of nominator]

Witnesses:

_____

_____

Petition for Appointment of Conservator

ATTORNEY OR PARTY WITHOUT ATTORNEY (Name and Address): TELEPHONE NO.:	FOR COURT USE ONLY
ATTORNEY FOR (Name):	

SUPERIOR COURT OF CALIFORNIA, COUNTY OF SACRAMENTO
STREET ADDRESS: 720 9TH STREET
MAILING ADDRESS:
CITY AND ZIP CODE: SACRAMENTO, CA 95814
BRANCH NAME:

CONSERVATORSHIP OF (NAME):

Proposed Conservatee

PETITION FOR APPOINTMENT OF CONSERVATOR OF THE ☐ **Person** ☐ **Estate** ☐ **Limited Conservatorship**	CASE NUMBER:

1. Petitioner (name): requests that

  a. (name and address):

  be appointed ☐ conservator ☐ limited conservator of the person of the proposed conservatee and Letters issue upon qualification.

  b. (name and address):

  be appointed ☐ conservator ☐ limited conservator of the estate of the proposed conservatee and Letters issue upon qualification.

  c. ☐ bond not be required for the reasons stated in attachment 1c.
  ☐ bond be fixed at $ _____ to be furnished by an authorized surety company or as otherwise provided by law (specify reasons if the amount is different from the minimum required by section 2320 of the Probate Code).
  ☐ deposits at (specify institution):
  in the amount of $ _____ be allowed. Receipts will be filed.

  d. ☐ authorization be granted under section 2590 of the Probate Code to exercise independently the powers specified in attachment 7.

  e. ☐ orders relating to the capacity of the proposed conservatee under sections 1873 or 1901 of the Probate Code be granted (specify orders, facts, and reasons in attachment 1e).

  f. ☐ orders relating to the powers and duties of the proposed conservator of the person under sections 2351-2358 of the Probate Code be granted (specify orders, facts, and reasons in attachment 1f).

  g. ☐ the proposed conservatee be adjudged to lack the capacity to give informed consent for medical treatment or healing by prayer and that the proposed conservator of the person be granted the powers specified in section 2355 of the Probate Code.

  h. ☐ (for limited conservatorship only) orders relating to the powers and duties of the proposed limited conservator of the person under section 2351.5 of the Probate Code be granted (specify powers and duties in attachment 1h).

  i. ☐ (for limited conservatorship only) orders relating to the powers and duties of the proposed limited conservator of the estate under section 1830(b) of the Probate Code be granted (specify powers and duties in attachment 1i).

(Continued on reverse)

Do NOT use this form for a temporary conservatorship.
Form Approved by the
Judicial Council of California
Revised Effective January 1, 1981
GC-310(81)

**PETITION FOR APPOINTMENT OF
CONSERVATOR**

CONSERVATORSHIP OF (NAME):	CASE NUMBER:
Proposed Conservatee	

PETITION FOR APPOINTMENT OF CONSERVATOR   Page 2 of 4

  j. ☐ *(for limited conservatorship only)* orders limiting the civil and legal rights of the proposed limited conservatee be granted *(specify limitations in attachment 1j).*

  k. ☐ other orders be granted *(specify in attachment 1k).*

2. The proposed conservatee is (name):
   (present address):   (telephone):

3. a. Jurisdictional facts. The proposed conservatee has no conservator within California and is a
     (1) ☐ resident of California and
         ☐ resident of this county.
         ☐ not a resident of this county but commencement of the conservatorship in this county is in the best interests of the proposed conservatee *(specify reasons in attachment 3a).*
     (2) ☐ non-resident of California but
         ☐ is temporarily living in this county, or
         ☐ has property in this county, or
         ☐ commencement of the conservatorship in this county is in the best interests of the proposed conservatee *(specify reasons in attachment 3a).*

   b. Petitioner is
      ☐ a creditor   ☐ not a creditor
      ☐ a debtor   ☐ not a debtor
      of the proposed conservatee.

   c. Proposed conservator is
      ☐ a nominee *(affix nomination as attachment 3c).*
      ☐ related to proposed conservatee as *(specify):*
      ☐ other *(specify):*

   d. Petitioner is
      ☐ the proposed conservatee.
      ☐ the spouse of the proposed conservatee.
      ☐ a relative of the proposed conservatee *(specify relationship):*
      ☐ a state or local public entity, officer, or employee.
      ☐ an interested person or friend of the proposed conservatee.
      ☐ the guardian of the proposed conservatee.

   e. Character and estimated value of the property of the estate
      Personal property: $
      Annual gross income from
         ☐ real property: $
         ☐ personal property: $
                         Total: $
      Real property: $

4. The proposed conservatee
   a. ☐ is not ☐ is a patient in or on leave of absence from a state institution under the jurisdiction of the State Department of Mental Health or the State Department of Developmental Services *(specify state institution):*

   b. ☐ is neither receiving nor entitled to receive ☐ is receiving or entitled to receive benefits from the Veterans Administration *(estimate amount of monthly benefit payable):* $

(Continued on next page)

CONSERVATORSHIP OF (NAME): Proposed Conservatee	CASE NUMBER:

PETITION FOR APPOINTMENT OF CONSERVATOR   Page 3 of 4

5. a. The proposed conservatee
☐ is an adult.
☐ will be an adult on the effective date of the order (date):
☐ is a married minor.
☐ is a minor whose marriage has been dissolved.

b. ☐ The proposed conservatee requires a conservator and is
(1) ☐ unable properly to provide for his or her personal needs for physical health, food, clothing, or shelter. Supporting facts are ☐ specified below ☐ specified in attachment 5b(1).

(2) ☐ substantially unable to manage his or her financial resources or resist fraud or undue influence. Supporting facts are ☐ specified below ☐ specified in attachment 5b(2).

c. ☐ The proposed conservatee voluntarily requests the appointment of a conservator (*specify facts showing good cause in attachment 5(c)*).

d. The proposed conservatee ☐ is ☐ is not developmentally disabled as defined in section 1420 of the Probate Code (*specify the nature and degree of the alleged disability in attachment 5d*). Petitioner is aware of the requirements of section 1827.5 of the Probate Code.

(Continued on reverse)

GC-310(81)

CONSERVATORSHIP OF (NAME):	CASE NUMBER
Proposed Conservatee	

PETITION FOR APPOINTMENT OF CONSERVATOR

6. The proposed conservatee
   a. ☐ will attend the hearing.
   b. ☐ is able but unwilling to attend the hearing, does not wish to contest the establishment of a conservatorship, does not object to the proposed conservator, and does not prefer that another person act as conservator.
   c. ☐ is unable to attend the hearing because of medical inability. An affidavit or certificate of a licensed medical practitioner or an accredited religious practitioner is affixed as attachment 6c.
   d. ☐ is not the petitioner, is out of state, and will not attend the hearing.

7. ☐ Granting the proposed conservator of the estate powers to be exercised independently under section 2590 of the Probate Code would be to the advantage and benefit and in the best interest of the conservatorship estate. Powers and reasons are specified in attachment 7.

8. ☐ There is no form of medical treatment for which the proposed conservatee has the capacity to give an informed consent. The proposed conservatee ☐ is ☐ is not an adherent of a religion that relies on prayer alone for healing as defined in section 2355(b) of the Probate Code.

9. ☐ Filed with this petition is a Petition for Appointment of Temporary Conservator *(see Judicial Council form GC-110)*.

10. ☐ the names, residence addresses, and relationships of the spouse and all relatives within the second degree of the proposed conservatee so far as known to petitioner are ☐ listed below ☐ listed in attachment 10.

RELATIONSHIP AND NAME	RESIDENCE ADDRESS
a. Spouse:	
b.	

11. ☐ Filed with this petition is a proposed Order Appointing Court Investigator *(see Judicial Council form GC-330)*.
12. ☐ Number of pages attached:
Dated: . . . .
                                                              (Signature of petitioner)

I declare under penalty of perjury under the laws of the State of California that the foregoing is true and correct and that this declaration is executed on (date): . . . . , at (place): . . . .

. . . .
(Type or print name)   (Signature of petitioner)

Completing the Petition

A few comments about the preparation of the petition might prove helpful. The legal assistant should first check the local rules in which the proceeding is being filed.

Question ld. In some counties you can ask for all the powers specified in section 2590, and they will be granted carte blanche. In Sacramento County you need to specify the particular powers requested and give the reason in a separate attachment. Powers previously granted under the old Probate Code are still good unless they had a termination date.

Question le. Normally you would not check this box, unless you want the conservatee to have some of the particular powers specified in those sections. Section 1901 grants the right to enter into marriage.

Question lf. If the conservator needs any of the powers specified in these sections (§§ 2351-2358), relating to care, medical treatment, education and welfare, the box should be checked and, if granted, the powers should be included in the letters.

Question lg. If the conservator believes the proposed conservatee is not able to give informed consent to medical treatment, say if the person is a total care patient, an invalid, or just not able to make decisions, this box should definitely be checked. If the box is checked the court investigator will comment on it, and if it seems inappropriate to him he may ask that counsel be appointed to look at that issue.

If the conservatee is not adjudicated to lack the capacity to give informed consent for medical treatment, he may so consent. The conservator is also authorized to give consent but that is not sufficient if the conservatee objects. In that event, if the box has not been checked and an adjudication is made that he lacks the capacity to give informed consent, and if the conservatee requires surgical or other medical treatment, it would be necessary to file another petition specifically for that purpose for a court order, at additional expense. (Prob. Code §2354(a)(b).) The form used immediately follows this section on questions.

Under Probate Code section 2354(c) the conservator may consent to medical treatment, based upon medical advice, that the case is emergency because (1) the treatment is required to alleviate severe pain or (2) the medical condition, if not immediately diagnosed and treated, will lead to serious disability or death.

Question 3a. The conservatee does not have to be a resident of the county where the petition is initiated, but the court could possibly move the conservatorship proceeding to another county if another petition is filed in another county.

Question 3e. How this is completed determines how the bond is set. It should be the conservator's best estimate. It is better to have the bond high than too low, if the conservator skips, which happens. The legal assistant should try to get as much information as possible about the assets of the conservatee.

If there is real property involved, the letters of conservatorship or order appointing conservator should be filed with the county recorder's office of the county where the real property is located, thus preventing the conservatee from making a bona fide sale to a third party.

Question 4. The code requires notice to the State Department of Mental Health or the State Department of Developmental Services. If they have a bill they are not barred by the statute of limitations unless they have been given notice, the notice starts the statute of limitations running.

Question 5(b)(2). The conservator should remember that the conservatee will be reading the answer and might not like what he reads; it should be carefully worded. The paralegal should be able to be of assistance here in choosing the language.

Question 5d. As mentioned *infra* under Limited Conservatorships, in some courts if you allege the person is developmentally disabled you must request a limited conservatorship, but not in Sacramento County.

The petition does not mention an affidavit of voter registration. The court investigator will determine and in his report comment on whether the conservatee is capable of completing an affidavit of voter registration as required by Probate Code section 1851(a).

Following is a form for *Petition for Authority to Give Consent for Medical Treatment*:

Petition for Authority to Give Consent for Medical Treatment

ATTORNEY OR PARTY WITHOUT ATTORNEY (NAME AND ADDRESS):	TELEPHONE NO.:	FOR COURT USE ONLY
ATTORNEY FOR (NAME):		

SUPERIOR COURT OF CALIFORNIA, COUNTY OF SACRAMENTO
STREET ADDRESS: 720 9TH STREET
MAILING ADDRESS:
CITY AND ZIP CODE: SACRAMENTO, CA 95814
BRANCH NAME:

CONSERVATORSHIP OF THE ☐ PERSON ☐ ESTATE OF (NAME):

Conservatee

PETITION FOR AUTHORITY TO GIVE CONSENT FOR MEDICAL TREATMENT	CASE NUMBER:

1. Petitioner (name): requests that

    a. the conservatee be adjudged to lack the capacity to give informed consent for medical treatment or healing by prayer.

    b. the conservator of the person be granted the exclusive authority to give consent for medical treatment or healing by prayer that the conservator in good faith based on medical advice determines to be necessary.

    c. the treatment be performed by ☐ a licensed medical practitioner ☐ an accredited practitioner of a religion that relies on prayer alone for healing.

    d. ☐ the order dated: made under section 1880 of the Probate Code be ☐ revoked
       ☐ modified as follows:

    e. ☐ other (specify):

    f. Letters of Conservatorship be reissued to include a statement that conservator has the powers requested in this petition.

2. There is no form of medical treatment for which the proposed conservatee has the capacity to give informed consent.

3. Conservatee ☐ is ☐ is not an adherent of a religion that relies on prayer alone for healing as defined in section 2355(b) of the Probate Code.

(Continued on reverse)

Form Approved by the
Judicial Council of California
Effective January 1, 1981
GC-380(81)

**PETITION FOR AUTHORITY TO GIVE
CONSENT FOR MEDICAL TREATMENT**

CONSERVATORSHIP OF (NAME):	CASE NUMBER:
Conservatee	

PETITION FOR AUTHORITY TO GIVE CONSENT FOR MEDICAL TREATMENT   Page 2

4. The conservatee
   a. ☐ will attend the hearing.
   b. ☐ is able but unwilling to attend the hearing and does not wish to contest this petition.
   c. ☐ is unable to attend the hearing because of medical inability. An affidavit or certificate of a licensed medical
      practitioner or an accredited religious practitioner is affixed as attachment 4c.
   d. ☐ is not the petitioner, is out of state, and will not attend the hearing.

5. Special notice ☐ has not been requested ☐ has been requested. Specify the names and addresses of persons
   requesting special notice in attachment 5.

6. ☐ Filed with this petition is a proposed Order Appointing Court Investigator which specifies duties to be performed
   prior to granting an order relating to medical consent *(see Judicial Council form GC-330).*

7. The names, residence addresses, and relationships of the spouse and all relatives within the second degree of
   the conservatee so far as known to petitioner are ☐ listed below ☐ listed in attachment 7.

   RELATIONSHIP AND NAME   RESIDENCE ADDRESS
   a. Spouse:

   b.

8. ☐ Number of pages attached:
Dated: . . . .
                                        _____
                                              (Signature of petitioner)

I declare under penalty of perjury under the laws of the State of California that the foregoing is true and correct
and that this declaration is executed on (date): . . . . at (place): . . . .

. . . . _____
               (Type or print name)   (Signature of petitioner)

Appointment of Conservator

Probate Code section 1800 provides for the appointment of a conservator of the person or estate, or both, of an adult or of the person of a minor who is married or whose marriage has been dissolved.

A conservator of the person may be appointed for any person who "is unable properly to provide for his or her personal needs for physical health, food, clothing or shelter . . . ." (Prob. Code §1801(a).)

A conservator of the estate may be appointed for a person who is "substantially unable to manage his or her own financial resources or resist fraud or undue influence . . . . Substantial inability may not be proved solely by isolated incidents of negligence or improvidence." (Prob. Code §1801(b).)

A person with sufficient capacity may himself petition for appointment of a conservator and nominate the conservator. The best time to nominate someone to act as conservator of one's person and/or property in the event one should ever become incapacitated, is when one is in good health and in full possession of one's faculties. "A prior nomination may be particularly appropriate if a person is old or infirm, about to undergo major surgery, or is exposed to a significant hazard. If there is no family, or if the person is not on good terms with some or all of the relatives who would normally be called on to care for him, the prior nomination when he is competent and free of undue influence gives him an opportunity to make his desires clear."* Once, however, one becomes ill, weak of mind, senile or lacking in capacity, the capacity of the proposed conservatee may be brought into question. The conservatee at the time of appointment may be too ill to appear in court and testify. In such event he may be the victim of a designing person more interested in his estate than in his best interests. Only someone who is trusted implicitly should be nominated and, in the case of property, someone who is fully qualified to care for one's property and financial interests.

The court must appoint the person so nominated unless it finds it is not in the nominator's best interests. (Prob. Code §1810.) The selection of a conservator is solely in the court's discretion, and while the court would not ignore the wishes of the nominator, the court could decide to appoint as conservator a person whom the conservatee would never have selected. Yet the best safeguard is a prior nomination and its advantage of "the benefit the nominator derives from feeling that he has placed himself and his affairs in friendly and competent hands, particularly if there is dissension in the family." (*Ibid.*)

---

*California Conservatorships (1968) (Cont. Ed. Bar) p. 18.

Notice

A citation must be issued and served with a copy of the petition on the conservatee (unless the conservatee is himself petitioning). The citation includes a statement of the legal standards by which the need for a conservator is adjudged, as stated in Probate Code section 1801. (Prob. Code §1824.)

At least 15 days before the hearing notice must be mailed to the spouse (if any) and relatives named in the petition, at their addresses stated therein. Notice shall also be mailed to the Director of Medical Health or the Director of Developmental Services if neither filed the petition, and to the Veterans Administration if the proposed conservatee is receiving or entitled to receive benefits. (Prob. Code §1822.)

Unless otherwise expressly provided, when a notice or other paper is required or permitted to be mailed, it shall be sent by first-class mail if within the United States or airmail if outside the United States. Mailing is complete upon deposit in the mail, postage prepaid, addressed to the person to whom mailed. (Prob. Code §1465.)

If service is made by mail as authorized by Code of Civil Procedure section 415.30, service is complete on the date a written acknowledgment of receipt is executed. (Prob. Code §1467.)

Proof of giving of notice may be made by the several means listed in section 1468, but is not limited to such means. The party entitled to notice may waive notice and the court should so find in its order, which is conclusive on all persons.

The forms for *Notice of Hearing* (with *Proof of Service* on the reverse side) and *Citation for Conservatorship* with *Proof of Service* follow:

Notice of Hearing, Guardianship or Conservatorship

ATTORNEY OR PARTY WITHOUT ATTORNEY (NAME AND ADDRESS):	TELEPHONE NO.:	FOR COURT USE ONLY
ATTORNEY FOR (NAME):		

SUPERIOR COURT OF CALIFORNIA, COUNTY OF SACRAMENTO
STREET ADDRESS: 720 9TH STREET
MAILING ADDRESS:
CITY AND ZIP CODE: SACRAMENTO, CA   95814
BRANCH NAME:

☐ GUARDIANSHIP ☐ CONSERVATORSHIP OF THE ☐ PERSON ☐ ESTATE OF
(NAME):
☐ Minor ☐ Conservatee

NOTICE OF HEARING
☐ **Guardianship** ☐ **Conservatorship** ☐ **Limited Conservatorship**

CASE NUMBER:

> **This notice is required by law. This notice does not require you to appear in court, but you may attend the hearing if you wish.**

1. NOTICE is given that (name):
   (representative capacity, if any):
   has filed (specify):

   reference to which is made for further particulars.

2. ☐ The petition includes an application for the independent exercise of powers under section 2590 of the Probate Code. Powers requested are ☐ specified below ☐ specified in attachment 2.

3. A hearing on the matter will be held

   on (date):   at (time): 9:00 A.M.   in ☐ Dept: ☐ Div: ☐ Rm.:

   located at (address of court):

   Dated: . . . . ☐ Clerk, by _____ , Deputy

                              ☐ Attorney _____
                                           (Signature)

   This notice was mailed on (date): . . . . , at (place): . . . ., California.

   (Continued on reverse)

Form Approved by the
Judicial Council of California
Revised Effective January 1, 1981
GC-020(81)

**NOTICE OF HEARING
GUARDIANSHIP OR CONSERVATORSHIP**

□ GUARDIANSHIP □ CONSERVATORSHIP OF (NAME): □ Minor □ Conservatee	CASE NUMBER:

NOTICE OF HEARING—GUARDIANSHIP OR CONSERVATORSHIP   Page 2
CLERK'S CERTIFICATE OF □ POSTING □ MAILING

I certify that I am not a party to this cause and that a true copy of the foregoing Notice of Hearing—Guardianship or Conservatorship

1. □ *(for sales under section 2543(c) of the Probate Code only)* was posted at (address):

2. □ was mailed, first class, postage fully prepaid, □ with a copy of the petition (title):

in a sealed envelope addressed to each person whose name and address is given below.
I certify that the notice was posted or mailed and this certificate was executed on (date): . . . .
at (place): . . . . , California.

Clerk, by . . . . , Deputy

PROOF OF SERVICE BY MAIL

I am over the age of 18 and not a party to this cause. I am a resident of or employed in the county where the mailing occurred. My residence or business address is:

I served the foregoing Notice of Hearing—Guardianship or Conservatorship □ with a copy of the petition (title):

by enclosing a true copy in a sealed envelope addressed to each person whose name and address is given below and depositing the envelope in the United States mail with the postage fully prepaid.

(1) Date of deposit: (2) Place of deposit (city and state):

I declare under penalty of perjury under the laws of the State of California that the foregoing is true and correct and that this declaration is executed on (date): . . . . at (place): . . . .

. . . .
(Type or print name)   (Signature of declarant)

NAME AND ADDRESS OF EACH PERSON TO WHOM NOTICE WAS MAILED

□ List of names and addresses continued on attachment.

Citation for Conservatorship and Proof of Service

ATTORNEY,OR PARTY WITHOUT ATTORNEY (NAME AND ADDRESS):	TELEPHONE NO.:	FOR COURT USE ONLY
ATTORNEY FOR (NAME):		

SUPERIOR COURT OF CALIFORNIA, COUNTY OF SACRAMENTO
STREET ADDRESS: 720 9TH STREET
MAILING ADDRESS:
CITY AND ZIP CODE: SACRAMENTO, CA   95814
BRANCH NAME:

CONSERVATORSHIP OF THE ☐PERSON ☐ESTATE OF (NAME):

Proposed Conservatee

CITATION FOR CONSERVATORSHIP ☐ **Limited Conservatorship**	CASE NUMBER:

THE PEOPLE OF THE STATE OF CALIFORNIA,

To (name):

1. You are hereby cited and required to appear at a hearing in this court

   on (date):   at (time): 9:00 A.M. in ☐ Dept   ☐ Div.   ☐ Rm.:

   located at (street address and city):

   and to give any legal reason why, according to the verified petition filed with this court, you should not be found
   to be ☐ unable to provide for your personal needs ☐ unable to manage your financial resources
   and by reason thereof, why the following person should not be appointed ☐ conservator ☐ limited conservator
   of your ☐ person ☐ estate (name):

2. A conservatorship of the person may be created for a person who is unable properly to provide for his or her
   personal needs for physical health, food, clothing or shelter. A conservatorship of the property (estate) may be
   created for a person who is unable to resist fraud or undue influence, or who is substantially unable to manage
   his or her own financial resources. "Substantial inability" may not be proved solely by isolated incidents of negligence
   or improvidence.

3. At the hearing a conservator may be appointed for your ☐ person ☐ estate. The appointment may affect or
   transfer to the conservator your right to contract, to manage and control your property, to give informed consent
   for medical treatment, to fix your place of residence, and to marry. You may also be disqualified from voting if
   you are found to be incapable of completing an affidavit of voter registration. The judge or the court investigator
   will explain to you the nature, purpose, and effect of the proceedings and answer questions concerning the explanation.

4. You have the right to appear at the hearing and oppose the petition. You have the right to hire an attorney of
   your choice to represent you. The court will appoint an attorney to represent you if you are unable to retain one.
   You must pay the cost of that attorney if you are able. You have the right to a jury trial if you wish.

5. *(for limited conservatorship only)* You have the right to oppose the petition in part by objecting to any or all of
   the requested duties or powers of the limited conservator.

Dated: . . . . Clerk, by _____ , Deputy

SEAL

(Proof of service on reverse)

Form Approved by the
Judicial Council of California
Revised Effective January 1, 1981
GC-320(81)

**CITATION FOR CONSERVATORSHIP
AND PROOF OF SERVICE**

CONSERVATORSHIP OF (NAME):	CASE NUMBER:
Proposed Conservatee	

PROOF OF SERVICE   Page 2
(Citation for Conservatorship)

1. I served the citation and petition as follows:

   a. Person cited (name):

   b. Person served (name):

   c. ☐ By delivery at ☐ home ☐ business   (1) date:
      (2) time: (3) address:

   d. ☐ By mailing (1) date:
                    (2) place:

2. Manner of service *(check proper box)*
   a. ☐ **Personal service.** By personally delivering copies to the person served. (CCP 415.10)
   b. ☐ **Mail and acknowledgment service.** By mailing (by first-class or airmail) copies to the person served, together with two copies of the form of notice and acknowledgment and a return envelope, postage prepaid, addressed to the sender. (CCP 415.30) **(Attach completed acknowledgment of receipt.)**
   c. ☐ **Service on person outside state** (CCP 415.40) *(specify manner of service)*:
   d. ☐ **Other manner authorized by court** ☐ specified below ☐ specified in attachment 2d.

3. At the time of service I was at least 18 years of age and not a party to this proceeding.

4. Fee for service: $

5. Person serving
   a. ☐ Not a registered California process server.
   b. ☐ Registered California process server.
   c. ☐ Employee or independent contractor of a registered California process server.
   d. ☐ Exempt from registration under Bus. & Prof. Code 22350(b).

   e. ☐ California sheriff, marshal, or constable.
   f. Name, address and telephone number and, if applicable, county of registration and number:

I declare under penalty of perjury under the laws of the State of California that the foregoing is true and correct and that this declaration is executed on (date): . . . . .
. . . .
at (place): . . . .

(For California sheriff, marshal or constable use only) I certify that the forgoing is true and correct and that this certificate is executed on (date): . . . .
at (place): . . . ., California.

_____   _____
(Signature)   (Signature)

The proposed conservatee must attend the hearing unless he is unable to do so by reason of medical inability, in which case such inability must be established by an affidavit or certificate of a doctor. Nor need the conservatee attend the hearing if the court investigator has reported that the conservatee is not willing to attend the hearing, does not wish to contest the conservatorship, and does not object to the proposed conservator, and the court makes an order that the conservatee need not attend. (Prob. Code §1825.)

Emotional or psychological instability is not considered good cause for not attending the hearing unless, by reason of such instability, attendance at the hearing is likely to cause serious and immediate psychological damage. (Prob. Code §1825(e).)

If the proposed conservatee is out of state when served, he/she need not be produced at the hearing. (Prob. Code §1825(a).)

The forms for *Declaration of Medical or Accredited Practitioner and Notification to Court of Address on Conservatorship* follow. The latter form is used in Sacramento County pursuant to local rule, to tell the court where the conservatee is. One of these forms must also be filed whenever the conservatee is moved.

A conservator subjects himself to possible removal, if he moves the conservatee without court approval in a temporary conservatorship; if the conservatee was injured as a result of the change, the conservator might be subject to liability.

Declaration of Medical or Accredited Practitioner

ATTORNEY OR PARTY WITHOUT ATTORNEY (Name and Address):	TELEPHONE NO.:	FOR COURT USE ONLY
ATTORNEY FOR (Name):		

SUPERIOR COURT OF CALIFORNIA, COUNTY OF SACRAMENTO
STREET ADDRESS: 720 9TH STREET
MAILING ADDRESS:
CITY AND ZIP CODE: SACRAMENTO, CA   95814
BRANCH NAME:

CONSERVATORSHIP OF THE ☐ PERSON ☐ ESTATE OF (NAME):

Proposed Conservatee

DECLARATION OF MEDICAL OR ACCREDITED PRACTITIONER	CASE NUMBER:

I, (name):   , hereby state:

1. a. ☐ I am a duly licensed medical practitioner, and the proposed conservatee is under my treatment. My office
   is located at (address):

   b. ☐ I am an accredited practitioner of a religion whose tenets and practices call for reliance on prayer alone
   for healing, which religion is adhered to by the proposed conservatee. The proposed conservatee is under
   my treatment. My office is located at (address):

2. The proposed conservatee is unable to attend the court hearing on the petition for appointment of a conservator
   set for (date):   and will continue to be unable to attend a court hearing
   ☐ until (date):   ☐ for the foreseeable future because of medical inability. Supporting
   facts are ☐ stated below ☐ stated in attachment 2.

I declare under penalty of perjury under the laws of the State of California that the foregoing is true and correct
and that this declaration is executed on (date): . . . . at (place): . . . .

_____
(Signature of declarant)

Emotional or psychological instability shall not be considered good cause for the absence unless, by reason of the instability, attendance at the hearing
is likely to cause serious and immediate physiological damage to the proposed conservatee.
Form Approved by the
Judicial Council of California   **DECLARATION OF MEDICAL OR**
Revised Effective January 1, 1981   **ACCREDITED PRACTITIONER**
GC-335(81)

Notification to Court of Address on Conservatorship or Guardianship

NAME AND ADDRESS OF ATTORNEY   TELEPHONE NO.:   FOR COURT USE ONLY

ATTORNEY FOR:

SUPERIOR COURT, STATE OF CALIFORNIA
COUNTY OF SACRAMENTO

☐ Guardianship   ☐ Conservatorship of the   ☐ Person   ☐ Estate of:

NOTIFICATION TO COURT OF ADDRESS ON CONSERVATORSHIP OR GUARDIANSHIP	CASE NUMBER

Medical Declaration Filed_____ Date Appointed _____ Date of Hearing _____

CONSERVATEE/WARD

Address _____ City _____ State _____ Zip Code _____

Area Code _____ Phone Number _____

ATTORNEY FOR CONSERVATEE/WARD

Name _____

Address _____ City _____ State _____ Zip Code _____

Area Code _____ Phone Number _____

CONSERVATOR/GUARDIAN

Name _____

Address _____ City _____ State _____ Zip Code _____

Area Code _____ Phone Number _____

ATTORNEY FOR CONSERVATOR/GUARDIAN

Name _____

Address _____ City _____ State _____ Zip Code _____

Area Code _____ Phone Number _____

COMPLETED BY

Name (Typed) _____ /Signature X _____

Address _____ City _____ State _____ Zip Code _____

Area Code _____ Phone Number _____

**NOTIFICATION TO COURT OF ADDRESS ON
CONSERVATORSHIP OR GUARDIANSHIP**

Probate Form 37
Adopted 5/1/78

Court Investigator's Interview

Upon receipt of the doctor's affidavit or certificate, or if the proposed conservatee is not willing to attend the hearing, the court investigator interviews the proposed conservatee and makes determinations of all the matters listed in Probate Code section 1826 and files his report at least 5 days before the hearing. The report is mailed to the attorney, if any, for the petitioner, the attorney, if any, for the proposed conservatee and other persons as ordered by the court.

The new law is more explicit as to the legal training and experience required of the court investigator, and the need to demonstrate sufficient knowledge of the law to inform conservatees and proposed conservatees of their rights, answer their questions, etc. (See Prob. Code §1454.)

Hearing, Orders, Letters

At the hearing, the petition may be opposed by the proposed conservatee or any interested person. A jury trial may be demanded. The proposed conservatee or anyone else may appear at the hearing to support or oppose the petition. Before the establishment of the conservatorship the court must consult with the proposed conservatee to determine his or her opinion as to the establishment of the conservatorship, the appointment of the proposed conservatee, and any order requested under sections 1870, *et seq.*

After hearing, an order appointing the conservator or conservators is made. Before letters of conservatorship may issue, however, a copy of the order must be served by mail on the conservatee. The order must contain the names, addresses and telephone numbers of the conservator, conservator's attorney, if any, and the court investigator, if any.

The forms for *Order Appointing Conservator, Proof of Service By Mail of Order,* and *Letters of Conservatorship* follow:

Order Appointing Conservator

ATTORNEY OR PARTY WITHOUT ATTORNEY (Name and Address):	TELEPHONE NO.:	FOR COURT USE ONLY
ATTORNEY FOR (Name):		

SUPERIOR COURT OF CALIFORNIA, COUNTY OF SACRAMENTO
STREET ADDRESS: 720 9TH STREET
MAILING ADDRESS:
CITY AND ZIP CODE: SACRAMENTO, CA 95814
BRANCH NAME:

CONSERVATORSHIP OF THE ☐ PERSON ☐ ESTATE OF (NAME):

Conservatee

ORDER APPOINTING CONSERVATOR ☐ Limited Conservatorship	CASE NUMBER:

1. The petition for appointment of conservator came on for hearing as follows (check boxes c, d, e, and f to indicate personal presence):
   a. Judge (name):

   b. Hearing date: Time: ☐ Dept.:   ☐ Div.:   ☐ Room:
   c. ☐ Petitioner (name):
   d. ☐ Attorney for petitioner (name):
   e. ☐ Attorney for person cited (name, address, and telephone):

   f. Person cited was ☐ present ☐ unable to attend ☐ able but unwilling to attend ☐ out of state.

2. THE COURT FINDS
   a. All notices required by law have been given.
   b. (Name):
      ☐ is unable properly to provide for his or her personal needs for physical health, food, clothing, or shelter.
      ☐ is substantially unable to manage his or her financial resources or to resist fraud or undue influence.
      ☐ has voluntarily requested appointment of a conservator and good cause has been shown for the appointment.
   c. Conservatee
      ☐ is an adult.
      ☐ will be an adult on the effective date of this order.
      ☐ is a married minor.
      ☐ is a minor whose marriage has been dissolved.
   d. ☐ There is no form of medical treatment for which the conservatee has the capacity to give an informed consent.
      ☐ Conservatee is an adherent of a religion defined in section 2355(b) of the Probate Code.
   e. ☐ Granting the conservator powers to be exercised independently under section 2590 of the Probate Code is to the advantage and benefit and in the best interest of the conservatorship estate.
   f. ☐ Conservatee is not capable of completing an affidavit of voter registration.
   g. ☐ Attorney (name):   has been appointed by the court as legal counsel to represent the conservatee in these proceedings. The cost for representation is $_____
      The conservatee has the ability to pay ☐ all ☐ none ☐ a portion of this sum (specify): $ _____
   h. ☐ Conservatee need not attend the hearing.
   i. ☐ The appointed court investigator is (name, address, and telephone):

   j. ☐ (for limited conservatorship only) The limited conservatee is developmentally disabled as defined in section 1420 of the Probate Code.

(Continued on reverse)

Do NOT use this form for a temporary conservatorship.
Form Approved by the
Judicial Council of California
Revised Effective January 1, 1981
GC-340(81)   **ORDER APPOINTING CONSERVATOR**

CONSERVATORSHIP OF (NAME):	CASE NUMBER:
Conservatee	

ORDER APPOINTING CONSERVATOR   Page 2

3. THE COURT ORDERS

   a. (name):
      (address):   (telephone):

      is appointed ☐ conservator ☐ limited conservator of the person of (name):
      and Letters shall issue upon qualification.

   b. (name):
      (address):   (telephone):

      is appointed ☐ conservator ☐ limited conservator of the estate of (name):
      and Letters shall issue upon qualification.

   c. ☐ Conservatee need not attend the hearing.

   d. ☐ Bond is not required.
      ☐ Bond is fixed at $_____ to be furnished by an authorized surety company or as otherwise
      provided by law.
      ☐ Deposits shall be made at (specify institution):   in the
      amount of $_____ and receipts filed.
   e. ☐ For legal services rendered, ☐ conservatee ☐ conservatee's estate ☐ parents of the minor ☐ minor's
      estate shall pay to (name):   the sum of $_____
      ☐ forthwith ☐ as follows (specify terms, including any combination of payors):

   f. ☐ Conservatee is disqualified from voting.
   g. ☐ Conservatee lacks the capacity to give informed consent for medical treatment and the conservator of the
      person is granted the powers specified in section 2355 of the Probate Code. ☐ The treatment shall be
      performed by an accredited practitioner of the religion defined in section 2355(b) of the Probate Code.
   h. ☐ The conservator of the estate is granted authorization under section 2590 of the Probate Code to exercise
      independently the powers specified in attachment 3h ☐ subject to the conditions provided.
   i. ☐ Orders relating to the capacity of the conservatee under sections 1873 or 1901 of the Probate Code as
      specified in attachment 3i are granted.
   j. ☐ Orders relating to the powers and duties of the conservator of the person under sections 2351-2358 of the
      Probate Code as specified in attachment 3j are granted.
   k. ☐ Orders relating to the conditions imposed under section 2402 of the Probate Code upon the conservator
      of the estate as specified in attachment 3k are granted.
   l. ☐ Other orders as specified in attachment 3l are granted.
   m.☐ The inheritance tax referee appointed is (name and address):

   n. ☐ (for limited conservatorship only) Orders relating to the powers and duties of the limited conservator of the
      person under section 2351.5 of the Probate Code as specified in attachment 3n are granted.
   o. ☐ (for limited conservatorship only) Orders relating to the powers and duties of the limited conservator of the
      estate under section 1830(b) of the Probate Code as specified in attachment 3o are granted.
   p. ☐ (for limited conservatorship only) Orders limiting the civil and legal rights of the limited conservatee are granted
      as specified in attachment 3p are granted.
   q. ☐ This order will be effective on the ☐ date signed ☐ date minor attains majority (date):

4. Number of boxes checked in item 3:
5. ☐ Number of pages attached:
Dated: . . . .   _____
                                         Judge of the Superior Court
                                   ☐ Signature follows last attachment

Proof of Service by Mail of Order Appointing Guardian or Conservator

ATTORNEY OR PARTY WITHOUT ATTORNEY (NAME AND ADDRESS):	TELEPHONE NO.	FOR COURT USE ONLY
ATTORNEY FOR (NAME):		

SUPERIOR COURT OF CALIFORNIA, COUNTY OF SACRAMENTO
STREET ADDRESS: 720 9TH STREET
MAILING ADDRESS:
CITY AND ZIP CODE: SACRAMENTO, CA 95814
BRANCH NAME:

☐ GUARDIANSHIP ☐ CONSERVATORSHIP OF THE ☐ PERSON ☐ ESTATE
OF (NAME):
☐ Minor ☐ Conservatee

PROOF OF SERVICE BY MAIL OF ORDER APPOINTING ☐ GUARDIAN ☐ CONSERVATOR	CASE NUMBER:

PROOF OF SERVICE BY MAIL
(Personal delivery also permitted. Probate Code, § 1466)

I am over the age of 18 and not a party to this cause. I am a resident of or employed in the county where the mailing occurred. My residence or business address is:

I served the Order Appointing ☐ Guardian ☐ Conservator by enclosing a true copy in a sealed envelope addressed to each person whose name and address is given below and depositing the envelope in the United States mail with the postage fully prepaid.

(1) Date of deposit: (2) Place of deposit (city and state):

I declare under penalty of perjury under the laws of the State of California that the foregoing is true and correct and that this declaration is executed on (date): . . . . at (place): . . . .

. . . .
(Type or print name)   (Signature of declarant)

NAME AND ADDRESS OF EACH PERSON TO WHOM NOTICE WAS MAILED

a. ☐ Ward 14 years of age or older:

b. ☐ Conservatee:

c.

☐ List of names and addresses continued in attachment.

Do NOT use this form for personal delivery permitted in lieu of mailing by section 1466 of the Probate Code.

Form Approved by the
Judicial Council of California
Revised Effective January 1, 1981
GC-030(81)

**PROOF OF SERVICE BY MAIL
OF ORDER APPOINTING
GUARDIAN OR CONSERVATOR**

Letters of Conservatorship

<table>
<tr><td>ATTORNEY OR PARTY WITHOUT ATTORNEY (Name and Address):</td><td>TELEPHONE NO.</td><td>FOR COURT USE ONLY</td></tr>
</table>

☐ IF RECORDED RETURN TO:

ATTORNEY FOR (Name):

SUPERIOR COURT OF CALIFORNIA, COUNTY OF SACRAMENTO
STREET ADDRESS: 720 9TH STREET
MAILING ADDRESS:
CITY AND ZIP CODE: SACRAMENTO, CA   95814
BRANCH NAME:

CONSERVATORSHIP OF (NAME):

Conservatee

LETTERS OF CONSERVATORSHIP
☐ Person ☐ Estate ☐ Limited Conservatorship

CASE NUMBER:

FOR RECORDER'S USE ONLY

STATE OF CALIFORNIA, COUNTY OF

1. ☐ (Name):   is the appointed
   ☐ conservator ☐ limited conservator of the ☐ person ☐ estate of
   (name):

2. ☐ (for conservatorship that was on December 31, 1980, a guardianship of an adult
   or of the person of a married minor) (name):
   was appointed the guardian of the ☐ person ☐ estate by order
   dated: and is now the conservator of the
   ☐ person ☐ estate of (name):

3. ☐ Other powers have been granted or conditions imposed as follows:
   a. ☐ exclusive authority to give consent for and to require the conservatee to
      receive medical treatment that the conservator in good faith based on
      medical advice determines to be necessary even if the conservatee objects,
      subject to the limitations stated in section 2356 of the Probate Code.
      ☐ This treatment shall be performed by an accredited practitioner of the
         religion whose tenets and practices call for reliance on prayer alone for healing of which
         the conservatee was an adherent prior to the establishment of the conservatorship.
      ☐ (applicable only if the court order limits the duration) This medical authority terminates on (date):

   b. ☐ powers to be exercised independently under section 2590 of the Probate Code as specified in attachment
      3b (specify powers, restrictions, conditions, and limitations).
   c. ☐ conditions relating to the care and custody of the property under section 2402 of the Probate Code
      as specified in attachment 3c.
   d. ☐ conditions relating to the care, treatment, education, and welfare of the conservatee under section 2358
      of the Probate Code as specified in attachment 3d.
   e. ☐ (for limited conservatorship only) powers of the limited conservator of the person under section 2351.5
      of the Probate Code as specified in attachment 3e.
   f. ☐ (for limited conservatorship only) powers of the limited conservator of the estate under section 1830(b)
      of the Probate Code as specified in attachment 3f.
   g. ☐ other (specify):

SEAL

Dated: . . . .

Clerk, by _____ , Deputy
☐ Number of pages attached:
(Continued on reverse)

This form may be recorded as notice of the establishment of a conservatorship of the estate as provided in section 1875 of the Probate Code.
Form Approved by the
Judicial Council of California
Effective January 1, 1981
GC-350(81)

LETTERS OF CONSERVATORSHIP

CONSERVATORSHIP OF (NAME):	CASE NUMBER:
Conservatee	

LETTERS OF CONSERVATORSHIP   Page 2

AFFIRMATION

I solemnly affirm that I will perform the duties of ☐ conservator ☐ limited conservator according to law.

Executed on (date): . . . ., at (place) . . . .

_____
(Signature of appointee)

CERTIFICATION

I certify that this document and any attachments is a correct copy of the original on file in my office, and that the letters issued to the person appointed above have not been revoked, annulled, or set aside, and are still in full force and effect.

Dated: . . . .   Clerk, by _____ , Deputy

SEAL

Bond

A bond in the amount required by the court must be posted before letters of conservatorship may be issued. If the proposed conservatee is the petitioner and he has waived the filing of a bond, the court may dispense with the filing of bond, or permit a lesser amount. (Prob. Code §2321.) Provision is made for the deposit of money in a savings and loan association, to be withdrawn only upon order of court, and waiving bond (Prob. Code §2328). Unless the court specifically requires, no bond is required of the conservator of the person. Bonds may be waived in small estates pursuant to Probate Code sections 2323 and 2628. In Sacramento County, in a conservatorship of the estate, the court usually requires at least a minimum bond of $4,000.

In lieu of a surety bond, a cash bond or an assigned interest in an account or accounts may be filed with the clerk of the court, returnable to the conservator on the termination of his service. Or personal assets of the conservatee may be deposited with a trust company and the bond of the conservator reduced (Prob. Code §2321). The conservator must file an inventory and appraisement of the estate, as of the date of appointment, within 90 days of the date of appointment. The property other than money must be appraised by an inheritance tax referee appointed by the court.

(If any conservatee is confined in a state hospital, the conservator must deliver a copy of the inventory to the State Department of Health in Sacramento.)

The conservatorship continues until the death of the conservatee or until terminated by an order of the court. The court may terminate the conservatorship if it is no longer required, i.e., if the conservator is then able to properly care for himself and his property. The petition for termination may be opposed by any relative or friend. The conservatorship of the estate terminates when the property of the estate has been exhausted.

Accounting

At the end of one year from the date of appointment the conservator must file an account and thereafter not less frequently than biennially an account must be presented to the court for settlement and allowance (Prob. Code §2620).

In Sacramento County the court sends a reminder 60 days before the hearing and the account is to be filed 30 days before the anniversary date.

Notice of hearing on the account is given 15 days prior to the hearing pursuant to Probate Code sections 1460 and 2621.

In most of the counties the investigator looks only at the care of the conservatee, not the account. In Sacramento County the investigator looks at the account and the return, and any variance or decrease in return.

Temporary Conservatorships (Prob. Code §§2250 *et seq.*)

If there are urgent matters requiring action by someone with authority to act, temporary letters of conservatorship may be granted, if a verified petition showing good cause therefor is filed, at the same time or after the petition for appointment of a conservator is filed — but not before. A second filing fee is required and bond must be posted. The power and authority and duties extend only to the temporary care, maintenance and support of the conservatee and his property. If the same person is appointed conservator, he may account for his administration in his first regular account; otherwise, he must account within 90 days of his appointment as conservator.

All the forms used in the "permanent" conservatorship which appear in the foregoing material are used for temporary conservatorships, except that separate forms are provided for the petition, letters and order appointing conservator. The forms needed for Temporary Conservatorships are:

*1. *Petition for Appointment of Temporary Guardian or Conservator;*

2. *Notice of Hearing Guardianship or Conservatorship;*

3. *Notification to Court of Address on Conservatorship or Guardianship* (used in Sacramento County);

4. *Declaration of Medical or Accredited Practitioner;*

5. *Citation for Conservatorship and Proof of Service;*

*6. *Order Appointing Temporary Guardian or Conservator;*

7. *Proof of Service by Mail of Order Appointing Guardian or Conservator;* and

*8. *Letters of Temporary Guardianship or Conservatorship.*

*Forms 1, 6 and 8, used only for temporary appointments, follow:

Petition for Appointment of Temporary Guardian or Conservator

ATTORNEY OR PARTY WITHOUT ATTORNEY (NAME AND ADDRESS):	TELEPHONE NO.:	FOR COURT USE ONLY
ATTORNEY FOR (NAME):		

SUPERIOR COURT OF CALIFORNIA, COUNTY OF SACRAMENTO
STREET ADDRESS: 720 9TH STREET
MAILING ADDRESS:
CITY AND ZIP CODE: SACRAMENTO, CA 95814
BRANCH NAME:

TEMPORARY ☐ GUARDIANSHIP ☐ CONSERVATORSHIP OF (NAME):

☐ Minor ☐ Conservatee

PETITION FOR APPOINTMENT OF TEMPORARY ☐ **GUARDIAN** ☐ **CONSERVATOR** ☐ Person ☐ Estate	CASE NUMBER:

1. Petitioner (name):   requests that
   a. (name and address):

      be appointed temporary ☐ guardian ☐ conservator of the person of the
      proposed ☐ ward ☐ conservatee and Letters issue upon qualification.
   b. (name and address):

      be appointed temporary ☐ guardian ☐ conservator of the estate of the
      proposed ☐ ward ☐ conservatee and Letters issue upon qualification.
   c. ☐ bond not be required for the reasons stated in attachment 1c.
      ☐ bond be fixed at $ _____ to be furnished by an authorized surety company or as
         otherwise provided by law (specify reasons if the amount is different from the minimum required by section
         2320 of the Probate Code).
      ☐ deposits at (specify institution):
         in the amount of $ _____ be allowed. Receipts will be filed.
   d. ☐ the powers specified in attachment 1d be granted in addition to the powers provided by law.
   e. ☐ an order be granted dispensing with notice to the proposed ☐ ward ☐ conservatee for the reasons stated
      in attachment 1e.
   f. ☐ other orders be granted (specify in attachment 1f).
2. The proposed ☐ ward ☐ conservatee is (name):
   (present address):   (telephone):

3. The proposed ☐ ward ☐ conservatee requires a temporary ☐ guardian ☐ conservator to ☐ provide for
   temporary care, maintenance, and support ☐ protect property from loss or injury because (facts are ☐ specified
   below ☐ specified in attachment 3):

(Continued on reverse)

**PETITION FOR APPOINTMENT OF
TEMPORARY GUARDIAN OR CONSERVATOR**

TEMPORARY ☐ GUARDIANSHIP ☐ CONSERVATORSHIP OF (NAME): ☐ Minor ☐ Conservatee	CASE NUMBER:

PETITION FOR APPOINTMENT OF TEMPORARY GUARDIAN OR CONSERVATOR   Page 2

4. The temporary ☐ guardianship ☐ conservatorship is required
   - ☐ pending the hearing on the petition for appointment of a general ☐ guardian ☐ conservator.
   - ☐ pending an appeal pursuant to section 2750 of the Probate Code.
   - ☐ during the suspension of powers of the ☐ guardian ☐ conservator.

5. Character and estimated value of the property of the estate
   - Personal property: $_____
   - Annual gross income from
     - ☐ real property: $_____
     - ☐ personal property: $_____
     - **Total:** $_____
   - Real property: $_____

6. ☐ CHANGE OF RESIDENCE OF PROPOSED CONSERVATEE
   a. ☐ Petitioner requests that the residence of the proposed conservatee be changed to (address):

        The proposed conservatee will suffer irreparable harm if his or her residence is not changed as requested and no means less restrictive of the proposed conservatee's liberty will suffice to prevent the harm because (precise reasons are ☐ stated below ☐ stated in attachment 6a):

   b. ☐ The proposed conservatee must be removed from the State of California to permit the performance of the following nonpsychiatric medical treatment essential to the proposed conservatee's physical survival. The proposed conservatee consents to this medical treatment. (Facts and place of treatment are ☐ specified below ☐ specified in attachment 6b.)

   c. (change of residence only) The proposed conservatee
      - ☐ will attend the hearing.
      - ☐ is able but unwilling to attend the hearing, does not wish to contest the establishment of a conservatorship, does not object to the proposed conservator, and does not prefer that another person act as conservator.
      - ☐ is unable to attend the hearing because of medical inability. An affidavit or certificate of a licensed medical practitioner or an accredited religious practitioner is affixed as attachment 6c.
      - ☐ is not the petitioner, is out of state, and will not attend the hearing.

   d. ☐ (change of residence only) Filed with this petition is a proposed Order Appointing Court Investigator (see Judicial Council form GC-330).

7. Petitioner believes the proposed ☐ ward ☐ conservatee ☐ will ☐ will not attend the hearing.

8. ☐ Number of pages attached:

Dated: . . . .

_____
(Signature of petitioner)

I declare under penalty of perjury under the laws of the State of California that the foregoing is true and correct and that this declaration is executed on (date): . . . . at (place): . . . .

. . . .   _____
(Type or print name)   (Signature of petitioner)

Order Appointing Temporary Guardian or Conservator

	FOR COURT USE ONLY
ATTORNEY OR PARTY WITHOUT ATTORNEY (Name and Address): TELEPHONE NO.:	

ATTORNEY FOR (Name):

SUPERIOR COURT OF CALIFORNIA, COUNTY OF SACRAMENTO
STREET ADDRESS: 720 9TH STREET
MAILING ADDRESS:
CITY AND ZIP CODE: SACRAMENTO, CA   95814
BRANCH NAME:

TEMPORARY ☐ GUARDIANSHIP ☐ CONSERVATORSHIP OF THE ☐ PERSON
☐ ESTATE OF (NAME):
☐ Minor ☐ Conservatee

ORDER APPOINTING TEMPORARY ☐ GUARDIAN ☐ CONSERVATOR

CASE NUMBER:

1. The petition for appointment of temporary ☐ guardian ☐ conservator came on for hearing as follows *(check boxes c and d to indicate personal presence)*:
   a. Judge (name):

   b. Hearing date: Time: ☐ Dept.:   ☐ Div.:   ☐ Room:

   c. ☐ Petitioner (name):
      ☐ Attorney for petitioner (name):

   d. ☐ Minor ☐ Conservatee (name):
      ☐ Attorney for ☐ minor ☐ conservatee (name):

2. THE COURT FINDS
   a. ☐ Notice of time and place of hearing has been given as directed by the court.
      ☐ Notice of time and place of hearing ☐ has been dispensed with ☐ should be dispensed with.

   b. ☐ It is necessary that a temporary ☐ guardian ☐ conservator be appointed to ☐ provide for temporary care, maintenance, and support ☐ protect property from loss or injury
      ☐ pending the hearing on the petition for appointment of a general ☐ guardian ☐ conservator.
      ☐ pending an appeal pursuant to section 2750 of the Probate Code.
      ☐ during the suspension of powers of the ☐ guardian ☐ conservator.

   c. ☐ To prevent irreparable harm, the residence of the conservatee must be changed. No means less restrictive of the conservatee's liberty will prevent irreparable harm.

   d. ☐ The conservatee must be removed from the State of California to permit the performance of nonpsychiatric medical treatment essential to the conservatee's physical survival. The conservatee consents to this medical treatment.

   e. ☐ The conservatee need not attend the hearing on change of residence or removal from the State of California.

(Continued on reverse)

Form Approved by the
Judicial Council of California
Effective January 1, 1981
GC-140(81)

**ORDER APPOINTING
TEMPORARY GUARDIAN OR CONSERVATOR**

TEMPORARY ☐ GUARDIANSHIP ☐ CONSERVATORSHIP (NAME): ☐ Minor ☐ Conservatee	CASE NUMBER:

ORDER APPOINTING TEMPORARY GUARDIAN OR CONSERVATOR   Page 2

3. THE COURT ORDERS
   a. (name):

      (address):   (telephone):

      is appointed temporary ☐ guardian ☐ conservator of the person

      of (name):   and Letters shall issue upon qualification.

   b. (name):

      (address):   (telephone):

      is appointed temporary ☐ guardian ☐ conservator of the estate

      of (name):   and Letters shall issue upon qualification.

   c. ☐ Notice of hearing is dispensed with.

   d. ☐ Bond is not required.
      ☐ Bond is fixed at $_____ to be furnished by an authorized surety company or as
      otherwise provided by law.
      ☐ Deposits shall be made at (specify institution):   in the
      amount of $_____ and receipts filed.

   e. ☐ The conservator is authorized to change the residence of the conservatee to (address):

   f. ☐ The conservator is authorized to remove the conservatee from the State of California to the following address
      to permit the performance of nonpsychiatric medical treatment essential to the conservatee's physical survival
      (address):

   g. ☐ The conservatee need not attend the hearing on change of residence or removal from the State of California.

   h. ☐ In addition to the powers granted by law, the temporary conservator is granted other powers. These powers
      are ☐ specified below ☐ specified in attachment 3h.

   i. ☐ Other orders as specified in attachment 3i are granted.

   j. ☐ Unless modified by further order of the court, this order expires on (date):

4. Number of boxes checked in item 3:
5. ☐ Number of pages attached:

Dated: . . . .   _____
                                                            Judge of the Superior Court
                                                          ☐ Signature follows last attachment

Letters of Temporary Guardianship or Conservatorship

ATTORNEY, OR PARTY WITHOUT ATTORNEY (NAME AND ADDRESS):	TELEPHONE NO.	FOR COURT USE ONLY

ATTORNEY FOR (NAME):

SUPERIOR COURT OF CALIFORNIA, COUNTY OF SACRAMENTO
STREET ADDRESS: 720 9TH STREET
MAILING ADDRESS:
CITY AND ZIP CODE: SACRAMENTO, CA 95814
BRANCH NAME

TEMPORARY ☐ GUARDIANSHIP ☐ CONSERVATORSHIP OF (NAME):

☐ Minor ☐ Conservatee

LETTERS OF TEMPORARY ☐ **GUARDIANSHIP** ☐ **CONSERVATORSHIP** ☐ **Person** ☐ **Estate**	CASE NUMBER

STATE OF CALIFORNIA, COUNTY OF

1. (Name):
   is appointed temporary ☐ guardian
   ☐ conservator of the ☐ person
   ☐ estate of (name):

2. ☐ Other powers have been granted or restrictions
   imposed on the temporary
   ☐ guardian ☐ conservator as
   ☐ specified below ☐ specified in attachment 2

3. These Letters shall expire
   ☐ thirty days after the appointment of the
   temporary ☐ guardian ☐ conservator
   (specify expiration date):
   or upon earlier notice of appointment of a
   general guardian or conservator.
   ☐ other date *(specify):*

Dated: . . . .

Clerk, by _____, Deputy

☐ Number of pages attached:

SEAL

---

4.   AFFIRMATION

I solemnly affirm that I will perform the duties of temporary ☐ guardian ☐ conservator according to law.

Executed on (date) . . . .

at (place): . . . .

(Signature of appointee)

5.   CERTIFICATION

I certify that this document and any attachments is a correct copy of the original on file in my office, and that the Letters issued to the person appointed above have not been revoked, annulled, or set aside and are still in full force and effect.

Dated: . . . .

Clerk, by _____, Deputy

SEAL

Form Approved by the
Judicial Council of California
Effective January 1, 1981
GC-150(81)

**LETTERS OF TEMPORARY
GUARDIANSHIP OR CONSERVATORSHIP**

Order Dispensing With Notice, Guardianship or Conservatorship

ATTORNEY OR PARTY WITHOUT ATTORNEY (NAME AND ADDRESS)   TELEPHONE NO | FOR COURT USE ONLY

ATTORNEY FOR (NAME)

SUPERIOR COURT OF CALIFORNIA, COUNTY OF SACRAMENTO
STREET ADDRESS   720 9TH STREET
MAILING ADDRESS
CITY AND ZIP CODE   SACRAMENTO, CA   95814
BRANCH NAME

☐ GUARDIANSHIP ☐ CONSERVATORSHIP OF (NAME):

☐ Minor ☐ Conservatee

ORDER DISPENSING NOTICE

CASE NUMBER

1. THE COURT FINDS that a petition for (specify):
   has been filed and

   a. ☐ all persons entitled to notice of hearing have ☐ waived notice ☐ consented to the appointment of the
   proposed ☐ guardian ☐ conservator.

   b. ☐ (for guardianship only) the following persons cannot with reasonable diligence be given notice (names):

   c. ☐ (for guardianship only) the giving of notice to the following persons is contrary to the interest of justice
   (names):

   d. ☐ good cause exists for dispensing with notice to the following persons referred to in section 1460(b) of the
   Probate Code (names):

   e. ☐ other (specify):

2. THE COURT ORDERS that notice of hearing on the petition for (specify):

   a. ☐ is not required except to persons requesting special notice under section 2700 of the Probate Code
   b. ☐ is dispensed with to the following persons (names):

Dated: ....

_____
Judge of the Superior Court

Form Approved by the
Judicial Council of California
Effective January 1, 1981
GC-021(81)
**ORDER DISPENSING WITH NOTICE
GUARDIANSHIP OR CONSERVATORSHIP**

LIMITED CONSERVATORSHIPS
Developmentally Disabled Adults

Legislation, effective January 1, 1981, provides for limited conservatorships for developmentally disabled adults. "Developmental disability" is defined as a disability originating before age 18, which continues, or can be expected to continue, indefinitely, and which constitutes a substantial handicap for the individual. The term includes "mental retardation, cerebral palsy, epilepsy, and autism" and handicapping conditions "closely related to mental retardation" or requiring similar treatment, but does not include other handicapping conditions "solely physical in nature."

If such persons are unable to retain legal counsel and request appointment of counsel in a particular matter, or do not retain legal counsel, the court shall appoint the public defender or private counsel in certain proceedings under the act. The proposed conservatee pays for the legal service if able to do so.

The limited conservatorship is to be utilized only as necessary to promote and protect the well-being of the individual, to encourage maximum self-reliance and independence, and shall be ordered only to the extent necessitated by the individual's proven mental and adaptive limitations.

"The conservatee of the limited conservatorship shall not be presumed to be incompetent and shall retain all legal and civil rights except those which by court order have been designated as legal disabilities and have been specifically granted to the limited conservator." (Prob. Code §1801.)

The same forms are used as for a regular conservatorship. Question 5d on the petition has boxes to be checked as to whether the person is or is not developmentally disabled. In some counties they take the position that if you check the box that the person is developmentally disabled, you have to file for a limited conservatorship. In Sacramento County you can check the box yes and still file for a regular conservatorship.

GUARDIANSHIPS
(Prob. Code §§1400, *et seq.*)

A guardian is a person appointed by the court to take care of the person or property of a minor. A guardian may not be appointed for a minor who is married or whose marriage has been dissolved, but a guardian may be appointed for a minor whose marriage has been adjudged a nullity. Certain nonprofit charitable corporations (incorporated in California) may be appointed as guardians. A trust company may be appointed as guardian of the estate only. The one whose person or property is to be cared for is called the "ward" of the guardian.

Parents are natural guardians of their children and need not be appointed by the court for the guardianship of the person of the child. A parent, however, cannot sell his child's property without court approval, or compromise or release a cause of action which the child has. A parent can receive $5,000 if the child's estate does not exceed $5,000. (Prob. Code §3401.) (See Probate Code sections 3410-3413 where the sole asset of the guardianship estate is money, or where the minor has no guardian and there is money belonging to the minor — not in excess of $20,000.)

Also, a parent may nominate a guardian of the person and/or estate of a child (by will or deed) to take effect upon that parent's death with the written consent of the other living parent unless the other parent is incapable of consent, if the other parent's consent would be required for adoption. (See Civ. Code §224.)

One who acts as a general guardian of a minor stands "in loco parentis," that is, in the place of a parent, and must act as a judicious parent would act, and, of course, such duties call for his or her personal attention.

A guardian ad litem is a special guardian, appointed by the court for a particular lawsuit.

Guardians are agents of the court and are appointed by the court. The Probate Code (§1510) provides that a relative or other person may file the petition. Also, a child over 14 years has the right to file a petition for appointment of a guardian, subject to court approval.

The attorney will probably be consulted by the person who wishes to be appointed as guardian of the minor. The legal assistant can obtain the information necessary to prepare the petition.

Guardianship Checklist

1. A Petition for Appointment of Guardian of Minor is filed in the superior court of the county in which the minor resides or has estate.
2. Prepare Notice of Hearing — Guardianship or Conservatorship. (Prob. Code §1511.) Notice is to be given at least 15 days before the hearing.
3. Petition is filed with county clerk; required fee paid.
4. Clerk signs Notice of Hearing — Guardianship.
5. Serve Notice of Hearing and copy of Petition on:
   (a) The person or persons who have custody of minor;

(b) The parents of the ward. Notice need not be given to parents or other relatives if minor has been relinquished to a licensed adoption agency or has been judicially declared free from custody and control of the parents, unless the court orders otherwise (Prob. Code §1511);

(c) The proposed ward if 14 years of age or older;

(d) The person nominated as guardian under Probate Code sections 1500 and 1501.

6. For hearing are prepared:
   (a) Order Appointing Guardian of Minor
       Original and office copy
       1 copy for bonding company if required
   (b) Letters of Guardianship
       Original and office copy
       1 copy to be certified for each bank account and securities

7. Notice is served on the above persons as provided by Code of Civil Procedure sections 415.10 (personal) or 415.30 (mail with acknowledgment) or as authorized by court. Notice is also served by mail or as authorized by court on:
   (a) The spouse, if any, named in the petition
   (b) The person having care of the proposed ward if other than the person having legal custody
   (c) The relatives named in the petition; if petition is for guardian of the estate only court may dispense with notice
   (d) Director of Mental Health or Director of Developmental Services or Director of Social Services if notice required by Probate Code sections 1461 or 1542
   (e) Veterans Administration if ward entitled to veterans' benefits

8. For hearing are prepared:
   (a) Order Appointing Guardian of Minor
       Original and office copy
       1 copy for bonding company if required
   (b) Letters of Guardianship
       Original and office copy
       1 copy to be certified for each bank account and securities
   (c) Guardian's bond. (Prob. Code §§2320, 2321.) The bond must be approved by the judge if it is not a surety company bond. A surety company bond must be in a sum equal to the value of the personal property and probable annual rents, issues and profits of all property belonging to the ward. If the bond is given by individuals, it must be in a sum equal to $2 \times$ the value of the personal property and $2 \times$ the value of the probable annual rents, issues and profits of property belonging to the ward.

The court investigator, probation officer, or domestic relations investigator in the county in which the petition for appointment of a guardian is pending makes an investigation of each case whenever requested by the court. (Prob. Code §1513.)

Termination of Guardianship

The guardianship of a minor terminates upon ward's attaining majority.(Prob. Code §1600.)

The marriage of a ward terminates guardianship of person (Prob. Code §1600) but not necessarily a guardianship of estate.

The guardian of a minor cannot be discharged for 1 year after the minor attains majority. (Prob. Code §2627(b).)

Prepare:

    affidavit for discharge and order

    1 original

    1 office copy

If a surety bond has been filed, the bonding company must be notified.

LPS CONSERVATORSHIPS

LPS conservatorships were established for gravely disabled persons under the Lanterman-Petris-Short Act in 1967. "Gravely disabled" is defined as "a condition in which a person, as a result of a mental disorder, is unable to provide for his basic personal needs for food, clothing, or shelter" or a person who has been found mentally incompetent under section 1370 of the Penal Code and where certain facts exist. (See Welf. & Inst. Code §5008, subd. (h)(2).) A conservator may be appointed when such a person is "unwilling to accept, or incapable of accepting, treatment voluntarily. . . ." (Welf. & Inst. Code, §5352.) The governing provisions are contained in Welfare and Institutions Code sections 5350-5368. The procedure for establishing, administering and terminating conservatorships are the same as provided in Probate Code sections 1400, *et seq.*, with the exceptions listed in Welfare & Institutions Code section 5350.

An LPS conservatorship may be established for a minor. The LPS conservatorship terminates automatically at the end of one year. It can be renewed if needed. If it is not needed at the end of the year, it can be terminated and a petition for conservatorship of the person filed, and the two combined.

The LPS conservator has a power which the conservator in a regular probate conservatorship does not have, i.e., the right to involuntarily detain the conservatee.

Chapter 18

CORPORATIONS

A survey of legal assistants working in corporation law indicates the obvious fact that there are many and varied tasks. Besides review of documents, which plays a large part in the position, the following are the tasks most frequently performed: checking availability of corporate name and reserving name; obtaining corporate seal, minute book, stock certificates; drafting minutes of directors meetings and drafting resolutions to be considered by directors. Also, drafting articles of incorporation, minutes of initial meetings, notice of shareholders meetings and corporate by laws.

These are the beginning tasks but indicate the wide range of direction there is in this field.

BACKGROUND

A corporation is a creation of law, a legal entity, formed for the convenience of its stockholders. A corporation may act only through its officers, members, or designated agents.

A *domestic corporation* is a corporation organized under the laws of the State of California. (Corp. Code §167.)

A *foreign corporation* is a corporation formed under the laws of another state. A foreign corporation may qualify to do business in California, through the Secretary of State's office. (See Corp. Code §2105.)

A corporation has a major advantage: its limited liability. The corporation is liable only to the extent of its assets. The individual shareholder is liable only to the extent of his investment in stock of the corporation.

It also has tax advantages. The corporation is taxed at a lesser rate than individuals. A Subchapter S corporation can pay its profits directly to its shareholders to avoid double taxation; losses can also be passed on to its shareholders. Shareholders are taxed on dividends received from the corporation.

There are two major types of corporations: (1) stock corporations, which issue stock and have shareholders and are formed with the intent of making a profit; (2) nonprofit corporations, without stockholders or owners, formed only for special purposes. They may or may not qualify for tax exemption. These corporations will be discussed in greater detail in this chapter, but first we turn to the stock corporations.

The General Corporation Law (Corp. Code §§100 *et seq.*), effective January 1, 1977, completely revised those provisions of the Corporations Code governing corporations for profit including foreign corporations qualified to do business in California.

The new General Corporation Law repealed the old law as to stock or business corporations but not with respect to nonprofit corporations, cooperative corporations, credit unions or savings and loan associations. Corporations formed prior to January 1, 1977, are not *required* to amend their articles of incorporation but may *elect* to be governed by the provisions of the new law not otherwise applicable by amending their articles to conform in their entirety to its requirements, and must include the statement, "This corporation elects to be governed by all of the provisions of the General Corporation Law effective January 1, 1977 not otherwise applicable to it under Chapter 23 thereof."

The General Corporation Law became applicable to state-chartered banks on January 1, 1979.

An attorney is usually retained for the purpose of incorporation, and a paralegal should be familiar with the procedure for incorporation, and also with forms of minutes and other corporate records. Forms are found in Mason's California Business Practice, Deering's California Codes, Annotated, as well as in other form books. The Secretary of State's office has a few sample forms available as guides.

STOCK CORPORATIONS

Reservation of Name

Incorporators usually have a name in mind for their corporation. Therefore the first step when incorporating is to reserve a name by writing to the Secretary of State's office in Sacramento. Any name may be chosen which is not the same as an established name of a corporation, or so close as to tend to deceive, or a name already reserved for use. (For exceptions see Corporations Code section 201.) The Secretary of State issues a certificate of reservation of corporate name; the fee is $4 (by mail); $6 (over the counter). (Gov. Code §12199.) The name may be reserved for 60 days. (Corp. Code §201.)

Articles of Incorporation
(Corp. Code §§200-202)

One or more natural persons may incorporate by preparing and executing Articles of Incorporation and filing them with the Secretary of State. The articles shall include (Corp. Code §202):

(1) Name of the corporation. (If the corporation is to be a "close" corporation as defined in Corporation Code section 158 (shares to be held by not more than 10 persons), name must contain the word, or abbreviation, of "corporation," "incorporated," or "limited.")

(2) Purpose for which the corporation is formed. One of the two following statements set forth in Corporations Code section 202 must be included, to wit:

(a) "The purpose of the corporation is to engage in any lawful act or activity for which a corporation may be organized under the General Corporation Law of California other than the banking business, the trust company business or the practice of a profession permitted to be incorporated by the California Corporations Code." or

(b) "The purpose of the corporation is to engage in the profession of _____ (with the insertion of a profession permitted to be incorporated by the California Corporations Code) and any other lawful activities (other than the banking or trust company business) not prohibited to a corporation engaging in such professions by applicable laws and regulations."

(3) A statement of purpose prescribed by the applicable provision of the Banking Law, if the corporation is subject to the Banking Law.

(4) If the corporation is subject to the Insurance Code as an insurer, it shall state that the business of the corporation is to be an insurer. No further or additional statement as to the purposes or powers shall be included except by way of limitation or if expressly required by any California law or federal statute or regulation.

(5) Name and address of the initial *agent for service of process* in accordance with Corporations Code section 1502, subdivision (b), which provides for designation of (1) a natural person residing in the state (with complete business or residence address) or (2) a corporation which has filed a certificate as provided in Corporations Code section 1505 (no address shall be set forth).

The prerequisites for a *corporation* which is to be designated for service of process are set forth in Corporations Code section 1505.

An agent designated for service may resign by filing a signed and acknowledged written statement of resignation, whereupon his authority to act as agent ceases. The Secretary of State forthwith gives notice to the corporation addressed to its principal executive office.

When an agent designated for service resigns, or dies, or if a corporate agent resigns, dissolves, withdraws from the state, forfeits its right to transact intrastate business, has its corporate rights, facts and privileges suspended, or ceases to exist, the corporation is required to designate a new agent. (Corp. Code §1504.)

(6) Total *number of shares of stock* the corporation is authorized to issue, if only one class is to be issued.

The concept of par value of shares is eliminated under the new law and therefore the articles should *not* contain a statement of the par value or aggregate par value, or that the shares are without par value.

(7) If corporation is to issue more than one *class of shares*, or if any class is to have two or more *series*, see Corporation Code section 202, subdivision (e)(1)(2)(3).

(8) *Optional provisions* for inclusion in the articles of incorporation are listed in Corporation Code section 204. The provisions in section 204, subdivision (2), shall not be effective unless they are expressly provided for in the articles. The names and addresses of the persons appointed to act as initial directors may be included. (Corp. Code 204, subd. (c).)

The first directors hold office until their successors are elected at an annual meeting of the shareholders and until their successors have been elected and qualified. (Corp. Code §301.)

The inclusion in the articles of the number of directors and the names and addresses of the first directors is optional rather than mandatory under the new law. If they are named, the articles are signed by one of the principals or any other person, who becomes the "incorporator," and after the articles are filed he can adopt bylaws specifying the number of directors and elect them.

FORMAT OF ARTICLES OF INCORPORATION

1. Prepare on 8½" × 11" or legal size paper
2. File the original (ribbon copy)
3. Type on one side of sheet only
4. Do not affix riders to the pages
5. Fasten with ordinary staples (not rivet-type) fasteners
6. Leave a space 2½" × 2½" in upper right hand corner or first page for filing stamp of Secretary of State

NUMBER OF COPIES

Original — file with Secretary of State
1 certified copy — to be retained at principal office of corporation
1 copy for minute book
1 office copy

(1 copy for exhibit for Application for Qualification of Securities, if stock is to be issued)

1 copy to be filed by the corporation in each county where the corporation holds property

A model of articles of incorporation of a stock corporation meeting minimum statutory requirements has been prepared by the Secretary of State's office and may be used as a *guide* for articles of incorporation, and is set out below:

Articles of Incorporation
OF
(CORPORATION NAME)

I

The name of this corporation is _____.

II

The purpose of this corporation is to engage in any lawful act or activity for which a corporation may be organized under the General Corporation Law of California other than the banking business, the trust company business or the practice of a profession permitted to be incorporated by the California Corporations Code.

III

The name and address is in the State of California of this corporation's initial agent for service of process is:

_____

IV

This corporation is authorized to issue only one class of shares of stock; and the total number of shares which this corporation is

authorized to issue is _____.

DATED:_____

_____
(Signature of incorporator)

_____
(Typed name of incorporator)

I hereby declare that I am the person who executed the foregoing Articles of Incorporation, which execution is my act and deed.

_____

[If a close corporation, add to paragraph I: "This corporation is a close corporation."]

In this form the incorporator signs twice and notarization is not necessary. (But see Corp. Code §200.) Questions as to the sufficiency of proposed articles of incorporation may be submitted to the Secretary of State's office for determination.

SIGNING OF ARTICLES OF INCORPORATION

Each incorporator, and each director named in the articles, must sign and acknowledge the articles of incorporation. (Corp. Code §200.)

FILING FEES FOR ARTICLES OF INCORPORATION

The fee for filing articles of incorporation providing for shares is $65. (Gov. Code §12201.)

The copy of the articles of incorporation returned by the Secretary of State will be stamped to show the filing date. The date of filing is the date received — unless the party submitting requests it be held. A document may be filed as of any future date specified up to 90 days after the document's receipt, if the document is actually received at least one business day prior to the date requested. A receipt will also be returned. The articles must be returned, or ascertainment made that the Secretary of State has actually filed the articles, before the corporation may function, as the corporation is not a corporation, and may not function, until the articles are filed. A check should be made to see that all the incorporators have signed, that their signatures have been acknowledged, that all exhibits incorporated by reference are attached, and that the corporate name is exactly the same in all places.

CERTIFIED COPY CHARGES

A charge of $3 is also made for each certified copy of the articles (if the applicant furnishes the copy); if the Secretary of State's office is requested to prepare the copy, the charge is $2 for certifying, plus an additional 30¢ per page. However, at the time of filing the articles (or any other document for which the filing charge is $15 or more), the Secretary of State will compare and certify up to 3 copies thereof without charge provided the copies are submitted with the original to be filed.

FRANCHISE TAX

At the time of filing the articles of incorporation any corporation not otherwise exempt (as nonprofit corporations, see Rev. & Tax Code §23701) must pay a franchise tax deposit of $200 (thereafter payable annually), as provided in Revenue and Taxation Code sections 23221 et seq. and 23153. (Credit unions and certain inactive gold mining corporations pay a $25 tax.) Remittances should be made payable to the Franchise Tax Board but should be mailed to the Secretary of State's office to expedite filing. Exempt corporations should apply directly to the Franchise Tax Board for a tax clearance certificate. Form FTB 3500 (Application for Exemption from Tax) may be obtained from the Franchise Tax Board, 1025 P Street, Sacramento,

California, or from the Secretary of State's office in Sacramento or Los Angeles.

Qualifying documents may be filed in either Los Angeles or Sacramento but when filed in Los Angeles office, must be presented in person by attorney, his client or a messenger, and are subject to a $5 special handling fee, as are documents presented over the counter in Sacramento.

Summary of Typical Fees for Incorporating

For a stock corporation (amount of stock issued without limit)

Filing articles of incorporation	$ 65.00
Franchise tax [for minimum amount of stock]	200.00
[3 certified copies of articles of incorporation are furnished free if sent at the same time as the articles of incorporation are mailed]	
	$265.00

Statement Required

Every domestic corporation is required to file a statement with the Secretary of State within 90 days after the filing of its original articles of incorporation and annually thereafter during the applicable filing period (the calendar month during which its original articles were filed and the 5 calendar months immediately preceding) containing:

1. The number of vacancies on the board, if any;

2. The names and complete business or residence addresses of its incumbent directors;

3. The names and complete business or residence addresses of its chief executive officer, secretary and chief financial officer;

4. The street address of its principal executive office;

5. If the address of its principal executive office is not in this state, the street address of its principal business office in this state, if any; and

6. A statement of the general type of business which constitutes the principal business activity of the corporation (for example, manufacture of aircraft; wholesale liquor distributor; retail department store).

Whenever any of the above information is *changed,* the corporation may file a *current* statement containing all this information and designating its agent for service required under Corporations Code section 1502(b). In order to *change* its agent for service of process, a similar statement must be filed. The Secretary of State may destroy any superseded statement.

The Secretary of State is required to mail a form for compliance with Corporations Code section 1502 approximately three months prior to the close of the applicable filing period. If the corporation fails to file its annual statement, the Secretary of State is required to mail a notice of delinquency to the corporation, in which the corporation is advised of the penalty ($250) for failure to timely file (60 days after mailing of notice of delinquency) and of its right to request relief because of reasonable cause or unusual circumstances justifying the failure to file or, if the Secretary of State does not grant relief, to pay the penalty under protest and file a claim with the Board of Control. If the statement is not timely filed, the name of the corporation is certified to the Franchise Tax Board and the penalty assessed.

Failure of the corporation to receive the form for compliance is not an excuse for failure to comply with the section. If the failure to provide notice of delinquency was due to an error of the Secretary of State, the Secretary of State will promptly decertify the corporation's name to the Franchise Tax Board and the Franchise Tax Board will abate the penalty. (Corp. Code §§1502 and 2204.)

Corporations Code section 2205 provides for suspension of corporate powers, rights and privileges where a corporation has failed to file a statement pursuant to section 1502 for an applicable filing period, has not filed such statement during the preceding 24 months, and was certified for penalty under section 2204 for the same filing period of the prior year.

The form of Statement follows:

Statement by Domestic Stock Corporation

P.O. Box 2830 Sacramento, CA 95812 Phone: (916) 445-2020	March Fong Eu Secretary of State	DO NOT WRITE IN THIS SPACE

STATE OF CALIFORNIA

STATEMENT BY DOMESTIC STOCK CORPORATION

THIS STATEMENT MUST BE FILED WITH
CALIFORNIA SECRETARY OF STATE (SEC. 1502, CORPORATIONS CODE)

PLEASE READ INSTRUCTIONS ON BACK OF FORM.

PLEASE TYPE OR USE BLACK INK WHICH WOULD BE SUITABLE FOR MICROFILMING.

FEE FOR FILING THIS STATEMENT – $5.00.

1.

DO NOT ALTER PREPRINTED NAME, IF ITEM 1 IS BLANK PLEASE ENTER CORPORATE NAME.

THE CORPORATION NAMED HEREIN, ORGANIZED UNDER THE LAWS OF THE STATE OF CALIFORNIA, MAKES THE FOLLOWING STATEMENT:

2. STREET ADDRESS OF PRINCIPAL EXECUTIVE OFFICE	SUITE OR ROOM	2A.	2B.
(DO NOT USE P.O. BOX NO.)		CITY	ZIP CODE
3. STREET ADDRESS OF PRINCIPAL BUSINESS OFFICE IN CALIF. (IF ANY)	SUITE OR ROOM	3A.	3B.
(DO NOT USE P.O. BOX NO.)		CALIF.	ZIP CODE
4. MAILING ADDRESS (OPTIONAL)	SUITE OR ROOM	4A.	4B.
		CITY AND STATE	ZIP CODE

NAMES OF THE FOLLOWING OFFICERS ARE:

5.	5A.	5B.	5C.
CHIEF EXECUTIVE OFFICER	BUSINESS OR RESIDENCE ADDRESS (DO NOT USE P.O. BOX)	CITY AND STATE	ZIP CODE
6.	6A.	6B.	6C.
SECRETARY	BUSINESS OR RESIDENCE ADDRESS (DO NOT USE P.O. BOX)	CITY AND STATE	ZIP CODE
7.	7A.	7B.	7C.
CHIEF FINANCIAL OFFICER	BUSINESS OR RESIDENCE ADDRESS (DO NOT USE P.O. BOX)	CITY AND STATE	ZIP CODE

8. NAMES AND COMPLETE BUSINESS OR RESIDENCE ADDRESS OF INCUMBENT DIRECTORS INCLUDING THOSE DIRECTORS WHO ARE ALSO OFFICERS. (Attach a supplemental list of directors if needed.)

A.			
NAME	BUSINESS OR RESIDENCE ADDRESS (DO NOT USE P.O. BOX)	CITY AND STATE	ZIP CODE
B.			
NAME	BUSINESS OR RESIDENCE ADDRESS (DO NOT USE P.O. BOX)	CITY AND STATE	ZIP CODE
C.			
NAME	BUSINESS OR RESIDENCE ADDRESS (DO NOT USE P.O. BOX)	CITY AND STATE	ZIP CODE
D.			
NAME	BUSINESS OR RESIDENCE ADDRESS (DO NOT USE P.O. BOX)	CITY AND STATE	ZIP CODE
E.			
NAME	BUSINESS OR RESIDENCE ADDRESS (DO NOT USE P.O. BOX)	CITY AND STATE	ZIP CODE

9. THE NUMBER OF VACANCIES ON THE BOARD, IF ANY [   ]

10.

AGENT FOR SERVICE OF PROCESS:

CALIFORNIA BUSINESS OR RESIDENCE ADDRESS IF AN INDIVIDUAL. ONLY ONE AGENT CAN BE NAMED. DO NOT INCLUDE ADDRESS IF AGENT IS A CORPORATION. (DO NOT USE P.O. BOX)

11. (EXPLANATION MUST BE BRIEF)

TYPE OF BUSINESS:

12. I DECLARE THAT I HAVE EXAMINED THIS STATEMENT AND TO THE BEST OF MY KNOWLEDGE AND BELIEF, IT IS TRUE, CORRECT AND COMPLETE.

DATE	TITLE	SIGNATURE OF CORPORATE OFFICER OR AGENT

FORM S/O 200

SECRETARY OF STATE
P.O. BOX 2830, SACRAMENTO 95812

INSTRUCTIONS FOR COMPLETING STATEMENT BY DOMESTIC STOCK CORPORATION

FILING PERIOD: All corporations must file within 90 days after filing articles of incorporation. Thereafter, corporations must file annually by the end of the calendar month of the anniversary date of its incorporation, or when the agent for service of process or his/her address is changed.

FILING FEE: All corporations must submit a five dollar ($5.00) filing fee with this statement. (Section 12210, Government Code.) Check or money order should be made payable to Secretary of State. Please do not send cash.

ITEMS 2-2B: The address to be entered is the STREET address of the corporation's principal executive office. Enter room or suite number and zip code. Do not use post office box number.

ITEMS 3-3B: Complete this item only if the address in Item 2 is outside California. The address to be entered is the STREET address of the corporation's principal office in CALIFORNIA, if any. Do not use post office box number.

ITEMS 4-4B: The address to be entered is the MAILING ADDRESS for the corporation.

ITEMS 5-7C Complete by entering the names and complete business or residence addresses of the corporation's chief executive officer (i.e., president), secretary, and chief financial officer (i.e., treasurer). The corporation must have these three officers in accordance with Section 312, Corporations Code. Any of the offices may be held by the same person unless the articles or bylaws provide otherwise. No list of additional officers should be submitted. Do not use post office box numbers.

ITEMS 8-8E: Enter the names and complete business or residence addresses of the incumbent directors. Do not use post office box numbers. Attach a supplemental list of directors if necessary.

ITEM 9: Enter the number of vacancies on the board, if any.

ITEM 10: Section 1502(b), Corporations Code, makes it mandatory that domestic corporations designate an agent for service of process. An agent for service of process is one who may accept papers in case of a law suit against the corporation. The agent may be an individual who is an officer or director of the corporation, or any other person. The person named as agent must be a resident of California. Only one individual may be named as agent for service of process. Or, the agent may be another corporation. However, a corporation named as agent for service of process for another corporation must have on file in this office, a certificate pursuant to Section 1505, Corporations Code. The certificate is required ONLY if a corporation is named as agent for service of process for other corporations. A CORPORATION CANNOT BE NAMED AS AGENT FOR SERVICE OF PROCESS FOR ITSELF. (For example, ABC Corporation cannot name ABC Corporation as its agent for service of process.)

At the agent is a person, enter name and complete business or residence address. If agent is another corporation, enter name of corporation only, and do not complete address portion. Only one agent for service of process is to be named.

ITEM 11: Complete by entering a statement of the general type of business which constitutes the principal business activity of the corporation. Explanation must be brief. (Examples: Manufacturer of aircraft. Wholesale liquor distributor. Retail department store.)

ITEM 12: Signature of corporate officer or agent is required to complete the form. Enter title and date signed.

(NOTE) ITEM 1: Do not alter the preprinted corporate name. If corporation name is not correct, please attach note of explanation. If space is blank enter exact corporate name and number, do not include your DBA name.

If the corporation has never done business and corporate officers have not been chosen, a statement of such fact should be set out in Item 8. In any case the name and address of the agent must be completed in Item 10. If the corporation does not maintain an actual office, the address in Item 2-B should be c/o one of the directors or the agent. It is required that a corporation file a statement even though it may not be actively engaged in business at the time the statement is due.

FAILURE TO FILE THIS FORM BY THE PREPRINTED DUE DATE IN ITEM 1 WILL RESULT IN THE ASSESSMENT OF A $250 PENALTY. (Section 2204, Corporations Code, and Section 25936, Revenue and Taxation Code.)

NOTE: Your canceled check is your receipt of filing. We suggest that you make a copy of this form before mailing, if you wish one for your files.

Amendment of Articles of Incorporation

Articles of incorporation may be amended. A fee of $15 is charged for filing the certificates of amendment. (See Corp. Code §§900-910; Gov. Code §12202.)

To accomplish an amendment after issuance of shares, a formal officers' certificate of amendment meeting the minimum requirements of Corporations Code section 905 must be filed. (See also, Corp. Code §907.) "The certificate of amendment must identify the particular provision to be amended strictly in accordance with the numerical or other designation given such provision in the articles, or by quoting the wording of the provision as it presently appears in the articles and must set forth the wording of that provision in full as amended. The certificate must also show that the amendment has been adopted by the board of directors and shareholders and must state the number of shares outstanding. The certificate must be signed and verified by the president and secretary, or corresponding officers of the corporation." (Sec/State Form LL-75 (12-79).)

The sample form issued by the Secretary of State is:

CERTIFICATE OF AMENDMENT
OF
ARTICLES OF INCORPORATION

JOHN DOE AND RICHARD ROE certify that:
1. They are the president and secretary, respectively, of ABC STOCK CORPORATION, a California Corporation.*
2. Article (insert correct designation) of the articles of incorporation of this corporation is amended to read as follows:
     (here set out the article as amended)
3. The foregoing amendment of articles of incorporation has been duly approved by the board of directors.
4. The foregoing amendment of articles of incorporation has been duly approved by the required vote of shareholders in accordance with Section 902 of the Corporations Code. The total number of outstanding shares of the corporation is _____. The number of shares voting in favor of the amendment equaled or exceeded the vote required. The percentage vote required was more than 50%.

JOHN DOE, President

RICHARD ROE, Secretary

---

*A certificate of amendment may be signed by the President, Chairman of the Board or Vice-President AND the Secretary, Assistant Secretary, Chief Financial Officer, Treasurer or Assistant Treasurer. The same two officers who sign the certificate of amendment must sign the declaration under penalty of perjury.

The undersigned declare under penalty of perjury that the matters set forth in the foregoing certificate are true of their own knowledge.

Executed at _____(City and State)_____ on _____(Date)_____ .

_____

JOHN DOE

_____

RICHARD ROE

Bylaws (Corp. Code §§211-213)

The bylaws may make provisions not in conflict with law or the corporation's articles of incorporation, including but not limited to:

1. Any provision referred to in subdivisions (b), (c) or (d) of section 204 [containing optional provisions for inclusion in articles of incorporation]

2. The time, place and manner of calling, conducting and giving notice of shareholders', directors' and committee meetings

3. Manner of execution, revocation and use of proxies

4. Qualifications, duties and compensation of directors; time of their annual election; requirements of a quorum for directors and for committee meetings

5. Appointment and authority of committees of the board

6. Appointment, duties, compensation and tenure of officers

7. Mode of determination of holders of record of its shares

8. Making of annual reports and financial statements to the shareholders. (See Corp. Code §212.)

Minute Book

Corporations Code section 1500 requires a corporation to keep minutes of the proceedings of its shareholders, board and committees of the board.

The minutes usually include:

1. The time and place of all such meetings

2. Whether a regular or special meeting, and if special, how authorized

3. The notice of the meeting given

4. Names of those present at the directors' meetings

5. The number of shares or members present represented at shareholders' or members' meetings

6. Proceedings of the meetings, including any votes taken by the board of directors.

Before the first meeting of the Board of Directors a Waiver of Notice and Consent to Holding of First Meeting of Board of Directors of the corporation should be signed by all the directors and placed in the minute book preceding the minutes of that meeting. This form might be drafted by the legal assistant but is usually contained in the kit.

If the initial Board of Directors is not named in the articles of incorporation, the incorporators are empowered under Corporations Code section 210 to do whatever is necessary, including adoption of bylaws.

The minimum and maximum number of directors is provided by Corporations Code section 212 and the number shall be set forth in the bylaws. In brief:

> 1 shareholder — 1 director, minimum
> 2 shareholders — 2 directors, minimum
> All others — 3 directors, minimum

The original or a copy of the bylaws must be kept in the corporation's principal executive office and be open to inspection by shareholders at all reasonable times during office hours. (Corp. Code §213.)

Stock

Corporations formed for purposes of profit will issue shares of stock, at the time of incorporation or later. The owners of the shares of stock have an interest in the corporation itself, that is, the owner has the right to participate in the profits and, if the corporation is dissolved, a right to share in the distribution of its assets. However, stockholders have no right to perform corporate acts; the directors control the business of the corporation.

If stock is to be issued at time of incorporation or later, after the corporation is formed, a Notice of Issuance of Shares Pursuant to Subdivision (h) of section 25102 of the California Corporations Code is obtained from the Corporation Commissioner's office and completed and mailed to his office, 1025 P Street, Sacramento, California 95814, with the required exhibits.

A fee of $25 should accompany the Notice. The form should be read carefully. It should be noted that an attorney *must* sign the Opinion of Counsel on the reverse side. The form follows:

Notice of Issuance of Shares

(Dept. of Corporations Use Only)	Dept. of Corporations File No., If Any
Fee Paid $ _____	
Receipt No. _____	(Insert File Number(s) of Previous Filings Before the Department, If Any)
	FEE: $25.00

TO THE COMMISSIONER OF CORPORATIONS OF
THE STATE OF CALIFORNIA

Notice of Issuance of Shares Pursuant to Subdivision (h) of
Section 25102 of the California Corporations Code

Name of Issuer

State of Incorporation

Address of Principal Place of Business
Number and Street   City   State   Zip Code

1. Is the issuer a "close corporation" as defined in Section 260.001, Title 10, California Administrative Code? ☐ Yes   ☐ No

   Instruction: Review Corporations Code Section 158 and Rule 260.001, Title 10, California Administrative Code.

2. Under the exemption provided by Section 25102(h), shares of voting common stock have been or are proposed to be issued pursuant to this Notice beneficially to not more than 10 persons, whose names are set forth below; together with the names of the corresponding record shareholders if other than the beneficial shareholders:

   _____   _____
   _____   _____
   _____   _____
   _____   _____
   _____   _____

3. Immediately after the issuance and sale of such shares, the above-named issuer had or will have only one class of stock outstanding which was or will be owned beneficially by no more than 10 persons.

   Instruction: Review Sections 260.102.4 and 260.102.5, Title 10, California Administrative Code.

4. The offer and sale of such shares was not nor will be accompanied by the publication of any advertisement and neither selling expenses nor promotional considerations were or will be given, paid or incurred in connection therewith.

260.102.8(7/80)

-1-

5. To the best knowledge of the issuer, its shareholders (or proposed shareholders) have not entered into or granted, and presently do not intend entering into or granting, a shareholders' agreement, voting agreement, irrevocable proxy or other arrangement the effect of which would cause the statements contained herein to be incorrect.

Instruction: Review Sections 260.001 and 260.102.4, Title 10, California Administrative Code.

6. Pursuant to the requirements of Section 260.102.6 of Title 10 of the California Administrative Code, all certificates evidencing such shares bear or will bear on their face the legend required by Section 260.141.11, and a copy of Section 260.141.11 has been or will be delivered to each issuee or transferee of the shares.

The undersigned officer of the issuer hereby declares that the foregoing is true under penalty of perjury. Executed at _____, _____ this _____ day of _____, 19__.

_____
Name

_____
Title

NOTE: If the officer signs this form in a jurisdiction which does not permit verifications under penalty of perjury, there must be attached a verification executed and sworn to before a notary public.

OPINION OF COUNSEL

I certify that I am an active member of the State Bar of California. On the basis of the facts stated in the foregoing Notice and other information, including representations as to the type of consideration received or to be received, supplied to me by officials and shareholders of the issuer and by proposed issuees, it is my opinion that the exemption from qualification with the Commissioner of Corporations provided by Subdivision (h) of Section 25102 of the California Corporations Code is available for the offer and sale of the shares referred to in this Notice.

_____   _____
Signature   Firm Name

_____   _____
Name of Member of the State Bar   Address   Tel. No.
of California

(This opinion of counsel must be signed by an active member of the State Bar of California. Type name of attorney, address, phone number and firm name, if any.)

NOTE: If the issuer is a non-California corporation, a Consent to Service of Process as prescribed in the Commissioner's Rule 102.8(b) must be filed concurrently.

Copies of Section 260.141.11 suitable for attachment to share certificates are available from the Department (see Item 6).

-2-

Those corporations intending to offer securities for sale must file an Application for Qualification of Securities Under the Corporate Securities Law of 1968 (commencing at Corp. Code §25000). Lengthy instructions accompany the form. Other rules are found in Title 10 of the California Administrative Code.

A form of Consent to Service of Process and a Customer Authorization of Disclosure of Financial Records may be required also.

Dissolution — Voluntary
(Corp. Code §§1900-1907)

The voluntary dissolution of California corporations is initiated by an election to dissolve. The election to dissolve may be made only by the vote or written consent of the shareholders holding at least 50 percent of the outstanding shares. If a business corporation has not issued shares, the election to dissolve may be made by the board of directors.

Once the election to dissolve has been made, a Certificate of Election to Dissolve must be prepared and filed in the Secretary of State's office. If the election was made by the board of directors (rather than the shareholders), the certificate must set forth the facts showing that the board of directors is entitled to make the election.

Corporations Code section 1900 also provides that a corporation may elect to wind up and dissolve where (1) an order of relief has been entered under a Chapter 7 bankruptcy proceeding, (2) a corporation has issued no shares, (3) the corporation has disposed of all its assets and has not conducted any business for five years preceding the adoption of the resolution to dissolve.

Brief Summary of Steps of Incorporation of Stock Corporation, for Legal Assistant

1. Check to see if the name desired is available. Send fee to Secretary of State and reserve name.
2. Within 60 days prepare articles of incorporation.
3. Arrange for signature and acknowledgment of articles.
4. Submit articles to Secretary of State with fees.
5. Make arrangements for a minute book (order kit).
6. Draft bylaws (or complete printed form).
7. Draft minutes of first meeting of directors (or complete printed form).
8. Prepare for first meeting of incorporators or board of directors.
9. If Subchapter S election, prepare minutes.
10. If stock is to be issued file Notice of Issuance of Shares of Stock.

11. Within 90 days of filing prepare and file statement to comply with Corporations Code section 1505.

See Function of Paralegal chart (Corporations) in Chapter 2.

NONPROFIT, NONSTOCK CORPORATIONS

Nonprofit, nonstock corporations are organized under the Nonprofit Corporation Law commencing at Corporations Code sections 5000, *et seq.*, and are of three basic types:

(1) Religious,
(2) Public benefit, which includes
    (a) Corporations organized for charitable or public purposes, planning tax exempt status under Revenue & Taxation Code section 2370ld or Internal Revenue Code section 501(c)(3)
    (b) Civic leagues or social welfare organizations, planning tax exempt status under Revenue & Taxation Code section 23701d or Internal Revenue Code section 501(c)(4).
(3) Mutual benefit (corporations other than religious, charitable, civic league or social welfare), planning tax exempt status under provisions other than Revenue & Taxation Code sections 23701d, 23701f, Internal Revenue Code sections 501(c)(3) or 501(c)(4). Upon dissolution, permits distribution of assets to members.

Duties a legal assistant may be called on to perform are on page 34. Also see Chapter 2, Functions of a Paralegal.

Categorization of Nonprofit Corporations

Corporations Code section 9912 makes all organizations formerly subject to prior nonprofit law, and corporations of a type so designated, subject either to the new (1) public benefit corporation law, (2) the mutual benefit corporation law, or (3) the new religious corporation law.

Any corporation organized "primarily or exclusively" for religious purposes is subject to the new religious corporation law (Corp. Code §§9110-9690). (Corp. Code §9912(a)(2).)

Any other corporation (such as a charity or public purpose nonprofit corporation) which has received an exemption under Revenue and Taxation Code section 23701d is subject to the new public benefit corporation law (Corp. Code §§5110-6910). A corporation which has all of its assets dedicated to charitable or public purposes and which, upon dissolution, must distribute its assets to a person or persons carrying on a similar purpose or purposes, is also subject to the new public benefit law (Corp. Code §9912(a)(4).

All other corporations (such as recreation or social clubs) are categorized as nonprofit mutual benefit corporations. (Corp. Code §9912(a)(5),(6).)

Statement

Each nonprofit corporation is required to file an annual statement (as do the stock corporations), pursuant to Corporations Code section 8210. The form follows:

Statement by Domestic Non-Profit Corporation

P.O. Box 2830 Sacramento, CA 95812 Phone: (916) 445-2020	**STATE OF CALIFORNIA**	March Fong Eu Secretary of State	DO NOT WRITE IN THIS SPACE

STATEMENT BY DOMESTIC NON-PROFIT CORPORATION

THIS STATEMENT MUST BE FILED WITH
CALIFORNIA SECRETARY OF STATE (SECTIONS 6210, 8210, 9660 CORPORATIONS CODE)

PLEASE READ INSTRUCTIONS ON BACK OF FORM.
PLEASE TYPE OR USE BLACK INK WHICH WOULD BE SUITABLE FOR MICROFILMING.
FEE FOR FILING THIS STATEMENT – $2.50.

DO NOT ALTER PREPRINTED NAME. IF ITEM 1 IS BLANK, PLEASE ENTER CORPORATE NAME

NOTICE OF NEW LAW:

EFFECTIVE JANUARY 1, 1980 ALL NON-PROFIT CORPORATIONS MUST FILE WITHIN 90 DAYS AFTER FILING ARTICLES OF INCORPORATION AN ANNUAL STATEMENT. THEREAFTER, CORPORATIONS MUST FILE ANNUALLY BY THE END OF THE CALENDAR MONTH OF THE ANNIVERSARY DATE OF ITS INCORPORATION. A TWO DOLLAR AND FIFTY CENT ($2.50) FILING FEE MUST ACCOMPANY THIS STATEMENT. THE LAW ALSO PROVIDES THAT THE FAILURE TO FILE THIS STATEMENT WILL RESULT IN THE ASSESSMENT OF A FIFTY DOLLAR ($50) PENALTY.

THE CORPORATION NAMED HEREIN, ORGANIZED UNDER THE LAWS OF THE STATE OF CALIFORNIA, MAKES THE FOLLOWING STATEMENT:

[Form fields: Street address of principal office, mailing address, names of officers — Chief Executive Officer, Secretary, Chief Financial Officer, Agent for Service of Process, declaration and signature lines.]

FORM S/C 105

SECRETARY OF STATE
P.O. BOX 2830, SACRAMENTO 95812

INSTRUCTIONS FOR COMPLETING STATEMENT BY DOMESTIC NON-PROFIT CORPORATION

FILING PERIOD: All Non-Profit Corporations must file within 90 days after filing articles of incorporation. Thereafter, corporations must file annually by the end of the calendar month of the anniversary date of its incorporation, or when the agent for service of process or his/her address is changed.

FILING FEE: All Non-Profit Corporations must submit a TWO DOLLAR-FIFTY CENT ($2.50) filing fee with this statement. (Section 12210(B) Government Code.) Check or money order should be made payable to Secretary of State. PLEASE DO NOT SEND CASH.

ITEMS 2-2B: The address to be entered is the STREET address of the corporation's principal office. Enter room or suite number and zip code. Do not use post office box number.

ITEMS 3-3B: The address to be entered is the MAILING ADDRESS for the corporation.

ITEMS 4-6C: Complete by entering the names and complete business or residence addresses of the corporation's chief executive officer (i.e., president, chairperson or other title), secretary, and chief financial officer (i.e., treasurer, chairperson or other title). No list of additional officers should be submitted. Do not use post office box numbers.

ITEM 7: Sections 6210, 8210 of the Corporations Code, makes it mandatory that domestic Non-Profit Corporations designate an agent for service of process. An agent for service of process is one who may accept papers in case of a law suit against the corporation. The agent may be an individual who is an officer or director of the corporation, or any other person. The person named as agent must be a resident of California. Only one individual may be named as agent for service of process. Or, the agent may be another corporation. However, a corporation named as agent for service of process for another corporation must have on file in this office, a certificate pursuant to Section 1505, Corporations Code. The certificate is required ONLY if a corporation is named as agent for service of process for other corporations. A CORPORATION CANNOT BE NAMED AS AGENT FOR SERVICE OF PROCESS FOR ITSELF. (For example, ABC Corporation cannot name ABC Corporation as its agent for service of process.)

If the agent is a person, enter name and complete business or residence address. If agent is another corporation, enter name of corporation only, and do not complete address portion. Only one agent for service of process is to be named.

ITEM 8: Signature of corporate officer or agent is required to complete the form. Enter title and date signed.

(NOTE) ITEM 1: Do not alter the preprinted corporate name. If corporation name is not correct, please attach note of explanation. If space is blank enter exact corporate name and number, do not include your DBA name.

If the corporation has never done business and corporate officers have not been chosen, a statement of such fact should be set out in Item 5. In any case the name and address of the agent must be completed in Item 7. It is required that a corporation file a statement even though it may not be actively engaged in business at the time the statement is due.

FAILURE TO FILE THIS FORM BY THE DUE DATE IN ITEM 1 WILL RESULT IN THE ASSESSMENT OF A PENALTY. (Sections 6810, 8810, Corporations Code, and Section 25936, Revenue and Taxation Code.)

NOTE: Your canceled check is your receipt of filing. We suggest that you make a copy of this form before mailing, if you wish one for your files.

Articles of Incorporation

The articles of incorporation shall contain

(a) The name of the corporation

(b) The name and address of the initial agent for service of process.

(c) The language specified in the respective code section stating that it is a nonprofit corporation and designating its type:

Nonprofit public benefit

"This corporation is a nonprofit public benefit corporation and is not organized for the private gain of any person. It is organized under the Nonprofit Public Benefit Corporation Law for (public or charitable [insert one or both]) purposes.

"[If the purposes include 'public' purposes, the articles shall, and in all other cases the articles may, include a further description of the corporation's purposes.]" (Corp. Code §5130(b).)

Nonprofit mutual benefit

"This corporation is a nonprofit mutual benefit corporation organized under the Nonprofit Mutual Benefit Corporation Law. The purpose of this corporation is to engage in any lawful act or activity for which a corporation may be organized under such law.

"[The articles may include a further description of the corporation's purposes.]" (Corp. Code §7130(b).)

Nonprofit religious

"This corporation is a religious corporation and is not organized for the private gain of any person. It is organized under the Nonprofit Religious Corporation Law (primarily or exclusively [insert one or both]) for religious purposes." [The articles may include a further description of the corporation's purposes.] (Corp. Code §9130(b).)

All three types of nonprofit corporations may include the following optional provisions in their articles of incorporation:

(1) Names and addresses of initial directors.

(2) Classes of members, if any, and rights, privileges, preferences, restrictions and conditions of each class.

(3) Provisions allowing any member to have more or less than one vote.

(4) Any other provision not in conflict with law for management of activities and conduct of affairs, including any provision required or permitted in the bylaws.

In addition, mutual benefit nonprofit corporations may include provisions concerning transfer of memberships, in accordance with section 7320. (Corp. Code §§5132(c), 7132(c)(2), 9132(c).)

The above provisions as to articles do not apply to nonprofit corporations existing on December 31, 1979, unless the corporation files an amendment to its articles electing to be governed under the new law.

The new law governs these corporations in all other respects. Therefore counsel for nonprofit corporations in existence before December 31, 1979, should review the articles of these corporations and consider whether amendment might not be needed or desirable. The legal assistant can, of course, assist in the review and amendment.

Sample Articles

Sample copies issued by the Secretary of State's office for each type of nonprofit corporation are included here, as guides:

1. *Religious*

ARTICLES OF INCORPORATION
OF
(CORPORATION NAME)

I

The name of this corporation is _____.

II

This corporation is a religious corporation and is not organized for the private gain of any person. It is organized under the Nonprofit Religious Corporation Law exclusively for religious purposes.

III

The name and address in the State of California of this corporation's initial agent for service of process is: _____.

IV

A. This corporation is organized and operated exclusively for religious purposes within the meaning of Section 501(c)(3) of the Internal Revenue Code.

B. Notwithstanding any other provision of these articles, the corporation shall not carry on any other activities not permitted to be carried on (a) by a corporation exempt from federal income tax under Section 501(c)(3) of the Internal Revenue Code or (b) by a corporation contributions to which are deductible under Section 170(c)(2) of the Internal Revenue Code.

C. No substantial part of the activities of this corporation shall consist of carrying on propaganda, or otherwise attempting to influence legislation, and the corporation shall not participate or intervene in any political campaign (including the publishing or distribution of statements) on behalf of any candidate for public office.

V

The property of this corporation is irrevocably dedicated to religious or charitable purposes and no part of the net income or assets of this corporation shall ever inure to the benefit of any director, officer or member thereof or to the benefit of any private person. Upon the dissolution or winding up of the corporation, its assets remaining after payment, or provision for payment, of all debts and liabilities of this corporation shall be distributed to a nonprofit fund, foundation or corporation which is organized and operated exclusively for religious or charitable purposes and which has established its tax exempt status under Section 501(c)(3) of the Internal Revenue Code.

DATED: _____.

_____
(Signature of Incorporator)

_____
(Typed Name of Incorporator)

I hereby declare that I am the person who executed the foregoing Articles of Incorporation, which execution is my act and deed.

_____
(Signature of Incorporator)

2. *Mutual Benefit*

ARTICLES OF INCORPORATION
OF
(CORPORATION NAME)

I

The name of this corporation is _____.

II

A. This corporation is a nonprofit mutual benefit corporation organized under the Nonprofit Mutual Benefit Corporation Law. The purpose of this corporation is to engage in any lawful act or activity for which a corporation may be organized under such law.

B. The specific purpose of this corporation is to _____.

III

The name and address in the State of California of this corporation's initial agent for service of process is: _____.

IV

Notwithstanding any of the above statements of purposes and powers, this corporation shall not, except to an insubstantial degree, engage in any activities or exercise any powers that are not in furtherance of the specific purposes of this corporation.

DATED: _____

_____
(Signature of Incorporator)

_____
(Typed name of Incorporator)

I hereby declare that I am the person who executed the foregoing Articles of Incorporation, which execution is my act and deed.

_____
(Signature of Incorporator)

3. *Nonprofit public benefit*

ARTICLES OF INCORPORATION
OF
(CORPORATION NAME)

I

The name of this corporation is _____.

II

A. This corporation is a nonprofit public benefit corporation and is not organized for the private gain of any person. It is organized under the Nonprofit Public Benefit Corporation Law for charitable purposes.

B. The specific purpose of this corporation is to _____.

III

The name and address in the State of California of this corporation's initial agent for service of process is: _____

IV

A. This corporation is organized and operated exclusively for charitable purposes within the meaning of Section 501(c)(3) of the Internal Revenue Code.

B. Notwithstanding any other provision in these articles, the corporation shall not carry on any other activities not permitted to be carried on (a) by a corporation exempt from federal income tax under Section 501(c)(3) of the Internal Revenue Code or (b) by a corporation contributions to which are deductible under Section 170(c)(2) of the Internal Revenue Code.

C. No substantial part of the activities of this corporation shall consist of carrying on propaganda, or otherwise attempting to influence legislation, and the corporation shall not participate or intervene in any political campaign (including the publishing or distribution of statements) on behalf of any candidate for public office.

V

The property of this corporation is irrevocably dedicated to charitable purposes and no part of the net income or assets of this corporation shall ever inure to the benefit of any director, officer or member thereof or to the benefit of any private person. Upon the dissolution or winding up of the corporation, its assets remaining after payment, or provision for payment, of all debts and liabilities of this corporation shall be distributed to a nonprofit fund, foundation or corporation which is organized and operated exclusively for charitable purposes and which has established its tax exempt status under Section 501(c)(3) of the Internal Revenue Code.

DATED: _____

_____
(Signature of Incorporator)

_____
(Typed name of Incorporator)

I hereby declare that I am the person who executed the foregoing Articles of Incorporation, which execution is my act and deed.

_____
(Signature of Incorporator)

Either the incorporator(s), or the directors if named in the articles, must sign the articles.

Amendment of Articles — Nonprofit Corporations

The requirements for amendment are found in Corporations Code sections 5810-5820 (nonprofit religious and public benefit corporations) and 7810-7820 (nonprofit mutual benefit corporations). The same form for amendment may be used for all three types and follows:

CERTIFICATE OF AMENDMENT
OF
ARTICLES OF INCORPORATION

JANE DOE AND RICHARD ROE certify that:

1. They are the president and the secretary, respectively, of ABC NON-PROFIT CORPORATION, a California Corporation.
2. Article _____(insert correct designation)_____ of the articles of incorporation of this corporation is amended to read as follows:
   (here set out the article as amended)
3. The foregoing amendment of articles of incorporation has been duly approved by the board of directors.
4. The foregoing amendment of articles of incorporation has been duly approved by the required vote of members.

_____
JANE DOE, President

_____
RICHARD ROE, Secretary

The undersigned declare under penalty of perjury that the matters set forth in the foregoing certificate are true of their own knowledge. Executed at ___(City and State)___ on ___(Date)___ .

_____

JANE DOE

_____

RICHARD ROE

A certificate of amendment may be signed by the President, Chairman of the Board or Vice-President AND the Secretary, Assistant Secretary, Chief Financial Officer, Treasurer or Assistant Treasurer. The same two officers who sign the certificate of amendment must sign the declaration under penalty of perjury.

See also Corporations Code section 5034 for definition of "Approval by (or Approval of) the Members."

Voluntary Dissolution

By a vote or written consent of a majority of all the members of the corporation, an election to dissolve may be made, following which a Certificate of Election to Dissolve must be filed with the Secretary of State. This document may be filed, if circumstances permit, at the same time the Certificate of Dissolution is filed after the business of the corporation has been wound up.

"If a nonprofit corporation, organized for charitable purposes (tax exempt under Revenue and Taxation Code Section 23701d) or holding assets under charitable trust holds any assets at the time of dissolution, the distribution of those assets must be approved by the Attorney General. See Corporations Code Sections 6716, 8716 and 9680.

"Before the final certificate of dissolution may be filed, a Tax Clearance Certificate must be obtained from the Franchise Tax Board, Tax Clearance Unit, Sacramento, California 95857, showing the corporation as having satisfied all franchise tax liability and the dissolution must be completed by the filing of said certificate on or before the expiration date shown on the tax clearance." (Sec/State Form LL-9 NP)

The Certificate of Dissolution should contain one of the following three statements:

"The corporation's known debts and liabilities have been adequately provided for by their assumption by (name and address)." or

"The corporation's known assets have been distributed to the persons entitled thereto." or

"The corporation is dissolved."

Tax Exemptions

A nonprofit corporation may have profits. Whether or not it is exempt from payment of federal or state income taxes, depends upon the uses of those profits. In any event, applications for exemption must be made, and the exempt status granted.

To obtain the California exemption, Form FTB 3500, Exemption Application, is used. The accompanying instructions for this form include sample Articles of Incorporation for the three types of nonprofit corporations (religious, mutual benefit, public benefit). These forms are also guides for provisions in the bylaws for unincorporated associations applying for exemption, and include requirements for organizations applying under Revenue and Taxation Code sections 23701d and 23701f, and organizations applying under sections other than 23701d and 23701f.

The bylaws must be structured properly to meet the requirements for exemption. The legal assistant should therefore be aware of and have these requirements in mind when preparing the bylaws, if exemption is to be claimed. The bylaws of the nonprofit corporation, rather than the articles as for a business corporation, usually set forth the rights of its members.

If a public benefit corporation anticipates a charitable tax exemption, the bylaws must contain a clause dedicating its assets to an appropriate nonprofit corporation or charitable organization upon its dissolution.

For a federal tax exemption, either Form 1023 is filed, for a 501(c)(3) exemption, or a Form 1024 for organizations described in 501(c) other than in 501(c)(3). Briefly, those organizations which may qualify under 501(c)(3) (Form 1023) are organizations operated exclusively for one or more of the following purposes: charitable, religious, educational, scientific, literary, testing for public safety, fostering national or international amateur sports competition (but only if no part of its activities involve the provisions of athletic facilities or equipment), or the prevention of cruelty to children or animals.

Some of the organizations which qualify under 501(c) but other than under 501(c)(3) are civic leagues and social welfare organizations, war veterans' organizations, labor, agricultural and horticultural organizations; business leagues, chambers of commerce, real estate boards, and boards of trade; social and recreation clubs, fraternal beneficiary societies and domestic fraternal societies. A number of other organizations also qualify under 501(c). Use Form 1024 for the latter named.

Instructions accompany the Forms 1023 and 1024, and Publication 557, How to Apply for and Retain Exempt Status of Your Organization, may be obtained from the Internal Revenue Service.

The legal assistant should check that all the Franchise Tax Board's requirements have been complied with so that the application is complete and will not be rejected. The legal assistant can make sure that the following are done correctly: application is signed by an authorized individual, *i.e.*, an elected officer or director or authorized representative (or trustee if the organization is a trust). The financial statements requested should be included or, if a new organization, a proposed budget. Income and expenses should be broken down. All organizing documents must be included, *i.e.*, the articles of incorporation (with endorsement stamp of Secretary of State) or bylaws or constitution (or trust instrument). If the application for exemption is filed at the same time as the articles, read item 4, "Filing the Application" on page 2 of the Instructions for Form FTB 3500. A detailed description of activities should be included.

Brief Summary of Steps of Incorporation of Nonprofit Corporation, for Legal Assistant

(1) Check availability of name, and reserve

(2) Draft and file articles of incorporation with Secretary of State

(3) Order kit (minute book, seal, membership certificates)

(4) Draft bylaws

(5) Draft minutes (or complete printed form if first meeting)

(6) Prepare for first meeting (adopting bylaws; electing officers; choosing accounting year; establishing bank account; authorizing appropriate actions)

(7) Apply for state income tax exemption with Franchise Tax Board

(8) Apply for federal income tax exemption with Internal Revenue Service

(9) File statement of officers and designation of agent for service of process

(10) If a public benefit nonprofit corporation, arrange for registration with Attorney General

(11) If a mutual benefit nonprofit corporation, and lobbying contemplated, arrange for registration with Fair Political Practices Commission

(12) If not otherwise exempt, apply for permit to issue memberships under federal and state securities laws

(13) Obtain any other licensing necessary for specific acts or solicitation of funds.

FOREIGN CORPORATIONS
(Corp. Code §§2100-2116.)

The California Corporations Commission under the Corporations Code regulates foreign corporations (corporations organized under laws of another state or country) transacting intrastate business in California.

Such corporations must file with the Secretary of State a form entitled "Statement and Designation by Foreign Corporation," which includes the information prescribed by Corporations Code section 2105:

(1) Its name and the state of its place of incorporation or organization.

(2) Address of its principal executive office.

(3) Address of its principal office in California.

(4) Name of agent within California upon whom process may be served; such designation to comply with Corporations Code section 1502(b). Either an individual person may be designated, with complete business or residence address, or a corporation which has complied with Corporations Code section 1505 and whose capacity has not terminated; no address for the corporation need be set forth. Under section 1505 the corporation must file a certificate with the Secretary of State which includes its address.

(5) Irrevocable consent to service on the agent and on the Secretary of State if agent or successor is no longer authorized to act or cannot be found at the address given.

(6) If the corporation is an insurer subject to the Insurance Code, must so state.

(7) A certificate by public official of place of incorporation that it is an existing corporation in good standing in that state; if it is an association, an officers' certificate similarly stating.

If a nonprofit corporation is to be qualified, the certificate must state that the corporation is a nonstock, nonprofit corporation.

A Certificate of Qualification is issued to the corporation.

All foreign corporations other than those wholly exempted have to file tax returns annually and pay a franchise tax on net taxable income derived from business done in California.

Name Reservation by Foreign Corporation

A foreign corporation (not an association) not transacting business in California may protect its name by registering its corporate name with the Secretary of State, pursuant to Corporations Code section 2101.

The corporation may register by filing:

(1) An application for registration signed by a corporate officer stating the name of the corporation, the state or place under the laws of which it is incorporated, the date of its incorporation, and that it desires to register its name under this section; and

(2) A certificate of an authorized public official of the state or place in which it is organized stating that such corporation is in good standing under those laws.

The registration may be renewed from year to year by filing an annual application and a certificate of good standing, between October 1 and December 31 in each year.

The foreign corporation does not need to file a Certificate of Qualification but must file an amended statement and designation as and when required by Corporations Code section 2107.

Also, a foreign corporation (and each foreign parent corporation) is required to file an officers' certificate annually, within 3 months and 15 days after the close of its income year ending on or after December 31, 1976, or within 30 days after filing its franchise tax return if an extension of time was granted. (See Corp. Code §2108.) That form follows:

Officers' Certificate — Foreign Corporation

STATE OF CALIFORNIA
OFFICERS' CERTIFICATE - FOREIGN CORPORATION
THIS STATEMENT MUST BE FILED WITH CALIFORNIA SECRETARY OF STATE (SEC. 2108, CORPORATIONS CODE).
P.O. BOX 2830, SACRAMENTO, CALIF. 95812   PHONE 916-445-2020

OFFICE USE ONLY

SEE REVERSE SIDE FOR REPRINT OF SECTION 2108 CORPORATIONS CODE

THE OFFICERS BELOW CERTIFY THE FOLLOWING:

1a.　Section 2115 does not apply to this corporation because it is:
(Please check appropriate box)

A non-profit corporation. ☐

An insurance company or trust company ☐

Listed on the New York or American Stock Exchange, or is a wholly owned
subsidiary of a corporation that is listed on the New York or American Stock Exchange. ☐

Other (show reason) _____

PLEASE PROCEED TO LINES 5 THROUGH 11 FOR SIGNATURES AND VERIFICATION. RETURN THIS FORM TO SECRETARY OF STATE.

1b.　IF SECTION 2115 DOES　　APPLY PLEASE CONTINUE.

2. As of the last record date for a shareholder's meeting, what percentage of outstanding voting stock
is held by persons having an address in California? _____ %

IF 40% OR LESS, PROCEED TO LINES 5 AND 6 FOR SIGNATURES AND VERIFICATION.
IF MORE, PLEASE CONTINUE.

3. Was all income of the corporation taxable for California franchise tax purposes or that such income would
have been so taxable if corporation had had sufficient income to be subject to more than minimum franchise
tax for the last income year?　　　　　　　　　　　　　　　　　　　　YES_____ NO_____

IF YES, PROCEED TO LINES 5 AND 6 FOR SIGNATURES AND VERIFICATION.
IF NO, PLEASE CONTINUE.

4. What is the corporation's property factor, payroll factor and sales factor computed as provided in Section 2115, Corporations Code?

(see reverse side of form)
(a)　Property Factor: _____ %

(b)　Payroll Factor: _____ %

(c)　Sales Factor: _____ %　AVERAGE OF a, b, c _____ %

THE PERSONS THAT SIGN ON LINES 5 AND 6 MUST ALSO SIGN ON LINES 10 AND 11. LINES 7, 8, 9 MUST ALSO BE COMPLETED.

5. Signed by _____　　　　　　　　　　　　　　Title _____
Signature of the Chairman of the Board, President or any Vice President (one of these officers must sign)

6. Signed by _____　　　　　　　　　　　　　　Title _____
Signature of the Secretary, Chief Financial Officer, Treasurer, Ass't. Secretary, or Ass't. Treasurer (one of these officers must sign)

Each of the undersigned declares under penalty of perjury that the matters
set forth in the foregoing certificate are true of their own knowledge.

DO NOT WRITE IN THIS SPACE

7. Executed at _____　　　8. _____
(City)　　　　　　　　　　　　　(State or Country)

9. On _____
(Date)

10. _____
Signature of person on line 5

11. _____
Signature of person on line 6

The Secretary of State may forfeit the right of any foreign Corporation to
transact intrastate business if it fails to file this certificate by the due date.

Form S/O 300

THERE IS NO FEE FOR FILING THIS CERTIFICATE

SECRETARY OF STATE
). BOX 2830, SACRAMENTO 95812

2108. (a) Each foreign corporation (other than a foreign association) qualified to transact intrastate business and each foreign parent corporation subject to Section 2115 shall file annually within three months and 15 days after the close of its income year ending on or after December 31, 1976 or within 30 days after the filing of its franchise tax return with the Franchise Tax Board if an extension of time for filing the return was granted, an officers' certificate setting forth:

(1) The percentage of its outstanding voting securities held of record, as of the last record date for a shareholder's meeting, by persons having addresses in this state, calculated as provided in Section 2115 and either

(2) That all the income of the corporation was taxable for California franchise tax purposes or that such income would have been so taxable if the corporation had had sufficient income to be subject to more than the minimum franchise tax; or

(3) Its property factor, payroll factor and sales factor computed as provided in Section 2115. This subdivision does not apply to a foreign corporation described in subdivision (e) of Section 2115. If the percentage in response to paragraph (1) is 40 percent or less, the officers' certificate need not include the information required by paragraph (2) or (3).

(b) The Secretary of State shall mail a form for compliance with this section to each foreign corporation qualified to transact intrastate business in reasonably sufficient time for such compliance. The form shall state the due date thereof and shall be mailed to the last address of the corporation according to the records of the Secretary of State. Neither the failure of the Secretary of State to mail the form nor the failure of the corporation to receive it is an excuse for failure to comply with this section.

(c) The Secretary of State need not mail a form to a foreign corporation exempted from subdivision (a) or a foreign corporation whose right to exercise its corporate powers, rights and privileges in this state were forfeited by the Franchise Tax Board pursuant to Section 23301 or 23301.5 of the Revenue and Taxation Code more than six months prior to the date the Secretary of State would otherwise have mailed the form pursuant to subdivision (b) and which right has not been revived on or prior to such date of mailing.

(d) The Secretary of State shall forfeit the right of any foreign corporation to transact intrastate business if it fails to file the statement required by this section for a period of six months after notice given to it by the Secretary of State that such filing is delinquent and that it will have its right to transact intrastate business forfeited unless it complies with this section.

(e) Neither the report required by this section nor the computation provided by Section 2115 shall have any effect with respect to the basis upon which the corporation reports its income for franchise tax purposes.

2115. (a) A foreign corporation (other than a foreign association but including a foreign parent corporation even though it does not itself transact intrastate business) is subject to this section if the average of the property factor, the payroll factor and the sales factor (as defined in Sections 25129, 25132 and 25134 of the Revenue and Taxation Code) with respect to it is more than 50 percent during its latest full income year and if more than one-half of its outstanding voting securities are held of record by persons having addresses in this state. The property factor, payroll factor and sales factor shall be those used in computing the portion of its income allocable to this state in its franchise tax return or, with respect to corporations the allocation of whose income is governed by special formulas or which are not required to file separate tax returns, which would have been so used if they were governed by such three-factor formula. The determination of these factors with respect to any parent corporation shall be made on a consolidated basis, including in a unitary computation (after elimination of inter-company transactions) the property, payroll and sales of the parent and all of its subsidiaries in which it owns directly or indirectly more than 50 percent of the outstanding shares entitled to vote for the election of directors, but deducting a percentage of such property, payroll and sales of any subsidiary equal to the percentage minority ownership, if any, in such subsidiary. For the purpose of this subdivision, any securities held to the knowledge of the issuer in the names of broker-dealers or nominees for broker-dealers shall not be considered outstanding.

(b) The following chapters and sections of this division shall apply to a foreign corporation subject to this section (to the exclusion of the law of the jurisdiction in which it is incorporated):

Chapter 1 (general provisions and definitions), to the extent applicable to the following provisions;

Section 301 (annual election of directors);

Section 303 (removal of directors without cause);

Section 304 (removal of directors by court proceedings);

Section 305, subdivision (c) (filling of director vacancies where less than a majority in office elected by shareholders);

Section 309 (directors' standard of care);

Section 316 (excluding paragraph (3) of subdivision (a) and paragraph (3) of subdivision (f) (liability of directors for unlawful distributions);

Section 317 (indemnification of directors, officers and others);

Sections 500 to 505, inclusive (limitations on corporate distributions in cash or property);

Section 506 (liability of shareholder who receives unlawful distribution);

Section 600, subdivisions (b) and (c) (requirement for annual shareholders' meeting and remedy if same not timely held);

Section 708, subdivisions (a), (b) and (c) (shareholder's right to cumulate votes at any election of directors);

Section 1001, subdivision (d) (limitations on sale of assets);

Section 1101 (provisions following subdivision (e) (limitations on mergers);

Chapter 12 (commencing with Section 1200) (reorganizations);

Chapter 13 (commencing with Section 1300) (dissenters' rights);

Sections 1500 and 1501 (records and reports);

Sections 1508 (action by Attorney General);

Chapter 16 (commencing with Section 1600) (rights of inspection).

(c) Subdivision (a) shall become applicable to any foreign corporation only upon the first day of the first income year of the corporation commencing on or after the 30th day after the filing by it of the report pursuant to Section 2108 showing that the tests referred to in subdivision (a) have been met or upon the entry of an order by a court of competent jurisdiction declaring that such tests have been met.

(d) Subdivision (a) shall cease to be applicable at the end of any income year during which a report pursuant to Section 2108 shall have been filed showing that at least one of the tests referred to in subdivision (a) is not met or an order shall have been entered by a court of competent jurisdiction declaring that one of such tests is not met, provided that such filing or order shall be ineffective if a contrary report or order shall be made or entered before the end of such income year.

(e) This section does not apply to any corporation with outstanding securities listed on any national securities exchange certified by the Commissioner of Corporations under subdivision (o) of Section 25100, or to any corporation if all of its voting shares (other than directors' qualifying shares) are owned directly or indirectly by a corporation not subject to this section.

REVENUE AND TAXATION CODE

25129. **Property factor**
The property factor is a fraction, the numerator of which is the average value of the taxpayer's real and tangible personal property owned or rented and used in this state during the income year and the denominator of which is the average value of all the taxpayer's real and tangible personal property owned or rented and used during the income year.

25132. **Payroll factor**
The payroll factor is a fraction, the numerator of which is the total amount paid in this state during the income year by the taxpayer for compensation, and the denominator of which is the total compensation paid everywhere during the income year.

25134. **Sales factor**
The sales factor is a fraction, the numerator of which is the total sales of the taxpayer in this state during the income year, and the denominator of which is the total sales of the taxpayer everywhere during the income year.

Fees — Foreign Corporations

STOCK or PROFIT CORPORATION:

Filing of Statement; issuing Certificate
of Qualification and Filing Designation
of Agent for Service of Process .... $ 350.00

Plus prepaid Franchise Tax (check or money
order remitted to Secretary of State's
office) 200.00

TOTAL .... $ 550.00

NONPROFIT, NONSTOCK CORPORATION:

Filing of Statement; issuing Certificate
of Qualification; and filing Designation
of Agent for Service of Process .... $ 15.00

Plus prepaid Franchise Tax (unless
exemption granted)* 200.00

TOTAL .... $ 215.00

*If the corporation is a nonprofit corporation of one of the types enumerated in Article 1 of Chapter 4 of the Bank and Corporation Franchise Tax Law, the accompanying tax exemption application, along with the required $10 application fee, may be submitted with the qualification papers in lieu of the minimum tax prepayment, but qualification will not be completed until the tax has been prepaid or exemption therefrom expressly granted by the Franchise Tax Board.

Amendments — Foreign Corporations

Any foreign corporation must file on a prescribed form an Amended Statement and Designation by Foreign Corporation, signed by a corporate officer, if it

(1) changes its name,

(2) changes the address of its principal office in California,

(3) changes the address of its principal executive office or its agent for the service of process,

(4) if the stated address of any natural person designated as agent is changed.

See Corporations Code section 2107 for further provisions.

Surrender of Right to Transact Intrastate Business

The Secretary of State's office has a form, *Certificate of Surrender of Right to Transact Intrastate Business,* under which a foreign corporation surrenders its right to engage in business within California. Corporations Code section 2112 provides that the *Certificate of Surrender* shall state:

(1) The name of the corporation as shown on the Secretary of State's records and the state or place of incorporation or organization;

(2) That it revokes its designation of agent for service of process;

(3) That it surrenders its authority to transact intrastate business;

(4) That it consents that process against it in any action upon any liability or obligation incurred within California prior to filing the certificate of withdrawal may be served upon the Secretary of State;

(5) A post office address to which the Secretary of State may mail a copy of the process served upon the Secretary of State, to be changed from time to time by filing a new statement signed by a corporate officer giving the new address or name or both.

The provisions for service of process on a foreign corporation are covered in Chapter 5, Commencing the Lawsuit.

Chapter 19

FAMILY LAW

The adoption of the Family Law Act in 1969 changed the law pertaining to marriage, divorce, separate maintenance, annulments, custody, support and community property. Divorce as such was eliminated, being replaced by a "dissolution of marriage." No longer is an action brought to terminate a marriage. A "proceeding" is initiated, and it is not adversary in nature. Parties to these proceedings are no longer "plaintiff" and "defendant" but "petitioner" and "respondent." Not a "complaint" but a "petition" is filed, not an "answer" but a "response."

While the new law is not without merit, it has by no means eliminated all the heartbreak involved at such times. The client is often emotionally distraught and needs and should be granted every consideration. Often marriages of 25 to 40 years' standing are being dissolved. Probably more often than not, financial difficulties confront one or both parties. Often a wife who has never been employed, and has no particular skills or training, maybe now in her fifties, is faced with the necessity of making a living for herself. The legal assistant as well as the attorney can offer moral support to the client and be of great help and comfort. Of course attorneys are frequently able to, and do, effect reconciliations. It is in this field that the simple act of caring, can be fruitful with intangible rewards for the legal assistant and might be said to be a "fringe benefit" of the profession.

A familiar complaint in a dissolution case is the seeming breakdown of client communications with the lawyer. Whether the complaint is justified or not, a legal assistant can be of assistance in keeping in close contact with the parties. A legal assistant can provide extremely valuable service in not only keeping track of the elements of the case including inventories and correspondence, but in reducing the tension for the client, fact gathering and keeping the attorney informed too. As always, the legal assistant can help conserve the time of the attorney by performing these tasks. This frees the attorney to plan strategy and settlements and prepare legal papers.

(See Chapter 2 for Function of Paralegal chart in Dissolutions.)

Petition and Summons

The dissolution proceeding is commenced by the filing of a petition, as in the ordinary civil action. Printed forms are used and the legal assistant should become familiar with the form of petition to find out what information is required.

This petition is filed in the superior court of the county in which the petitioner is a resident. The petitioner, or the respondent, must have been a resident in California for six months and of the county in which the proceeding is brought three months next preceding the commencement of the proceeding.

Where neither party complied with the residence requirements at the commencement of the proceedings, the petition (or responsive pleading requesting decree of dissolution) may be amended. The date of the amended petition or responsive pleading is deemed to be the date of commencement of the proceedings.

If an appearance has been made, notice of the amended petition or responsive pleading must be given as prescribed by the rules. If no appearance has been made, notice may be given by mail to the last known address of the other party, or by personal service, provided that the intent of the party to so amend upon satisfaction of the residence requirements of subdivision (a) of section 4530 is set forth in the initial petition or pleading in the manner provided by Judicial Council rules.

In a proceeding under the Family Law Act, if both parties move from the county rendering the decree, the court has discretion to order the proceedings transferred to the county of residence of either party.

A decree of dissolution (or of legal separation) may be obtained on the ground of "irreconcilable differences, which have caused the irremediable breakdown of the marriage" or incurable insanity. "Irreconcilable differences" are those grounds "which are determined by the court to be substantial reasons for not continuing the marriage and which make it appear that the marriage should be dissolved." (Civ. Code §§4506, 4507.)

The use of the printed forms *Petition (Family Law)* and *Summons (Family Law)* adopted by the Judicial Council of California is mandatory, as are most of the family law forms. The original summons is issued at the time of filing the petition, as in any other civil action.

In those counties having a conciliation court (see Code Civ. Proc. §§1730 *et seq.*), the petitioner must sign and file, concurrently with the petition, a Confidential Counseling Statement (in the form prescribed by Rule 1284 of the California Rules of Court).

Copies of the Family Law *Petition* and *Summons* follow:

Petition (Family Law)

ATTORNEY OR PARTY WITHOUT ATTORNEY (NAME AND ADDRESS): TELEPHONE NO.:	FOR COURT USE ONLY
ATTORNEY FOR (NAME):	

SUPERIOR COURT OF CALIFORNIA, COUNTY OF
STREET ADDRESS:
MAILING ADDRESS:
CITY AND ZIP CODE:
BRANCH NAME:

MARRIAGE OF
PETITIONER:

RESPONDENT:

PETITION FOR	CASE NUMBER:

PETITION FOR
☐ **Dissolution of Marriage**   ☐ **And Declaration Under Uniform Child**
☐ **Legal Separation**   **Custody Jurisdiction Act**
☐ **Nullity of Marriage**

1. RESIDENCE (Dissolution only)   ☐ Petitioner   ☐ Respondent
   has been a resident of this state for at least six months and of this county for at least three months immediately preceding the filing of this Petition for Dissolution.

2. STATISTICAL FACTS   a. Date of marriage: c. Period between marriage and separation
                     b. Date of separation: Years: Months:

3. DECLARATION REGARDING MINOR CHILDREN OF THIS MARRIAGE
   a. ☐ There are no minor children.
   b. ☐ The minor children are:

Name	Birthdate	Age	Sex

   c. IF THERE ARE MINOR CHILDREN, COMPLETE EITHER (1) or (2)
       (1) ☐ Each child named in 3b is presently living with ☐ Petitioner ☐ Respondent
            at (address):

   and during the last five years has lived in no state other than California and with no person other than petitioner or respondent or both.

   Petitioner has not participated in any capacity in any litigation or proceeding in any state concerning custody of any minor child of this marriage.

   Petitioner has no information of any pending custody proceeding or of any person not a party to this proceeding who has physical custody or claims to have custody or visitation rights concerning any minor child of this marriage.

       (2) ☐ A completed Declaration Under Uniform Custody of Minors Act is attached.
                        (Continued on reverse)

The declaration under penalty of perjury must be signed in California, or in a state that authorizes use of a declaration in place of an affidavit; otherwise an affidavit is required.

Form Adopted by Rule 1281   **PETITION**
Judicial Council of California   **(FAMILY LAW)**   CC 4503, 5158, CRC 1215
Revised Effective January 1, 1980

4. DECLARATION REGARDING COMMUNITY AND QUASI-COMMUNITY ASSETS AND OBLIGATIONS AS PRESENTLY KNOWN
   a. ☐ There are no such assets or obligations subject to disposition by the court in this proceeding.
   b. ☐ All such assets and obligations have been disposed of by written agreement.
   c. ☐ All such assets and obligations are listed in the property declaration to be filed with this petition.
   d. ☐ All such assets and obligations are listed below:

5. ☐ Petitioner requests confirmation of the following as separate assets and obligations:
   ITEM   CONFIRM TO

6. Petitioner requests
   a. ☐ Dissolution of the marriage based on
      (1) ☐ irreconcilable differences. CC 4506(1)
      (2) ☐ incurable insanity. CC 4506(2)

   b. ☐ Legal separation of the parties based on
      (1) ☐ irreconcilable differences. CC 4506(1)
      (2) ☐ incurable insanity. CC 4506(2)

   c. ☐ Nullity of void marriage based on
      (1) ☐ incestuous marriage. CC 4400
      (2) ☐ bigamous marriage. CC 4401

   d. ☐ Nullity of voidable marriage based on
      (1) ☐ petitioner's age at time of marriage. CC 4425(a)
      (2) ☐ prior existing marriage. CC 4425(b)
      (3) ☐ unsound mind. CC 4425(c)
      (4) ☐ fraud. CC 4425(d)
      (5) ☐ force. CC 4425(e)
      (6) ☐ physical incapacity. CC 4425(f)

7. Petitioner requests that the court grant the relief or judgment specified in item 6, make injunctive and other orders as may be proper, and that
   a. ☐ Visitation rights be determined and child custody be awarded
      ☐ Petitioner ☐ Respondent ☐ Other (specify): . . . .
   b. ☐ Child support be awarded ☐ Petitioner ☐ Respondent
   c. ☐ Spousal support be awarded ☐ Petitioner ☐ Respondent
   d. ☐ Property rights be determined.
   e. ☐ Attorney's fees and costs be awarded ☐ Petitioner ☐ Respondent
   f. ☐ Wife's former name be restored (specify): . . . .

Petitioner declares under penalty of perjury that the foregoing, including any attachment, is true and correct and that this declaration is executed at (place): . . . . , California, on (date): . . . .

_____
(Signature of Petitioner)

. . . .
(Type or print name of attorney)

_____
(Signature of Attorney for Petitioner)

Summons (Family Law)

ATTORNEY OR PARTY WITHOUT ATTORNEY (NAME AND ADDRESS):	TELEPHONE NO.:	FOR COURT USE ONLY

ATTORNEY FOR (NAME):

SUPERIOR COURT OF CALIFORNIA, COUNTY OF
STREET ADDRESS:
MAILING ADDRESS:
CITY AND ZIP CODE:
BRANCH NAME:

MARRIAGE OF
PETITIONER:

RESPONDENT:

SUMMONS (FAMILY LAW)	CASE NUMBER:

NOTICE!	¡AVISO!
You have been sued. The court may decide against you without your being heard unless you respond within 30 days. Read the information below. If you wish to seek the advice of an attorney in this matter, you should do so promptly so that your response or pleading, if any, may be filed on time.	Usted ha sido demandado. El tribunal puede decidir contra Ud. sin audiencia a menos que Ud. responda dentro de 30 días. Lea la información que sigue. Si Usted desea solicitar el consejo de un abogado en este asunto, debería hacerlo inmediatamente, de esta manera, su respuesta o alegación, si hay alguna, puede ser registrada a tiempo.

1. TO THE RESPONDENT

The petitioner has filed a petition concerning your marriage. If you fail to file a response within 30 days of the date that this summons is served on you, your default may be entered and the court may enter a judgment containing injunctive or other orders concerning division of property, spousal support, child custody, child support, attorney fees, costs, and such other relief as may be granted by the court. The garnishment of wages, taking of money or property, or other court authorized proceedings may also result.

Dated: . . . .   Clerk, By _____, Deputy

(SEAL)

2. NOTICE TO THE PERSON SERVED. You are served
   a. ☐ As an individual
   b. ☐ On behalf of Respondent

   Under:
   ☐ CCP 416.60 (Minor)
   ☐ CCP 416.70 (Ward or Conservatee)
   ☐ CCP 416.90 (Individual)
   ☐ Other (specify):

   c. ☐ By personal delivery on (Date):

(See reverse for Proof of Service)

The response (printed form rule 1282) and other permitted papers must be in the form prescribed by the California Rules of Court. They must be filed in this court with the proper filing fee and proof of service of a copy of each on petitioner. The time when the 30 days to respond begins may vary depending on the method of service. For example, see CCP 413.10-415.50.

Form Adopted by Rule 1283
Judicial Council of California
Revised Effective January 1, 1980

**SUMMONS
(FAMILY LAW)**

CC 4503
CCP 412.20
CRC 1216

PROOF OF SERVICE

(Use separate proof of service for each person served)

1. I served the Summons (Family Law) and Petition (Family Law) on respondent (name):
   a. with (1) ☐ blank Confidential Counseling Statement   (5) ☐ completed and blank Property Declarations
         (2) ☐ Order to Show Cause and Application   (6) ☐ Other (specify):
         (3) ☐ blank Responsive Declaration
         (4) ☐ completed and blank Income and
              Expense Declarations
   b. ☐ By leaving copies with (name and title or relationship to person served):
   c. ☐ By delivery at ☐ home ☐ business
         (1) Date of: (3) Address:
         (2) Time of:
   d. ☐ By mailing
         (1) Date of: (2) Place of:

2. Manner of service: (Check proper box)
   a. ☐ **Personal service.** By personally delivering copies to the person served. (CCP 415.10)
   b. ☐ **Substituted service on natural person, minor, incompetent.** By leaving copies at the dwelling house, usual place of abode, or usual place of business of the person served in the presence of a competent member of the household or a person apparently in charge of the office or place of business, at least 18 years of age, who was informed of the general nature of the papers, and thereafter mailing (by first-class mail, postage prepaid) copies to the person served at the place where the copies were left. (CCP 415.20(b)) **(Attach separate declaration or affidavit stating acts relied on to establish reasonable diligence in first attempting personal service.)**
   c. ☐ **Mail and acknowledgment service.** By mailing (by first-class mail or airmail) copies to the person served, together with two copies of the form of notice and acknowledgment and a return envelope, postage prepaid, addressed to the sender. (CCP 415.30) **(Attach completed acknowledgment of receipt.)**
   d. ☐ **Certified or registered mail service.** By mailing to address outside California (by registered or certified airmail with return receipt requested) copies to the person served. (CCP 415.40) **(Attach signed return receipt or other evidence of actual delivery to the person served.)**
   e. ☐ Other. (Specify code section):
         ☐ Additional page is attached.

3. The notice to the person served (Item 2 on the copy of the summons served) was completed as follows (CCP 412.30, 415.10, and 474):
   a. ☐ As an individual
   b. ☐ On behalf of Respondent
         Under: ☐ CCP 416.60 (Minor) ☐ Other (specify):
                ☐ CCP 416.70 (Ward or Conservatee)
                ☐ CCP 416.90 (Individual)
   c. ☐ By personal delivery on (Date): . . . .
4. At the time of service I was at least 18 years of age and not a party to this action.
5. Fee for service: $ . . . .
6. Person serving
   a. ☐ Not a registered California process server.   e. ☐ California sheriff, marshal, or constable.
   b. ☐ Registered California process server.   f. Name, address and telephone number and
   c. ☐ Employee or independent contractor of a   if applicable, county of registration and number:
         registered California process server.
   d. ☐ Exempt from registration under Bus. & Prof.
         Code 22350(b)

I declare under penalty of perjury that the foregoing   (For California sheriff, marshal or constable use only)
is true and correct and that this declaration is executed   I certify that the foregoing is true and correct and that
on (date): . . . .   this certificate is executed on (date): . . . .
at (place): . . . . , California.   at (place): . . . ., California.

_____   _____
(Signature)   (Signature)

A declaration under penalty of perjury must be signed in California or in a state that authorizes use of a declaration in place of an affidavit; otherwise an affidavit is required.

Service and Response

A copy of the *Petition (Family Law)* and of the *Summons (Family Law)* are served on the respondent, in the manner provided for service of summons in other civil actions. (See Service of Documents, *supra.*) Also, in those counties having a conciliation court, the petitioner must at the same time serve upon the respondent a blank form of the *Confidential Counseling Statement*. Proof of service must be made in the manner provided for proof of service of summons in civil actions generally.

A respondent may appear in the case by filing, within 30 days after the service of the summons and petition, a *Response (Family Law)*, a printed mandatory form, or a printed form of *Appearance, Stipulation and Waivers (Family Law)*. The latter form contains language that the proceeding may be treated as an uncontested matter in the same manner as if respondent's default had been entered. Likewise, in those counties having a conciliation court, the respondent who files a response shall, concurrently with the filing thereof, sign and file a *Confidential Counseling Statement,* in the form prescribed by Rule 1284.

A copy of each of the Family Law *Response, Appearance, Stipulation and Waivers, and Confidential Counseling Statement* forms follows:

Response (Family Law)

<table>
<tr><td colspan="2">ATTORNEY OR PARTY WITHOUT ATTORNEY (NAME AND ADDRESS):</td><td>TELEPHONE NO.:</td><td>FOR COURT USE ONLY</td></tr>
<tr><td colspan="4">ATTORNEY FOR (NAME):</td></tr>
</table>

SUPERIOR COURT OF CALIFORNIA, COUNTY OF
STREET ADDRESS:

MAILING ADDRESS:

CITY AND ZIP CODE:

BRANCH NAME:

MARRIAGE OF

PETITIONER:

RESPONDENT:

RESPONSE ☐ **REQUEST FOR**	☐ **Dissolution of Marriage** ☐ **Legal Separation** ☐ **Nullity of Marriage**	☐ **And Declaration Under Uniform Child Custody Jurisdiction Act**	CASE NUMBER:

1. RESIDENCE (Dissolution only) ☐ Petitioner ☐ Respondent
has been a resident of this state for at least six months and of this county for at least three months immediately preceding the filing of this Petition for Dissolution.

2. STATISTICAL FACTS   a. Date of marriage: c. Period between marriage and separation
                    b. Date of separation: Years: Months:

3. DECLARATION REGARDING MINOR CHILDREN OF THIS MARRIAGE
    a. ☐ There are no minor children.
    b. ☐ The minor children are:

Name	Birthdate	Age	Sex

c. IF THERE ARE MINOR CHILDREN, COMPLETE EITHER (1) or (2)
   (1) ☐ Each child named in 3b is presently living with ☐ Petitioner ☐ Respondent
       at (address):

and during the last five years has lived in no state other than California and with no person other than petitioner or respondent or both.

Respondent has not participated in any capacity in any litigation or proceeding in any state concerning custody of any minor child of this marriage.

Respondent has no information of any pending custody proceeding or of any person not a party to this proceeding who has physical custody or claims to have custody or visitation rights concerning any minor child of this marriage.

   (2) ☐ A completed Declaration Under Uniform Custody of Minors Act is attached.

(Continued on reverse)

The declaration under penalty of perjury must be signed in California, or in a state that authorizes use of a declaration in place of an affidavit; otherwise an affidavit is required.

Form Adopted by Rule 1282
Judicial Council of California
Revised Effective January 1, 1980

**RESPONSE
(FAMILY LAW)**

CC 4355; CRC 1215

4. DECLARATION REGARDING COMMUNITY AND QUASI-COMMUNITY ASSETS AND OBLIGATIONS AS PRESENTLY KNOWN

    a. ☐ There are no such assets or obligations subject to disposition by the court in this proceeding.

    b. ☐ All such assets and obligations have been disposed of by written agreement.

    c. ☐ All such assets and obligations are listed in the property declaration to be filed with this response.

    d. ☐ All such assets and obligations are listed below:

5. ☐ Respondent requests confirmation of the following as separate assets and obligations:

ITEM   CONFIRM TO

6. ☐ Respondent contends there is a reasonable possibility of reconciliation.

7. ☐ Respondent denies the grounds set forth in item 6 of the petition.

8. ☐ Respondent requests

    a. ☐ Dissolution of the marriage based on

        (1) ☐ irreconcilable differences. CC 4506(1)

        (2) ☐ incurable insanity. CC 4506(2)

    b. ☐ Legal separation of the parties based on

        (1) ☐ irreconcilable differences. CC 4506(1)

        (2) ☐ incurable insanity. CC 4506(2)

    c. ☐ Nullity of void marriage based on

        (1) ☐ incestuous marriage. CC 4400

        (2) ☐ bigamous marriage. CC 4401

    d. ☐ Nullity of voidable marriage based on

        (1) ☐ respondent's age at time of marriage. CC 4425(a)

        (2) ☐ prior existing marriage. CC 4425(b)

        (3) ☐ unsound mind. CC 4425(c)

        (4) ☐ fraud. CC 4425(d)

        (5) ☐ force. CC 4425(e)

        (6) ☐ physical incapacity. CC 4425(f)

9. Respondent requests that the court grant the relief or judgment specified in item 8, make injunctive and other orders as may be proper, and that

    a. ☐ Visitation rights be determined and child custody be awarded

        ☐ Petitioner ☐ Respondent ☐ Other (specify): . . . .

    b. ☐ Child support be awarded ☐ Petitioner ☐ Respondent

    c. ☐ Spousal support be awarded ☐ Petitioner ☐ Respondent

    d. ☐ Property rights be determined.

    e. ☐ Attorney's fees and costs be awarded ☐ Petitioner ☐ Respondent

    f. ☐ Wife's former name be restored (specify): . . . .

Respondent declares under penalty of perjury that the foregoing, including any attachment, is true and correct and that this declaration is executed at (place): . . . . , California, on (date): . . . .

                                                         _____

                                                        (Signature of Respondent)

. . . .   _____

          (Type or print name of attorney)   (Signature of Attorney for Respondent)

Appearance, Stipulation and Waivers

ATTORNEY OR PARTY WITHOUT ATTORNEY (NAME AND ADDRESS):	TELEPHONE NO.:	FOR COURT USE ONLY
ATTORNEY FOR (NAME):		

SUPERIOR COURT OF CALIFORNIA, COUNTY OF
STREET ADDRESS:
MAILING ADDRESS:
CITY AND ZIP CODE:
BRANCH NAME:

MARRIAGE OF
PETITIONER:

RESPONDENT:

APPEARANCE, STIPULATION AND WAIVERS	CASE NUMBER:

1. ☐ Respondent makes a general appearance.
2. ☐ Respondent has previously made a general appearance.
3. ☐ Respondent is a member of the military services of the United States of America and waives all rights under the Soldiers and Sailors Civil Relief Act of 1940, as amended, and does not contest this proceeding.
4. ☐ The parties stipulate that this cause may be tried as an uncontested matter.
5. ☐ The parties waive their rights to notice of trial, findings of fact and conclusions of law, motion for new trial, and the right to appeal.
6. ☐ This matter may be tried by a commissioner sitting as a temporary judge.
7. ☐ A written settlement agreement has been entered into between the parties.
8. ☐ A stipulation for judgment will be submitted to the court at the uncontested proceeding.
9. ☐ None of these stipulations or waivers shall apply unless the court approves the written settlement agreement or stipulation for judgment.
10. ☐ Other (specify):

11. Total number of boxes checked (specify):

Dated: . . . . _____
(Signature of Petitioner)

Dated: . . . . _____
(Signature of Respondent)

Dated: . . . .

. . . . _____
(Type or print name)   (Signature of Attorney for Petitioner)

Dated: . . . .

. . . . _____
(Type or print name)   (Signature of Attorney for Respondent)

Form Approved by Rule 1282 50
Judicial Council of California
Effective January 1, 1980

APPEARANCE, STIPULATION AND WAIVERS
(FAMILY LAW)

Confidential Counseling Statement

Name, Address and Telephone No. of Attorney(s)	Space Below for Use of Court Clerk Only

Attorney(s) for . . . .

SUPERIOR COURT OF CALIFORNIA, COUNTY OF . . . .

In re the marriage of	CASE NUMBER
Petitioner:	☐ **Petitioner's** ☐ **Respondent's**
and	**CONFIDENTIAL COUNSELING STATEMENT**
Respondent:	**(MARRIAGE)**

I understand that conciliation services are available to me through the court in this county.

☐ I would like marriage counseling.

☐ I would like to talk with a trained person about my present family situation.

☐ I do not desire counseling at this time.

Mailing address of requesting party:

Name:

Street:

City/State/Zip

Mailing address of other party:

Name:

Street:

City/State/Zip

Date:

(Signature)

Form Adopted by Rule 1284 of
The Judicial Council of California   **CONFIDENTIAL COUNSELING STATEMENT (MARRIAGE)**
Effective January 1, 1975

A respondent may also appear in the case by filing, within 30 days after the service of the summons and petition, either

1. A notice of motion to quash the proceedings pursuant to California Rules of Court, Rule 1230:
   a. Lack of legal capacity to sue
   b. Prior judgment or other action pending between same parties for same cause
   c. Residence requirements not met
   d. Limitations of Civil Code section 4426 not met *or*
2. Notice of motion to quash service of summons or notice of filing of a petition for writ of mandate pursuant to California Rules of Court, Rule 1234 (see Code Civ. Proc. §418.10), *or*
3. Notice of motion to transfer the proceeding. (See Code Civ. Proc. tit. IV §§392 *et seq.*)

After denial of any of the motions or the petition for writ of mandate immediately above, the respondent must file a *Response (Family Law)* within the time allowed by the court; otherwise, the case will be treated as an uncontested case.

The only pleading permitted by a petitioner is the *Petition (Family Law)*; the only pleading permitted by a respondent is the *Response (Family Law)* above. Amendments to pleadings, amended pleadings, and supplemental pleadings may be served and filed as provided by law for civil actions generally. (See Code Civ. Proc. §471.5-473, Rule 205.) There need be no reply by petitioner if respondent has filed a response. No default may be entered because one of the parties did not reply to an amended pleading. (Rule 1215.) Demurrers and cross-complaints may not be filed.

Either the court on its own motion, or the petitioner or the respondent, may file a motion to strike from the petition or response any matter not specifically required in the forms. (See Rules 1281 and 1282.) A notice of motion to strike by the respondent does not extend the time for filing a response by the respondent. The motion to strike is governed by California Rules of Court, Rule 1229. (Code of Civil Procedure sections 435 and 453 do not apply.)

Uncontested Cases

If the respondent did not file a *Response (Family Law)* (either within 30 days of service of the petition and summons or within the time allowed by court after motion) or if an *Appearance, Stipulation and Waivers (Family Law)* form was filed (in which it is stipulated that the proceeding may be treated as an uncontested matter in the same manner as if respondent's default had been taken and entered), respondent's default may be entered.

However, the court must, in addition to any statement or findings of facts made by a referee, require proof of the grounds alleged, and the proof, if not taken by the court, shall be by affidavit; the personal appearance of the affiant is required only when it appears: (1) reconciliation of the parties is reasonably possible; (2) a proposed child custody order is not in the best interests of the child; (3) a proposed child support order is less than a noncustodial parent is capable of paying; or (4) a personal appearance of any party or interested person would be in the best interests of justice.

The affidavit must contain a stipulation by the affiant that he or she understands that proof will be by affidavit and that he or she will not appear before the court unless so ordered by the court.

(See Civ. Code §4511, and Code Civ. Proc §585.)

Petitioner files a form of *Request to Enter Default (Family Law)*. It contains a declaration of mailing of the document to respondent's attorney or respondent himself at his last known address, a memorandum of costs, and a declaration that respondent is not in the military service of the United States. An address of the respondent must be given or a default cannot be entered. (Cal. Rules of Court, Rule 1240.) The form follows:

Request to Enter Default (Family Law)

ATTORNEY OR PARTY WITHOUT ATTORNEY (NAME AND ADDRESS):	TELEPHONE NO.	FOR COURT USE ONLY
ATTORNEY FOR (NAME):		

SUPERIOR COURT OF CALIFORNIA, COUNTY OF
STREET ADDRESS:
MAILING ADDRESS:
CITY AND ZIP CODE:
BRANCH NAME:

MARRIAGE OF
PETITIONER:

RESPONDENT:

REQUEST TO ENTER DEFAULT	CASE NUMBER:

1. TO THE CLERK: Please enter the default of the respondent who has failed to respond to the petition.
2. A completed ☐ Income and Expense Declaration ☐ Property Declaration is attached.
3. A completed ☐ Income and Expense Declaration ☐ Property Declaration is *not* attached because (check at least one of the following)
   (1) ☐ There have been no changes since the previous filing.
   (2) ☐ The issues subject to disposition by the court in this proceeding are the subject of a written agreement.
   (3) ☐ There are no issues of child custody, child or spousal support, division of community property or attorney fees and costs subject to determination by this court.
   (4) ☐ The petition does not request money, property, costs or attorney fees.

Dated:

. . . . _____
(Type or print name)   Signature of (Attorney for) Petitioner

3. DECLARATION
   a. ☐ No mailing is required because service was by publication and the address of respondent remains unknown.
   b. ☐ A copy of this Request to Enter Default including any attachments was mailed to the respondent's attorney of record or, if none, to respondent's last known address as follows
      (1) Date of mailing: (2) Addressed as follows:

   c. I declare under penalty of perjury that the foregoing is true and correct and that this declaration is executed on (date): . . . . at (place): . . . ., California

. . . . _____
(Type or print name)   (Signature of declarant)

FOR COURT USE ONLY
Default entered as requested on (date):   Clerk, by:
Default NOT entered. Reason:

(See reverse for Memorandum of Costs and Declaration of Nonmilitary Status)

The declaration under penalty of perjury must be signed in California or in a state that authorizes use of a declaration in place of an affidavit; otherwise an affidavit is required. (CCP 2015.5)

Form Adopted by Rule 1286   **REQUEST TO ENTER DEFAULT**
Judicial Council of California   **(FAMILY LAW)**
Revised Effective January 1, 1980   CCP 585,587

4. MEMORANDUM OF COSTS

   a. ☐ Costs and disbursements are waived.
   b. Costs and disbursements are listed as follows

  (1) ☐ Clerk's fees .... $ ....

  (2) ☐ Process server's fees .... $ ....

  (3) ☐ Other (specify) .... $ ....

                                       $ ....

                                       $ ....

                                       $ ....

     TOTAL .... $ ....

I am the attorney, agent, or party who claims these costs. To the best of my knowledge and belief the foregoing items of cost are correct and have been necessarily incurred in this cause or proceeding.

I declare under penalty of perjury that the foregoing is true and correct and that this declaration is executed on (date): .... at (place): .... , California.

....
(Type or print name)   (Signature of declarant)

5. DECLARATION OF NONMILITARY STATUS

Respondent is not in the military service or in the military service of the United States as defined in Section 101 of the Soldiers' and Sailors' Relief Act of 1940, as amended, and not entitled to the benefits of such act.

I declare under penalty of perjury that the foregoing is true and correct and that this declaration is executed on (date): .... at (place): .... , California.

....
(Type or print name)   (Signature of declarant)

Contested Proceedings

The contested proceeding is set for trial as in civil actions. (See Setting for Trial in Chapter 8, The Trial, *supra*.)

Financial Declaration

If there is property subject to disposition by the court, the petitioner must file a *Property Declaration (Family Law)*. Part A need not be completed if the matter is to be disposed of as by a default, or as an uncontested matter.

However, no *Property Declaration* need be filed if the petition for dissolution contains no demand for money, property, costs, or attorney's fees and the decree of dissolution is entered by default. (Civ. Code §4364.)

Once the *Request to Enter Default (Family Law)* (and *Property Declaration* if required as above) are filed, local rules should be consulted as to setting the case for hearing. In Sacramento County, for instance, the case could be set for hearing by phoning a specified department of the superior court.

The form of *Property Declaration (Family Law)* follows:

Property Declaration (Family Law)

ATTORNEY OR PARTY WITHOUT ATTORNEY (NAME AND ADDRESS):	TELEPHONE NO.:	FOR COURT USE ONLY
ATTORNEY FOR (NAME):		

SUPERIOR COURT OF CALIFORNIA, COUNTY OF
STREET ADDRESS:
MAILING ADDRESS:
CITY AND ZIP CODE:
BRANCH NAME:

MARRIAGE OF
PETITIONER:

RESPONDENT:

☐ **PETITIONER'S** ☐ **RESPONDENT'S** ☐ **COMMUNITY & QUASI-COMMUNITY PROPERTY DECLARATION** ☐ **SEPARATE PROPERTY DECLARATION**	CASE NUMBER:

INSTRUCTIONS

When this form is attached to Petition or Response, values and your proposal regarding division need not be completed. Do not list community, including quasi-community, property with separate property on the same form. Quasi-community property must be so identified. For additional space, use the form "Continuation of Property Declaration."

ITEM NO.	BRIEF DESCRIPTION	GROSS FAIR MARKET VALUE	AMOUNT OF DEBT	NET FAIR MARKET VALUE	PROPOSAL FOR DIVISION AWARD TO	
					PETITIONER	RESPONDENT
		$	$	$	$	$
1. REAL ESTATE						
2. HOUSEHOLD FURNITURE, FURNISHINGS, APPLIANCES						
3. JEWELRY, ANTIQUES, ART, COIN COLLECTIONS, etc.						
4. VEHICLES, BOATS, TRAILERS						
5. SAVINGS, CHECKING, CREDIT UNION, CASH						

(Continued on reverse)

The declaration under penalty of perjury must be signed in California or in a state that authorizes use of a declaration in place of an affidavit; otherwise an affidavit is required.

Form Adopted by Rule 1285.55
Judicial Council of California
Effective January 1, 1980

**PROPERTY DECLARATION
(FAMILY LAW)**

ITEM NO.	BRIEF DESCRIPTION	GROSS FAIR MARKET VALUE	AMOUNT OF DEBT	NET FAIR MARKET VALUE	PROPOSAL FOR DIVISION AWARD TO	
					PETITIONER	RESPONDENT
		$	$	$	$	$
6.	LIFE INSURANCE (CASH VALUE)					
7.	EQUIPMENT, MACHINERY, LIVESTOCK					
8.	STOCKS, BONDS, SECURED NOTES					
9.	RETIREMENT, PENSION, PROFIT-SHARING, ANNUITIES					
10.	ACCOUNTS RECEIVABLE, UNSECURED NOTES, TAX REFUNDS					
11.	PARTNERSHIPS, OTHER BUSINESS INTERESTS					
12.	OTHER ASSETS AND DEBTS					
13.	TOTAL FROM CONTINUATION SHEET					
14.	TOTALS					

15. ☐ A Continuation of Property Declaration is attached and incorporated by reference.

. . . . (Type or print name of attorney) . . . . . .   ——————————————
                                                                        (Signature of attorney)

I declare under penalty of perjury that, to the best of my knowledge, the foregoing is a true and correct listing of assets and obligations and that the amounts shown are correct; and that this declaration was executed on (date): . . . . at (place): . . . ., California.

. . . .   ——————————————
          (Type or print name)   (Signature)

Income and Expense Declaration (Family Law)

ATTORNEY OR PARTY WITHOUT ATTORNEY (NAME AND ADDRESS):	TELEPHONE NO.	FOR COURT USE ONLY
ATTORNEY FOR (NAME):		

SUPERIOR COURT OF CALIFORNIA, COUNTY OF
STREET ADDRESS:
MAILING ADDRESS:
CITY AND ZIP CODE:
BRANCH NAME:

MARRIAGE OF
PETITIONER:

RESPONDENT:

INCOME AND EXPENSE DECLARATION ☐ PETITIONER ☐ RESPONDENT	CASE NUMBER

GROSS MONTHLY INCOME	Petitioner	Respondent	DEDUCTIONS FROM GROSS INCOME	Petitioner	Respondent
1. Salary & wages (Include commissions, bonuses and overtime)	$	$	12. State income taxes	$	$
2. Pensions & retirement	$	$	13. Federal income taxes	$	$
3. Social Security	$	$	14. Social Security	$	$
4. Disability and unemployment benefits	$	$	15. State disability insurance	$	$
5. Public assistance (Welfare, AFDC payments, etc.)	$	$	16. Medical and other insurance	$	$
6. Child/spousal support	$	$	17. Union and other dues	$	$
7. Dividends and interest	$	$	18. Retirement and pension fund	$	$
8. Rents (gross receipts, less cash expenses; attach schedule)	$	$	19. Savings plan	$	$
9. Contributions to household expenses from other sources	$	$	20. Other deductions (Specify)	$	$
10. Income from all other sources (gross receipts, less cash expenses; attach schedule)	$	$	21. TOTAL DEDUCTIONS	$	$
			11. TOTAL GROSS MONTHLY INCOME (from line 11)	$	$
			21. TOTAL DEDUCTIONS (From line 21)	$	$
11. TOTAL GROSS MONTHLY INCOME	$	$	22. NET MONTHLY INCOME (line 11 minus line 21)	$	$

23. Withholding information   a. Number of exemptions claimed: b. Marital status

24. Certain property under the control of the parties

	Petitioner	Respondent		Petitioner	Respondent
a. Cash & checking accounts	$	$	c. Stocks, bonds, life insurance, other liquid assets	$	$
b. Savings & credit union accounts	$	$	d. TOTAL (24a,b,c)	$	$

The declaration under penalty of perjury must be signed in California or in a state that authorizes use of a declaration in place of an affidavit; otherwise an affidavit is required.

Form Adopted by Rule 1285.50
Judicial Council of California
Revised Effective January 1, 1980

INCOME & EXPENSE DECLARATION (FAMILY LAW)

25. List the name, age, and relationship of all members of the household whose expenses are included below

MONTHLY EXPENSES	Petitioner	Respondent			Petitioner	Respondent
26. Residence payments			34.	Child/spousal support (prior marriage)	$	$
a. Rent or mortgage	$	$				
b. Taxes & insurance	$	$	35.	School	$	$
c. Maintenance	$	$	36.	Entertainment	$	$
27. Food & household supplies	$	$	37.	Incidentals	$	$
28. Utilities & telephone	$	$	38.	Transportation & auto expenses (insurance, gas, oil, repair)	$	$
29. Laundry & cleaning	$	$	39.	Installment payments (Insert total and itemize below at 42)	$	$
30. Clothing	$	$				
31. Medical & dental	$	$				
32. Insurance (life, health accident, etc.)	$	$	40.	Other: (specify)	$	$
33. Child care	$	$	41.	TOTAL MONTHLY EXPENSES	$	$

42. ITEMIZATION OF INSTALLMENT PAYMENTS OR OTHER DEBTS ☐ Continued on attachment 42.

CREDITOR'S NAME	FOR	MONTHLY PAYMENT	BALANCE
		$	$

43. ☐ ATTORNEY FEES HAVE BEEN REQUESTED.

a. I have paid my attorney for fees and costs the sum of $ . . . .   b. My arrangement for attorney fees and costs is:

_____   _____
(Print or type name of Attorney)   (Signature of Attorney)

I declare under penalty of perjury that the foregoing, including any attachment, is true and correct and that this declaration is executed at (place): . . . ., California, on (date): . . . .

_____   _____
(Print or type name of Declarant)   (Signature of Declarant)

There is also a form *Continuation of Property Declaration (Family Law)*, which is not reproduced here.

Property Declaration — Division of Property

Prior to 1970, the court had discretion to divide the property of the parties in proportion to their fault.

The law was changed to provide generally that in the absence of a written agreement of the parties, or oral stipulation in open court, the court shall value the assets and liabilities as near as practicable to the time of trial and divide the community property and quasi-community property equally (with certain exceptions noted; see Civil Code section 4800). Consideration must be given to the net to each party after taxes, in order to divide the assets equally.

Property which either of the parties owned before the marriage is separate property; the income (interest, rents, etc.) and profit from such separate property is also separate property. An inheritance or gift is likewise separate property. The court cannot award the separate property to the other party. Separate property, and joint tenancy property, should be listed under question 5 of the *Petition (Family Law)*.

Community property is generally property (other than separate property) acquired after marriage; earnings of both parties are community property. (See the landmark case of *Marvin v. Marvin* (1976) 18 Cal.3d 660, re nonmarital "community" property.)

Quasi-community property is defined in Civil Code section 4803 and includes real or personal property, whether situated in California or elsewhere, "heretofore and hereafter" acquired:

"(a) By either spouse while domiciled elsewhere which would have been community property if the spouse who acquired the property had been domiciled in this state at the time of its acquisition.

"(b) In exchange for real or personal property, wherever situated, which would have been community property if the spouse who acquired the property so exchanged had been domiciled in this state at the time of its acquisition."

Quasi-community property would therefore include earnings of each spouse while married but living outside California and assets traceable to such earnings.

Special problems arise when separate and community or quasi-community property has been commingled or the value of separate property has been enhanced by community services or property. For example, suppose the parties used community funds to make improvements on a parcel of real property that is separate property; suppose the husband is a general contractor or a handyman, who remodels a house owned by his wife as separate property.

Property may have been changed, transmuted, from separate to community, or vice versa, or commingled. Complex situations may exist if the parties cannot agree, and the party claiming separate property has the burden of proof to show that it is his.

Considerable expertise may be required to determine whether property is separate or community. Inquiry should be made of the client at the outset as to the *source* of all property. If the legal assistant has any question, the attorney should be consulted; the services of an accountant could be required.

The Property Declarations of the parties are significant documents in the dissolution proceedings. Careful thought should be given to their completion — by the clients, the legal assistants, and the attorneys.

Income and Expense Statement

The client is not apt to bring with him or her all the information needed. The legal assistant should urge the client to take the time necessary to get the information needed to complete this section as accurately as possible. In discussing valuations with the client, the legal assistant can at the same time assemble information that will be needed for the property settlement agreement. A form of agreement may be found in the *Legal Secretary's Handbook.* (Parker & Son Publications, Inc.) A table of forms for marital settlement agreements may be found in CEB's *1978 Supplement to California Marital Termination Settlements.*

Records of expenses should be carefully checked by the client. The amounts should be reasonable, and not "padded." Amounts which appear excessive in relation to the parties' income may arouse the judge's suspicion of the client's accuracy, if not truthfulness. Checkbooks, charge accounts, any records of cash expenses maintained, provide verification and make reasonable estimates possible.

In some locales verification of salaries is required (*i.e.*, by W-2 forms, income tax returns, payroll stubs, etc.).

Under "(e) Other debts and obligations," attorney fees should be included as a debt, along with other community debts.

The client should be cautioned *not* to include the value of any separate property under (f).

Bank accounts: The client should be able to readily determine the amounts in checking and savings bank accounts, credit unions, etc. The legal assistant should determine whether interest entries have been brought up to date, and how title is held, *i.e.*, trustee account, joint tenancy.

Retirement or pension fund: Ask the client to bring in any retirement plan brochure, determine years of employment and wages, age.

A claim to a pension fund is based on a formula of years of marriage and life expectancies. The nonemployee is entitled to one-half the portion attributable to the marriage before separation. The pension plan must be joined in the action. (See Joinder — Pension Plan.) Information will have to be obtained from the plan, after joinder. An actuary will probably be needed to determine the value of the rights in the pension fund.

After a value for the pension fund is fixed, assets equivalent to that value can be awarded to the other spouse. In *Gilmore v. Gilmore* (1981) 29 Cal.3d 418, the California Supreme Court has ruled that after a dissolution of a marriage the person who has earned pension benefits but has not yet retired must still pay a former spouse a share of the benefits. The court said that "a unilateral choice to postpone retirement cannot be manipulated so as to impair a spouse's interest in those retirement benefits." If the employee is retired, a portion of the monthly payment can be awarded to the nonemployee spouse.

Railroad Retirement Act: The Supreme Court has ruled that benefits are not divisible as community property. (*Hisquierdo v. Hisquierdo* (1979) 99 S.Ct. 802.)

Military Retirement Pay: A United States Supreme Court decision has held that federal law governing military retirement pay precludes state courts from dividing such pay in divorce proceedings pursuant to state community property laws. (*McCarty v. McCarty* (1981) 49 U.S. Law Week 4850.)

See Mason, California Family Law Handbook, Chapter 10, pages 131 *et seq.*, for a discussion of pension and retirement benefits.

Life insurance policies: The legal assistant should check with the life insurance companies involved as to the cash surrender values of life insurance policies. In fixing value, possible dividends should also be considered. If the policy was in existence at the time of marriage, the difference, *i.e.*, presumable increase, in its cash values should be computed.

Even term policies with no cash surrender value may have intrinsic value if the insured is no longer insurable. The legal assistant should ascertain dates, amounts, names of insured and named beneficiary of all insurance policies. If possible, the actual policies should be reviewed.

Stocks and bonds: A stockbroker can supply the current market value of any stocks and bonds. The difference between the highest and lowest selling price on the valuation date is usually split in fixing value. The legal assistant should also ascertain how title is held.

Real estate: Real estate may have to be appraised, either by an inheritance tax referee, as in San Francisco and Los Angeles, or an independent appraiser hired.

Comparable sales in the area may provide adequate basis for valuation. Substantial properties would justify the cost of an expert appraiser. If only a modest home is involved, it should not be necessary to employ the highest qualified expert.

If the sale of the home is imminent, an argument can be made that the costs of the sale, and any capital gains tax, be deducted from the equity. An order might be obtained for payment of the appraiser's fee from the sale price.

Sales have tax effects on the parties, and the benefit of a tax accountant's advice is frequently beneficial.

Court rulings also have tax effects and therefore testimony of a tax accountant is desirable to fully advise the court before a ruling is made. Transfers of property ordered by the court are not subject to gift tax. Adverse tax effects may generate a malpractice claim if the client was not fully informed beforehand.

The field of taxation is becoming increasingly complex, and the average practitioner, client or judge cannot be expected to be tax experts, but they should be mindful that their actions during the dissolution proceeding may have present or future income or estate tax consequences. Being a tax expert is now a full-time occupation.

To illustrate, suppose a wife were to be awarded some rental units with no cash flow, or even, what is becoming more prevalent, negative cash flow. Does she have the means to make the payments? If she does, is it in her best interests to hold such a property? If she did not have the means to make the payments, immediate sale would be necessary to avoid foreclosure. Suppose that in addition it has a low adjusted basis. (By "adjusted basis" is meant the cost plus improvements minus depreciation taken; sales price minus adjusted basis is subject to capital gains.) How much would the capital gains tax be? How high is the mortgage? Would she net any money at all?

Good will: One of the parties may own a business or have a professional practice. Then the value of the good will of that business or practice must be determined. While good will is an intangible asset, it is regarded as property, with a value. "The 'good will' of a business is the expectation of continued public patronage." (Bus. & Prof. Code §14100.) As defined in *In re Lyons* (1938) 27 Cal.App.2d 293, 297-298, good will is " 'the advantage or benefit which is acquired by an establishment beyond the mere value of the capital stock, funds, or property employed therein, in consequence of the general public patronage and encouragement which it receives from constant or habitual customers, on account of its local position, or common celebrity, or reputation for skill . . . . [Citation.] . . . it is the probability that the old customers will resort to the old place. It is the probability that the business will continue in the future as in the past, adding to the profits of the concern and contributing to the means of meeting its engagements as they come in.' ''

Good will is determined on the facts and circumstances of each case and must exist at the time of the dissolution. Valuation is sometimes based on net income, net earnings, or accounts receivable. (See *In re Marriage of Foster,* 42 Cal.App.2d 577, 580, re methods of valuation of a medical practice.)

If one of the parties is in business, a CPA may be needed to establish the value of the business; if a professional practice is involved, the assets, accounts receivable and good will have to be valued. Time of valuation should approximate the time of trial.

Household furniture and furnishings: Hopefully the parties can agree as to the fair market value of household furniture and furnishings and an appraisal not be needed. The cost of an appraisal may exceed the difference of the parties' values. Cost of furniture has little relationship to present value because furniture depreciates rapidly.

Ordinarily the valuation of an expert is required to establish the value of antiques, works of art, unusual jewelry. Preferably this is done with the understanding and agreement of counsel that the appraiser's report will be admitted into evidence and that he need not testify at the trial, adding to the expense. Art galleries may be of assistance.

Automobiles: The value of an automobile can be determined by examining the retail and wholesale *Kelly's Blue Book* values; often the value is fixed halfway between. If the firm does not own a copy of *Kelly's Blue Book*, the legal assistant can usually get this information over the phone from an automobile dealer.

The legal assistant should also get a description of the automobile and ascertain how title is held.

Social security benefits: If a wife or husband is entitled to social security for his or her own employment, the benefits are separate property and are not includible. However, if either party has a right to social security only as a spouse of the other, it is community property and should be included.

Personal injury damages: Effective January 1, 1980, money or other property received by a married person in satisfaction of a judgment for damages for personal injury — or pursuant to an agreement for settlement or compromise of a claim for damages — is the separate property *if the cause of action arose* while the spouses were living separate and apart or after a decree of legal separation or interlocutory or final judgment of dissolution. This change applies retroactively in any case where marital property rights have not been adjudicated by a decree of dissolution or legal separation which has become final. (Civ. Code §§4800 and 5126) (Previously personal injury damages were separate property when *received* after a decree of legal separation or interlocutory or final judgment of dissolution, or while spouses were living separate and apart.)

Educational Loans: Educational loans are to be assigned to the spouse receiving the education in the absence of extraordinary circumstances rendering such an assignment unjust. (Civ. Code §4800.4.)

Assignment of Contracts

Where an attorney represents a client in an action for dissolution or legal separation, the attorney is required to give written notice to his or her client that although an obligation based on a contract is assigned to one party, if the party to whom the contract was assigned defaults on the contract, the creditor may have a cause of action against the other party. (Civ. Code §4800.6.)

Tax Considerations

In preparing a property settlement agreement counsel must look at the tax effects. Certainly if the tax ramifications threaten to be too complicated for the attorney, he will consult an accountant to avoid any claim of malpractice. The parties should be fully informed as to the tax consequences of their settlement. A better look at the tax situation can be taken in arriving at an agreement than through a court decision.

If co-owned property is divided equally, no gain or loss ensues. If property is transferred to settle rights a taxable gain or a loss *may* result. The gain or loss is equal to the difference between the appraised value (amount property is worth when transferred) and the basis.

If the community property is divided unequally, pursuant to an agreement, a gift tax situation could arise. A transfer will not be subject to a gift tax if it is made pursuant to a written agreement, the final judgment of dissolution is entered within two years of the effective date of the agreement, and the transfer is made to settle their respective marital or property rights or is a reasonable allowance for the support of their children. (IRC §2516.)

If the parties jointly own 600 shares of ABC stock, and each gets 300 shares without a sale of the stock, no capital gain or loss is involved and they keep its original tax basis. If they sell the same stock and divide the proceeds equally, each has a gain or loss.

If each spouse keeps his or her *separate* property, no tax is involved; otherwise, gift taxes might become payable.

Often the principal residence must be sold, and tax questions arise. (See IRC 121 and Rev. & Tax. Code §17155.) A look must be taken, then, at how each spouse is individually affected tax-wise, what they can deduct, their future tax brackets, tax liability incurred, payment of tax, and their after-tax net.

The legal assistant who may be drafting property settlement agreements is not ordinarily expected to be a tax expert but must be aware of at least some of the more common tax consequences that occur. The greater the tax expertise of the legal assistant, the greater his/her value to the attorney.

Some items are deductible by one spouse and the same must be reported as income by the other spouse. Who gets the tax advantage, if any, is the question that must be asked. Capital gain taxes and/or income taxes must both be considered. For instance, what about spousal support payments?

Spousal support payments:

Deductible by the paying spouse from gross income.

Taxable as income to the receiving spouse.

Items paid pursuant to the decree (such as rent, utility bills):

Itemized deduction for the spouse who makes payments. ("Itemized deductions" must be distinguished from deductions from gross income as for alimony. The fact that an item may be taken as an itemized deduction may be of no value to the spouse who is going to be taking the standard deduction in any event; of course, circumstances can change that too.)

Taxable as income to the spouse whom the payments benefit.

Life insurance premiums on a policy on life of Husband (H) where Wife (W) is owner and irrevocable beneficiary and decree specifies that W shall be the owner:

Deductible by H as spousal support from gross income.

Taxable to W as income. (Minus value to W unless and until she collects, however.)

House payments (mortgage payments, taxes, insurance) paid by H on former residence of H and W, pursuant to decree:

(a) *W sole owner:*

Payments are treated as spousal support from H and deductible from H's gross income.

Taxable income to W, but interest and taxes may be an itemized deduction by W.

(b) *H sole owner and W lives in home rent free, pursuant to decree:*

H cannot deduct fair rental value as spousal support. H may deduct interest and taxes if he itemizes.

Life insurance premiums paid by H on a policy not owned by W and on which W is only a contingent beneficiary:

Not deductible by H as spousal support.

Not included in W's income.

H and W own former residence as tenants in common (without right of survivorship) and both are personally and equally liable for mortgage:

H pays mortgage (principal and interest), insurance and taxes. H may deduct one-half as spousal support and if H itemizes deductions he may deduct one-half the real estate taxes and interest.

W includes one-half the mortgage payments, insurance and taxes in taxable income. If W itemizes deductions, W may deduct one-half real estate taxes and interest. Insurance is nondeductible.

H and W own home as joint tenants with right of survivorship or as tenants by the entirety, and both are personally and equally liable for mortgage:

Pursuant to agreement made part of the divorce decree H pays spousal support from which W is to pay the mortgage payments. H may deduct one-half of each principal and interest payment as spousal support from gross income. If H itemizes, he may deduct one-half of the interest and *all* the property taxes.

If W itemizes deductions, W may deduct one-half the interest payment.

Child Support Payments

The parent making child support payments may not deduct them. Payments for care, support and education may not be deducted. The custodial parent need not report child support payments as income. Counsel should consider these facts in deciding on amount of spousal support and child support.

Another consideration is, who is going to be eligible to claim the dependency exemption(s) for the child or children? As a general rule, exemption turns on who has custody for most of the year, but there are exceptions.

The noncustodial parent may claim medical expenses paid from support payments he/she made, if he/she itemizes deductions, subject to medical deduction limitations, if he/she is entitled to claim the child as dependent.

The noncustodial parent may take the exemption if the noncustodial parent paid at least $600 for the child's support during the year, and the decree (or separation agreement) permits.

However, the noncustodial parent can claim the exemption in any event if it can be proved he or she provided $1,200 or more during the year and the custodial parent cannot prove he or she supplied a greater amount.

If the noncustodial spouse pays both spousal support and child support pursuant to the decree, and pays a lesser amount than the total, the payments apply first to child support (nondeductible) and then spousal support (deductible).

For example, Husband (H) pays $300 a month child support and $200 a month spousal support. If H makes payments for a year, H may deduct $2,400 spousal support and Wife (W) must report $2,400 income. H may not deduct the $3,600 child support.

If H pays a total of only $5,000 during the year, $3,600 is child support and $1,400 is spousal support. H may deduct only $1,400 as spousal support and W reports $1,400 income.

For a discussion of child support payments, see Mason, *California Family Law Handbook*, pages 159, *et seq.*

The attorney's fee for the divorce is not deductible. The following are deductible:

A. cost of tax advice paid by the person receiving the benefit,

B. legal fees for securing or collecting spousal support. (Attorney should itemize his charges so client can determine what is deductible.)

In the year the final decree of divorce is filed, each of the parties must file as an unmarried person.

The legal assistant may wish to obtain a copy of IRS Publication 504, Tax Information for Divorced or Separated Individuals, available without charge from IRS offices.

Stipulation for Judgment

A stipulation for judgment in the form prescribed by Rule 1287 may be submitted to the court for signature at the time of the hearing on the merits. At the end of the document, immediately above the space reserved for the judge's signature, the following language must be included:

"The foregoing is agreed to by:

[signature]	[signature]
(Petitioner)	(Respondent)
[signature]	[signature]
(Attorney for Petitioner)	(Attorney of Respondent)

The approved form, *"Interlocutory Judgment of Dissolution of Marriage (Family Law)"* follows:

Interlocutory Judgment of Dissolution of Marriage (Family Law)

ATTORNEY OR PARTY WITHOUT ATTORNEY (NAME AND ADDRESS):	TELEPHONE NO.:	FOR COURT USE ONLY
ATTORNEY FOR (NAME):		

SUPERIOR COURT OF CALIFORNIA, COUNTY OF
STREET ADDRESS:
MAILING ADDRESS:
CITY AND ZIP CODE:
BRANCH NAME:

MARRIAGE OF
PETITIONER:

RESPONDENT:

INTERLOCUTORY JUDGMENT OF DISSOLUTION OF MARRIAGE	CASE NUMBER:

1. This proceeding came on for ☐ default or uncontested ☐ contested hearing as follows

    a. Date: ☐ Dept.: ☐ Div.: ☐ Room:

    b. Judge (name): ☐ Temporary judge

    c. ☐ Petitioner present in court ☐ Attorney present in court (name):

    d. ☐ Respondent present in court ☐ Attorney present in court (name):

    e. ☐ Claimant present in court ☐ Attorney present in court (name):

2. The court acquired jurisdiction of the respondent on (date):
    a. ☐ Respondent was served with process.
    b. ☐ Respondent appeared.

3. THE COURT ORDERS
    a. An interlocutory judgment be entered and the parties are entitled to have their marriage dissolved.

    b. After six months from the date the court acquired jurisdiction of the respondent a final judgment of dissolution may be entered upon proper application of either party or on the court's own motion, unless a dismissal signed by both parties is filed. The final judgment shall include such other and further relief as may be necessary to a complete disposition of this proceeding, but entry of the final judgment shall not deprive this court of its jurisdiction over any matter expressly reserved to it in this or the final judgment until a final disposition is made of each such matter.

    c. Jurisdiction is reserved to make such other and further orders as may be necessary to carry out the provisions of this judgment.

4. ☐ THE COURT FURTHER ORDERS
    a. ☐ Wife's former name be restored (specify):
    b. ☐ Other:

Dated: . . . . _____
                                                   Judge of the Superior Court

5. Total number of pages attached: ☐ Signature follows last attachment

---

THIS INTERLOCUTORY JUDGMENT DOES NOT CONSTITUTE A FINAL DISSOLUTION OF MARRIAGE AND THE PARTIES ARE STILL MARRIED. ONE OF THE PARTIES MUST SUBMIT A REQUEST FOR FINAL JUDGMENT ON THE FORM PRESCRIBED BY RULE 1288. NEITHER PARTY MAY REMARRY UNTIL A FINAL JUDGMENT OF DISSOLUTION IS ENTERED.

ALTHOUGH AN OBLIGATION BASED ON A CONTRACT IS ASSIGNED TO ONE PARTY AS PART OF THE DIVISION OF THE COMMUNITY, IF THE PARTY TO WHOM THE OBLIGATION WAS ASSIGNED DEFAULTS ON THE CONTRACT, THE CREDITOR MAY HAVE A CAUSE OF ACTION AGAINST THE OTHER PARTY.

No attachment permitted on less than a full page. Cal Rule of Ct 201(b)

Form Adopted by Rule 1287
Judicial Council of California
Revised Effective January 1, 1981

**INTERLOCUTORY JUDGMENT OF
DISSOLUTION OF MARRIAGE
(FAMILY LAW)**

CC 4512, 4514

Notice of Entry of Interlocutory Judgment

The form of *Notice of Entry of Judgment* (Rule 1290) should be prepared and submitted to the court in triplicate with carbons intact, completed except for signatures, and showing the names and addresses of the parties' attorneys or the parties' last-known addresses. The clerk serves the notice on the parties. The form follows:

Notice of Entry of Judgment (Family Law)

ATTORNEY OR PARTY WITHOUT ATTORNEY (NAME AND ADDRESS):	TELEPHONE NO.:	FOR COURT USE ONLY
ATTORNEY FOR (NAME):		

SUPERIOR COURT OF CALIFORNIA, COUNTY OF
STREET ADDRESS:
MAILING ADDRESS:
CITY AND ZIP CODE:
BRANCH NAME:

MARRIAGE OF
PETITIONER:

RESPONDENT:

NOTICE OF ENTRY OF JUDGMENT	CASE NUMBER:

You are notified that the following judgment was entered on (date):

1. ☐ Interlocutory Judgment of Dissolution of Marriage

> THE INTERLOCUTORY JUDGMENT TO WHICH THIS NOTICE REFERS DOES NOT CONSTITUTE A FINAL DISSOLUTION OF MARRIAGE AND THE PARTIES ARE STILL MARRIED. ONE OF THE PARTIES MUST SUBMIT A REQUEST FOR A FINAL JUDGMENT ON THE FORM PRESCRIBED BY RULE 1288. NEITHER PARTY MAY REMARRY UNTIL A FINAL JUDGMENT OF DISSOLUTION IS ENTERED.

2. ☐ Final Judgment of Dissolution of Marriage
3. ☐ Final Judgment of Legal Separation
4. ☐ Final Judgment of Nullity

Dated: . . . .   Clerk, By _____ , Deputy

CLERK'S CERTIFICATE OF MAILING

I certify that I am not a party to this cause and that a copy of the foregoing was mailed first class, postage prepaid, in a sealed envelope addressed as shown below, and that the mailing of the foregoing and execution of this certificate occurred at (place): . . . . , California,

on (date): . . . .   Clerk, By _____ , Deputy

Form Adopted by Rule 1290
Judicial Council of California
Revised Effective January 1, 1980

**NOTICE OF ENTRY OF JUDGMENT
(FAMILY LAW)**

An appeal may be taken from an interlocutory judgment, including the provisions determining the separate, community or quasi-community property, regardless of whether the court has reserved jurisdiction to divide all or a portion of the community or quasi-community property.

Request for Final Judgment

After the lapse of six months from the date of service of summons and petition upon respondent and 60 days from the date of mailing of the *Notice of Entry of Judgment (Family Law)*, a form of *Request and Declarations for Final Judgment of Dissolution of Marriage (Family Law)* should be filed. At the same time a *Notice of Entry of Judgment (Family Law)* form should be submitted to the court, as was done at the time of obtaining the interlocutory judgment. An original and a copy of the *Final Judgment (Family Law)* form should also be submitted to the court.

Commencing January 1, 1981, every final judgment declaring a marriage or nullity or dissolving a marriage contains the following language:

"Notice, Please review your will. Unless a provision is made in the property settlement agreement, this court proceeding does not affect your will and the ability of your former spouse to take under it." (Civ. Code §4352.)

If after executing a will or codicil on or after January 1, 1981, a testator's marriage is dissolved or declared a nullity by a final judgment and if the testator and his or her former spouse have executed a property settlement agreement waiving and renouncing all rights to inherit from the other, or to receive property under a will executed prior to the agreement, the former spouse of the testator and the lineal descendants of the former spouse shall be deemed to have predeceased the testator.

"Lineal descendants" in this section (Prob. Code §80) includes all lineal descendants of the former spouse of the testator who are not also lineal descendants of the testator. However, these provisions are not applicable if the testator's death occurs during the remarriage to the former spouse.

The filing of an appeal or a motion for new trial does not stay the granting of a final judgment as to the dissolution of marriage status, unless the appealing or moving party specifies an objection in the notice of appeal or motion for new trial. However, such objections are precluded unless first made at time of trial. (Civ. Code §4514.)

Where the parties first filed for summary dissolution but later revoked and filed for dissolution under section 4503 within 90 days thereafter, the period of time between the filing of the joint petition and date of its revocation is deducted in calculating the permissible date for entry of final judgment. (Code of Civil Proc. §4514(c).)

Government Code section 26859 requires that at the time of entry of final judgment in a dissolution proceeding, legal separation or nullity decree, the petitioner pay a fee of $2 to the county clerk. The county clerk in turn sends a copy of the final decree to the Bureau of Vital Statistics, from which a statewide index is compiled.

When the final judgment has been entered, the clerk of the court will mail a copy of the *Notice of Entry of Judgment (Family Law)* to the address on the form and return a copy of the *Final Judgment (Family Law)* conformed to the original. Copies of the *Request and Declarations for Final Judgment of Dissolution of Marriage (Family Law)* and *Final Judgment (Family Law)* follow:

Request and Declaration for Final Judgment of Dissolution of Marriage

ATTORNEY OR PARTY WITHOUT ATTORNEY (NAME AND ADDRESS)	TELEPHONE NO.:	FOR COURT USE ONLY

ATTORNEY FOR (NAME)

SUPERIOR COURT OF CALIFORNIA, COUNTY OF
STREET ADDRESS:
MAILING ADDRESS:
CITY AND ZIP CODE:
BRANCH NAME:

MARRIAGE OF
PETITIONER:

RESPONDENT:

REQUEST AND DECLARATION FOR FINAL JUDGMENT OF DISSOLUTION OF MARRIAGE	CASE NUMBER

1. The court acquired jurisdiction of the respondent on (date):

2. An Interlocutory Judgment of Dissolution of Marriage was entered on (date):

3. Since entry of the Interlocutory Judgment the parties have not become reconciled and have not agreed to dismiss this proceeding. No motion or other proceeding to set aside or annul, and no appeal from that part of the interlocutory judgment granting dissolution of the marriage, is pending and undetermined, and that part of the judgment has become final.

4. I request that final judgment of dissolution of marriage be entered.
   a. ☐ Endorsed copies of a Joint Petition for Summary Dissolution and a Notice of Revocation are attached and I request entry of final judgment pursuant to Civil Code section 4514(b).
   b. ☐ I request judgment be entered effective (nunc pro tunc)
      (1) As of (date):
      (2) For the following reason:

5. ☐ Other request (specify):

6. I declare under penalty of perjury that the foregoing is true and correct and that this declaration is executed on (date): . . . . at (place): . . . . , California.

. . . .   _____
(Type or print name)   (Signature of declarant)

. . . .   _____
(Type or print name)   (Signature of attorney for declarant)

The declaration under penalty of perjury must be signed in California, or in a state that authorizes use of a declaration in place of an affidavit; otherwise an affidavit is required.

Form Adopted by Rule 1288
Judicial Council of California
Revised Effective January 1, 1980

**REQUEST AND DECLARATION FOR FINAL
JUDGMENT OF DISSOLUTION OF MARRIAGE
(FAMILY LAW)**

CC 4514, 4515

Final Judgment (Family Law)

ATTORNEY OR PARTY WITHOUT ATTORNEY (Name and Address):	TELEPHONE NO.:	FOR COURT USE ONLY
ATTORNEY FOR (Name):		

SUPERIOR COURT OF CALIFORNIA, COUNTY OF

STREET ADDRESS:
MAILING ADDRESS:
CITY AND ZIP CODE:
BRANCH NAME:

MARRIAGE OF
PETITIONER:
RESPONDENT:

FINAL JUDGMENT OF	☐ **DISSOLUTION OF MARRIAGE** ☐ **LEGAL SEPARATION** ☐ **NULLITY** ☐ **DISSOLUTION OF MARRIAGE—STATUS ONLY**	CASE NUMBER:

1. The court acquired jurisdiction of the respondent on (date):

2. THE COURT ORDERS

     a. ☐ A final judgment of dissolution be entered, and the parties are restored to the status of unmarried persons.
     b. ☐ A judgment of legal separation be entered.
     c. ☐ A judgment of nullity be entered on the ground of (specify):

     and the parties are declared to be unmarried persons.

3. ☐ THE COURT FURTHER ORDERS

     a. This judgment be entered nunc pro tunc as of (date):
     b. Wife's former name be restored (specify):
     c. ☐ Other:

Dated: . . . .   ————————————
                                           Judge of the Superior Court

                                 ☐ Signature follows last attachment.

4. Total number of pages attached:

NOTICE

PLEASE REVIEW YOUR WILL. UNLESS A PROVISION IS MADE IN THE PROPERTY SETTLEMENT AGREEMENT, THIS COURT PROCEEDING DOES NOT AFFECT YOUR WILL AND THE ABILITY OF YOUR FORMER SPOUSE TO TAKE UNDER IT.

IF YOU FAIL TO PAY ANY COURT ORDERED CHILD SUPPORT, AN ASSIGNMENT OF YOUR WAGES WILL BE OBTAINED WITHOUT FURTHER NOTICE TO YOU.

No attachment permitted on less than a full page. Cal Rule of Ct 201(b)

Form Adopted by Rule 1289   **FINAL JUDGMENT**
Judicial Council of California   **(FAMILY LAW)**   CC 4514, 4515
Revised Effective January 1, 1981

Joinder of Parties

The Family Law Act provides for joinder of parties who claim an interest in the proceeding. Such parties are called "claimants." The persons who may seek joinder are listed in California Rules of Court, Rule 1252, to wit:

a. Petitioner or respondent may ask for order of joinder of a person who has or claims custody or physical control of any of the minor children of the marriage or who controls or claims to control any property subject to jurisdiction of court in the proceeding.

b. The party himself who claims custody or physical control may apply for the order.

c. A person who has been served with an order temporarily restraining use of property in his possession or control or to which he claims to own or affecting the custody of minor children of the marriage.

A *Notice of Motion and Declaration for Joinder (Family Law)* is served and filed and specifies a hearing date not more than 20 days from the date of filing the notice. (See Rule 1291.20.) If the court orders that a person be joined, it will issue an *Order re Joinder (Family Law)* (see Rule 1291.30) and a *Summons (Joinder) (Family Law)* (See Rule 1291.40). The claimant must then be served with:

1. *Notice of Motion and Declaration re Joinder (Family Law)* and the accompanying pleading setting forth the claim,

2. *Order re Joinder (Family Law)* and the,

3. *Summons (Joinder).*

The *Responsive Declaration to Motion for Joinder Consent Order of Joinder (Family Law)* is in response to the above documents.

The forms follow:

Notice of Motion and Declaration for Joinder (Family Law)

ATTORNEY OR PARTY WITHOUT ATTORNEY (NAME AND ADDRESS):	TELEPHONE NO.:	FOR COURT USE ONLY
ATTORNEY FOR (NAME):		

SUPERIOR COURT OF CALIFORNIA, COUNTY OF
STREET ADDRESS:
MAILING ADDRESS:
CITY AND ZIP CODE:
BRANCH NAME:

MARRIAGE OF
PETITIONER:

RESPONDENT:

NOTICE OF MOTION AND DECLARATION FOR JOINDER	CASE NUMBER:

NOTICE OF MOTION

1. TO ☐ Petitioner ☐ Respondent

2. A hearing on this motion for joinder will be held as follows

    a. date: time: in ☐ Dept.:   ☐ Div.:   ☐ Rm.:

    b. Address of court:

    c. ☐ Petitioner ☐ Respondent ☐ Claimant will apply to this court for an order joining claimant as a party to this proceeding on the grounds set forth in the Declaration below.

3. The pleading required by California Rules of Court rule 1253 accompanies this notice of motion.

Dated: . . . .

. . . .
(Type or print name)   (Signature)

DECLARATION FOR JOINDER

4. Facts showing that each person sought or seeking to be joined possesses or controls or claims to own any property subject to disposition by this court, or that such person has or claims custody, physical control or visitation rights with respect to any minor child of the marriage, are (specify):

(Continued on reverse)

The declaration under penalty of perjury must be signed in California, or in a state that authorizes use of a declaration in place of an affidavit; otherwise an affidavit is required.

Form Adopted by Rule 1291.10
Judicial Council of California
Revised Effective January 1, 1980

NOTICE OF MOTION AND DECLARATION FOR JOINDER (FAMILY LAW)

CC 4363

5. Facts showing that it would be appropriate for this court to determine the particular issue in the proceeding are:

6. Facts showing that each person sought or seeking to be joined is either indispensable to a determination of the particular issue or necessary to the enforcement of any judgment rendered on the issue are:

I declare under penalty of perjury that the foregoing, including any attachment, is true and correct and that this declaration is executed at (place): . . . . , California, on (date): . . . .

. . . . _____
(Type or print name)   (Signature of declarant)

Summons (Joinder)

Name, Address and Telephone No of Attorney(s)

Space Below for Use of Court Clerk Only

ATTORNEY(S) FOR . . . .

SUPERIOR COURT OF CALIFORNIA, COUNTY OF . . . .

. . . .
(Insert post office and street address of court or branch court)

In re the marriage of

Petitioner:

and

Respondent:

CASE NUMBER

SUMMONS (JOINDER)

NOTICE! You have been sued. The court may decide against you without your being heard unless you respond within 30 days. Read the information below.

¡AVISO! Usted ha sido demandado. El tribunal puede decidir contra Ud. sin audiencia a menos que Ud. responda dentro de 30 dias. Lea la información que sigue.

1. TO THE PETITIONER/RESPONDENT. CLAIMANT (See footnote*).

    a. A pleading has been filed pursuant to an order joining (Name of Claimant):

    as a party in this proceeding You may file an appropriate written pleading within **30** days of the date that this summons is served on you

    b If you fail to file a written response within such time, your default may be entered and the court may enter a judgment containing the relief requested in the pleading, court costs, and such other relief as may be granted by the court which could result in the garnishment of wages, taking of money or property, or other relief

    c. **If you wish to seek the advice of an attorney in this matter, you should do so promptly so that your pleading, if any, may be filed on time.**

Dated . . . ., Clerk, By _____, Deputy

(SEAL)

2. ☐ **NOTICE TO THE PERSON SERVED:** You are served

    a. ☐ As an individual defendant.

    b. ☐ As (or on behalf of) the person sued under the fictitious name of: . . . .

    c ☐ On behalf of: . . . .

    Under: ☐ CCP 416.10 (Corporation)   ☐ CCP 416.60 (Minor)

             ☐ CCP 416.20 (Defunct Corporation)   ☐ CCP 416.70 (Incompetent)

             ☐ CCP 416.40 (Association or Partnership)   ☐ CCP 416.90 (Individual)

             ☐ Other

* A written pleading must be in the form required by the California Rules of Court It must be filed in this court with the proper filing fee and proof of service of a copy on each party to the proceeding The time when a summons is deemed served on a party may vary depending on the method of service For example, see CCP 413.10 through 415 40

Form Adopted by Rule 1291 40 of
The Judicial Council of California
Revised Effective January 1, 1975

(See reverse side for Proof of Service)

SUMMONS (JOINDER)

PROOF OF SERVICE

(See Instruction Sheet and use separate proof of service for each person served)

I served the summons and ☐ (Title of pleading) . . . .
☐ Notice of Motion and Declaration re Joinder (Marriage),
☐ Order re Joinder (Marriage),   ☐ Order to Show Cause (Marriage),
☐ **Blank** Responsive Declaration,   ☐ **Blank** Financial Declaration, as follows:

1. Name: 4. Date and time of delivery:

2. Person served and title: 5. Mailing date, type of mail and place of mailing:

3. Person with whom left and title or relationship to person served: 6. Address, city and state (when required, indicate whether address is home or business):

7. Manner of service: (Check proper box)

☐ **(Personal service)** By personally delivering copies to the person served. (CCP 415.10.)

☐ **(Substituted service on corporation, unincorporated association (including partnership), or public entity)** By leaving, during usual office hours, copies in the office of the person served with the person who apparently was in charge and thereafter mailing (by first-class mail, postage prepaid) copies to the person served at the place where the copies were left (CCP 415.20(a).)

☐ **(Substituted service on natural person, minor, incompetent, or candidate)** By leaving copies at the dwelling house, usual place of abode, or usual place of business of the person served in the presence of a competent member of the household or a person apparently in charge of his office or place of business, at least 18 years of age, who was informed of the general nature of the papers, and thereafter mailing (by first-class mail, postage prepaid) copies to the person served at the place where the copies were left (CCP 415.20(b). **Attach separate declaration or affidavit stating acts relied on to establish reasonable diligence in first attempting personal service.)**

☐ **(Mail and acknowledgment service)** By mailing (by first-class mail or airmail) copies to the person served, together with two copies of the form of notice and acknowledgment and a return envelope, postage prepaid, addressed to the sender (CCP 415.30 **Attach written acknowledgment of receipt.)**

☐ **(Certified or registered mail service)** By mailing to address outside California (by registered or certified airmail with return receipt requested) copies to the person served (CCP 415.40 **Attach signed return receipt or other evidence of actual delivery to the person served.)**

☐ **(Other—CCP 413.10, 413.30, 417.10–417.30—Attach separate page if necessary):**   ☐ Additional page is attached

8. The following notice appeared on the copy of the summons served (CCP 412.30 or 474):

☐ You are served as an individual defendant.
☐ You are served as (or on behalf of) the person sued under the fictitious name of
☐ You are served on behalf of:
Under: ☐ CCP 416.10 (Corporation)   ☐ CCP 416.60 (Minor)   ☐ Other:
         ☐ CCP 416.20 (Defunct corporation)   ☐ CCP 416.70 (Incompetent)
         ☐ CCP 416.40 (Association or partnership) ☐ CCP 416.90 (Individual)

9. At the time of service I was at least 18 years of age and not a party to this action.

10. Fee for service $. . . . . . Mileage $. . . . . Notary $. . . . . Total $

(To be completed in California by process server, other than a sheriff, marshal or constable*)	(To be completed in California by sheriff, marshal or constable*)
☐ Not a registered California process server (CCP 417.40).	I certify that the foregoing is true and correct and that this certificate was executed on (Insert date) . . . .
☐ Registered: . . . . County, Number:	at (Insert place) . . . . , California. (Type or print name, title, county and, when applicable, Municipal or Justice Court District)
I declare under penalty of perjury that the foregoing is true and correct and that this declaration was executed on (Insert date) . . . . at (Insert place) . . . . , California. (Type or print name, address, and telephone no.)	

Signature: Signature:

This declaration or certificate of service must be executed within California (CCP 2015.5) A proof of service executed outside California must be made by affidavit

Responsive Declaration to Motion for Joinder Consent Order of Joinder (Family Law)

ATTORNEY OR PARTY WITHOUT ATTORNEY (NAME AND ADDRESS):	TELEPHONE NO	FOR COURT USE ONLY
ATTORNEY FOR (NAME):		

SUPERIOR COURT OF CALIFORNIA, COUNTY OF
STREET ADDRESS
MAILING ADDRESS
CITY AND ZIP CODE
BRANCH NAME

MARRIAGE OF
PETITIONER:

RESPONDENT:

CLAIMANT:

RESPONSIVE DECLARATION TO MOTION FOR JOINDER ☐ **CONSENT ORDER OF JOINDER**	CASE NUMBER:

1. ☐ Petitioner ☐ Respondent

    a. ☐ Consents to the requested joinder and stipulates to an order joining claimant as a party to this proceeding.
    b. ☐ Does not consent to the requested joinder of claimant as a party to this proceeding.

2. ☐ The statements contained in the Declaration for Joinder are incorrect or insufficient as follows (specify):

I declare under penalty of perjury that the foregoing is true and correct and that this declaration was executed at (place) . . . . , California, on (date) . . . .

. . . .
(Type or print name)

. . . .
(Signature of declarant)

(See reverse for order)

The declaration under penalty of perjury must be signed in California, or in a state that authorizes use of a declaration in place of an affidavit, otherwise an affidavit is required

Form Adopted by Rule 1291.20
Judicial Council of California
Revised Effective January 1, 1980

RESPONSIVE DECLARATION TO MOTION FOR JOINDER
CONSENT ORDER OF JOINDER
(FAMILY LAW)

CONSENT ORDER

3. ☐ Petitioner ☐ Respondent having consented and good cause appearing,
   IT IS ORDERED that
   a. The claimant is joined as a party to this proceeding.
   b. The clerk file the original of the submitted pleadings.
   c. ☐ Summons (Joinder) be issued and claimant be served with a copy of the motion for joinder with pleading attached and a copy of the summons (Joinder).
   d. ☐ The hearing on the motion for joinder is taken off calendar for (date):

Dated: . . . .   _____
                                                                        Judge of the Superior Court

Joinder — Pension Plans

The judgment in the dissolution will not be enforceable against an employee pension benefit plan unless the plan is joined as a party to the proceeding (Civ. Code §4351), in accordance with the provisions of Civil Code Section 4363.1.

A *Request for Joinder of Employee Pension Benefit Plan and Order (Family Law)* must be filed with the court. After the court grants the order the following must be served upon a trustee or administrator of the plan:

1. *Pleading on Joinder — Employee Pension Benefit Plan (Family Law)*

2. Copy of *Request for Joinder of Employee Pension Benefit Plan and Order (Family Law)*

3. Copy of the *Summons (Joinder) (Family Law)* and

4. Blank copy of *Notice of Appearance and Response of Employee Pension Benefit Plan (Family Law)*.

If the *Notice of Appearance* is not filed in 30 days, default may be taken as provided in Civil Code section 4363.1(c).

The forms follow:

Pleading on Joinder — Employee Pension Benefit Plan (Family Law)

ATTORNEY OR UNREPRESENTED PARTY (NAME AND ADDRESS): TELEPHONE NO.:	FOR COURT USE ONLY
ATTORNEY FOR (Name):	

SUPERIOR COURT OF CALIFORNIA, COUNTY OF

MARRIAGE OF

PETITIONER

RESPONDENT

CLAIMANT

PLEADING ON JOINDER—EMPLOYEE PENSION BENEFIT PLAN	CASE NUMBER

TO THE CLAIMANT: You have been joined as a party claimant in this proceeding because an interest is claimed in the employee pension benefit plan that is or may be subject to disposition by this court. The party who obtained the order for your joinder declares

1. Information concerning the employee covered by the plan
   a. Name:
   b. Employer (Name):
   c. ☐ Name of labor union representing employee:
   d. ☐ Employee identification number:
   e. ☐ Other (Specify):

2. Petitioner's
   a. ☐ Attorney (Name, address and telephone number):

   b. ☐ Address and telephone number, if unrepresented by an attorney:

3. Respondent's
   a. ☐ Attorney (Name, address and telephone number):

   b. ☐ Address and telephone number, if unrepresented by an attorney:

4. Petition for dissolution ☐ and response states
   a. Date of marriage:
   b. Date of separation:

5. ☐ Response states
   a. Date of marriage:
   b. Date of separation:

6 Interlocutory judgment
   a. ☐ has not been entered
   b. ☐ was entered on (Date):
      (1) ☐ and disposes of each spouse's interest in the employee pension benefit plan.
      (2) ☐ and does not dispose of each spouse's interest in the employee pension benefit plan.

(Continued on reverse)

Form adopted by Rule 1291.35
Judicial Council of California
Effective January 1, 1979

**PLEADING ON JOINDER—
EMPLOYEE PENSION BENEFIT PLAN
(FAMILY LAW)**

CC 4363.1

7. The following relief is sought

   a. ☐ An order determining the nature and extent of both employee and nonemployee spouse's interest, in employee's benefits under the plan.

   b. ☐ An order restraining claimant from making benefit payments to employee spouse pending the determination and disposition of nonemployee spouse's interest, if any, in employee's benefits under the plan.

   c. ☐ An order directing claimant to notify nonemployee spouse when benefits under the plan first become payable to employee.

   d. ☐ An order directing claimant to make payment to nonemployee spouse of said spouse's interest in employee's benefits under the plan when they become payable to employee.

   e. ☐ Other (Specify):

   f. Such other orders as may be appropriate.

_____

Signature of (Attorney for) ☐ petitioner ☐ respondent

Dated: . . . .

(Type or print name)

Request for Joinder of Employee Pension Benefit Plan and Order (Family Law)

ATTORNEY OR UNREPRESENTED PARTY (NAME AND ADDRESS). TELEPHONE NO.	FOR COURT USE ONLY
ATTORNEY FOR (Name)	

SUPERIOR COURT OF CALIFORNIA, COUNTY OF

MARRIAGE OF

PETITIONER

RESPONDENT

CLAIMANT

REQUEST FOR JOINDER OF EMPLOYEE PENSION BENEFIT PLAN AND ORDER	CASE NUMBER

TO THE CLERK

1. Please join as a party claimant to this proceeding (Name of employee pension benefit plan)

2. The pleading on joinder is submitted with this application for filing

Dated

Signature of (Attorney for)

[ ] Petitioner   [ ] Respondent

(Type or print name)

ORDER OF JOINDER

3. IT IS ORDERED

    a. The following is joined as a party claimant to this proceeding (Name of employee pension benefit plan):

    b. The pleading on joinder be filed
    c. Summons be issued
    d. Claimant be served with a copy of the pleading on joinder, a copy of this request for joinder and order, the summons and a blank Notice of Appearance and Response of Employee Pension Benefit Plan.

J. A. Simpson, County Clerk

Dated: Clerk, By   , Deputy

Claimant means a person joined or sought or seeking to be joined as a party to the proceeding. The pleading on joinder must be submitted for filing with this request for joinder and order. This form may only be used to request joinder of an employee pension benefit plan as defined in CC 4363 3

Form adopted by Rule 1291 15
Judicial Council of California
Revised Effective January 1, 1979

**REQUEST FOR JOINDER OF
EMPLOYEE PENSION BENEFIT PLAN AND ORDER
(FAMILY LAW)**

CC 4351, 4363–4363 3

Summons (Joinder) (Family Law)

ATTORNEY OR UNREPRESENTED PARTY: TELEPHONE NO.:	FOR COURT USE ONLY
ATTORNEY FOR (Name):	

SUPERIOR COURT OF CALIFORNIA, COUNTY OF

MARRIAGE OF

PETITIONER

RESPONDENT

CLAIMANT

SUMMONS (JOINDER)	CASE NUMBER:

NOTICE! You have been sued. The court may decide against you without your being heard unless you respond within 30 days. Read the information below.

If you wish to seek the advice of an attorney in this matter, you should do so promptly so that your response or pleading, if any, may be filed on time.

¡AVISO! Usted ha sido demandado. El tribunal puede decidir contra Ud. sin audiencia a menos que Ud. responda dentro de 30 dias. Lea la información que sigue.

Si Usted desea solicitar el consejo de un abogado en este asunto, deberia hacerlo inmediatamente, de esta manera, su respuesta o alegación, si hay alguna, puede ser registrada a tiempo.

1. ☐ TO THE ☐PETITIONER ☐RESPONDENT ☐CLAIMANT
   A pleading has been filed pursuant to an order joining (Name of claimant):

   as a party in this proceeding. If you fail to file an appropriate pleading within **30** days of the date this summons is served on you, your default may be entered and the court may enter a judgment containing the relief requested in the pleading, court costs and such other relief as may be granted by the court, which could result in the garnishment of wages, taking of money or property or other relief.

2. ☐ TO THE CLAIMANT EMPLOYEE PENSION BENEFIT PLAN
   A pleading on joinder has been filed pursuant to the clerk's order joining (Name of employee pension benefit plan):

   as a party claimant in this proceeding. If the Employee Pension Benefit Plan fails to file an appropriate pleading within **30** days of the date this summons is served on it, a default may be entered and the court may enter a judgment containing the relief requested.

Dated: Clerk, By _____ , Deputy

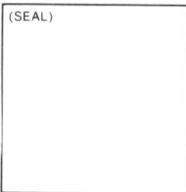

3. NOTICE TO THE PERSON SERVED: You are served

(SEAL)

    a. ☐ As an individual.

    b. ☐ As (or on behalf of) the person sued under the fictitious name of:

    c. ☐ On behalf of:

       Under: ☐ CCP 416.10 (Corporation)   ☐ CCP 416.60 (Minor)
              ☐ CCP 416.20 (Defunct Corporation)   ☐ CCP 416.70 (Incompetent)
              ☐ CCP 416.40 (Association or Partnership) ☐ CCP 416.90 (Individual)
              ☐ Other: ☐ CCP 4363.1 (Employee Pension Benefit Plan)

    d. ☐ By personal delivery on (Date):

A written pleading must be in the form required by the California Rules of Court. It must be filed in this court with any necessary filing fee and proof of service of a copy on each party to the proceeding. The time when a summons is deemed served on a party may vary depending on the method of service. For example, see CCP 413.10 through 415.50.

Form adopted by Rule 1291.40   **(See reverse for proof of service)**
Judicial Council of California   **SUMMONS (JOINDER)**
Revised Effective January 1, 1979   **(FAMILY LAW)**

PROOF OF SERVICE—SUMMONS (JOINDER)
(Use separate proof of service for each person served)

1. I served the
   a. Summons and (1) ☐ Request for Joinder of Employee Pension Benefit Plan and Order, Pleading on Joinder-Employee Pension Benefit Plan, blank Notice of Appearance and Response of Employee Pension Benefit Plan
      (2) ☐ Notice of Motion and Declaration Re Joinder (3) ☐ Order   Re Joinder
      (4) ☐ Pleading-Joinder (Specify title):
      (5) ☐ Other:
   b. On (Name of party or claimant):
   c. By serving (1) ☐ Party or claimant.   (2) ☐ Other (Name and title or relationship to person served):

   d. ☐ By delivery at ☐ home   ☐ business (1) Date of:
      (2)   Time of: (3) Address:

   e. ☐ By mailing (1) Date of: (2) Place of:
2. Manner of service: (Check proper box)
   a. ☐ **Personal service.** By personally delivering copies. (CCP 415.10)
   b. ☐ **Substituted service on corporation, unincorporated association (including partnership), or public entity.** By leaving, during usual office hours, copies in the office of the person served with the person who apparently was in charge and thereafter mailing (by first-class mail, postage prepaid) copies to the person served at the place where the copies were left. (CCP 415.20(a))
   c. ☐ **Substituted service on natural person, minor, incompetent, or candidate.** By leaving copies at the dwelling house, usual place of abode, or usual place of business of the person served in the presence of a competent member of the household or a person apparently in charge of the office or place of business, at least 18 years of age, who was informed of the general nature of the papers, and thereafter mailing (by first-class mail, postage prepaid) copies to the person served at the place where the copies were left. (CCP 415.20(b)) **(Attach separate declaration or affidavit stating acts relied on to establish reasonable diligence in first attempting personal service.)**
   d. ☐ **Mail and acknowledgment service.** By mailing (by first-class mail or airmail) copies to the person served, together with two copies of the form of notice and acknowledgment and a return envelope, postage prepaid, addressed to the sender. (CCP 415.30) **(Attach completed acknowledgment of receipt.)**
   e. ☐ **Certified or registered mail service.** By mailing to address outside California (by registered or certified airmail with return receipt requested) copies to the person served. (CCP 415.40) **(Attach signed return receipt or other evidence of actual delivery to the person served.)**
   f. ☐ Other (Specify code section):
      ☐ Additional page is attached.
3. The notice to the person served (Item 3 on the copy of the summons served) was completed as follows (CCP 412.30, 415.10 and 474):
   a. ☐ As an individual.
   b. ☐ As the person sued under the fictitious name of:
   c. ☐ On behalf of:
      Under: ☐ CCP 416.10 (Corporation)   ☐ CCP 416.60 (Minor)
             ☐ CCP 416.20 (Defunct corporation) ☐ CCP 416.70 (Incompetent)
             ☐ CCP 416.40 (Association or   ☐ CCP 416.90 (Individual)
                       partnership)   ☐ CCP 4363.1 (Employee Pension Benefit Plan)
   d. ☐ By personal delivery on (Date):
4. At the time of service I was at least 18 years of age and not a party to this action.
5. Fee for service: $ . . . .
6. Person serving
   a. ☐ Not a registered California process server.   e. Name, address and telephone number, and, if
   b. ☐ Registered California process server.   applicable, county of registration and number:
   c. ☐ Exempt from registration under Bus. & Prof.
        Code 22350(b).
   d. ☐ California sheriff, marshal, or constable.

I declare under penalty of perjury that the foregoing is true and correct and that this declaration is executed on (Date): . . . . at (Place): . . . . , California.

(For California Sheriff, Marshal, or Constable use only)
I certify that the foregoing is true and correct and that this certificate is executed on (Date): . . . . at (Place): . . . . , California

_____   _____
        (Signature)   (Signature)

A declaration under penalty of perjury must be signed in California or in a state that authorizes use of a declaration in place of an affidavit; otherwise an affidavit is required.

Notice of Appearance and Response of Employee Pension Benefit Plan (Family Law)

ATTORNEY OR UNREPRESENTED PARTY (NAME AND ADDRESS)   TELEPHONE NO.   FOR COURT USE ONLY

ATTORNEY FOR (Name)

SUPERIOR COURT OF CALIFORNIA, COUNTY OF

MARRIAGE OF

PETITIONER

RESPONDENT

CLAIMANT

NOTICE OF APPEARANCE ☐ AND RESPONSE OF EMPLOYEE PENSION BENEFIT PLAN	CASE NUMBER

1. An appearance in this proceeding is entered by claimant employee pension benefit plan (Name).

2. Service on claimant may be made as follows

 a. ☐ Attorney for claimant (Name, address and telephone number):

 b. ☐ Other (Name, title, address and telephone number):

3. ☐ Claimant responds to the pleading on joinder and states that the allegations of the pleading are

 a. ☐ correct

 b. ☐ incorrect as set forth in ☐ attachment 3b or ☐ as follows (Specify):

Dated: Claimant: . . . .

. . . . (Type or print name and title) . . . .   By _____   (Signature)

Claimant means a person joined or sought or seeking to be joined as a party to the proceeding
A copy of this notice must be served upon the party requesting joinder and a proof of service filed with the court

Form adopted by Rule 1291 25
Judicial Council of California
Revised Effective January 1, 1979

**NOTICE OF APPEARANCE AND RESPONSE
OF EMPLOYEE PENSION BENEFIT PLAN
(FAMILY LAW)**   CC 4351 4363–4363 3

Support of Spouse or Children and Attorney Fees

If temporary or permanent support of the petitioner or children is requested, or temporary custody of the children or attorney fees, or an injunctive order, is sought, the following Judicial Council forms must be filed:

1. *Order to Show Cause (Family Law)* (Rule 1285.10)
2. *Application for Order and Supporting Declaration (Family Law)* (Rule 1285.20)
3. *Responsive Declaration to Order to Show Cause or Notice of Motion (Family Law)* (Rule 1285.40)
4. *Property Declaration (Family Law)* (Rule 1285.50) is usually required, since the finances of the parties are usually relevant, and Rule 1243 requires that it be filed when it is relevant.

(The forms in paragraphs 1, 2 and 3 are set forth hereinbelow.)

The father and mother have equal responsibility to support and educate the child, taking into consideration their respective earnings and earning capacities. The court is required to make appropriate findings with regard to the basis of its order. (Civ. Code, §4700.)

When considering the earning capacity of each spouse in fixing spousal support, the court is to take into account "the extent to which the supported spouse's present and future earning capacity is impaired by periods of unemployment that were incurred during the marriage to permit the supported spouse to devote time to domestic duties." (Civ. Code §4801.)

The duty to support owed by a noncustodial parent for support of a minor child shall not be affected by a failure or refusal by the custodial parent to implement the rights of the noncustodial parent as to custody or visitation. (Civ. Code §4382.)

Under new Civil Code sections 4801.6 and 4801.7 courts are authorized, upon a showing of good cause, to order assignments of salary or wages sufficient to make payments of spousal support previously ordered, either to the person to whom the spousal support was ordered to be paid, or a county clerk, court officer or county officer designated by the court. (Ch. 866.)

Generally speaking, as to court-ordered child or spousal support payments, money held, controlled, or in process of distribution by a public agency for retirement or pension purposes, or the right to or payment of disability, death or other specified benefits, is no longer exempt from execution of judgment and is subject to garnishment, attachment or other process, and subject to assignment to a court or county officer. The right to benefits under the State Teacher's Retirement System is no longer exempt; neither is money from a private retirement plan or self-employed retirement plans and individual annuities and accounts. Specified unemployment insurance benefits are an exception. (See ch. 173, AB 145, Stats. 1980, amending Civ. Code §4701, Code Civ. Proc. §690.18, Educ. Code §22005, and Gov. Code §21201.)

If the respondent does not reply, the judge may make a determination in the matter without allowing the respondent to present any testimony or other evidence. The *Responsive Declaration* should be filed in advance of the hearing since if it is not filed until the date of the hearing the other party would not have an opportunity to properly respond to the matters raised in the documents.

The responding party may not, by filing this response, seek affirmative relief; to do so, he must file his own *Order to Show Cause, Notice of Motion,* and *Property Declaration.*

Attorneys' Fees

If attorney's fees are desired, they should be requested in the *Petition* or in the *Response.* But to obtain attorney's fees during the pendency of the action, an *Order to Show Cause* and supporting documents must be filed as explained above.

Order to Show Cause (Family Law)

ATTORNEY OR PARTY WITHOUT ATTORNEY (NAME AND ADDRESS):	TELEPHONE NO.:	FOR COURT USE ONLY
ATTORNEY FOR (NAME):		

SUPERIOR COURT OF CALIFORNIA, COUNTY OF
STREET ADDRESS:
MAILING ADDRESS:
CITY AND ZIP CODE:
BRANCH NAME

MARRIAGE OF
PETITIONER:

RESPONDENT:

ORDER TO SHOW CAUSE ☐ **FOR MODIFICATION** ☐ **ORDER SHORTENING TIME**	☐ **Child Custody** ☐ **Visitation** ☐ **Child Support** ☐ **Spousal Support** ☐ **Attorney Fees and Costs** ☐ **Injunctive Order** ☐ **Other (Specify):**	CASE NUMBER:

1. TO (Name):

2. YOU ARE ORDERED TO APPEAR IN THIS COURT AS FOLLOWS TO GIVE ANY LEGAL REASON WHY THE RELIEF SOUGHT IN THE ATTACHED APPLICATION SHOULD NOT BE GRANTED

   a. date: time: in ☐Dept.:   ☐ Div.:   ☐Rm.:

   b. Address of court:

3. IT IS FURTHER ORDERED that
   a. The following documents shall be served with this order
      (1) Application for Order and Supporting Declaration
      (2) ☐ Income and Expense Declaration
      (3) ☐ Property Declaration
      (4) ☐ Points and authorities
      (5) ☐ Other (specify):

   b. ☐ the application for an order shortening time is granted and this order may be served on or before (Date):
   c. ☐ Other (specify):

4. Total number of boxes checked in item 3:

Dated: . . . . _____
                                                  Judge of the Superior Court

Form Adopted by Rule 1285
Judicial Council of California
Effective January 1, 1980

ORDER TO SHOW CAUSE
(FAMILY LAW)

CC 4159 4170 4155 1 21 4809

Application for Order and Supporting Declaration (Family Law)

MARRIAGE OF (last name—first names of parties)	CASE NUMBER:

APPLICATION FOR ORDER AND SUPPORTING DECLARATION OF ☐ **PETITIONER** ☐ **RESPONDENT**
☐ **CLAIMANT** requests the following relief.

1. ☐ CHILD CUSTODY   ☐ TO BE ORDERED PENDING THE HEARING
     a. Child   b. Request custody to   c. ☐ Modify existing order
        (1) Name   (2) Age   (1) filed on (date):
                                                               (2) ordering (specify):

2. ☐ CHILD VISITATION   ☐ TO BE ORDERED PENDING THE HEARING
     a. ☐ Reasonable
     b. ☐ Other (specify):   c. ☐ Modify existing order
                                                   (1) filed on (date):
                                                   (2) ordering (specify):

3. ☐ CHILD SUPPORT
     a. Child   b. Support requested   c. ☐ Modify existing order
        (1) Name   (2) Age   (1) Monthly amount   (1) filed on (date):
                                             $ (2) ordering (specify):
                                                                           $

4. ☐ SPOUSAL SUPPORT
     a. ☐ Amount requested (monthly): $ b. ☐ Modify existing order
     c. ☐ Terminate existing order   (1) filed on (date):
        (1) filed on (date):   (2) ordering (specify):
        (2) ordering (specify):

5. ☐ ATTORNEY FEES AND COSTS
     a. ☐ Fees: $ b. ☐ Costs: $

6. ☐ RESIDENCE EXCLUSION AND RELATED ORDERS   ☐ TO BE ORDERED PENDING THE HEARING
     ☐ Petitioner ☐ Respondent must move out and must not return to the family dwelling at (address):

     ☐ Taking only clothing and personal effects needed until the hearing.

7. ☐ STAY AWAY ORDERS   ☐ TO BE ORDERED PENDING THE HEARING
     ☐ Petitioner ☐ Respondent must stay at least . . . . yards away from the following places:
     a. ☐ applicant's residence (address optional):
     b. ☐ applicant's place of work (address optional):
     c. ☐ the children's school (address optional):
     d. ☐ other (specify):

8. ☐ RESTRAINT ON PERSONAL CONDUCT   ☐ TO BE ORDERED PENDING THE HEARING
     a. ☐ Petitioner ☐ Respondent shall not contact, molest, attack, strike, threaten, sexually assault, batter,
        telephone or otherwise disturb my peace
        ☐ and the following family or household members (name):

(Continued on reverse)

Form Adopted by Rule 1285.20
Judicial Council of California
Revised Effective January 1, 1981

**APPLICATION FOR ORDER
AND SUPPORTING DECLARATION
(FAMILY LAW)**

Civil Code
Section 4359

APPLICATION FOR ORDER AND SUPPORTING DECLARATION (FAMILY LAW)

9. ☐ PROPERTY RESTRAINT   ☐ TO BE ORDERED PENDING THE HEARING
    a. ☐ Petitioner   be restrained from transferring, encumbering, hypothecating, concealing or
    b. ☐ Respondent   in any way disposing of any property, real or personal, whether community,
    c. ☐ Claimant   quasi-community, or separate, except in the usual course of business or for
                 the necessities of life.
               ☐ and applicant be notified of any proposed extraordinary expenditures and
               an accounting of such be made to the court.

10. ☐ PROPERTY CONTROL   ☐ TO BE ORDERED PENDING THE HEARING
    a. ☐ Petitioner ☐ Respondent be given the exclusive temporary use, possession and control of the follow-
    ing property we own or are buying:

    b. ☐ Petitioner ☐ Respondent be ordered to make the following payments on liens and encumbrances
    coming due while the order is in effect:

Debt	Amount of Payment	Pay To

11. ☐ LAW ENFORCEMENT AGENCIES
    I request that copies of orders be given to the following law enforcement agencies having jurisdiction over
    the locations where violence is likely to occur:

Law Enforcement Agency	Address

12. ☐ OTHER RELIEF (specify):

13. ☐ Facts in support of relief requested and change of circumstances for any modification are (specify):
    ☐ contained in the attached declaration

I declare under penalty of perjury under the laws of the State of California that the foregoing, including any attachment,
is true and correct and that this declaration is executed on (date): . . . .
at (place): . . . .

. . . . (Type or print name) . . . .   _____
            (Type or print name)   (Signature of applicant)

Responsive Declaration to Order to Show Cause or Notice of Motion (Family Law)

ATTORNEY OR PARTY WITHOUT ATTORNEY (Name and Address):	TELEPHONE NO.:	FOR COURT USE ONLY
ATTORNEY FOR (Name):		

SUPERIOR COURT OF CALIFORNIA, COUNTY OF

STREET ADDRESS:

MAILING ADDRESS:

CITY AND ZIP CODE:

BRANCH NAME:

MARRIAGE OF

PETITIONER:

RESPONDENT:

RESPONSIVE DECLARATION TO ORDER TO SHOW CAUSE OR NOTICE OF MOTION	

HEARING	DATE	TIME	DEPT., ROOM OR DIVISION	CASE NUMBER

1. ☐ CHILD CUSTODY AND SUPPORT   b. ☐ I consent to the following order:
   a. ☐ I consent to the order requested.

2. ☐ CHILD VISITATION   b. ☐ I consent to the following order:
   a. ☐ I consent to the order requested.

3. ☐ CHILD SUPPORT   b. ☐ I consent to the following order:
   a.   I consent to the order requested.

4. ☐ SPOUSAL SUPPORT   b. ☐ I consent to the following order:
   a. ☐ I consent to the order requested.
   c. ☐ I do not consent to the order requested.

5. ☐ ATTORNEY FEES   b. ☐ I consent to the following order:
   a. ☐ I consent to the order requested.
   c. ☐ I do not consent to the order requested.

6. ☐ RESIDENCE EXCLUSION   b. ☐ I consent to the following order:
   a. ☐ I consent to the order requested.
   c. ☐ I do not consent to the order requested.

7. ☐ STAY AWAY ORDERS   b. ☐ I consent to the following order:
   a. ☐ I consent to the order requested.
   c. ☐ I do not consent to the order requested.

(Continued on reverse)

Form Adopted by Rule 1285.40
Judicial Council of California
Revised Effective January 1, 1981

RESPONSIVE DECLARATION TO ORDER TO SHOW CAUSE OR NOTICE OF MOTION (FAMILY LAW)

**RESPONSIVE DECLARATION TO ORDER TO SHOW CAUSE
OR NOTICE OF MOTION**
(FAMILY LAW)
Page two

8. ☐ RESTRAINT ON PERSONAL CONDUCT   b. ☐ I consent to the following order:
    a. ☐ I consent to the order requested.
    c. ☐ I do not consent to the order requested.

9. ☐ PROPERTY RESTRAINT   b. ☐ I consent to the following order:
    a. ☐ I consent to the order requested.
    c. ☐ I do not consent to the order requested.

10. ☐ PROPERTY CONTROL   b. ☐ I consent to the following order:
    a. ☐ I consent to the order requested.
    c. ☐ I do not consent to the order requested.

11. ☐ OTHER RELIEF, AS REQUESTED IN ITEM 11 OF THE APPLICATION
    a. ☐ I consent to the order requested.   b. ☐ I consent to the following order:
    c. ☐ I do not consent to the order requested.

12. ☐ SUPPORTING INFORMATION
    ☐ contained in the attached declaration.

I declare under penalty of perjury under the laws of the State of California that the foregoing, including any attachment, is true and correct and that this declaration is executed on (date): . . . . at (place): . . . .

. . . . (Type or print name) . . . .   _____
            (Type or print name)   (Signature of Declarant)

Custody of Children

Reportedly over a million marriages per year are ending in divorce or annulment in the United States and at least one million minor children are involved in these breakups yearly.

California law relating to the custody of these children is found in Civil Code sections 4600 *et seq.*

Over the years the custody law has changed. Originally the pendulum swung in favor of the father having exclusive custody. Then the law swung the other way, favoring custody of children of "tender years" in the mother. In 1972 the preference of custody was deleted from section 4600. Custody was then to be awarded "to either parent according to the best interests of the child."

Legislation effective January 1, 1980, created a presumption that *joint* custody (defined as legal custody) is in the best interests of the child where the parents have agreed to joint custody or so agree in open court, and would also specifically authorize such an award in other cases, as designated. (Civ. Code §4600.5(a).) "Joint custody" is to mean "an order awarding custody of the minor child or children to both parents and providing that physical custody shall be shared by the parents i~ such a way as to assure the child or children of frequent and continuing contact with both parents; provided, however, that such order may award joint legal custody without awarding *joint physical* custody." (Civ. Code §4600.5(c).)

The court may require the parents to submit to the court a plan for implementation of the joint custody order. An order for joint custody may be modified or terminated upon the petition of one or both parents or on the court's own motion if it is in the best interests of the child's welfare. A change of circumstances does not warrant a change of custody; the *criteria* is always the best interests of the child.

If either party so requests, the court will direct that an investigation be made to assist the court in determining whether an award of joint custody is appropriate. (Civ. Code §4600.5(b).)

The cold hard fact is that no award of custody is a good substitute for a home with both parents in which love and harmony abides. Nevertheless, the legislature and the courts must necessarily deal with the situation presented, once a maritial dissolution is filed, at least to do what *seems* best for the children under all the circumstances. A child cannot physically be in two places at the same time. And someone must have the legal right to make certain decisions that affect the child's life until he or she is of age.

Under section 4600 custody is to be awarded in the following order of preference: "(a) To both parents jointly pursuant to Section 4600.5 or to either parent. In making an order for custody to either parent, the court shall consider, among other factors, which parent is more likely to allow the child or children frequent and continuing contact with the noncustodial parent, and shall not prefer a parent as custodian because of that parent's sex.''

Under Civil Code section 4600 the court cannot award custody to anyone other than a parent, without the parents' consent, unless it first makes a finding that an award of custody to a parent would be detrimental to the child and the award to the nonparent is required to serve the best interests of the child. Such an allegation — other than as a statement of ultimate fact — may not, however, appear in the pleadings.

Section 232 of the Civil Code details the procedure for declaring a child free from parental custody and control, upon a finding that the parent or parents are, and will remain, incapable of supporting or controlling the child in a proper manner because of mental deficiency or mental illness, based upon the testimony of two physicans and surgeons, as specified. This section also authorizes such a finding upon the testimony of licensed psychologists, as specified.

Other reasons for giving the custody to persons other than the parents include abandonment, cruel treatment or neglect, use of alcohol, drugs, moral depravity, conviction of felonies of a nature to prove unfitness, mentally ill or developmentally disabled parents, or where a child has been cared for in one or more foster homes and return to parents would be detrimental to the child.

Mediation

Civil Code section 4607 provides that where custody or visitation is a contested issue, the matter shall be set for mediation prior to or concurrent with the setting of the matter for hearing.

The purpose is to reduce acrimony between the parties and to develop an agreement assuring a child or children's continuing contact with the parents after the marriage is dissolved.

The proceedings are held in private; the mediator may exclude counsel. The agreement reached as a result of mediation is reported to the court and counsel.

The petition form used in Sacramento County follows:

Petition for Mediation

SUPERIOR COURT OF CALIFORNIA, COUNTY OF SACRAMENTO

**READ INSTRUCTIONS FIRST
ON BACK OF FORM**

In Re the Marriage of:

_____

_____
                                    Petitioner

_____
                                    Respondent

PETITION FOR MEDIATION
Civil Code Section 4607

Court # D _____

A controversy exists between the above named parties concerning:
☐ Child Custody   ☐ Child Visitation

Petitioner's Address:

WORK PHONE _____

NUMBER   STREET   CITY   ZIP CODE   HOME PHONE

Respondent's Address:

WORK PHONE _____

NUMBER   STREET   CITY   ZIP CODE   HOME PHONE

CHILDREN IN THE HOME

NAME	AGE	NAME	AGE
1. _____ _____		4. _____ _____	
2. _____ _____		5. _____ _____	
3. _____ _____		6. _____ _____	

The children of this controversy reside with: ☐ Petitioner   ☐ Respondent

Name of Petitioner's attorney: _____   Phone: _____

Attorney's Address _____
    NUMBER   STREET   SUITE   CITY   ZIP CODE

Name of Respondent's Attorney: _____   Phone: _____

Attorney's Address _____
    NUMBER   STREET   SUITE   CITY   ZIP CODE

Any information I have provided above and any attachment to this Petition is furnished in good faith in the hope of settling the controversy. I declare under penalty of perjury that the foregoing information is true and correct.

Dated _____ , at (city) _____ , California

SIGN HERE _____▶ _____ ◀_____ SIGN HERE
                 PETITIONER'S/RESPONDENT'S SIGNATURE

ORDER: Mediation of the controversy is ordered. Date:_____

_____
JUDGE OF THE SUPERIOR COURT

APPLICATION INSTRUCTIONS

Read the following instructions before filling out the application form.

1. Type or write legibly in ink. Provide all information requested.

2. Use business address only when home address is unavailable.

3. Sign the Petition, submit the Petition to the Court for the Judge's order.

4. Forward one copy of the Petition signed by the Judge and endorsed by the County Clerk to the Office of Family Court Services - 901 G Street, Room 131, Sacramento, California 95814.

   Additional endorsed copies of the petition should be forwarded to the other party and attorneys of record.

5. When received by the Office of Family Court Services, we will notify both parties about your appointment. If you have any questions, phone 440-5633, between 8:30 a.m., and 4:00 p.m., Monday through Friday.

6. Appointments are set on weekdays only. There are no evening appointments available.

Temporary Restraining Orders

If temporary spousal support or child support or attorney's fees are desired pending trial, an *Order to Show Cause* is obtained, usually at the same time as filing the petition. A temporary restraining order may also be sought. If so, the hearing must be not later than 15 days from the date the court issues the Order; the court can extend to 20 days upon a showing of good cause. (Code Civ. Proc. §527.)

An *Application and Order and Declaration in Support of Order to Show Cause* is presented to the judge at the time the Order is requested.

The adverse party must be served at least 10 days before the hearing with conformed copies of the following documents (or 2 days before the hearing if a temporary restraining order has been granted):

1. *Order to Show Cause (Family Law)*
2. *Application for Order and Supporting Declaration (Family Law)*
3. *Income and Expense Declaration,* and a blank copy of the form
4. Blank form of *Responsive Declaration to Order to Show Cause or Notice of Motion (Family Law)*
5. *Temporary Restraining Orders (Family Law).*

Code of Civil Procedure section 527 expressly authorizes a court to grant a temporary restraining order without notice when it appears from facts shown by affidavit or by the verified complaint that great or irreparable injury would result to the applicant before the matter could be heard on notice and, except when applying for an order under Code of Civil Procedure section 546 or Civil Code sections 4357, 4359 or 7020, the applicant or his attorney certifies under oath:

(i) that within a reasonable time prior to the application he informed the opposing party or his attorney at what time and where the application would be made;

(ii) that he in good faith attempted to inform the opposing party and his attorney but was unable to so inform the opposing party or his attorney, specifying the efforts made to contact them, or

(iii) that for reasons specified he should not be required to so inform the opposing party or his attorney.

Forms 1, 2, 4 and 5 above and *Order After Hearing (Family Law)* follow:

Order to Show Cause (Family Law)

ATTORNEY OR PARTY WITHOUT ATTORNEY (NAME AND ADDRESS): TELEPHONE NO.:	FOR COURT USE ONLY
ATTORNEY FOR (NAME):	

SUPERIOR COURT OF CALIFORNIA, COUNTY OF
STREET ADDRESS:
MAILING ADDRESS:
CITY AND ZIP CODE:
BRANCH NAME:

MARRIAGE OF
PETITIONER:

RESPONDENT:

ORDER TO SHOW CAUSE ☐ **FOR MODIFICATION** ☐ **ORDER SHORTENING TIME**	☐ **Child Custody** ☐ **Visitation** ☐ **Child Support** ☐ **Spousal Support** ☐ **Attorney Fees and Costs** ☐ **Injunctive Order** ☐ **Other (Specify):**	CASE NUMBER:

1. TO (Name):

2. YOU ARE ORDERED TO APPEAR IN THIS COURT AS FOLLOWS TO GIVE ANY LEGAL REASON WHY THE RELIEF SOUGHT IN THE ATTACHED APPLICATION SHOULD NOT BE GRANTED

   a. date: time: in ☐Dept.:   ☐ Div.:   ☐Rm.:

   b. Address of court:

3. IT IS FURTHER ORDERED that
   a. The following documents shall be served with this order
      (1) Application for Order and Supporting Declaration
      (2) ☐ Income and Expense Declaration
      (3) ☐ Property Declaration
      (4) ☐ Points and authorities
      (5) ☐ Other (specify):

   b. ☐ the application for an order shortening time is granted and this order may be served on or before (Date):
   c. ☐ Other (specify):

4. Total number of boxes checked in item 3:

Dated: . . . .   _____
                                            Judge of the Superior Court

Form Adopted by Rule 1285
Judicial Council of California
Effective January 1, 1980

**ORDER TO SHOW CAUSE
(FAMILY LAW)**

CC 4359, 4370, 4455, 4801, 4809

Application for Order and Supporting Declaration (Family Law)

MARRIAGE OF (last name—first names of parties)	CASE NUMBER

APPLICATION FOR ORDER AND SUPPORTING DECLARATION OF ☐ **PETITIONER** ☐ **RESPONDENT** ☐ **CLAIMANT** requests the following relief.

1. ☐ CHILD CUSTODY
   a. Child
      (1) Name   (2) Age

   ☐ TO BE ORDERED PENDING THE HEARING
   b. Request custody to
   c. ☐ Modify existing order
      (1) filed on (date):
      (2) ordering (specify):

2. ☐ CHILD VISITATION
   a. ☐ Reasonable
   b. ☐ Other (specify):

   ☐ TO BE ORDERED PENDING THE HEARING
   c. ☐ Modify existing order
      (1) filed on (date):
      (2) ordering (specify):

3. ☐ CHILD SUPPORT
   a. Child
      (1) Name   (2) Age

   b. Support requested
      (1) Monthly amount
      $
   c. ☐ Modify existing order
      (1) filed on (date):
      (2) ordering (specify):
      $

4. ☐ SPOUSAL SUPPORT
   a. ☐ Amount requested (monthly): $
   c. ☐ Terminate existing order
      (1) filed on (date):
      (2) ordering (specify):

   b. ☐ Modify existing order
      (1) filed on (date):
      (2) ordering (specify):

5. ☐ ATTORNEY FEES AND COSTS
   a. ☐ Fees: $ b. ☐ Costs: $

6. ☐ RESIDENCE EXCLUSION AND RELATED ORDERS   ☐ TO BE ORDERED PENDING THE HEARING
   ☐ Petitioner ☐ Respondent must move out and must not return to the family dwelling at (address):

   ☐ Taking only clothing and personal effects needed until the hearing.

7. ☐ STAY AWAY ORDERS   ☐ TO BE ORDERED PENDING THE HEARING
   ☐ Petitioner ☐ Respondent must stay at least . . . . .yards away from the following places:
   a. ☐ applicant's residence (address optional):
   b. ☐ applicant's place of work (address optional):
   c. ☐ the children's school (address optional):
   d. ☐ other (specify):

8. ☐ RESTRAINT ON PERSONAL CONDUCT   ☐ TO BE ORDERED PENDING THE HEARING
   a. ☐ Petitioner ☐ Respondent shall not contact, molest, attack, strike, threaten, sexually assault, batter, telephone or otherwise disturb my peace
      ☐ and the following family or household members (name):

(Continued on reverse)

Form Adopted by Rule 1285.20
Judicial Council of California
Revised Effective January 1, 1981

**APPLICATION FOR ORDER
AND SUPPORTING DECLARATION
(FAMILY LAW)**

Civil Code
Section 4359

APPLICATION FOR ORDER AND SUPPORTING DECLARATION (FAMILY LAW)

9. ☐ PROPERTY RESTRAINT   ☐ TO BE ORDERED PENDING THE HEARING
   a. ☐ Petitioner   be restrained from transferring, encumbering, hypothecating, concealing or
   b. ☐ Respondent   in any way disposing of any property, real or personal, whether community,
   c. ☐ Claimant   quasi-community, or separate, except in the usual course of business or for
                the necessities of life.
       ☐ and applicant be notified of any proposed extraordinary expenditures and
        an accounting of such be made to the court.

10. ☐ PROPERTY CONTROL   ☐ TO BE ORDERED PENDING THE HEARING
   a. ☐ Petitioner ☐ Respondent be given the exclusive temporary use, possession and control of the follow-
       ing property we own or are buying:

   b. ☐ Petitioner ☐ Respondent be ordered to make the following payments on liens and encumbrances
       coming due while the order is in effect:
       Debt   Amount of Payment   Pay To

11. ☐ LAW ENFORCEMENT AGENCIES
   I request that copies of orders be given to the following law enforcement agencies having jurisdiction over
   the locations where violence is likely to occur:
   Law Enforcement Agency   Address

12. ☐ OTHER RELIEF (specify):

13. ☐ Facts in support of relief requested and change of circumstances for any modification are (specify):
   ☐ contained in the attached declaration

I declare under penalty of perjury under the laws of the State of California that the foregoing, including any attachment, is true and correct and that this declaration is executed on (date):. . . . . at (place): . . . .

. . . . (Type or print name) . . . .   _____
                                     (Signature of applicant)

Responsive Declaration to Order to Show Cause or Notice of Motion (Family Law)

ATTORNEY OR PARTY WITHOUT ATTORNEY (Name and Address):	TELEPHONE NO.:	FOR COURT USE ONLY
ATTORNEY FOR (Name):		

SUPERIOR COURT OF CALIFORNIA, COUNTY OF
STREET ADDRESS:
MAILING ADDRESS:
CITY AND ZIP CODE:
BRANCH NAME:

MARRIAGE OF
PETITIONER:

RESPONDENT:

RESPONSIVE DECLARATION TO ORDER TO SHOW CAUSE OR NOTICE OF MOTION

HEARING	DATE	TIME	DEPT., ROOM OR DIVISION	CASE NUMBER:

1. ☐ CHILD CUSTODY AND SUPPORT
   a. ☐ I consent to the order requested.
   b. ☐ I consent to the following order:

2. ☐ CHILD VISITATION
   a. ☐ I consent to the order requested.
   b. ☐ I consent to the following order:

3. ☐ CHILD SUPPORT
   a. I consent to the order requested.
   b. ☐ I consent to the following order:

4. ☐ SPOUSAL SUPPORT
   a. ☐ I consent to the order requested.
   c. ☐ I do not consent to the order requested.
   b. ☐ I consent to the following order:

5. ☐ ATTORNEY FEES
   a. ☐ I consent to the order requested.
   c. ☐ I do not consent to the order requested.
   b. ☐ I consent to the following order:

6. ☐ RESIDENCE EXCLUSION
   a. ☐ I consent to the order requested.
   c. ☐ I do not consent to the order requested.
   b. ☐ I consent to the following order:

7. ☐ STAY AWAY ORDERS
   a. ☐ I consent to the order requested.
   c. ☐ I do not consent to the order requested.
   b. ☐ I consent to the following order:

(Continued on reverse)

Form Adopted by Rule 1285.40
Judicial Council of California
Revised Effective January 1, 1981

RESPONSIVE DECLARATION TO ORDER TO SHOW CAUSE OR NOTICE OF MOTION (FAMILY LAW)

**RESPONSIVE DECLARATION TO ORDER TO SHOW CAUSE
OR NOTICE OF MOTION**
(FAMILY LAW)
Page two

8. ☐ RESTRAINT ON PERSONAL CONDUCT   b. ☐ I consent to the following order:
   a. ☐ I consent to the order requested.
   c. ☐ I do not consent to the order requested.

9. ☐ PROPERTY RESTRAINT   b. ☐ I consent to the following order:
   a. ☐ I consent to the order requested.
   c. ☐ I do not consent to the order requested.

10. ☐ PROPERTY CONTROL   b. ☐ I consent to the following order:
   a. ☐ I consent to the order requested.
   c. ☐ I do not consent to the order requested.

11. ☐ OTHER RELIEF, AS REQUESTED IN ITEM 11 OF THE APPLICATION
   a. ☐ I consent to the order requested.   b. ☐ I consent to the following order:
   c. ☐ I do not consent to the order requested.

12. ☐ SUPPORTING INFORMATION
   ☐ contained in the attached declaration.

I declare under penalty of perjury under the laws of the State of California that the foregoing, including any attachment, is true and correct and that this declaration is executed on (date): . . . . at (place): . . . .

. . . .   _____
        (Type or print name)   (Signature of Declarant)

Temporary Restraining Orders (Family Law)

MARRIAGE OF (last name—first names of parties)	CASE NUMBER:

TEMPORARY RESTRAINING ORDERS
(FAMILY LAW ATTACHMENT)

1. ☐ RESTRAINT ON PERSONAL CONDUCT
   a. ☐ Petitioner ☐ Respondent shall not contact, molest, attack, strike, threaten, sexually assault, batter, telephone or otherwise disturb the peace of (name):
   ☐ and the following family or household members (name):

2. ☐ RESIDENCE EXCLUSION AND RELATED ORDERS
   ☐ Petitioner ☐ Respondent must move out and must not return to the family dwelling at (address):

   ☐ Taking only clothing and personal effects needed until the hearing.

3. ☐ STAY AWAY ORDERS
   ☐ Petitioner ☐ Respondent must stay at least . . . . yards away from the following places:
   a. ☐ Residence of (name):
       (address optional)
   b. ☐ Place of work of (name):
       (address optional)
   c. ☐ The children's school (address optional):

   d. ☐ Other (specify)

4. ☐ PROPERTY RESTRAINT
   a. ☐ Petitioner   is restrained from transferring, encumbering, hypothecating, concealing, or in any
   b. ☐ Respondent   way disposing of any property, real or personal, whether community, quasi-
   c. ☐ Claimant   community, or separate, except in the usual course of business or for the necessities
                       of life.
                       ☐ and applicant is to be notified of any proposed extraordinary expenditures and
                          an accounting of such be made to the court.

5. ☐ PROPERTY CONTROL
   a. ☐ Petitioner ☐ Respondent is given the exclusive temporary use, possession and control of the following property the parties own or are buying:

   b. ☐ Petitioner ☐ Respondent is ordered to make the following payments on liens and encumbrances coming due while the order is in effect:

Debt	Amount of Payment	Pay To

THESE ORDERS SHALL EXPIRE AT THE DATE AND TIME OF THE COURT HEARING UNLESS EXTENDED BY THE COURT.

VIOLATION OF THIS TEMPORARY RESTRAINING ORDER IS A MISDEMEANOR, PUNISHABLE BY A $500 FINE, SIX MONTHS IN JAIL, OR BOTH. THIS ORDER SHALL BE ENFORCED BY ALL LAW ENFORCEMENT OFFICERS.

(Continued on reverse)

Form Adopted by Rule 1285.05
Judicial Council of California
Effective January 1, 1981

**TEMPORARY RESTRAINING
ORDERS
(FAMILY LAW)**

TEMPORARY RESTRAINING ORDERS
(FAMILY LAW)
Page two

6. ☐ MINOR CHILDREN
☐ Petitioner ☐ Respondent shall not remove the minor children
☐ from the State of California
☐ other (specify):

7. ☐ By the close of business on the date of this order a copy of this order and any Proof of Service shall be delivered to the law enforcement agencies listed below as follows:
☐ the Clerk of the Court shall mail.
☐ the applicant shall deliver.
☐ the applicant's attorney shall deliver.

Law Enforcement Agency   Address

8. ☐ OTHER ORDERS

9. This order is effective when made. Law enforcement agencies shall enforce it immediately upon receipt. If proof of service on the restrained person has not been received by the law enforcement agency, the law enforcement agency shall advise the restrained person of the terms of this order.

Dated: . . . . _____
(Judge of the Superior Court)

CLERK'S CERTIFICATE OF MAILING
I certify that I am not a party to this cause and that a copy of the foregoing was mailed first class, postage prepaid, in a sealed envelope addressed as shown in item 7, and that the mailing of the foregoing and execution of this certificate occurred at (place): . . . . , California, on (date): . . . .

Clerk, by _____ , Deputy

Order After Hearing (Family Law)

ATTORNEY OR PARTY WITHOUT ATTORNEY (NAME AND ADDRESS)	TELEPHONE NO	FOR COURT USE ONLY
ATTORNEY FOR (NAME)		

SUPERIOR COURT OF CALIFORNIA, COUNTY OF
STREET ADDRESS
MAILING ADDRESS
CITY AND ZIP CODE
BRANCH NAME

MARRIAGE OF
PETITIONER

RESPONDENT

CLAIMANT

ORDER AFTER HEARING ☐ **MODIFICATION**	☐ Child Custody ☐ Child Support ☐ Attorney Fees and Costs ☐ Injunctive Order	☐ Visitation ☐ Spousal Support ☐ Joinder ☐ Other (Specify):	CASE NUMBER

1. This proceeding came on for hearing as follows

    a. Date: ☐ Dept.   ☐ Div.   ☐ Room:

    b. Judge (Name):   ☐ Temporary Judge
    c. ☐ Petitioner present in court   ☐ Attorney present in court (Name):
    d. ☐ Respondent present in court   ☐ Attorney present in court (Name):
    e. ☐ Claimant present in court   ☐ Attorney present in court (Name):
    f. ☐ On the Order to Show Cause filed
        Date: By:

    g. ☐ On the Motion filed
        Date: By:

2. ☐ Evidence was presented ☐ the parties entered into a stipulation, and the matter was submitted.
3. IT IS ORDERED ☐ Pending trial or until further order of this court
               ☐ Existing orders shall continue in effect, except as modified by this order
    a. ☐ Custody and support of the minor children of the parties are fixed as follows

		Monthly		
Child (Name and age):	Custody to:	Child Support: $	Payable by:	Payable on:

    b. ☐ Petitioner ☐ Respondent ☐ Claimant shall have
        (1) ☐ reasonable visitation rights with the minor children
        (2) ☐ the following visitation rights:

    c. ☐ Petitioner ☐ Respondent shall pay as spousal support
        (1) To ☐ Petitioner ☐ Respondent ☐ Other (specify):
        (2) Amount: $
        (3) Payable:

(Continued on reverse)

Form Approved by Rule 1291.30
Judicial Council of California
Effective January 1, 1980

**ORDER AFTER HEARING
(FAMILY LAW)**

rule 1253(b)

d. ☐ Petitioner ☐ Respondent shall pay on account to attorney (name):

    (1) ☐ Fees: $ payable:
    (2) ☐ Costs: $ payable:

e. ☐ Petitioner is excluded from   f ☐ Respondent is excluded from
    (1) ☐ The family dwelling at (address):   (1) ☐ The family dwelling at (address):

    (2) ☐ Respondent's dwelling at (address):   (2) ☐ Petitioner's dwelling at (address):

    (3) Effective (date and time):   (3) Effective (date and time):

g. ☐ Petitioner is restrained from molesting   h. ☐ Respondent is restrained from molesting
    or disturbing the peace of respondent   or disturbing the peace of petitioner
    ☐ and any person under the care,   ☐ and any person under the care,
    custody or control of respondent.   custody or control of petitioner.

i. ☐ Petitioner ☐ Respondent ☐ Claimant
is restrained from transferring, encumbering, hypothecating, concealing, or in any way disposing of any property, real or personal, whether community, quasi-community, or separate, except in the usual course of business or for the necessities of life.

j. ☐ Claimant is joined as a party to this proceeding
    (1) Claimant (name):
    (2) ☐ The clerk shall file the original of the submitted pleading.
    (3) ☐ Summons (Joinder) be issued and claimant be served with a copy of the motion for joinder with pleading attached, a copy of this order and a copy of the Summons (Joinder).

k. ☐ Decision on all other issues is reserved to time of trial.
l. ☐ Other (specify):

Dated: . . . .
              Judge of the Superior Court

4. Total number of boxes checked in item 3:

5. Approved as conforming to court order.

Dated: . . . .
         Signature of Attorney for

Modification Orders

The same *Order to Show Cause* form may be used to obtain a modification of a prior order. "RE MODIFICATION" must be typed in the caption.

The form should be accompanied by the same *Application for Order and Declaration and a Supportive Declaration re Modification* form, as well as a *Property Declaration* form if the matter is related to support.

Contempt Orders

In the event of noncompliance with a court order, such as for attorney's fees, custody, visitation, property, or child support, the other party may go back to court and seek a contempt order. (See Civ. Code §4380.)

Contempt proceedings are closely akin to criminal proceedings. Therefore the person cited need not take the stand. He cannot be adjudged in contempt for not appearing in person at the hearing as long as his attorney appears. The *Order to Show Cause* should be personally served, though the court has power to direct certain other modes of service.

The party filing the *Order to Show Cause* must establish: "(1) a lawful court order was made, (2) the citee had knowledge of the order, (3) the citee had ability to comply, (4) there was disobedience of the order and (5) the citee's disobedience was willful. [*In re Liu* (1969) 273 Cal.App.2d 135]." (Mason, *California Family Law Handbook*, p. 219.)

The form used is *Order to Show Cause and Declaration for Contempt (Family Law)* [Rule 1285.60], and follows:

Order to Show Cause and Declaration for Contempt (Family Law)

ATTORNEY OR PARTY WITHOUT ATTORNEY (NAME AND ADDRESS):	TELEPHONE NO	FOR COURT USE ONLY
ATTORNEY FOR (NAME):		

SUPERIOR COURT OF CALIFORNIA, COUNTY OF
STREET ADDRESS
MAILING ADDRESS
CITY AND ZIP CODE
BRANCH NAME

MARRIAGE OF
PETITIONER

RESPONDENT

ORDER TO SHOW CAUSE AND DECLARATION FOR CONTEMPT	CASE NUMBER

NOTICE!	¡AVISO!
A contempt proceeding is criminal in nature. If the court finds you in contempt, the possible penalties include jail sentence and fine.	Un procedimiento de contumacia es de índole criminal. Si la corte le encuentra en contumacia, los castigos posibles incluyen sentencia en la cárcel y multa.
You are entitled to the services of an attorney who should be consulted promptly in order to assist you. If you cannot afford an attorney, the court may appoint an attorney to represent you.	Usted tiene el derecho de los servicios de un abogado a quien se le debe consultar enseguida para que pueda asistirle. Si usted no está en condiciones de pagar los servicios de un abogado, la corte le podrá nombrar un abogado que le represente.

1. TO CITEE (Name):

2. YOU ARE ORDERED TO APPEAR IN THIS COURT AS FOLLOWS TO GIVE ANY LEGAL REASON WHY THIS COURT SHOULD NOT FIND YOU GUILTY OF CONTEMPT AND PUNISH YOU FOR WILLFULLY DISOBEYING ITS ORDERS AS SET FORTH IN THE DECLARATION BELOW AND REQUIRE YOU TO PAY, FOR THE BENEFIT OF THE MOVING PARTY, THE ATTORNEY FEES AND COSTS OF THIS PROCEEDING

   a. date: time: in ☐ Dept.:   ☐ Div.:   ☐ Rm.:

   b. Address of court:

Dated: . . . .

                                                  Judge of the Superior Court

DECLARATION

3. Citee has willfully disobeyed certain orders of this court as set forth in this declaration
   a. Citee had knowledge of the order in that (specify):

   b. Citee was able to comply with each order when it was disobeyed.

4. Based on the instances of disobedience described in this declaration, there have been
   a. ☐ No prior applications
   b. ☐ Prior applications as follows (specify applications and dispositions):

(Continued on reverse)

A copy of the moving party's Income and Expense Declaration must be attached when attorney fees are requested. The declaration under penalty of perjury must be signed in California, or in a state that authorizes use of a declaration in place of an affidavit; otherwise an affidavit is required

Form Adopted by Rule 1285.60
Judicial Council of California   **ORDER TO SHOW CAUSE AND DECLARATION FOR CONTEMPT**
Revised Effective January 1, 1980   **(FAMILY LAW)**

5. Each order disobeyed and each instance of disobedience is described as follows
   a. ☐ Orders for child support, spousal support, attorney fees, and court or other litigation costs:

DATE DUE	TYPE OF ORDER AND DATE FILED	PAYABLE TO	AMOUNT ORDERED	AMOUNT PAID	AMOUNT DUE
			$	$	$

☐ Continued on attachment 5a.

Recapitulation of orders for:		TOTAL AMOUNT ORDERED	TOTAL AMOUNT PAID	TOTAL AMOUNT DUE
Child support		$	$	$
Spousal support				
Attorney fees				
Court and other costs				
Total		$	$	$

   b. ☐ Injunctive or other order (Describe each order and disobedience with particularity)
       ☐ contined on attachment 5b.

   c. ☐ Other material facts:

I declare under penalty of perjury that the foregoing declaration, including any attachment, is true and correct and that this declaration was executed at (place): . . . ., California, on (date): . . . . . .

. . . . _____
         (Type or print name)   (Signature)

Summary Dissolutions

Parties who meet the jurisdictional requirements may file a joint petition for summary dissolution of their marriage where (1) there are no children of the relationship of the parties born before or during the marriage or adopted by the parties during the marriage, and the wife, to her knowledge, is not pregnant, (2) they have no interest in any real property, (3) they have no unpaid debts over $3,000 (excluding debts for automobiles), (4) they waive rights to spousal support, (5) they have not been married more than 5 years, (6) market value of their personal property (excluding encumbrances and automobiles) does not exceed $10,000 and neither party has separate property assets (excluding encumbrances and automobiles) exceeding $10,000 and other prescribed conditions exist. (Civ. Code, §4550.)

Commencing January 1, 1983, and on January 1 of each odd-numbered year thereafter, the limitations on value of obligations and assets will be adjusted pursuant to a specified formula.

At any time before an application for final judgment is filed, either party may file a notice of revocation, a copy of which must be sent by first-class mail, postage prepaid, to the other party's last known address.

When six months from date of filing the joint petition has expired, either party may apply for a final judgment. The clerk is required to send a notice of entry of final judgment to each of the parties at their last known address. Entry of the final judgment is a final adjudication of rights and constitutes a waiver of rights to spousal support, appeal, to request findings of fact and conclusions of law, and to move for a new trial.

The judgment may be set aside as to all matters except the status of the marriage upon proof the parties did not meet the specified jurisdictional requirements.

Legal Separation (Formerly Separate Maintenance)

The Family Law Act (Civ. Code, §4508(b)) provides for "legal separation." No provision is made for an action for "separate maintenance." Unlike the old law, a legal separation may not be granted *unless both parties consent,* except after a default. About half the number of legal separation proceedings are being filed, as compared to the actions filed for separate maintenance.

Two situations where a legal separation might be recommended are (1) for religious reasons, where divorce is against one's faith (but if one party files for legal separation the spouse can ask for dissolution), or (2) for economic reasons, where one spouse is retired from the military.

Procedures for support of spouse and children and obtaining money for attorneys' fees are identical to those for dissolution of marriage.

Nullity Proceeding (formerly Annulment)

Void Marriages — A marriage is no longer "annulled," but it may be declared void as of the time it was entered into. California marriages are considered void if made between:

1. Parents and children, ancestors and descendants of every degree
2. Brothers and sisters, of half or whole blood
3. Uncles and nieces
4. Aunts and nephews, or
5. A marriage by a person having an already existing valid marriage (unless the former spouse is absent and not known to be living for five years preceding the marriage, or generally believed to be dead at the time the marriage was contracted). However, this second marriage is valid until it is adjudged a nullity.

Voidable Marriages — Marriages which may be declared null are set forth in Civil Code section 4425. Such marriages must be declared a nullity within the time specified in Civil Code section 4426 *or they become valid* and can henceforth be dissolved only by a dissolution as in other valid marriages.

Briefly, the marriage may be declared a nullity if any of the following conditions existed at the time of the marriage:

1. Lack of capability of consenting thereto (age of consent, see Civ. Code §4101), unless after attaining age of consent, such party for any time freely cohabited. Time limit: within four years after attaining age of consent, or by a parent or guardian before reaching age of consent.

2. When husband or wife of either party was living and marriage was then in force, although believed dead. Time limit: any time within life of the other, or by former husband or wife.

3. Unsound mind of either party, unless came to reason and freely cohabited. Time limit: By the party injured, or relative or guardian of the party of unsound mind, at any time before death of either party.

4. Consent to marry obtained by fraud, unless after fraud discovered, cohabited freely: Time limit: By the party injured, within four years after discovery of the fraud.

5. Consent obtained by force unless cohabited freely afterwards: Time limit: by the injured party, within four years after the marriage.

6. Physical incapacity which continues and appears to be incurable. Time Limit: By injured party, within four years after the marriage.

Residence Requirements for Void or Voidable Marriages

The requirements for six months' residence in California and three months in the county where the proceeding is filed, do not apply.

Procedure

The procedure is the same except that no interlocutory or final judgments are involved.

Nonmarital Relationships

Census figures reportedly indicate that eight times as many couples were living together in 1970 as ten years earlier. One could question the accuracy of these figures on the premise that couples live together more *openly* than previously, using their own names, with no "Mr. and Mrs." tags. Be that as it may, no doubt a substantial number of couples living together today are not married.

The landmark decision of *Marvin v. Marvin* (1976) 18 Cal.3d 660, has changed the outlook for "family" law. In the *Marvin* case plaintiff (Michelle Marvin) and defendant (Lee Marvin) lived together for seven years in a nonmarital situation. The plaintiff claimed she rendered services as a "companion, homemaker and cook." When they split she sued to enforce an oral contract under which she claimed they were to combine earnings and share all property accumulated. All property during the time they lived together had been acquired in defendant's name. The trial court granted judgment to the defendant and the California Supreme court reversed, holding that the fact that a man and woman live together without marriage, and engage in a sexual relationship, does not in itself invalidate agreements between them relating to their earnings, property, or expenses and that agreements between nonmarital partners fail only to the extent that they rest upon an explicit consideration of meretricious sexual services.

Suffice it to say here that parties entering into such a cohabitation arrangement would seem to be well advised to have a written cohabitation agreement, in the same manner that couples enter into premarital agreements as to their property, particularly when they are both persons with substantial assets.

A form of Cohabitation Agreement may be found in Mason, *California Family Law Handbook*, in Chapter 2 on Cohabitation, pages 23-25.

Nonmarital arrangements can have some adverse economic effects. See cases cited in the same reference, at pages 26-29.

Domestic Violence Prevention Act
(Code Civ. Proc. §§540, *et seq.*)

Generally, this act would "(a) permit family or household members to petition for a temporary restraining order to prevent domestic violence; (b) permit the court to restrain any party from molesting, abusing, threatening, sexually assaulting or doing similar acts to specifically named family or household members; (c) permit the court to order a party to vacate a dwelling if that party assaults or threatens to assault other members of the household; (d) expand the authority of the court to issue further orders relating to custody and visitation of children, monetary compensation of victims for losses suffered due to domestic violence, medical or psychiatric treatment of either party, or to an award of attorney's fees and costs to the prevailing party; (e) extend the duration of such orders from 30 days to 90 days, with the court retaining authority to renew such orders; (f) provide for the delivery of the order by the petitioner or the petitioner's attorney, and mailing by the county clerk and (g) require local law enforcement agencies to maintain a file on all such orders filed with them."

This act would also "(a) expand the court's authority to issue orders to vacate a dwelling to include circumstances where one party assaults or threatens to assault the other party; (b) empower the courts to enjoin a party from specified behavior which the court determines is necessary to effectuate its orders as specified; (c) authorize the courts to issue such orders as part of an interlocutory or final judgment of dissolution or separation to cover a period not exceeding one year; (d) require the transmission of such orders to law enforcement agencies who would keep them on file for reference when responding to domestic violence scenes; and (e) authorize the court to determine the temporary use, possession and control of real or personal property of the parties and the payment of any liens or encumbrances coming due during the pendency of the order."

This act further amended Code of Civil Procedure section 527. Upon the filing of plaintiff's affidavit that the defendant could not be served on time, the court may reissue any temporary restraining order previously issued pursuant to Code of Civil Procedure section 546 and dissolved for failure to serve. The reissued order is to state a date for its expiration. No fee is to be charged unless the order has been dissolved three times previously.

A booklet, "Instructions for Orders Prohibiting Domestic Violence" is available, prepared by Judicial Council. The following is an excerpt from this booklet:

"What Are Domestic Violence Forms:

Form 1. *Application and Declaration (Domestic Violence)*

This four page form tells the judge the facts of your case and what orders you want the court to make.

Form 2. *Order to Show Cause and Temporary Restraining Order (Domestic Violence)*

The judge signs this order to tell the defendant to come to court for the court hearing. It usually will contain one or more court orders that take effect immediately and stay in effect until the hearing.

Form 3. *Responsive Declaration (Domestic Violence)*

The defendant may file this form to say that he (or she, of course) objects to the orders you have asked the court to make. The form has room for the defendant's side of the story.

Form 4. *Order Prohibiting Domestic Violence*

This is the form signed by the court following the hearing. It will expire in ninety days unless the court extends it.

Form 5. *Proof of Service*

This form is used to show a defendant has been served with legal papers as required by law.

Form 6. *Application and Order for Re-Issuance of Order to Show Cause (Domestic Violence)*

If you cannot have the defendant served before the hearing as ordered by the court, complete and file this form to continue your temporary orders in effect and obtain a new hearing date. This form must go to law enforcement agencies so they will know your temporary orders did not expire.

Form 7. *Other Forms*

If you want an order about the custody of minor children of you and the defendant, you will need a Declaration Under Uniform Custody of Minors Act. If you want an order for defendant to pay money, you will need an Income and Expense Declaration (Family Law) to give the judge information about your finances and those of the defendant. The sample forms in this book tell you when you need these additional forms.

You will need four copies of each form: one for a worksheet, the original to file with the court, a copy to be delivered to the defendant, and a copy to keep for yourself. In addition, you will need extra copies for forms 2 and 4. Get two for each law enforcement agency you will want to have enforcing your orders, and an extra to keep for yourself.''

These forms appear immediately below:

Declaration Under Uniform Custody of Minors Act

Name, Address and Telephone No. of Attorney(s)

Space Below for Use of Court Clerk Only

Attorney(s) for . . . .

SUPERIOR COURT OF CALIFORNIA, COUNTY OF SAN DIEGO

In re the marriage of

Petitioner:

and

Respondent:

CASE NUMBER

DECLARATION UNDER UNIFORM CUSTODY OF MINORS ACT

1. The number of minor children subject to this proceeding is . . . . The name, place of birth, birthdate and sex of each child, the present address, periods of residence and places where each child has lived within the past five (5) years, and the name, present address and relationship to the child of each person with whom the child has lived during that time are: (See footnote *)

Child's Name:		Place of Birth:	Birthdate:	Sex:
A.				

Period of Residence:	Address:	Person Child Lived With: (Name and Present Address)	Relationship:
to present			
to			
to			
to			

Child's Name:		Place of Birth:	Birthdate:	Sex:
B.				

Period of Residence:	Address:	Person Child Lived With: (Name and Present Address)	Relationship:
to present			
to			
to			
to			

Total Number of Continuation Pages Attached . . . . .

* Singular includes plural. Declaration under penalty of perjury must be signed in California (CCP 2015.5.) Affidavit is required when signed outside California. When declaration applies to more than two children, attach additional page (CRC 201 (b)).

Form Approved by the Judicial Council of California Effective January 1, 1975

DECLARATION UNDER UNIFORM CUSTODY OF MINORS ACT

CC 5158
D-6 Co. Clk. (6-76)

2. ☐ I have not participated as a party, witness, or in any other capacity in any other litigation or custody proceeding, in this or any other state, concerning custody of a child subject to this proceeding.

☐ I have participated as a party, witness, or in some other capacity in other litigation or custody proceeding, in this or some other state, concerning custody of a child subject to this proceeding, as follows:

a. Name of each child:

b. Capacity of declarant:

c. Court and state:

d. Date of court order or judgment (if any):

3. ☐ I have no information of any custody proceeding pending in a court of this or any other state concerning a child subject to this proceeding, other than that set out in item 2.

☐ I have the following information concerning a custody proceeding pending in a court of this or some other state concerning a child subject to this proceeding, other than that set out in item 2:

a. Name of each child:

b. Nature of proceeding:

c. Court and state:

d. Status of proceeding:

4. ☐ I do not know of any person not a party to this proceeding who has physical custody or claims to have custody or visitation rights with respect to any child subject to this proceeding.

☐ I know that the following named person not a party to this proceeding has physical custody or claims custody or visitation rights with respect to a child subject to this proceeding:

a. Name and address of person: b. Name and address of person: c. Name and address of person:

☐ Has physical custody	☐ Has physical custody	☐ Has physical custody
☐ Claims custody rights	☐ Claims custody rights	☐ Claims custody rights
☐ Claims visitation rights	☐ Claims visitation rights	☐ Claims visitation rights

a. Name of each child: b. Name of each child: c. Name of each child:

I declare under penalty of perjury that the foregoing, including any attachments, is true and correct and that this declaration is executed on (Date) . . . . at (Place) . . . . ,California.

. . . .
(Type or print name)   (Signature of Declarant)

NOTICE TO DECLARANT: You have a continuing duty to inform this court of any information you obtain of any custody proceeding, in this or in any other state, concerning a child subject to this proceeding.

Application and Declaration (Domestic Violence)

PLAINTIFF (name):	CASE NUMBER:
DEFENDANT (name):	

☐ Plaintiff's ☐ Defendant's **APPLICATION AND DECLARATION FOR ORDER PROHIBITING DOMESTIC VIOLENCE**

Read the Instructions for Order Prohibiting Domestic Violence before completing this form.

1. Plaintiff and defendant are *(check at least one)*:

   a. ☐ married and no Family Law proceeding is pending between us.
   b. ☐ formerly married.
   c. ☐ related to each other by blood, marriage or adoption.
   d. ☐ not related but regularly live in the same household.
   e. ☐ not related but during the last six months regularly lived in the same household.

2. Plaintiff and defendant *(check one)*:

   a. ☐ live in the same household.

   b. ☐ lived in the same household until *(give date and describe reason one of you moved out)*:

3. (Name): . . . . .has intentionally or recklessly *(check at least one)*:
   a. ☐ caused bodily injury or attempted bodily injury to me or a household member.

   b. ☐ made me or another household member afraid of immediate serious bodily injury.

Explain in detail. It is important to be specific. Give as many facts as you know. If more space is needed, attach additional pages or use item 17 on the last page of this form.
   (1) When:

   (2) By whom:
   (3) To whom:

   (4) What was done and how:

   (5) Describe injury, if any:

(Continued on reverse)

**APPLICATION AND DECLARATION
(DOMESTIC VIOLENCE)**
C.C.P. §§ 540-553

APPLICATION AND DECLARATION
(DOMESTIC VIOLENCE)
Page two of four

4. ☐ I have asked for restraining orders against the defendant before. The orders were ☐ granted ☐ denied.
Explain:

I REQUEST THE COURT TO MAKE THE ORDERS INDICATED BY THE CHECK MARKS IN THE BOXES BELOW.

5. ☐ **RESTRAINING ORDERS** ☐ **To be ordered pending the hearing**
   a. (Name): . . . . shall not contact, molest, attack, strike, threaten, sexually assault, batter, telephone or otherwise disturb my peace ☐ and the following family or household members (name):

   b. (Name): . . . . , who is not their parent, must not take or conceal the following children (name):

6. ☐ **RESIDENCE EXCLUSION AND RELATED ORDERS** ☐ **To be ordered pending the hearing**
   (Name): . . . . must move out and must not return to (address):

   a. ☐ taking only personal clothing and personal effects.
   b. ☐ I wish the court to make the residence exclusion effective immediately. I have a legal right to live at the address above because of the attached document or following fact (specify):

7. ☐ **STAY AWAY ORDERS** ☐ **To be ordered pending the hearing**
   (Name): . . . . must stay at least . . . . . . yards away from the following places:
   a. ☐ my residence (address optional):

   b. ☐ my place of work (address optional):

   c. ☐ the children's school (address optional):

   d. ☐ other (specify) (address optional):

8. ☐ **CHILD CUSTODY AND VISITATION** ☐ **To be ordered pending the hearing**

   a. ☐ **CUSTODY** Attach Declaration Under Uniform Custody of Minors Act if an order relating to custody is sought. Exclusive care, custody and control of the minor children listed in the attached declaration should be awarded as follows:

Name of child	Age	Award to (name)

   b. ☐ **VISITATION**
   (Name): . . . . should be awarded visitation as follows:
   (1) ☐ none.
   (2) ☐ reasonable visitation.
   (3) ☐ visitation with the following restrictions (specify):

   c. Facts showing the need for this custody and visitation order are (specify):

(Continued)

PLAINTIFF (name):	CASE NUMBER
DEFENDANT (name):	

APPLICATION AND DECLARATION
(DOMESTIC VIOLENCE)
Page three of four

If an order for child support, attorney fees or costs is requested, attach a completed Income and Expense Declaration (Family Law).

9. ☐ **CHILD SUPPORT**
   (Name): . . . . .should be ordered to pay support as specified:

   Child's name   Age   Monthly amount to be paid

10. ☐ **PROPERTY CONTROL**   ☐ **To be ordered pending the hearing**
    a. I request that I be given the exclusive temporary use, possession and control of the following property we own or are buying:

    I need the use of the specified property because:

    b. (Name): . . . . .should be ordered to make the following payments on liens and encumbrances coming due while the order is in effect:
    Debt   Pay to   Amount of payment

11. ☐ **ATTORNEY FEES AND COSTS**
    (Name): . . . . should be ordered to pay attorney fees and costs as follows:

12. ☐ **RESTITUTION**
    I request that (name): . . . . should be ordered to pay the following lost earnings and other actual expenses caused directly by the violence complained of:
    Type of loss   Pay to   Amount of claim

13. ☐ **COUNSELING**
    I request and stipulate to an order, upon agreement of both parties, that either or both of us participate in counseling.

(Continued on reverse)

APPLICATION AND DECLARATION

(DOMESTIC VIOLENCE)

Page four of four

14. ☐ **EXTENSION OF ORDERS**

I will request the court to set a hearing date for extension or modification of the restraining orders granted at the hearing.

15. **LAW ENFORCEMENT AGENCIES**

I request that copies of orders be given to the following law enforcement agencies having jurisdiction over the locations where violence is likely to occur:

Law Enforcement Agency	Address

16. ☐ I request that time for service of the Order to Show Cause and accompanying papers be shortened so that they may be served not less than *(specify number):*_____ days before the time set for the hearing. I need to have the order shortening time because of the facts contained in this application. *Add additional facts if necessary:*

17. ☐ Other orders *(specify other orders you request to help carry out the orders previously requested):*

18. ☐ Additional facts in support of this application are:
    ☐ contained in the attached declaration.

I declare under penalty of perjury under the laws of the State of California that the foregoing is true and correct and that this declaration is executed on (date):. . . . . at (place):. . . . .

_____   _____
(Type or print name)   (Signature of applicant)

Order to Show Cause and Temporary Restraining Order

ATTORNEY OR PARTY WITHOUT ATTORNEY (NAME AND ADDRESS):	TELEPHONE NO.	FOR COURT USE ONLY

ATTORNEY FOR (NAME):

SUPERIOR COURT OF CALIFORNIA, COUNTY OF

STREET ADDRESS:

MAILING ADDRESS:

CITY AND ZIP CODE:

BRANCH NAME:

PLAINTIFF:

DEFENDANT:

ORDER TO SHOW CAUSE AND TEMPORARY RESTRAINING ORDER (DOMESTIC VIOLENCE ACT / UNIFORM PARENTAGE ACT)	CASE NUMBER:

To (name):

YOU ARE ORDERED TO APPEAR IN THIS COURT AS FOLLOWS TO GIVE ANY LEGAL REASON WHY THE ORDERS SOUGHT IN THE ATTACHED APPLICATION SHOULD NOT BE GRANTED.

Date: Time: in ☐ Dept.:   ☐ Div.:   ☐ Room:

at the street address of the court, shown above.

FAILURE TO ATTEND THE HEARING MAY RESULT IN FURTHER ORDERS BEING MADE AGAINST YOU. YOU HAVE THE RIGHT TO APPEAR AND OPPOSE THE APPLICATION, WITH OR WITHOUT AN ATTORNEY.

TEMPORARY RESTRAINING ORDER

UNTIL THE TIME OF HEARING, IT IS ORDERED

1. ☐ (Name): . . . . shall not contact, molest, attack, strike, threaten, sexually assault, batter, telephone or disturb the peace of (name): . . . .

   ☐ and the following family and household members (names):

2. ☐ (Name): . . . . must move out and must not return to (address):

   ☐ and take only personal clothing and personal effects.

3. ☐ (Name): . . . . is ordered to stay at least . . . . yards away from the following places:

   (a) ☐ Residence of (name): . . . . (address optional):

   (b) ☐ Place of work of (name): . . . . (address optional):

   (c) ☐ The children's school (address optional):

   (d) ☐ Other (specify) (address optional):

4. ☐ Exclusive care, custody and control of the minor children:

   Name of child   Birthdate

is temporarily awarded to (name):

THESE ORDERS SHALL EXPIRE AT THE DATE AND THE TIME OF THE HEARING SHOWN IN THE BOX ABOVE UNLESS EXTENDED BY THE COURT.

VIOLATION OF THIS TEMPORARY RESTRAINING ORDER IS A MISDEMEANOR, PUNISHABLE BY A $500 FINE, SIX MONTHS IN JAIL, OR BOTH. THIS ORDER SHALL BE ENFORCED BY ALL LAW ENFORCEMENT OFFICERS IN THE STATE OF CALIFORNIA.

(TEMPORARY RESTRAINING ORDER CONTINUED ON REVERSE OF THIS PAGE)

Form Adopted by Rule 1296 10
Judicial Council of California
Revised Effective January 1, 1981

**ORDER TO SHOW CAUSE
AND TEMPORARY RESTRAINING ORDER
(DOMESTIC VIOLENCE / UNIFORM PARENTAGE)**

C.C.P. § 540-553

PLAINTIFF (name):	CASE NUMBER:
DEFENDANT (name):	

ORDER TO SHOW CAUSE AND TEMPORARY RESTRAINING ORDER
(DOMESTIC VIOLENCE / UNIFORM PARENTAGE)

5. ☐ **OTHER ORDERS** *(specify):*

6. By the close of business on the date of this order a copy of this order and any proof of service shall be given to the law enforcement agencies listed below as follows:
   a. ☐ the Clerk of the Court shall mail.
   b. ☐ applicant shall deliver.
   c. ☐ applicant's attorney shall deliver.

   Law enforcement agency   Address

7. The following documents shall be personally served on the defendant prior to the hearing: (1) Application and Declaration (Domestic Violence); (2) Blank Responsive Declaration (Domestic Violence); (3) Other *(specify):*

8. The documents referred to in item 7 shall be served at least
   a. ☐ ten days before the hearing.
   b. ☐ (specify number). . . . . . days before the hearing.

9. This order is effective when made. Law enforcement agencies shall enforce it immediately upon receipt. If proof of service on the defendant has not been received by the law enforcement agency, the law enforcement agency shall advise the restrained person of the terms of this order.

. . . .   _____
(Type or print name)   (Signature of Judge)

CLERK'S CERTIFICATE OF MAILING

I certify that I am not a party to this cause and that a copy of the foregoing was mailed first class, postage prepaid, in a sealed envelope addressed as shown in item 6, and that the mailing of the foregoing and execution of this certificate occurred at (place):. . . . . , California,

on (date) . . . .   Clerk, by _____ , Deputy

Responsive Declaration to Order to Show Cause (Domestic Violence)

ATTORNEY OR PARTY WITHOUT ATTORNEY (NAME AND ADDRESS):	TELEPHONE NO.:	FOR COURT USE ONLY
ATTORNEY FOR (NAME)		

SUPERIOR COURT OF CALIFORNIA, COUNTY OF
STREET ADDRESS
MAILING ADDRESS
CITY AND ZIP CODE
BRANCH NAME
PLAINTIFF
DEFENDANT

RESPONSIVE DECLARATION TO ORDER TO SHOW CAUSE (DOMESTIC VIOLENCE)	

HEARING	DATE	TIME	DEPT., ROOM OR DIVISION	CASE NUMBER

This response will be considered by the judge at the time of the court hearing. You must still obey the orders granted pending the hearing.

1. I respond to the **Application and Declaration (Domestic Violence)** as follows:

2. ☐ **RESTRAINING ORDERS**　　　　　　　　　　b. ☐ I consent to the following order:
    a. ☐ I consent to the order requested.
    c. ☐ I do not consent to the order requested.

3. ☐ **RESIDENCE EXCLUSION AND RELATED ORDERS**　　b. ☐ I consent to the following order:
    a. ☐ I consent to the order requested.
    c. ☐ I do not consent to the order requested.

4. ☐ **STAY AWAY ORDERS**　　　　　　　　　　b. ☐ I consent to the following order:
    a. ☐ I consent to the order requested.
    c. ☐ I do not consent to the order requested.

5. ☐ **CHILD CUSTODY**　　　　　　　　　　　b. ☐ I consent to the following order:
    a. ☐ I consent to the order requested.

6. ☐ **CHILD VISITATION**　　　　　　　　　　b. ☐ I consent to the following order:
    a. ☐ I consent to the order requested.

7. ☐ **CHILD SUPPORT**　　　　　　　　　　　b. ☐ I consent to the following order:
    a. ☐ I consent to the order requested.
    c. ☐ I do not consent to the order requested.

8. ☐ **PROPERTY CONTROL**　　　　　　　　　　b. ☐ I consent to the following order:
    a. ☐ I consent to the order requested.
    c. ☐ I do not consent to the order requested.

(Continued on reverse)

Form Adopted by Rule 1296.20
Judicial Council of California
Effective July 1, 1980

**RESPONSIVE DECLARATION TO
ORDER TO SHOW CAUSE
(DOMESTIC VIOLENCE)**

RESPONSIVE DECLARATION TO ORDER TO SHOW CAUSE
(DOMESTIC VIOLENCE)
Page two

9. ☐ **ATTORNEY FEES**
   a. ☐ I consent to the order requested.
   c. ☐ I do not consent to the order requested.
                 b. ☐ I consent to the following order:

10. ☐ I request the court to order the payment of my attorney fees if I prevail.

11. ☐ **RESTITUTION**
   a. ☐ I consent to the order requested.
   c. ☐ I do not consent to the order requested.
                 b. ☐ I consent to the following order:

12. ☐ **COUNSELING**
   a. ☐ I do not consent to counseling.
                 b. ☐ I consent and stipulate to an order to counseling.

13. ☐ **OTHER ORDERS**
   a. ☐ I consent to other orders as requested in item 16 of the application.
   c. ☐ I do not consent to the order requested.
                 b. ☐ I consent to the following order:

14. ☐ I request the court to order payment of my out of pocket expenses incurred as the result of an ex parte temporary restraining order issued without sufficient supporting facts. The expenses are:
       Item   Amount

15. ☐ I request the following additional orders:

16. ☐ **EXTENSION OF ORDERS**
I request and stipulate that the orders to which I have consented be extended not to exceed one year.

17. ☐ **SUPPORTING INFORMATION**
☐ contained in the attached declaration.

I declare under penalty of perjury that the foregoing, including any attachment, is true and correct and that this declaration is executed on (date): . . . . at (place): . . . . , California.

. . . .
(Type or print name)   (Signature of Declarant)

The declaration under penalty of perjury must be signed in California, or in a state that authorizes use of a declaration in place of an affidavit; otherwise an affidavit is required.

Order Prohibiting Domestic Violence

ATTORNEY OR PARTY WITHOUT ATTORNEY (NAME AND ADDRESS)	TELEPHONE NO	FOR COURT USE ONLY

ATTORNEY FOR (NAME)

SUPERIOR COURT OF CALIFORNIA, COUNTY OF
STREET ADDRESS
MAILING ADDRESS
CITY AND ZIP CODE
BRANCH NAME
PETITIONER/PLAINTIFF
RESPONDENT/DEFENDANT

ORDER PROHIBITING DOMESTIC VIOLENCE (FAMILY LAW—DOMESTIC VIOLENCE PREVENTION—UNIFORM PARENTAGE)	CASE NUMBER

1. This proceeding came on for hearing as follows:

    a. Date: ☐ Dept. ☐ Div. ☐ Room

    b. Judge (Name): ☐ Temporary Judge
    c. ☐ Petitioner/Plaintiff present ☐ Attorney present (Name):
    d. ☐ Respondent/defendant present ☐ Attorney present (Name):

After hearing on the application of applicant (name):

IT IS ORDERED THAT (name):

2. shall not contact, molest, attack, strike, threaten, sexually assault, batter, telephone, or disturb the peace of (name):

3. ☐ and shall move from and not return to (address):

    ☐ and take only personal clothing and personal effects

4. ☐ and stay at least _____ yards away from the following places:
    a. ☐ Residence of (name): (address optional.)

    b. ☐ Place of work of (name): (address optional.)

    c. ☐ Other (specify):

5. ☐ (Name): shall not take or conceal the following children:

6. ☐ Exclusive care, custody and control of the following minor children is temporarily awarded as follows:
    Name of child   Birthdate   Awarded to

7. ☐ Visitation is awarded as follows:

(Continued on reverse)

NOTICE: THIS ORDER SHALL BE ENFORCED BY ALL LAW OFFICERS IN THE STATE OF CALIFORNIA. VIOLATION OF THIS ORDER IS A CRIME, PUNISHABLE BY A $500 FINE OR SIX MONTHS IN JAIL, OR BOTH.

Form Adopted by Rule 1296.30
Judicial Council of California
Revised effective January 1, 1981   **ORDER PROHIBITING DOMESTIC VIOLENCE**
(FAMILY LAW—DOMESTIC VIOLENCE—UNIFORM PARENTAGE)   C C P § 540-553

ORDER PROHIBITING DOMESTIC VIOLENCE
(FAMILY LAW—DOMESTIC VIOLENCE—UNIFORM PARENTAGE)
Page two

8. ☐ Child support is awarded as follows:

9. ☐ (Name): . . . . is given exclusive use, possession, and control of the
following property:

☐ (Name): . . . . shall make the following payments coming due while this
order is in effect:

Debt	Payable to	Amount of payment

10. ☐ This matter is continued to (date): . . . . for consideration of
extension or modification of these orders.

11. ☐ By the close of business on the date of this order a copy of this order and any Proof of Service shall be
delivered to the law enforcement agencies listed below as follows:
☐ the Clerk of the Court shall mail.
☐ the applicant shall deliver.
☐ the applicant's attorney shall deliver.

Law Enforcement Agency	Address

12. This order is effective when made. Law enforcement agencies shall enforce it immediately upon receipt. If proof
of service on the restrained person has not been received by the law enforcement agency, the law enforcement
agency shall advise the restrained person of the terms of this order.

13. ☐ Other orders:

14. **THIS ORDER, EXCEPT FOR ANY AWARD OF CHILD CUSTODY, VISITATION, OR MONEY, SHALL EXPIRE AT
MIDNIGHT ON (DATE):** . . . . **UNLESS A COURT ORDER EXTENDS IT.**

Dated: . . . . _____

_____
Judge of the Superior Court

CLERK'S CERTIFICATE OF MAILING

I certify that I am not a party to this cause and that a copy of the foregoing was mailed first class, postage prepaid,
in a sealed envelope addressed as shown in item 11, and that the mailing of the foregoing and executive of this
certificate occurred at (place): . . . ., California

on (date): . . . . Clerk, by _____ , Deputy

Proof of Service

<table>
<tr><td>ATTORNEY OR PARTY WITHOUT ATTORNEY (NAME AND ADDRESS)

ATTORNEY FOR (NAME)</td><td>TELEPHONE NO.:</td><td>FOR COURT USE ONLY</td></tr>
<tr><td colspan="2">SUPERIOR COURT OF CALIFORNIA, COUNTY OF

PLAINTIFF

DEFENDANT</td><td></td></tr>
<tr><td colspan="2" align="center">PROOF OF SERVICE</td><td>CASE NUMBER:</td></tr>
</table>

Instructions—Personal Service

Attach a completed Proof of Service to the original or a true copy of the document served and submit it to the clerk for filing.

1. I served a copy of the following documents *(Put a check in the box before the title of each document you served):*

DOMESTIC VIOLENCE

a. ☐ Application and Declaration for Order Prohibiting Domestic Violence AND Order to Show Cause and Temporary Restraining Order (Domestic Violence)

b. ☐ Blank Responsive Declaration to Order to Show Cause (Domestic Violence)

c. ☐ Instructions for Orders Prohibiting Domestic Violence

d. ☐ Order Prohibiting Domestic Violence

EMANCIPATION

i. ☐ Petition for Declaration of Emancipation

j. ☐ Petition for Rescission of Declaration of Emancipation

HARASSMENT

e. ☐ Instructions for Lawsuits to Prohibit Harassment, Petition for Injunction Prohibiting Harassment, Order to Show Cause (Harassment)

f. ☐ AND Temporary Restraining Order

g. ☐ Blank Response to Petition for Injunction Prohibiting Harassment

h. ☐ Injunction Prohibiting Harassment

OTHER

k. ☐ *(Specify):*

2. Person served (name):

3. By personally delivering copies to the person served, as follows:
   (1) Date . . . . (2) Time: . . . .
   (3) Address . . . .

4. At the time of service I was **at least 18 years of age and not a party to this cause.**

5. I declare under penalty of perjury that the foregoing is true and correct and that this declaration is executed on
   (date): . . . . at (place): . . . ., California.

6. . . . .   _____
   (Type or print name)   (Signature)

(See reverse for Proof of Service by Mail)

The declaration under penalty of perjury must be signed in California; or in a state that authorizes use of a declaration in place of an affidavit; otherwise an affidavit is required

Form Approved by Rule 1296.40
Judicial Council of California
Effective July 1, 1980   **PROOF OF SERVICE**

PROOF OF SERVICE

TITLE OF CASE	CASE NUMBER:

INSTRUCTIONS—SERVICE BY MAIL

Most of the documents listed on the reverse must be served by personal delivery. They cannot be mailed.

Attach a completed Proof of Service to the original or to a true copy of the document served and submit it to the clerk for filing. An unsigned copy of the Proof of Service should be attached to and served with the document served.

7. I am over the age of 18 and **not a party to this cause**. I am a resident of or employed in the county where the mailing occurred. My residence or business address is:

8. I served a copy of the following documents *(list documents):*

by placing a true copy of each document, in the United States mail, in a sealed envelope with postage fully prepaid, as follows:

a. Date of deposit:

b. Place of deposit (city and state):

c. Addressed as follows:

9. I declare under penalty of perjury that the foregoing is true and correct and that this declaration is executed on (date): . . . . , at (place): . . . ., California.

10. . . . . _____
(Type or print name)   (Signature)

PROOF OF SERVICE

Application and Order for Re-Issuance of Order to Show Cause

ATTORNEY OR PARTY WITHOUT ATTORNEY (Name and Address):	TELEPHONE NO.:	FOR COURT USE ONLY
ATTORNEY FOR (Name):		

SUPERIOR COURT OF CALIFORNIA, COUNTY OF
STREET ADDRESS:
MAILING ADDRESS:
CITY AND ZIP CODE:
BRANCH NAME:

PLAINTIFF:

DEFENDANT:

APPLICATION AND ORDER FOR RE-ISSUANCE OF ORDER TO SHOW CAUSE (DOMESTIC VIOLENCE)	CASE NUMBER:

1. Declarant was unable to have the defendant served as required prior to the hearing date and requests the court to re-issue the order to show cause and temporary restraining order originally issued as follows:
   a. Order to show cause was issued on (date):
   b. Order to show cause was last set for hearing on (date):
   c. Order to show cause has been re-issued previously (number of times):

I declare under penalty of perjury under the laws of the State of California that the foregoing, including any attachment, is true and correct and that this declaration is executed on (date): . . . . at (place): . . . .

. . . . (Type or print name) . . . .   (Signature) . . . .

ORDER

2. IT IS ORDERED that the order to show cause issued as shown in item 1 above is re-issued and reset for hearing as follows:

   date: time: ☐ Dept.:   ☐ Div.:   ☐ Room:
   at the street address of the court shown above.

   b. By the close of business on the date of this order a copy of this order and any proof of service shall be given to the law enforcement agencies named in item 6 of the Order to Show Cause as follows:
   ☐ the Clerk of the Court shall mail.
   ☐ the applicant shall deliver.
   ☐ the applicant's attorney shall deliver.

   c. A copy of this order shall be attached to documents to be served on the defendant, as directed in item 7 of the order to show cause, and shall also be served on the defendant.

   d. All other orders contained in the order to show cause remain in full force and effect unless modified by this order. **THE ORDER TO SHOW CAUSE AND THIS ORDER EXPIRE ON THE DATE AND TIME OF THE HEARING SHOWN IN THE BOX ABOVE UNLESS EXTENDED BY THE COURT.**

Dated: . . . .
                                          Judge of the Superior Court

CLERK'S CERTIFICATE OF MAILING

I certify that I am not a party to this cause and that a copy of the foregoing was mailed first class, postage prepaid, in a sealed envelope addressed as shown in item 6 of the order to show cause, and that the mailing of the foregoing and execution of this certificate occurred at . . . . , California.

on (date): . . . . Clerk, by _____ , Deputy

The word "plaintiff" includes petitioner and "defendant" includes respondent.

Adopted by Rule 1296.15
Judicial Council of California
Effective January 1, 1981
APPLICATION AND ORDER FOR RE-ISSUANCE OF ORDER TO SHOW CAUSE (DOMESTIC VIOLENCE)
     C.C.P § 527(b)

Chapter 20

LANDLORD AND TENANT

(Code Civ. Proc. §§116.2, 1159-1179a.)

Legal Assistant Role

Actions in this chapter provide many opportunities for the legal assistant to take part in the legal process. Most of the eleven steps in the procedure found later in this chapter may be performed by the legal assistant under the direction of the attorney.

UNLAWFUL DETAINER

An unlawful detainer action is a special civil proceeding by which a landlord seeks possession of property occupied by a tenant, often because of nonpayment of rent. Under Code of Civil Procedure section 1161, such an action may also be brought for failure of the tenant to perform conditions of lease, holding over after expiration of term, subletting contrary to terms of lease, or after commission of waste, nuisance or unlawful use of premises. Also, a tenant may seek possession from a subtenant.

Jurisdiction in Unlawful Detainer Actions

The court in which the suit is filed depends upon the amount of the rent and the total amount owing. In actions to recover possession of real property where rent is charged, and the amount of the last rental charged is $1,000 per month or less, and the total damages $15,000 or less, the case may be filed either in the municipal or justice court (the jurisdiction of municipal and justice courts is concurrent); for rents and amounts above these limits, the action must be filed in the superior court.

The giving of certain notices is prerequisite to the filing of certain unlawful detainer actions. Also, the terms of a rental agreement may contain express agreements as to the length of notice required.

Rent Default

Let us assume that a tenant has not paid his rent. What is to be done? A three-day Notice to Pay Rent or Quit is prepared and served on the tenant. The owner may have done this before consulting an attorney. If not, the legal assistant can draft the notice. The notice may not be served until a date after the day the rent is due.

The amount of the rent due must be stated in the notice.

The tenant has a full three days to pay the rent or move. The day of service is not counted, and if the third day falls on a holiday, the three-day period is extended an additional day. (Time is counted in the same manner for 30-day notices.)

Let us suppose the tenant offers to pay part of the rent due and promises to pay the balance owing on a certain date. If the landlord accepts the amount of the rent offered, and if the tenant then fails to pay the balance as promised, the landlord should not file an unlawful detainer action without first serving and filing another three-day notice to pay rent or quit.

A suggested form of three-day notice to pay rent or quit follows:

Three Days' Notice to Pay Rent or Quit

TO:_____
Tenant(s) in Possession

Address:_____ Apartment No._____

City_____ State_____ Zip_____

Demand is hereby made upon you for payment of rent of the above-described premises. WITHIN THREE DAYS after the service on you of this notice you are hereby required to pay the rent on the above-described premises, of which you now hold possession, amounting to _____ Dollars ($____), being the rent due for the period from _____, _____, to _____, _____, or you are hereby required to deliver up possession of said premises to the undersigned within three days after service on you of this notice or the undersigned will institute legal proceedings against you to declare a forfeiture of the lease under which you occupy said premises and to recover possession of said premises and to recover TREBLE RENTS and DAMAGES for the unlawful detention of said premises.

The undersigned elects to and does declare a forfeiture of the lease if the rent is not paid within the three days.

DATED:_____, _____.

_____
(signature)
Owner/Agent

[The exact amount of the rent due must be stated.]

Forfeiture of Lease

The above notice contains language that if the rent is not paid the owner will institute legal proceedings to declare a forfeiture of the lease. This makes it possible for the owner in the subsequent unlawful detainer action to have a forfeiture of the lease declared. What does this mean? Suppose a tenant has a year's lease on an apartment and is not paying his rent as agreed. If the court in the unlawful detainer action not only restores the premises to the owner but declares a forfeiture of the lease, the tenant has no further obligation to perform the conditions of the lease — although he still owes for any back rent, or taxes. In a tight rental market where the owner might have difficulty renting, the owner might possibly want to try to collect future rent from the tenant after he has moved.

However, as a practical matter, ordinarily the owner will not attempt to do this. If he has a tenant who is not meeting his agreement to pay rent while he is living there, he is unlikely to collect any rent from the tenant after he has moved. Chances are the landlord will simply try to rent the apartment once the tenant moves, and forget about the rent the tenant owes. In other words, he will want a forfeiture of the lease.

For a discussion of lease forfeiture, see article, "Hardship and the Decision to Elect a Forfeiture: The Landlord's Dilemma," by Edward L. Felman in the August 1980 issue of the California State Bar Journal.

If the tenant fails to pay rent within three days after service of the notice, then a complaint in unlawful detainer may be prepared and served. It is at this point that the landlord-client is apt to consult an attorney, assuming he did not ask the attorney for advice when his problem arose. Therefore the legal assistant is also likely to become involved in the proceedings at this point, at the time of preparation of the complaint (see Complaint for Unlawful Detainer, *infra*) or at time of preparation of answer, in representation of defendant.

Periodic Tenancy

If for any reason the landlord desires to have the tenant move, a 30-day notice to quit must be given. This is true whether there is a written agreement for a month-to-month tenancy or whether there is only an oral agreement by which the rent is paid monthly. (See Civ. Code §1944.) A form of 30-day notice to quit follows. Note that it contains a provision that the rent is due and payable to the date of termination of tenancy under the notice.

Thirty-Day Notice to Terminate Tenancy

TO:_____

Tenant(s) in Possession

Address:_____ Apartment No._____

City_____ State_____ Zip_____

NOTICE IS HEREBY GIVEN that you are hereby required to quit and deliver up to me the possession of the above-described premises now held and occupied by you at the expiration of thirty (30) days after the service on you of this notice.

YOU ARE FURTHER NOTIFIED that the purpose and intent of this notice is to terminate said tenancy at the expiration of said thirty days' period and that if at the expiration of said period you fail to quit and deliver up possession of said premises, legal proceedings for unlawful detainer will be instituted against you to recover possession of said premises.

The rent shall be due and payable to and including the date of termination of your tenancy under this notice.

DATE:_____, _____.

(Signature)_____

Owner/Agent

If the tenancy is by a written agreement which provides for a seven-day notice to quit, the notice to quit may be for seven days rather than thirty. The language in the notice should be changed accordingly.

The seven-day notice, unlike the 30-day notice, must be given to coincide with the expiration of the term of the tenancy. (Civ. Code §1946.) Therefore service should be made no later than eight days prior to the expiration of the term, to give a full seven days' notice. A tenant terminating on October 31, 1979, for example, should be served no later than October 24. A seven-day notice follows:

NOTICE TO QUIT

TO: BENNETT BUSHMAN, Tenant in Possession.

TAKE NOTICE that you are hereby required to quit and deliver up to me the possession of the premises now held and occupied by you, being the premises known as 1400 — 22nd Street, Sacramento, California, at the expiration of your month-to-month tenancy of said premises commencing on the 1st day of October, 1979, and ending on the 31st day of October, 1979.

THIS IS INTENDED as a seven-days' notice to quit, for the purpose of terminating your tenancy as aforesaid.

Dated this 22nd day of October, 1979.

_____

Owner

If the landlord is seeking forfeiture of the lease if the rent is not paid, the notice must so state. However, if the landlord has been in the habit of accepting rent when it was past due, he may have waived the condition of prompt payment of rent and may not seek forfeiture of lease on that ground, without first giving notice of intention to enforce that condition in the future.

Expiration of Term

No notice to quit is required if the landlord wishes to terminate the tenancy of a tenant holding over at the expiration of his lease for a specified period, as, for example, a lease for six months or a year.

In the absence of specific provisions of the lease controlling, where a lease for a year expires but the tenant holds over and pays a month's rent which the landlord accepts, thereafter the tenant is on a month-to-month tenancy and 30-day notice is required. Other terms of the lease remain binding.

A provision for automatic renewal or extension for full term of the lease is prohibited unless it appears in eight-point boldface type. (Civ. Code §1945.5.)

Breach of Lease

If a tenant has failed to perform a condition of his lease (such as no pets), a three-day notice to quit is required. If the breach is one that can be performed during the three-day period (*i.e.*, the tenant could get rid of a pet), the notice must be in the alternative, that is, to perform *or* quit. When the condition cannot be remedied, the notice need not be in the alternative, and the reason for terminating the lease need not be stated.

Waste or Nuisance

Under Code of Civil Procedure section 1161, subdivision 4, any tenant "committing waste . . . contrary to the conditions or covenants of his lease, or maintaining, committing, or permitting the maintenance or commission of a nuisance upon the demised premises or using such premises for an unlawful purpose, thereby terminates the lease, and the landlord, or his successor in estate, shall upon service of three days' notice to quit upon the person or persons in possession, be entitled to restitution of possession. . . ." The code does not contain a definition of "waste."

"Nuisance" is defined in Civil Code section 3479 as "anything which is injurious to health, or is indecent or offensive to these senses, or an obstruction to the free use of property" and has been held to include disturbance of other tenants by loud noise, quarreling loudly, or using vile and obscene language, drunkenness, or loud music.

Many forms of notice are available. In volume 14, California Forms of Pleading and Practice, at pages 342-343, Form No. 6 is a composite form designed for use against a tenant who continues in possession after a noncurable breach of covenant; assigning or subletting or committing waste on the demised premises, contrary to the conditions or covenants of his lease; and maintaining, committing or permitting the maintenance or commission of a nuisance on the demised premises, or using a premises for an unlawful purpose.

Tenancy at Will

When a tenant holds a piece of property by agreement at the will of the landlord, tenancy can be terminated under Civil Code section 789 by the giving of a thirty-day notice to quit.

* * *

*Summary of Notices Prerequisite to Complaint
for Unlawful Detainer:*

Code of Civil
Procedure,
§1161:

Subdivision:

1. Expiration of term of lease	No notice required
2. Rent default	3-day notice to pay rent or quit
3. Breach of lease	3-day alternative notice to perform or quit (if condition can be performed)
	or
	3-day notice to quit (if condition cannot be performed)
4. Commission of waste or nuisance	3-day notice to quit

Civil Code,
§789:
Tenancy at will   30-day notice to quit

Civil Code,
§1944:
Periodic Tenancy   30-day notice to quit

Service of Notice

The notice may be served on the tenant personally. If the tenant is absent from his place of residence and from his usual place of business, he may be served by leaving a copy with someone of suitable age and discretion at either place and sending a copy through the mail to the tenant at his residence. If place of residence and business cannot be ascertained or a suitable person cannot be found, the notice may be served by

1. Posting a copy in a conspicuous place on the property *and*
2. Delivering a copy to a person there residing *and*
3. Sending a copy through the mail addressed to the tenant at the place where the property is situated. (Code Civ. Proc. §1162.)

Complaint in Unlawful Detainer

After service of the required notices a complaint and summons are prepared. The summons is a special mandatory form for use in unlawful detainer actions, obtainable from the county clerk, and is served in the same manner as any other summons in a civil proceeding.

A default may be taken if no answer is filed within five days after date of service (of complaint or amended complaint). An extension of time to answer under Code of Civil Procedure section 1054 shall not exceed 10 days without the consent of the adverse party. (Code Civ. Proc. §1167.5.) A cross-complaint is not permitted in any proceeding for unlawful detainer.

If an answer is filed, the case must be set for trial in accordance with local rules. The case is entitled to priority in setting for trial.

Complaint in Unlawful Detainer

```
 1   ROBERT REINERT
     Attorney at Law
 2   945 Beacon St.
     Sacramento, CA 95814
 3   (916) 234-5678

 4   Attorney for Plaintiff

 5

 6

 7

 8        MUNICIPAL COURT, SACRAMENTO MUNICIPAL COURT DISTRICT,

 9          COUNTY OF SACRAMENTO, STATE OF CALIFORNIA

10

11   RALPH REYNOLDS,              )       NO.
                                  )
12             Plaintiff,         )
                                  )
13        v.                      )   COMPLAINT IN UNLAWFUL DETAINER
                                  )
14   BERT GILROY,                 )
                                  )
15             Defendant.         )
     _____)
16

17        Plaintiff complains of defendant and alleges that:

18        1.  Plaintiff is, and at all times herein mentioned

19   was, the owner of the premises commonly known as 4100 X Street,

20   Sacramento, California.

21        2.  The above designated premises are within the

22   Sacramento Municipal Court District.

23        3.  On or about May 1, 1978, by written agreement,

24   plaintiff leased to defendant Apartment No. 3 on said premises

25   for a month-to-month term at a monthly rental of $180 payable

26   in advance on the 1st day of each month commencing May 1, 1978.

27   A copy of said written agreement is attached hereto and incor-

28   porated herein.
```

1

1   4. On or about May 1, 1978, pursuant to said agreement,

2 defendant went into possession of said premises and ever since

3 has been and now is in possession thereof.

4   5. Defendant has failed to pay rent as follows: $180

5 for the rental period of September 1, 1978, through September 30,

6 1978, and $180 for the rental period October 1, 1978, through

7 October 31, 1978.

8   6. On October 11, 1978, plaintiff caused to be served

9 upon defendant a 3-day notice to pay rent or quit. A copy of

10 said notice is attached hereto and incorporated herein.

11   7. More than three days have elapsed since the service

12 of said notice but no part of said rent has been paid, and

13 plaintiff is entitled to possession of the premises.

14   8. The reasonable value of the use and occupancy of

15 the premises is $6.00 per day.

16   9. By the terms of said written agreement, defendant

17 agreed to pay the reasonable attorney's fee if action were com-

18 menced to recover possession of the premises or to collect rent.

19   WHEREFORE, plaintiff prays for judgment against

20 defendant as follows:

21   1. Restitution of the premises.

22   2. Damages for all unpaid rent and for treble damages

23 for each day commencing three days after service of the 3-day

24 notice to pay rent or quit.

25   3. Attorney's fees.

26   4. Costs of suit.

27   5. Such further relief as the court may deem proper.

28

                           Attorney for Plaintiff

2

1   I, RALPH REYNOLDS, state;

2   I am the plaintiff in the above-entitled matter.

3   I have read the foregoing complaint and know the

4   contents thereof; the same is true of my own knowledge, except

5   as to those matters which are therein stated on information and

6   belief and, as to those matters, I believe it to be true.

7   Executed on October 18, 1978, at Sacramento, California.

8   I declare under penalty of perjury that the foregoing

9   is true and correct.

10

11   _Ralph Reynolds_

12

13

14

15

16

17

18   [Rental agreement would be Exhibit A but

19   is not reproduced here.]

20

21

22

23

24

25

26

27

28

                              3

Summary of Procedure in Unlawful Detainer Actions

The procedure in unlawful detainer actions is basically the same as in other civil litigation, but there are some variations. The legal assistant can be useful in this field as in other areas of civil litigation. Documents can be drafted by the legal assistant as follows under the general supervision of the attorney and subject to his review.

1. If plaintiff served the three-day Notice to Pay Rent or Quit, collect from him the original notice and the proof of service, and also the original rental agreement made with defendant.

2. Prepare original complaint (verified by plaintiff) and copy to serve on defendant, plus 2 copies for file (one to be endorsed-filed).

3. Prepare original summons (special summons for unlawful detainer action) and a copy for each defendant and a copy for the file.

Note that the summons for an unlawful detainer action requires the defendant to make an appearance within 5 days from the date of service of the copy of the summons and complaint upon him. (Code Civ. Proc. §1167.) The five-day requirement also applies to time to answer an amended complaint or to amend the answer under subdivisions (2), (3), (5) or (6) of Code of Civil Procedure section 586.

4. File the complaint, have summons issued, and serve copy of summons and complaint on defendant, in the same manner as in any other civil action.

5. If defendant fails to make an appearance within 5 days after service of the summons and complaint upon him, his default may be taken in the usual manner.

6. Prepare a declaration for judgment for plaintiff's signature.

7. Prepare a writ of possession and mail to the clerk requesting that the writ be completed and issued.

8. Contact the marshal's office or the sheriff's office to determine the amount of cash deposit required. (A deposit is required for eviction costs, costs of moving and storage of the defendant's possessions.)

9. Prepare instructions for the marshal.

10. Mail the instructions, original writ and adequate copies to the levying officer. He will give the tenant written notice to vacate the premises within 10 days otherwise all of his possessions on the premises will be removed and stored at the defendant's expense. The initial moving and storing expenses must be advanced by the plaintiff although chargeable to the defendant.

11. To regain possession of his property, the tenant must pay all of the costs of moving and storage.

"Rent" is payable to the date of judgment. In an unlawful detainer action filed after the expiration of a three-day notice to pay rent or quit, the plaintiff will be awarded either (1) damages and rent found due or (2) punitive, or "treble damages," in an amount not exceeding three times the amount of damages and rent found due, if malice can be shown. (Code Civ. Proc. §1174(b).)

Notice of Trial

Five days' notice of trial must be given in an unlawful detainer action or, if notice is served by mail (whether by clerk of court or other party), service must be made not less than 10 days prior to the trial date. Code of Civil Procedure section 1013 (extending time if service be by mail) does not extend such notice of trial for unlawful detainer actions. Proof of such service must be made either by the clerk's certificate pursuant to Code of Civil Procedure section 1013a(3) or by the party's affidavit or certificate pursuant to Code of Civil Procedure section 1013a(1) or (2) or other competent evidence. (Code Civ. Proc. §594.)

JUDGMENT

Rent default: The landlord is entitled to recover all delinquent rent due and unpaid at time of trial, and *may* be granted damages from the date of the unlawful detention to the date of judgment. Judgment for punitive damages, up to an amount three times the rent or damages, may be awarded, in the discretion of the trial court, if malice is found. (See Code Civ. Proc. §1174.)

Procedure After Judgment

If the tenant remains in possession after judgment is entered, an application to the court for a writ of possession must be made. (Code Civ. Proc. §682(5).)

The following notice appears on a writ of restitution of the premises (Writ of Execution (Possession of Real Property)) pursuant to an action for unlawful detainer:

> Personal property remaining on the premises at the time of its restitution to the landlord will be sold or otherwise disposed of in accordance with Section 1174 of the Code of Civil Procedure unless the tenant or the owner pays the landlord the reasonable cost of storage and takes possession of the personal property not later than 15 days after the time the premises are restored to the landlord.

There is a fee for issuance of the writ. Instructions to the levying officer must be prepared; a fee is required by the levying officer.

The procedure for restoring the premises is set forth in Code of Civil Procedure section 1174. The procedure is the same as for a writ of attachment in Code of Civil Procedure, section 488.310, subdivision (d), in addition, where a copy of the writ of possession is posted on the property, another copy of the writ must be mailed to the defendant at his residence or business address last known or to his attorney, or if no such address is known, at the premises.

If the tenant does not vacate within five days from the date of service or, if the writ if posted, within five days from the date of mailing of the additional notice, the enforcing officer shall remove the tenant from the premises and place the plaintiff in possession thereof.

The landlord shall store defendant's possessions in a place of safe-keeping, as provided in subdivision (g) of Code of Civil Procedure section 1174.

An attachment may be sought for the amount of rent that will be due from the date of the complaint to the estimated date of judgment and an estimated amount authorized by Code of Civil Procedure section 482.110 for costs and attorney fees and may, in the discretion of the court, include an additional amount for rent from date of filing of complaint until the estimated date of judgment or possession. (See Code Civ. Proc. §483.020.)

Appeal

The defendant may appeal but proceedings on the judgment are not stayed unless the judge so directs.

Reference

Reference books for Unlawful Detainer; for comprehensive treatment:

Goddard and Hunt, California Landlord and Tenant.

California Forms of Pleading and Practice, vol. 14.

Legal Aspects of Real Estate Transactions (Cal. Cont. Ed. Bar 1956), Ch. 20, Termination of a Proceeding Involving Tenancy, §§53-56, 75, 84.

California Eviction Defense Manual, Moskovitz, Honigsberg, & Finkelstein (1971) (Regents of the Univ. of Cal.)

See Function of Paralegal chart in chapter 2 for an outline of duties in unlawful detainer actions.

Chapter 21

ADOPTIONS

(Civil Code §§221 *et seq.*)

California law provides for four types of adoptions:
1. Independent adoption;
2. Agency (relinquishment) adoption;
3. Step-parent adoption and
4. Adult adoption

LEGAL ASSISTANT ROLE

Adoption is another area where the legal assistant may be of a great amount of assistance to the attorney. In this field, the law is not complex but the arrangements and paper work are extensive. Traditionally legal secretaries have actually done the work with the attorney overseeing the result and making court appearances. The legal assistant will find in this chapter most of the duties within his/her capacities.

INDEPENDENT ADOPTIONS

This chapter deals with independent adoptions, probably the most common type of adoption likely to be handled by a private practitioner and paralegal. An independent adoption is one in which the parent or parents of the child to be adopted consent to its adoption by specific individuals. The child is placed directly by the natural parents with an adopting family. The persons desiring to adopt such a child must petition the superior court in the county of their residence.

PROCEDURE

What is the general procedure? The following outline provides a quick look at what should be done by a paralegal assisting an attorney (and by others) in an adoption:
1. Pending the filing of the petition, certified copies of the documents required must be collected, such as:

707

    a. Proof of death of one or both natural parents.

    b. Certified copies of all prior marriage records of both petitioners.

    c. Certified copies of all terminations of prior marriages of petitioners (death, divorce, or annulment).

    d. Certified copy of marriage record of petitioners.

    e. Certified copy of birth record of minor child to be adopted.

    f. Birth certificates of adopting parents.

2. The mother voluntarily signs a consent to release of her child from the hospital, but this is not the consent to adoption.

3. A petition for adoption is prepared and the original filed in the county clerk's office. The legal assistant can draft this form. (A form of petition may be found in Deering's Annotated Civil Code following section 226 thereof.) Consult local court rules. In Los Angeles County the first paragraph of the petition must allege the minor's existing name, e.g.: "The name by which the minor who is the subject of this petition was registered at birth is_____." The petition must contain:

    a. Sex and date of birth of the minor

    b. Name child had prior to adoption (or, if a licensed agency joins in petition, name may appear in the joinder signed by the agency).

The caption shall *not* contain the name of the child, but shall contain the names of the petitioners.

4. The consent of the biological parents should be obtained. (See Civil Code §§7000-7018, The Uniform Parentage Act, for presumptions concerning the natural father.)

    Children cannot be adopted without the consent of the mother and of the presumed father — if living — with the exception that if the custody of a child has been given by judicial decree to one parent, and the other parent has willfully failed to pay for the care and support of the child for a period of one year, only the parent having custody need consent to the adoption, but only after the parent not having custody has been personally served with a copy of a citation to appear in court.

    If the other parent cannot be personally served because his whereabouts are unknown, a citation may be served by way of publication.

    The consent of a child who is over 12 years of age must also be obtained. (Civ. Code §225.)

    No consent is required:

a. If juvenile court or other court has declared child free from custody of parents.

b. If child has been deserted without provision for identification.

c. If child has been relinquished for adoption to an authorized adoption agency.

Parents who are minors can consent to the adoption of their children.

Civil Code section 224.1 provides that when a minor is in the custody of a public agency or a licensed adoption agency, and the persons whose consent to adoption is required are deceased, the State Department of Social Services, or the licensed adoption agency, may bring an action asking the court for an order establishing that the agency so requesting has the right of custody and control and the authority to place the minor for adoption. The agency bringing the action must give notice as prescribed by the court to all known relatives of the minor up to and including the third degree of lineal and collateral consanguinity (as defined in Probate Code sections 252 and 253).

5. Serve a citation on a nonconsenting natural parent when required by Civil Code section 224.

6. A letter is written to the State Department of Social Services sending them:

a. A copy of the petition for adoption with notation as to filing date and the court docket number.

b. All documentary evidence which has been collected. (See above.)

c. Information as to parental consent, if any.

d. Addresses and telephone numbers of petitioners and minor child.

e. Information as to any action taken to free child from parental control or custody.

f. Addresses and telephone numbers of natural parent or parents.

7. The Department of Social Services sends its report to the attorney's office. (The Department has 180 days within which to prepare its report.) The Department makes it own arrangements with petitioners for home study and obtains the required consents of the natural parents.

8. The State Department of Social Services will file its original report in the court record and send a copy to the attorney. When the report is received, the court should be notified and the matter set for hearing.

9. At the hearing the adopting parents and child must be present. The hearing is closed. The attorney will take with him an Agreement

for Adoption and a Decree of Adoption for the signature of the judge. In the Agreement for Adoption the adopting parents agree that they will treat the child as their own child and agree to the adoption; this document is signed at the time of the hearing. An itemized Declaration and Report of Expenses of petitioners in connection with birth and placement of child, pursuant to Civil Code section 224r, must also be filed, no later than the hearing date.

10. After the hearing a copy of the Decree of Adoption and Agreement for Adoption is sent to the State Department of Social Services. The Decree of Adoption shall contain the new name of the minor but shall *not* contain the name the child had prior to adoption.

11. A new birth certificate from the Department of Vital Statistics is obtained. A fee is charged if the filing fee has not been paid. The Department should be given the original name of the child, its birthdate, its birthplace, new name, date of adoption, court action number, and complete names of petitioners. This can be done immediately after the decree of adoption has been made; or the court will notify the Department at a later date.

12. A closing letter is sent to the client, with a bill, returning any original documents belonging to the clients and sending them the new birth certificate.

A procedural checklist is set forth in volume 1, page 48, Adoptions, California Forms of Pleading and Practice (published by Matthew Bender Company). The legal assistant should, of course, follow up as each step is completed, by preparing for the next step.

See chapter 2 for Function of Paralegal Chart for adoptions.

NOTE:

Section 225m is included in the Civil Code making it unethical for an attorney to represent both the prospective adopting parents and the natural parents of the child being adopted unless a written consent is obtained from both parties. This provision does not apply to a stepparent adoption or when an organization licensed by the State Department of Social Services joins in the petition.

On the following pages are some sample pleadings (petition, agreement, and decree) for independent and stepparent adoptions.

Petition for Adoption

```
 1  ANDREW, LINCOLN
    1234 N St.
 2  Sacramento, CA 95814
    447-9302
 3
    Attorney for Petitioners
 4

 5

 6

 7
                    SUPERIOR COURT OF CALIFORNIA
 8
                       COUNTY OF SACRAMENTO
 9

10  In the Matter of the       )    NO. 314256    Dept. _____
    Petition of                )
11                             )
       RALPH ARTHUR BARNES and )    PETITION FOR ADOPTION
12     PEARL ALICE BARNES,     )
                               )       (Independent)
13          Adopting Parents.  )
    _____)
14

15

16         Petitioners allege:

17         1.  The name by which the minor who is the subject of

18  this petition was registered at birth is BABY GIRL JONES.

19         2.  The petitioners are husband and wife and reside in

20  the County of Sacramento, State of California, and desire to

21  adopt BABY GIRL JONES, the above-named minor child who was born

22  in Sacramento, California, on July 1, 1981.  The petitioners are

23  adult persons and more than ten years older than said minor.

24         3.  The parents entitled to sole custody of the child

25  have placed the child directly with the petitioners for adoption

26  and are prepared to consent to the child's adoption by peti-

27  tioners.

28                               1
```

1

2   4. The child is a proper subject for adoption. The

3 petitioners' home is suitable for the child and they are able

4 to support and care properly for the child. The petitioners

5 agree to treat the child in all respects as their own lawful

6 child.

7   5. Each petitioner hereby consents to the adoption

8 of the child by the other.

9   WHEREFORE, petitioners pray that the Court adjudge

10 the adoption of the child by petitioners, declaring that each

11 petitioner and the child thenceforth shall sustain toward each

12 other the legal relation of parent and child, and have all the

13 rights and be subject to all the duties of that relation; and

14 that the child be known as JENNIFER ROSE BARNES.

15   Dated: September 1, 1981.

16

17 *Ralph Arthur Barnes*   Petitioner

18

19 *Dear Alice Barnes*   Petitioner

20

21 *Andrew Lincoln*

Attorney for Petitioner

22

23

24

25 [Add verification by petitioners]

26

27

28

Agreement for Adoption

1   [If the child being adopted were over 12 years of age, a
2   CONSENT OF CHILD would be added to this form.]

3

4

5

6

7

8   SUPERIOR COURT OF CALIFORNIA

9   COUNTY OF SACRAMENTO

10

11   In the Matter of the   )   NO. 134256   Dept. ____
     Petition of   )
12   )
     RALPH ARTHUR BARNES and   )   AGREEMENT FOR ADOPTION
13   PEARL ALICE BARNES,   )
)
14   Adopting Parents.   )
)
15   _____

16   We, the undersigned petitioners, having petitioned the

17   above-entitled Court for the approval of the adoption of BABY

18   GIRL JONES, do hereby agree with the State of California and

19   with the said minor child that the said minor child shall be

20   adopted and treated in all respects as our own lawful child

21   should be treated and that said minor child shall enjoy all of

22   the rights of a natural child of our own issue, including the

23   right of inheritance, and that each of us hereby agrees to the

24   adoption of said minor child by the other.

25   Dated at Sacramento, California, this 10th day of

26   August, 1981.

27   *Ralph Arthur Barnes*
                                        Husband
28   *Pearl Alice Barnes*
                                        Wife

Decree of Adoption

<pre>
 1   ANDREW LINCOLN
     1234 X St.
 2   Sacramento, CA 95814
     447-9302
 3
     Attorney for Petitioners
 4

 5

 6

 7

 8   SUPERIOR COURT OF CALIFORNIA

 9   COUNTY OF SACRAMENTO

10

11   In the Matter of the   )   NO. 134256 Dept. ___
     Petition of   )
12   )
            RALPH ARTHUR BARNES and)   DECREE OF ADOPTION
13   PEARL ALICE BARNES,   )
)   (Independent)
14   Adopting Parents.   )
)
15   _____)

16   The petition of RALPH ARTHUR BARNES and PEARL ALICE

17   BARNES, husband and wife, for the adoption of the minor child

18   named in the petition herein, came on regularly this day for

19   hearing, Andrew Lincoln appearing as attorney for petitioners,

20   and the petitioners and the said minor child appearing in person,

21   and said persons having been examined separately by the Court,

22   and it appearing that the Sacramento County Department of Adop-

23   tions heretofore filed its written report recommending the grant-

24   ing of said petition, and evidence to the satisfaction of the

25   Court having been introduced, the Court finds that:

26   All of the allegations in said petition are true;

27   that petitioners were married on March 4, 1975, and ever since

28   have been and now are husband and wife; each of them is an adult
</pre>

1

1 | person and more than ten years older than said minor child;
2 | the minor child who is the subject of this petition is a
3 | female child born on July 1, 1981, in the City of Sacramento,
4 | County of Sacramento, State of California.
5 | That the consents required by law under the facts
6 | of this case have been given and filed in the manner required
7 | by law.
8 | The petitioners have executed the requisite consent
9 | and agreement that the said child shall be adopted and treated
10 | in all respects as their own lawful child and the Court, being
11 | satisfied that the interests and welfare of the minor child will
12 | be promoted by the adoption proposed, and that the petition
13 | should be granted; now, therefore,
14 | IT IS ORDERED that the petition is granted and that
15 | said minor child is now the adopted child of petitioners, RALPH
16 | ARTHUR BARNES and PEARL ALICE BARNES, and shall be in the cus-
17 | tody of said petitioners and be regarded and treated in all
18 | respects as their own lawful child; that they shall sustain
19 | toward the child and the child toward them the legal relation of
20 | parents and child, and each respectively shall have all of the
21 | rights and be subject to all of the duties of natural parent and
22 | child; and that the name of said child henceforth shall be
23 | JENNIFER ROSE BARNES.
24 | Dated: October 6, 1981.
25 | _William Cooper_
26 | Judge
27 |
28 |

2

Petition for Adoption (Stepparent)

```
 1    IVAN TAYLOR
      3030 Howe Ave., Suite 116
 2    Sacramento, CA 95821
      Telephone:  488-1234
 3
      Attorney for Petitioner
 4

 5

 6

 7

 8              SUPERIOR COURT OF THE STATE OF CALIFORNIA

 9                  FOR THE COUNTY OF SACRAMENTO

10

11    In the Matter of the Adoption   )     No.
      Petition of                     )
12                                     )     PETITION FOR ADOPTION
             WILLIAM ROBERT JACKSON,   )
13                                     )          (Stepparent)
                     Adopting Parent.  )
14    _____)

15

16          Petitioner, WILLIAM ROBERT JACKSON, alleges:

17                             I

18          The name by which the minor who is the subject of this

19    petition was registered at birth is MARGARET ANNE PUTNAM.

20                            II

21          The above named minor child was born in the City of

22    Sacramento, County of Sacramento, California, on July 29, 1980.

23                            III

24          Petitioner is an adult person and desires to adopt said

25    child.  Petitioner is the husband of ALICE JACKSON, the mother of

26    said child, who retains her right of custody of the child.  Peti-

27    tioner and said spouse and said minor child reside in the County

28    of Sacramento, State of California.

                             1
```

IV

The mother of the child, ALICE JACKSON, was married to the petitioner on August 30, 1981, at Carson City, Nevada, and is prepared to consent to the child's adoption by the petitioner, retaining all of her rights to custody and control.

V

That ALICE JACKSON is the natural mother of said minor, and under the provisions of the Civil Code of the State of California, her consent alone is required for this adoption.

VI

The child is a proper subject for adoption, the petitioner's home is suitable for the child, and he is able to support and care for the child properly. The interest of the child will be promoted by this adoption. The petitioner agrees to treat the child in all respects as his own lawful child.

WHEREFORE, petitioner prays that the Court adjudge the adoption of the child by petitioner, declaring that the petitioner and the child thenceforth shall sustain toward each other the legal relation of parent and child, and have all the rights and be subject to all the duties of that relation; and that the child shall be known as MARGARET ANNE JACKSON.

DATED: September 15, 1981.

WILLIAM ROBERT JACKSON, Petitioner

IVAN TAYLOR
Attorney for Petitioner

-2-

Decree of Adoption (Stepparent)

```
1   IVAN TAYLOR
    3030 Howe Ave., Suite 116
2   Sacramento, CA 95821
    Telephone:  488-1234
3
    Attorney for Petitioner
4

5

6

7

8           SUPERIOR COURT OF THE STATE OF CALIFORNIA

9               FOR THE COUNTY OF SACRAMENTO

10

11  In the Matter of the Adoption  )    NO.
    Petition of                    )
12                                 )
        WILLIAM ROBERT JACKSON,    )    DECREE OF ADOPTION
13                                 )
              Adopting Parent.     )       (Stepparent)
14  _____)

15

16          The petition of WILLIAM ROBERT JACKSON for the adoption

17  of the minor child named in the petition herein, came on regular-

18  ly this day for hearing, IVAN TAYLOR appearing as attorney for

19  petitioner; and the petitioner, his wife, and the said minor

20  child having appeared before the Court, and the Court having

21  examined them, each separately, and the matter being submitted,

22  the Court finds:

23          1.  All of the allegations contained in the petition

24  are true; that the petitioner and ALICE JACKSON, the natural

25  mother, were married on August 30, 1981, and they are now husband

26  and wife; that petitioner is over the age of twenty-one years;

27  that the minor child was born on July 29, 1980, and now resides

28  in the County of Sacramento, State of California, with the
```

1

1 petitioner and her mother.

2   2. That under the provisions of the Civil Code of the

3 State of California, the consent of the natural mother, ALICE

4 JACKSON, alone is required for this adoption.

5   3. That the petitioner has executed an agreement that

6 the child shall be treated in all respects as the lawful child

7 of the petitioner.

8   4. That the child is a proper subject for adoption,

9 and the petitioner's home is suitable for the child; and that the

10 interests of the child will be promoted by her adoption by the

11 petitioner; now, therefore,

12   IT IS ORDERED that said child be adopted by the peti-

13 tioner and that these persons hereafter shall sustain toward each

14 other all legal obligations of parent and child, and shall have

15 all the rights and be under all of the duties of such relation-

16 ship, including all legal rights and duties of custody, support,

17 and inheritance.

18   IT IS FURTHER ORDERED that the child hereafter shall

19 bear the family name of the petitioner and shall be known as

20 MARGARET ANNE JACKSON.

21   DATED: October ___, 1981.

22   _Benjamin Mitchell_

23   JUDGE OF THE SUPERIOR COURT

24

25

26

27

28

2

CALIFORNIA PARALEGAL'S GUIDE

Chapter 22

BANKRUPTCY

BACKGROUND

In the calendar year 1980, a total of 410,695 nonbusiness or personal bankruptcy estates were filed, up 79.5 percent from the same period a year earlier. Individuals filed 86.9 percent of all bankruptcy cases. This represents an all-time high for nonbusiness estates. Bankruptcy filings had been declining since 1975, but started climbing in late 1979.

An increase in the percentage of Chapter 13 nonbusiness estates under the new law has been noted. In the calendar year 1979, a total of 40,195 Chapter 13 estates were filed. In 1980, this number rose to 103,982, an increase of 107.2 percent.

In California, in the calendar year 1980, there were a total of 45,317 filings, of which 8,551 were Chapter 13 filings and 35,847 were Chapter 7 filings, according to the Administrative Office of the United States Courts.

Legal Assistants and Bankruptcy

The services of a legal assistant are very useful to a successful bankruptcy practice. Section 330 of the new Bankruptcy Code seems to recognize the value of such services by promising compensation therefor. Section 330 provides in part: "(a) After notice to any parties in interest and to the United States trustees and a hearing, and subject to sections 326, 328, and 329 of this title, the court may award to a trustee, to an examiner, to a professional person employed under section 327 or 1103 of this title, or to the debtor's attorney -

"(1) reasonable compensation for actual, necessary services rendered by such trustee, examiner, professional person, or attorney, as the case may be, *and by any paraprofessional person employed by such trustee, professional person, or attorney,* as the case may be, based on the time, the nature, the extent, and the value of such services, and *the cost of comparable services other than in a case under this title:* and

"(2) reimbursement for actual, necessary expenses." (Emphasis added.)

Knowledge and understanding of the bankruptcy law on the part of the legal assistant is of prime importance. Let us first examine the background of bankruptcy law.

Bankruptcy a Federal Law

Bankruptcy is exclusively a federal jurisdiction. There are not and cannot be any state bankruptcy laws. The United States Constitution provides that "The Congress shall have power . . . to establish . . . uniform laws on the subject of bankruptcies throughout the United States." (Art. I, §8, cl. 45.) The first bankruptcy law dates back to 1800. Bankruptcy acts were passed in 1800, 1841 and 1898, at which time bankruptcy really was developed; the law was amended in 1938.

A new bankruptcy act (Public Law 95-598) became law on October 1, 1979. It repealed the Bankruptcy Act of 1898 and enacted the Bankruptcy Reform Act of 1978. Cases commenced before October 1, 1979, are governed by the old law.

The law is divided into four titles:

Title I codifies and enacts Title 11 of the United States Code, entitled "Bankruptcy."

Title II amends Title 28 of the United States Code and the Federal Rules of Evidence relating to the bankruptcy courts, judges and trustees.

Title III amends additional United States laws to conform to the new act.

Title IV repeals the Bankruptcy Act of 1898 and amends and provides effective dates and transitional provisions.

Bankruptcy Courts and Judges

A United States Bankruptcy Court is created in each judicial district, as an *independent* adjunct to the respective district court. However, the bankruptcy courts existing on September 30, 1979 (and appointed by the district court) shall continue through the transition period, October 1, 1979 - March 31, 1984.

Bankruptcy judges are to be appointed by the President with the advice and consent of the Senate for a term of 14 years.

A referee, upon the expiration of his appointed term, shall have the title of "United States bankruptcy judge," unless he is found to be not qualified by the Chief Judge of the Circuit Court after consultation with a merit screening committee.

Appeals

Under the old law all appeals were taken to the district court.

Under the new law an appeal may (1) be taken to the district court, or (2) the circuit courts of appeal may designate panels of three bankruptcy judges of districts located within that district to hear appeals from judgments, orders and decrees of the bankruptcy court, or (3) an appeal may be taken directly to the circuit court of appeal.

Rules of the Bankruptcy Court

The old rules remain effective until repealed or superseded by new rules. Cases filed before October 1, 1979, are in any event subject to the old rules. In the meantime, Interim Rules have been issued as guidelines only and are not binding unless adopted as local rules or applied judicially.

What is bankruptcy?

A "debtor" (the term "bankrupt" is no longer used) is a person legally declared unable to pay his debts. The object of a bankruptcy proceeding is to liquidate assets in an orderly fashion, that is, turn the debtor's assets, his property, into cash to be distributed pro rata to his creditors, in proportion to the amount owed to each. At the same time, since its purpose in so doing is to provide the debtor a "fresh start," certain assets are declared to be exempt so that the debtor will be able to start afresh. He may become a debtor only once every six years.

Who may become a debtor?

Under a Chapter 7 proceeding, a debtor is any person, partnership or corporation, so long as the person, or the partnership or corporation, has debts, with the *exceptions* of:

railroads
banks (savings and cooperatives, foreign or domestic)
building and loan associations
insurance companies, domestic and foreign
savings and loan associations
homestead associations
credit unions

The Voluntary Petition

A voluntary petition may be filed by any of the aforementioned debtors but must be accompanied by an alphabetical list of creditors and their addresses (Form 1051). Schedules and a statement of financial affairs must be filed within 10 days thereafter.

The commencement of a voluntary proceeding constitutes an "order for relief" (under the old law called "adjudication").

The Involuntary Petition

An involuntary bankruptcy proceeding may be initiated against a person eligible to become a debtor under Chapter 7 (liquidation or "straight" bankruptcy) or 11 (business reorganization) only (except a farmer or a corporation that is not a moneyed, business or commercial corporation (e.g., church)) by three or more creditors with claims aggregating $5,000 over and above any lien on the debtor's property; if fewer than 12 hold claims, by any one creditor if claims aggregate $5,000. (§303.)

In an involuntary proceeding, the debtor may accept service and consent to an order for relief. If he defaults, an order for relief is made upon his default; if he contests, after hearing the petition will either be dismissed, or an order for relief will be filed.

The court may require the petitioners to file a bond; but only after notice and a hearing, and for cause. (§303(e), (i).)

At the trial the appraisal must either show that the debtor is generally not paying his debts as they become due or that a custodian was appointed within 120 days before the date of filing.

Sanctions are provided in section 303(i). The court may grant the debtor costs, an attorney's fee and damages, if the court dismisses the petitioner other than by consent. The court may grant punitive damages as well as damages against the petitioners if it finds they filed in bad faith.

Automatic Stay

The filing of a petition in any bankruptcy proceeding operates as a stay of any pending action by a creditor or continuation or commencement of any litigation against the debtor (including setoffs (§362(a)(7)) — with stated exceptions, listed in section 362(b). They include:

(1) Criminal actions;

(2) Collection of alimony, maintenance or support from property not in estate;

(3) Acts to perfect interests in property;

(4) Enforcement of a governmental unit's police or regulatory power and judgments other than a money judgment, obtained in such an action;

(5) Commodity futures contracts;

(6) Commencement of action by Secretary of Housing and Urban Development to foreclose a mortgage or deed of trust when insured by National Housing Act and covering property consisting of 5 or more living units;

(7) Issuance of a notice of tax deficiency.

Section 1110 refers to certain aircraft equipment and assets and section 1168 to rolling stock equipment for which a stay does not operate under conditions specified in said section.

The stay also prohibits creditors from moving against certain co-debtors and from commencing or continuing any civil action to collect the debt, with certain exceptions specified in section 1301.

Utilities are stayed (§366) from discontinuing service or discriminating against a debtor unless neither the trustee nor the debtor, within 20 days after the date of the order for relief, furnishes adequate assurance of payment, by way of a deposit or other security, for service after such date. If a debtor's account with a utility is current, probably they would not wish to discontinue service in any event.

The purpose of the new code is to insulate the debtor from harassment or efforts to collect. Creditors may not contact the debtor once a petition is on file — no phone calls or letters.

The creditor should first obtain from the bankruptcy court a copy of all the papers filed. If he then desires to communicate with the debtor, to have his debt reaffirmed or whatever, he should have his attorney write the debtor's attorney. The debtor may be contacted directly only if he has no attorney but is acting in pro per. A record should be kept of all correspondence and attempts to communicate with debtor's attorney. If the debtor's attorney fails to respond, a complaint may have to be filed. The automatic stay stops when the discharge is granted.

If a secured creditor wants to foreclose, or if an owner of rentals needs to evict, he must first commence an adversary proceeding to lift the stay. Although he may not have received a formal notice of the bankruptcy, if he has reason to know of the bankruptcy and takes ordinary action to collect rent, i.e., such as serving a 3-day notice to pay rent or quit, asking the tenant to pay his rent, filing an unlawful detainer action for nonpayment of rent (or for other reason), he becomes subject to being held in contempt of court and fined. An unlawful detainer action or other action already commenced against the tenant before the bankruptcy petition was filed, is likewise stayed by the automatic stay. Upon filing the adversary proceeding to lift the stay, the bankruptcy court could authorize an unlawful detainer action to be filed in a state court, or to proceed if already filed. The trustee might abandon the leasehold interest (see Abandonment of Assets, *infra*), in which event the owner could proceed in a state court to at least recover possession of his rental unit — though not any back rent owing.

A claim for back rent should be filed in the bankruptcy court, although chances are that it will not be paid, since the amount owed would probably be included within the $7,900 federal exemption expected to be taken by nonhomeowners.

Further, if a tenant makes payments of back rent within 90 days of filing for bankruptcy, the owner may be compelled to deliver this money to the trustee under a presumption of insolvency (see Preferences, *infra*) for the benefit of all the creditors.

(On the other hand, the apartment owner who finds himself in financial difficulty may be able to obtain sufficient relief under a Chapter 11 reorganization to preserve his investment.)

A stay may be lifted 30 days after a request unless the court orders the stay continued pending, or as a result of, a final hearing and determination.

The automatic stay may be vacated if "adequate protection" cannot be provided by the debtor to the creditor. "Adequate protection" is described in section 361 as periodic cash payments if stay is decreasing value of property (§361(1)); additional or replacement liens (§361(2)); compensation other than administrative expense the "indubitable equivalent" of the creditor's interest in the property. (§361(3).) The trustee has the burden of proof on the issue of "adequate protection" (§363(e)).

CHAPTER 7 BANKRUPTCY

The Bankruptcy Petition and Schedules

The legal assistant will in all probability work with the client in completing the bankruptcy schedules.

The bankruptcy proceeding is commenced by the filing of a bankruptcy "Petition, Schedules and Statement of Financial Affairs," available from stationery stores. An original and three copies of the petition,, schedules, and statement of affairs are required. A joint petition (of husband and wife) may be filed under Chapters 7 (liquidation), 11 (reorganization) and 13 (adjustment of debts). The same combined form may be used for execution by a sole petitioner or by joint petitioners. In joint petition cases separate schedules and statements of financial affairs may be filed, depending upon the exemptions chosen and the separate assets of each spouse, among other criteria. Extra forms of schedules and statement of financial affairs may be purchased separately (Blumberg forms).

Filing fees

The filing fee for a Chapter 7 (liquidating or straight bankruptcy) or Chapter 13 for bankruptcy (adjustment of debts) is increased to $60 for an individual or a husband and wife filing jointly.

The legal assistant should make certain that a retainer letter is sent by the attorney to the client specifying the services the fee will cover. The client should understand that the fee covers only the bankruptcy proceeding itself, and not any litigation which might develop as a result of the filing of the proceeding (unless, of course, that is in the agreement, in which event the fee would have been adjusted accordingly). Ordinarily the fee set is limited to the bankruptcy proceeding, since extensive litigation cannot be foreseen.

Schedule A, "Statement of All Liabilities of Debtor." The instructions on this and the other forms should be read carefully. It is important to the debtor-client that all his/her debts be listed. All claims against the debtor or his property as of the date of the filing of the petition must be listed. It is also important to give the last known address of all creditors so that notices will be certain to reach them. The legal assistant should check all addresses carefully.

If a creditor disputes the amount of the debt as listed, the burden is on the creditor to contend and prove a different amount. The claim he files should set out the variance. The claim should show the balance owing on the date of filing the claim. Valuations are not made at the creditors' meetings.

In a straight bankruptcy it may not matter, however, since none of the debt may be paid, but in a Chapter 13 proceeding it could be important.

Schedule A-1, "Creditors Having Priority." The debts having priority are listed alongside the schedule. Some of the debts having priority are (§507):

1. Administrative expenses allowed under section 503(b) (including wages, salaries, or commissions), fine, penalty or reduction in credit relating to tax; certain creditors' expenses.

2. Unsecured claims allowed under section 502(f) (in involuntary cases).

3. Unsecured claims for wages earned up to $2,000 within 90 days before proceeding was filed, or the date of cessation of the debtor's business, whichever occurs first (§507(3)).

4. Claims for contributions to employee benefit plans for services rendered within 180 days before filing of petition or the date of cessation of the debtor's business, whichever occurs first, to the extent of "(i) the number of employees covered by such plan multiplied by $2,000; less (ii) the aggregate amount paid to such employees under paragraph (3) of this subsection, plus the aggregate amount paid by the estate on behalf of such employees to any other employee benefit plan."

5. Unsecured claims up to $900 arising from deposits for purchase, lease or rental of property or purchase of services for the personal family or household use of such individuals that were not delivered or provided prior to the date the proceeding was filed.

6. Unsecured claims for certain government taxes (in income, property taxes, withholding, employment, excise, customs duty) as specified in section 507(6).

If the trustee attempts to provide "adequate protection" to the holder of a secured claim by placing a lien on the debtor's property and if nevertheless the creditor has a claim arising from the stay of action, then that creditor's claim has priority over every other claim. This provision was not in the old law.

Schedule A-2, "Creditors Holding Security." All "secured" debts are listed in this schedule.

A "secured" creditor has a lien on the property of the debtor to which the lien is applicable. A "lien" is defined in section 101(28) to mean a "charge against or interest in property to secure payment of a debt or performance of an obligation. 'Security interest' is defined as a "lien created by an agreement." (§101(37).) [Definitions of terms used in the new bankruptcy law are found in section 101 thereof.]

Redemptions

Consumer debts for "personal, family, or household use" are recognized only to the fair market value of the collateral, if such property is exempt under section 522 or has been abandoned under section 554.

In other words, say the debtor has, for example, purchased furniture for $2,000, on which he now owes $1,400, which is appraised in the debtor's estate at the fair market value of $500. (True, under California law the household furnishings would be exempt from liquidation. But the furnishings may also be subject to repossession.) He may keep his furniture by paying off the $500. (§722.) The balance of $900 owed becomes an unsecured debt, dischargeable in bankruptcy.

The legal assistant should inquire of the debtor whether he/she still has in his/her possession the goods which secure a debt to which the seller retained title, e.g., household furnishings.

Fair market value is what a willing buyer would pay for the goods.

As to secured debts, the same conditions as to reaffirmation apply. And the automatic stay operates until the discharge date, unless the creditor seeks relief in court from the stay. However, after the discharge date, the creditor may pick up the asset, as say a car. Or the creditor can retain his lien, until the debtor misses a payment.

If the creditor *does* repossess the car and sells it, he cannot move against the debtor for attorney fees or repossession fees as may have been provided in the contract; the contract has been eliminated except for the security interest.

Schedule A-3, "Creditors Having Unsecured Claims Without Priority." Probably most of the debts will fall into this category. Care should be taken by the legal assistant that *all* debts get listed. *If a debt is not listed in the schedules, it risks not being discharged.*

If the creditor acknowledges having actual notice of the Chapter 13 proceeding, or the debtor can prove he did, the debt may be discharged in the proceeding. If a creditor actually receives notice of the first date set for a meeting of creditors, he has actual notice of the bankruptcy.

Schedule B lists all the property of the debtor — real, personal, or other. In *Schedule B-1, "Real Property,"* all interests in real property are detailed as indicated. In *Schedule B-2, "Personal Property,"* all personal property is listed as indicated in the various categories described in the left margin. All other property of the debtor not listed in Schedules B-1 or B-2 are included in Schedule B-3.

"Property Not Otherwise Scheduled."

Wages earned at the date of filing but not paid are an asset. The portion of a pay check attributable to salary earned after the date of filing is not included with assets.

The client may not realize that some things he owns are assets, or he may have forgotten about them temporarily. Many people have been required to make a deposit with a utility company, for instance, to obtain service, or may have forgotten about a small savings account somewhere. The legal assistant should carefully review with the client items of personal effects such as jewelry or household items, which are also sometimes overlooked.

Claims

Creditors should file proof of claims for the debts (secured or unsecured) listed on the schedules, including those designated as nondischargeable, or exempt, or for any claim they have which was omitted. If a debt is a real property debt, the claim should be filed for the full amount, not the amount of the delinquency only.

Governmental agencies file claims; IRS files claims and keeps them current.

If a judgment had been obtained against a debtor, an abstract of judgment should be recorded, whether or not the debtor owns real property.

Claims must be timely filed (see §726). Time limits are found in the Rules of Bankruptcy Procedure applicable in each district. In the Eastern District of California, for example, claims must be filed in either a Chapter 7 or Chapter 13 proceeding within 6 months after the date set for the meeting of creditors.

In a Chapter 11 case, the code specifies (§1111) that a claim is deemed filed for any claim or interest listed in the schedules — unless the claim or interest is scheduled as disputed, contingent or unliquidated.

Co-ownership of assets by debtor

Any contact with the coowner should be made through his attorney, the same as with the principal debtor.

In a Chapter 13 proceeding, an automatic stay operates to protect the co-owner as well as the debtor, unless the coowner became liable on or secured such debt in the ordinary course of his business, or the case is closed, dismissed or converted to a Chapter 7 or 11 proceeding. (§1301(a).)

Relief from this stay might be granted under section 1301(c) after notice and hearing if the individual received consideration for the claim, the plan does not propose to pay the creditor's claim, or the creditor's interest would be irreparably harmed by the stay.

Under specified circumstances (§363(b)(1)-(4)), the trustee may sell property of the debtor and a coowner, without the coowner's consent, but only after giving such coowner (or a debtor's spouse in the case of commercial property) the right to purchase the property at the price at which the sale was to be consummated (§363(i)). If the trustee does sell the property to another party, he is required to pay the coowner the value of his interest, less costs and expenses of sale but not including any compensation to the trustee (§363(j)).

Schedule B-4, "Property Claimed as Exempt."   All property of the debtor which is exempt from bankruptcy should be entered here.

The debtor's exemptions are listed in section 522. The debtor may now choose between the federal exemptions or his own state's exemptions. However, states are given the right to deny this option, and a few have done so, leaving only that state's exemptions available to the debtor, or making the federal exemption mandatory. Therefore the legal assistant should check the home state law. At this writing Florida, Louisiana and Virginia have eliminated the federal exemption.

Where the husband and wife are filing jointly, whether one may elect the federal exemption and the other claim the state exemption, has been open to question. In Sacramento, the husband and wife filing jointly have had to choose between the federal and state exemptions.

If they filed separately, one might elect the federal, the other the state. However, a state law, effective Jan. 1, 1982, prohibits exemptions of both federal and state law to be claimed. (Code Civ. Proc. §690 (1981 ch. 455))

The client should be made fully aware of his options of exemptions (if any) and full consideration given to the choices available, in discussion had with the attorney and legal assistant, to determine the choices most advantageous to the client and in his best interests, under all the circumstances.

A California debtor with substantial equity in a home (and who has on file a declaration of homestead) could be expected to choose the California exemption in view of California's $45,000 homestead exemption. A spouse with children can take the full exemption as this gives him status of head of the household.

A high percentage of persons filing in bankruptcy do not own any real property, however, or have only a small equity, and may be well advised to choose the federal exemption in view of the $7,900 general exemption (§522(d)(5) $400 "grubstake exemption" plus unused $7,500 household exemption) regardless of the nature of the asset. (See *infra*, Federal Exemptions, ¶(5).)

A debtor entitled to disability benefits might also be apt to choose the California exemptions. Before claiming any item exempt such as jewelry or an automobile, an appraisal may have to be made. The legal assistant can arrange to have such appraisals made.

Valuation should be as of date of filing the petition in bankruptcy. The value of an automobile might be, and often is, based on the average between the high and low book value (Kelly's Blue Book) on cars. A used furniture dealer may be asked to provide his estimate of what he would pay for the furniture.

Federal Exemptions

Under federal law the debtor may exempt from bankruptcy the following basic exemptions:

(1) $7,500 Household exemption (interest in real or personal property used as a residence, a cooperative, or burial plot — for debtor or dependent)

(2) $1,200 Motor vehicle

(3) $ 200 Household furnishings, household goods, wearing apparel, appliances, books, animals, crops, or musical instruments held primarily for personal, family or household use

(4) $ 500 Jewelry

(5) $ 400 Interest in *any* property, *plus any unused amount of exemption in (1) above* (referred to as the "grubstake exemption")

(6) $ 750 Implements, professional books, or tools of the trade of the debtor or the trade of a dependent of the debtor

(7)   Professionally prescribed health aids

Additional exemptions are provided in section 522 for unmatured life insurance contracts, and rights to receive certain types of property. When claiming insurance policies exempt, the numbers of the insurance policies, as well as the names of the companies, should be set out.

California Exemptions — Alternative to Federal Exemptions

The exemptions available to California debtors include:

(1) $45,000 Homestead exemption. (See Civ. Code §1240.) A complete legal description of the real property should be given. Homestead exemptions are governed by state law. The declaration of homestead should have been filed before the petition in bankruptcy was filed. The legal assistant can check on this.

(2) $ 500 Interest in motor vehicle over and above encumbrances (Code Civ. Proc. §690.2)

(3) $ 2,500 Tools, implements, uniforms, furnishings, books, equipment, one commercial fishing boat and net, 1 commercial motor vehicle reasonably necessary to and actually used in a commercial activity. (Code Civ. Proc. §690.4.) (See *Sun Ltd. v. Casey* (1979), 96 Cal.App. 38, 157 Cal. Rptr. 576.)

(4) $ 1,000 Savings and loan deposits (Code Civ. Proc. §690.7)

(5) $ 1,500 Credit union deposits (Fin. Code §15406)

(6)   Necessary household furnishings and appliances and wearing apparel, including 1 piano, 1 radio, 1 TV, provisions and fuel sufficient for 3 months, 1 shotgun, 1 rifle. Works of art are not exempt unless of or by the debtor and resident family. (Code Civ. Proc. §690.1)

(7)   Other personal property ordinarily and reasonably necessary to, personally owned and used by, the debtor exclusively in the exercise of the trade, calling or profession by which he earns his livelihood (Code Civ. Proc. §690.4)

(8)   Church pews (Code Civ. Proc. §690.25)

(9)   1 cemetery lot (Code Civ. Proc. §690.24)

(10)   Cash surrender value of a life insurance policy if provisions do not exceed $500 year (Code Civ. Proc. §690.9)

(11)   Benefits from health or disability insurance not exceeding $500 year (Code Civ. Proc. §690.11), all benefits from worker's compensation (Code Civ. Proc. §690.15), unemployment insurance (Code Civ. Proc. §690.175), pension plans (Code Civ. Proc. §690.18), and public assistance (Code Civ. Proc. §690.19)

". . . [T]he prevailing policy in California is to construe exemption statutes liberally in favor of debtors." (*Independence Bank v. Heller,* 275 Cal.App.2d 84 [at p. 88]; 79 Cal. Rptr. 868 (1969); see also *Sun Ltd. v. Elana Casey* (1979), 96 Cal.App.3d 38, 157 Cal. Rptr. 576.)

The forms include a *"Summary of Debts and Property"* listed in Schedules A and B. Also included is a *"List of Creditors"* to be used:

"a)   when a creditor's list is needed to enable late filing of schedules and statement of financial affairs under Rule 108(b), Rule 13-107(b) and Interim Rule 1007(d);

"b)   in a chapter 11 case as a list of 10 largest creditors, Interim Rule 1007(a);

"c)   in a chapter 11 case as part of a list of creditors and equity security holders, Interim Rule 1007(b);

"d)   whenever local rules require separate lists of creditors (usually preferred in alphabetical order)," — and a "Statement Pursuant to Rule 219(b)."

Preferences

Creditors in bankruptcy are on an equal basis and the debtor may not show a "preference" for one creditor over another. Therefore any transfer of property by a debtor to a creditor for or on account of an antecedent debt prior to filing in bankruptcy is open to question. Transfers may not be made while the debtor was insolvent.

Under the new law, a presumption of insolvency is established for any transfer made within 90 days preceding the date of filing of the petition (§547(f)) and the trustee may avoid any such transfer during this period.

Further, if the creditor was an "insider" (as defined in §101(25)) the trustee may avoid any transfer made between 90 days and 1 year before date of filing the petition, in which event the trustee must also show that the insider had reasonable cause to believe the debtor was insolvent at the time of transfer. There is no presumption of insolvency for these transfers, as for transfers within 90 days. (§547(b)(4).)

The transfer must have enabled the creditor to receive more than (1) he would have received under a case under Chapter 7, (2) if transfer had not been made, or (3) if the creditor received payment to the extent provided by the title (§547(b)(5)).

Reaffirmation

If a creditor wants a reaffirmation agreement, he must contact the debtor's attorney, not the debtor himself. If the debtor's attorney agrees, a confirming letter should be written. All communications should be documented, so the creditor can present proof if the debtor should renege on his agreement.

A debtor may tell a creditor he will pay his debt, reaffirm the debt, orally or in writing, may personally make payments on the debt; nevertheless, there is no *legal* reaffirmation of the debt unless the court approves a reaffirmation at the discharge hearing.

Any reaffirmation agreement must be made after the bankruptcy proceeding was filed and before discharge. The debtor has the right to rescind the agreement within 30 days after he makes it. After the debtor has signed a reaffirmation agreement, the creditor should request a hearing date and the creditor should make sure the debtor's attorney knows the agreement is in the file. The original agreement will be presented to the judge for his approval and the creditor need not attend, although it might prove beneficial if he did appear to look after his interest. As a practical matter, three or four creditors should perhaps retain the same attorney.

The debtor must appear at the discharge hearing, where he will be advised that he does not need to reaffirm and will be told of the consequences of reaffirmation.

To approve the court must find that the agreement is in the best interests of the debtor and does not impose undue hardship or that it is a good faith settlement of litigation under section 523 (nondischargeable debts) or is an agreement for redemption of "tangible personal property intended primarily for personal, family, or household use" under section 722.

Meetings of Creditors

The first meeting of creditors is set for not less than 20 nor more than 40 days after the order of relief. The court gives all creditors at least 10 days' notice by mail of the first meeting of creditors (and of proposed sales of property and other matters, as provided in Rule 203, Rules of Bankruptcy Procedure).

Provision is also made for a meeting of any equity security holders. The judge may not preside at or attend either of these meetings; the clerk of the bankruptcy court presides.

The debtor must appear to be examined, under oath, at the first meeting of the creditors held, either by the creditors, any indenture trustee, or any trustee or examiner (§343). No court reporter is present unless specific arrangements are made in advance.

The clerk of the court who conducts the proceedings asks if there are any creditors present who wish to vote for a trustee. If no one responds, then the trustee present is asked if he would like to proceed.

Unless the debtor is representing himself, the attorney for the debtor must be present and ask questions of the debtor, such as:

1. Have you listed all your property?
2. Have you listed all your debts?
3. Do you have any interest in real property?
4. Are you expecting an inheritance from any deceased person's estate?
5. Do you have any income tax refunds owing to you?
6. What is the reason for your filing bankruptcy?
7. Do you own an automobile?
8. Where are you now employed?

If a husband and wife are both debtors, the attorney may ask the questions of one, and then ask the other, if his/her answer would have been substantially the same to the questions.

After the attorney concludes the trustee is asked if he has any questions, who proceeds to ask any questions he may have.

The clerk asks if there are any creditors present who wish to be heard. If no one responds, the clerk may say, "I see none."

Chapters 7 and 11: If a claim is not filed before the first date set for the meeting of creditors, the debtor or trustee may file a claim in the name of the creditor, in which event the court gives notice to the creditor and trustee. The creditor is not estopped from filing his own claim pursuant to Rule 302 or 3001, which supersedes the claim filed by the debtor. (Interim Rule 3004, adapted from Rule 303, conforming to 11 U.S.C., §501(c).)

Discharge

A date 60 days from the date of first meeting of creditors is fixed by the bankruptcy court as the last day for filing objections to the petitioner's discharge as a debtor. (The rules require that it shall be a date not less than 30 days nor more than 90 days after the first date set for the first meeting of creditors.)

The bankruptcy court, in some jurisdictions at least, sends out the notice of hearing of the first meeting of creditors and the notice of the last day for filing objections at the same time.

Nondischargeable Debts

The following debts are nondischargeable in bankruptcy (§523):

1. Tax or customs duty.

2. Certain debts not listed on schedule in time to permit timely filing of proof of claim.

3. Alimony and child support.

4. Willful and malicious injury to another entity or property of another entity.

5. Fines, penalties or forfeitures.

6. Educational loans unless the loan became due 5 years before the petition was filed or exception would impose undue hardship. Whether there is undue hardship is decided by the judge, upon petition.

7. Debts listed in a prior bankruptcy petition for which the debtor was denied or waived discharge.

8. A debt incurred for business by use of a false financial statement.

9. A debt incurred for fraud or defalcation while acting as a fiduciary, embezzlement, or larceny.

The creditor must make a request of a determination of dischargeability for 8 and 9 above.

If the creditor is granted judgment because the debtor obtained a loan through fraudulent representation, he is entitled to a reasonable attorney fee (§523(d)).

"No asset" cases

A notice of no dividend may be given when it appears from the schedules that there are no assets from which a dividend can be paid; the notice of the first meeting of creditors may include a statement that there are no assets from which a dividend can be paid and that therefore it is unnecessary to file claims, and that if sufficient assets become available for the payment of a dividend, the court will give further notice and an opportunity to file a claim. In that event a complaint objecting to the debtor's discharge must be filed as of the date of the first meeting of creditors held. (Rules 203(b), 404(b).)

The debtor must appear in person at the hearing. (§524(d).)

Abandonment of Assets

The trustee may abandon property that is burdensome to the estate or of inconsequential value. For example, a trustee might decide to abandon an automobile if the low book value is within $500 of the debt owing, in which event the trustee would file an application to abandon. An asset is not abandoned *to* anyone, the bankruptcy court just abandons its interest. After the judge signs an order for abandonment, the bankruptcy estate has no interest in the vehicle.

The creditor with a surety interest should take no action before an order of abandonment is signed. However, the creditor with security interest in a car might be well advised to appear at the first meeting of creditors and inquire whether there is a current policy of comprehensive insurance on the vehicle and request that the trustee be provided with a copy of the policy.

Scheduled assets that are not administered before the case is closed are deemed abandoned, unless the court otherwise orders.

CHAPTER 11 BANKRUPTCY

A straight liquidation bankruptcy is no longer available to businesses. Instead, they are permitted to reorganize under Chapter 11. The debtor submits a list of the 10 largest creditors. A committee of creditors having unsecured claims is appointed by the court, ordinarily consisting of the persons who hold the seven largest claims and who are willing to serve (§1102). An attorney representing a client with a significant claim should attend the first meeting of creditors and participate in the election of the creditors. (An attorney representing the committee may not represent any particular client.) The debtor remains in possession of its property and business, unless a request is made by a party in interest for the appointment of a trustee. After motion and a hearing a trustee may be appointed by the court for cause, including fraud, dishonesty, incompetency or gross mismanagement of the debtor's affairs as specified in section 1104.

Once appointed, the committee meets with the debtor and reviews his obligations and works with him to formulate a plan. They may propose alternate plans to the debtor's proposal. Property may be sold by the committee, liquidated. They attempt to insure that the creditors will not be harmed by a Chapter 11 proceedings.

Claims should be filed by the creditors, before approval of disclosure statement.

CHAPTER 13 BANKRUPTCY

A Chapter 13 proceeding is a voluntary proceeding, and is an alternative to a Chapter 7 straight bankruptcy liquidation. (An involuntary petition may not be filed under Chapter 13.)

Chapter 13 provides for the adjustment of debts of individuals with regular income. An "individual with regular income" means a person "whose income is sufficiently stable and regular to enable such individual to make payment under a plan under chapter 13 of this title, other than a stock broker or a commodity broker.'' (§101, subd. 24.)

In short, Chapter 13 provides an opportunity to develop a plan for full or partial, and orderly, repayment of debts, under court supervision, over an extended period of time.

A Chapter 13 proceeding may not be filed unless an individual's unsecured debts are less than $100,000 and noncontingent, liquidated, secured debts less than $350,000. Creditors might improve their chances of collection from a delinquent debtor by encouraging him to file a Chapter 13 proceeding, thereby avoiding a straight bankruptcy in which chances of collection are greatly reduced.

The legal assistant can make certain that the attorney has advised the client of the option to file under Chapter 13, as this is legal advice which the client who is considering filing for bankruptcy should be given. A malpractice claim could conceivably arise if an attorney fails to give this advice.

In essence, under a Chapter 13 proceeding, the debtor turns over all or a portion of his future earnings and income to a trustee necessary for the repayment plan over a period up to 3 years or, if approved by the court, up to 5 years.

The debtor has exclusive right to propose a repayment plan. The plan must provide for payment of claims only out of future income or a combination of future income and proceeds from a partial liquidation.

The plan must comply with the code and the requirements of the court. The plan must be offered in ''good faith.'' (In the Sacramento area (and possibly others) ''good faith'' has been interpreted to mean ''best effort.'') The plan must be workable, i.e., it should appear that the funds to pay the creditors, whether it be 10 cents or 100 cents on the dollar, will be available.

The trustee administers the plan; the debtors pay the trustee as agreed and the trustee disburses payments to creditors and assists them if need be, as well as helping the debtor with his financial problems. The trustee has authority to make temporary and reasonable adjustments of the plan.

Except for a medical emergency, the debtor must seek court approval before seeking credit while under the plan.

The court may hold hearings to consider cancelling any unwanted or unnecessary controls of the debtor, by returning merchandise or discontinuing services. A husband and wife may file jointly if one does not qualify.

Small proprietary businesses also may take advantage of the Chapter 13 repayment plan and thereby avoid closing their businesses and liquidating their assets. The same debt ceilings apply to them. (Under the old law only a "wage earner" was eligible for Chapter 13 relief.) The debtor continues to run his business but not without pressure from creditors. As with the individual, he may need to seek court approval of any unusual business expenses or purchases.

Maintenance and support obligations as defined in section 523(a)(5) are the only debts not dischargeable under a Chapter 13 plan.

A Chapter 13 proceeding might be denied if the debtor did not make his first payments under the plan or if it appears that the plan cannot continue for whatever reasons. The debtor's situation might worsen due to unforeseen developments.

If the Chapter 13 proceeding fails, the debtor may decide to file a Chapter 7 proceeding, in which event the better practice seems to be to dismiss the Chapter 13 and to file a Chapter 7, so that additional or subsequent debts may be added.

Debts incurred subsequent to the filing of a Chapter 13 proceeding, whether made with or without the trustee's permission, are subject to the plan. If the creditor knew of the Chapter 13 proceeding at the time the debt was incurred, he is provided for in the plan and tied to the conditions in the plan; however, if the creditor did not know of the Chapter 13 proceeding, he is not tied to the conditions of the plan.

Practice may vary from area to area. In the Eastern District of California, for instance, the debtor is told he cannot obtain credit without the trustee's consent. Any debt incurred without the trustee's permission is not dischargeable.

See Chapter 2 for Function of Paralegal chart in Bankruptcy.

CALIFORNIA PARALEGAL'S GUIDE

Chapter 23

WORKERS' COMPENSATION

By Therese M. Nichols, Legal Assistant

Chief Judge Arthur Vanderbilt once wrote that an administrative agency "is as far toward the judicial end of the spectrum as it is possible to go without being an outright court."

Administrative agencies have grown in number in federal, state and local governments, regulating many areas of activity, such as public utilities, unemployment insurance, unfair labor practices, and social security.

The Workers' Compensation Appeals Board is one of these agencies and regulates compensation for employees injured in the scope of their employment. The decisions of the Board, as of those of other agencies, are subject to judicial review.

In this chapter are described (1) the role of the legal assistant in the field of workers' compensation, (2) the benefits provided by workers' compensation, and (3) the forms used in this field. A chart of functions of the legal assistant in workers' compensation appears in Chapter 2, Utilization of Paralegals; it is recommended that this chart be read in conjunction with this chapter.

For the statutory basis for Workers' Compensation Claims see Labor Code §§3200-6208. For a thorough, practical treatment of this subject see *California Employer-Employee Benefits Handbook*, by David O'Brien, Winter Brook Pub. Co. (6th ed. 1981).

THE ROLE OF THE LEGAL ASSISTANT IN THE WORKERS' COMPENSATION FIELD OF LAW

The Workers' Compensation Appeals Board is an administrative agency and as such non-attorneys are not precluded from appearing before it for the purpose of representing an injured employee, lien claimant or insurance carrier. Unlike most other fields of law (except for Social Security hearings, retirement hearings and other administrative hearings), the legal assistant may participate at a hearing, may attend a deposition and may partake in settlement negotiations.

The legal assistant (or paralegal) is, of course, not allowed to appeal a case to the Court of Appeal or the Supreme Court of California. Only attorneys licensed in the State of California may represent a party (or parties) in a case on appeal. However, at the appellate level, the legal assistant can be of help to the attorney in preparing a petition for writ of review and in legal research for the reply brief.

Along with the above legal limitations as to the paralegal's role, the attorney may add other restrictions to the paralegal's duties. An employer, attorney or insurance carrier may or may not allow a legal assistant to represent a client at a hearing. The preference may be to have an attorney handle all the litigation. The legal assistant remains, nevertheless, extremely valuable.

The following is a sample of various positions demonstrating the legal assistant's utilization:

1. *Legal assistant to an applicant's attorney*   The duties are usually outlined by the attorney and the extent (or limitation) of the legal activities are delineated by the attorney for whom the legal assistant works. The legal assistant may interview the clients, request and review the medical records and reports, schedule evaluations with physicians, attend pre-trial conferences and hearings and/or participate in settlement negotiations with the defense attorney or insurance carrier.

As a legal assistant to a defense attorney, the duties are very similar to those above stated, except as to the necessity of interviewing the clients. Again, any limitations to the legal assistant's participation stem directly from the attorney's wishes.

2. *Adjuster for an insurance company or a defense firm.*   The adjuster may be the most important individual in a workers' compensation case before the file is forwarded to an attorney for litigation. If an injured employee has not sought representation, the adjuster has significant control over the employee's rights and extent of benefits. To reach an equitable decision, the adjuster may wish to schedule a medical evaluation, obtain medical records and, upon receipt of the medical report(s), may request a disability rating. In some instances, the adjuster will handle a claim "all the way," when the injured employee does not have legal representation or his case does not proceed through the entire litigation route. The rehabilitation benefits of a claimant will be assessed by the adjuster as to date of rehabilitation, choice of rehabilitation counselors and supervision of the rehabilitation program. Some firms utilize rehabilitation adjusters whose duties en-

compass only the rehabilitation aspect of a workers' compensation case. Because the adjusters' involvement in a workers' compensation may be quite extensive, it is necessary that their knowledge of the laws governing this field be extensive.

3. *Freelance legal assistant.* This endeavor is still very infrequent, but there are firms comprised solely of legal assistants (with an attorney on hand for the appellate work) who handle workers' compensation cases, combined sometimes with social security and retirement cases. The legal assistants approach a workers' compensation case much as attorneys would, since an attorney's actions are well outlined by the Workers' Compensation Appeals Board.

4. *As representative of lien claimants.* The medical care provider has the right under workers' compensation to request reimbursement for any medical care expended for the treatment of an injured employee. Toward that recovery a representative may be required to handle the lien. A lien claimant representative will file a lien on the claimant's behalf and will attend conferences or hearings for the purpose of obtaining reimbursement of the lien as filed. Similarly, a representative may be at a conference or hearing on behalf of the Employment Development Department for the purpose of obtaining reimbursement for the State Disability Insurance or unemployment benefits provided to an injured employee while he is temporarily disabled.

In summary, the legal assistant in the workers' compensation field is an essential individual who can operate independently, or at best individually in an area of law which lends itself very well to the legal assistant's role.

(See Function of Paralegal, Workers' Compensation, in Chapter 2, Utilization of Paralegals.)

Appeals

A petition to review an order or award of the Workers' Compensation Appeals Board (WCAB) shall be accompanied by proof of service of

(1) 2 copies on the WCAB
(2) 1 copy on each party who entered an appearance in the action before the WCAB and whose interest is adverse to the party filing the petition.

If the claim is made in the petition that the decision is not supported by substantial evidence, the petition must fairly state the material evidence relevant to the points at issue.

Exhibits required to be attached to the petition include copies of

(1) Each order, decision, or award to be reviewed

(2) The workers' compensation judge's finding and decision including the judge's report and recommendation on the petition for reconsideration.

Within 20 days after service of the petition, the WCAB and any real party in interest may serve and file or join in the filing of an answer and brief, which must be served on all adverse parties.

Within 10 days after service of an answer, the petitioner may serve and file a reply, which must be served upon all adverse parties.

(Cal. Rules of Court, Rule 57.)

A petition for a statutory writ of review of an agency (e.g., an order of the Workers' Compensation Appeals Board) is not considered on its merits until the responsive filings provided for by rule have been received, or the time for such response has expired. After considering the petition, the court will summarily deny it, or issue a writ returnable at an indicated date and time. A temporary stay of the order sought to be reviewed is sometimes appropriate. If a stay is desired, a request should be submitted with the petition.

SUMMARY OF WORKERS' COMPENSATION BENEFITS

What Is An Industrial Injury?

An industrial injury may be an injury or a disease. It may include damage to artificial limbs, dentures or braces. It must be caused or aggravated by work or working conditions. An injury need not come from a single event. It can develop over a period of time (i.e., a series of micro-trauma) and be considered "cumulative." An injury need not be a physical injury: emotional injuires may also be covered. An aggravation of a preexisting injury may also come within the scope of this program.

The concept of workers' compensation is broad as to who is an employee and what is an injury. A rule of liberal construction permeates the entire system.

Are Public Employees Covered Under This Program?

Yes. The Workers' Compensation Law applies to almost all employees in California: State, County, City, School District and other local government employees. There are special benefits for certain groups of public employees in addition to the basic benefits received by employees in private business or industry.

What Injured Employees Should Do

First, report injury to the supervisor. The law states that the employer must be notified of the industrial injury or illness. It is then the employer's reponsibility to provide necessary medical treatment and other benefits. The supervisor will provide the forms to fill out. The forms must be completed as accurately as possible. If an injury is not reported promptly (within 30 days) or if the injured employee unreasonably refuses medical care, the rights to benefit may be lost.

For information on a particular case, the supervisor or personnel officer should be contacted. He or she will refer the inquiry to the claims representative who is handling the file.

What Benefits Are Provided?

The benefits in the ordinary workers' compensation case are:
(1) medical care and treatment;
(2) temporary disability indemnity;
(3) permanent disability indemnity; and
(4) rehabilitation.

These benefits are *different* from the recovery often received in a personal injury action in the regular civil courts. The two systems should not be confused. Another difference is that fault is not a prime consideration here.

The law also provides a program of rehabilitation which is considered where an injured employee has been determined to be a Qualified Injury Worker (no longer able to perform his previous occupation, in need of retaining and recognized by a doctor to require such a program.)

Medical Care and Treatment

An injured employee is entitled to receive all medical, surgical, hospital services and supplies, and prescriptions necessary to cure or relieve the effects of the industrial injury (for example, nursing care and such things as crutches and artifical limbs). Reasonable transportation expense incidental to treatment is also reimbursed. The employer, or his representative, has initial control of the medical program, but an injured employee obtains control after thirty days. The right to medical benefits may continue throughout a lifetime.

Temporary Disability

Temporary disability (TD) payments are to help the injured employee in meeting daily expenses while recovering from an injury or until a condition is reached where further inprovement is not expected. At this point the employee still may not be able to return to work, but *temporary* disability payments will stop and the employee may be entitled to *permanent* disability payments. At this point the injured employee is said to be "permanent and stationary" (P&S).

Payments normally start on the fourth day after injury. When the temporary disability lasts for an extended period (over 21 days), or causes hospitalization as a bed patient or patient receives hospital surgical care (on an outpatient basis), the first days of disability will be paid for. Disability payments are never made for the actual day of injury. The employer must tell the employee when his benefits will start and when they will stop, and why. If the employer denies a claim, he must tell the employee promptly.

Payments are based upon earnings. Payments will be a fraction of the regular salary and there are limits in the amount of the weekly payments. The current maximum amount for temporary disability payments is $175 a week.

An employee able to work part-time, although suffering a partial loss of earnings because of his injury, may be entitled to partial payments.

Permanent Disability

In some cases of industrial injury a permanent disability may result. The employee then receives permanent disability indemnity (PD) payments.

Where the effects of any injury cause a loss of earning power, or impairment of the normal use of a member, or a competitive handicap in the open labor market, there is at least a "partial permanent disability" and the employee will be entitled to compensation based upon the degree of this disability. Some disability may be "apportioned" to nonindustrial causes or to other injuries.

The degree of disability is "rated" in terms of "percent of permanent disability." The higher the rating percentage, the longer benefits will be paid. PD payments are based on the earnings or earning capacity of the disabled employee and have limits, just as for temporary disability payments. The current normal maximum is $70 a week.

The Permanent Disability Rating Schedule is utilized to compute a rating. It provides a method of uniformly evaluating a disability in percentage terms. It takes into consideration the nature of the injury, the age and occupation of the employee at the time of the injury and his ability to compete in the open labor market. If the disability is very serious and rates over 70 percent, a lifetime pension may be provided at a reduced rate after regular payments have ceased.

An employee does not have to be off the job to receive PD payments. He can be retired or working full time and still receive them.

In such circumstances they are in addition to regular income. Sometimes, there are offsets applied to retirement benefits and/or social security.

Death Benefits

When the industrial injury results in death, the benefit to the surviving spouse in cases of total dependency is $50,000. If there is a surviving spouse and one or more dependent minor children, the award can be as much as $75,000. A burial allowance is provided for. These benfits are normally in addition to those provided under the retirement system. The law also makes provision for those only partly dependent upon the deceased employee for support.

Subsequent Injuries Fund

An employee with a prior injury or disability who is injured at work may be entitled to benefits from the Subsequent Injuries Fund if the combined effect of the work injury and the earlier disability equals a rating of 70 percent or more and if:

1. The prior disability was to an eye, arm, hand, leg or foot and the new injury is to the opposite and corresponding member and rates five percent or more.

2. The prior disability is to any part of the body and the second injury is one which rates 35 percent or more. Employers are liable only for the disability caused by an industrial injury and not for any preexisting handicap (whether industrial, congenital or degenerative in nature). Thus, there is no financial penalty for hiring a handicapped employee. The employer pays the normal award for the injury at work. The cost resulting from the earlier disability is paid by the Subsequent Injuries Fund.

Special Provisions for Public Employees

Many special provisions exist for public employees. Sick leave may apply as it would in nonindustrial cases. Usually, there are offsets against sick leave and other accumulated time so that the employee may receive the equivalent of his full pay for an extended period. Extended leave (so-called "4800 time" or "4850 time") is provided for many public safety employees. State employees may receive industrial disability leave (IDL) benefits.

Presumptions of industrial causation apply to certain injuries for some public employees. Hernia, heart trouble, pneumonia and tuberculosis may be presumptive factors for certain employees.

Possible Penalties

Serious and Willful Misconduct.   Where the injury was caused by the "serious and willful misconduct" of the employer, the compensation award may be increased by an additional 50 percent of the recovery, up to $10,000. These are very difficult cases to prove and usually require a knowing violation of a formal safety order. If the injured employee was guilty of serious and willful misconduct, his benefits may be reduced by one-half.

Delay in Making Payments.   If benefits are unreasonably delayed or refused, the award may be increased. Interest and penalty are payable where compensation awarded by the Board has not been paid when due.

Discrimination.   It is unlawful for an employer to discharge, threaten to discharge, or discriminate against an employee because he is going to file an application or testify before the Workers' Compensation Appeals Board or because he has done so.

Intoxication.   Compensation benefits can be lost if an employee is injured by reason of his own intoxication, where the injury is intentionally self-inflicted; or arises out of an altercation in which he is the initial physical aggressor.

How Does the Employee Claim These Benefits?

The first benefits are received from the moment the employer sends the injured employee to a doctor. Most minor compensation cases are worked out between the injured employee and his employer. This is particularly true where the only benefits needed are for medical care and perhaps temporary disability.

If a dispute exists as to the amount of permanent disability, or the need for further temporary disability payments, a judge is needed to decide the dispute. This is the job of the Workers' Compensation Appeals Board (WCAB) and its judges. To bring the matter to the Board's attention, an application is filed.

Filing an application.   A proceeding is normally started by filling out an application and mailing or bringing it to an office of the WCAB. Copies of the application then must be served on the employer and his representative.

Time limits.   The application must be filed within one year from date of injury; or within one year after the employee has a disability and knows (or reasonably ought to know) that the disability resulted from his employment; or within one year after the last furnishing of benefits by the employer. An application for death benefits must normally be filed within one year after the date of death.

Where there is *new and further disability* after initial benefits, a claim may be filed within five years from the date of the injury. However, the original application still must have been filed in time, or the injury recognized through a voluntary furnishing of benefits on the part of the employer or his insurance carrier.

Pretrial conferences. After an application is filed, a conference pretrial is scheduled before a WCAB judge. Notice of the time and place is given to all parties. Unless agreement can be reached at that level, the issues are outlined and the case is set for hearing at that time.

Hearings. The judge will schedule a hearing based upon the need for testimony of witnesses and allowing time for examination and cross-examination. When that determination has been made, the hearing will be scheduled for a given amount of time; notice will be served on all parties as to time, date and place. At the hearing, the parties may present evidence supporting or opposing the claim with the assistance of medical witnesses, lay witnesses and/or medical reports in their possession.

These hearings somewhat parallel court trials but at the WCAB a jury is never called upon.

Compromises. Sometimes the parties to a disputed claim may want to agree upon a total sum in return for which the claim will be dropped, similar to a "settlement out of court." Any such "compromise and release" (C&R) must be approved by the WCAB. Once the employer is released from liability by approval of the C&R, the employee's claim is ended. Only in rare instances will further proceedings be entertained. Other informal settlement processes are available, including informal rating and stipulated awards.

What About Legal Assistance?

In most cases of minor injuries the injured employee will be capable of handling the matter on his own. The "pro per" (in propria persona, i.e., by one's self) approach is usually followed if medical care has been provided by the employer and temporary disability payments have been received. When all those benefits have been provided on a voluntary basis by the employer, there is no need to file an application with the WCAB. If a dispute arises from the claim of the injured employee, for instance, anticipated permanent disability, halt in temporary disability payments, halt in medical care or pending rehabilitation benefits, it may be necessary to call upon the WCAB to resolve the impasse. When an injured employee does not seem to overcome whatever impasse he has reached in his case, he may wish to consult with an attorney or legal assistant. The fees awarded the attorney or representative are set by the WCAB. They are usually 9 percent to 12 percent of the recovery made by the injured employee. If a case is not concluded successfully, the attorney or representative will not receive a fee.

USING WORKERS' COMPENSATION CASE FORMS

The Application for Adjudication of Claim is the first form needed to start the litigation process. It is filed with the Workers' Compensation Appeals Board and is endorsed and served upon the employer, the workers' compensation insurance carrier and/or the attorney representing the insurance carrier.

The Application for Adjudication of Claim (death case) is filed with the Workers' Compensation Appeals Board in the event the injured employee dies at the time of the injury or pursuant to the industrial injury sustained. This form is utilized when a widow, widower and/ or dependents are claiming benefits arising out of such an industrially caused death.

Upon receiving an endorsed copy of either of the two forms of Adjudication of Claim, the applicant is to serve copies on all parties in the case.

The Notice and Request for Allowance of Lien is filed by a doctor, medical facility or medical insurance carrier to insure that the amounts expended for the injured employee's care will be considered for payment at the conclusion of a workers' compensation case.

The Answer is filed by the insurance carrier or its attorney following its receipt of the Application. It serves to outline the areas of agreed liability and the denials of the allegations contained in the Application from the applicant.

The Declaration of Readiness to Proceed is the form filed with the Workers' Compensation Appeals Board requesting a Conference Pretrial, a Rating Pretrial or a Hearing. It is very similar to a Memorandum that Civil Case is at Issue utilized in civil cases.

The Notice of Conference is served by the Workers' Compensation Appeals Board upon all parties to the case to be heard at the conference level. It usually does not state the length of time to be allotted to the conference since most conferences usually last thirty minutes. The date, time and judge's name are stated on the notice.

The Notice of Hearing is served by the Workers' Compensation Appeals Board upon all parties to the case to be heard at the hearing level. The date, time of hearing, duration of the hearing and name of the judge are stated on the notice.

The Stipulations with Request for Award may be submitted by either the applicant (or his representative) or the defense. By this document, both parties agree to obtain conclusion of a case via the approval of a Workers' Compensation Judge. Stipulations usually provide for future medical care. Generally, the awarded permanent disability is paid to the injured worker on a weekly basis of $70 per week.

The Compromise and Release may be submitted by either the applicant (or his representative) or the defense. The parties agree to a lump-sum settlement releasing the insurance carrier of any future liability for the care and medical treatment of the injured employee. It is ratified by a Workers' Compensation Judge via his Order Approving the Compromise and Release.

See the following pages for samples of these forms:

Application for Adjudication of Claim (injury)
Application for Adjudication of Claim (death)
Notice and Request for Allowance of Lien
Answer
Declaration of Readiness to Proceed
Notice of Conference
Notice of Hearing
Stipulations with Request for Award
Compromise and Release

Application for Adjudication of Claim (Injury)

STATE OF CALIFORNIA
DEPARTMENT OF INDUSTRIAL RELATIONS

SEE REVERSE SIDE
FOR INSTRUCTIONS

DIVISION OF INDUSTRIAL ACCIDENTS—WORKERS' COMPENSATION APPEALS BOARD

APPLICATION FOR ADJUDICATION OF CLAIM   CASE No.

Mr. Mrs. Miss_____
(INJURED EMPLOYEE)

Social Security No._____

_____ (INJURED EMPLOYEE'S ADDRESS)

_____
(APPLICANT, IF OTHER THAN INJURED EMPLOYEE)

_____
(APPLICANT'S ADDRESS AND ZIP CODE)

vs.

_____
(EMPLOYER)

_____
(APPLICANT'S TELEPHONE NUMBER)

_____
(EMPLOYER'S ADDRESS)

_____
(EMPLOYER'S INSURANCE CARRIER OR STATE IF SELF-INSURED OR
PERMISSIBLY UNINSURED)

_____
(ADDRESS OF INSURANCE CARRIER, IF ANY)

IT IS CLAIMED THAT:

1. The injured employee, born_____, while employed as a_____
   (DATE OF BIRTH)   (OCCUPATION AT TIME OF INJURY)

   on _____at _____, _____, by the employer
         (DATE OF INJURY)   (CITY)   (STATE)

   sustained injury arising out of and in the course of employment to _____
                                                          (STATE WHAT PARTS OF BODY WERE INJURED)

2. The injury occurred as follows: _____
                          (EXPLAIN WHAT EMPLOYEE WAS DOING AT TIME OF INJURY AND HOW INJURY WAS RECEIVED)

3. Actual earnings at time of injury were: _____
                          (GIVE WEEKLY OR MONTHLY SALARY OR HOURLY RATE AND NUMBER OF HOURS WORKED PER WEEK)

   _____
   (SEPARATELY STATE VALUE PER WEEK OR MONTH OF TIPS, MEALS, LODGING OR OTHER ADVANTAGES REGULARLY RECEIVED)

4. The injury caused disability as follows: _____
                          (SPECIFY LAST DAY OFF WORK DUE TO THIS INJURY AND BEGINNING AND ENDING DATES OF ALL PERIODS OFF DUE TO THIS INJURY)

5. Compensation was paid ____ $_____ $_____ _____ _____
                          (YES) (NO)   (TOTAL PAID)   (WEEKLY RATE)   (DATE OF LAST PAYMENT)

6. Medical treatment was received ____ ____ _____ All treatment was furnished by the employer or
                                   (YES) (NO) (DATE OF LAST TREATMENT)

   insurance company ____ ____ other treatment was provided or paid for by_____
                      (YES) (NO)   (NAME PERSON OR AGENCY PROVIDING OR PAYING FOR MEDICAL CARE)

   Doctors not provided or paid for by employer or insurance company, who treated or examined for this injury are

   _____
   (STATE NAMES AND ADDRESSES OF SUCH DOCTORS AND NAMES OF HOSPITALS TO WHICH SUCH DOCTORS ADMITTED INJURED)

7. Unemployment Insurance or Unemployment Compensation Disability benefits have been received since the date of
   injury ____ ____
          (YES) (NO)

8. Other cases have been filed for industrial injuries by this employee as follows: _____
                                                            (SPECIFY CASE NUMBER AND CITY WHERE FILED)

9. This application is filed because of a disagreement regarding liability for: Temporary disability indemnity_____
   Permanent disability indemnity_____ Reimbursement for medical expense_____ Medical treatment_____
   Compensation at proper rate_____ Other_____ Specify: _____
   and applicant requests a hearing and award of the same, and for all other appropriate benefits provided by law.

   Dated at_____, California, _____
                    (CITY)   (DATE)

_____
(APPLICANT'S ATTORNEY)

_____
(APPLICANT'S SIGNATURE)

_____
(ADDRESS AND TELEPHONE NUMBER OF ATTORNEY)

DIA WCAB FORM 1 (REV. 4-75)

*Please file signed original and six copies
and print or type names and addresses*

INSTRUCTIONS

FILING AND SERVICE OF A DECLARATION OF READINESS (DIA/WCAB Form 9) IS PREREQUISITE TO THE SETTING OF A CASE FOR HEARING.

Effect of Filing Application

Filing of this application constitutes the beginning of formal proceedings against the defendant parties named in your application.

Service of Documents

Copies of this application will be served by the Workers' Compensation Appeals Board on all parties. If you file any other documents you must mail or deliver a copy of the document to all parties in the case. Attorneys or agents filing an application shall serve a copy upon Defendants, with proof of service submitted to the Appeals Board.

Filling Out Application

All blanks in the application should be completed. Where the information is unknown, place "unknown" in the blank.

Assistance in Filling Out Application

You may request the assistance of the Division of Industrial Accidents in filling out the application.

Right to Attorney

You may be represented in the case by an attorney or agent or you may represent yourself. The attorney's fee will be set by the Board at the time the case is decided, and is payable out of the award made to the applicant.

IMPORTANT!

If any applicant is under 18 years of age, it will be necessary to file Petition for Appointment of Guardian ad Litem. Forms for this purpose may be obtained at the office of the Workers' Compensation Appeals Board.

Application for Adjudication of Claim (Death)

Please file signed original and six copies and print or type names and address

STATE OF CALIFORNIA
AGRICULTURE AND SERVICES AGENCY
DEPARTMENT OF INDUSTRIAL RELATIONS
DIVISION OF INDUSTRIAL ACCIDENTS
WORKERS' COMPENSATION APPEALS BOARD

SEE REVERSE SIDE
FOR INSTRUCTIONS

APPLICATION FOR ADJUDICATION OF CLAIM (Death Case)   CASE No. _____

Mr. Mrs. Miss _____
              (APPLICANT)

_____ (APPLICANT'S ADDRESS)

_____

_____ (DECEASED EMPLOYEE'S NAME AND SOCIAL SECURITY NUMBER)

          VS.

_____
          (EMPLOYER)

_____ (EMPLOYER'S ADDRESS)

_____ (EMPLOYER'S INSURANCE CARRIER OR STATE IF SELF-INSURED OR PERMISSIBLY UNINSURED)

_____ (ADDRESS OF INSURANCE CARRIER, IF ANY)

IT IS CLAIMED THAT:

1. Deceased employee born _____, while employed as a _____
                 (DATE OF BIRTH)   (OCCUPATION AT TIME OF INJURY)

   on _____, at _____, _____, by the employer sustained injury arising
      (DATE OF INJURY)   (CITY)   (STATE)

   out of and in the course of employment to _____
                                         (STATE WHAT PARTS OF BODY WERE INJURED)

2. The injury occurred as follows: _____
                                (EXPLAIN WHAT EMPLOYEE WAS DOING AT TIME OF INJURY AND HOW INJURY WAS RECEIVED)

   _____ resulting in death on _____,
                                                  (DATE OF DEATH)

3. Actual earnings at time of injury were: _____
                             (GIVE WEEKLY OR MONTHLY SALARY OR HOURLY RATE AND NUMBER OF HOURS WORKED PER WEEK)

4. The injury caused disability as follows: _____
                            (SPECIFY LAST DAY OFF WORK DUE TO THIS INJURY AND BEGINNING AND ENDING DATES OF ALL PERIODS OFF DUE TO THIS INJURY)

5. Compensation was paid ____ ____ $_____ $_____ _____
            (YES)   (NO)   (TOTAL PAID)   (WEEKLY RATE)   (DATE OF LAST PAYMENT)

6. Medical treatment was received ____ ____ _____ All treatment was furnished by the employer or
                     (YES)   (NO)   (DATE OF LAST TREATMENT)

   insurance company ____ ____ other treatment was provided or paid for by _____
          (YES)   (NO)

   Doctors not provided or paid for by employer or insurance company, who treated or examined for this injury are:

   _____
         (STATE NAMES AND ADDRESSES OF SUCH DOCTORS AND NAMES OF HOSPITALS TO WHICH SUCH DOCTORS ADMITTED INJURED)

7. Defendants have paid burial expense. ____ ____ TOTAL PAID _____
                                (YES)   (NO)

8. The employee left surviving him the following dependents:

NAME	DATE OF BIRTH (if under 18)	RELATIONSHIP TO THE EMPLOYEE	ADDRESS

WHEREFORE, applicant requests a hearing and an award of: Death benefit____ Burial expense____ Compensation
accrued and unpaid____ Unpaid Medical bills____ Other____ Specify: _____
_____ and all other appropriate benefits provided by law.
                        Dated at _____, California, _____
                                   (CITY)   (DATE)

_____
(APPLICANT'S ATTORNEY)

_____
(ADDRESS AND TELEPHONE NUMBER OF ATTORNEY)

_____
(APPLICANT'S SIGNATURE)

DIA WCAB FORM 2 (REV. 11-74)

DIA WCAB FORM 2 (REV. 11-74)

INSTRUCTIONS

FILING AND SERVICE OF A DECLARATION OF READINESS (DIA/WCAB Form 9) IS PRE REQUISITE TO THE SETTING OF A CASE FOR HEARING.

Effect of Filing Application

Filing of this application constitutes the beginning of formal proceedings against the defendant parties named in your application.

Service of Documents

Copies of this application will be served by the Workers' Compensation Appeals Board on all parties. If you file any other documents you must mail or deliver a copy of that document to all parties in the case. Attorneys or agents filing an application shall serve a copy upon defendants, with proof of service submitted to the Appeals Board.

Filling Out Application

All blanks in the application should be completed. Where the information is unknown, place "unknown" in the blank.

Assistance in Filling Out Application

You may request the assistance of the Division of Industrial Accidents in filling out the application.

Right to Attorney

You may be represented in the case by an attorney or agent or you may represent yourself. The attorney's fee will be set by the Board at the time the case is decided, and is payable out of the award made to the applicant.

IMPORTANT!

If any applicant is under 18 years of age, it will be necessary to file Petition for Appointment of Guardian ad Litem. Forms for this purpose may be obtained at the office of the Workers' Compensation Appeals Board.

Notice and Request for Allowance of Lien

WORKERS' COMPENSATION APPEALS BOARD
STATE OF CALIFORNIA

CASE NO.————————

NOTICE AND REQUEST FOR ALLOWANCE OF LIEN

	LIEN CLAIMANT		ADDRESS
VS.			

EMPLOYEE		ADDRESS

EMPLOYER		ADDRESS

INSURANCE CARRIER		ADDRESS

The undersigned hereby requests the Workers' Compensation Appeals Board to determine and allow as a lien the sum of

————————————————————————————— Dollars ($—————————————) against

any amount now due or which may hereafter become payable as compensation to————————————————————
EMPLOYEE

on account of injury sustained by him on————————————————————.
DATE

This request and claim for lien is for: (Mark appropriate box)

☐ The reasonable expense incurred by or on behalf of said employee for medical treatment to cure or relieve from the effects of said injury; or

☐ The reasonable medical expense incurred to prove a contested claim; or

☐ The reasonable value of living expenses of said employee or of his dependents, subsequent to the injury, or

☐ The reasonable living expenses of the wife or minor children, or both, of said employee, subsequent to the date of injury, where such employee has deserted or is neglecting his family; or

☐ The reasonable fee for interpreter's services performed on————————————————.
DATE

☐

☐

NOTE: ITEMIZED STATEMENTS MUST BE ATTACHED

The undersigned declares that he delivered or mailed a copy of this lien claim to each of the above-named parties on

ATTORNEY FOR LIEN CLAIMANT		DATE

ADDRESS OF ATTORNEY FOR LIEN CLAIMANT		LIEN CLAIMANT

EMPLOYEE'S CONSENT TO ALLOWANCE OF LIEN

I consent to the requested allowance of a lien against my compensation.

ATTORNEY FOR EMPLOYEE		EMPLOYEE

DEPARTMENT OF INDUSTRIAL RELATIONS
DIVISION OF INDUSTRIAL ACCIDENTS

DIA WCAB FORM 6 (REV 8-75)
⟨𝕆 OSP

Answer

DIA WCAB FORM 10 (REV. 2-75)
D OSP ⬤⬤⬤ 13

STATE OF CALIFORNIA

DEPARTMENT OF INDUSTRIAL RELATIONS
DIVISION OF INDUSTRIAL ACCIDENTS

WORKERS' COMPENSATION APPEALS BOARD

ANSWER of _____

_____
(INJURED EMPLOYEE)

Case No. _____

vs.

Date of alleged injury: _____

_____
(CORRECT NAME OF EMPLOYER)

_____
(EMPLOYER'S ADDRESS)

_____
(CORRECT NAME OF INSURANCE CARRIER)

_____
(INSURANCE CARRIER'S ADDRESS)

_____
(CERTIFICATE NUMBER IF SELF-INSURED)

ANSWERING DEFENDANTS deny the allegations of the Application as indicated below with such explanations as expressly set forth and admit all other material allegations.

DENIALS
(MARK X IF ALLEGATION IS DENIED)

EXPLAIN BELOW

_____ Employment

_____ Occupation

_____ Injury

(IF DENIAL IS BASED ON DATE OR PART OF BODY INJURED, EXPLAIN FULLY)

_____ Insurance coverage

(CHECK IF EMPLOYER HAS BEEN NOTIFIED TO APPEAR AND DEFEND)

_____ Liability for self
procured treatment

_____ Liability for future
medical treatment

_____ Medical-legal costs

_____ Earnings

_____ Periods of disability

(GIVE LAST DAY WORKED AND CORRECT DATE OF RETURN TO WORK)

_____ Permanent disability

(IF APPORTIONMENT IS CLAIMED, SO STATE)

IT IS FURTHER ALLEGED:

1. Defendants have paid disability indemnity in the total amount of $_____ at the rate of $_____ a week

beginning _____ through _____ plus _____ .

2. Affirmative defenses and other matters: _____

_____

_____

Defendants do not waive the right to raise additional issues in accordance with the provisions of law and the Rules of Practice if other issues develop.

Estimated time for trial: _____

All defendants medical reports have been filed _____

Additional reports will be filed before trial _____

Dated at _____, California, _____
(CITY)   (DATE)

_____
(EMPLOYER OR INSURANCE CARRIER)

By: _____

_____
(ADDRESS AND TELEPHONE NUMBER OF ATTORNEY)

Declaration of Readiness to Proceed

STATE OF CALIFORNIA
DEPARTMENT OF INDUSTRIAL RELATIONS
DIVISION OF INDUSTRIAL ACCIDENTS

WORKERS' COMPENSATION APPEALS BOARD

CASE No.

_____ } *Applicant*

vs.

_____ *Defendants*

DECLARATION OF READINESS TO PROCEED

NOTICE: "Any objection to the proceedings requested by a Declaration of Readiness to proceed shall be filed and served within ten (10) days after service of the declaration."
(Rule 10416)

The (☐ Employee or applicant) requests that this case be set for hearing at
☐ Defendant
☐ Lien Claimant

_____.
(Place)

on the ☐ Rating Pretrial (or) ☐ Conference Pretrial (or) ☐ Regular calendar and with respect to readiness therefor states:

[COMPLETE ONLY ONE OF THESE PARAGRAPHS **]**

☐
Rating Pretrial is requested because the employee's condition following injury is permanent and stationary as shown by the report of Dr._____
dated_____, filed and served on_____ (or) to be filed and served on or about_____.

☐
Conference Pretrial is requested to frame issues, record stipulations, join necessary parties,
(or)_____.
(Other)

☐
Regular Hearing is requested. At the present time the principal issues are—

☐ Compensation Rate
☐ Temporary Disability
☐ Permanent Disability
☐ Other_____

☐ Reimbursement for Self-procured Medical Treatment
☐ Future Medical Treatment

Employee ☐ is (or) ☐ is not presently receiving compensation payments.

I expect to present_____witnesses, including_____medical witnesses, and estimate the time required for the hearing will be_____hours.

All medical reports in my possession have been filed and served as required by WCAB Rules of Practice and Procedure.

Adverse parties ☐ have (or) ☐ have not served me with medical reports.

Copies of this Declaration have been served this date as shown on the reverse side.

Name (Print or type)_____

Declarant's Signature_____

Address_____ Phone_____

Date_____

(SEE REVERSE SIDE FOR INSTRUCTIONS AND SERVICE.)

DIA/WCAB FORM 9 (REV. 3-78)

SERVICE

Type or print names and addresses of parties, including attorneys and representatives served with a copy of this Declaration.

_____   _____
_____   _____
_____   _____
_____   _____
_____   _____
_____   _____
_____   _____
_____   _____
_____   _____
_____   _____

INSTRUCTIONS

1. This Declaration must be completed and filed before any case will be set for hearing.

2. Unless notified otherwise, no witness other than the applicant need attend Pretrial Hearings.

3. The party producing a non-English-speaking witness must arrange for the presence of a disinterested interpreter.

4. Continuances are not favored and none will be granted after the filing of this Declaration without a clear and timely showing of good cause.

5. The Appeal Board favors the presentation of medical evidence in the form of written reports.

OFFICES OF THE DIVISION OF INDUSTRIAL ACCIDENTS

BAKERSFIELD	225 Chester Avenue (93301)	327-7591
BELL GARDENS	6450 Garfield Avenue (90201)	771-8650
EUREKA	619 Second Street (95501)	443-4003
FRESNO	2550 Mariposa Street (93721)	488-5051
LONG BEACH	230 E. Fourth Street (90802)	590-5001
LOS ANGELES	107 S. Broadway (90012)	620-2680
OAKLAND	1111 Jackson Street (94607)	464-0500
POMONA	300 S. Park Avenue (91766)	623-4301
REDDING	2115 Akard Avenue (96001)	246-6551
SACRAMENTO	1006 - 4th Street (95814)	445-9812
SALINAS	21 W. Laurel Drive (93901)	449-5461
SAN BERNARDINO	303 W. Third Street (92401)	383-4341
SAN DIEGO	1350 Front Street (92101)	237-7321
SAN FRANCISCO	455 Golden Gate Avenue (94102)	557-0680
SAN JOSE	111 N. Market St. (95113)	277-1246
SANTA ANA	28 Civic Center Plaza (92701)	558-4121
SANTA BARBARA	411 E. Canon Perdido (93101)	966-1527
SANTA MONICA	819 Broadway (90401)	451-8901
SANTA ROSA	750 Mendocino Avenue (95401)	542-3146
STOCKTON	31 E Channel Street (95202)	948-7757
VAN NUYS	8155 Van Nuys Blvd. (91402)	782-4061
VENTURA	5810 Ralston Street (93003)	647-0442

WORKERS' COMPENSATION APPEALS BOARD
455 GOLDEN GATE AVENUE, SAN FRANCISCO 94102

Notice of Conference

WORKERS COMPENSATION APPEALS BOARD
STATE OF CALIFORNIA

Case. No.

Applicant	NOTICE OF CONFERENCE
vs.	☐ Change of Time or Place
Defendants	

It has been determined that this case is subject to Workers' Compensation Appeals Board conference procedures, These procedures will be completed prior to referral to the calendar for trial as requested in the Declaration of Readiness to Proceed filed herein.

You are hereby notified that captioned case is set for a conference before a Workers' Compensation Judge of the Workers' Compensation Appeals Board of the State of California at 1006 - 4th Street, Second Floor, Sacramento, CA. 95814:

CONTINUANCES ARE NOT FAVORED AND WILL BE GRANTED ONLY UPON CLEAR SHOWING OF GOOD CAUSE.

NOTE TO INSURED EMPLOYERS: Your Attendance at this hearing may not be necessary. Ask your insurance company.

Attendance by the applicant is required. If you have any questions concerning this Notice of Conference, please telephone (916) 445-9812.

Served by mail on persons shown
on the Official Address Record:

Date:_____

By: _____

NOTE: By this procedure the Workers' Compensation Appeals Board will endeavor to handle this case expeditiously and inexpensively so that appropriate benefits may flow to the injured worker at the earliest possible time and to permit early, prompt, and inexpensive resolution of disputes.

IMPORTANT: READ REVERSE SIDE OF THIS FORM.

Notice of Hearing

WORKERS' COMPENSATION APPEALS BOARD
STATE OF CALIFORNIA

Case. No.

Notice of Hearing

Applicant

vs.

Defendants

☐ Trial Calendar

☐ Conference Calendar

☐ Rating Calendar

☐ Settlement Calendar

☐ Standby Referee

☐ Cross Examination

    ☐ Rater

    ☐ Doctor

☐ Change of Time or Place

☐

You are hereby notified that the above entitled case is set for hearing before the Workers' Compensation Appeals Board of the State of California at

DEPARTMENT OF INDUSTRIAL RELATIONS
DIVISION OF INDUSTRIAL ACCIDENTS
WORKMEN'S COMPENSATION APPEALS BOARD
1006 Fourth Street
Sacramento. California 95814

CONTINUANCES ARE NOT FAVORED AND WILL BE GRANTED ONLY UPON CLEAR SHOWING OF GOOD CAUSE.

NOTE TO INSURED EMPLOYERS: Your attendance at this hearing may not be necessary. Ask your insurance company.

Dated_____

SERVICE BY MAIL ON
PARTIES AS SHOWN ON
OFFICIAL ADDRESS RECORD
EFFECTED ON ABOVE DATE.

By_____

_____
Referee, WORKERS' COMPENSATION APPEALS BOARD

DEPARTMENT OF INDUSTRIAL RELATIONS
DIVISION OF INDUSTRIAL ACCIDENTS

DIA WCAB FORM 12 (REV. 10-75)
Ⓤ OSF

Stipulations with Request for Award

WORKERS' COMPENSATION APPEALS BOARD

STATE OF CALIFORNIA

Applicant

Case No.

Stipulations with Request for Award

vs.

Defendants

The parties hereto stipulate to the issuance of an Award and/or Order, based upon the following facts, and waive the requirements of Labor Code Section 5313:

1. _____ , born _____ , while
              (Employee)

employed within the State of California as _____ on _____ ,
                                      (Occupation)   (Date of Injury)

by _____ whose compensation insurance carrier was
                (Employer)

_____ sustained injury arising out of and in the course of employment _____ .
                                                                    (Parts of body injured)

2. The injury caused temporary disability for the period _____

through _____ for which indemnity is payable at $_____ per

week, less credit for such payments previously made.

3. The injury caused permanent disability of _____ %, for which indemnity is payable at $_____

per week beginning _____ , in the sum of $_____ , less credit for such

payments previously made.

An informal rating has   has not   been previously issued.
               (Select one)

4. There is   is not   may be need for medical treatment to cure or relieve from the effects of said injury.
   (Select one)

DEPARTMENT OF INDUSTRIAL RELATIONS
DIVISION OF INDUSTRIAL ACCIDENTS

WORKERS COMPENSATION APPEALS BOARD

STATE OF CALIFORNIA

5. Medical-legal expenses are payable by defendant as follows:

6. Applicant's attorney request a fee of $

7. Liens against compensation are payable as follows:

8. Other stipulations:

Dated

Applicant

Social Security Number of Applicant

Address of Applicant

Attorney for Applicant

Address of Attorney for Applicant

Address of Employer

Address of Insurance Company

Attorney or Authorized Representative for Defendant

Address of Attorney or Authorized Representative

WORKERS' COMPENSATION APPEALS BOARD
STATE OF CALIFORNIA

AWARD

AWARD IS MADE in favor of _____ against

_____ of:

(A) Temporary disability indemnity in accordance with paragraph 2 above,

(B) Permanent disability indemnity in accordance with paragraph 3 above,

> Less the sum of $_____ payable to applicant's attorney as the reasonable value of services rendered.

> Less liens in accordance with Paragraph 7 above,

(C) Further medical treatment in accordance with Paragraph 4 above,

(D) Reimbursement for medical-legal expenses in accordance with Paragraph 5 above,

(E)

_____
Dated:

_____
Referee
WORKERS' COMPENSATION APPEALS BOARD

Copy served on all persons listed on
Official Address Record.

Date: _____

By: _____
        (Signature)

DIA WCAB FORM 3 (REV. 5-75)   (Page 3)   DEPARTMENT OF INDUSTRIAL RELATIONS
                                                                DIVISION OF INDUSTRIAL ACCIDENTS

Compromise and Release

COMPROMISE AND RELEASE
PLEASE SEE INSTRUCTIONS ON
REVERSE OF PAGE 2 BEFORE
COMPLETING FORM.

STATE OF CALIFORNIA
DEPARTMENT OF INDUSTRIAL RELATIONS
DIVISION OF INDUSTRIAL ACCIDENTS
WORKERS' COMPENSATION APPEALS BOARD

CASE NO. ....

SOCIAL SECURITY NO. ....

(Mr.) (Mrs.) (Miss) ....

               VS.   APPLICANT   ADDRESS

....

            CORRECT NAME OF EMPLOYER   ADDRESS

....

          CORRECT NAME OF INSURANCE CARRIER   ADDRESS

The parties hereto, for the purpose of compromise only, hereby submit the following agreed statements of fact:

1. ...., employee herein, born on ....

   claims that he was employed on the............day of....................., 19........at..

                                                (MONTH)   (YEAR)   (CITY)   (STATE)

   as a..by .... then insured as to

                  (OCCUPATION)   (NAME OF EMPLOYER)

   workers' compensation liability by.. and that

                                 (STATE NAME OF CARRIER OR WHETHER SELF-INSURED)

   he sustained an injury arising out of and in the course of his employment as follows: ....

   ....

   ....

2. The actual weekly wages of the employee at the time of injury were $........................, while the average weekly wages

   were $........................ .

3. The employee's present disability is..

                                  (STATE PRESENT DISABILITY RESULTING FROM THE INJURY)

   and the employee............returned to work........................ .

                                  (IF SO. STATE WHEN)

4. (a) Temporary disability indemnity has been paid to the employee in the sum of $........................at $........................per week

        beginning........................to and including........................ . The amount due and unpaid to the employee is $........................ .

   (b) Permanent disability indemnity has been paid to the employee in the sum of $........................covering period ....to........ .

5. The parties hereby agree to settle any and all claims on account of said injury by the payment of the sum of $........................
   in addition to any sums heretofore paid by the employer or the insurer to the employee, said sum to be payable as follows:

   ....

   ....

   ....

6. Medical and hospital expenses have been paid $........................by the employee and $........................by the employer or carrier.

   Unpaid bills amount to $........................ . Future medical and hospital expense is estimated at $........................ . Unpaid and

   future medical and hospital expense is to be assumed as follows: ....

   ....

7. Name and address of employee's attorney, if any ....

8. Said attorney requests a fee of $ .... Amount of attorney fee previously paid, if any, $ ....

9. Reason for Compromise ....

....

10. The undersigned request that this Compromise Agreement and Release be approved.

11. Upon approval of this Compromise Agreement by the Workers' Compensation Appeals Board or a Referee, and payment in accordance with the provisions hereof, said employee releases and forever discharges said employer and insurance carrier from all claims and causes of action, whether now known or ascertained, or which may hereafter arise or develop as a result of said injury, including any and all liability of said employer and said insurance carrier and each of them to the dependents, heirs, executors, representatives, administrators or assigns of said employee.

12. It is agreed by all parties hereto that the filing of this document is the filing of an application on behalf of the employee, and that the W.C.A.B. may in its discretion set the matter for hearing as a regular application, reserving to the parties the right to put in issue any of the facts admitted herein, and that if hearing is held with this document used as an application the defendants shall have available to them all defenses that were available as of the date of filing of this document, and that the W.C.A.B. may thereafter either approve said Compromise Agreement and Release or disapprove the same and issue Findings and Award after hearing has been held and the matter regularly submitted for decision.

13. For the purpose of determining the lien claim filed herein for the unemployment compensation disability benefits or unemployment compensation benefits and extended duration benefits which have been paid under or pursuant to the California Unemployment Insurance Code, the parties propose the following division of the sum agreed upon for settlement and release of this case:

$ .... for temporary disability covering the period .... to ....

$ .... for accrued medical expense paid or incurred by the employee.

$ .... for future medical care.

$ .... for permanent disability.

(The above segregation must be fair and reasonable and must be based on the real facts of the case. There should be no attempt made to deprive the lien claimant of a reasonable recovery consistent with all the amounts involved. W.C.A.B. Rule 10886 requires proof of service of a copy of this agreement on such Lien Claimant.)

WITNESS *the signature hereof this* .... *day of* .... *, 19* ...... *, at* ....

....

                    WITNESSES
        THE INJURED APPLICANT'S SIGNATURE MUST BE ATTESTED BY TWO
        DISINTERESTED PERSONS OR ACKNOWLEDGED BEFORE A NOTARY PUBLIC

            STATE OF CALIFORNIA   }
                                         } SS.
    .... County of .... }

On this .... *day of* .... *, A.D. 19* ...... *, before me,* ....,
a Notary Public in and for the said County and State, residing therein, duly commissioned and sworn, personally appeared

....

known to me to be the person .... *whose name* ....
subscribed to the within Instrument, and acknowledged to me that ...... *he* ...... *executed the same.*
     IN WITNESS WHEREOF, *I have hereunto set my hand and affixed my official seal the day and year in this Certificate first above written.*

                                                    ....
                                                    Notary Public in and for said County and State of California

INSTRUCTIONS

1. Do not use this form in death cases. Use Form 16. Do not use in third-party cases. Use 17.

2. If the injured employee be under 18 years of age and a guardian ad litem has not been previously appointed, a petition for appointment of guardian ad litem and trustee must accompany this agreement.

3. The guardian must sign this agreement on behalf of an injured employee who is under 18 years of age. If the minor is above the age of 14, such minor should also sign this agreement.

4. Attach all medical reports not heretofore submitted to the Workers' Compensation Appeals Board and advise when other reports were filed.

5. Please use space below for additional information.

**Offices of Division of Industrial Accidents
(Workers' Compensation)**

225 Chester Ave.
Bakersfield, CA 93301
(805) 395-2723

6450 Garfield Ave.
Bell Gardens, CA 90201
(213) 771-8650

619 Second St., Rm. 108
Eureka, CA 95501
(707) 443-4003

2550 Mariposa Ave.
State Building #4078
Fresno, CA 93721
(209) 445-5051

P.O. Box 2620
Long Beach, CA 90802
(2828 Junipero Ave.
Signal Hill)
(213) 595-8381

107 S. Broadway, Rm. 4107
Los Angeles, CA 90012
(213) 620-2730
(Central South) (213) 620-4890

1111 Jackson St., Rm. 3000
Oakland, CA 94607
(415) 464-0500

Pomona, CA 91766
(300 S. Park Ave., Rm. 420)
(714) 623-4301

2115 Akard, Rm. 15
Redding, CA 96001
(916) 246-6551

1006 Fourth, St., 2d Floor
Sacramento, CA 95814
(916) 445-9812

21 W. Laurel Drive, Suite 69
Salinas, CA 93906
(408) 443-3060

San Bernardino, CA 92401
(303 W. Third St., Rm. 400)
(714) 383-4341

1350 Front St., Rm. 3047
San Diego, CA 92101
(714) 237-7321

P.O. Box 603
San Francisco, CA 94101
(525 Golden Gate Ave.)
Headquarters: (415) 557-3542
District Office: (415) 557-3314

111 N. Market St., Rm. 1020
San Jose, CA 95113
(408) 552-1246

28 Civic Center Plaza, Rm. 451
Santa Ana, CA 92701
(714) 558-4121

411 E. Canon Perdido, Rm. 1
Santa Barbara, CA 93101
(805) 966-1527

Santa Monica Office:
11804 W. Olympic Blvd.
Los Angeles, CA 90064
(213) 478-2593

750 Mendocino Ave., Suite 4
Santa Rose, CA 95401
(707) 542-3146

P.O. Drawer 60
Stockton, CA 95201
(31 E. Channel St., Rm. 344)
(209) 948-7757

P.O. Box 4810
Van Nuys, CA 91402
(Panorama City)
(8155 Van Nuys Blvd.,
12th Floor)
(213) 782-4061

5810 Ralston St.
Ventura, CA 93003
(805) 654-4670

CALIFORNIA PARALEGAL'S GUIDE

Chapter 24

UNEMPLOYMENT INSURANCE

A party to an unemployment insurance matter may choose an attorney or a non-attorney to represent him at an administrative hearing involving such case. Therefore, the "representative" discussed in this chapter may be either a paralegal or an attorney.

To understand the documentary evidence involved in an unemployment insurance matter and how such a case arises the paralegal should be familiar with the claim process. Therefore, that process will be discussed prior to explaining the appeal procedure.

A typical unemployment insurance matter begins when an employee quits his job or is discharged (as distinguished from being laid off). He then proceeds to the nearest field office of the Employment Development Department to file a claim for unemployment insurance benefits.

Over a period of a few days to a few weeks the following events will most likely take place. The claimant (the former employee) will fill out an Initial Claim Statement by checking various boxes, stating such matters as how his last job ended, whether he is able to work, whether he is attending school, etc. A Claimant's Separation Statement will be prepared wherein the claimant will write a full and complete explanation as to how his last employment terminated. The claimant will be interviewed by a Department representative concerning all aspects of his entitlement to benefits. The representative will write up a summary of this interview on a Record of Claim Status Interview. The representative will also probably telephone the claimant's last employer and ask questions as to why the employment relationship terminated. This interview also will be summarized on the form.

A UI Claim Filing Form will be sent to the last employer. This form will contain a statement written by the claimant as to how the employment relationship ended. The employer is asked to complete his part of the form and return it to the Department within ten days, explaining in detail the circumstances surrounding the claimant's quit or discharge.

When the Department has completed its evaluation of the above material it will issue a Notice of Determination/Ruling. This document will state whether the claimant is or is not entitled to benefits and whether the employer's reserve account is or is not subject to charges for its proportionate share of the benefits that may be paid to the claimant. This document also tells the claimant and employer that if they believe that the conclusion reached in the notice is contrary to law, an appeal to an Administrative Law Judge may be filed within 20 days. An appeal may be filed either by a letter or by a form provided for the purpose and available at the offices listed at the end of this chapter. The appeal form has an entry to show whether the appellant is representing himself or, if represented by someone else, who that person is. Complete grounds or reasons for the appeal should be stated therein.

If an appeal is filed, the documents mentioned above are transmitted by the Department to the appropriate Office of Appeals of the California Unemployment Insurance Appeals Board. The case is calendared in its proper order for hearing for a particular day and before a named Administrative Law Judge. At least ten days before the hearing date, a Notice of Hearing is sent to the parties and their representative. This notice states the time and place of hearing and the issues to be considered at the hearing.

Accompanying the Notice of Hearing is an Appeal Information pamphlet. This document spells out how to prepare for the hearing and how the hearing will be conducted. The most important portions of that pamphlet are here set forth:

TIME AND PLACE OF HEARING

The time and place of hearing is shown in the center of the Notice of Hearing. Where the claimant and the employer, or witnesses for either, cannot attend the same place of hearing because the travel would require one hour or more each way, the Office of Appeals may schedule a phone hearing or hold two hearings.

A request to the Office of Appeals for a different date, time, or place of the hearing is discouraged and *will not* be granted unless you have "good cause." Any request for a change must be made immediately upon learning the need for the change.

Importance of Hearing

The Administrative Law Judge will decide the appeal on the testimony given by parties and witnesses and documents submitted at the hearing. If there are any witnesses or documents relating to your client's case, bring them to the hearing. A witness who can give a firsthand account of what happened is better than presenting secondhand testimony.

ATTENDANCE OF WITNESSES

If you wish a witness to testify, you may arrange for him to attend voluntarily. If you wish the Office of Appeals to serve by mail to a witness a written "Notice to Attend Hearing", then write or phone the Office of Appeals immediately and give:

1. The *case number, date,* and *location* of hearing assigned to the appeal;
2. The *name* and *address* of the person you desire to attend;
3. A statement why this person is necessary — what relevant information can be given substantiating your case.

Or you may request a subpoena which is *your* responsibility to personally serve on the witness reasonably prior to the date of hearing. If a witness does not appear in response to a "Notice to Attend Hearing" and that witness's testimony is necessary to properly decide your case, the Administrative Law Judge may issue a subpoena for that witness to attend a subsequent hearing. Witness fees ($12) and mileage (20¢ one way) are claimed through the Administrative Law Judge assigned the case.

If you wish a particular person employed by the Department to appear at the hearing, notify the Office of Appeals immediately.

Where a witness resides in a location too far to commute to the scheduled place of hearing, arrangements may be made to obtain the testimony of the witness by telephone or through another Office of Appeals, if a request is made immediately to the Office of Appeals for such arrangements.

DECLARATION/STATEMENT UNDER PENALTY OF PERJURY

Where the claimant or employer, or witness is unable to attend a hearing, a declaration/statement under penalty of prejury will be considered as evidence if received before the end of the hearing. *Evidence given in person at a hearing is given more consideration by the Administrative Law Judge and the Appeals Board than a declaration/ statement.*

A declaration/statement under penalty of perjury must be in writing and contain:

1. The case number, *date* and *place* of hearing (shown on the Notice of Hearing).
2. A through explanation of what occurred, giving names, dates and places. Letters, medical statements, pay vouchers, etc., may be attached which will be returned after the hearing, if requested.
3. At the end of the statement the following declaration should be written or typed: "I certify under penalty of perjury that the foregoing is true."
4. Below this declaration, the person making the statement must sign and give the date he signed and place where signed.

Mail the declaration/statement to the Office of Appeals that is shown on the Notice of Hearing either before the date set for the hearing or bring it to the hearing.

GETTING RECORDS FOR THE HEARING

Records used for the hearing will be those from the Department and those presented by the parties. Instruct your client to bring all documents which will support his or her position, such as letters, medical statements, pay vouchers, employment contracts and correspondence. An employer who intends to introduce business records into evidence should have at the hearing the original (and a copy if the original is to be returned) and to have a person who can explain how records were prepared.

If a necessary document or record is in the possession of someone else, an affidavit for production may be obtained from the Office of Appeals. When this form is properly filled out and mailed or delivered to the Office of Appeals, and if the document is relevant, a Notice to Produce or a subpoena for the production of the record will be issued for the hearing. (See 'Attendance of Witnesses' above on service and claim for witness fee.)

INTERPRETER

If an interpreter will be needed for the client or witness, advise the Office of Appeals *immediately*, and one will be provided.

RIGHT TO HAVE A REPRESENTATIVE

The Administrative Law Judge will ask questions of parties and their witnesses to determine the truth and will assist unrepresented parties in phrasing questions. A claimant has the right to have a representative present, either an attorney or a non-attorney. Free legal services may be available in the community. Representation by a skilled paralegal may be considered. If a charge is made by the representative, the claimant must pay his fees. Should the claimant question the amount of the fee, notify the Administrative Law Judge who will determine the maximum amount payable.

FAILURE TO APPEAR AT THE HEARING

The person appealing should attend the hearing; otherwise the appeal shall be dismissed. If the opposing party does not attend the hearing, the appeal will be decided on the evidence received at the hearing. "Good cause" for failure to appear must be established for any reopening of the matter under appeal.

DISMISSAL FOR LATE APPEAL

If the claimant did not file his or her appeal within twenty (20) calendar days after the Department's determination was mailed or handed to him or her, the claimant must show "good cause" for the delay. Otherwise, the appeal shall be dismissed. Therefore, the claimant should be prepared to explain at the hearing why the appeal was late.

WITHDRAWAL OF APPEAL

The appellant may withdraw his appeal by written request to the Office of Appeals at any time before the hearing or before a decision is issued, or by oral request at the time of hearing.

RIGHTS OF THE PARTY AT THE HEARING

Each party has these rights:
1. To testify in his own behalf;
2. To be represented by a representative of his own choosing;
3. To present documents, records and written declarations/ statements;
4. To have his own witnesses testify;
5. To question opposing parties and witnesses;
6. To explain or rebut evidence against him;
7. To request a continuance when surprised by a new issue or unexpected evidence;
8. To make a statement at the end of the hearing as to how the evidence and the law supports his position and to submit such a statement in writing at the close of the hearing.

CONDUCT OF HEARING

The Administrative Law Judge has the sole authority for the conduct of the hearing. In conducting the hearing he will:

1. Explain the issues and the meaning of terms the parties do not understand;
2. Explain the order in which persons will testify, ask questions and give rebuttal;
3. Assist parties in asking questions of other witnesses;
4. Question parties and witnesses to obtain necessary facts;
5. Determine on his own motion or the request of a party if testimony and documents being offered should be received and considered;
6. Require parties to give a proper background or foundation for secondary evidence, documents and opinion testimony;
7. Take official or judicial notice of well-established matters of common knowledge and public records.

THE DECISION

The decision of the Administrative Law Judge, in most cases, should be mailed to the claimant, within ten days after the hearing. The decision will set forth the facts found from the evidence, the reasons for the decision, and the decision.

Attached to the decision will be an explanation on how to request from the Office of Appeals a reopening of the matter or to file an appeal to the Unemployment Insurance Appeals Board should the claimant disagree with the Administrative Law Judge's decision. If an appeal is taken, the Appeals Board generally will decide the matter solely on the record made at the Administrative Law Judge's hearing, together with oral or written argument, if any, presented to the Board. Contact the field office where claim is on file regarding the payment of benefits.

PARTIES TO AN APPEAL

Either the claimant or the employer, if adversely affected by a determination made by the Employment Development Department, may file an appeal to an Administrative Law Judge.

Department representatives who attend the hearing have the right to present written and oral evidence and to question other parties and witnesses and may be questioned by the claimant and the employer.

The Department as well as the claimant or the employer may appeal from an Administrative Law Judge's decision to the Unemployment Insurance Appeals Board.

Independence of the Administrative Law Judge

Under the Unemployment Insurance Code, the Unemployment Insurance Appeals Board and its Administrative Law Judges in deciding appeals are completely independent of the Employment Development Department.

A concise statement of the hearing procedure is contained in Appeals Procedure, a publication of the Unemployment Insurance Appeals Board, as follows:

Procedure in Presenting Cases

The Appeals Board recognizes the fact that most claimants and employers have not previously attended a court or administrative hearing. Therefore, the procedure is explained at the outset. The Rules of the Board require the administrative law judge to inform parties the order in which evidence will be given and to explain the issues which will be considered at the hearing. (Board Rule 5038.) When the hearing is convened, the administrative law judge also identifies the case by name and number, introduces himself and the reporter and states the names of the parties.

The administrative law judge generally admits into evidence or takes official notice of those records of the Department which give a history of the case and which are necessary to a disposition of the issue; you will be given an opportunity to rebut statements in Department records with which you disagree. Usually the appellant or petitioner, having shown disagreement with the Department action by filing an appeal or petition, presents his case first. Thereafter, the respondent gives his evidence. An opportunity to ask questions of all witnesses and parties and to present additional evidence is then allowed.

Role of the Administrative Law Judge

The administrative law judge may question any party or witness and order into evidence any relevant information in possession of the Department. (Board Rule 5038.) Because of his expertise and his obligation to make certain that all relevant evidence is presented, the administrative law judge takes an active role in developing all the material facts in possession of the parties and their witnesses. He may conduct a large part of the examination of parties as witnesses. This results in a saving of time and cost to the parties and the Board. Any party or his representative may examine his own witnesses or the other party, if desired.

The Admissibility of Evidence

Section 1952 of the Code provides that "The Appeals Board and its representatives and referees are not bound by common law or statutory rules of evidence or by technical or formal rules of procedure but may conduct the hearings and appeals in such manner as to ascertain the substantial rights of the parties."

Appeals Board Rule 5038 provides that all testimony shall be taken only on oath or affirmation or under penalty of perjury. Any relevant evidence shall be admitted if it is the type of evidence on which responsible persons are accustomed to rely in the conduct of serious affairs. During the hearing each party shall have the right to call and examine parties and witnesses; to introduce exhibits; to question opposing parties and witnesses on any matter relevant to the issues even though that matter was not covered in the direct examination; to impeach any witness; and to offer rebuttal evidence. An employer who intends to introduce business records into evidence should have at the hearing a person who can explain how such records were prepared.

You should bring to the hearing all evidence (witnesses and documents) which you believe has a bearing on your case.

Subpoenas for Witnesses and Records

Either before or after a case is set for hearing any party may request the administrative law judge to issue a subpoena for witnesses or records. A request for a subpoena to compel the attendance of a witness must show a need therefor. A request for a subpoena to produce books, papers, memoranda or other records must be by affidavit and describe the matters desired and show the materiality thereof to the issues in the case. Forms are available in all Offices of Appeals and Department field benefits offices. Assistance in preparing the request will be provided if desired.

Obtaining Department Records and Witnesses

Section 1095 of the Code provides that any information in the possession of the Department that is necessary for a worker or an employer to safeguard his rights under the Code must be made available to him. These records may be examined by the parties in the field offices of the Department during normal office hours. Any party may examine the claim records which the Department sent with the appeal prior to the date of hearing by making arrangements with the Office of Appeals. You also can examine Department records on the day of hearing at the place of hearing prior to commencement of your hearing. If any party desires a record of the Department to be presented as evidence in a hearing or needs an employee of the Department as a witness in his case, the administrative law judge will issue a "Notice to Produce" to the Department which will cause it to bring the record or the employee to the hearing.

Contentions and Argument

At the conclusion of the hearing, reasonable time, if requested, will be granted to the parties to make their contentions known by oral argument. If written argument is requested, the parties shall be advised as to the time and manner of filing. (Board Rule 5044.)

After hearing the evidence and listening to oral argument, if any, the administrative law judge closes the hearing and takes the case under submission. However, a hearing may be reopened if an error or omission is called to the attention of the administrative law judge before the decision is issued.

The Decision of the Administrative Law Judge

If no request has been made to reopen a case, the administrative law judge promptly issues a decision. The decision will generally set forth (1) the issues and the facts that were found to be true after evaluating the evidence; (2) the applicable statutory, regulatory, court and Appeals Board legal principles involved, and an application of the legal principles to the facts; and (3) the conclusion and decision concerning the action of the Department.

Copies of the decision are mailed to all parties. Each decision is accompanied by an explanation of further appeal rights. After the decision has been mailed or served, it cannot be changed except to correct clerical errors. It may be reopened by an administrative law judge if one of the parties shows good cause for failure to attend the hearing. (Board Rule 5045.)

*   *   *   *

The most common issues presented in unemployment insurance hearings involve discharges, whether or not discharge is for misconduct, voluntary quits, whether or not the quit was for good cause, whether a claimant is able to work and is available for work, whether a claimant has, without good cause, refused suitable employment or failed to apply for suitable employment, and whether the claimant has made a false statement or withheld information to obtain benefits.

Section 1256 of the California Unemployment Insurance Code (hereinafter "code") contains the provisions dealing with misconduct and voluntary quit. That section provides: "An individual is disqualified for unemployment compensation benefits if the director finds that he left his most recent work voluntarily without good cause or that he has been discharged for misconduct connected with his most recent work.

"An individual is presumed to have been discharged for reasons other than misconduct in connection with his work and not to have voluntarily left his work without good cause unless his employer has given written notice to the contrary to the director within five days after the termination of service, setting forth facts sufficient to overcome the presumption. The presumption provided by this section is rebuttable.

"An individual whose employment is terminated under the compulsory retirement provisions of a collective bargaining agreement to which the employer is a party, shall not be deemed to have left his work without good cause."

The term "most recent work" had not been defined in the law but there was a long-standing administrative interpretation that it meant the work a claimant last performed prior to and nearest to a claim for benefits, including part-time work. *Tomlin v. California Unemployment Insurance Board* (1978) 82 Cal.App.3d 642, held that it was not the last part-time work claimed but the "primary or principal or full-time employment" or "significant or regular employment." The *Tomlin* decision caused confusion. The legislature has added section 1256.3 to the Unemployment Insurance Code defining "most recent work" as that in which a claimant last performed "compensated services" (1) prior to and nearest the date of filing a new, reopened, or additional claim for benefits, or (2) during the calendar week for which a continued claim is filed.

The criteria for determining misconduct is set forth in *Maywood Glass Co. v. Stewart* (1959) 170 Cal.App.2d 719 [339 P.2d 947]. It is held therein that the term "misconduct" is limited to conduct evincing such wilful or wanton disregard of an employer's interest as is found in deliberate violations or disregard of standards of behavior which the employer has the right to expect of his employee, or in carelessness or negligence of such degree or recurrence as to manifest equal culpability, wrongful intent or evil design or to show an intentional and substantial disregard of the employer's interest or of the employee's duties and obligations to his employer. On the other hand, mere inefficiency, unsatisfactory conduct, failure in good performance as the result of inability or incapacity, inadvertencies or ordinary negligence in isolated instances, or good faith errors in judgment or discretion are not deemed "misconduct" within the meaning of the statute. The burden of proof in establishing misconduct is upon the employer.

In a voluntary quit situation, it is held in Precedent Benefit Decision No. P-B-27 that there is good cause for the voluntary leaving of work where the facts disclose a real, substantial, and compelling reason of such nature as would cause a reasonable person genuinely desirous of retaining employment to take similar action.

Evenson v. California Unemployment Insurance Appeals Board (1976) 62 Cal.App.3d 1005 [133 Cal.Rptr. 488], has the following to say about "good cause" (page 1016): "Voluntary termination must be based on serious and exigent circumstances. . . . In general, 'good cause,' as used in an unemployment compensation statute, means such a cause as justifies an employee's voluntarily leaving the ranks of the employed; the quitting must be for such a cause as would, in a similar situation, reasonably motivate the average able-bodied and qualified worker to give up his or her employment with its certain wage rewards in order to enter the ranks of the unemployed. (81 C.J.S., Social Security and Public Welfare, §167, p. 253.)"

Section 1253 of the code deals with able and available and provides: "An unemployed individual is eligible to receive unemployment compensation benefits with respect to any week only if the director finds that: * * *(c) He was able to work and available for work for that week."

Ability to work deals in general with physical or health matters. A person is not entitled to benefits if he is not able to work so that there is no reasonable prospect of obtaining employment.

In Precedent Benefit Decision No. P-B-17, it is held that to be considered available for work a claimant must be ready, willing and able to accept suitable employment in a labor market where there is a demand for his services. However, he is not available for work if through personal preference or force of circumstances he imposes unreasonable restrictions on suitable work, such as limitations on hours, days, shifts or wages, which materially reduce the possibilities of obtaining employment.

A landmark decision was issued by the California Supreme Court on "availability for work" in 1977. *Sanchez v. Unemployment Insurance Appeals Board* (1977) 20 Cal.3d 55 (141 Cal. Rptr. 146), holds that availability does not require that a claimant be willing to accept work which he has good cause to refuse, if a substantial field of employment remains. The burden of proof as to good cause is with the claimant. The burden of proof as to a substantial field of employment is with the Department.

The suitable employment and false statement provisions are contained in section 1257 of the code. That section provides: "An individual is also disqualified for unemployment compensation benefits if:

"(a) He or she willfully, for the purpose of obtaining unemployment compensation benefits, either made a false statement or representation, with actual knowledge or the falsity thereof, or withheld a material fact in order to obtain any unemployment compensation benefits under this division."

"(b) He or she, without good cause, refused to accept suitable employment when offered to him, or failed to apply for suitable employment when notified by a public employment office."

In interpreting former subdivision (a), the Appeals Board, in Precedent Benefit Decision No. P-B-72, had the following to say about the meaning of "wilful" and "material":

"The claimant herein did withhold information with respect to the job offer at the time she filed her continued claim. The question then arises as to whether her failure to inform the Department was wilful. The term wilful has been defined by the Califonria courts as follows:

" 'After indulging in this mental process, if an act is done as the result of it, it is a wilful act.' (*People v. Sheldon* (1886), 68 Cal. 434, 9 P. 457)

" 'To do a thing wilfully is to do it knowingly.' (*People v. Swiggy*, 69 Cal. App. 574, 581, 232 P. 174; 4 Words and Phrases, Second Series, p. 1304; Pen. Code, section 7 subds. 1 and 5; *People v. Calvert* (1928), 93 Cal. App. 569, 269 P. 969)

" ' "Wilful" ordinarily signifies intention, and that, we think, is its signification here. It does not imply any malice or wrong toward the other party.' (*Benkert v. Benkert* (1867), 32 Cal. 467)

. . . .

"As to the materiality of the information withheld, it is our opinion that the application of section 1257(a) is not dependent upon whether the information withheld would have necessarily resulted in ineligibility or disqualification for benefits under other appropriate sections of the code. It is sufficient that the claimant believed, or should have known, that the facts withheld would raise a question as to her entitlement to benefits."

Section 1258 of the code states the meaning of "suitable employment." That section provides: "Suitable employment' means work in the individual's usual occupation or for which he is reasonably fitted, regardless of whether or not it is subject to this division.

"In determining whether the work is work for which the individual is reasonably fitted, the director shall consider the degree of risk involved to the individual's health, safety, and morals, his physical fitness and prior training, his experience and prior earnings, his length of unemployment and prospects for securing local work in his customary occupation, and the distance of the available work from his residence, and such other factors as would influence a reasonably prudent person in the individual's circumstances.''

The foregoing discussion of various issues merely touches the highlights. To thoroughly study and reseach these matters, the following source material should be consulted:

Unemployment Insurance Code.

Deering's Annotated Unemployment Insurance Code.

West's Annotated Unemployment Insurance Code.

Regulations of the Employment Development Department.

Rules of the Appeals Board.

Index Digest of Selected Benefit Decisions.

Index Digest of Precedent Decisions.

The Regulations of the Department and the Rules of the Appeals Board can be found in Title 22 of the California Administrative Code.

For information or assistance, contact any of the Offices of Appeals listed below. Appeals Board interpretations of the law are available during office hours at all Offices of Appeals.

LOS ANGELES OFFICE OF
APPEALS
1300 WEST OLYMPIC BLVD.,
5TH FLOOR
LOS ANGELES, CA 90015
PHONE: (213) 744-2250

INGLEWOOD OFFICE OF
APPEALS
2930 WEST IMPERIAL HWY,
2ND FLOOR
INGLEWOOD, CA 90303
PHONE: (213) 757-3131

VAN NUYS OFFICE OF
APPEALS
14435 SHERMAN WAY,
2ND FLOOR
P.O. BOX 9203
VAN NUYS, CA 91409
PHONE: (213) 781-9100

SAN DIEGO OFFICE OF
APPEALS
6160 MISSION GORGE RD.,
SUITE 210
P.O. BOX 81489
SAN DIEGO, CA 92138
PHONE: (714) 237-7596

SAN FRANCISCO OFFICE OF
APPEALS
745 FRANKLIN ST.,
ROOM 402
P.O. BOX 7667
SAN FRANCISCO, CA 94120
PHONE: (415) 557-3030

OAKLAND OFFICE OF
APPEALS
5850 SHELLMOUND ST.,
1ST FLOOR
EMERYVILLE, CA 94608
PHONE: (415) 464-0695

LONG BEACH OFFICE OF
APPEALS
4140 LONG BEACH BLVD.,
3RD FLOOR
P.O. BOX 550
LONG BEACH, CA 90801
PHONE: (213) 426-2157

UPLAND OFFICE OF APPEALS
600 NORTH MOUNTAIN AVE.,
B-100
P.O. BOX 5002
UPLAND, CA 91786
PHONE: (714) 985-9891

SAN JOSE OFFICE OF
APPEALS
1500 E. HAMILTON AVE.,
SUITE 200
CAMPBELL, CA 95008
PHONE: (408) 277-1561

SACRAMENTO OFFICE OF
APPEALS
2131 S STREET
SACRAMENTO, CA 95816
PHONE: (916) 445-2343

FRESNO OFFICE OF
APPEALS
2550 MARIPOSA STREET,
ROOM 4067
FRESNO, CA 93721
PHONE: (209) 445-5363

Chapter 25

CRIMINAL LAW

Only a comparatively small number of attorneys specialize in "criminal" cases; the bulk of the law practice of most attorneys consists of "civil" law cases. However, any lawyer may be called upon to handle an occasional criminal case, if only when a regular client finds himself charged with a crime.

Representation of those accused of crime — involving as it does their "life, liberty and pursuit of happiness" — is exacting of the attorney's abilities. If an appeal is taken, the burden of the "paper work" and procedure falls on the prosecution, the district attorney's office. Some documents, such as an application for permission to prepare a settled statement, the agreed statement of facts, or subpoenas for witnesses, may need to be prepared. Accuracy of the title of the case, the name of the witness, and the time and place of appearance may be even more vital than in subpoenas in civil cases, since a person's life, or freedom, may hinge upon the testimony of one of the witnesses.

And when the attorney does handle that occasional criminal case, the paralegal aide is apt to be the one who receives the first call from the person under arrest (or his relative or friend). And anyone under arrest is apt to be upset and anxious to be released. The paralegal should be certain to get the name of the person in jail, the name and address of the jail, or the name, relationship and telephone number of the person calling, and also determine at least the basic details, such as the nature of the charge, the time and place of arrest, and whether the arrest was made with or without a warrant.

A person under arrest may be limited in the number of calls he can make or have difficulty in phoning, so do not suggest that he phone back later but make every effort to locate the employer-attorney if he is out of the office at the time of the call, and to assist as much as possible. Presumably the attorney-employer will have previously issued general instructions to cover such an emergency. The attorney will want to see the client as soon as possible after the arrest and vice versa.

Bail

Since the first objective of the person arrested usually is to be set free, he must obtain "bail." "Bail" may be defined as security (money or bond) given by or on behalf of the person in custody as a guarantee that he will appear at all times lawfully required; if he fails to appear the bail is forfeited and a bench warrant may be issued for his arrest.

The amount of the bail on either a felony or misdemeanor charge may be set in the warrant of arrest. If the defendant has appeared before a judge, his bail will have been fixed at that time. However, if the defendant has been arrested on a capital offense and the proof of his guilt is evident or the presumption of his guilt is great, he cannot be admitted to bail. (Pen. Code §1268a.)

A paralegal or legal assistant is well advised to maintain an up-to-date bail schedule for the particular county of his employment, which can be obtained from the clerk of the criminal department, the local county bar association, or a bail bondsman.

The law pertaining to bail generally has been changed. The new law (ch. 873, Stats. 1979) became operative January 1, 1981, and remains in effect until December 31, 1985. The Office of Criminal Justice Planning, in consultation with the State Bar and Judicial Council, will issue a report of the impact of the bill.

A defendant who has been arrested for a misdemeanor may be released from custody upon deposit of 10 percent of the amount of bail fixed (unless the bail is under $150) *and* upon execution of a release agreement *and* an appearance bond. (Pen. Code §1269d.) *In addition or in lieu thereof* (other than a release upon own recognizance) when the court finds it necessary to assure the defendant's appearance in court, the court may require the defendant to agree to any or all of the following conditions: (1) to report at reasonable intervals to a person designated by the court, who shall inform the court if the defendant does not report as ordered; (2) to notify the court if he or she changes his or her place of residence; (3) to secure the permission of the court before leaving the state; (4) to submit the name and address of his or her employer, or any change thereof, to the court. (Pen. Code §1269d.)

The Judicial Council prescribes a uniform statewide release agreement form, bond form, and receipt form.

Defendants arrested or charged with an offense other than a capital offense, may be released on their own "recognizance" without any bail, if the magistrate believes they will surrender to custody. (Pen. Code §1270.) However, such defendants must sign a release agreement as specified in Penal Code section 1318 which includes: (1) defendant's promise to appear at all times and places ordered by the court, (2) defendant's promise not to leave the state without leave of court, (3) agreement to waive extradition if defendant fails to appear and is apprehended outside California; and (4) acknowledgment of information as to consequences and penalties for violation of the conditions of release.

Defendants arrested on out-of-county warrants may likewise be released on their own recognizance unless the court makes a finding upon the record that such release will not reasonably assure the appearance of the defendant as required. (Pen. Code §1270.)

If the defendant does not have sufficient funds to post cash bail, a bail bond is necessary (Pen. Code §1287) and a bail bondsman should be requested to see the person under arrest, immediately.

Crimes are classified as *felonies* (more serious crimes punishable by death or imprisonment in a state prison) or *misdemeanors* (any crime less than a felony, punishable by imprisonment in a county jail, such as petty theft, drunken driving, reckless driving, hit-and-run, assault and battery.) Also, Penal Code section 17 provides that when a crime punishable by a prison sentence is also punishable by a fine or imprisonment in the county jail, in the discretion of the court, it "shall be deemed a misdemeanor under the circumstances specified in Penal Code section 17(b)." This is known as a "wobbler." (See Holland, *"Conviction" Defined*, an article on the importance and significance of sentencing, and the effect of conviction, appearing in 40 State Bar Journal, page 636.)

The following outline of procedure is set forth only to provide the paralegal with a general idea of the basic procedure involved in criminal cases, not as a summary either of the procedure or the law.

Misdemeanors

When the charge is triable in the inferior courts (municipal or justice courts), the "accusatory pleading" is a written complaint. On a misdemeanor charge, the defendant will either have been cited, or arrested and bail arranged; therefore he is not in custody. After the arrest is made, the accused is brought before a magistrate for *arraignment*, his first court appearance.

The defendant must be given a "reasonable time to answer". (Pen. Code §990.) The defendant may either enter a *plea* or a *demurrer*. (Pen. Code §1002 *et seq.*) (No preliminary examination is held on a misdemeanor charge.)

Penal Code section 1016 provides for six different pleas. The defendant may plead guilty, or not guilty and enter one or more of the other permissible pleas.

Penal Code section 1004 sets forth the grounds for demurrer. The demurrer in a criminal case is the same in principle and format as a demurrer in a civil case. (See Demurrers, ch. 5.) Trial will be held in either a municipal or justice court.

If the defendant pleads guilty, the court must appoint a time for pronouncing judgment not less than 6 hours and up to 5 days after the plea of guilty, but the defendant may waive this time requirement and be sentenced at the time of arraignment. (Pen. Code §1449.)

The misdemeanor is handled from beginning to end in the Municipal Court.

Felonies

The "accusatory pleading" in prosecutions for felonies in superior courts is *usually* an *information* filed by the district attorney, but may be an *indictment* (a "true bill") by the grand jury.

1. *Information*

The arrest may be made with a warrant when a complaint has been made which convinces the magistrate that reasonable cause exists that the accused committed the offense. (Pen. Code §§806, 813.) Or an accused may be arrested without a warrant.

Preliminary arraignment

In either case, the accused is brought before a magistrate for *preliminary arraignment*. If the arrest was made without a warrant the accused must be taken before a magistrate for preliminary arraignment "without unnecessary delay" and, in any event, within two days after his arrest, excluding Sundays and holidays (Pen Code §825) and a complaint charging his offense must be filed.

The preliminary arraignment serves to correctly identify the accused; to personally inform the accused in open court of the charge against him and of his right to counsel, and to protect him from unlimited detention before formal proceedings are commenced against him. (Pen. Code §825.)

Defendant may enter any of the pleas provided in Penal Code section 1016 the same as on misdemeanor charges.

If a guilty plea is received, and the magistrate and prosecuting officer consent, a preliminary examination is waived and the defendant certified to the superior court for sentence without trial. But the court cannot accept a plea of guilty unless the offense charged is a felony not punishable with death and unless the defendant is represented by counsel. (Pen Code §859a.) If an indigent criminal is eligible for a Public Defender, the court will appoint a Public Defender. If the defendant, represented by counsel, pleads guilty, he is certified to the superior court for sentencing.

Prehearing Conference

In Sacramento and in almost every California county a prehearing conference (really a pre-preliminary hearing conference) is held where a not guilty plea is entered, where the defendant is not in custody. The purpose is to try to resolve the case without the necessity of trial. Procedure varies from county to county and the legal assistant should check out the procedure in his/her own county.

At the conference plea bargaining may be arranged, that is, the defendant could agree to plead guilty to an offense lesser than the one charged, or to only one of the charged offenses, in return for an agreement that the prosecution will obtain, seek or not oppose a certain disposition. Of course, the plea has to be voluntary and have a factual basis.

While the public is often critical of this process, time and money is saved for the state, and the judicial process does not get hopelessly behind. As a practical matter, without it, the court system would have to be enlarged immeasurably or the cases could not get heard.

Preliminary hearing or examination

If the defendant pleads not guilty, a date is set for the *preliminary examination* (not less than 2 days, excluding Sundays and holidays from the date of setting. (Pen. Code §859b.)

Section 859b of the Penal Code has been amended to give the right to a preliminary examination to the People and to the defendant within 10 court days of the date the defendant is arraigned or pleads, whichever occurs later, and, if the defendant is in custody, the preliminary arraignment cannot be continued beyond 10 court days thereafter unless the defendant personally waives such right.

The *main purpose* of the preliminary examination is the same as that of the grand jury's, to determine whether the charges are supported and whether there is sufficient cause to hold the defendant to answer, before subjecting him to a trial. (Pen. Code § 872.) If the magistrate does so decide, the district attorney has the duty to file in the superior court of the county an *information* against the defendant, within 15 days after the commitment. (Pen. Code §739.)

A defendant may request that the hearing be closed to the public. However, the victim of the crime, particularly the victim of a sexual assault, may be attended by a person of their choice.

If the defendant is held to answer in the superior court, a pretrial conference will be held, and plea bargaining may take place at the pretrial conference.

The indictment

Grand juries are provided for by Penal Code section 888: "A grand jury is a body of the required number of persons . . . sworn to inquire of public offenses committed or triable within the county." Their main duty in modern times is to inquire into the conduct of public officers and institutions. Since their purpose is inquiry and investigation of charges which may prove to be unsupported, the charges are not disclosed, and the deliberations of the grand jury are "secret," or at least as secret as possible, since certain persons necessarily may appear (such as the district attorney or his deputy, special counsel and investigators, a reporter, a judge, witnesses). The accused does not appear, because the grand jury does not function as a court. Prohibitions against disclosure by grand jurors are prescribed by statutes. A grand jury might be used in cases of rape or child molestation.

If the grand jury believes that if all the evidence taken, if unexplained or uncontradicted, would warrant a conviction by a trial jury, the grand jury must find an *indictment* (return a "true bill"). After the indictment is filed, if the accused is not in custody, a bench warrant is issued for his arrest.

After his arrest, the accused is still entitled to a preliminary examination, before arraignment in the superior court. (*Hawkins v. Superior Court* (1978) 22 Cal.3d 584.)

Criminal actions are brought against defendants in the name of the People of the State of California. In the superior courts the People are represented by the district attorney as the prosecutor; if the defendant does not have means for counsel of his own choice, he is entitled to representation by the Public Defender's office or by an attorney appointed by the court.

Motions

There are quite a number of motions which may be made in criminal cases. The forms of the motions are the same as in civil cases (see Motions, *supra*, in Chapter 8, The Trial), and with points and authorities.

Motion to Suppress — "1538.5"

A most important and frequently used motion is the motion to suppress evidence, known as the "1538.5." The theory behind this motion is that the police have illegally obtained certain evidence and therefore the prosecution should not be able to use it.

In the Municipal Court the motion is heard at the hearing. In the Superior Court it is heard prior to the trial unless for some extraordinary reason the defense attorney did not know about the grounds before trial.

Evidence seized after issuance of a search warrant has a presumptive legitimacy. So the defense must prove why it was illegal to seize it. To do this, the defense would attach points and authorities to a motion showing reason why it is illegal.

On the other hand, if there was no warrant, the burden is automatically shifted to the prosecution, who must prove the search was legitimate. The defense then does not have to prove the seizure was illegitimate. The district attorney will usually file points and authorities and the defense will file rebuttal points and authorities. Testimony is taken on the motion to suppress. Most motions can be argued on legal points alone.

Motion to Dismiss

Another common motion is the motion to dismiss pursuant to Penal Code section 995. This motion is exclusive to the superior court.

The defendant in the superior court may have been brought there after a preliminary hearing in the municipal court, or he may have been indicted by the grand jury.

A court reporter is present at both the preliminary examination and a grand jury. The defense attorney can therefore review the transcript and decide the charge is not supported and file a "995" motion.

Trial

The accused is entitled to have a jury trial. Juries for criminal trials are formed in the same manner as juries for civil actions, as provided in Penal Code section 1046.

Any citizen of the United States of 18 years of age or over, who meets the residency requirements of electors of California, is in possession of his/her natural faculties and of ordinary intelligence and not decrepit, and possessed of sufficient knowledge of the English language, may be called upon for jury duty. (Code Civ. Proc. §198.)

Counsel question the prospective jurors selected and may excuse a certain number of persons (the number depending upon the type of case) without giving an excuse or reason. This is called a "*peremptory challenge.*" Other prospective jurors are "*excused for cause.*" Twelve jurors are selected. The process is called "*impaneling*" a jury.

At the beginning of a jury trial each attorney may make an opening statement to the jury, summarizing what is intended to be proven. Testimony is taken and written evidence introduced as plaintiff's exhibits and defendant's exhibits. The exhibits of one party may be designated numerically (Pl. Ex. 1, Pl. Ex. 2, etc.) and the exhibits of the other party by letters. (Def. Ex. A, Def. Ex. B, etc.) During the trial objections may be made by counsel to questions asked. The judge may exclude improper evidence. Closing arguments to the jury are made by counsel. The judge reads the instructions — usually prepared by counsel — to the jury. They are checked "given" or "given as modified." Some instructions may be "refused" by the judge. (See Jury Instructions, ch. 6, The Trial.) The judge may advise the jury to acquit, but the jury is not bound by the advice. (Pen. Code §1118.) After receiving its instructions, the jury "retires" for deliberations. In California, a three-fourths vote is needed for a decision in a civil case; in a criminal case the verdict must be unanimous.

Sentencing

Concurrent and consecutive sentences: An individual convicted of more than one crime will be sentenced for each crime. If his sentences for both crimes run *concurrently*, he will be serving time for both crimes at the same time. If they run *consecutively*, he will serve out one sentence, and then the second, and so on. The judge makes the decision as to how the sentences shall run, subject to the statutory law.

For example, under Penal Code section 669 as it now reads, any defendant committed to prison on a life sentence which is ordered to run consecutive to any determinate term of imprisonment imposed under the sections enumerated therein, will serve the determinate term of imprisonment first and without credit toward the person's eligibility for parole.

APPEALS — CRIMINAL CASES

(Rules 30-45, California Rules of Court)

Appeals from the superior courts in criminal cases may be taken by the defendant as provided in Penal Code sections 1237 and 1237.5 and, by the People, in Penal Code section 1238. (See Penal Code section 1466 for cases in which appeals from inferior courts to superiors courts may be taken in criminal proceedings.)

If the defendant's case is appealed, the People are represented by the Attorney General's office and the defendant appears either (1) by his own privately paid counsel, (2) in his own behalf (in propria persona), or (3) by court-appointed counsel paid by the court.

The rules governing appeals in civil cases are applicable to appeals in criminal cases, except where other express provision is made. (See Rules 30-45, Cal. Rules of Court.) Those provisions are summarized here as follows:

Notice of appeal

In a criminal case the defendant files a written notice of appeal with the clerk of the superior court within 60 days after the rendition of the judgment or the making of the order. (See Rule 31, Cal. Rules of Court.)

If the judgment of conviction was entered upon a plea of guilty or *nolo contendere,* see Rule 31(d), Cal. Rules of Court, for requirements on appeal.

Notification re appeal

Clerk of superior court forthwith mails a photocopy to the clerk of the reviewing court and a notification of the filing of the notice of appeal to each party other than the appellant. (Rule 31(c), Cal. Rules of Court.)

Stay of execution of judgment of conviction

Application for a stay of execution of a judgment of conviction must first be made to the superior court. (See Rule 32(a), Cal. Rules of Court.)

Bail

Application for bail or reduction of bail must likewise first be made to the superior court. (See Rule 32(b), Cal. Rules of Court.)

Automatic appeal on judgment of death

The record on appeal contains the entire record of the action. (Rule 33(c), Cal. Rules of Court.)

Clerk's Transcript

The clerk's transcript (original and 2 copies) is prepared upon the filing of the notice of appeal. When a judgment of death has been rendered, an additional copy is prepared for the district attorney and each defendant. (Rule 35(a), Cal. Rules of Court.)

Reporter's Transcript

Where a reporter's transcript is required, the clerk notifies the reporter immediately upon filing of the notice of appeal. Within 20 days thereafter the reporter is required to deliver to the clerk the required number of copies (same number as are required for the clerk's transcript), unless the time is extended pursuant to subdivision (d) of rule 35. (Upon affidavit showing good cause, the reviewing court may extend the time up to 60 days. See Rule 35, subdivision (c).)

Briefs

Time requirements for filing of briefs in the reviewing court are the same as in civil cases, except that time for filing a brief may not be extended by stipulation of parties. (See chapter 10 on Appeals — Civil.)

The time for filing briefs — civil or criminal — will not be extended by the court for good cause. In determining good cause, "only circumstances related to the case (e.g., settlement negotiations, pendency of related litigation, or extraordinarily voluminous record) or to counsel personally (e.g., illness or other unpredictable emergency) will be considered. Vacation schedules or the press of other work are not good cause."

Briefs may by typed or printed, at the option of the party. (Rule 37(b), Cal. Rules of Court.)

The number of copies required is the same as in civil cases. (See Appeals — Civil, chapter 10.)

Every brief of the defendant must be served on both the district attorney and the Attorney General and a copy delivered to the county clerk for the judge who presided at the trial in the superior court. Proof of such service must be made before the brief may be filed.

The respondent's brief is filed by the Attorney General's office and a copy is served on the appellant. The respondent's brief is likewise served on the district attorney and a copy sent to the county clerk for delivery to the judge who presided at the trial, prior to the filing of the brief, and proof of such service must be included with the brief.

Habeas Corpus — Bail

A helpful booklet entitled "Internal Operating Practices and Procedures" (Aug. 1979) which covers all the California Courts of Appeal may be obtained from the Administrative Office of the Courts, State Building, 3d Floor, 350 McAllister St., San Francisco, California 94102, without charge. The following is quoted from the Internal Operating Practices for San Francisco. The legal assistant should check the procedure in the Court of Appeal in which the action is filed.

1. *Habeas Corpus*

Many petitions for writs of habeas corpus are denied without being calendared for oral argument. If the petition fails to state a prima facie case for relief, it is summarily denied. If it contains allegations setting forth prima facie grounds for relief and documentation is available, but not included with the petition, the court is empowered to obtain information concerning any matter of record pertaining to the case by ordering the custodian of the record to produce the same, or a certified copy thereof, to be filed with the clerk of the court. (Cal. Rules of Court, rule 60.)

Matters of record may conclusively refute allegations contained in a petition and result in the denial of the petition. Also, points and authorities in opposition to a petition may be requested from a custodial officer before any ruling on the petition. In a proper case, bail may be allowed pending disposition of the petition.

When it appears that a prima facie case for relief has been made and no factual issue is presented, it is the practice of the Court of Appeal to order the custodial officer to show cause why the relief prayed for should not be granted. The return of the custodial officer to the order to show cause may be followed by the filing of a traverse to the return, and oral argument, unless argument is waived. The matter is then submitted for decision and decided in due course by a written opinion.

In instances where a prima facie case for relief has been made out, but a factual issue exists, the court will usually issue a writ of habeas corpus, returnable before a superior court judge sitting in the appellate district, or appoint a referee to conduct a hearing and make findings on the factual issues. If the latter procedure is followed, the referee submits his report to the court, and his findings will be adopted as the findings of the court or rejected. Depending upon the findings of the referee, the court may deny the petition, issue an order to show cause, or issue a writ.

2. *Bail on Appeal*

Bail on appeal is rarely granted by the reviewing court. Any application to a Court of Appeal must be accompanied by proof of service upon the prosecutor and the Attorney General, and include a showing that a proper application for bail or a reduction of bail was made to the superior court and that the court unjustifiably denied the application. (Cal. Rules of Court, rule 32(b).) Applications to the appellate court should be limited to situations where it can be established that the trial court abused its discretion when it denied bail or fixed excessive bail, or where the trial court could have allowed bail in an exercise of its discretion, but declined to exercise its discretion. If the trial court has failed to exercise discretionary power to grant or deny bail on appeal, the Court of Appeal will direct the trial court to exercise discretion. If it determines that the trial court has abused its discretion by denying bail or by fixing bail in an excessive amount, the Court of Appeal may fix bail at a reasonable amount, to be deposited with the trial court.

3. *Writs of Prohibition and Mandate*

Counsel should always forward a copy of the preliminary or grand jury transcript with any petition for a writ pursuant to section 999a of the Penal Code.

* * * *

Paralegal Functions

While, except on appeal, criminal cases do not involve all the paper work of civil cases, the paralegal can be helpful — and influential — in a criminal case.

Before the attorney conducts his *voir dire* examination of the jurors, the legal assistant can do much by way of investigation of the prospective jurors. The attorney tries to pick jurors who will hopefully be more favorable to his case. The more he can learn about them, the better educated his judgment is. The paralegal can learn much by telephone or other means without questioning the jurors' friends or neighbors, which would alert the jurors that inquiries were being made and might make them hostile.

The paralegal can also assist in scheduling and briefing the witnesses, who may have to wait before being called to the stand. The legal assistant should attempt to schedule the witnesses to avoid inconveniencing them and wasting their time. Any unavoidable delay should be explained and prepared for (where possible).

The legal assistants will let witnesses know what is going on in the trial and brief them as to any problems developing at the trial. The witness is more apt to be cooperative if he understands the significance of his or her testimony, and how it meshes into the whole picture.

The legal assistant should see to it that each witness presents a proper appearance, or at least avoids extremes. The witness should answer "Yes" or "No" and not go into a long dissertation, except that he may ask the judge for permission to explain if he feels a "Yes" or "No" answer does not permit him to answer truthfully. Neither should he guess, or try to figure out the helpful answer. If he is uncertain of his recollection, he can precede an answer with a statement such as "To the best of my memory," or "As I recall." The witness should be instructed not to answer if either attorney objects to a question until the judge rules on the objection.

Legal assistant with social welfare background (Master Social Work) specializing in criminal law have found roles combining social work and criminal law. They interview the criminal and may make recommendations as alternatives to incarceration, showing why it is not the best policy to send them to jail. Arguments are made for diversion out of the criminal justice system to the mental health system where appropriate.

These paralegals have also done legal research on issues such as parole and sentencing. They thereby develop an expertise in sentencing, rather than the expertise of the attorney in pleas. A whole range of sentencing can be brought into play, as to misdemeanors, felonies, prior records. They can often work with the probation officer, who may join in their recommendation, which is preferable.

The legal assistant can also be useful at a bail reduction hearing, in verifying needed information.

A pilot program substituting paralegals for deputy public defenders in several courts was recently instituted in Los Angeles County, and is viewed as the first step toward developing a paralegal career ladder in county service.

Tasks listed as appropriate for a paralegal in felony arraignments are "bail review hearings, assisting clients in preparing information for parole hearings, and coordination of cases set for preliminary hearings in the various divisions of Municipal Court . . ." (Los Angeles Daily Journal, Aug. 17, 1981.)

In criminal law proceedings the paralegal may encounter the following abbreviations:

aka	also known as
a.d.w.	assault with a deadly weapon
arrgt.	arraignment
b/w	bench warrant
burg.	burglary
C.Y.A.	California Youth Authority
forg.	forgery
g.t.	grand theft
h.c.	habeas corpus
H. & S. Code	Health and Safety Code
indict.	indictment
misd.	misdemeanor
o.r.	on recognizance
p. & s.	probation and sentence
t/w	time waived

CALIFORNIA PARALEGAL'S GUIDE

Chapter 26

ETHICS FOR LEGAL ASSISTANTS

"The longing for justice is men's eternal longing for happiness.
It is happiness that man cannot find as an isolated individual
and hence seeks in society. Justice is social happiness."
                    Kelsen, General Theory of Law and State.

A basic tenet of the law in our free and democratic society is
protection of individual rights and respect for the dignity of the individual.

Our lawyers are the guardians of that law. "[I]n the critical periods
of history the members of [the legal] profession have stood for the
protection of individual liberties . . . . By oath sworn and tradition
inherited, the lawyer assumes a major responsibility for the ends of
the society in which he lives. These are commonly called justice, truth,
honor, and integrity."*

To fulfill their role they must understand their function and maintain
the highest standards of ethical conduct. To this end the American Bar
Association promulgated standards of professional conduct in its Code
of Professional Responsibility. The State Bar of California has established Rules of Professional Conduct for its members. These ethics are
the compass of the legal profession. Breaches of these rules are punishable as provided by law, but "in the last analysis it is the desire
for the respect and confidence of the members of his profession and
of the society which he serves that should provide to a lawyer the
incentive for the highest possible degree of ethical conduct"° And with
the maintenance of the highest personal and professional integrity is
attained "the greatest treasure of all — a clear conscience, and with
it the sure and certain knowledge deep within you that among the

---

*Stone, Handbook of Law Study (Little, Brown & Co.) pp. 156, 157.
°Preamble, American Bar Association Code of Professional Responsibility.

vicissitudes of your busy personal and professional life you are an honest man.''**

The lawyer's ethical conduct commands the respect of the legal assistant for the lawyer and his chosen profession. And the legal assistant — as well as anyone else working within the legal profession — should be imbued with a high regard for the law, and should seek to promote respect for that law, that it may be effective and survive.

*   *   *

Ethics for the Paralegal or Legal Assistant

Guided by the lengthy problems and discussions of ethics by attorneys and their Codes, especially in the work of state bar associations and the American Bar Association, the National Association of Legal Assistants, Inc., adopted the following Code of Ethics and Professional Responsibility on May 1, 1975:

Code of Ethics and Professional Responsibility of National Association of Legal Assistants, Inc.

Preamble

It is the responsibility of every legal assistant to adhere strictly to the accepted standards of legal ethics and to live by general principles of proper conduct. The performance of the duties of the legal assistant shall be governed by specific canons as defined herein in order that justice will be served and the goals of the profession attained.

The canons of ethics set forth hereafter are adopted by the National Association of Legal Assistants, Inc., as a general guide, and the enumeration of these rules does not mean there are not others of equal importance although not specifically mentioned.

Canon 1. A legal assistant shall not perform any of the duties that lawyers only may perform nor do things that lawyers themselves may not do.

Canon 2. A legal assistant may perform any task delegated and supervised by a lawyer so long as the lawyer is responsible to the client, maintains a direct relationship with the client, and assumes full professional responsibility for the work product.

Canon 3. A legal assistant shall not engage in the practice of law by giving legal advice, appearing in court, setting fees, or accepting cases.

**From speech by Frank K. Richardson, Associate Justice, Supreme Court of California

Canon 4. A legal assistant shall not act in matters involving professional legal judgment as the services of a lawyer are essential in the public interest whenever the exercise of such judgment is required.

Canon 5. A legal assistant must act prudently in determining the extent to which a client may be assisted without the presence of a lawyer.

Canon 6. A legal assistant shall not engage in the unauthorized practice of law and shall assist in preventing the unauthorized practice of law.

Canon 7. A legal assistant must protect the confidences of a client, and it shall be unethical for a legal assistant to violate any statute now in effect or hereafter to be enacted controlling privileged communications.

Canon 8. It is the obligation of the legal assistant to avoid conduct which would cause the lawyer to be unethical or even appear to be unethical, and loyalty to the employer is incumbent upon the legal assistant.

Canon 9. A legal assistant shall work continually to maintain integrity and a high degree of competency throughout the legal profession.

Canon 10. A legal assistant shall strive for perfection through education in order to better assist the legal profession in fulfilling its duty of making legal services available to clients and the public.

Canon 11. A legal assistant shall do all other things incidental, necessary, or expedient for the attainment of the ethics and responsibilities imposed by statute or rule of court.

Canon 12. A legal assistant is governed by the American Bar Association Code of Professional Responsibility.

*   *   *

Affirmation of Responsibility

The National Federation of Paralegal Associations had adopted an "Affirmation of Responsibility," which is the code of ethics for its members. The "Affirmation" sets forth self-regulating guidelines for paralegals in the delivery of legal services, and affirms their responsibility to the public, and their dedication to the development of the paralegal profession. The "Affirmation" is printed here in its entirety, with the permission of the National Federation of Paralegal Associations:

"PREAMBLE
The National Federation of Paralegal Associations recognizes and accepts its commitment to the realization of the most basic right of a free society, equal justice under the law.

In examining contemporary legal institutions and systems, the members of the paralegal profession recognize that a redefinition of the traditional delivery of legal services is essential in order to meet the needs of the general public. The paralegal profession is committed to increasing the availability and quality of legal services.

The National Federation of Paralegal Associations has adopted this Affirmation of Professional Responsibility to delineate the principals of purpose and conduct toward which paralegals should aspire. Through this Affirmation, the National Federation of Paralegal Associations places upon each paralegal the responsibility to adhere to these standards and encourages dedication to the development of the profession.

I.   PROFESSIONAL RESPONSIBILITY

A paralegal shall demonstrate initiative in performing and expanding the paralegal role in the delivery of legal services within the parameters of the unauthorized practice of law statutes.

Discussion: Recognizing the professional and legal responsibility to abide by the unauthorized practice of law statutes, the Federation supports and encourages new interpretations as to what constitutes the practice of law.

II.   PROFESSIONAL CONDUCT

A paralegal shall maintain the highest standards of ethical conduct.

Discussion: It is the responsibility of a paralegal to avoid conduct which is unethical or appears to be unethical. Ethical principles are aspirational in character and embody the fundamental rules of conduct by which every paralegal should abide. Observance of these standards is essential to uphold respect for the legal system.

III.   COMPETENCE AND INTEGRITY

A paralegal shall maintain a high level of competence and shall contribute to the integrity of the paralegal profession.

Discussion: The integrity of the paralegal profession is predicated upon individual competence. Professional competence is each paralegal's responsibility and is achieved through continuing education, awareness of developments in the field of law and aspiring to the highest standards of personal performance.

IV.   CLIENT CONFIDENCES

A paralegal shall preserve client confidences and privileged communications.

Discussion: Confidential information and privileged communications are a vital part of the attorney, paralegal and client relationship. The importance of preserving confidential and privileged information is understood to be an uncompromising obligation of every paralegal.

V. SUPPORT OF PUBLIC INTERESTS

A paralegal shall serve the public interests by contributing to the availability and delivery of quality legal services.

Discussion: It is the responsibility of each paralegal to promote the development and implementation of programs that address the legal needs of the public. A paralegal shall strive to maintain a sensitivity to public needs and to educate the public as to the services that paralegals may render.

VI. PROFESSIONAL DEVELOPMENT

A paralegal shall promote the development of the paralegal profession.

Discussion: This Affirmation of Professional Responsibility promulgates a positive attitude through which a paralegal may recognize the importance, responsibility and potential of the paralegal contribution to the delivery of legal services. Participation in professional associations enhances the ability of the individual paralegal to contribute to the quality and growth of the paralegal profession.

* * *

American Bar Association Code of Professional Responsibility

Inasmuch as a paralegal must reflect the high standards of the attorney who is the employer, a brief look at the Code of Professional Responsibility of the American Bar Association points up some of the possible problem areas of ethics. Comments are based on details of the Code. (A complete replacement of the ABA Code of Professional Responsibility is under consideration at this writing.)

Canon 1. A lawyer should assist in maintaining the integrity and competence of the legal profession. Comment: Every person in our society should have ready access to the services of a lawyer and be protected from those who are not qualified to be lawyers. A lawyer (and paralegals) should maintain high standards and encourage fellow professionals to do likewise. (NALA Canon, 7, 9; NFPA ¶s Aff. I, III.)

Canon 2. A lawyer should assist the legal profession in fulfilling its duty to make legal counsel available. Comment: Important functions of the legal profession are to educate laymen to recognize their problems, to facilitate the process of the intelligent selection of lawyers, and to assist in making legal services fully available. Educational programs, lectures and civic programs should be encouraged for lawyers, but one who participates should shun personal publicity. (NFPA Aff. ¶ V.)

It is well to keep up with changes in this Canon as the Bar is changing its views on advertising. A paralegal may become involved in preparation of such material and should consult the latest ruling of the Bar association.

Canon 3. A lawyer should assist in preventing the unauthorized practice of law. Comment: A lawyer delegates tasks to paralegals, secretaries, clerks, and others. Such delegation is proper if the lawyer maintains a direct relationship with his client, supervises the delegated work and has complete professional responsibility for the work product. (See NALA Canons 3, 6; NFPA Aff. ¶ I.)

Canon 4. A lawyer should preserve the confidences and secrets of a client. Comment: "Both social amenities and professional duty should cause a lawyer [and, needless to say, legal assistants] to shun indiscreet conversations concerning clients."

Clients come to attorneys to be served in their deepest needs and troubles. It is as important that the client inform his attorney as to all the pertinent facts, as it is important that a patient tell a doctor of all his pains and symptoms. The client therefore often discloses much personal information, relying on the attorney to hold this information confidential. The lawyer may not violate the confidence so reposed in him. Under the lawyer-client privilege he cannot be compelled to divulge such information. The lawyer himself, or through an employee, may reveal such confidences only with the consent of the client and after full disclosure to the client, with the exceptions provided in Disciplinary Rule 4-101.

It is common knowledge that much confidential information from clients is a matter of written record within the file and necessarily exposed to employees including of course legal assistants. Obviously the attorney must depend upon his employees to keep this information confidential.

The foundation of sound personal relationships, and societal institutions, is mutual trust. If clients were to lose faith in attorneys to keep their confidences, if attorneys could not depend upon their employees not to reveal what they should not, then the framework of the legal profession, and of the legal order, would indeed be threatened. (See also, Disciplinary Rules 4-101, NALA Canon 7; NFPA Aff. ¶ IV.)

Canon 5. A lawyer should exercise independent professional judgment on behalf of a client. Comment: A legal assistant must deal with the same kind of questions such as interest in property in which a firm's client has an interest, and suggestions of gifts from a client. "If a client voluntarily offers to make a gift to his lawyer [or legal assistant], the lawyer may accept the gift, but before doing so, he should urge that his client secure disinterested advice. . . ." (NALA Canon 4.)

Canon 6. A lawyer should represent a client competently. Comment: Applying also to the paralegal or legal assistant, a lawyer should keep abreast of current legal literature, participating in continuing education programs, and careful training of younger associates. He should not accept employment in any area of the law in which he is not qualified, except that he may accept it in good faith of becoming qualified with proper study. (See NALA Canon 9; NPPA Aff. ¶ III.)

Canon 7. A lawyer should represent a client zealously within the bounds of the law. Comment: The legal profession, of which the legal assistant is part of the "team," has a duty to assist the public to secure and protect legal rights and benefits. "[E]ach member of our society is entitled to have his conduct judged and regulated in accordance with the law; to seek any lawful objective through legally permissible means; and to present for adjudication any lawful claim, issue, or defense." (See NALA Canons 2, 5 and 8.)

Canon 8. A lawyer should assist in improving the legal system. Comment: The fair administration of justice requires the availability of competent lawyers, according to the ABA Canon 8 — EC 8-3. As a member of the legal team, the legal assistant can, by fulfilling his or her responsibilities, take part in this fair administration of justice. The latter, following the admonitions to the attorneys, should also "participate in proposing and supporting legislation and programs to improve the system . . ." (See NALA Canon 10; NFPA Aff. ¶ II.)

Canon 9. A lawyer should avoid even the appearance of professional impropriety. Comment: An important admonition to remember applies to both the lawyer and his paralegal employee: "When explicit ethical guidance does not exist, a lawyer should determine his conduct by acting in a manner that promotes public confidence in the integrity . . . of the legal system. . . ." (See NALA Canons 8 and 11.)

State of California Rules of Professional Conduct

The State Bar Association of California has developed Rules of Professional Conduct approved by the California Supreme Court. The substance of the Rules is similar to that of the American Bar Association. California attorneys who are not members of the ABA are not bound by the ABA Code of Professional Responsibility but by their own Rules; the attorneys of each state are bound by the ethical codes of their own state bar associations.

Similarly, each state may enact its own law — but not in conflict with federal law. Neither California, nor any other state to date to the writer's knowledge, has enacted any legislation governing paralegals. Some State Bars have adopted guidelines for paralegals. The Supreme Court of Kentucky adopted a Paralegal Code governing lawyers who employ paralegals effective January 1, 1980. New York's State Bar in June 1976 adopted "Guidelines for the Utilization by Lawyers of the Services of Legal Assistants." Some of the other states have adopted similar guidelines. (See Legal Assistants Update '80, published by the American Bar Association, 1155 East 60th St., Chicago, Ill. 60637.) The California State Bar has not set up any such guidelines.

Therefore the California paralegal looks to the California Rules of Professional Conduct, the Business and Professions Code, the ABA Canons of Ethics, and codes of ethics of paralegal associations, for some guidelines to function. The California paralegal acts only under the supervision of an active member of the State Bar. The adequacy of that supervision is left to the attorney's professional responsibility and competence, and ultimately, if need be, to State Bar disciplinary bodies and the courts.

Every legal assistant should be thoroughly familiar with the California State Bar Act (Bus. & Prof. Code §§6000-6206) and Rules of Professional Conduct. The legal assistant is the agent of the attorney and his or her acts reflect upon the attorney and can cause the attorney to be in violation of the State Bar Act or Rules of Professional Conduct and subject to disciplinary action, or an action for malpractice. In short, an attorney could lose his license, or have it suspended, as a result of a legal assistant's act, or failure to act. For, as explained above it is the attorney who is charged with the ultimate responsibility. (This is aside from considerations of unauthorized practice of law where paralegals are directly held to account. Rule 3-101, *infra*.)

This is not to say that the blame for all disciplinary actions or malpractice suits can be traced to the legal assistant, but to say that the legal assistant who acts knowledgably, responsibly and conscientiously can and should afford the busy attorney a goodly measure of protection.

Today's attorney lives in an era when the practice of law is increasingly demanding. Both procedural and substantive law are more complex. At the same time the general public, including the lawyer's own clients, are cause-conscious. The days of stigma at being involved in litigation are fast disappearing, if not gone.

Consequently, the legal assistant must be more aware. Important changes in the rules listed have been made, and standards issued, which are set out below, as well as inclusion of some of the other rules which might involve the legal assistant, and some new rules.

Rule 2-101. Professional Employment.   (This rule is prospective and does not apply to alleged violations of the Rules in effect prior to January 1, 1975.)

Under the new rule an attorney may seek professional employment from a former, present or potential client "by any means consistent with these rules." An attorney may respond to inquiries from potential clients.

Rule 2-101(A) defines "communication" as "a message concerning the availability for professional employment of a member or a member's firm." An attorney may advertise his availability for professional employment but such "communication" of his availability shall not contain any untrue statement or any matter, "or present or arrange any matter in a manner or format, which is false, deceptive, or which tends to confuse, deceive or mislead the public;" or omit facts necessary to prevent misleading the public.

No such communication may be transmitted by an attorney *or his agent* in person or by telephone to a potential client and must not be "transmitted in any manner which involves intrusion, coercion, duress, compulsion, intimidation, threats or vexatious or harassing conduct."

Under this new rule communications made by written or electronic media must be retained for one year and, upon request, made available to the State Bar.

The State Bar Act (Bus. & Prof. Code §6152) makes it unlawful for an "agent, runner or capper" (defined in Bus. & Prof. Code §6151) to solicit any business "in and about the state prisons, county jails, city jails, city prisons, or other places of detention of persons, city receiving hospitals, city and county receiving hospitals, county hospitals, justice courts, municipal courts, superior courts, or in any public institution or in any public place or upon any public street or highway or in and about private hospitals, sanitariums or in and about any private institution or upon private property of any character whatsoever."

Nor may an attorney accept employment offered or obtained through the acts of an "agent, runner or capper" which if performed by a member of the State Bar, would be in violation of paragraphs (A) and (B) of Rule 2-101.

The Board of Governors of the State Bar adopted standards pursuant to Rule 201(D) as to the communications which will be presumed to violate (A) or (B), to wit: "(1) A 'communication' which contains guarantees, warranties or predictions regarding the result of legal action is presumed to violate Rule 2-101, Rules of Professional Conduct.

"(2) A 'communication' which contains testimonials about or endorsements of a member is presumed to violate Rule 2-101, Rules of Professional Conduct.

"(3) A 'communication' which is delivered in person or by telephone to a potential client who is in such a physical, emotional or mental state that he or she would not be expected to exercise reasonable judgment as to the retention of counsel, is presumed to violate Rule 2-101, Rules of Professional Conduct.

"(4) A 'communication' which is transmitted at the scene of an accident or at or en route to a hospital, emergency care center or other health care facility is presumed to violate Rule 2-101, Rules of Professional Conduct."

The leading case on attorney advertising is *Bates v. State Bar of Arizona* (1977) 97 S.Ct. 2691, and its reading by the legal assistant is recommended. The *Bates* case held that an advertisement publicizing attorneys' "legal clinic" and claiming that such attorneys offered services at "very reasonable" prices was not misleading and fell within the scope of First Amendment protection. The court states (page 2703): "The only services that lend themselves to advertising are the routine ones, the uncontested divorce, the simple adoption, the uncontended personal bankruptcy, the change of name, and the like — the very services advertised by appellants. Although the precise service demanded in each task may vary slightly, and although legal services are not fungible, these facts do not make advertising misleading so long as the attorney does the necessary work at the advertised price."

New *Rule 2-102* permits participation in group, prepaid and voluntary legal services organizations, programs and activities, as well as in a lawyer referral service conforming to specified Minimum Standards for such services.

Splitting of fees between attorneys for merely referring a client is unethical. (*Altschul v. Sayble* (1978) 83 Cal.App.3d 153.)

Rule 2-103, Professional Notices, Letterheads, Offices and Law Lists and *Rule 2-104, Recommendation of Professional Employment*, have been repealed, effective April 1, 1979.

It would not seem to be in violation of the California Rules for a law firm to *identify* an employee such as a paralegal, office manager, librarian or investigator by name and title on letterhead or card, so long as there was nothing false or misleading.

In this connection, the American Bar Association's Commission on Ethics and Professional Responsibility issued Informal Opinion 1185 (Legal Assistant on Business Card) on May 31, 1979, and is set forth in part:

"You have inquired whether it is ethically proper to designate a paralegal employee, whose duties consist of interviewing witnesses, obtaining copies of hospital records, court records and other contacts outside the office, as a 'Legal Assistant' on a business card. It is the opinion of the Committee that this would be proper, assuming that the duties which are performed by the individual are those which can

properly be performed by a layman under the direction of a lawyer.
* * * Formal Opinion 316 is to the same effect.

"Informal Opinion 909 permits the designation on a business card
of an employee of a law firm who does investigation work for that
firm as an 'Investigator.' By the same reasoning, it would appear to
be proper to designate a legal assistant on such a business card, provided that the designation is accurate, and the duties involved are
properly performed under the direction of the lawyer. In this connection, all of the strictures set forth at some length in Informal Opinion
909 in regard to investigators would be equally applicable to Legal
Assistants."

Rule 2-107(B) lists the facts for determining reasonableness of fees.

Rule 3-101. Aiding Unauthorized Practice of Law. Section (A)
of this rule provides: "A member of the State Bar shall not aid any
person, association, or corporation in the unauthorized practice of
law."

Business and Professions Code section 6125, *et seq.*, proscribe the
unlawful practice of law; section 6126 states that *any person* advertising
himself as practicing or entitled to practice law *or otherwise practicing
law* who is not an active member of the State Bar is guilty of a
misdemeanor.

From the above we see that not only is the attorney who *aids* any
person in the unauthorized practice of law subject to disciplinary action,
censure or suspension under Rule 3-101, but the paralegal himself/
herself who is found guilty under section 6126 of practicing law is
guilty of a misdemeanor. (And can be given a county jail sentence up
to 6 months or a fine up to $500, or both (Pen. Code §19)). Obviously
no paralegal would deliberately subject himself/herself to the possibility of such penalties.

What acts, then, constitute unauthorized practice of law? That is
the question.

ABA Ethical Consideration 3-5 provides in part: "It is neither
necessary nor desirable to attempt the formulation of a single, specific
definition of what constitutes the practice of law." The writer would
agree with this. Chaos could result.

Most of the many tasks of the paralegal do not come into conflict
with rules of ethics and professional behavior. That a paralegal cannot
represent a litigant in a court trial seems clear enough. That a paralegal
cannot give advice to clients seems clear enough (or fairly clear).
Paralegals constantly have to guard against giving legal advice. Clients
sometimes press hard for answers that, if given, could constitute legal
advice, or be so construed. The line between advice and information
is often very fine, indeed. Diplomacy and caution are required.

But there are some gray areas, and emergency situations arise. The attorney cannot always be reached for consultation and the paralegal is required to act. To quote an old bromide, he/she must then "use common sense where good judgment permits it." Some situations just can *not* wait. The paralegal treads a veritable mine field at times.

A footnote to EC 3-5 quoted above reads: "What constitutes unauthorized practice of the law in a particular jurisdiction is a matter for determination by the courts of that jurisdiction," and contains a reference to ABA Opinion 198 (1939).

Rule 3-102 Financial Arrangements with Non-lawyers. Comment: An attorney may not, directly or indirectly, share legal fees except with another attorney and as provided in Rule 3-102. In other words, he may not enter into an agreement with a lay person — including a legal assistant — to split the fees in a case. (See Canon 3, Disciplinary Rule 3-102.)

Paragraphs (B) and (C), the substance of which was found in other prior rules, have been added to Rule 3-102. In brief, a member of the State Bar may not compensate or give or promise anything of value to secure employment for the member or a firm's member by a client, or as a reward. Nor may an attorney compensate, or give or promise anything to the press, radio, television or other communication medium in anticipation of or in return for publicity — except that incidental provision of food or beverages is not itself a violation.

Rule 5-102. Avoiding the Representation of Adverse Interests.

An attorney should not attempt to represent parties whose interests are adverse. (See *Briggs Estate* (1956) 139 Cal.App.2d 802.) This situation sometimes comes about when an attorney has been representing two persons jointly, as a husband and wife who then decide to file for dissolution. Both parties may request him to represent each of them in the dissolution proceeding, perhaps in the hope of reducing attorney fees, or perhaps they are in agreement as to division of property, child custody, etc. This dual representation is at best unwise. At the point when one party becomes dissatisfied, possibly because the other party has not lived up to their agreement, or other reason, problems begin, with additional expense, maybe an appeal, and quite possibly a claim of inadequate representation because of dual representation.

New *Rule 5-105. Communication of Written Settlement Offer*, is set forth in full: "A member of the State Bar shall promptly communicate to the member's client all amounts, terms and conditions of any written offer of settlement made by or on behalf of an opposing party. As used in this rule, 'client' includes a person employing the member of the State Bar who possesses the authority to accept an offer of settlement, or, in a class action, who is a representative of the class.''

Rule 6-101. Failure to Act Competently.

The State Bar Act does not specify either negligence or gross negligence as grounds for discipline. However, cases have held that negligence or inattention may amount to an "act involving moral turpitude, dishonesty or corruption" proscribed by section 6106 of the act. (See cases annotated 7 Cal.Jur.2d, Attorneys at Law, §53, fns. 54, 55.)

Causes for discipline have included acceptance of fees for which little if any services were rendered; misinforming clients as to progress made in their cases; using for private purposes money advanced by clients for court costs.

In *Glenn v. State Bar* (1919) 14 Cal.2d 318, the court held that the practice of having a client sign a blank form of verification before preparation of the pleading was reprehensible.

In one Wisconsin case a court entertained disciplinary proceedings based upon an attorney's naming himself or his associate as the executor, or as the attorney for executor, in a will drafted by him. It has been held permissible for a lawyer to "insert in a will a provision appointing himself as executor, or directing the executor to employ him as counsel for the estate, where the testator is entirely competent, the attorney-client relationship is a longstanding one, and the suggestion to name the attorney originates with the testator." (Annot. 57 A.L.R.3d at p. 704.)

The attorney should be careful not to misrepresent to his client; the legal assistant should do likewise. At the outset of a case promises of success should not be made, regardless of how favorable the case appears to be. Care should be taken not to mislead the client.

Agreements with clients should be in writing and worded with care.

One area in which the legal assistant can promote good public relations between the bar and the general public is in *keeping clients informed*. Clients should be promptly advised of developments in their cases. Unexpected delays should be explained to them. Their letters and questions should be responded to with alacrity. Correct information should be given.

Probate is one field giving rise to claims of delay against an attorney. A legal assistant working in probate should be able to move the probate proceeding along. Any necessary delay should be explained to the client. No unnecessary delays should be permitted to occur.

A client may sustain damages from delayed probate. An estate if not properly administered leaves the door open for claims of malpractice. An estate can be liable for penalty and interest payments for unpaid taxes. Money can be lost to the estate by not planning timing of payment of expenses and improperly taking deductions, by failure to consider tax consequences to the estate in various ways, to confirm title to assets or discover assets, distinguishing between income and principal of receipts and disbursements, to explain to the personal representative his responsibility, to consider possible tax benefits to beneficiaries, among others.

Clients also sustain damages when an attorney fails to have a complaint filed on their behalf before the statute of limitation expires. Or when a client's case is dismissed for failure to bring to trial. The alert legal assistant should prevent such happenings.

Attorneys are held to "the strictest observance at all times of the principles of truth, honesty, and fairness, especially in their criticism of the courts, to the end that the public confidence in the due administration of justice be upheld, and the dignity and usefulness of the courts maintained." (*In re Humphrey* (1917) 174 Cal. 290, 296.)

Rule 7-103. Communicating with an adverse party represented by counsel. Comment: Rule 7-103 provides: "A member of the State Bar shall not communicate directly or indirectly with a party whom he knows to be represented by counsel upon a subject of controversy, without the express consent of such counsel. This rule shall not apply to communications with a public officer, board, committee or body." The legal assistant, as the attorney's agent, is likewise bound by this same prohibition.

The purpose of the rule is to permit an attorney to function properly in his representation and to prevent the opposing counsel from impeding his proper performance. If opposing counsel is present with the client, he can correct any errors or the effect of the communication and protect his client.

This rule seems quite clear. Yet disciplinary actions have arisen as a result of its violation. If a party has retained counsel, neither the attorney — nor the legal assistant as an agent of the attorney — may contact that party. He may neither telephone nor write or in any other matter communicate with such person, without the express consent of counsel. A party is represented by counsel if he has counsel of record.

See *Mitton v. State Bar* (1969) 71 Cal.2d 525; *Abeles v. State Bar* (1973) 9 Cal.3d 603.

(See ABA Canon 7, EC 7-18.)

Rule 7-105. Trial Conduct.

This rule provides in part: "A member of the State Bar shall not intentionally misquote to a judge or judicial officer the language of a book, statute or decision; nor shall he, with knowledge of its invalidity and without disclosing such knowledge, cite as authority a decision that has been overruled or a statute that has been repealed or declared unconstitutional.''

The legal assistant who furnishes legal research to an attorney for a trial (or for other purpose) should be certain to first Shepardize a case. Quotations should be checked *at the source*. Quotations in a case from another case should not be relied on; usually they are correct but not *always;* check it out. Supplements to statutes should be checked for repeals, amendments or additions.

While the rule refers only to *intentional* misquotations, and the citation of overruled decisions or repealed statutes *with knowledge of their invalidity,* which are matters of evidence and proof, the attorney does not want to be subjected to the possibility of a disciplinary action. The appearance of impropriety must be avoided. At the very least, the attorney would be embarrassed at being wrong. It appears as sloppy practice, whatever the reason.

Neither may the attorney conceal pertinent letters or documents from the court. The paralegal who assists in the preparation of exhibits, documents and information for trial should be certain the attorney is fully informed as to all evidentiary material, whether or not adverse to his client.

Rule 7-107. Contact with Witnesses.

An attorney may not directly or indirectly cause a witness to secrete himself or leave the area of the court's jurisdiction to make himself unavailable as a witness.

Rule 8-101. Preserving the identity of funds and property of a client. Comment: Money received from clients as advances for costs or expenses, or money received for the benefit of a client, should be deposited in a separate trust account designated as ''Trust Account'' or ''Clients' Funds Account'' or similar labeling. Other office funds should not be commingled.

This rule against commingling was adopted to prevent any loss of a client's money, as a safeguard against any such danger. Funds are commingled when they may be used for an attorney's personal expenses or income subject to claims of the attorney's creditors.

The rule is violated when an attorney withdraws funds from a trust account for his personal use. (*Seavey v. State Bar* (1935) 4 Cal.2d 73.) Nor may an attorney, without knowledge or consent of his client, unilaterally determine his own fee and withdraw the fee from funds held in trust for his client.

Rule 8-101 provides in part: ''(2) Funds belonging in part to a client and in part presently or potentially to the member of the State Bar or firm of which he is a member must be deposited therein and the portion belonging to the member of the State Bar or firm of which he is a member must be withdrawn at the earliest reasonable time after the member's interest in that portion becomes fixed.'' The attorney's portion may not be withdrawn while any dispute with the client remains unresolved.

Clients should be notified promptly of receipt of funds (or securities or properties) for their benefit and prompt payment or delivery should be made.

(Disciplinary Rule 9-102.)

Actual deposits and withdrawals into a trust account might conceivably be made by the legal assistant or other staff member rather than by the attorney himself; that fact does not excuse the attorney since he is presumed to have reasonable supervision over staff. (*Black v. State Bar* (1972) 7 Cal.3d 676.)

Restitution to a client is not a defense, though it may have a bearing on the discipline.

*   *   *   *

A professional legal assistant or paralegal has an important calling which demands the highest standards of personal integrity and competence. The more seriously one accepts such a career goal, the more meaningful will be one's work in providing those aspects of legal service as she or he is qualified to perform. ''Continuation of the American concept that we are to be governed by rules of law requires that the people have faith that justice can be obtained through our legal system.'' (ABA Canon 9.) To this end, the paralegal assistant has a necessary and vital role within the legal profession.

*   *   *   *

Chapter 27

VOCABULARY AND LATIN PHRASES

FOREIGN WORDS AND PHRASES

Foreign and Latin phrases were once widely used in law; the modern trend in legal writing is to avoid them. But certain phrases immediately convey a lengthy legal principle to lawyers and remain in use for their economy of expression. Other writers may delight in the use of such phrases. Some words and phrases of foreign derivation have been so widely used as to have become a part of our own language. These words are no longer italicized (underscored in typewritten material). The trend is to avoid italicization, but the authorities are far from being in complete agreement. The list below is offered as a guide only.

A

ab initio	From the beginning
action in personam	An action against a person
action in rem	An action as to rights in property, as a foreclosure or partition action
addendum	Anything added
ad hoc	For this particular purpose, e.g., an ad hoc committee is formed to accomplish a particular purpose
ad hominem	Appeal to principles and passions instead of logic and truth, is an *ad hominem* argument
ad infinitum	Without limit

ad litem	A person who acts for the purposes of the particular litigation only, as a person appointed by the court to bring an action on behalf of a minor is called a guardian ad litem
ad valorem	According to the valuation
a fortiori	With stronger reason
alias	Another name used by person
alibi	Accused's claim that he was in another place at time of commission of crime
aliunde	Testimony from another source to explain a written instrument is evidence *aliunde*
alter ego	Another self, another part of self (a corporation is the shareholders' alter ego where the corporate entity is disregarded)
amicus curiae	Friend of the court (an amicus curiae brief may be filed by permission of court by someone with interest in the case other than a party to the action)
anno Domini	The year of our Lord
ante	Before
a posteriori	Inductive reasoning, from effect to cause; opposite of a priori
a priori	Reasoning from cause to effect; opposite of *a posteriori*
apropos	Appropriate to the occasion
arguendo	By way of argument
assumpsit	A form of action for nonperformance of an implied contract, a promise

B

bona fide	Good faith

C

causa mortis	An act done in contemplation of death, as a transfer of property
causa sine qua non	A prerequisite
caveat emptor	Let the buyer beware
certiorari	A writ issued by a higher court to a lower court to send up the record in a proceeding

cestui que trust	The beneficiary of a trust, the legal control of which is vested in a trustee
chose	A thing
chose in action	A right to recover money or other personal property by a court proceeding
circa	About
compos mentis	Mentally competent
consortium	In law, the right to receive certain things from a marriage, as support, companionship
contra	Against
contra bonos mores	Contrary to good morals and public policy
contra pacem	Literally, against the peace; a formal allegation
coram nobis	A writ permitting court to correct errors of fact, fraud or coercion
coram non judice	A judgment which exceeds the issues litigated, and therefore null and void
corpus	The main body of a thing, a principal sum, e.g., a trust corpus
corpus delicti	The body, i.e., the essence of a crime
corpus juris	A comprehensive body of law

E

ex contractu	Arising by way of contract
ex delicto	From the crime
ex officio	By virtue of his office (as county clerks are ex officio clerks of the superior courts)
ex parte	Relating to one party only (italicize if in name of case, as *Ex parte Miller*)
ex post facto	A law is an ex post facto law if it applies retroactively to acts committed before its enactment, to detriment of accused, forbidden by the Constitution
expressio unius est exclusio alterius	The express mention of one thing implies the exclusion of another different thing
ex proprio vigore	Of its own innate vigor or force
ex rel.	By or on the information of someone, used in names of cases, as *United States ex rel. Walters*
ex tempore	Without premeditation

F

flagrante delicto	To be caught in *flagrante delicto* is to be caught in the act or commission of the crime

H

habeas corpus	A writ directed to a person having custody of another to produce that person in court

I

ibid.	Where in a text or footnote reference a complete case citation, or a citation of a secondary authority, appears, and upon the same page and without intervening citations another reference is made to the case, *ibid.* is a sufficient citation. First reference: *Guaranty Trust Co. v. York*, 326 U.S. 99, 108; second reference to the same case, also on page 108, can use *ibid.*
id.	Where a second reference is to the same case or secondary authority but to a different page, can use *id.* In the above example, if reference is to page 108, would be "*Id.* at p. 109." *Id.* may never be used in citing statutory and quasi-statutory materials.
in forma pauperis	To sue as a poor man, hence, to be relieved from costs (as in a bankruptcy proceeding)
infra	Below, meaning the latter is referred to in the document thereinafter, as opposed to *supra*
in haec verba	In the same words
in loco parentis	In the place of a parent
in pari delicto	Where two parties suing each other are equally guilty or in fault and are therefore denied recovery
in pari materia	Equality of things
in propria persona	In one's own behalf or character (where one acts as his own attorney in a lawsuit)
In re	In the matter of (in California used in titles of habeas corpus cases)
inter alia	Among other things

inter alios	Among other persons
inter vivos	Between living persons (a transfer of property made during the life of the donor is a transfer *inter vivos*)
ipso facto	As the result of the mere fact or act itself
in toto	In its entirety

L

laches	Neglect to enforce a right at a proper time under the law
laissez faire	To leave to do; leave alone, not interfere
lex	The law
lis pendens	Notice of a pending suit (in California required to be filed in a quiet title action and condemnation action)
loc. cit.	Where cited; in the place cited

M

mala fides	In bad faith
mala prohibita	Acts wrongful because the law prohibits them
malum in se	Evil in itself
mandamus	A writ issuing out of a court directing a person to do some act by virtue of his office
mens rea	Guilty mind, criminal intent necessary for commission of crime
modus operandi	Usual mode of operation (as of a criminal)

P

per curiam	A ''by the court''opinion, i.e., an opinion by the entire court, as distinguished from one authorized by one judge and concurred in by others
per diem	By the day
per se	Considered by itself
per stirpes	By stocks (as descendants take by right of representation, as opposed to per capita)
petit larceny	A small larceny; a petty theft (in California petty theft includes all thefts not grand thefts)
post-mortem	After death

praecipe; prǝcipe	Command; written order to the clerk of the court to issue a writ
prima facie	On its face; evidence which appears sufficient in law to establish fact, in absence of contrary evidence
pro forma	As a matter of form
pro rata	In proportion (as in bankruptcy the assets of the debtor may be distributed pro rata to the bankrupt's debtors, i.e., in proportion to their debts)
pro tanto	To a certain extent
pro tempore	For the time being (as a judge who is not a regular judge of a particular court sits as a judge "pro tem" in that court)

Q

quaere	Query; doubtful point of law
quantum	The amount
quasi	Almost; quasi-judicial
quid pro quo	A term denoting the consideration for a contract

R

raison d'etre	Reason for being
reductio ad absurdum	Reducing a contention to an absurdity
res gestae	Transaction; the subject matter
res judicata	The matter having been decided by a court of competent jurisdiction

VOCABULARY

For the most part an attempt has been made here to explain the meaning of the words, rather than to define them.

A

| abscond | To depart secretly; to withdraw and hide oneself (i.e., the embezzler absconds with the money). |
| absolve | To set free, or release, as from some obligation or from the consequences of guilt. |

abstract of title	A record of the title to a piece of land, showing how the title has passed from owner to owner, and whether or not the property is free and clear of encumbrances.
accessory before the fact	A person who instigates, or contributes to, but who does not actually take part in, the commission of a crime.
account stated	An account rendered by the creditor, and by the debtor assented to as correct, either expressly, or by implication of law from the failure to object.
acquitted	Not guilty — cleared of charges.
adjudged	Same as adjudicated — to order or decree.
administer	The management and disposal, under legal authority, of the estate of a deceased person.
administrator (M) administratrix (F)	One who by order of the court carries out the administration necessary in an estate where the decedent left no will.
affiant	One who makes a sworn statement; person making an affidavit.
affidavit	A sworn statement; a written declaration under oath.
agreement	An exchange of promises, written or oral.
alibi	The plea or fact of having been, at the alleged time of commission of an act, elsewhere than at the alleged place of commission.
allegation	A formal averment in a complaint, a positive assertion.
answer	In law, a document filed in reply to a complaint or cross-complaint.
appeal	To make application for trial of a cause to a higher court.
appellant	One who appeals a decision.
appraisal	A valuation of property (real property, furniture, etc.).
appurtenances and hereditaments	Things, rights, etc., that pertain to the land, and title to which goes with the land. "Hereditaments" are particularly things that may be inherited.

arraignment	The formal calling of an accused person into court, reading the accusatory pleading to him, and asking him whether he is guilty or not guilty.
assignee	One to whom material is assigned.
assignor	The one who assigns, e.g., you might assign an interest in an estate.
assigns (noun)	Those to whom one may assign, e.g., creditors.
attachment	Writ issued by court commanding sheriff to attach property rights, credits or effects of defendant to satisfy demands of plaintiff, usually pending a trial to determine the validity of plaintiff's claim at trial.

B

bankruptcy	State of impoverishment — a law to liquidate property.
beneficiary	The recipient under a will, trust.
bequeath	To give personal property by will.
bequest	The personal property given by will.
bona fide	In good faith, genuine.
book account	Detailed statement of the transaction between parties; a record of goods sold or services rendered.

C

certified copy	Copy of an instrument made from records in a recorder's (or county clerk's) office, and certified to by the recorder (or county clerk) as being an exact copy of the paper on file or of record.
certificate	A declaration in writing.
certiorari, writ of	A writ from a superior court to call up for review the records of an inferior court or a body acting in a quasi-judicial capacity.
chattels	Personal property.
code	A collection of laws (as Government Code, Civil Code, Code of Civil Procedure, Probate Code).
codicil	An addition to a will.

collateral	Material security.
community property	Usually (in California) all property acquired after marriage other than separate property.
complainant	The party making complaint.
complaint	Legal paper filed in court setting forth a cause of action.
conveyance	An instrument conveying title.
corpus delicti	Body or element of the crime, i.e., the facts forming its basis.
corroborate	To make more certain, to confirm.
council	A deliberative body, e.g., a city council.
counsel (noun)	One who gives advice; advice; an attorney.
counterclaim	An opposing claim filed in response to a complaint as part of an answer.
covenant	A promise in a contract or other legal paper.
cross-complaint	A document setting up adverse claims against complainant.
cross-defendant	The person who must defend the cross-complaint (one of the cross-defendants, at least, will be also the plaintiff or complainant).
cross-examination	Examination of witness by other side.

D

decedent	A deceased (dead) person.
decree	An order of the court.
default	Failing to answer or reply, as to a complaint.
defendant	The adverse party to a complaint or the one who must defend.
delict	An offense or transgression against law; the behavior of that individual against whom a sanction as a consequence of his behavior is directed.
demurrer	A document setting up that while truth may be stated, the subject is insufficient for legal action.
deponent	One who gives written testimony to be used in court.
devise	To give real property by will.

devisee	One to whom real property is given by will.
dictum, dicta (pl.)	An authoritative statement; judicial opinion on point other than precise issue involved in case; an expression of an opinion in a case which is influential because of its sound reasoning.
direct examination	First testimony of witness.
disbursements	Money paid out, as for expenses.

E

eminent domain	The power of the state to take private property for public use.
encumbrances	Liens.
equitably	Justly or impartially.
escrow	Deeds or other documents are placed ''in escrow,'' i.e., in the hands of a disinterested party, usually a title company, to be delivered upon the fulfillment of certain conditions.
executed	Signed, finished, or completed, as a person executed his will.
executor (M) executrix (F)	One who by order of court and appointment carries out the terms of a will (i.e., is named in will).
exhibit	A document entered as evidence in a case.
ex parte	On one side only; by or for one party; done for, in behalf of, or on the application of, one party only. A judicial proceeding is said to be ''ex parte'' when it is taken or granted at the instance and for the benefit of one party only.

F

fee simple	An absolute title to property, with no limitations or restrictions.
felony	A serious crime (in California punishable by death or imprisonment in a state prison).
foreclosure suit	A suit brought to foreclose a mortgage, i.e., to close out a mortgagor's interest if he has defaulted on his payments on the mortgage.

G

garnishee	Trustee or one warned by legal process in respect to the interest of third parties in property held by him.
garnishment	A proceeding wherein a party who owes money to, or holds personal property of, a defendant is ordered to withhold such money or personal property so that it may be applied to payment of the defendant's debts.
grantee	A person to whom a grant is made.
grantor	A person who makes a grant.
guardian ad litem	A guardian for a specific suit.

H

habeas corpus	A writ of habeas corpus may be issued by a court, ordering anyone holding or detaining another to bring the detained or imprisoned person into court for a hearing regarding the lawfulness of the detention.
heirs	Those who inherit under the law, by virtue of their relationship to the deceased.
holographic	Written by hand (a holographic will).

I

immaterial	Not pertinent or of no substance, as immaterial testimony.
incompetent	One unable to handle his own affairs, mentally incompetent, etc.
indictment	An accusation of a public offense in writing presented by the Grand Jury to the court.
injunction	Prohibitory writ issued by court to restrain one or more defendants to a suit from doing or permitting his servants, etc. to do an act which is inequitable to rights of other parties to actions.
instrument	A written document.
intestate	One who dies not having made a valid will before death.
inure	To take effect or to result.
invalid	Void; of no force or effect under the law.
irrelevant	Not pertaining.

J

judgment	A decree or a decision of the court.
judicial	Of or pertaining or appropriate to the administration of justice, or courts of justice, as judicial power.
jurat	Part of sworn statement where officer certifies that the same was sworn to before him.
jury	A body of persons sworn to give a true answer or verdict upon some matter submitted to them.

L

larceny	The unlawful taking of personal property without the consent of the other (stealing or theft).
lease	A rental agreement between the landlord and tenant.
legatee	One to whom property is bequeathed in a will.
lesee	Person to whom a lease is given (the tenant).
lessor	One who leases (the landlord).
libel	Libel is written, defamatory statements (slander is spoken).
lien	Hold or claim which one person has upon property of another as security for some debt or charge.
liquidated	to discharge or pay off, as for damages. Debts are "liquidated" when they are paid.
lis pendens	Notice of a pending suit.
litigate	To contest in law — to make the subject of a lawsuit.
litigation	Legal action, a lawsuit.

M

mandamus, writ of (mandate)	Writ issued by court of competent jurisdiction to compel a lower court, municipality, corporation, or person, to perform some public duty.
metes and bounds	Used in describing the measurements and boundaries of a piece of property.

misdemeanor	Any crime less than a felony (in California punishable by imprisonment in a county jail).
mortgage	A conveyance of property as security for a debt.

N

nonsuit	A judgment given against a plaintiff because of his failure to prosecute his case or his inability to establish a prima facie case at the trial.
norm	An authoritative rule or standard; an ideal standard binding upon the members of a group and serving to guide, control, or regulate proper and acceptable behavior.
notary public	A public officer who certifies deeds, and other writings.
nuncupative	Oral, not written, will.

P

partition	Dividing of lands held by joint tenants, or tenants in common, into distinct portions. In a less technical sense, any division of real or personal property between coowners or coproprietors.
perjury	False swearing.
petition	A pleading similar to a complaint. A petition for writ of mandate, for example, might be filed in a superior court or it might be filed in an appellate court (Courts of Appeal or Supreme Court of California) as an original proceeding. Parties are called "petitioner" and "respondent" instead of "plaintiff" and "defendant."
petitioner	One who petitions the court.
plaintiff	One who instigates a lawsuit.
plea	An argument.
praecipe	A written order to clerk of court to issue writ.
precedent	A judicial decision serving as a rule for future determination in similar cases.
premises	Property; also, the facts of a case.

probate proceeding	Term is broadly used to refer to any proceeding within the jurisdiction of the probate court, including those for probate of wills, administration of estates of decedents and incompetents, and guardianship of minors.
probative	Serving to prove, as evidence.
procedure	The method of doing things.
proceedings	Steps taken in completion of a lawsuit to judgment.
prohibition, writ of	Writ issued by court of competent jurisdiction to certain person preventing him from doing certain things.
propria persona (pro per)	By oneself or for oneself. Person who represents himself in court, acts as his own attorney, appears "in propria persona."
pro rata	Proportionately, according to share or liability.
prosecutor	One who conducts an official prosecution before the court.

Q

quiet title	A suit to "quiet title" or "quiet title proceedings" may be brought to perfect the title to property.
quo warranto	Writ by which government commences action to recover office or franchise from person or corporation in possession of it.

R

rehearing	A second or new hearing (as of an argument on appeal) by the same court and upon the pleadings already in the case.
remand	To send back, as to send back a case to a lower court for further consideration.
remittitur	The returning or sending back by a court of appeal of the record and proceedings in a cause after its decision thereon, to the court from which it was appealed.
rescind	To cancel.
rescission (noun)	To have annulled or cancelled.

residuary clause	The clause in a will by which the testator disposes of property remaining after special devises and bequests.
residue	The balance of an estate remaining after payment of all debts and devises and bequests.
restraining order	A court order temporarily restraining a party from committing a certain act until the court can decide whether or not an injunction should be issued.

S

separate	Individual property (in California, property owned before marriage, or property acquired after marriage by gift, or inherited, etc.).
situated	Located at.
stipulation	An agreement, between parties to an action, usually through counsel; also, any condition in an agreement.
subpoena	An order of court directing witness to appear and testify in court at an appointed time or for taking a deposition.
subpoena duces tecum	Order of court directing witness to appear and testify and bring papers, files and records into court.
summons	An order of court directing defendant to appear and answer conplaint within 10 days if served in county, 30 days if elsewhere.
supersedeas, writ of	Written order of court staying further proceedings in a case.
supra	Above, previously stated.

T

testament	Will.
testate	One dies "testate" who dies having made a valid will before death.
testator (M) testatrix (F)	One who makes a will.
therefor	For that (e.g., "pay therefor," "and good cause appearing therefor").

therefore — For that reason (e.g., "Now, therefore, it is hereby ordered," etc.).

U

unlawful detainer — The unjustifiable retention of the possession of lands by one whose original entry was lawful and of right, but whose right to the possession has terminated and who refuses to quit, as in the case of a tenant holding over after the termination for possession by the landlord.

V

venue — Place of trial, county in which court is located.

verily — In very truth.

vindicate — To justify or successfully defend.

voucher — Receipt or evidence of payment.

W

with prejudice — Voluntary dismissal of suit "with prejudice" as part of settlement of litigation is as conclusive of rights of parties as if suit had been prosecuted to final adjudication adverse to plaintiff.

without prejudice — Without effect upon or detrimental to any rights that existed prior to a certain act; declaration that no rights or privileges of the party concerned to be considered as waived or lost except as expressly conceded.

witness — One who testified or one who saw certain things.

writ — Order issued by court of competent jurisdiction, returnable to same, commanding the performance or nonperformance of some act, as a writ of execution, writ of attachment, writ of mandate, writ of certiorari, writ of supersedeas, writ of prohibition.

COMMON MEDICAL TERMS

Listed below are frequently used medical terms, for a quick reference for spelling.

abdomen
abdominal
aberration
abscission
acidification
acidulate
adenoid
anaesthesia
antispasmodic
aorta
appendicitis
appendix vermiformis
arteriosclerosis
bifurcation
bronchitis
cauterization
cerebellum
cerebritis
cerebrum
cirrhosis
clavicle
coccyx
coronary
cranial
diaphragm
dorsi
duodenum
embolism
entomology

epidermis
epiglottis
epilepsy
Eustachian
femur
fibrosis
fibula
frontal
gastritis
germicide
granulation
hemorrhage
humerus
interstitial
intracranial
jugular
larynx
locomotor ataxia
lumbar
malignancy
mandible
metacarpal
metatarsal
myocarditis
myopia
nephritis
neuralgia
neurasthenia
paraplegia

paresis
parietal
patella
pectoral
pelvic
pelvis
pericarditis
peritonitis
phalanges
pleurisy
rhinitis
sacrum
scapula
sciatica
sclerosis
sclerotic
sclerotitis
talus
therapeutical
thrombosis
tibia
trachea
trachoma
ulceration
ulna
varicose
ventricle
vertebrae
viscera

For comprehensive list of medical terms, refer to Blakiston's New Gould Medical Dictionary.

MISCELLANEOUS LEGAL CONCEPTS

There are many legal concepts that require more than a phrase to properly define them. A few of these concepts follow, with extended definitions:

Ratio Decidendi

The *ratio decidendi* is the reason for making the decision. To determine exactly what a case decides, it is necessary to direct attention to the legal reason for the decision. Thus the *ratio decidendi* is the underlying principle of the case, without which no judgment could have been given.

Res Judicata

The higher norm (the statute or a norm of common law) determines, to a greater or lesser extent, the creation and the contents of the lower norm (the decision of the court). If the plaintiff or the defendant believes that the decision of the court does not correspond to the general norms of statutory or customary law, he may appeal to a higher court (on grounds permitted for an appeal). The higher court can replace the decision by another decision which — according to the opinion of the higher court — conforms to the general norm (the statute or a norm of common law). "This is the typical process by which the legal order endeavors to guarantee the legality of the judicial process."* But this process must end somewhere — and it does, with the decision of the court of last resort, "an authority whose decision cannot be annulled or changed anymore. With this decision, the case becomes *res judicata.*"** That adjudication controls litigation thereafter, i.e., when the litigation is identical in that (1) the same thing is sued for, (2) the cause of action is the same, (3) the parties are the same and (4) the character of the parties is the same (suing or defending, and in the same capacity). Then the decision cannot be litigated further.

But there never exists any absolute guarantee that the lower norm (the final decision of the court) corresponds to the higher norm (statute, custom, constitution).

For example, in *Leung Gim v. Brownell* (9th Cir. 1956) 238 F.2d 27, the court held that a dismissal of a complaint for lack of subject matter jurisdiction was res judicata barring a second action in the same court upon the same subject matter.

In a 1980 mandate action, a finding in a former action that a nonresident defendant was not subject to California process was held res judicata in a subsequent action brought by the same plaintiffs against the same defendant, which concededly had not changed its relationship to California since the former decision was made. The defendant was held entitled to an order quashing service of summons in the current action.

---

*Kelsen, op. cit. supra, p. 154.
**Kelsen, op. cit. supra, p. 154.

Stare Decisis

Each new decision becomes law according to the doctrine of stare decisis. In this way the system grows continuously through contributions made by every case which enunciates a new rule. The court's decision stands until overruled (either by a later decision of its own or of a higher court) as an authoritative interpretation of the statute and a *precedent* for subsequent decisions.

The rule of stare decisis comes into play in that it expresses the principle that the court decisions should stand as precedents for future guidance. The maxim *"stare decisis et non quieta movere"* means to adhere to precedents and not to disturb things that are established. If there is no statute covering a matter, precedents are not the law, but the highest evidence of the law. The case becomes the law in deciding any future case which involves the exact same principle of law. When the same general principle of law is found embodied in a long line of decisions, you can reasonably assume it will be relied on in future decisions.

It is these precedents which the lawyers (and paralegals) must look for when trying to discover what the law is on a given point, and in attempting to determine whether a statute is valid and how it should be interpreted.

Sometimes a decision of a California case in point cannot be located. Decisions of courts of other states may be urged. These decisions, however, are not stare decisis to California courts, although careful attention and respect be accorded.

A decision issued 50 or 100 years ago upon a point not since considered is not necessarily stare decisis, if proof can be made to the satisfaction of a court that the decision is no longer acceptable in the light of present-day conditions. Also, later decided cases, although not overruling the earlier case, may show a *trend* in a different direction. The dicta in these cases is often helpful in proving this trend.

The doctrine of stare decisis applies with special force to decisions involving property rights, especially real property and rights vested therein. Obviously, where parties have invested money and acquired real property interests on the basis of a decision rendered by a court, injustice would result from the disturbance of such a decision. Therefore the decision of the case is in all probability stare decisis as a rule of property.

Decisions of the Courts of Appeal are stare decisis to superior courts in making their decisions in similar cases, unless of course a decision of a Court of Appeal was thereafter superseded by a decision of the California Supreme Court.

Courts of Appeal are obligated to give full consideration and respect to sister Courts of Appeal, but the decision of one Court of Appeal is not stare decisis to all the other Courts of Appeal. But a decision of the California Supreme Court is stare decisis to cases decided thereafter by the Courts of Appeal.

Similarly, California Courts of Appeal and the California Supreme Court must accord full respect to decisions of federal courts, but only the decisions of the United States Supreme Court are stare decisis decisions to all the courts.

Equity

Laws are usually broad rules laid down to cover a multitude of situations, and sometimes a strict application of a law to a particular case would result in injustice. The conditions of the case may be novel; the law cannot anticipate every case that might arise under a law. Therefore, there may not be a precedent that will fit the case at hand; equity steps in to bring about justice in that case. The present system of equity has been said to be the result of a struggle between the courts to supplement and remedy the deficiencies of the law.

We do not have separate courts to hear cases "in equity" as opposed to cases "in law." The forms of the actions and the procedure are the same. California Code of Civil Procedure section 307 states that there is but one form of civil action "for the enforcement or protection of private rights and the redress or prevention of private wrongs." Nevertheless, there are distinctions between legal and equitable cases.

An in-depth discussion of those distinctions cannot be provided here. In law schools semester courses are taught on the subject of equity. Perhaps an idea of what equity is can best be provided by the following summary of its origin from the case of *Dalton v. Vanderveer*, 29 N.Y.S. 342, at page 343: ". . . The origin of the high court of chancery in England was wholly due to the inability, and, to a limited extent, the unwillingness, of the common-law courts to entertain and give relief in every case, and thus meet all the requirements of justice. The common-law courts paid such deference to forms and precedents that they became slaves to them. . . . They adhered to certain precise writs and rigid forms of action which were not sufficiently comprehensive to give adequate redress in some cases of injustice and wrong, or to give any redress in many others. In such cases the aggrieved person was remediless, except he could get a hearing of the king himself. Petitions by those in such cases were, therefore, frequently presented to the king, asking for relief [by] him as a matter of grace, because it could not be got of his courts. From the fact that the king usually referred such petitions to his secretary, called his 'chancellor,' they came in course of time to be presented to the chancellor directly by the suitors themselves; and thus, gradually and at a time which history cannot enable us to precisely fix, the court of chancery became to be established. . . . Thus, side by side there existed the court of chancery and the common-law courts, each with a distinct jurisdiction, the test of chancery's jurisdiction in any given case being that the suitor could either get no relief, or could not get adequate relief, in a court of common law; and, therefore, necessarily there also grew up, not only two distinct systems of practice in these courts, but also two distinct systems of substantive jurisprudence, that in the court of chancery being the system which we call 'equity'. . . . The court of chancery is gone, but the system of equity jurisprudence remains, and is still administered, but by the same court which also administers the common-law system. . . . "

CALIFORNIA PARALEGAL'S GUIDE

APPENDIX

Examination for Certified Legal Assistant

In England, paralegals are known as "legal executives." The Institute of Legal Executives provides two levels of proficiency: associates and legal executives. Only the latter may use the professional letters "F. Inst. L. Ex." Thus in England the paralegal is clearly defined.

"Obviously the issue of certification is central to your present state of development," writes L. W. Chapman, Director General, the Institute of Legal Executives. "It was this that this Institute was set up to provide in 1963. From our point of view, little can be achieved without it."

The CLA (Certified Legal Assistant) exam was developed by the Certifying Board of the National Association of Legal Assistants, which is comprised of five experienced legal assistants; two prominent members in the field of education; and two respected attorneys who are members of the American Bar Association. It is a voluntary examination and entitles persons who successfully pass the examination to use of the CLA designation (a duly registered service mark). The exam was established in an effort to meet the high standards of professional and ethical conduct in the paralegal profession.

Eligibility for examination. An applicant must meet one of the following requirements:

(1) Graduation from an ABA-approved training course or training course for legal assistants, plus 1 year of practical experience;

(2) Graduation from an unapproved training course or from an unaccredited school plus 3 years' experience as a legal assistant;

(3) A bachelor's degree in any field plus 3 years' experience as a legal assistant;

(4) Certification as a Professional Legal Secretary and five years law related experience under the supervision of a member of the bar (this requirement expires in 1986);

(5) Seven years of law-related experience under the supervision of a member of the bar (this provision expires in 1986).

The two-day examination covers the following general areas:

(1) Communications — Grammar, accurate understanding of words commonly used, information letters to client, memos, nonverbal communications, concise writing, basic requirements for corporate minutes, proper signatures.

(2) Ethics and Human Relations — Authorized practice, ethical rules, practice rules, delegation of authority, consequences of delegation, working with people, confidentiality.

(3) Interviewing Techniques — General considerations for interviewing situation, initial roadblocks, manner of questions, special handling situations, use of checklists for specific matters, requesting documents from clients.

(4) Analyzing and categorizing facts and evidence; legal assistant's relationship with the lawyer, legal secretary, client, other law firms and the courts; reactions to specific situations; handling telephone situations.

(5) Law Office Management — Docket control, timekeeping, billing, word processing, information retrieval, personnel management, equipment, office layout, chargeable expenses, bookkeeping principles, management principles.

(6) Legal Research — Principles of legal research, sources of the law, finding tools, court reports, Shepardizing, research procedure.

(7) Legal Terminology — Latin phrases, legal phrases or terms in general, utilizing and understanding of common legal terms.

(8) Substantive Law — The American legal system; history, branches of government; the Constitution.

In addition, four sets of general questions must be selected and completed from the following areas: Real Estate, Estate Planning and Probate, Litigation, Bankruptcy, Contracts, Tax Law, Corporate Law, Administrative Law, and Criminal Law.

Continuing legal education is required to retain the designation.

Certainly the CLA test is a comprehensive examination which tests the applicant's knowledge in a broad spectrum of legal fields.

National Associations

National Association of Legal Assistants, Inc., 3005 East Skelly Drive, Suite 122, Tulsa, Oklahoma 74105.

Its membership is comprised of individuals throughout the United States. This organization seeks to promote the profession of the legal assistant. Its primary goals include promulgation of its Code of Professional Responsibility for Legal Assistants, continuing legal education, and the adoption of a national certification procedure for paralegals. It formulated and administers the examination for Certified Legal Assistant.

It also assists in the establishment of guidelines for the legal assistant, educates the public for the advancement and improvement of the profession and broadens public understanding of the function of the legal assistant. It presents annual workshops and regional seminars. Currently a number of educational efforts are in process.

National Federation of Paralegal Associations, Ben Franklin Station, P.O. Box 14103, Washington, D.C. 20044

A professional organization of state and local paralegal associations; an organized communications network offering a forum for paralegals practicing in all sectors, including public and private law firms, legal services, financial institutions, the courts, trade associations, and the federal, state and local governments.

Its general objective is to advance, foster and promote the paralegal profession; it seeks to advance the educational standards of the profession and to conduct research, seminars, experiments, investigations, studies or other work relative to the paralegal profession. It publishes an Affirmation of Responsibility (its code of ethics). The Federation at this writing has 24 member associations and 61 sustaining members throughout the United States, representing more than 5,000 people.

National Paralegal Institute, 2000 P St., N.W., Washington, D.C. 20005; Western office: 1714 Stockton, San Francisco, California, 94133. A national organization whose purpose is to promote the utilization and training of paralegals and other lay people in law-related work in the public sector.

Associations of Legal Assistants — California:

East Bay Association of Legal Assistants, P.O. Box 424, Oakland, CA 94604

California Alliance of Paralegal Associations (state organization), P.O. Box 26668, San Francisco, CA 94126

California Public Sector Paralegal Association, 1446 West 19th St., Merced, CA 95340

Los Angeles Paralegal Association, P.O. Box 24350, Los Angeles, CA 90024

Paralegal Association of San Mateo Co., Care of Linda Vetter, 250 Wheeler, Redwood City, CA 94061

Sacramento Association of Legal Assistants, P.O. Box 453, Sacramento, CA 95802, President: Linda Dougherty

San Diego Association of Legal Assistants, P.O. Box 1649, San Diego, CA 92112

San Francisco Association of Legal Assistants, P.O. Box 26668, San Francisco, CA 94126

California Institutions Offering Legal Assistant Training Programs:

American College of Paramedical Arts and Sciences, 1800 North Broadway, Santa Ana. CA 92706

American Legal Services Institute, c/o 2719 Canada Blvd., Glendale, CA 91208

American River College, 4700 College Oak Dr., Sacramento, CA 95841

California College of Paralegal Studies, 6832 Van Nuys Blvd., Van Nuys, CA 91405

California State College, San Bernardino, Paralegal Studies, Department of Political Science, 5500 State College Parkway, San Bernardino, CA 92407

California State University, Dominguez Hills, Public Paralegal Certificate Program, School of Social & Behavioral Sciences, Carson, CA 90747

California State University, Chico, Department of Political Science, 725 Butte Hall, Chico, CA 95929

California State University, Fullerton, State College Blvd., Fullerton, CA 92634

California State University, Hayward, Paralegal Studies Program, 25800 Carlos Bee Blvd., Hayward, CA 94542

California State University at Los Angeles, 5151 State University Drive, Los Angeles, CA 90032

Canada College, 4200 Farm Hill Blvd., Redwood City, CA 94061

Cerritos College, 11110 East Alondra Blvd., Norwalk, CA 90650

City College of San Francisco, 51 Phelan Avenue, San Francisco, CA 94112

Coast Community College District including Orange Coast College, 2701 Fairview Road, Costa Mesa, CA 92626

Coastline Community College, 10231 Slater Ave., Fountain Valley, CA 92708

Criss College of Business (In cooperation with Glendale University College of Law), 220 North Glendale Ave., Glendale, CA 91206

Dominican College of San Rafael, San Rafael, CA 94901

Empire College, 37 Old Courthouse Square, Santa Rosa, CA 95400

Fresno City College, 1101 East University Avenue, Fresno, CA 93741

Fullerton College, 321 E. Chapman Avenue, Fullerton, CA 92634

Glendale College of Legal Arts, 220 North Glendale Ave., Glendale, CA 91206

Golden Gate University, Center for Management Development, 536 Mission St., San Francisco, CA 94105

Golden West College, 15744 Golden West, Huntington Beach, CA 92647

Humphreys College, 6650 Inglewood Drive, Stockton, CA 95207

Imperial Valley College, P.O. Box 158, Imperial, CA 92251

Lake Tahoe Community College, Legal Assistant Certificate, 2659 Lake Tahoe Blvd., P.O. Box 14445, South Lake Tahoe, CA 95702

Lone Mountain City College, 2800 Turk Blvd., San Francisco, CA 94118

Los Angeles City College, 855 North Vermont Ave., Los Angeles, CA 90029

Los Angeles Southwest College, Legal Assistant Program, 1600 West Imperial Highway, Los Angeles, CA 90047

Merritt College, 12500 Campus Drive, Oakland, CA 94619

Orange Coast College, 2701 Fairview Road, Costa Mesa, CA 92626

Pacific College of Legal Careers, 580 University Ave., Sacramento, CA 95825

Pacific Legal Arts Academy, 1387 Del Norte Road, Camarillo, CA 93010

Paralegal Training and Resource Center, 655 Sutter St., San Francisco, CA 94102

Pasadena City College, 1570 E. Colorado Blvd., Pasadena, CA 91106

Pepperdine University, Legal Studies Program, 8035 S. Vermont Avenue, Los Angeles, CA 90044

Rio Hondo College, Paralegal Program, 3600 Workman Mill Road, Whittier, CA 90608

Rutledge College of San Diego, 3580 Aero Court, San Diego, CA 92123

San Bernardino Valley College, Legal Administration Program, 701 South Mt. Vernon Ave., San Bernardino, CA 92403

San Francisco City College, San Francisco, CA 94112

San Francisco State University, Paralegal Studies Program, 1600 Holloway Ave., San Francisco, CA 94132

San Jose State University, Continuing Education, San Jose, CA 95192

Santa Ana College, Seventeenth at Bristol, Santa Ana, CA 92706

Sawyer College of Business, 6832 Van Nuys Blvd., Van Nuys, CA 91405

Skyline College, 3300 College Drive, San Bruno, CA 94066

Sonoma State University, Office of Extended Education, Rohnert Park, CA 94928

South Bay Community Law Center, 387 Third Ave., Chula Vista, CA 92010

Southwestern College, 900 Otay Lakes Road, Chula Vista, CA 92010

St. Mary's College, P.O. Box 52, Moraga, CA 94575

University of California, University Extension, Davis, CA 95616

UCLA Attorney Assistant Training Program, UCLA Extension, 10955 Le Conte Ave., Rm. 214, Los Angeles, CA 90024

U.C. Santa Cruz Extension, Laurel Community Center, 301 Center St., Santa Cruz, CA 95064

U.C. Santa Cruz Extension, Palo Alto Municipal Court, Room 1, 270 Grant Ave., Palo Alto, CA 93406

University of California at Berkeley, University Extension, 2223 Fulton Street, Berkeley, California 94720

University of California, Irvine University Extension, Irvine, CA 92717

University of LaVerne, 1950 3d St., LaVerne, CA 91750

University of San Diego, Box 231, DeSales Hall, Alcala Park, San Diego, CA 92110

University of Santa Clara, Institute for Paralegal Education, Bannan Hall, Room 261, Santa Clara, CA 95053

University of Southern California, Law Center, University Park, Los Angeles, CA 90007

University of West Los Angeles, School of Paralegal Studies, 10811 Washington Blvd., Culver City, CA 90230

Valley College of Paralegal Studies, 10911 Riverside Drive, North Hollywood, CA 91602

Ventura County Community College, 71 Day Road, Ventura, CA 93003

West Valley Community College:

    Mission campus: 3585 Monroe Street, Santa Clara, CA 95051
    Campbell campus: 44 E. Latimer, Campbell, CA 95008
    Saratoga campus: 14000 Fruitvale, Saratoga, CA 95070

INDEX OF FORMS AND TABLES

SUBJECT INDEX